THE
NEW AMERICAN NATION
1775–1820

A Twelve-Volume Collection of Articles on the Development of the Early American Republic

Edited by

PETER S. ONUF
UNIVERSITY OF VIRGINIA

A GARLAND SERIES

THE NEW AMERICAN NATION
1775–1820

Volume

1

★

THE REVOLUTION IN AMERICAN THOUGHT

Edited with an
Introduction by

PETER S. ONUF

GARLAND PUBLISHING, INC.
NEW YORK & LONDON
1991

3 -11 - 92

Introduction © 1991 by Peter S. Onuf

Library of Congress Cataloging-in-Publication Data

The Revolution in American thought / edited with an introduction by
Peter S. Onuf.
    p.   cm. — (New American nation, 1776–1815 ; v. 1)
    Includes bibliographical references.
    ISBN 0-8153-0436-6 (alk. paper)
    1. United States—Politics and government—Revolution, 1775–1783. 2.
United States—Intellectual life—18th century. I. Onuf, Peter S. II. Series.
    E. 164.N45   1991 vol. 1
    [E210]
    973s—dc20   91-13170
    [973]   CIP

Printed on acid-free, 250-year-life paper.
Manufactured in the United States of America

THE NEW AMERICAN NATION, 1775–1820

EDITOR'S INTRODUCTION

This series includes a representative selection of the most interesting and influential journal articles on revolutionary and early national America. My goal is to introduce readers to the wide range of topics that now engage scholarly attention. The essays in these volumes show that the revolutionary era was an extraordinarily complex "moment" when the broad outlines of national history first emerged. Yet if the "common cause" brought Americans together, it also drove them apart: the Revolution, historians agree, was as much a civil war as a war of national liberation. And, given the distinctive colonial histories of the original members of the American Union, it is not surprising that the war had profoundly different effects in different parts of the country. This series has been designed to reveal the multiplicity of these experiences in a period of radical political and social change.

Most of the essays collected here were first published within the last twenty years. This series therefore does *not* recapitulate the development of the historiography of the Revolution. Many of the questions asked by earlier generations of scholars now seem misconceived and simplistic. Constitutional historians wanted to know if the Patriots had legitimate grounds to revolt: was the Revolution "legal"? Economic historians sought to assess the costs of the navigation system for American farmers and merchants and to identify the interest groups that promoted resistance. Comparative historians wondered how "revolutionary" the Revolution really was. By and large, the best recent work has ignored these classic questions. Contemporary scholarship instead draws its inspiration from other sources, most notable of which is the far-ranging reconception and reconstruction of prerevolutionary America by a brilliant generation of colonial historians.

Bernard Bailyn's *Ideological Origins of the American Revolution* (1967) was a landmark in the new historical writing on colonial politics. As his title suggests, Bailyn was less interested in constitutional and legal arguments as such than in the "ideology" or political language that shaped colonists' perception of and responses to British imperial policy. Bailyn's great contribution was to focus attention on colonial political culture; disciples and critics alike followed his lead as they explored the impact—and limits—of "republicanism" in specific colonial settings. Meanwhile, the social historians who had played a leading role in the transformation of colonial historiography were extending their work into the late colonial period and were increasingly interested in the questions of value, meaning, and behavior that were raised by the new political history. The resulting convergence points to some of the unifying themes in recent work on the revolutionary period presented in this series.

A thorough grounding in the new scholarship on colonial British America is the best introduction to the history and historiography of the Revolution. These volumes therefore can be seen as a complement and extension of Peter Charles Hoffer's eighteen-volume set, *Early American History*, published by Garland in 1987. Hoffer's collection includes numerous important essays essential for understanding developments in independent America. Indeed, only a generation ago—when the Revolution generally was defined in terms of its colonial origins—it would have been hard to justify a separate series on the "new American nation." But exciting recent work—for instance, on wartime mobilization and social change, or on the Americanization of republican ideology during the great era of state making and constitution writing—has opened up new vistas. Historians now generally agree that the revolutionary period saw far-reaching and profound changes, that is, a "great transformation," toward a more recognizably modern America. If the connections between this transformation and the actual unfolding of events often remain elusive, the historiographical quest for the larger meaning of the war and its aftermath has yielded impressive results.

To an important extent, the revitalization of scholarship on revolutionary and early national America is a tribute to the efforts and expertise of scholars working in other professional disciplines. Students of early American literature have made key contributions to the history of rhetoric, ideology, and culture; political scientists and legal scholars have brought new clarity and sophistication to the study of political and constitutional thought and practice in the founding period. Kermit L. Hall's superb Garland series, *United States Constitutional and Legal History* (20 volumes, 1985), is another fine resource for students and scholars interested in the founding. The sampling of recent work in various disciplines offered in these volumes gives a sense of the interpretative possibilities of a crucial period in American history that is now getting the kind of attention it has long deserved.

Peter S. Onuf

INTRODUCTION

The most exciting recent work on the American Revolution focuses on the evolution of political thought and practice. Challenging the interpretations of Charles Beard, Arthur Schlesinger, Sr., and other progressive historians who emphasized the primacy of material interests in the decision for independence, neo-Whig writers such as Edmund S. Morgan insisted that the Patriots' constitutional claims deserved to be taken seriously. The neo-Whigs' new insights reflected their sophisticated understanding of Anglo-American culture as well as a more balanced assessment of the actual costs of the British navigation system.

The culmination of neo-Whig revisionism came with the publication of Bernard Bailyn's influential *Ideological Origins of the American Revolution* (1967). Building on Caroline Robbins's study of eighteenth-century British oppositionists, Bailyn drew the diverse sources of radical thought into a coherent world view. Like the commonwealthmen, Patriot pamphleteers were self-conscious "republicans," obsessed with the destruction of liberty by civic corruption and despotic power. *Ideological Origins* reinvigorated the study of political and constitutional ideas by offering a compelling account of their uses in the process of revolutionary mobilization. Here, in what Robert Shalhope dubbed "The Republican Synthesis," was the apparent resolution of the historiographical split between "materialists" and "idealists." Ideas-in-action were social facts; the Revolutionaries' language mediated economic interests, social tensions, and principled commitments.

If Bailyn alerted his fellow Americanists to the importance of an Anglo-American republican tradition, J. G. A. Pocock traced Revolutionary political ideas back to the revival of classical thought in Renaissance Florence. His *Machiavellian Moment* (1975) is the great monument of republicanist scholarship, remarkable both for its conceptual sophistication as well as its capaciousness. While the republican revival provided the narrative framework for his study, Pocock's account accommodated a more forward-looking "commercial republicanism" as well as a strain of Calvinist evangelical thought that was particularly prevalent in the American colonies.

The republican synthesis has not gone unchallenged. Beginning in the late 1960s social historians operating within a neo-progressive paradigm began to question the appeal of republican arguments beyond educated elite groups. On closer examination, however, the premises of popular political action proved to be surprisingly congenial with elite republicanism: both were characterized by the idealization of the old order and a commitment to traditional corporatist values. A more recent and forceful challenge to the republican synthesis, represented here by Isaac Kramnick, asserted that the Revolutionaries were Lockean "liberals" whose deepest commitments were not to neoclassical conceptions of the republic, but rather to individual rights and private property. The neo-liberals rehabilitated Louis Hartz's seminal *Liberal Tradition in America* (1955) and combined it with a sophisticated understanding of the impulses and assumptions of enterprising Anglo-Americans.

The jury may still be out on the relative importance of "republican" and "liberal" language in the political discourse of the Revolutionary era: the current state of the debate can be assessed by proceeding to Volume 5, *The Federal Constitution*. Of course, the debate itself encourages a reductionist polarization of views that obscures the subtlety and complexity of the antagonists' positions. But one clearly salutary effect of this historiographical tempest has been to encourage some of the finest Revolutionary historians of the last generation to take ideas and language seriously. Ideological historians look for socio-political resonance and for connections between high politics and everyday life. Essays in this and later volumes thus explore the relations between the history of family and gender relations and the independence movement. And even while historians and political theories seek to assign priority to one strain of thought or another, they have illuminated a multiplicity of contemporaneous perspectives. These studies have in turn helped us understand how Americans of the Revolutionary generation saw themselves acting in history. The historical narratives that the Revolutionaries first constructed inaugurated a still-unfolding historiographical tradition.

Peter S. Onuf

ADDITIONAL READING

Bernard Bailyn. *The Ideological Origins of the American Revolution.* Cambridge: Harvard University Press, 1967.

Ruth H. Bloch. *Visionary Republic: Millenial Themes in American Thought, 1756–1800.* New York: Cambridge University Press, 1985.

Lester H. Cohen. *The Revolutionary Histories: Contemporary Narratives of the American Revolution.* Ithaca, NY: Cornell University Press, 1980.

Jack P. Greene, ed. *The Reinterpretation of the American Revolution*. New York: Harper & Row, 1968.

Louis Hartz. *The Liberal Tradition in America: An Interpretation of American Political Thought since the Revolution*. New York: Harcourt, Brace & World, 1955.

Cathy D. Matson and Peter S. Onuf. *A Union of Interests: Political and Economic Thought in Revolutionary America*. Lawrence: University Press of Kansas, 1990.

Edmund S. Morgan. *Inventing the People: The Rise of Popular Sovereignty in England and America*. New York: W. W. Norton, 1988.

—— and Helen M. Morgan. *The Stamp Act Crisis: Prologue to Revolution*. New York: Collier Books, 1953.

J. G. A. Pocock. *The Machiavellian Moment: Florentine Political Thought and the Atlantic Republican Tradition*. Princeton, NJ: Princeton University Press, 1975.

Caroline Robbins. *The Eighteenth Century Commonwealthman: Studies in the Transmission, Development and Circumstance of English Liberal Thought from the Restoration of Charles II until the War with the Thirteen Colonies*. Cambridge: Harvard University Press, 1959.

Gerald Stourzh. *Alexander Hamilton and the Idea of Republican Government*. Stanford, CA: Stanford University Press, 1970.

Alfred F. Young, ed. *The American Revolution: Explorations in the History of American Radicalism*. DeKalb: Northern Illinois University Press, 1976.

CONTENTS

Volume 1—The Revolution in American Thought

Winthrop D. Jordan, "Familial Politics: Thomas Paine and the Killing of the King, 1776," *Journal of American History*, 1973–74, 60(2):294–308.

Gerald Stourzh, "Reason and Power in Benjamin Franklin's Political Thought," *American Political Science Review*, 1953, 47:1092–1115.

Pauline Maier, "Reason and Revolution: The Radicalism of Dr. Thomas Young," *American Quarterly*, 1976, 28(2):229–249.

Lester H. Cohen, "Explaining the Revolution: Ideology and Ethics in Mercy Otis Warren's Historical Theory," *William and Mary Quarterly*, 1980, 37(2) (Third Series):200–218.

ACKNOWLEDGMENTS

Volume 1—The Revolution in American Thought

Louis Hartz, "American Political Thought and the American Revolution," *American Political Science Review*, 1952, 46(2):321–342. Reprinted with the permission of the American Political Science Association. Courtesy of Yale University Law Library.

Donald S. Lutz, "The Relative Influence of European Writers on Late Eighteenth-Century American Political Thought," *American Political Science Review*, 1984, 78(1):189–197. Reprinted with the permission of the American Political Science Association. Courtesy of Yale University Law Library.

Robert E. Shalhope, "Toward a Republican Synthesis: The Emergence of an Understanding of Republicanism in American Historiography," *William and Mary Quarterly*, 1972, 29(1) (Third Series):49–80. Originally appeared in the *William and Mary Quarterly*. Courtesy of Yale University Sterling Memorial Library.

Robert E. Shalhope, "Republicanism and Early American Historiography," *William and Mary Quarterly*, 1982, 39(2) (Third Series):334–356. Originally appeared in the *William and Mary Quarterly*. Courtesy of Yale University Sterling Memorial Library.

Linda K. Kerber, "The Republican Ideology of the Revolutionary Generation," *American Quarterly*, 1985, 37(4):474–495. Reprinted with the permission of the author, and the American Studies Association as publisher. Courtesy of Yale University Sterling Memorial Library.

Jean Yarbrough, "Federalism in the Foundation and Preservation of the American Republic," *Publius*, 1976, 6(3):43–60. Reprinted with the permission of the North Texas State University. Courtesy of *Publius*.

James T. Kloppenberg, "The Virtues of Liberalism: Christianity, Republicanism, and Ethics in Early American Political Discourse," *Journal of American History*, 1987, 74(1):9–33. Reprinted with the permission of the *Journal of American History*. Courtesy of Yale University Sterling Memorial Library.

J. G. A. Pocock, "Virtue and Commerce in the Eighteenth Century," *Journal of Interdisciplinary History*, 1972, 3(1):119–134. Reprinted with the permission of the Massachusetts Institute of Technology and the editors of the *Journal of Interdisciplinary History*. Courtesy of Yale University Sterling Memorial Library.

Ralph Lerner, "Commerce and Character: The Anglo-American as New-Model Man," *William and Mary Quarterly*, 1979, 36(1) (Third Series):3–26. Originally appeared in the William and Mary Quarterly. Courtesy of Yale University Sterling Memorial Library.

Isaac Kramnick, "Republican Revisionism Revisited," *American Historical Review*, 1982, 87(3):629–664. Reprinted with the permission of the

The American
Political Science Review

| VOL. XLVI | JUNE, 1952 | NO. 2 |

AMERICAN POLITICAL THOUGHT AND
THE AMERICAN REVOLUTION

LOUIS HARTZ

Harvard University

I

"The great advantage of the American," Tocqueville once wrote, "is that he has arrived at a state of democracy without having to endure a democratic revolution. . . ."[1] Fundamental as this insight is, we have not remembered Tocqueville for it, and the reason is rather difficult to explain. Perhaps it is because, fearing revolution in the present, we like to think of it in the past, and we are reluctant to concede that its romance has been missing from our lives. Perhaps it is because the plain evidence of the American revolution of 1776, especially the evidence of its social impact that our newer historians have collected, has made the comment of Tocqueville seem thoroughly enigmatic. But in the last analysis, of course, the question of its validity is a question of perspective. Tocqueville was writing with the great revolutions of Europe in mind, and from that point of view the outstanding thing about the American effort of 1776 was bound to be, not the freedom to which it led, but the established feudal structure it did not have to destroy. He was writing too, as no French liberal of the nineteenth century could fail to write, with the shattered hopes of the Enlightenment in mind. The American revolution had been one of the greatest of them all, a precedent constantly appealed to in 1793. In the age of Tocqueville there was ground enough for reconsidering the American image that the Jacobins had cherished.

Even in the glorious days of the eighteenth century, when America suddenly became the revolutionary symbol of Western liberalism, it had not been easy to hide the free society with which it started. As a matter of fact, the liberals of Europe had themselves romanticized its social freedom, which put them in a rather odd position; for if Reynal was right in 1772, how could Condorcet be right in 1776? If America was

[1] Alexis de Tocqueville, *Democracy in America*, ed. F. Bowen (Boston, 1873), Vol. 2, p. 123.

321

from the beginning a kind of idyllic state of nature, how could it suddenly become a brilliant example of social emancipation? Two consolations were being extracted from a situation which could at best yield only one. But the mood of the Americans themselves, as they watched the excitement of Condorcet seize the Old World, is also very revealing. They did not respond in kind. They did not try to shatter the social structure of Europe in order to usher in a Tenth and Final Epoch in the history of man. Delighted as they were with the support that they received, they remained, with the exception of a few men like Paine and Barlow, curiously untouched by the crusading intensity we find in the French and the Russians at a later time. Warren G. Harding, arguing against the League of Nations, was able to point back at them and say, "Mark you, they were not reforming the world."[2] And James Fenimore Cooper, a keener mind than Harding, generalized their behavior into a comment about America that America is only now beginning to understand: "We are not a nation much addicted to the desire of proselytizing."[3]

There were, no doubt, several reasons for this. But clearly one of the most significant is the sense that the Americans had themselves of the liberal history out of which they came. In the midst of the Stamp Act struggle, young John Adams congratulated his colonial ancestors for turning their backs on Europe's class-ridden corporate society, for rejecting the "canon and feudal law."[4] The pervasiveness of Adams' sentiment in American thought has often been discussed, but what is easily overlooked is the subtle way in which it corroded the spirit of the world crusader. For this was a pride of inheritance, not a pride of achievement; and instead of being a message of hope for Europe, it came close to being a damning indictment of it. It saturated the American sense of mission, not with a Christian universalism, but with a curiously Hebraic kind of separatism. The two themes fought one another in the cosmopolitan mind of Jefferson, dividing him between a love of Europe and fear of its "contamination"; but in the case of men like Adams and Gouverneur Morris, the second theme easily triumphed over the first. By the time the crusty Adams had gotten through talking to politicians abroad, he had buried the Enlightenment concept of an oppressed humanity so completely beneath the national concept of a New World that he was ready to predict a great and ultimate struggle between America's youth and Europe's decadence. As for Morris, our official ambassador

[2] *Rededicating America* (Indianapolis, 1920), p. 137.
[3] In J. L. Blau (ed.), *Social Theories of Jacksonian Democracy* (New York, 1947), p. 58.
[4] "Dissertation on the Canon and Feudal Law," in John Adams, *Works*, ed. C. F. Adams (Boston, 1856), Vol. 3, pp. 447–465.

to France in 1789, he simply inverted the task of the Comintern agent. Instead of urging the French on to duplicate the American experience, he badgered them by pointing out that they could never succeed in doing so. "They want an American constitution," he wrote contemptuously, "without realizing they have no Americans to uphold it."[5]

Thus the fact that the Americans did not have to endure a "democratic revolution" deeply conditioned their outlook on people elsewhere who did; and by helping to thwart the crusading spirit in them, it gave to the wild enthusiasms of Europe an appearance not only of analytic error but of unrequited love. Symbols of a world revolution, the Americans were not in truth world revolutionaries. There is no use complaining about the confusions implicit in this position, as Woodrow Wilson used to complain when he said that we had "no business" permitting the French to get the wrong impression about the American revolution. On both sides the reactions that arose were well-nigh inevitable. But one cannot help wondering about something else: the satisfying use to which our folklore has been able to put the incongruity of America's revolutionary role. For if the "contamination" that Jefferson feared, and that found its classic expression in Washington's Farewell Address, has been a part of the American myth, so has the "round the world" significance of the shots that were fired at Concord. We have been able to dream of ourselves as emancipators of the world at the very moment that we have withdrawn from it. We have been able to see ourselves as saviours at the very moment that we have been isolationists. Here, surely, is one of the great American luxuries that the twentieth century has destroyed.

II

When the Americans celebrated the uniqueness of their own society, they were on the track of a personal insight of the profoundest importance. For the nonfeudal world in which they lived shaped every aspect of their social thought: it gave them a frame of mind that cannot be found anywhere else in the eighteenth century, or in the wider history of modern revolutions.[6]

[5] Quoted in D. Walther, *Gouverneur Morris* (New York and London, 1934), p. 76.

[6] The term "feudal," of course, has a technical reference to the medieval period. What Tocqueville and Adams largely had in mind, and what I refer to here, is the decadent feudalism of the later period—the "corporate" society of Europe, as some historians of the eighteenth century have put it. It has often been noted that the nonexistence of a feudal tradition—save for scattered remnants of which most, to be sure, were abolished by the American revolution—has been the great distinguishing feature of American civilization. But no interpretation of American politics or American political thought has as yet been inspired by this observation. It is obvious that the development of liberalism without feudalism, the development of Locke, as it were, without the antagonism of Filmer

3

One of the first things it did was to breed a set of revolutionary thinkers in America who were human beings like Otis and Adams rather than secular prophets like Robespierre and Lenin. Despite the European flavor of a Jefferson or a Franklin, the Americans refused to join in the great Enlightenment enterprise of shattering the Christian concept of sin, replacing it with an unlimited humanism, and then emerging with an earthly paradise as glittering as the heavenly one that had been destroyed. The fact that the Americans did not share the crusading spirit of the French and the Russians, as we have seen, is already some sort of confirmation of this, for that spirit was directly related to the "civil religion" of Europe and is quite unthinkable without it. Nor is it hard to see why the liberal good fortune of the Americans should have been at work in the position they held. Europe's brilliant dream of an impending millennium, like the mirage of a thirst-ridden man, was inspired in large part by the agonies it experienced. When men have already inherited the freest society in the world, and are grateful for it, their thinking is bound to be of a solider type. America has been a sober nation, but it has also been a comfortable one, and the two points are by no means unrelated.

Sam Adams, for example, rejects the hope of changing human nature: in a mood of Calvinist gloom, he traces the tyranny of England back to "passions of Men" that are fixed and timeless.[7] But surely it would be unreasonable to congratulate him for this approach without observing that he implicitly confines those passions to the political sphere—the sphere of Parliaments, ministers, and Stampmasters—and thus leaves a social side to man which can be invoked to hold him in check. The problem was a different one for Rousseau and Marx, who started from the view that the corruption of man was complete, as wide as the culture in which he lived, with the result that revolutions became meaningless unless they were based on the hope of changing him. Here, obviously, is a place where the conclusions of political thought breathe a different spirit from the assumptions on which they rest. Behind the shining optimism of Europe, there are a set of anguished grievances; behind the sad resignation of America, a set of implicit satisfactions.

One of these satisfactions, moreover, was crucially important in developing the sober temper of the American revolutionary outlook. It was

---

and Maistre, is bound to raise a whole series of peculiar problems. One of the reasons for our failure to examine these problems is undoubtedly to be found in the academic separation of American from European history. Any attempt to follow up the nonfeudal nature of the American experience requires the interchangeable use of American and European data and the formulation of issues that tend to be unfamiliar to the American specialist.

[7] Samuel Adams, *Writings*, ed. F. H. Cushing (New York, 1904–08), Vol. 2, p. 164.

the high degree of religious diversity that prevailed in colonial life. This meant that the revolution would be led in part by fierce Dissenting ministers, and their leadership destroyed the chance for a conflict to arise between the worldly pessimism of Christianity and the worldly ambitions of revolutionary thought. In Europe, especially on the Continent, where reactionary church establishments had made the Christian concept of sin and salvation into an explicit pillar of the *status quo*, liberals were forced to develop a political religion, as Rousseau saw, if only in answer to it. The Americans not only avoided this compulsion; they came close, indeed, to reversing it. Here, above all in New England, the clergy was so militant that it was Tories like Daniel Leonard who were reduced to blasting it as a dangerous "political engine," a situation whose irony John Adams caught when he reminded Leonard that "in all ages and countries" the church is "disposed enough" to be on the side of conservatism.[8] Thus the American liberals, instead of being forced to pull the Christian heaven down to earth, were glad to let it remain where it was. They did not need to make a religion out of the revolution because religion was already revolutionary.

Consider the case of Rev. William Gordon of Roxbury. In 1774, when all of Boston was seething with resentment over the Port Bill, Gordon opened one of his sermons by explicitly reminding his congregation that there were "more important purposes than the fate of kingdoms" or the "civil rights of human nature," to wit, the emancipation of men from the "slavery of sin and Satan" and their preparation "for an eternal blessedness." But the Sons of Liberty did not rise up against him; they accepted his remarks as perfectly reasonable. For instead of trying to drug Bostonians with a religious opiate, Gordon proceeded to urge them to prepare for open war, delivering a blast against the British that the Tories later described as a plea for "sedition, rebellion, carnage, and blood."[9] When Christianity is so explosive, why should even the most ardent revolutionary complain if heaven is beyond his grasp?

Of course, the Gordons and the Mayhews of America were quite unaware that their work had this significance—the indirect significance of keeping political thought down to earth. If anything impressed them in their role as religious figures, it was undoubtedly the crusade they were carrying forward against the "popery" of the Anglican Tories—in other

[8] John Adams, *Works*, Vol. 4, p. 55.
[9] J. Thornton (ed.), *The Pulpit of the American Revolution* (Boston, 1876), pp. 196–7.
The point I am making here about America in contrast to Europe is much the same point that Halevy makes about England in contrast to the Continent. We must not, of course, confuse French and English thought on this score. But the role of nonconformity in discouraging the rise of political religions was actually more marked in America than it was in England.

words, what mattered to them was not that they were helping America to avoid the eighteenth century, but that they were helping it to duplicate the seventeenth. However, their achievement on the first count was actually far more important than their achievement on the second. The revolutionary attack on Anglicanism, with its bogy of a Bishop coming to America and its hysterical interpretation of the Quebec Act of 1774, was half trumped up and half obsolete; but the alliance of Christian pessimism with liberal thought had a deep and lasting meaning. Indeed, the very failure of the Americans to become seventeenth-century prophets like the English Presbyterians enhances this point considerably. For when we add to it the fact that they did not become latter-day prophets like the Jacobins and the Marxists, they emerge, if we wish to rank them with the great revolutionaries of modern history, as in a curious sense the most secular of them all.

Perhaps it was this secular quality that Joel Barlow was trying to describe when he declared, in a Fourth of July oration in Boston in 1778, that the "peculiar glory" of the American revolution lay in the fact that "sober reason and reflection have done the work of enthusiasm and performed the miracles of Gods."[10] In any case, there was something fateful about it. For if the messianic spirit does not arise in the course of a country's national revolution, when is it ever going to arise? The post-revolutionary age, as the experience of England, France, and even in some sense Russia shows, is usually spent trying to recuperate from its effects. The fact that the Americans remained politically sober in 1776 was, in other words, a fairly good sign that they were going to remain that way during the modern age which followed; and if we except the religiosity of the Civil War, that is exactly what happened. There have been dreamers enough in American history, a whole procession of "millennial Christians," as George Fitzhugh used to call them; but the central course of our political thought has betrayed an unconquerable pragmatism.

Sir William Ashley, discussing the origins of the "American spirit," once remarked that "as feudalism was not transplanted to the New World, there was no need for the strong arm of a central power to destroy it."[11] This is a simple statement, but, like many of Ashley's simple statements, it contains a neglected truth. For Americans usually assume that their attack on political power in 1776 was determined entirely by the issues of the revolution, when as a matter of fact it was pre-

[10] Quoted in H. Niles (ed.), *Principles and Acts of the Revolution in America* (New York, 1876), p. 56.

[11] *Surveys Historic and Economic* (London and New York, 1900), p. 406.

cisely because of the things they were not revolting against that they were able to carry it through. The action of England inspired the American colonists with a hatred of centralized authority; but had that action been a transplanted American feudalism, rich in the chaos of ages, then they would surely have had to dream of centralizing authority themselves.

They would, in other words, have shared the familiar agony of European liberalism—hating power and loving it too. The liberals of Europe in the eighteenth century wanted, of course, to limit power; but confronted with the heritage of an ancient corporate society, they were forever devising sharp and sovereign instruments that might be used to put it down. Thus while the Americans were attacking Dr. Johnson's theory of sovereignty, one of the most popular liberal doctrines in Europe, cherished alike by Bentham and Voltaire, was the doctrine of the enlightened despot, a kind of political deism in which a single force would rationalize the social world. While the Americans were praising the "illustrious Montesquieu" for his idea of checks and balances, that worthy was under heavy attack in France itself because he compromised the unity of power on which so many liberals relied. Even the English Whigs, men who were by no means believers in monarchical absolutism, found it impossible to go along with their eager young friends across the Atlantic. When the Americans, closing their eyes to 1688, began to lay the axe to the concept of parliamentary sovereignty, most of the Whigs fled their company at once.

A philosopher, it is true, might look askance at the theory of power the Americans developed. It was not a model of lucid exposition. The trouble lay with their treatment of sovereignty. Instead of boldly rejecting the concept, as Franklin was once on the verge of doing when he said that it made him "quite sick," they accepted the concept and tried to qualify it out of existence. The result was a chaotic series of forays and retreats in which a sovereign Parliament was limited, first by the distinction between external and internal taxation, then by the distinction between revenue and regulation, and finally by the remarkable contention that colonial legislatures were as sovereign as Parliament was. But there is a limit to how much we can criticize the Americans for shifting their ground. They were obviously feeling their way; and they could hardly be expected to know at the time of the Stamp Act what their position would be at the time of the first Continental Congress. Moreover, if they clung to the concept of sovereignty, they battered it beyond belief, and no one would confuse their version of it with the one advanced by Turgot or even by Blackstone in Europe. The meekness of the American sovereign testifies to the beating he had received. Instead of putting up a fierce and embarrassing battle against the limits of natural law and the separation of powers, as he usually did in the theories of Europe, he accepted those limits with a vast docility.

If we look at what happened to America's famous idea of judicial control when the physiocrats advanced it in France, we will get an insight into this whole matter. Who studies now the theory of legal guardianship with which La Rivière tried to bind down his rational and absolute sovereign? Who indeed remembers it? American students of the judicial power rarely go to Cartesian France to discover a brother of James Otis—and the reason is evident enough. When the physiocrats appealed to the courts, they were caught at once in a vise of criticism: either they were attacked for reviving the feudal idea of the *parlements* or they were blasted as insincere because they had originally advanced a despot to deal with the feudal problem. They had to give the idea up.[12] But in America, where the social questions of France did not exist and the absolutism they engendered was quite unthinkable, the claim of Otis in the Writs of Assistance Case, that laws against reason and the Constitution were "void" and that the "Courts must pass them into disuse," met an entirely different fate.[13] It took root, was carried forward by a series of thinkers, and blossomed ultimately into one of the most remarkable institutions in modern politics.

The question, again, was largely a question of the free society in which the Americans lived. Nor ought we to assume that its impact on their view of political power disappeared when war and domestic upheaval finally came. Of course, there was scattered talk of the need for a "dictator," as Jefferson angrily reported in 1782;[14] and until new assemblies appeared in most places, Committees of Public Safety had authoritarian power. But none of this went deep enough to shape the philosophic mood of the nation. A hero is missing from the revolutionary literature of America. He is the Legislator, the classical giant who almost invariably turns up at revolutionary moments to be given authority to lay the foundations of the free society. He is not missing because the Americans were unfamiliar with images of ancient history, or because they had not read the Harringtons or the Machiavellis and Rousseaus of the modern period. Harrington, as a matter of fact, was one of their favorite writers. The Legislator is missing because, in truth, the Americans had no need for his services. Much as they liked Harrington's republicanism, they did not require a Cromwell, as Harrington thought he did, to

---

[12] Cf. M. Einaudi, *The Physiocratic Doctrine of Judicial Control* (Cambridge, Mass., 1938).

[13] Quoted in John Adams, *Works*, Vol. 2, p. 522.

[14] Thomas Jefferson, *Writings*, ed. P. L. Ford (New York, 1892–99), Vol. 3, p. 231.

erect the foundations for it. Those foundations had already been laid by history.

The issue of history itself is deeply involved here. On this score, inevitably, the fact that the revolutionaries of 1776 had inherited the freest society in the world shaped their thinking in a most intricate way. It gave them, in the first place, an appearance of outright conservatism. We know, of course, that most liberals of the eighteenth century, from Bentham to Quesnay, were bitter opponents of history, posing a sharp antithesis between nature and tradition. And it is an equally familiar fact that their adversaries, including Burke and Blackstone, sought to break down this antithesis by identifying natural law with the slow evolution of the past. The militant Americans, confronted with these two positions, actually took the second. Until Jefferson raised the banner of independence, and even in many cases after that time, they based their claims on a philosophic synthesis of Anglo-American legal history and the reason of natural law. Blackstone, the very Blackstone whom Bentham so bitterly attacked in the very year 1776, was a rock on which they relied.

The explanation is not hard to find. The past had been good to the Americans, and they knew it. Instead of inspiring them to the fury of Bentham and Voltaire, it often produced a mystical sense of Providential guidance akin to that of Maistre—as when Rev. Samuel West, surveying the growth of America's population, anticipated victory in the revolution because "we have been prospered in a most wonderful manner."[15] The troubles they had with England did not alter this outlook. Even these, as they pointed out again and again, were of recent origin, coming after more than a century of that "salutary neglect" which Burke defended so vigorously. And in a specific sense, of course, the record of English history in the seventeenth century and the record of colonial charters from the time of the Virginia settlement provided excellent ammunition for the battle they were waging in defense of colonial rights. A series of circumstances had conspired to saturate even the revolutionary position of the Americans with the quality of traditionalism—to give them, indeed, the appearance of outraged reactionaries. "This I call an innovation," thundered John Dickinson, in his attack on the Stamp Act, "a most dangerous innovation."[16]

Now here was a frame of mind that would surely have troubled many of the illuminated liberals in Europe, were it not for an ironic fact. America piled on top of this paradox another one of an opposite kind,

[15] The Pulpit of the American Revolution, p. 311.
[16] John Dickinson, Writings, ed. P. L. Ford (Philadelphia, 1895), p. 316.

and thus as it were, by misleading them twice, gave them a deceptive sense of understanding.

Actually, the form of America's traditionalism was one thing, its content quite another. Colonial history had not been the slow and glacial record of development that Bonald and Maistre loved to talk about. On the contrary, since the first sailing of the *Mayflower*, it had been a story of new beginnings, daring enterprises, and explicitly stated principles—it breathed, in other words, the spirit of Bentham himself. The result was that the traditionalism of the Americans, like a pure freak of logic, often bore amazing marks of anti-historical rationalism. The clearest case of this undoubtedly is to be found in the revolutionary constitutions of 1776, which evoked, as Franklin reported, the "rapture" of European liberals everywhere. In America, of course, the concept of a written constitution, including many of the mechanical devices it embodied, was the end-product of a chain of historical experience that went back to the Mayflower Compact and the Plantation Covenants of the New England towns: it was the essence of political traditionalism.[17] But in Europe just the reverse was true. The concept was the darling of the rationalists—a symbol of the emancipated mind at work.

Thus Condorcet was untroubled. Instead of bemoaning the fact that the Americans were Blackstonian historicists, he proudly welcomed them into the fraternity of the illuminated. American constitutionalism, he said, "had not grown, but was planned"; it "took no force from the weight of centuries but was put together mechanically in a few years." When John Adams read this comment, he spouted two words on the margin of the page: "Fool! Fool!"[18] But surely the judgment was harsh. After all, when Burke clothes himself in the garments of Siéyès, who can blame the loyal rationalist who fraternally grasps his hand? The reactionaries of Europe, moreover, were often no keener in their judgment. They made the same mistake in reverse. Maistre gloomily predicted that the American Constitution would not last because it was created out of the whole cloth of reason.

But how then are we to describe these baffling Americans? Were they rationalists or were they traditionalists? The truth is, they were neither, which is perhaps another way of saying that they were both. For the war between Burke and Bentham on the score of tradition, which made a great deal of sense in a society where men had lived in the shadow of feudal institutions, made comparatively little sense in a society where

[17] Cf. B. F. Wright, Jr., "The Early History of Written Constitutions in America," in *Essays in History and Political Theory in Honor of Charles Howard McIlwain* (Cambridge, Mass., 1936), pp. 344 ff.

[18] Quoted in J. Shapiro, *Condorcet and the Rise of Liberalism* (New York, 1934), p. 223.

for years they had been creating new states, planning new settlements, and, as Jefferson said, literally building new lives. In such a society a strange dialectic was fated to appear, which would somehow unite the antagonistic components of the European mind; the past became a continuous future, and the God of the traditionalists sanctioned the very arrogance of the men who defied Him.

This shattering of the time categories of Europe, this Hegelian-like revolution in historic perspective, goes far to explain one of the enduring secrets of the American character: a capacity to combine rock-ribbed traditionalism with high inventiveness, ancestor worship with ardent optimism. Most critics have seized upon one or the other of these aspects of the American mind, finding it impossible to conceive how both can go together. That is why the insight of Gunnar Myrdal is a very distinguished one when he writes: "America is . . . conservative . . . . But the principles conserved are liberal and some, indeed, are radical."[19] Radicalism and conservatism have been twisted entirely out of shape by the liberal flow of American history.

III

What I have been doing here is fairly evident: I have been interpreting the social thought of the American revolution in terms of the social goals *it did not need to achieve*. Given the usual approach, this may seem like a perverse inversion of the reasonable course of things; but in a world where the "canon and feudal law" are missing, how else are we to understand the philosophy of a liberal revolution? The remarkable thing about the "spirit of 1776," as we have seen, is not that it sought emancipation but that it sought it in a sober temper; not that it opposed power but that it opposed it ruthlessly and continuously; not that it looked forward to the future but that it worshipped the past as well. Even these perspectives, however, are only part of the story, misleading in themselves. The "free air" of American life, as John Jay once happily put it, penetrated to deeper levels of the American mind, twisting it in strange ways, producing a set of results fundamental to everything else in American thought. The clue to these results lies in the following fact: the Americans, though models to all the world of the middle class way of life, lacked the passionate middle class consciousness which saturated the liberal thought of Europe.

There was nothing mysterious about this lack. It takes the contemptuous challenge of an aristocratic feudalism to elicit such a consciousness; and when Richard Price glorified the Americans because they were men

[19] *An American Dilemma* (New York, 1944), p. 7.

of the "middle state," men who managed to escape being "savage" without becoming "refined,"[20] he explained implicitly why they themselves would never have it. Franklin, of course, was a great American bourgeois thinker; but it is a commonplace that he had a wider vogue on this score in Paris and London than he did in Philadelphia; and indeed there is some question as to whether the Europeans did not worship him more because he seemed to exemplify Poor Richard than because he had created the philosophy by which Poor Richard lived. The Americans, a kind of national embodiment of the concept of the bourgeoisie, have, as Mr. Brinkmann points out,[21] rarely used that concept in their social thought, and this is an entirely natural state of affairs. Frustration produces the social passion, ease does not. A triumphant middle class, unassailed by the agonies that Beaumarchais described, can take itself for granted. This point, curiously enough, is practically never discussed, though the failure of the American working class to become class conscious has been a theme of endless interest. And yet the relationship between the two suggests itself at once. Marx himself used to say that the bourgeoisie was the great teacher of the proletariat.

There can, it is true, be quite an argument over whether the challenge of an American aristocracy did not in fact exist in the eighteenth century. One can point to the great estates of New York where the Patroons lived in something resembling feudal splendor. One can point to the society of the South where life was extraordinarily stratified, with slaves at the bottom and a set of genteel planters at the top. One can even point to the glittering social groups that gathered about the royal governors in the North. But after all of this has been said, the American "aristocracy" could not, as Tocqueville pointed out, inspire either the "love" or the "hatred" that surrounded the ancient titled aristocracies of Europe.[22] Indeed, in America it was actually the "aristocrats" who were frustrated, not the members of the middle class, for they were forced almost everywhere, even in George Washington's Virginia, to rely for survival upon shrewd activity in the capitalist race. This compulsion produced a psychic split that has always tormented the American "aristocracy"; and even when wealth was taken for granted, there was still, especially in the North, the withering impact of a colonial "character" that Sombart himself once described as classically bourgeois.[23] In Massachusetts Governor Hutchinson used to lament that a "gentleman" did

[20] *Observations on the Importance of the American Revolution* (London, 1785), p. 69.

[21] *Encyclopedia of Social Sciences* (New York, 1937), Vol. 2, p. 645. By the same logic, we have never had a "Liberal Party" in the United States.

[22] *Democracy in America*, Vol. 1, p. 58.

[23] W. Sombart, *Quintessence of Capitalism* (London, 1915), p. 306.

not meet even with "common civility" from his inferiors.[24] Of course, the radicals of America blasted their betters as "aristocrats," but that this was actually a subtle compliment is betrayed in the quality of the blast itself. Who could confuse the anger of Daniel Shays with the bitterness of Francis Place even in the England of the nineteenth century?

Thus it happened that fundamental aspects of Europe's bourgeois code of political thought met an ironic fate in the most bourgeois country in the world. They were not so much rejected as they were ignored, treated indifferently, because the need for their passionate affirmation did not exist. Physiocratic economics is an important case in point. Where economic parasites are few, why should men embark on a passionate search for the productive laborer? Where guild restrictions are comparatively slight and continental tariffs unknown, why should they embrace the ruthless atomism of Turgot? America's attack on the English Acts of Trade was couched in terms of Locke, not in terms of Quesnay; and though Franklin and Jefferson were much taken by the "modern economics," they did not, here as in certain other places, voice the dominant preoccupation of American thought. It had often been said, of course, that the Americans were passionately "laissez faire" in their thinking; but this is to confuse either bourgeois ease with bourgeois frustration or a hatred of absolute power with the very economic atomism which, in physiocratic terms, was allied to it. Turgot himself saw that the Americans did not long to smash a feudal world into economic atoms any more than they longed for a unified sovereign to accomplish this feat. A lover of the Americans who, like most European liberals, could not quite imagine life outside the *ancien régime*, he complained bitterly on both counts. His complaint on the count of sovereignty is legendary, but his complaint on the count of laissez faire has, alas, been entirely forgotten. This is because John Adams replied to the one in his *Defence of the Constitutions* but did not mention the other. And yet it appears in the same place, in Turgot's famous letter to Richard Price: *On suppose partout le droit de regler le commerce . . . tant on est loin d'avoir senti que la loi de la liberté entière de tout commerce est un corrollaire du droit de proprieté.*[25]

The lament of Turgot reveals that America's indifference to the bourgeois fixations of Europe had in itself a positive meaning: the failure to develop a physiocratic conscience led to a quiet and pragmatic outlook

---

[24] Quoted in V. Parrington, *Main Currents in American Thought* (New York, 1927–30), Vol. 1, p. 200.

[25] The letter, dated 1778, is printed in Price's *Observations*, p. 95. For a general discussion of the problem, see O. and M. Handlin, *Commonwealth: Massachusetts* (New York, 1947), and L. Hartz, *Economic Policy and Democratic Thought* (Cambridge, Mass., 1948).

on the question of business controls. This is the outlook that characterizes a whole mass of early economic legislation that American historians are now beginning to unearth in what should have been, reputedly, the most "laissez faire" country in the world.[26] But it is in connection with materialism and idealism, utilitarianism and natural law, that the inverted position of the Americans comes out most clearly. There was no Bentham, no Helvetius among the superlatively middle-class American thinkers. On the contrary, they stuck with Puritan passion to the dogma of natural law, as if an outright hedonism were far too crass for consideration. In a purely political sense this may be interesting, for the Americans, at least during the Stamp Act phase of their struggle, were fighting that corrupt system of parliamentary representation which in England Benthamism later rose to assail. But it is in terms of the wider significance of utility as an attack on feudal norms, as an effort to make of "business a noble life," as Crane Brinton has put it,[27] that America's indifference to it takes on its deepest meaning. Benjamin Franklins in fact, the Americans did not have to become Jeremy Benthams in theory. Unchallenged men of business, they did not have to equate morality with it. And this has been a lasting paradox in the history of American thought. The American tradition of natural law still flourishes after a century and a half of the most reckless material exploitation that the modern world has seen. A persistent idealism of mind, reflected in Emerson's remark that utilitarianism is a "stinking philosophy," has been one of the luxuries of a middle class that has never been forced to become class conscious.

But this is not all. If the position of the colonial Americans saved them from many of the class obsessions of Europe, it did something else as well: it inspired them with a peculiar sense of community that Europe had never known. For centuries Europe had lived by the spirit of solidarity that Aquinas, Bossuet, and Burke romanticized: an organic sense of structured differences, an essentially Platonic experience. Amid the "free air" of American life, something new appeared: men began to be held together, not by the knowledge that they were different parts of a corporate whole, but by the knowledge that they were similar participants in a uniform way of life—by that "pleasing uniformity of decent competence" which Crèvecoeur loved so much.[23] The Americans themselves were not unaware of this. When Peter Thacher proudly announced

[26] Some of the finest work on this subject is being done by Professor Carter Goodrich of Columbia. See his recent articles in the *Political Science Quarterly*.

[27] *Encyclopedia of Social Sciences*, Vol. 15, p. 199.

[28] M. G. Jean de Crèvecoeur, *Letters from an American Farmer* (London, 1926), p. 40.

that "simplicity of manners" was the mark of the revolutionary colonists,[29] what was he saying if not that the norms of a single class in Europe were enough to sustain virtually a whole society in America? Richard Hildreth, writing after the levelling impact of the Jacksonian revolution had made this point far more obvious, put his finger directly on it. He denounced feudal Europe, where "half a dozen different codes of morals," often in flagrant contradiction with each other, flourished "in the same community," and celebrated the fact that America was producing "one code, one moral standard, by which the actions of all are to be judged. . . ."[30] Hildreth knew that America was a marvellous mixture of many peoples and many regions, but he also knew that it was characterized by something more marvellous even than that: the power of the liberal norm to penetrate them all.

Now a sense of community based on a sense of uniformity is a deceptive thing. It looks individualistic, and in part it actually is. It cannot tolerate internal relationships of disparity, and hence can easily inspire the kind of advice that Professor Nettels once imagined a colonial farmer giving his son: "Remember that you are as good as any man— and also that you are no better."[31] But in another sense it is profoundly anti-individualistic, because the common standard is its very essence, and deviations from that standard inspire it with an irrational fright. The man who is as good as his neighbors is in a tough spot when he confronts all of his neighbors combined. Thus William Graham Sumner looked at the other side of Professor Nettels's colonial coin and did not like what he saw: "public opinion" was an "impervious mistress. . . . Mrs. Grundy held powerful sway and Gossip was her prime minister."[32]

Here we have the "tyranny of the majority" that Tocqueville later described in American life; here too we have the deeper paradox out of which it was destined to appear. Freedom in the fullest sense implies both variety and equality; but history, for reasons of its own, chose to separate these two principles, leaving the one with the old society of Burke and giving the other to the new society of Paine. America, as a kind of natural fulfillment of Paine, has been saddled throughout its history with the defect which this fulfillment involves, so that a country like England, in the very midst of its ramshackle class-ridden atmosphere, seems to contain an indefinable germ of liberty, a respect for the privacies of life, that America cannot duplicate. At the bottom of the

[29] Quoted in *Principles and Acts of the Revolution in America*, cited above (n. 8), p. 46.
[30] *Theory of Politics* (New York, 1854), p. 262.
[31] C. Nettels, *Roots of American Civilization* (New York, 1938), p. 315.
[32] Quoted in A. G. Keller (ed.), *The Challenge of Facts and Other Essays* (New Haven, 1914), p. 318.

American experience of freedom, not in antagonism to it but as a constituent element of it, there has always lain the inarticulate premise of conformity, which critics from the time of Cooper to the time of Lewis have sensed and furiously attacked. "Even what is best in America is compulsory," Santayana once wrote, "—the idealism, the zeal, the beautiful happy unison of its great moments."[33] Thus while millions of Europeans have fled to America to discover the freedom of Paine, there have been a few Americans, only a few of course, who have fled to Europe to discover the freedom of Burke. The ironic flaw in American liberalism lies in the fact that we have never had a real conservative tradition.

One thing, we might suppose, would shatter the unprecedented sense of uniform values by which the colonial American was beginning to live: the revolution itself. But remarkably enough, even the revolution did not produce this result; John Adams did not confront Filmer, as Locke did, or Maistre, as the followers of Rousseau did. He confronted the Englishmen of the eighteenth century; and most of these men, insofar as the imperial struggle went, themselves accepted the Lockean assumptions that Adams advanced. Nor did the American Tories, with the fantastic exception of Boucher, who stuck to his thesis that Filmer was still "unrefuted," confront him with a vision of life completely different from his own. Samuel Seabury and Joseph Galloway accepted the Lockean principles, even sympathized with the American case, insisting only that peaceful means be used to advance it. Among their opponents, indeed, there were few who would fundamentally deny the "self-evident" truths the Americans advanced in 1776. The liberals of Europe always had a problem on their hands, which they usually neglected, to be sure, of explaining how principles could be "self-evident" when there were obviously so many people who did not believe them. Circumstance nearly solved this problem for the Americans, giving them, as it were, a national exemption from Hume's attack on natural law—which may be one of the reasons why they almost invariably ignored it. When one's ultimate values are accepted wherever one turns, the absolute language of self-evidence comes easily enough.

This then is the mood of America's absolutism: the sober faith that its norms are self-evident. It is one of the most powerful absolutisms in the world, more powerful even than the messianic spirit of the Continental liberals which, as we saw, the Americans were able to reject. That spirit arose out of contact with an opposing way of life, and its very intensity betrayed an inescapable element of doubt. But the American absolutism, flowing from an honest experience with universality, lacked

---

[33] G. Santayana, *Character and Opinion in the United States* (New York, 1924), p. 210.

even the passion that doubt might give. It was so sure of itself that it hardly needed to become articulate, so secure that it could actually support a pragmatism which seemed on the surface to belie it. American pragmatism has always been deceptive because, glacier-like, it has rested on miles of submerged conviction, and the conformitarian ethos which that conviction generates has always been infuriating because it has refused to pay its critics the compliment of an argument. Here is where the joy of a Dewey meets the anguish of a Fenimore Cooper; for if the American deals with concrete cases because he never doubts his general principles, this is also the reason he is able to dismiss his critics with a fine and crushing ease. But this does not mean that America's General Will always lives an easy life. It has its own violent moments—rare, to be sure, but violent enough. These are the familiar American moments of national fright and national hysteria when it suddenly rises to the surface with a vengeance, when civil liberties begin to collapse, and when Cooper is actually in danger of going to jail as a result of the Rousseauian tide. Anyone who watches it then can hardly fail to have a healthy respect for the dynamite which normally lies concealed beneath the free and easy atmosphere of the American liberal community.

When we study national variations in political theory, we are led to semantic considerations of a delicate kind, and it is to these, finally, that we must turn if we wish to get at the basic assumption of American thought. We have to consider the peculiar meaning that American life gave to the words of Locke.

There are two sides to the Lockean argument: a defense of the state that is implicit, and a limitation of the state that is explicit. The first is to be found in Locke's basic social norm, the concept of free individuals in a state of nature. This idea untangled men from the myriad associations of class, church, guild, and place, in terms of which feudal society defined their lives; and by doing so, it automatically gave to the state a much higher rank in relation to them than ever before. The state became the only association that might legitimately coerce them at all. That is why the liberals of France in the eighteenth century were able to substitute the concept of absolutism for Locke's conclusions of limited government and to believe that they were still his disciples in the deepest sense. When Locke came to America, however, a change appeared. Because the basic feudal oppressions of Europe had not taken root, the fundamental social norm of Locke ceased in large part to look like a norm and began, of all things, to look like a sober description of fact. The effect was significant enough. When the Americans moved from that concept to the contractual idea of organizing the state, they were not conscious of having already done anything to fortify the state, but were conscious only that they were about to limit it. One side of Locke became virtually the whole of him. Turgot ceased to be a modification of Locke, and became, as he was for John Adams, the destruction of his very essence.

It was a remarkable thing—this inversion of perspectives that made the social norms of Europe the factual premises of America. History was on a lark, out to tease men, not by shattering their dreams, but by fulfilling them with a sort of satiric accuracy. In America one not only found a society sufficiently fluid to give a touch of meaning to the individualist norms of Locke, but one also found letter-perfect replicas of the very images he used. There was a frontier that was a veritable state of nature. There were agreements, such as the Mayflower Compact, that were veritable social contracts. There were new communities springing up *in vacuis locis*, clear evidence that men were using their Lockean right of emigration, which Jefferson soberly appealed to as "universal" in his defense of colonial land claims in 1774. A purist could argue, of course, that even these phenomena were not enough to make a reality out of the pre-social men that liberalism dreamt of in theory. But surely they came as close to doing so as anything history has ever seen. Locke and Rousseau themselves could not help lapsing into the empirical mood when they looked across the Atlantic. "Thus, in the beginning," Locke once wrote, "all the world was America. . . ."[34]

In such a setting, how could the tremendous, revolutionary social impact that liberalism had in Europe be preserved? The impact was not, of course, missing entirely; for the attack on the vestiges of corporate society in America that began in 1776, the disestablishment of the Anglican church, the abolition of quitrents and primogeniture, the breaking up of the Tory estates, tinged American liberalism with its own peculiar fire.[35] Nor must we therefore assume that the Americans had wider political objectives than the Europeans, since even their new governmental forms were, as Becker once said, little more than the "colonial institutions with the Parliament and king left out."[36] But after these cautions have been taken, the central point is clear. In America the first half of Locke's argument was bound to become less a call to arms than

[34] *Second Treatise on Civil Government* (Oxford, 1947), p. 29.
[35] The distinctive nature of these reforms is that they were a fulfillment of the past rather than, as in Europe, a revolt against it. The elimination of feudal vestiges in a society already under the dominion of liberalism is an entirely different matter from the introduction of liberalism in a society still heavily ridden by feudal forms. America's "social revolution" thus is not to be compared with the great social revolutions of Europe. I am reserving this general problem for another discussion.
[36] C. L. Becker, *Freedom and Responsibility in the American Way of Life* (New York, 1945), p. 16.

a set of preliminary remarks essential to establishing a final conclusion: that the power of the state must be limited. Observe how it is treated by the Americans in their great debate with England, even by original thinkers like Otis and Wilson. They do not lavish upon it the fascinated inquiry that we find in Rousseau or Priestley. They advance it mechanically, hurry through it, anxious to get on to what is really bothering them: the limits of the British Parliament, the power of taxation. In Europe the idea of social liberty is loaded with dynamite; but in America it becomes, to a remarkable degree, the working base from which argument begins.

Here, then, is the master assumption of American political thought, the assumption from which all of the American attitudes discussed in this essay flow: the reality of atomistic social freedom. It is instinctive to the American mind, as in a sense the concept of the polis was instinctive to Platonic Athens or the concept of the church to the mind of the middle ages. Catastrophes have not been able to destroy it, proletariats have refused to give it up, and even our Progressive tradition, in its agonized clinging to a Jeffersonian world, has helped to keep it alive. There has been only one major group of American thinkers who have dared to challenge it frontally: the Fitzhughs and Holmeses of the pre-Civil War South who, identifying slavery with feudalism, tried to follow the path of the European reaction and of Comte. But American life rode roughshod over them—for the "prejudice" of Burke in America was liberal and the positive reality of Locke in America transformed them into the very metaphysicians they assailed. They were soon forgotten, massive victims of the absolute temper of the American mind, shoved off the scene by Horatio Alger, who gave to the Lockean premise a brilliance that lasted until the crash of 1929.[37] And even the crash, though it led to a revision of the premise, did not really shatter it.

It might be appropriate to summarize with a single word, or even with a single sentence, the political outlook that this premise has produced. But where is the word and where is the sentence one might use? American political thought, as we have seen, is a veritable maze of polar contradictions, winding in and out of each other hopelessly: pragmatism and absolutism, historicism and rationalism, optimism and pessimism, materialism and idealism, individualism and conformism. But, after all, the human mind works by polar contradictions; and when we have evolved an interpretation of it which leads cleanly in a single direction, we may be sure that we have missed a lot. The task of the cultural analyst is

[37] I have sketched the main lines of this interpretation of Southern thought in "The Reactionary Enlightenment: Southern Political Thought before the Civil War," *Western Political Quarterly*, Vol. 5, pp. 31–50 (March, 1952).

not to discover simplicity, or even to discover unity, for simplicity and unity do not exist, but to drive a wedge of rationality through the pathetic indecisions of social thought. In the American case that wedge is not hard to find. It is not hidden in an obscure place. We find it in what the West as a whole has always recognized to be the distinctive element in American civilization: its social freedom, its social equality. And yet it is true, for all of our Jeffersonian nationalism, that the interpretation of American political thought has not been built around this idea. On the contrary, instead of interpreting the American revolution in terms of American freedom, we have interpreted it in terms of American oppression, and instead of studying the nineteenth century in terms of American equality, we have studied it in terms of a series of cosmic Beardian and Parringtonian struggles against class exploitation. We have missed what the rest of the world has seen and what we ourselves have seen whenever we have contrasted the New World with the Old. But this is a large issue, which brings us not only to the Progressive historians but to the peculiar subjectivism of the American mind that they reflect, and it is beyond the scope of our discussion here.

IV

The liberals of Europe in 1776 were obviously worshipping a very peculiar hero. If the average American had been suddenly thrust in their midst, he would have been embarrassed by the millennial enthusiasms that many of them had, would have found their talk of classes vastly overdone, and would have reacted to the Enlightenment synthesis of absolutism and liberty as if it were little short of dishonest doubletalk. Bred in a freer world, he had a different set of perspectives, was animated by a different set of passions, and looked forward to different goals. He was, as Crèvecoeur put it, a "new man" in Western politics.

But, someone will ask, where did the liberal heritage of the Americans come from in the first place? Didn't they have to create it? And if they did, were they not at one time or another in much the same position as the Europeans?

These questions drive us back to the ultimate nature of the American experience, and, doing so, confront us with a queer twist in the problem of revolution. No one can deny that conscious purpose went into the making of the colonial world, and that the men of the seventeenth century who fled to America from Europe were keenly aware of the oppressions of European life. But they were revolutionaries with a difference, and the fact of their fleeing is no minor fact: for it is one thing to stay at home and fight the "canon and feudal law," and it is another to leave it far behind. It is one thing to try to establish liberalism in the Old

World, and it is another to establish it in the New. Revolution, to bor-r⁓w the words of T. S. Eliot, means to murder and create, but the American experience has been projected strangely in the realm of creation alone. The destruction of forests and Indian tribes—heroic, bloody, legendary as it was—cannot be compared with the destruction of a social order to which one belongs oneself. The first experience is wholly external and, being external, can actually be completed; the second experience is an inner struggle as well as an outer struggle, like the slaying of a Freudian father, and goes on in a sense forever.[38] Moreover, even the matter of creation is not in the American case a simple one. The New World, as Lord Baltimore's ill-fated experiment with feudalism in the seventeenth century illustrates, did not merely offer the Americans a virgin ground for the building of a liberal system: it conspired itself to help that system along. The abundance of land in America, as well as the need for a lure to settlers, entered so subtly into the shaping of America's liberal tradition, touched it so completely at every point, that Sumner was actually ready to say, "We have not made America, America has made us."[39]

It is this business of destruction and creation which goes to the heart of the problem. For the point of departure of great revolutionary thought everywhere else in the world has been the effort to build a new

[38] Note the words of Goethe:

> Amerika, du hast es besser
> Als unser Kontinent, das Alte
> Hast keine verfallene Schloesser
> Und keine Basalte.
> Dich stoert nicht im Innern
> Zu lebendiger Zeit
> Unnuetzes Erinnern
> Und vergeblicher Streit.

[39] In *The Challenge of Facts and Other Essays,* p. 304. It will be seen that this analysis coincides to some extent with the much debated philosophy of Frederick Jackson Turner. The mistake of Turner was to miss the importance of the liberal ideas that the American settlers brought with them from the Old World and the East; nevertheless he seized upon an important truth when he emphasized the raw environment that they found. That feudalism could be established in Canada does not alter the fact that liberalism could be established much more easily in America because feudalism did not already exist. B. F. Wright, Jr., one of the earliest of the Turner critics, noted the significance of this factor of a new environment. Moreover, it cannot be denied that the abundance of land in America ʰelped to support a system of liberal individualism by giving it a solid economic basis. Turner, in other words, seized upon a half-truth, and the argument over his theory has tended to obscure it. The American liberal community arose out of what must be accounted one of the happiest coincidences of modern history: the interplay between the philosophy of liberalism and an almost actualized state of nature. I am indebted to Mr. Rush Welter for originally suggesting to me that the interpretation of American thought advanced here, based on the nonexistence of a feudal tradition, might serve to confirm in part Turner's famous and controversial insight.

society on the ruins of an old society, and this is an experience America has never had. Tocqueville saw the issue clearly, and it is time now to complete the sentence of his with which we began this essay: "The great advantage of the American is that he has arrived at a state of democracy without having to endure a democratic revolution; *and that he is born free without having to become so.*"

Born free without having to become so: this idea, especially in light of the strange relationship which the revolutionary Americans had with their admirers abroad, raises an obvious question. Can a people that is born free ever understand peoples elsewhere that have to become so? Can it ever lead them? Or to turn the issue around, can peoples struggling for a goal understand those who have inherited it? This is not a problem of antitheses such, for example, as we find in Locke and Filmer. It is a problem of different perspectives on the same ideal. But we must not for that reason assume that it is any less difficult of solution; it may in the end be more difficult, since antitheses define each other and hence can understand each other, but different perspectives on a single value may, ironically enough, lack this common ground of definition. Condorcet might make sense out of Burke's traditionalism, for it was the reverse of his own activism, but what could he say about Otis, who combined both concepts in a synthesis that neither had seen? America's experience of being born free has put it in a strange relationship to the rest of the world.

The Relative Influence of European Writers on Late Eighteenth-Century American Political Thought

DONALD S. LUTZ
University of Houston

Drawing upon a comprehensive list of political writings by Americans published between 1760 and 1805, the study uses a citation count drawn from these 916 items as a surrogate measure of the relative influence of European writers upon American political thought during the era. Contrary to the general tendencies in the recent literature, the results here indicate that there was no one European writer, or one tradition of writers, that dominated American political thought. There is evidence for moving beyond the Whig-Enlightenment dichotomy as the basis for textual analysis, and for expanding the set of individual European authors considered to have had an important effect on American thinking. Montesquieu, Blackstone, and Hume are most in need of upgrading in this regard. The patterns of influence apparently varied over the time period from 1760 to 1805, and future research on the relative influence of European thinkers must be more sensitive to this possibility.

The bicentennial of the American founding era has led to renewed interest in the origins and nature of American political thought. One aspect of this interest has been heightened concern with a thorny question that has exercised historians and political scientists for a good number of years—the relative influence of European thinkers on the American founders as they designed their political institutions at the state and national levels.

Shalhope (1972, 1982) has summarized the debate in two historiographical essays. What he calls the "orthodox" view held that John Locke's ideas dominated American political thought until Thomas Jefferson introduced the republican thought of the English Civil War authors during the post-Confederation period. Two writers frequently cited as prominent among the many holding to the orthodox view are Hartz (1955) and Becker (1958).

On the other hand, Robbins (1947), Rossiter (1953), and Adair (1956) were prominent in dissenting from the orthodox view and in pointing out the non-Lockean roots of our political tradition. In her book, *The Eighteenth Century Commonwealthman* (1959), Robbins argued for the importance of the English libertarian heritage to colonial and revolutionary Americans. Men such as Harrington, Milton, Sidney, Neville, Moles-

worth, and Trenchard and Gordon, she argued, had a central and continuing influence on early American political thought. The quickening interest in the topic on the part of historians produced many important contributions that did not directly support Robbins's work, but the work of others, including Main (1961), Levy (1960), Elkins and McKitrick (1961), Handlin and Handlin (1961), Miller (1961) and Pocock (1965, 1975) fleshed out the importance of English Whig thought.

Just when a new synthesis seemed needed, it was provided by Bailyn (1965, 1967; but see Pocock, 1981). Bailyn identified five major sources from which American colonists drew their political thinking—the writings of classical antiquity, the writings of Enlightenment rationalism, the tradition of English common law, the political and social theories of New England Puritanism (especially covenant theory), and the writers identified by Robbins as being associated with the English Civil War and Commonwealth period. According to Bailyn, this last group, the radical English Whigs, generated the perspective that brought order and synthesis to the other strands of writing, and more than any other source "shaped the mind of the American Revolutionary generation." Wood (1969) wrote a monumental study describing how this synthesis of ideas informed the events surrounding the writing of the constitutions between 1776 and 1789, and a new orthodoxy seemed firmly in place.

However, this new orthodoxy was soon subjected to methodological modifications that have called into question the supposed monolithic character of the republican synthesis stressed by Bailyn and Wood. The post-Bailyn tendency to

Received: March 1, 1983
Revision received: May 10, 1983
Accepted for publication: July 3, 1983

An earlier version of this article was presented at a Covenant Workshop sponsored by the Center for the Study of Federalism at Temple University, May, 1982.

189

use categories of European writers, sometimes referred to as "traditions," has continued to breed confusion as new categories are "discovered" or assembled. For example, Wills (1978) adds the Scottish Enlightenment as distinct from Bailyn's more general use of Enlightenment. Lundberg and May (1976) correctly note that the term Enlightenment is too broad and hides a great deal of variance in the authors subsumed by the category. They are led to break it into the First Enlightenment (with the likes of Montesquieu, Locke, and Pufendorf), the more radical Second Enlightenment (which includes Voltaire, Diderot, and Helvetius among others), and the Third Enlightenment (typified by Beccaria, Rousseau, Mably, and Raynal). Wills's Scottish Enlightenment becomes the category "Scottish Common Sense" in their schema, and they add the categories Deists and Near-Deists, Devotional and Apologetic, and Romantic. Lundberg and May, on the other hand, do not mention the categories of Common Law, Puritanism, or classical antiquity.

Nor does the use of general categories solve the problem of where many of the major European thinkers belong. Wills places Hume within the Scottish Common Sense tradition, Lundberg and May place him within the Second Enlightenment, and it is not entirely clear where Bailyn places him. Lundberg and May place Hobbes among the English Deists and Near-Deists, whereas Bailyn never clearly places him. Bailyn makes Locke an Enlightenment figure, Lundberg and May place Locke in the First Enlightenment, yet Wills correctly notes that Locke was very often linked by American readers with Algernon Sidney, the great Whig theorist. Without agreement on either a stable set of categories, or the placement of major writers in them, analysis of the relative influence of such "traditions" is problematic.

The prominent alternative of using close textual analysis on major American political writers still generally eschews arguing in terms of broad categories and focuses instead upon specific European writers. The unfortunate tendency here is to identify a single source as dominant. For example, investigations of the texts by Thomas Jefferson have variously concluded that he reflects the dominant influence of the Scottish Enlightenment (Wills, 1979), John Locke (Mahowy, 1979), or the negative influence of Montesquieu (Appleby, 1982). Madison either borrowed many of his ideas from Hume (Adair, 1956-1957), Locke (Devine, 1975), republicanism (Morgan, 1974), or, like Jefferson, wrote in reaction to Montesquieu (Morgan, 1974). We can even still be treated to close textual analysis that completely denies the influence of Whig political ideas on early American political thought (Schmitt & Webking, 1979).

Method of Analysis

If we are to make significant progress toward unravelling this matter of relative influence, it is essential that we move beyond close textual analysis that assumes discipleship on the part of the person whose text is under examination. It will no longer do to examine a text from the American founding era without considering the possibility of multiple influences. This requires more comprehensive identification of those who are candidates for having influenced American political writing. Otherwise we are left with the relatively fruitless debates between those who find one dominant influence as opposed to another, when there is a reasonable probability that the pattern of influence will be multiple and vary from text to text—even in those written by the same author. The purpose of this essay is to advance such a systematic identification of European writers who need to be taken into account.

Contrary to the general tendencies in the recent scholarly literature, the results here indicate that there was no one European writer, or one tradition of thought, that dominated American political reading and writing during the late 1700s. If there was one man read and reacted to by American political writers of all factions during all the stages of the founding era, it was probably not Locke but Montesquieu. As for the relative influence of the various intellectual traditions, the method used here cannot support either the radical English Whigs or the Enlightenment writers as more important—they look about equal in influence. However, there is strong evidence for moving beyond a Whig-Enlightenment dichotomy as the basis for debate on this issue. Debate in the future should include biblical and common law sources as well, just as the number of individual authors deemed important should probably be enlarged and their relative importance reassessed.

Several surrogate measures of influence have already been attempted. One was to examine the educational background of prominent American political writers such as Madison, Hamilton, and Jefferson (Myers, 1981; Wills, 1978). These attempts are limited to a few men, only a few texts, and marred by the assumption that exposure to one or two college instructors was decisive. Another surrogate measure was the examination of the library holdings of a few dozen prominent Americans (Colbourn, 1965). This approach suffered from the assumption that the critical men have been identified and was seriously marred by the assumption that all books in a person's collection were equally valuable to him. A more ambitious approach was to examine all of the booksellers' catalogues from the era, plus the institutional libraries (mainly colleges), library companies, and private libraries (Lundberg & May, 1976). Although a major advance, this expanded effort had the one major problem of not being able to tell us how widely a given volume was actually read. A more useful surrogate measure would be a count of how many times a given volume or author was cited, quoted, or paraphrased, since this would not only help to answer how widely a book was read but also how highly regarded it was.

Approximately ten years ago this author set out with Charles S. Hyneman to read comprehensively the political writings of Americans published between 1760 and 1805. This period was defined as the "founding era" during which the theory and institutions informing the state and national constitutions took final form. Reviewing an estimated 15,000 items, and reading closely some 2,200 items with explicitly political content, we identified and rated those with the most significant and coherent theoretical content. Included were all books, pamphlets, newspaper articles, and monographs printed for public consumption. Excluded was anything that remained private and so did not enter public consciousness, such as letters and notes. Essentially we exhausted all those items reproduced in collections published by historians, the newspapers available in the Library of Congress, the early American imprints held by the Lilly Library at Indiana University, the Huntington Library in San Marino, California, and the Library of Congress. Finally, we examined the two volumes of Shipton and Mooney, *National Index of American Imprints*, for items in the Evans collection of early American imprints on microcard.

The resulting sample has 916 items, which include 3,154 references to 224 different individuals. The sample includes all of the Anti-Federalist pieces identified by Storing (1981) plus 33 more, for a total of 197 Anti-Federalist pieces. It also includes 190 items written by Federalists. Most of these items are identified in Storing (1976); the rest can be found in Hyneman and Lutz (1983), which lists 515 pieces. Although not exhaustive, the sample is by far the largest ever assembled, and neither excludes nor emphasizes any point of view. Excluding the proceedings of legislatures and conventions, upon which the sample does not draw, the sample represents approximately one-third of all public political writings longer than 2,000 words published between 1760 and 1805. Also, the distribution of published writings during the era is roughly proportional to the number of citations for each decade.

A citation for purposes of the study is defined as any footnote, direct quote, attributed paraphrasing, or use of a name in exemplifying a concept or position. The primary assumption is that a citation indicates familiarity with the author being cited. Furthermore, it is assumed that the citation is made because potential readers are also likely to be so familiar. Thus, a citation count indirectly provides a sense of the relative frequency with which European authors were read.

Bailyn (1967) has pointed out that such citations and references in the political literature of the founding era often give the appearance of being more window dressing and that often they betray an incomplete understanding of the author or work being cited. Even in those instances where this is true, there must be some familiarity with the cited text on the part of the person writing the pamphlet, as well as some assumed familiarity on the part of potential readers of the pamphlet, if the window dressing is to make any sense. In short, using a citation count has an advantage over close textual analysis in that we can assume familiarity with the text being cited, whether or not the citation is theoretically serious, or whether or not the author has complete command of the text he is citing.

Another advantage is that a citation count need not distinguish between positive and negative citations; to cite another author in order to attack him still shows that the work has been read, and it also shows influence insofar as the cited author's categories of thought are being used. Locke responded negatively to Filmer. Hume responded negatively to Locke. Madison responded positively to certain aspects of Locke and Hume, and negatively to certain aspects of Montesquieu. In each case it is reasonable to assume that a negative citation represents as much familiarity as a positive citation with a cited work, and it is this familiarity we are seeking to establish.

Thus, "influence" is used here in a broad sense. Only close textual analysis can establish the presence of specific ideas in a text, and comparative textual analysis the probable source of the ideas. A weakness of the citation-count method is that it cannot distinguish among citations that represent the borrowing of an idea, the adapting of an idea, the approval of an idea, the opposition to an idea, or an appeal to authority. An advantage of a citation count is that this inability to distinguish the nature of a citation does not matter if all one is trying to do is systematically establish which European writers were consulted and with what frequency. The overview that results provides a good basis for guiding those engaged in close textual analysis to look for influences that might otherwise be missed. A citation count is also a good way of testing the adequacy of the various schemes that have been developed for categorizing European writers by those interested in the relative influence of various intellectual traditions on American political theory.

The basic categorization scheme used is that developed by Bailyn (1967). Although Bailyn's is one of the most prominent categorization schemes and is relatively noncontroversial, there is still room for argument. Where should Locke and Hume be placed? We might view them in one way today, but early American writers emphasized different works by them than we do, and thus viewed them in a way that might be difficult for us to appreciate. To minimize controversy, a citation count both by category and by major individual authors is provided.

The Pattern of Citations for the Entire Founding Era

If we ask what book was most frequently cited by Americans during the founding era, the answer somewhat surprisingly is: the Book of Deuteronomy. From Table 1 we can see that the biblical tradition is most prominent among the citations. Anyone familiar with the literature will know that most of these citations come from sermons reprinted as pamphlets; hundreds of sermons were reprinted during the era, amounting to at least 10% of all pamphlets published. These reprinted sermons accounted for almost three-fourths of the biblical citations, making this nonsermon source of biblical citations roughly as important as the Classical or Common Law categories. Since our concern in this essay is with sorting out the relative influence of European thinkers, the problem of how to count biblical citations is not important. It is relevant, nonetheless, to note the prominence of biblical sources for American political thought, since it was highly influential in our political tradition, and is not always given the attention it deserves (Lutz, 1980).

References to writers identified with the European Enlightenment are fairly constant throughout the 45-year founding era, but the mix of writers within this category changes significantly over the years. One major conclusion suggested by this study is that the relative prominence of a writer usually varies over time, and when discussing relative influence, we should, for example, distinguish the Revolutionary era from the era surrounding the writing of the United States Constitution.

For example, Montesquieu and Locke are very prominent during the 1760s, when the percentage of Enlightenment citations is highest. Together they account for over 60% of all references to Enlightenment thinkers. During the 1770s these two account for over 75% of all references to Enlightenment thinkers. However, the references to the two are structured in an interesting manner. References to Locke in the 1770s are found heavily in pieces justifying the break with England, whereas Montesquieu is cited heavily in pieces dealing with constitutional design. As the writing of state and national constitutions continues in the 1780s, Montesquieu increases in importance to the point where he accounts for almost 60% of all Enlightenment references. Meanwhile, Locke's rate of citation falls off drastically, never to return to prominence. After the writing of the national Constitution, references to Montesquieu also fall off and are limited primarily to pieces related to the writing of state constitutions during the 1790s. This pattern should not surprise us at all upon reflection. Locke is profound when it comes to the bases for establishing a government and for opposing tyranny, but has little to say about institutional design. Therefore his influence most properly lies in justifying the revolution and the right of Americans to write their own constitu-

Table 1. Distribution of Citations by Decade (%)

	1760s	1770s	1780s	1790s	1800-05	% of Total Number
Bible	24	44	34	29	38	34
Enlightenment	32	18	24	21	18	22*
Whig	10	20	19	17	15	18
Common Law	12	4	9	14	20	11
Classical	8	11	10	11	2	9
Peers	6	2	3	6	5	4
Other	8	1	1	2	2	2
	100%	100%	100%	100%	100%	100%
N	216	544	1306	674	414	3154

*If we break Bailyn's Enlightenment category into the three sub-categories described by Lundberg and May, the results are not significantly altered. The "First Enlightenment," dominated by Montesquieu, Locke, and Pufendorf, comprises 16% of all citations. The more radical writers of the "Second Enlightenment," men like Voltaire, Diderot, and Helvetius, garner 2% of the citations. The "Third Enlightenment," typified by Beccaria, Rousseau, Mably, and Raynal, receives 4% of the citations, to bring the total back to the 22% listed here.

Table 2. Most Cited Thinkers by Decade[a]

	1760s	1770s	1780s	1790s	1800-05	% of Total Number
Montesquieu	8	7	14	4	1	8.3
Blackstone	1	3	7	11	15	7.9
Locke	11	7	1	1	1	2.9
Hume	1	1	1	6	5	2.7
Plutarch	1	3	1	2	0	1.5
Beccaria	0	1	3	0	0	1.5
Trenchard & Gordon	1	1	3	0	0	1.4
Delolme	0	0	3	1	0	1.4
Pufendorf	4	0	1	0	5	1.3
Coke	5	0	1	2	4	1.3
Cicero	1	1	1	2	1	1.2
Hobbes	0	1	1	0	0	1.0
	33	25	37	29	32	32.4
Others	67	75	63	71	68	67.6
	100%	100%	100%	100%	100%	100.0%
N	216	544	1306	674	414	3154

[a]This table is limited to those who were cited at least 32 times, which is 1% of the total of 3,154 citations. The extra decimal point in the last column is to allow more precise recovery of the number of citations over the era, whereas all other percentages are rounded off to the nearest whole number to ease the viewing of the table. The use of 0% indicates fewer than .5% of the citations for a given decade.

tions rather than in the *design* of any constitution, state or national. Locke's influence has been exaggerated in the latter regard, and finding him hidden in passages of the U.S. Constitution is an exercise that requires more evidence than has hitherto ever been provided.

Montesquieu's prominence during the period of constitution writing is supplemented by the relative prominence of two other Enlightenment writers—Beccaria and deLolme (usually written Delolme). It is also during this period of constitution writing that a host of English Whig writers becomes prominent. "Cato" (Trenchard and Gordon), Hoadley, Bolingbroke, Price, Burgh, Milton, Rollin, Molesworth, Priestly, Macaulay, Sidney, Somers, Harrington, and Rapin were most heavily cited during the late 1770s and the 1780s. They are joined by other Enlightenment writers including Robertson, Grotius, Rousseau, Pope, Raynal, Mably, Burlamaqui, and Vattel. All in all, during the period of constitution writing the Enlightenment and Whig authors were cited about equally as a group, with the references to the Whigs spread over about three times as many authors. There is no Whig author to compare with Montesquieu for sheer volume or dominance of the category. Indeed, Montesquieu is almost without peer during the founding era for prominence, except for Blackstone.

Blackstone is the second most prominent secular writer during the founding era. He is cited well over two and a half times as often as Locke. Whereas Locke's pattern is toward relative prominence early during the founding era, falling off after the 1770s, Blackstone's pattern is that of increasing frequency of citation after the 1770s to achieve prominence late in the founding era. Hume follows a similar pattern. Both Blackstone and Hume are strong on governmental process and the operation and interaction of institutions. There is a certain logic, then, in their becoming prominent during the portion of the founding era when the operation, adjustment, and evolution of political institutions becomes of greater concern than their design. This is not to say that the matters of foundation and institutional design are never discussed by Blackstone and Hume, since they are. And the two are cited in this regard during the early years of the founding era. These two also become vehicles for extending Locke's visibility indirectly. Blackstone himself cites Locke a number of times, and certain of his institutional and procedural concepts seem to be grounded in Locke insofar as they are congruent with Locke's principles, or logically implied by Locke. Hume, on the other hand, was one of Locke's most severe critics. To a certain extent his work is in opposition to Locke and can be viewed as running contrary to some of the implications contained in Locke's writing.

There does not seem to be at this time any basis for explaining the pattern followed by citations to

Table 3. Ordering of Most Cited Thinkers, 1760-1805[a]

	(%)		(%)
1. Montesquieu	8.3	19. Shakespeare	.8
2. Blackstone	7.9	20. Livy	.8
3. Locke	2.9	21. Pope	.7
4. Hume	2.7	22. Milton	.7
5. Plutarch	1.5	23. Tacitus	.6
6. Beccaria	1.5	24. Coxe	.6
7. Trenchard & Gordon	1.4	25. Plato	.5
8. Delolme	1.4	26. Abbé Raynal	.5
9. Pufendorf	1.3	27. Mably	.5
10. Coke	1.3	28. Machiavelli	.5
11. Cicero	1.2	29. Vattell	.5
12. Hobbes	1.0	30. Petyt	.5
13. Robertson	.9	31. Voltaire	.5
14. Grotius	.9	32. Robison	.5
15. Rousseau	.9	33. Sidney	.5
16. Bolingbroke	.9	34. Somers	.5
17. Bacon	.8	35. Harrington	.5
18. Price	.8	36. Rapin	.5

[a]Includes all thinkers cited at least sixteen times (.5% out of the total number of 3,154 citations). These 36 names account for 47.8% of all citations.

Pufendorf and Coke during the era. The classics are cited rather consistently, although there is a sharp drop toward the end of the founding era. The category "Peers" is a bit of a misnomer; about a fifth of these citations concern Americans dead by the time they were cited, although all but a few wrote during the 1700s. The term "Peers" is used instead of "Americans" because during the 1760s almost all of the citations in this category are to members of the English Parliament or to articles and essays written by men in England. After 1770, about a third of the references are to documents such as a state constitution or a resolution passed by a state legislature. There is not one of prominence among those cited, in the sense that no one is cited very often. Benjamin Franklin gets a few references, as do Thomas Paine and

Thomas Jefferson, but it is a very diverse category.

The Pattern of Citations from 1787 to 1788

Tables 4 and 5 illustrate the pattern of citations surrounding the debate on the U.S. Constitution. The items from which the citations for these two tables are drawn come close to exhausting the literature written by both sides. The Bible's prominence disappears, which is not surprising since the debate centered upon specific institutions about which the Bible had little to say. The Anti-Federalists do drag it in with respect to basic principles of government, but the Federalists' inclination to Enlightenment rationalism is most evident here in their failure to consider the Bible

Table 4. Distribution of Citations:
Federalist Versus Antifederalist

	Federalist (%)	Antifederalist (%)	Total for 1780s (%)
Bible	0	9	34
Enlightenment	34	38	24
Whig	23	29	19
Common Law	8	12	9
Classical	33	9	10
Peers	1	2	3
Other	1	1	1
	100	100	100
N	164	364	1306

Table 5. Twenty Most Cited Thinkers: Federalist Versus Antifederalist

	Federalist (%)	Antifederalist (%)	Total for 1780s (%)
Montesquieu	29	25	14
Blackstone	7	9	7
Locke	0	3	1
Hume	3	1	1
Plutarch	7	0	1
Beccaria	0	4	3
Trenchard & Gordon	2	2	3
Delolme	0	6	3
Pufendorf	0	1	1
Coke	0	1	1
Cicero	0	1	1
Robertson	0	0	1
Licurgus	6	1	1
Mably	7	2	2
Grotius	5	0	1
Temple	5	1	1
Price	0	2	1
Addison	0	2	.5
Vattel	0	1	.5
Sidney	1	0	.5
	72	62	44.5
Other	28	38	55.5
	100	100	100.0
N	164	364	1306

relevant. Surprisingly, both sides use Enlightenment and Whig authors in about the same proportion.

Montesquieu is almost twice as prominent during the debate over the national Constitution as he is for the decade as a whole, and three to three-and-a-half times as prominent as he is for the entire era. Grotius and Mably are the only other Enlightenment figures mentioned prominently by the Federalists, whereas the Anti-Federalists use Delolme, Beccaria, Mably, Price, Vattel, Pufendorf, and Locke to their advantage. Among Whig writers, the Federalists favor Trenchard and Gordon, Temple, and Sidney, whereas the Anti-Federalists favor Price, Addison, and Trenchard and Gordon about equally. Despite these differences, the most interesting finding is how similar the Federalists and Anti-Federalists are in their citation patterns. Not only do we *not* find the Federalists inclined toward Enlightenment writers and the Anti-Federalists away from them, the Federalists sometimes cite Enlightenment writers while attacking them. For example, there is a lot of arguing against Montesquieu's dictum that republics must be small and homogeneous if they are to survive, while the Anti-Federalists cite Montesquieu with approval on this point.

The debate surrounding the adoption of the Constitution was fought out mainly in the context of Montesquieu, Blackstone, the English Whigs, and major writers of the Enlightenment. The Federalists also have a third of their references to classical thinkers, while the Anti-Federalists have an average level of such citations. The classical thinkers provided exemplars of practices, leaders, and behavior—often negative ones—but generally were not drawn upon for concepts, terms, and institutional analyses that are most appropriate to such a debate. Hence the Federalists cited most heavily Plutarch, not Aristotle, Plato, or Cicero.

Conclusions

There is hardly an historian or political scientist working in this area who would be surprised by the presence of Montesquieu in the citations, but his prominence turns out to be so great, and his appeal so wide across all factions, it is surprising that so little beyond Spurlin (1940) has been written about him in the American context. It is time to consider as carefully the influence of Montesquieu on specific political texts as we have sought the influence of Locke.

The prominence of Blackstone would come as a surprise to many, and he is the prime candidate for the writer most likely to be left out in any list of influential European thinkers. His work is not readily available in inexpensive form, but like Montesquieu he was cited frequently by all sides. A trenchant reference to Blackstone could quickly end an argument. Such a respected writer deserves a much closer look by those studying American political thought.

There is good reason to treat Locke's influence with greater care. Even though the motto *Locke et praeterea nihil* as it applies to eighteenth-century American political thought has been thoroughly discredited by historians, there is probably still a tendency to overestimate his importance. Furthermore, the Locke we read today was not the Locke generally read then. Today we are likely to read his *Second Treatise*, whereas during the founding era Americans were much more likely to read *An Essay Concerning Human Understanding*. References to Locke's *Second Treatise* often indicate a relative lack of understanding—as if they are relying more upon general hearsay that upon a direct reading. Indeed, Lundberg and May (1976) demonstrate that the two treatises had only about one-third the availability of *An Essay Concerning Human Understanding* from the libraries and booksellers of the era. The availability of the *Second Treatise* about matches that of Addison's *Evidences of the Christian Religion*, Pope's *Essay on Man*, or Wollaston's *The Religion of Nature Delineated*. There is no question that Locke was important for American political thought, but it needs to be placed in context and his influence more carefully assessed.

There is evidence that Hume should be considered about equal in influence to Locke, and that Hume is more important for theory surrounding the writing of constitutions when it comes to content. The Hume read then is also not the Hume we are likely to read today. Citations to his work come overwhelmingly from *The History of England* rather than from his *Essays and Treatises on Several Subjects* or his *Dialogues Concerning Natural Religion*. There is no doubt that his Essays and Treatises was highly influential on some Federalist minds, however, such as Madison's and Hamilton's, and the availability of this work precisely matched that of Locke's two treatises. Hume deserves a much more careful look. Beyond this, we need to pay more attention to a whole host of Enlightenment, Whig, and Common Law theorists. The 36 names listed in Table 3 are all possible candidates.

It is interesting that the writers of the so-called Scottish Enlightenment—Francis Hutcheson, David Hume, Adam Smith, Thomas Reid, and Adam Ferguson—are, with only one exception, not very prominent among the citations. In the case of Hume, we may today read him as a member of such a category, but Bailyn and others are probably correct when they say that Americans during the founding era often saw him as an exponent of Whig republicanism, or else as a covert Tory.

Finally, the patterns of influence apparently varied over time. The current literature is not sensitive to this possibility, and too often a close textual analysis of one or two documents written in, say, 1776 or 1788, allows the establishment of one European author's influence to stand for the entire era. We need to consider the extent to which the debate surrounding the adoption of the U.S. Constitution reflected different patterns of influence than did the debates surrounding the writing and adoption of the state constitutions, or the Revolutionary writing surrounding the Declaration of Independence. Examining more carefully the differences and similarities in such patterns should lead us to a firmer understanding of the intellectual divisions within American political thought at the time, divisions that increasingly appear to be more complex than is usually credited in recent political science literature.

References

Adair, D. "That politics may be reduced to a science": David Hume, James Madison, and the tenth Federalist. *Huntington Library Quarterly,* 1965-1957, *20,* 343-360.

Appleby, J. What is still American in the political philosophy of Thomas Jefferson? *William and Mary Quarterly,* 3d. Ser., 1982, *39,* 287-309.

Bailyn, B. (Ed.). *Pamphlets of the American Revolution, 1750-1776.* Cambridge, Mass.: Belknap Press, 1965.

Bailyn, B. *The ideological origins of the American Revolution.* Cambridge, Mass.: Belknap Press, 1967.

Becker, C. *The Declaration of Independence: a study in the history of ideas.* New York: Vintage, 1922.

Colbourn, H. T. *The lamp of experience.* Chapel Hill: University of North Carolina Press, 1965.

Devine, F. E. Absolute democracy or indefeasible right: Hobbes versus Locke. *The Journal of Politics,* 1975, *37,* 736-765.

Elkins, S., & McKitrick, E. The founding fathers: young men of the revolution. *Political science Quarterly,* 1961, *82,* 38-57.

Hamowy, R. Jefferson and the Scottish enlightenment: a critique of Garry Wills' *Inventing America: Jefferson's Declaration of Independence. William and Mary Quarterly,* 3d. Ser., 1979, *36,* 503-523.

Handlin, O., & Handlin, M. James Burgh and American revolutionary theory. Massachusetts Historical Society, *Proceedings,* 1961, *73,* 38-57.

Hartz, L. *The liberal tradition in America.* New York: Harcourt, Brace & Jovanovich, 1955.

Hyneman, C. S., & Lutz, D. S. (Eds.). *American political writing during the funding era, 1760-1805.* Indianapolis: Liberty Press, 1983.

Levy, L. *Legacy of suppression: freedom of speech and press in early American history.* Cambridge, Mass.: Harvard University Press, 1960.

Lundberg, D., & May, H. F. The enlightened reader in America. *American Quarterly,* 1976, *28* (special issue), 262-293.

Lutz, D. S. From covenant to constitution in American political thought. *Publius: The Journal of Federalism,* 1980, *10,* 101-133.

Main, J. T. *The Antifederalists.* Chapel Hill: University of North Carolina Press, 1961.

Miller, P. From the covenant to the revival. In J. W. Smith & A. L. Jamison (Eds.), *Religion in American life.* Vol. 1: *The shaping of American religion.* Princeton, N.J.: Princeton University Press, 1961.

Morgan, R. J. Madison's theory of representation in the tenth Federalist. *The Journal of Politics,* 1974, *36,* 852-885.

Myers, M., Jr. A source for eighteenth-century Harvard master's questions. *William and Mary Quarterly,* 3d. Ser., 1981, *38,* 261-267.

Pocock, J. G. A. Machiavelli, Harrington, and English political ideologies in the eighteenth century. *William and Mary Quarterly,* 3d Ser., 1965, *22,* 549-583.

Pocock, J. G. A. *The Machiavellian moment.* Princeton, N.J.: Princeton University Press, 1975.

Pocock, J. G. A. *The Machiavellian moment* revisited: a study in history and ideology. *Journal of World History,* 1981, *53,* 49-72.

Robbins, C. Algernon Sidney's *Discourses concerning government:* textbook of revolution. *William and Mary Quarterly,* 3d. Ser., 1947, *4,* 267-296.

Robbins, C. *The eighteenth century commonwealthman.* Cambridge, Mass.: Harvard University Press, 1959.

Rossiter, C. *Seedtime of the republic.* New York, 1953.

Schmitt, G. J., & Webking, R. H. Revolutionaries, Antifederalists, and Federalists: comments on Gordon Wood's understanding of the American founding. *The Political Science Reviewer,* 1979, *9,* 195-229.

Shalhope, R. E. Toward a republican synthesis: the emergence of an understanding of republicanism in American historiography. *William and Mary Quarterly,* 3d. Ser., 1972, *29,* 49-80.

Shalhope, R. E. Republicanism and early American historiography. *William and Mary Quarterly,* 3d. Ser., 1982, *39,* 334-356.

Shipton, C. K., and Mooney, J. E. (Eds.). *National index of American imprints through 1800: the short-title Evans* (2 vols.). Barre, Mass.: American Antiquarian Society and Barre Publishers, 1969.

Spurlin, P. M. *Montesquieu in America, 1760-1801.* Baton Rouge: Louisiana State University Press, 1940.

Storing, H. J. The "other" Federalist Papers. *The Political Science Reviewer,* 1976, *6,* 215-247.

Storing, H. J., with Dry, M. *The complete Anti-Federalist.* Chicago: University of Chicago Press, 1981.

Wills, G. *Inventing America: Jefferson's Declaration of Independence.* Garden City, N.J.: Doubleday, 1978.

Wood, G. S. *The creation of the American republic, 1776-1787.* Chapel Hill: University of North Carolina Press, 1969.

Toward a Republican Synthesis: The Emergence of an Understanding of Republicanism in American Historiography

Robert E. Shalhope*

THE effect upon American intellectual history of the symbolic statement, *Locke et praeterea nihil*, has been both profound and unfortunate.[1] That popular formula has helped to obscure an understanding of early American thought by obstructing a full appreciation of the vital shaping role of republicanism. Only within the last decade have historians clearly discerned the unique and dynamic qualities of republicanism in the period 1760 to 1789. Their efforts represent the culmination of a long, slow process, and implications arising from this work have yet to be extended to other periods of American history. It should prove fruitful, then, to trace this evolution of ideas in order to perceive those important strands of thought that can be drawn together into a tentative synthesis. Hopefully, this "republican synthesis" will shed new light upon early American history and provide insights for future research.

A brief explication of the ideas of George M. Dutcher reveals the older view of republicanism in America.[2] Dutcher, in an essay published

* Mr. Shalhope is a member of the Department of History, University of Oklahoma. The author wishes to thank his colleagues David W. Levy and Robert A. Nye for their suggestions on points of analysis in the article.

[1] In the present essay this phrase denotes the frame of reference that for so long dominated studies of American thought and may be referred to as the "orthodox" position of republicanism. Stanley Katz claims that *"Locke et praeterea nihil*, it now appears, will no longer do as a motto for the study of eighteenth-century Anglo-American political thought." "The Origins of Constitutional Thought," *Perspectives in American History*, III (1969), 474. J. G. A. Pocock believes that "it is clear that the textbook account of Augustan political thought as *Locke et praeterea nihil* badly needs revision." "Machiavelli, Harrington, and English Political Ideologies in the Eighteenth Century," *William and Mary Quarterly*, 3d Ser., XXII (1965), 551.

[2] Scholarly works propounding the traditional position are legion. Dutcher's essay is singled out only because it presents the orthodox view so succinctly and is cited so often by later authors. Other examples include Merle Curti, *The Growth*

in 1940, maintained that Americans in 1776 had little if any knowledge
of past republics and that consideration of these was "clearly irrelevant to
the discussion of the origins of republican institutions in America."[3] After
discussing the ideas of the English Civil War, Dutcher contended that
"republican and democratic ideas of that revolutionary period passed into
unpopularity and oblivion with the Restoration in 1660, not to be revived
and repopularized until the nineteenth century."[4] While Dutcher felt
that Americans did draw upon the English Bill of Rights and the ideas
of John Locke, he held that between the English Civil War and the
American Revolution "republican ideas were practically taboo and no
direct contribution to their development was made except by Algernon
Sidney."[5] Believing this, Dutcher could confidently affirm that "available
evidence indicates clearly that republican government in America developed in 1775 and 1776 from political necessity and not from political
theory or public agitation, exactly as in England in 1649, and apparently,
without any recognition of the precedent."[6] He then concluded that
"popular acceptance of republican government and devotion to it were,
however, primarily the work of the twelve years from 1789 to 1801.... It
was the genius of Jefferson, in the great struggle between the Federalists
and his followers, that focused American opinion against monarchy and
in favor of republicanism."[7]

The salient characteristics of the orthodox view emerge from Dutcher's essay: Republican authors of importance were those of the English
Civil War, but their ideas were dead until after the American Revolu-

---

of American Thought (New York, 1943); Zera S. Fink, The Classical Republicans:
An Essay in the Recovery of a Pattern of Thought in Seventeenth Century England
(Evanston, Ill., 1945); Correa Moylan Walsh, The Political Science of John Adams:
A Study in the Theory of Mixed Government and the Bicameral System (New
York, 1915); Randolph Greenfield Adams, Political Ideas of the American Revolu-
tion (Durham, N. C., 1922); Andrew C. McLaughlin, The Foundations of Ameri-
can Constitutionalism (New York, 1932); C. Edward Merriam, A History of
American Political Thought (New York, 1903); Benjamin Fletcher Wright, Ameri-
can Interpretations of Natural Law: A Study in the History of Political Thought
(Cambridge, Mass., 1931); and Carl Becker, The Declaration of Independence: A
Study in the History of Political Ideas (New York, 1922).

³ "The Rise of Republican Government in the United States," Political Science
Quarterly, LV (1940), 199-216. The quotation is on pp. 199-200.

⁴ Ibid., 203.

⁵ Ibid., 204.

⁶ Ibid., 205.

⁷ Ibid., 215.

tion; John Locke's ideas dominated American thought; and the great impetus to republicanism came from Thomas Jefferson in the post-Confederation period. Scholars assumed that republicanism represented simply a form of government; no hint of republicanism as a dynamic ideology assuming moral dimensions and involving the very character of American society appeared in these early studies.

Seven years after the appearance of Dutcher's article Caroline Robbins published an essay initiating an approach which would gradually erode the orthodox position. She contended that Sidney's ideas did not die with him in 1683, but instead were taken up by radical whigs such as Robert Molesworth, John Toland, Thomas Gordon, John Trenchard, Richard Baron, and Thomas Hollis.[8] While these men did not affect English politics, they did manage to transmit their libertarian heritage to America where it acquired great vitality.

Robbins felt that radicals or revolutionaries could find greater sustenance in Sidney's *Discourses* than in Locke's more temperate *Essays*. By the 1770s Englishmen, eager for accommodation and harmony, came to view Sidney either as irrelevant or dangerous and thus his ideas lost their popularity. The opposite took place in America: As tension mounted between mother country and colony Sidney's belief in restricted sovereignty and resistance to power became critical elements in American thought. These ideas emanated from his contention that the people were sovereign and must protect that sovereignty against incursions by their leaders. Since power always corrupted, the people must erect safeguards to ensure that magistrates did not encroach upon their sovereignty and thus deprive them of their liberties. Robbins delivered a trenchant observation when she noted that "the debt of English reformers to America, and of America to the men who failed to impose their ideas on England in 1689, has not yet been properly assessed. English and American intellectual history from 1640 to 1840 needs rewriting between the covers of one book."[9] While it would be years before other scholars took up this challenge, Robbins made an important contribution to scholarship by initiating a move toward understanding English libertarian thought and indicating its influence in America.

In 1950 Robbins added substance to her earlier insight in a discussion

[8] "Algernon Sidney's *Discourses Concerning Government:* Textbook of Revolution," *Wm. and Mary Qtly.*, 3d Ser., IV (1947), 267-296.
[9] *Ibid.*, 273.

of Thomas Hollis (1720-1774), who spent the greater part of his life disseminating throughout the world books, medals, and coins that would foster liberty.[10] It was, however, a peculiar kind of liberty that he desired to stimulate; his was the liberty of ancient republics reflected in the writing of Milton, Marvell, and others. The great fear in Hollis's mind was that the vast new prosperity being enjoyed by England would be her downfall just as luxury had caused the political decline of the ancient republics. Public virtue and private frugality seemed to be the only way to avoid this impending danger. The best way for a people to maintain their liberties was to guard them carefully and have frequent parliamentary elections in order to enforce restraints upon their rulers.

Robbins made it explicit that Hollis's peculiar brand of liberty struck a responsive chord in America. That these ideas reached America was certain; the question of what shape they assumed there she left unanswered; her primary concern, after all, was to understand the English Commonwealthmen. Nonetheless, she had made another contribution through further explication of libertarian thought and by noting its passage to America.

Historians directing their efforts to American thought received a boost from an essay on the Tenth *Federalist* by Douglass Adair in which he maintained that the work of Charles A. Beard and other progressive historians had cast a shadow over study of the Constitution—and by implication over all of early American history—by minimizing the importance of ideas and ideological factors.[11] Adair held that political ideas and philosophies were central to the writing of both *Federalist* Number Ten and the Constitution and that Madison's Tenth *Federalist* was "eighteenth-century political theory directed to an eighteenth-century problem; and it is one of the great creative achievements of that intellectual movement that later ages have christened 'Jeffersonian democracy.' "[12] Adair's

---

[10] "The Strenuous Whig, Thomas Hollis of Lincoln's Inn," *Wm. and Mary Qtly.*, 3d Ser., VII (1950), 406-453. The editors of the *Quarterly* noted that this essay was one of a series being printed to better illuminate the relationship between whig thought and the American Revolution. These included Robbins's earlier essay on Algernon Sidney; Peter Laslett, "Sir Robert Filmer: The Man versus the Whig Myth," *ibid.*, V (1948), 523-546; Lucy Martin Donnelly, "The Celebrated Mrs. Macaulay," *ibid.*, VI (1949), 173-207; and Felix Gilbert, "The English Background of American Isolationism in the Eighteenth Century," *ibid.*, I (1944), 138-160.

[11] "The Tenth Federalist Revisited," *ibid.*, VIII (1951), 48-67.

[12] *Ibid.*, 67.

essay assumes importance not because it clearly delineated eighteenth-century American thought, but because it helped to shift attention toward ideological factors in the creation of the Constitution and in the understanding of early American society.

It must be emphasized that historians, while beginning to analyze intellectual factors, were still wrestling with separate and distinct strands of thought that lacked an integrative frame of reference. Carl Cone mentioned English radical thought in a book published in the early 1950s, but the relationship between English and American ideas remained unclear.[13] Historians could gain from Cone's work the knowledge that Price—and by implication other English radicals—exerted a great influence upon American thought, but the nature of that thought and the form it took in America remained vague. The fact that scholarship relative to English and American thought progressed along parallel rather than convergent paths caused this lack of clarity to persist.[14]

This predicament became obvious in 1954 with the appearance of essays by Neal Riemer and Caroline Robbins. Riemer contended that James Madison was best understood in the light of his complete dedication to republicanism rather than through any pursuit of economic interests.[15] He presented a sophisticated analysis of Madison's struggles with problems confronting and confounding those who would establish a republican form of government and offered sound evidence that "Republican ideology—not economic interest, not social class, not sectional outlook—[was] the key to his [Madison's] political thought and actions."[16] While Riemer

[13] *Torchbearer of Freedom: The Influence of Richard Price on Eighteenth Century Thought* (Lexington, Ky., 1952).

[14] This same vagueness permeated Clinton Rossiter's massive *Seedtime of the Republic: The Origins of the American Tradition of Political Liberty* (New York, 1953). Rossiter claimed that *Cato's Letters*, written by John Trenchard and Thomas Gordon, were far more influential in America than Locke's *Two Treatises on Civil Government* and that Locke's role had been greatly overemphasized (p. 141), yet he vacillated between this position and one lauding Locke's influence (pp. 328, 358). In an article published the same year and also incorporated in the book Rossiter portrayed Richard Bland as "the whig in America" yet made no mention of libertarian thought. Bland was a Lockean whig, not at all like Trenchard or Gordon. "Richard Bland: The Whig in America," *Wm. and Mary Qtly.*, 3d Ser., X (1953), 33-79. Clearly Rossiter recognized, or at the very least suspected, the libertarian influence, yet its impact in America remained blurred.

[15] "The Republicanism of James Madison," *Pol. Sci. Qtly.*, LXIX (1954), 45-64; Riemer, "James Madison's Theory of the Self-Destructive Features of Republican Government," *Ethics*, LXV (1954), 34-43.

[16] Riemer, "Republicanism of Madison," *Pol. Sci. Qtly.*, LXIX (1954), 63.

recognized that republicanism was a motivating force in Madison's life, he did not discuss the content of that ideology. To Riemer, as to those before him, republicanism represented only the allegiance to a specific form of government. Riemer also tended to reinforce the orthodox belief that republicanism gained its greatest strength from Jeffersonian democracy, for while he substituted Madison for Jefferson, the result was identical. Thus, although Riemer ably refuted Beard and supported an emphasis upon republicanism, just what "republicanism" was remained unclear.

In an essay on Francis Hutcheson Caroline Robbins refined her analysis of radical English thought, but at the same time moved further away from its American implications.[17] Hutcheson was intimately associated with Robert Molesworth, whom Robbins described as "the catalytic agent in the transfusion of the ideas of the English classical republicans with the philosophic and political theories of his own time."[18] Through Molesworth and others—Benjamin Hoadley, Trenchard, Gordon, Moyle—Hutcheson soaked himself in the dissenting tradition, which struggled to keep alive the ideas of Harrington, Sidney, Marvell, and others of the Commonwealth period. Hutcheson's friendship with Molesworth began at the very time when the latter was supporting the right of resistance, agitating for an equitable redistribution of parliamentary seats, and struggling against the corruption and luxury he perceived around him. Molesworth's *An Account of Denmark* taught Hutcheson that people who did not constantly guard their liberties were bound to lose them.

Hutcheson's *System of Moral Philosophy* constituted his greatest philosophical contribution, for in that work he revealed his controlling belief that virtue and happiness were closely related and that virtue must be cultivated above all else in any society. He wholeheartedly endorsed the right of resistance to a power which was subverting the good society, since he believed that governments existed only to further the common good, not to exalt a few.

In evaluating Hutcheson's significance Robbins emphasized that his thought represented the product of the total environment into which he

---

[17] " 'When It Is That Colonies May Turn Independent': An Analysis of the Environment and Politics of Francis Hutcheson (1694-1746)," *Wm. and Mary Qtly.*, 3d Ser., XI (1954), 214-251.

[18] *Ibid.*, 239.

had been born and in which he lived rather than being reflective of his single genius. She explicitly demonstrated the emergent dissenting tradition in England and the "mind set" being transferred to America. The outlines of republicanism as it would emerge in America could be seen in Hutcheson's analysis of moral philosophy; while Robbins did not make this point, her work contributed fertile ideas that could be taken up by scholars when they directed their attention to America and accordingly to the form dissenting thought would take in a different culture.

Two other works published in 1954 began to draw a connection between English and American thinkers, but again the exact nature of the thought and the connection lacked clarity. Through a study of the political and religious reform societies flourishing in England, Nicholas Hans identified English radicals such as Joseph Priestley, Price, and others, and demonstrated concrete connections between these men and Benjamin Franklin and Jefferson.[19] In his *Benjamin Franklin and American Foreign Policy* (Chicago, 1954) Gerald Stourzh hinted that many of the ideas commonly circulating in America were drawn from English radicals, but he did not develop this insight. Both works underscored the fact that a frame of reference regarding English radical ideas and American revolutionary thought was yet to be established.

An essay by Cecelia Kenyon exhibited this same handicap, although it is a tribute to the brilliance of this scholar that she was able to study the institutional nature of antifederalist thought as incisively as she did without the benefit of this frame of reference.[20] Kenyon's analysis represented a major step toward understanding the ideological nature of the dispute between the Federalists and antifederalists, which had been so badly obscured by Beard and his followers. Kenyon viewed the fundamental issue separating these two groups as the question of whether a republican government could be extended over a vast area. To her the antifederalists, rather than being the democrats pictured by Beard, were conservative "men of little faith" who drew upon the thought of Montesquieu and clung tenaciously to the ideas of the past; rather it was the Federalists who "created a national framework which would accommodate

---

[19] "Franklin, Jefferson, and the English Radicals at the End of the Eighteenth Century," American Philosophical Society, *Proceedings*, LXXXVIII (1954), 406-426.
[20] "Men of Little Faith: The Anti-Federalists on the Nature of Representative Government," *Wm. and Mary Qtly.*, 3d Ser., XII (1955), 3-43.

the later rise of democracy."[21] While Kenyon shed new light upon the dispute between the Federalists and antifederalists, there were two problems to which she did not address herself. First, she identified the antifederalists solely with Montesquieu rather than making any connection with the dissenting tradition. Second, she did not see that both the Federalists and antifederalists drew their ideas from a common source, and thus she failed to inquire into what caused the Federalists to deviate from the original mode of thought while the antifederalists clung so desperately to the ways of the past. Her insight into institutional thought revealed a great need for an understanding of republican ideology as it emerged in America; such a comprehension would allow the scholar to deal with both the Federalists and the antifederalists within a common framework.

In an essay dealing with James Madison and the Tenth *Federalist* in which he explicitly held the Federalists to have been motivated by ideological rather than economic factors, Douglass Adair implied the existence of such a common frame of reference.[22] Adair contended that Madison's use of history in the Constitutional Convention did not represent "mere rhetorical-historical window-dressing, concealing substantially greedy motives of class and property" and analyzed Madison's intellectual struggle with Montesquieu, showing how, drawing upon David Hume, he worked to fashion a republican form of government that encompassed the entire nation.[23] In his Tenth *Federalist* Madison turned Montesquieu on his head by showing that stability—that most precarious commodity in a republican government—could be better achieved in a large geographic area by checking factions against each other within a vitalized federalism.

It remained to be demonstrated why Madison felt the need for a vitalized federalism; to show that he thought as a political scientist and not as a class-conscious elitist did not explain why he behaved as he did. Nonetheless, Adair's article represented an important step toward a republican synthesis, because it established Madison's concern for re-

[21] *Ibid.*, 43.

[22] " 'That Politics May Be Reduced to a Science': David Hume, James Madison, and the Tenth *Federalist*," *Huntington Library Quarterly*, XX (1956-1957), 343-360.

[23] *Ibid.*, 347. It is clear that Adair did not recognize the libertarian heritage, but, nonetheless, he did see that Madison worked from a body of knowledge shared with antifederalists.

publicanism and showed that he reasoned within this context. What was still lacking was a sophisticated understanding of the context; republicanism was yet to be clearly defined other than simply as a form of government. It was still not perceived as a pervasive political ideology.

H. Trevor Colbourn drew much closer to an understanding of American republicanism in an essay dealing with Thomas Jefferson's vital interest in history.[24] Colbourn pointed out that Jefferson was not drawn equally to all history, but rather to "Whig history." An avid scholar of Thomas Gordon's translation of Tacitus, Catherine Macaulay's *History of England, Cato's Letters,* and the writings of James Burgh, Jefferson immersed himself in whig thought. Drawing upon this persuasion in his *Summary View of the Rights of British America,* Jefferson held that Americans, by resisting British tyranny, stood for their rights as transplanted Englishmen just as the dissenting radicals stood against the corruption and decadence that seemed to be taking England away from her true ideals. Thus Colbourn identified a persistent and enduring motivating force in Jefferson's life—and certainly by implication in the lives of thousands of other Americans—long before he forged "Jeffersonian democracy." While Colbourn did not make explicit reference to the libertarian heritage or to American republicanism—neither being clearly discernible at this point in scholarly research—his essay did provide the rudiments of an understanding by historians that a republican political ideology was developing in pre-Revolutionary America. American historiography still lacked a clear definition of the heritage upon which Americans drew and the shape republicanism would assume, but the former was not long in coming.

In 1959 Caroline Robbins published *The Eighteenth-Century Commonwealthman.*[25] This book represents a turning point in the effort to understand American republicanism since Robbins fully developed her earlier observations and precisely delineated the English libertarian heritage upon which Americans drew so heavily. Through a discussion of the ideas of individual Commonwealthmen from Neville through Joseph Priestley, Robbins revealed the libertarian thrust which was responsible for keeping alive the ideas of Harrington, Nedham, Milton, Ludlow, Sidney, Neville,

[24] "Jefferson's Use of the Past," *Wm. and Mary Qtly.,* 3d Ser., XV (1958), 56-70.
[25] *The Eighteenth-Century Commonwealthman: Studies in the Transmission, Development, and Circumstances of English Liberal Thought from the Restoration of Charles II until the War with the Thirteen Colonies* (Cambridge, Mass., 1959).

and Marvell. These "Real Whigs," who admired the Leveller inheritance but tempered it with an admiration for the English Constitution, could only view the development of the Cabinet as a threat to the balance of the Constitution. They believed in the separation of powers of the three branches and rotation in office, and urged parliamentary reform, the redistribution of seats, and annual parliaments. They struggled for freedom of thought and for the sovereignty of the people in the face of what they considered increasing corruption and tyranny by both the monarch and Parliament.

While no attempt will be made to summarize the entirety of this work, certain strains of thought that shed light upon American republicanism should be mentioned. Robert Molesworth's *An Account of Denmark* constituted one of the strongest warnings that people must constantly guard their liberties. The quickest way to forfeit cherished liberties was to fail to call ministers and kings to account. Molesworth's clearest warning, however, was against an institution that would be the bane of republicanism: the standing army. The people must be ever wary of the establishment of a standing army, for it was through such a device that kings and ministers most often deprived the people of their rights. In its stead militias composed of the people were the safest method to defend a country against both foreign enemies and domestic tyrants.

These same ideas permeated the work of John Trenchard and Thomas Gordon. In *Cato's Letters* and *The Independent Whig*—both of which circulated widely in America and were to be of the utmost importance in the creation of American republicanism—the authors emphasized the necessity for discussing everything political as well as religious. They believed that all men were naturally good and that citizens became restless only when oppressed. Every man should act according to his own conscience, judge when a magistrate had done ill, and should possess the right of resistance. Without this right man could not defend his liberty. *Cato* paired liberty and equality, and the preservation and extension of liberty became all important. Since the greatest danger to the liberty and thus to the equality of the people came from their leaders, the people must constantly be wary of men coming to power, being corrupted by it, and stealthily usurping power and liberty from the people.

For the development of an understanding of American republicanism, Robbins's book is of utmost importance, for it thoroughly explored the thought upon which Americans drew and began the essential historical shift away from Locke. A prominent scholar would later note this shift and observe that "the state of nature, doctrine of consent, and theory of natural rights were not as important, before 1776, as the ideas of mixed government, separation of powers, and a balanced constitution. The preservation of individual liberty through careful engineering of governmental structure was the dominant concern of political theorists in the new world and the old."[26] With this set of ideas, moreover, there evolved a peculiar way of viewing society, its people, and its rulers. It was this peculiar view of society that demanded study, since this constituted the heart of American republicanism.

The same year that Robbins's book appeared Colbourn published an article dealing with John Dickinson that demonstrated the growing historical awareness of the English experience.[27] As in his earlier article on Jefferson, Colbourn showed Dickinson's reliance upon whig history and the whig interpretation of the English past: Dickinson was particularly drawn to *Cato's Letters*, which described the failure of the eighteenth-century English to reclaim their Saxon heritage. "Instead," Colbourn observed, "contemporary England was frequently shown racing toward economic, moral, and political collapse, ridden with corruption, and afflicted with an unrepresentative Parliament."[28] Dickinson's reading of the libertarians gave him a "disturbing portrait of a mother country on the high road to ruin, oblivious of her ancestral liberties, and mostly unaware that the way to salvation lay in a return to Saxon simplicity, with annually elected and uncorrupted parliaments, and a people's militia rather than a dangerous and expensive standing army."[29]

The composite picture drawn by these writers received reinforcement through Dickinson's personal observation during his tenure at the Middle Temple, and so his anxiety over conditions in England in the 1750s could only turn to outright alarm in the 1760s when English colonial policy appeared to change drastically. Dickinson's reading, now reinforced

---

[26] Katz, "Origins of Constitutional Thought," *Perspectives*, III (1969), 474.

[27] "John Dickinson, Historical Revolutionary," *Pennsylvania Magazine of History and Biography*, LXXXII (1959), 271-292. Colbourn is clearly aware of Robbins's interpretation by this point and notes that her "forthcoming book" would discuss writers of the whig persuasion who were influential in America (p. 273, n. 6).

[28] *Ibid.*, 283.

[29] *Ibid.*

through correspondence with Catherine Macaulay and James Burgh, heightened this anxiety since it appeared that the mother country was now attempting to spread her own decadence and corruption to America. These views shaped Dickinson's response to British actions throughout the 1760s and 1770s and permeated his writing. A consistent theme ran throughout his work: Americans were Englishmen struggling to maintain English (Saxon) liberties against usurpers.

The significance of this essay for the emergence of an understanding of republicanism lies in the clear connection made between the libertarian persuasion and American thought and action. This was, however, simply a beginning, since it still remained necessary to clarify the form republicanism assumed in America. It could not be presumed that English libertarian ideas transferred to the colonies intact, and so the process of transformation and clarification they underwent in America still existed to challenge scholars.

In the early 1960s historians more clearly delineated the nexus between English libertarian thought and the American experience while making tentative gestures toward understanding the dynamics of that thought. Leonard Levy discussed the American reliance upon *Cato's Letters* in his analysis of freedom of speech and the press in early America while Jackson Turner Main made the libertarian heritage central to his discussion of the antifederalists.[30] Main, believing that the antifederalists drew upon "left-wing Whiggism," tied them to the libertarian heritage and cogently discussed *Cato's Letters* and the work of James Burgh. He recognized the Commonwealthman's suspicion of the evil effects of power and the consequent warning for the people to maintain a vigilant watch over their elected leaders. From these basic beliefs, he maintained, stemmed the antifederalists' desire to keep power responsive to the people through frequent elections, rotation in office, and reliance upon the lower house of the legislature where leaders could be more closely watched. Oppression could be avoided by tying the government more closely to the people and by denying it easily abused powers.

Although Main made excellent use of the libertarian heritage and aided in clarifying its connection to American thought, he also tended to obscure future research on republicanism. By tying the antifederalists

[30] Levy, *Legacy of Suppression: Freedom of Speech and Press in Early American History* (Cambridge, Mass., 1960); Jackson Turner Main, *The Antifederalists: Critics of the Constitution, 1781-1788* (Chapel Hill, N. C., 1961).

to the Commonwealthmen Main attempted to make the former great democrats. However, in so doing he clouded a more important issue: What was the Federalists' response to this same body of thought? This question could only appear irrelevant to Main since he did not believe that the Federalists drew upon this persuasion. Main inadvertently read history backward: He observed that the antifederalists drew heavily upon the libertarians and that the Federalists did not and concluded that only the antifederalists responded to these ideas. The problem was that he observed Federalist behavior after the fact—that is, after they had begun a transformation in their thought and had altered libertarian ideas—and thus Main failed to attain a full understanding of the influence of republicanism in America by making it the sole possession of one faction instead of an ideology that permeated all of American society.

In the same year that Main's work appeared Stanley Elkins and Eric McKitrick, Oscar and Mary Handlin, and Perry Miller published essays that contributed to the emergence of a republican synthesis.[31] The Elkins and McKitrick article posed the important question of why the Federalists and antifederalists split; the Handlins presented a superb analysis of the thought of James Burgh and its impact in America; and Miller's essay injected a vital word of caution for historians to avoid becoming too secular in their analyses of early America.

Elkins and McKitrick, while never explicitly discussing republicanism, maintained that the variance between the Federalists and antifederalists did not hinge upon disagreements over "democracy," but rather over differences in their willingness to see republican government extended beyond state boundaries. The chief disparity lay "in the Federalists' conviction that there was such a thing as national interest and that a government could be established to care for it which was fully in keeping with republican principles."[32] The authors added to an understanding

[31] Stanley Elkins and Eric McKitrick, "The Founding Fathers: Young Men of the Revolution," *Pol. Sci. Qtly.*, LXXVI (1961), 181-216; Oscar and Mary Handlin, "James Burgh and American Revolutionary Theory," Massachusetts Historical Society, *Proceedings*, LXXIII (1961), 38-57; Perry Miller, "From the Covenant to the Revival," in James Ward Smith and A. Leland Jamison, eds., *Religion in American Life*. Vol. I: *The Shaping of American Religion* (Princeton, N. J., 1961), 322-368.

[32] Elkins and McKitrick, "Founding Fathers," *Pol. Sci. Qtly.*, LXXVI (1961), 201.

of the Confederation period by indicating that for the Federalists this was indeed a "critical period," because, imbued with a vision of a prospering republican nation and committed to its survival, they felt that the government must be restructured if this was to be the case. The authors—while not casting direct light upon republicanism—noted that both sides adhered to a single ideology and so directed attention to the need to analyze both the Federalists and antifederalists within the same intellectual framework.

Oscar and Mary Handlin studied James Burgh's impact upon American revolutionary theory and posited that Burgh's perceptive insights into the evils of eighteenth-century English society caused him to be avidly read by Americans. He and his coterie of friends believed that the corruption they saw all about them had perverted politics. Burgh's concern with moral issues led him into a moral view of politics and the belief that the prerequisite to change was a nationwide moral regeneration. All of his writings rang with the call for a rebirth. The essential first step in such a process—the only way to save England from tyranny or anarchy—was to institute a government that truly represented all the people.

The Handlins believed that the ease and assurance with which Americans employed Burgh's ideas was the result of "a significant congruence between Burgh's ideas on government and those which the colonists had developed out of other sources in other ways."[33] This observation disclosed a concept of importance: While Americans made great use of Burgh's thought, his ideas did not cross the Atlantic intact. Americans adapted his conceptions—ideas about consent, constitution, liberty—to their specific and concrete problems, so that even when the same words were used, and the same formal principles adhered to, novel circumstances transformed their meaning. The Handlins considered Burgh a significant aid in discerning those elements of distinctiveness: "Precisely because he was not a great theorist, he reflected the attitudes of a particular time and place. By virtue of his situation, he was as close to American thought as any European of his time; and the differences between his ideas and those of the colonists who read him illuminated an important facet of the development of the 'American mind.'"[34] Thus, the Handlins suggested a critical element for understanding American

[33] Handlin and Handlin, "James Burgh," Mass. Hist. Soc., *Proceedings*, LXXIII (1961), 52.
[34] *Ibid.*, 57.

republicanism: Americans drew fully upon English ideas—especially libertarian ones—but while doing so, created a unique mode of thought. While the Handlins did not address themselves to the concept of republicanism, their essay did lend support to the thesis that a unique ideology emerged in America, an ideology that historians would soon recognize as republicanism.

Perry Miller's essay "From the Covenant to the Revival" is of great importance in understanding republicanism in America, for by carefully examining the Puritan jeremiad Miller cautioned scholars not to become too secular in their search for the dynamic qualities of the American mind. While not addressing himself directly to republican ideology, Miller discussed elements that permeated it, especially the belief that America was unique—a city on a hill—and constantly in need of re-vitalization. This dark view of the present, accompanied by a desperate sense of urgency, pervaded the "republican jeremiads" of John Taylor of Caroline and other later republicans. These constituted legacies of Puritan thought which Miller knew to be a vital part of the American mind that emerged between the Revolution and the Civil War. Puritanism, with its heavy emphasis upon regeneration, strenuous morality, and a sense of community, prepared the way for republicanism.

In 1962 Cecelia Kenyon made another contribution to the emerging republican synthesis.[35] Her "old-fashioned" interpretation of the American Revolution maintained that one of the profound changes wrought by that movement was the establishment of republican governments in place of monarchical ones.[36] She then noted another change that provided perceptive insight into American thought: Americans developed an ideo-

[35] It should not be presumed that the "emerging republican synthesis" represented a goal toward which the authors under discussion consciously strove; nor should it be presumed to be the only "synthesis" that could be drawn from research being undertaken throughout the 1950s and 1960s. Merrill Jensen's *The New Nation: A History of the United States During the Confederation, 1781-1789* (New York, 1950); Elisha P. Douglass's *Rebels and Democrats: The Struggle for Equal Political Rights and Majority Rule During the American Revolution* (Chapel Hill, N. C., 1955); and Jack P. Greene's *The Quest for Power: The Lower Houses of Assembly in the Southern Royal Colonies, 1689-1776* (Chapel Hill, N. C., 1963) are only a few of the outstanding treatments of the period that do not fit the republican synthesis. Greene presents an excellent analysis of the "neo-whig" school of Revolutionary historiography in "The Flight from Determinism: A Review of Recent Literature on the Coming of the American Revolution," *South Atlantic Quarterly*, LXI (1962), 235-259.

[36] "Republicanism and Radicalism in the American Revolution: An Old-Fashioned Interpretation," *Wm. and Mary Qtly.*, 3d Ser., XIX (1962), 153-182.

logical attachment to republicanism. Good government had come to mean republican government. If this ideological attachment to republicanism represented a break with the past, it also carried with it far-reaching consequences for the future, since the "ideological habit thus acquired has been extended to other areas and has become a major factor in American political thinking. Like republicanism, socialism, imperialism, and colonialism are all terms which have become stereotypes for Americans, frequently exercising a powerful ideological force at odds with our alleged pragmatism."[37] These observations regarding the doctrinaire quality of American republicanism added a significant perspective to the study of that ideology and its role in early American society.

Two years after the appearance of Kenyon's article Richard Buel published an essay central to an understanding of the emergence of republicanism.[38] Discussing the same problem as Kenyon—democracy—Buel contended that Americans relied on sources in addition to Montesquieu whom her research had stressed nearly to the exclusion of all others. Buel, believing that historians had despaired unduly of finding a point of departure from which to assess the meaning of the revolutionary experience, maintained that the English dissenting tradition constituted the common initial frame of reference for American intellectuals.[39]

Just as the Commonwealthmen found themselves forced to rely heavily upon the power of the people, so too did Americans; and "like all eighteenth-century English thinkers the provincial leadership sought to control power by limiting and dividing it."[40] While this principle was not unique, the scope with which Americans applied it certainly was. Most important, "rather than confine the balance of the constitution to the autonomous composition of the supreme power, to the parliamentary components of king, Lords, and Commons, Americans turned to a conception of balance between two broad, countervailing forces in political society, the rulers and the ruled."[41] Only in such an elaboration of the relationship between rulers and ruled could Americans define an arrange-

---

[37] *Ibid.*, 167.

[38] "Democracy and the American Revolution: A Frame of Reference," *Wm. and Mary Qtly.*, 3d Ser., XXI (1964), 165-190.

[39] *Ibid.*, 166-167. Buel's discussion of the "dissenting tradition" was drawn specifically from Robbins's work.

[40] *Ibid.*, 168.

[41] *Ibid.*

ment "whereby society might benefit from the exercise of power without suffering from its corresponding abuses."[42]

The people expressed their power over their rulers through representation, and Buel presented a cogent analysis of this process as well as its implications, the most important of which was that Americans entered the Revolution with the assumption that the "power the people did possess was not designed to facilitate the expression of their will in politics but to defend them from oppression."[43] Here Buel revealed a valuable point: Americans entered the Revolution armed with a common set of assumptions stemming from a negative view of government. Government was something to be carefully watched and restricted, not a dynamic force in society.

While Buel's analysis of the common point of departure in American Revolutionary thought constituted an important contribution, his concluding remarks were even more provocative. He believed that the dissenting tradition, which undergirded American thought, underwent subtle transformations as Americans found themselves forced to respond to the logic of revolutionary events. With this observation Buel cut to the heart of the problem which had eluded so many previous scholars: What caused men starting with a common intellectual heritage to pursue separate paths? While Buel did not answer this, his essay, by establishing an initial point of departure, made it easier for future scholars to pose more penetrating questions in directing their own research. Further, Buel's essay provided an additional impetus for scholars to turn their attention toward the unique frame of mind that emerged when power seemed not to be balanced between a triumvirate of king, Lords, and Commons, but between the people and their rulers.

This frame of mind became much clearer in 1965 with the publication of the initial volume of Bernard Bailyn's *Pamphlets of the American Revolution, 1750-1776* (Cambridge, Mass., 1965), the most important single statement of the new synthesis.[44] Bailyn finally made clear the shape English dissenting thought had assumed in America and the implications for American society of the intellectual life of the Revolution. Viewing

[42] *Ibid.*
[43] *Ibid.*, 189.
[44] Two years later the introduction to this volume, "The Transforming Radicalism of the American Revolution," appeared in slightly expanded form as *The Ideological Origins of the American Revolution* (Cambridge, Mass., 1967).

the intellectual history of the years from 1763 to 1776 as "the story of the clarification and consolidation under the pressure of events of a view of the world and of America's place in it only vaguely and partially seen before," Bailyn analyzed the sources of this world view.[45] He mentioned the classical influence, the Enlightenment rationalism of Locke and others, the common law, and New England Puritanism, but considered these to be disparate strands, some of which were contradictory. The thought that brought these fragments into a coherent whole emanated from the English Civil War and Commonwealth period, but while Americans respected this thought, they identified with the "early eighteenth-century transmitters of this tradition of seventeenth-century radicalism."[46] This single "peculiar strain of thought" provided the framework within which Enlightenment abstractions and common law precedents, covenant theology and classical analogies were brought together into a comprehensive theory of politics.

Bailyn believed the theory of politics which emerged in the pre-Revolutionary years rested "on the belief that what lay behind every political scene, the ultimate explanation of every political controversy, was the disposition of power." To the colonist power meant "the dominion of some men over others, the human control of human life: ultimately force, compulsion." Colonial discussions of power "centered on its essential characteristic of aggressiveness: its endlessly propulsive tendency to expand itself beyond legitimate boundaries," but what "gave transcendent importance to the aggressiveness of power was the fact that its natural prey, its necessary victim, was liberty, or law, or right." The emergent colonial persuasion saw society "divided into distinct, contrasting, and innately antagonistic spheres: the sphere of power and the sphere of liberty or right. The one was brutal, ceaselessly active, and heedless; the other was delicate, passive, and sensitive. The one must be resisted, the other defended, and the two must never be confused."[47]

The meaning imparted to events after 1763 by this integrated group of attitudes lay behind the colonists' rebellion: British actions seemed to fit into a growing "logic of rebellion." The colonists saw an ominous

[45] Bailyn, ed., *Pamphlets,* 20.

[46] *Ibid.,* 29. These "transmitters" were Robbins's Commonwealthmen. It should be noted that Bailyn does not eliminate Locke's influence, he simply places it within its proper context. *Locke et praeterea nihil* becomes *Locke et multum praeterea.*

[47] *Ibid.,* 38-39.

attempt to spread British corruption into America by deceit. Their belief that British actions stemmed from corruption "gave a radical new meaning to their [American] claims; it transformed them from constitutional arguments to expressions of a world regenerative creed."[48] Americans must preserve the light of liberty. It would be treason for them not to revolt.

Bailyn applied the ideas inherent in this new philosophy to American society as it emerged from the Revolution and noted its effect upon various segments of American life: Americans began to question established religion, slavery, and the deferential society found in America. There emerged a faith in the idea that a better world "could be built where authority was distrusted and held in constant scrutiny; where the status of men flowed from their achievements and from their personal qualities, not from distinctions ascribed to them at birth; and where the use of power over the lives of men was jealously guarded and severely restricted. It was only where there was this defiance, this refusal to truckle, this distrust of all authority, political or social, that institutions would express human aspirations, not crush them."[49] Thus, in an attempt to better explain the American Revolution, Bernard Bailyn provided brilliant insight into the development of American republicanism, since the unique frame of mind that developed in the Revolutionary period would be a dynamic force in the development of American society in later years as well.

In the same year that Bailyn published his *Pamphlets* other works appeared that served to broaden historians' comprehension of the libertarian heritage and its role in the American experience even further.[50] H. Trevor Colbourn brought his research to fruition with the publication of *The Lamp of Experience*.[51] He amplified his earlier discussions of

[48] *Ibid.*, 82. The idea of regeneration becomes a key element in republicanism and helps to explain the doctrinaire attitude identified earlier by Kenyon.

[49] *Ibid.*, 202.

[50] Libertarian thought reached a wider audience with the publication of David L. Jacobson, ed., *The English Libertarian Heritage, From the Writings of John Trenchard and Thomas Gordon in* The Independent Whig *and* Cato's Letters (Indianapolis, 1965). This comprised a volume in the Bobbs-Merrill American Heritage Series which attempts to bring primary sources within the reach of a greater number of students.

[51] *The Lamp of Experience: Whig History and the Intellectual Origins of the American Revolution* (Chapel Hill, N. C., 1965).

Jefferson and Dickinson to show how a great many Americans were influenced by whig history. While Bailyn's research provided a sharper picture of the unique frame of mind that existed in America, Colbourn's work was more valuable when looking beyond the Revolutionary period. His chapter on Thomas Jefferson indicated that this frame of mind constituted a continuing dynamic with Jefferson until his death. This was an important contribution, for it indicated that this mode of thought continued well beyond the Revolutionary period and revealed the need to pursue it into the 1820s.

Works by Alan Heimert and Edmund S. Morgan appeared within a year of one another and gave yet another dimension to the evolving synthesis.[52] Heimert's *Religion and the American Mind* developed the thesis that two streams of thought—evangelical and rational—represented the divisions into which American Protestantism had been divided by the Great Awakening. He contended that these streams were "part of a process, wherein competing intellectuals [sought] to make their ideologies efficacious in the lives of Americans, and in their communities" and suggested, but did not develop, the idea that these divisions continued past the Revolution.[53] Were these divisions to be applied to republicanism in the 1780s, an added dimension could be given to the struggle between the Federalists and the antifederalists—both operated within a single ideology, but differed over means to maintain it within their society. James Madison—the rationalist—wanted to change the structure while John Taylor of Caroline—the evangelical—desired a rebirth of the spirit of the people within the existing structure. This schism in American thought needs to be developed in a later period, for while Heimert did indicate that the religious ideas of the Calvinists after the Great Awakening were caught up in the Jeffersonian party of the 1800s, his focus remained too narrow. Rather than dealing solely with the Jeffersonian political party Heimert might have done better to expand his analysis to deal with republican political ideology since this was clearly not the exclusive possession of any particular party or group.

— Morgan suggested that American policies and thought from 1760 to

---

[52] Alan Heimert, *Religion and the American Mind: From the Great Awakening to the Revolution* (Cambridge, Mass., 1966); Edmund S. Morgan, "The Puritan Ethic and the American Revolution," *Wm. and Mary Qtly.*, 3d Ser., XXIV (1967), 3-43.

[53] Heimert, *Religion and the American Mind,* ix.

the 1790s were affected, not to say guided, by a set of values he termed the Puritan Ethic. This ethic encouraged frugality and a suspicion of luxury, distrusted prosperity, and called for a constant renewal of virtue. Morgan's central ideas dovetailed nicely with those of Perry Miller and Alan Heimert and gave another dimension to the study of republicanism through the revelation of the affinity of ideas between Puritanism and republicanism.[54]

In 1967 Bailyn made still another contribution when he applied his ideas regarding the ideological origins of the Revolution to the unique form that politics assumed in America.[55] Bailyn demonstrated how Americans translated the libertarian persuasion into a style of politics; the Commonwealthman's dominating concern lest power usurp liberty became the American's controlling concept in politics. "What in England were theoretical dangers decried by an extremely vocal but politically harmless opposition, appeared in the colonies to be real dangers that threatened an actual and not a theoretical disbalancing of the mixed constitution in favor of an executive engrossment, with all the evils that were known to follow from that destructive event."[56] On the other hand, the possibility that "democracy" might "overreach its proper boundaries and encroach upon the area of power properly entrusted to the first order of the constitution, seemed continuously to be at the edge of realization. Both fears seemed realistic; neither merely theoretical; neither merely logical." Thus did Bailyn hint that in order to protect republicanism in the future it might be necessary to restrain the democracy, not the executive.[57] Bailyn's excellent portrait of American politics in the Revolutionary period provided the nucleus for analyses of post-Revolutionary political life.

The publication of Gordon Wood's *The Creation of the American Republic, 1776-1787* constituted another landmark in the creation of a republican synthesis. Wood drew already present strains of thought into

[54] The similarities between these two persuasions are striking and a thorough analysis of them should prove rewarding. Gordon Wood considers republicanism to be "a more relaxed, secularized version" of Puritanism. *The Creation of the American Republic, 1776-1787* (Chapel Hill, N. C., 1969), 418.

[55] Bernard Bailyn, "Origins of American Politics," *Perspectives*, I (1967), 9-120. This appeared under the same title in book form one year later (New York, 1968).

[56] *Ibid.*, 120.

[57] *Ibid.* With this insight Bailyn laid the groundwork for a discussion of both Federalists and antifederalists within the same ideological framework.

a masterful synthesis of the "Whig science of politics" and added original contributions that carried American thought to 1787. Throughout the whole he drew a brilliant portrait of republicanism by emphasizing the deeply felt American belief that "they had created a new world, a republican world." For them "republicanism meant more . . . than simply the elimination of a king and the institution of an elective system. It added a moral dimension, a utopian depth, to the political separation from England—a depth that involved the very character of their society." Wood maintained that "Americans had come to believe that the Revolution would mean nothing less than a reordering of eighteenth-century society and politics as they had known and despised them—a reordering that was summed up by the conception of republicanism." He devoted his volume to considering that "reordering."[58]

Wood was the first author both to clearly recognize the dynamic qualities of republicanism and effectively define and analyze these qualities. He penetrated the unique persuasion that permeated American society. Americans believed that what either made republics great or ultimately destroyed them was not force of arms, but the character and spirit of the people. Public virtue became preeminent. A people noted for their frugality, industry, temperance, and simplicity were good republican stock. Those who wallowed in luxury could only corrupt others. Easily acquired wealth had to be gained at the expense of others; it was the whole body politic that was crucial, for the public welfare was the exclusive end of good government and required constant sacrifice of individual interests to the greater needs of the whole. Thus the people, conceived of as a homogeneous body (especially when set against their rulers), became the great determinant of whether a republic lived or died. The essential prerequisite for good government was the maintenance of virtue. Those forces which might sap or corrupt virtue were unrepublican and were to be purged before they destroyed the good society.

By identifying this persuasion Wood opened the way for his interpretation of the years following the Revolution. Having noted that republicanism involved the whole character of society, Wood argued that the social dimension of republicanism was precisely the point of the Revolution and that which provided the dynamic for later action.

[58] Wood, *Creation of the American Republic,* 47-48.

Americans were anxiety-ridden over whether they were the stuff out of which republicans were made, and they continually called for moral reformation. They experienced constant concern over the need to maintain public virtue and ardently believed that republicanism must ever maintain a regenerative character.

It is within this context—the shaping and omnipresent force of republicanism—that Wood explained the formation of the American system of government and traced the intellectual twists and turns of the years leading up to the Constitution. Thus the creation of the Articles of Confederation and the battle between the Federalists and antifederalists is played out within this controlling intellectual framework. Wood explored the piecemeal manner in which Americans evolved their own peculiar theory of politics, a theory that resulted from their attempts to institutionalize their experiences and to fashion a government in accord with the way they saw man and society. "The Americans of the Revolutionary generation had constructed not simply new forms of government, but an entirely new conception of politics, a conception that took them out of an essentially classical and medieval world of political discussion into one that was recognizably modern."[59]

Wood's book is crucial to the formation of a republican synthesis, for as he noted, the approach of many historians to the American Revolution "had too often been deeply ahistorical; there had been too little sense of the irretrievability and differentness of the eighteenth-century world." The ahistorical character of a great many studies of the Revolution and the Constitution—and by implication of later periods as well—resulted from "a failure to appreciate the distinctiveness of the political culture in which the revolutionary generation operated."[60] It is the great contribution of Wood's book to provide insight into this distinctive culture so that others may begin their studies with an understanding of the intellectual milieu in which eighteenth-century Americans lived rather than assuming that words like "democracy," "virtue," "tyranny," and "republicanism" have a timeless application.

With the publication of Wood's book the main outlines of a republican synthesis became clear: Americans, drawing heavily upon English libertarian thought, created a unique attitude toward government and society

[59] *Ibid.*, viii.
[60] *Ibid.*

that literally permeated their culture. A consensus, holding the concept of republicanism to stand for the new world Americans believed they had created, quickly formed. This unique persuasion, outlined so skillfully by Bailyn, Wood, and others, caused anxiety for eighteenth-century Americans and bafflement for twentieth-century historians because it placed so much stress upon intangibles such as "virtue" and "character." Republicanism meant maintaining public and private virtue, internal unity, social solidarity, and it meant constantly struggling against "threats" to the "republican character" of the nation. This led to an ofttimes paranoid outlook on the part of many Americans who were constantly fearful lest irresponsible or vicious fellow citizens were at work to corrupt their society. This anxiety resulted from the firmly held belief that republics were short-lived due to their innate susceptibility to internal subversion and external attack.

. Vague and supple as the concept of republicanism may be, historians who ignore it do so at great risk if their goal is an understanding of early American society. What is most important, indeed vital, to bear in mind if republicanism is to stimulate further research is the fact that Americans quickly formed a pervasive ideological attachment to the concept. It was not the creation of any single political party or faction and certainly was not restricted to the Jeffersonians or "Old Republicans" —an insight that may be applied to the pre-Revolutionary period as well since research following Bailyn has not sufficiently explored the possibility that both whigs and tories responded to the same ideological stimuli. Equally as important is the observation that republicanism represented a general consensus solely because it rested on such vague premises. Only one thing was certain: Americans believed that republicanism meant an absence of an aristocracy and a monarchy. Beyond this, agreement vanished—what form a republican government should assume and, more important, what constituted a republican society created disagreement and eventually bitter dissension.

This was a consensus that promoted discord rather than harmony, for if republicanism remains a difficult concept for historians to define today, eighteenth-century Americans found it deceptively simple. Different groups or factions in various sections of the nation defined "republicanism" as they perceived it and could only view their opponents as dangerously antirepublican. The Jeffersonian-Republicans and the Federalists, each firmly believing themselves to be the true servants of republicanism, attacked one another for being a subversive force which would corrupt and destroy republican America.[61] It is a mistake to interpret Thomas Jefferson as the champion of republicanism and his Federalist opponents as its great foes. To do so is to accept only Jefferson's version of the argument.

The works of Gerald Stourzh and James M. Banner are recent examples that both break new ground and revise older interpretations of the early national period.[62] Stourzh, by examining Alexander Hamilton's actions within this fresh framework, has been able to cast new light upon the man and his policies. "Regard to reputation" became for Hamilton what "corruption through power" was to most radical whigs in England and republicans in America. In essence, Hamilton, while operating within the same ideological framework as his fellow Americans, did not behave similarly to other republicans. This is an important point to bear in mind with reference to the use of republicanism as a historical tool; the concept should not become a catchall to be superimposed upon everything and everybody. To do so would oversimplify history and place the historian in a straitjacket. To say that Americans were republicans is not to say that they all behaved alike; historians should not create "republican automatons." As John Howe pointed out, "Republicanism was obviously subject to a variety of readings when individuals as diverse as Alexander Hamilton and Thomas Jefferson, John Adams and John Taylor could each claim allegiance to it."[63] Stourzh's study is the first to reexamine a prominent and oft-studied figure from this fresh vantage point; hopefully, his will not be the last.

Just as Stourzh took a new approach to an old problem, so too did Banner when he reexamined the impetus leading to the Hartford Con-

[61] Marshall Smelser clearly identified this passion, but attributed it to differences of political and social principles and to state and sectional rivalries. "The Jacobin Phrenzy: Federalism and the Menace of Liberty, Equality, and Fraternity," *Review of Politics,* XIII (1951), 457-482; Smelser, "The Federalist Period as an Age of Passion," *American Quarterly,* X (1958), 391-419; Smelser, "The Jacobin Phrenzy: The Menace of Monarchy, Plutocracy, and Anglophilia, 1789-1798," *Rev. of Pol.,* XXI (1959), 239-258. For a perceptive analysis which places this turmoil within the republican synthesis see John R. Howe, Jr., "Republican Thought and the Political Violence of the 1790s," *Amer. Qtly.,* XIX (1967), 147-165.

[62] Gerald Stourzh, *Alexander Hamilton and the Idea of Republican Government* (Stanford, Calif., 1970); James M. Banner, Jr., *To the Hartford Convention: The Federalists and the Origins of Party Politics in Massachusetts, 1789-1815* (New York, 1970).

[63] Howe, "Republican Thought," *Amer. Qtly.,* XIX (1967), 153.

vention. By proving the Massachusetts Federalists' adherence to republicanism, Banner provided a sophisticated reinterpretation of the Hartford Convention and effectively demonstrated that republican ideology was not restricted to either the South or the Jeffersonians. Out of this commitment to republicanism emerged a political party; Banner maintained that the New England Federalists who pressed for the convention did so out of a belief that it was the only way to preserve American republicanism from corruption at the hands of the Jeffersonians.

The research of Banner and Stourzh, with that of Linda Kerber, David H. Fischer, and others, demonstrated that the Federalists have been too long stereotyped as latent monarchists whom the Jeffersonians had to dispatch for the good of American society.[64] While she does not analyze the ideology of the Federalists with the perceptivity of Banner, Kerber clearly reveals their organic view of society and the consequent fear and distrust of the Jeffersonians emanating from that conception of the social order. Fischer's book demonstrates that the "young Federalists" adapted to the changing political styles and attempted to retain their conception of government and society while operating within the confines of the new politics.

The emergence of the republican synthesis requires that a key development of the 1790s—the rise of political parties—be wholly reviewed. This phenomenon may well have emerged as a natural result of the prior existence of a widely held ideology. Banner noted that the Federalist party emerged in Massachusetts after the growth and definition of a political ideology, not before. His perceptive study of the social, economic, religious, and psychological processes working in Massachusetts to create an ideology and then a political party might well be expanded to the entire process of the formation of parties in early America. This takes on added significance upon noting the distinctions between parties as they developed in America and their English counterparts as described by Lewis Namier, Richard Pares, and others.[65] The English conception of government—that

[64] Linda K. Kerber, *Federalists in Dissent: Imagery and Ideology in Jeffersonian America* (Ithaca, N. Y., 1970); David Hackett Fischer, *The Revolution of American Conservatism: The Federalist Party in the Era of Jeffersonian Democracy* (New York, 1965).

[65] Sir Lewis Namier, *The Structure of Politics at the Accession of George III*, 2 vols. (London, 1929); Sir Lewis Namier and John Brooke, *The House of Commons, 1754-1790*, 3 vols. (London, 1964); Richard Pares, *King George III and the Poli-*

the general government existed not to legislate but simply to govern—
caused political parties to vie for office and little else. In America the
government of necessity played a far more dynamic role and thus the
competing parties believed it necessary to gain power in order to shape
society; government actually legislated in the United States.[66]

Within this context Joseph Charles's observation that "the fundamental issue of the 1790's was no other than what form of government
and what type of society were to be produced in this country" reveals
perceptive insight.[67] Charles's "fundamental issue" should become the
measure by which early American leaders are analyzed rather than as
Federalists or Jeffersonians. To lump all Jeffersonian or Federalist leaders
together in their respective party obscures the subtle—and at times
gross—nuances of difference existent within those political camps.[68] Viewed
from this perspective Madison might well be seen as in many ways
ideologically closer—especially with respect to the role of government in
society—to Hamilton than to Jefferson and Jefferson's affinity to John
Taylor of Caroline would also become clearer.[69]

Just as the republican synthesis can contribute to an understanding
of the emergence of political institutions, so too might it help to reveal
the social dynamics of early American society; the search for the foundations of American democracy may gain much from this viewpoint. Within
this perspective the progressive and neo-whig schools of thought no longer

---

ticians (Oxford, 1953); Betty Kemp, *King and Commons, 1660-1832* (London,
1957); John B. Owen, *The Rise of the Pelhams* (London, 1957).

[66] Bailyn presents a stimulating analysis of this point in *Origins of American
Politics,* esp. 101-105.

[67] *The Origins of the American Party System: Three Essays* (Chapel Hill, N. C.,
1956), 6. Elements of thought which made up American reactions to historical
process may have been even more subtle than indicated by Charles. For provocative
essays on this subject see Leo Marx, *The Machine in the Garden: Technology and
the Pastoral Ideal in America* (New York, 1964); and David Bertelson, *The Lazy
South* (New York, 1967).

[68] While aiding in bringing James Madison to his rightful place in American
intellectual development, Adrienne Koch blurs distinctions far more subtle and
sophisticated than simply the differences between the "practical" Madison and the
"idealistic" Jefferson. *Jefferson and Madison: The Great Collaboration* (New
York, 1950).

[69] While a good number of Federalists and Jeffersonians could profitably be reexamined in light of this new perspective, Gordon Wood's brief but incisive hint
that John Taylor of Caroline had an extremely perceptive understanding of American society requires amplification. *Creation of the American Republic,* 587-592.

need to polarize historical research. J. R. Pole's perceptive studies—especially with regard to the breakdown of a deferential society in America—have drawn the essence from each of these approaches and presented a cogent analysis of early American culture that blends nicely with Bailyn and Wood: American society, operating within the ideology of republicanism, underwent constant transformations as it moved from a deferential society toward a democratic one.[70]

Closely related is the ability to observe the social psychology of polarization within American society. It is fascinating to observe the thought of Theodore Sedgwick of Massachusetts and John Taylor of Virginia since, while both men operated within the controlling confines of the single ideology republicanism, each came to view the other and his followers as a dangerous enemy. The parallels in their thought are striking. Each perceived his own style of life as beneficial to America, believed that it should be emulated by others, and therefore considered the other subversive of the good society. Each man even contemplated the secession of his section in order to preserve republicanism as he defined it. This is a provocative phenomenon that should yield fruitful results to the historian who investigates it.

Recent work by a number of social historians raises an intriguing problem related to the social dynamics and polarization of American society. Their research indicates that American society was becoming more stratified at the very point in time when republican ideology was becoming more popular and egalitarian. Kenneth A. Lockridge maintains that by the time of the Revolution much of New England was "becoming more and more an old world society: old world in the sense of the size of farms, old world in the sense of an increasingly wide and articulated social hierarchy, old world in that 'the poor' were ever present and in increasing numbers."[71] He concludes that this sense of becoming like the

---

[70] Pole's approach is most succinctly presented in "Historians and the Problem of Early American Democracy," *Amer. Hist. Rev.*, LXVII (1961-1962), 626-646. The concept of deference is central to both Bailyn's and Wood's discussions of early American society.

[71] Kenneth Lockridge, "Land, Population and the Evolution of New England Society 1630-1790," *Past and Present*, No. 39 (Apr. 1968), 62-80. The quotation is from p. 80. Lockridge expands his ideas in *A New England Town: The First Hundred Years, Dedham, Massachusetts, 1636-1736* (New York, 1970). Similar views may be found in Charles S. Grant, *Democracy in the Connecticut Frontier Town of Kent* (New York, 1961); and in James A. Henretta, "Economic De-

old world was one of the strains that led to an acceptance of the rhetoric of the Revolution, but believes that the egalitarianism of the Revolution and the later migration out of New England eased the "overcrowded" condition of the area, thus allowing it to escape class tension and conflict.

Stephan Thernstrom's research indicates that the stratification process identified in the pre-Revolutionary period by Lockridge continued on unabated, indeed with increased intensity, through the nineteenth century. His study of Newburyport reveals a working-class people "unable to escape a grinding regimen of manual labor: this was the sum of the social mobility achieved by Newburyport's unskilled laborer by 1880."[72] Yet, these people seemed to accept the "mobility ideology" and, by inference, the prevailing republicanism. These studies reveal a great need to analyze the social-intellectual processes at work within a society that is undergoing stratification while at the same time accepting an increasingly egalitarian ideology.[73]

There is pressing need to carry the synthesis forward past 1800. A number of studies employ the concept of republicanism in some manner or other: Roger H. Brown's *The Republic in Peril: 1812* (New York, 1964), Robert Remini's *Martin Van Buren and the Making of the Democratic Party* (New York, 1959), and Marvin Meyers's *Jacksonian Persuasion: Politics and Belief* (Stanford, Calif., 1957) among others presently appear as scattered and isolated bits of a theme that need to be brought together.

---

velopment and Social Structure in Colonial Boston," *Wm. and Mary Qtly.*, 3d Ser., XXII (1965), 75-92.

[72] *Poverty and Progress: Social Mobility in a Nineteenth Century City* (Cambridge, Mass., 1964), 163. Thernstrom expands his views in "Urbanization, Migration, and Social Mobility in Late Nineteenth-Century America," in Barton J. Bernstein, ed., *Towards a New Past: Dissenting Essays in American History* (New York, 1968), 158-175. His view of increasing stratification is supported by Douglas T. Miller, *Jacksonian Aristocracy: Class and Democracy in New York, 1830-1860* (New York, 1967); and Sam Bass Warner, Jr., *The Private City: Philadelphia in Three Periods of Its Growth* (Philadelphia, 1968). While not touching upon stratification or ideology, Daniel H. Calhoun does present a provocative study of social change in this same period in his *Professional Lives in America: Structure and Aspiration, 1750-1850* (Cambridge, Mass., 1965).

[73] Though not addressing himself specifically to this matter, Michael B. Katz presents a fascinating study of the upper class in control of education in Massachusetts, the ideology they attempted to implement through the schools, and the lower-class response. This approach needs to be applied to the relationship between stratification and republicanism. *The Irony of Early School Reform: Educational Innovation in Mid-Nineteenth Century Massachusetts* (Cambridge, Mass., 1968).

Just as the ideas of Bailyn, Wood, and others provided a frame of reference for the Revolutionary and early national periods, so too can republicanism become a unifying theme in this later period.[74] The ideology would very likely not perform the same functions as it had earlier; rather than being the dynamic shaping force of the Revolutionary years, republicanism may well have assumed a static, doctrinaire quality to which people clung mindlessly in times of social malaise. It may have provided stale answers for fresh questions and thus have assumed a stagnant—indeed stultifying—character. Nonetheless, its role needs to be examined since it can offer a synthetic framework for scattered studies and provide the opportunity to approach the dynamics of an ideology in stable as well as fluid times and thus the transformations it undergoes over time.

If this new understanding of republicanism is to prove valuable a word of caution must be heeded. Jackson Turner Main has warned scholars that intellectual history of the sort represented by a study of republicanism may become a dead end.[75] If an explication of republicanism is the sole end of a scholar, such could prove to be the case, but if one recognizes republicanism as ideology, then new doors of scholarship are opened. Research needs to be directed toward a definition of ideology, its functions, its origins, and its special language.[76]

[74] In a narrative of the activities of the "Quids" Norman Risjord attempts to trace the descent of republican ideas of the 1790s to the Calhounites in the 1830s. *The Old Republicans: Southern Conservatives in the Age of Jefferson* (New York, 1965). His book is seriously flawed, however, because he misunderstands republicanism. While extremely vague, Risjord appears to consider republicanism to be the product of the Jeffersonian party and to be epitomized by the Virginia and Kentucky Resolutions. To consider the Quids to be the "missing link" between republican ideas of the 1790s and Calhoun not only seriously constricts republicanism, but fails to take into account the fact that Calhoun's ideas were anathema to republicans (even the southern ones Risjord studies) in the 1820s and 1830s. Richard H. Brown presents a more perceptive analysis of republican thought and politics in the Jacksonian era in "The Missouri Crisis, Slavery and the Politics of Jacksonianism," *So. Atlantic Qtly.*, LXV (1966), 55-72.

[75] Jackson Turner Main's review of Wood, *Creation of the American Republic, Wm. and Mary Qtly.*, 3d Ser., XXVI (1969), 604-607.

[76] The concept of ideology is itself the subject of much disagreement among social scientists. As employed in this essay ideology denotes the "unconscious tendency underlying religious and scientific as well as political thought: the tendency at a given time to make facts amenable to ideas, and ideas to facts, in order to create a world image convincing enough to support the collective and the individual sense of identity." Erik H. Erikson, *Young Man Luther: A Study in Psychoanalysis*

Some recent students of ideology contend that strain rather than interest serves as the impetus to the creation of an ideological system; that is, ideologies should be viewed as symptoms of strains present in a culture rather than as reflections of the interests of particular groups or factions.[77] Thus the identification of a particular ideology should be taken as a symptom of social dislocation in the society within which it is found. Further, ideology needs to be viewed as "symbolic action" rather than as an actual reflection of reality.[78] Indeed, a prominent sociologist believes that it is the absence of an understanding of symbolic action that has "reduced sociologists to viewing ideologies as elaborate cries of pain." They have failed to construe the import of ideological assertions by simply failing to recognize it as a problem. He feels that sociologists have viewed the simplified language of ideologies as just that. "Either it deceives the uninformed (interest theory) or it excites the unreflective (strain theory). That it might draw its power from its capacity to grasp, formulate, and communicate social realities that elude the tempered

---

and History (New York, 1958), 22. For analyses of varying definitions and usages of the term see Ben Halpern, " 'Myth' and 'Ideology' in Modern Usage," History and Theory, I (1961), 129-149; Karl Lowenstein, "The Role of Ideologies in Political Change," International Social Science Bulletin, V (1953), 51-74; David W. Minar, "Ideology and Political Behavior," Midwest Journal of Political Science, V (1961), 317-331; and Jay W. Stein, "Beginnings of 'Ideology,' " So. Atlantic Qtly., LV (1956), 163-170. For an understanding of the emergence of the idea of ideology see George Lichtheim, The Concept of Ideology, and Other Essays (New York, 1967). Norman Birnbaum includes a 46-page, double-columned bibliography of works dealing with ideology in his "The Sociological Study of Ideology (1940-60): A Trend Report and Bibliography," Current Sociology, IX (1960), 91-172.

[77] Talcott Parsons, The Social System (Glencoe, Ill., 1951); Winston White, Beyond Conformity (Glencoe, Ill., 1961); Francis X. Sutton et al., The American Business Creed (Cambridge, Mass., 1956); Clifford Geertz, "Ideology as a Cultural System," in David E. Apter, ed., Ideology and Discontent (Glencoe, Ill., 1964), 47-76.

[78] The symbolic action concept, which has been skillfully employed by social scientists in various ways, originated with Kenneth Burke and is most clearly discussed in his The Philosophy of Literary Form: Studies in Symbolic Action (Baton Rouge, La., 1941). Making sophisticated use of Burke's insight, Gene Wise notes that "language to Burke is action. Further, it is 'symbolic' action in that it expresses men's efforts to communicate with their environment and to create symbols to order that communication. Language, in whatever form and of whatever quality, is interpreted by Burke as a series of humanly-created 'strategies' for responding to selectively-perceived 'situations.' " "Political 'Reality' in Recent American Scholarship: Progressives versus Symbolists," Amer. Qtly., XIX (1967), 306. It is within this context that republicanism should be viewed as symbolic action.

language of science, that it may mediate more complex meanings than its literal reading suggests, is not even considered." Simple language may not be a label but a trope. More precisely, it "appears to be a metaphor, or at least an attempted metaphor."[79]

Historians need to take up these insights and apply them to the study of republicanism, for in this manner they may be able to more fully understand the strains American society underwent in its infancy. Further, rather than viewing cries about "corruption," "tyranny," "virtue," "regeneration," and "republicanism" as simple language used as weapons by competing interests—and thus dismissing what a man said while paying attention to his actions or his socio-economic status—scholars might do well to view these terms as the symbolic action of early Americans. These people encountered reality strategically and refracted reality rather than reflected it.[80]

Banner, with reference to the Federalists' use of such terms as "tyrant," "Jacobin," and others, maintains that "to dismiss these impassioned charges of corruption, despotism, and conspiracy as so much partisan hyperbole would be seriously to misinterpret the central thrust of the Massachusetts Federalist ideology. If Jeffersonian policy was neither tyrannical nor cabalistic, neither was it in the best interests of New England as the Federalists of Massachusetts—farmers, merchants, lawyers, clerics, and artisans—defined them."[81] Banner's insight—which should similarly be applied to Jeffersonian rhetoric—indicates that republican language may well hold a key to understanding American society in this period.

Viewed in these terms an understanding of republicanism becomes a tool that aids the historian in his attempt to gain access into the social, economic, political, and religious life of a period. Hopefully, an understanding of republicanism might open the door to provocative new insights about American society.

[79] Geertz, "Ideology as Cultural System," in Apter, ed., *Ideology and Discontent*, 57-58.

[80] Wise offers a stimulating discussion of "refraction" and "reflection" which indicates that his "symbolist" approach should prove fruitful to those interested in republican ideology. From this point of view "the individual does not so much *reflect* the world, as he *refracts* his selectively-perceived environment." In this approach "the external world is the raw material which the human being uses to shape (not fully according to *his* own purposes, but not quite according to *its* either) into that which can be understood, communicated with, manipulated." "Political 'Reality,' " *Amer. Qtly.*, XIX (1967), 323.

[81] Banner, *To the Hartford Convention*, 45.

Republicanism and Early American Historiography

Robert E. Shalhope

WITHIN the last several decades a dramatic reorientation has taken place in interpretation of the Revolutionary and early national periods. This new perspective is the result of scholars' recognition of the vital function of republicanism in early American society. As an increasingly sophisticated comprehension of republicanism continues to transform our understanding of the Revolution and its aftermath, it has the potential to collapse the idealist-materialist dichotomy in the progressive-whig dialogue that has dominated twentieth-century American historiography.

More than any other historian, Bernard Bailyn was the progenitor of this new appreciation of republicanism. His work, along with that of Gordon S. Wood and J.G.A. Pocock, among others, established the initial perception of republicanism that has become so familiar.[1] These authors argue that colonial American spokesmen, drawing deeply on the libertarian thought of the English commonwealthmen, embraced a distinctive set of political and social attitudes and that these attitudes permeated their society.[2] Believing that history revealed a continual struggle between the spheres of liberty and power, the American Revolutionaries quickly formed a consensus in which the concept of republicanism epitomized the new social and political world they believed they had created. Preserving a republican polity meant protecting liberty from the ceaseless aggression of power. In addition, Americans believed that what made republics great or

Mr. Shalhope is a member of the Department of History at the University of Oklahoma. The author wishes to acknowledge the kind assistance of David W. Levy of the University of Oklahoma whose perceptive reading of the manuscript helped immeasurably in clarifying a number of points of analysis.

[1] Bailyn, *The Ideological Origins of the American Revolution* (Cambridge, Mass., 1967), and *The Origins of American Politics* (New York, 1967); Wood, *The Creation of the American Republic, 1776-1787* (Chapel Hill, N.C., 1969); Pocock, *The Machiavellian Moment: Florentine Political Thought and the Atlantic Republican Tradition* (Princeton, N.J., 1975). Pocock discusses important distinctions in the ways these three authors view republicanism in his *"The Machiavellian Moment Revisited: A Study in History and Ideology," Journal of World History*, LIII (1981), 49-72.

[2] Essential to understanding this thought is Caroline Robbins, *The Eighteenth-Century Commonwealthman: Studies in the Transmission, Development and Circumstance of English Liberal Thought from the Restoration of Charles II until the War with the Thirteen Colonies* (Cambridge, Mass., 1959).

ultimately destroyed them was not the force of arms but the character and spirit of the people. Public virtue, as the essential prerequisite for good government, was all-important. A people practicing frugality, industry, temperance, and simplicity were sound republican stock, while those who wallowed in luxury were corrupt and would corrupt others. Since furthering the public good—the exclusive purpose of republican government—required the constant sacrifice of individual interests to the greater needs of the whole, the people, conceived of as a homogeneous body (especially when set against their rulers), became the great determinant of whether a republic lived or died. Thus republicanism meant maintaining public and private virtue, internal unity, social solidarity, and vigilance against the corruptions of power. United in this frame of mind, Americans set out to gain their independence and then to establish a new republic.

This perspective has exerted a tremendous influence on the historical profession. Its primary themes pervade recent work on early America.[3] Many scholars have elaborated on these basic concepts, and have applied to various aspects of late eighteenth- and early nineteenth-century America insights found in or inferred from the writings of Bailyn, Wood, and Pocock. These efforts have shed fresh light on old historical problems and opened up inviting new avenues of research.

If historians now commonly recognize that republicanism represented a secular faith for Americans, who found in it identity and meaning for their lives, precisely what that meaning was, and whether it bore the same significance for Americans in all social ranks and in every region, remains open to question. Many scholars have either raised serious questions about the broad view of republicanism sketched above or gone beyond it. The result is an increasingly diverse and at times seemingly inconsistent body of literature that casts republicanism in an enigmatic role. Gone are the clarity and simplicity of the "republican synthesis" of nearly a decade ago.[4] In its place is a problematic and complex web of interpretations that requires analysis.

I

Bailyn's introduction to *Pamphlets of the American Revolution* quickly established a new paradigm for interpreting the Revolution.[5] The breach

[3] Representative examples include Pauline Maier, *From Resistance to Revolution: Colonial Radicals and the Development of American Opposition to Britain, 1765-1776* (New York, 1972); Richard Buel, Jr., *Securing the Revolution: Ideology in American Politics, 1789-1815* (Ithaca, N.Y., 1972); Mary Beth Norton, *The British-Americans: The Loyalist Exiles in England, 1774-1789* (Boston, 1972); Alan Rogers, *Empire and Liberty: American Resistance to British Authority, 1755-1763* (Berkeley and Los Angeles, Calif., 1974); and Lance Banning, *The Jeffersonian Persuasion: Evolution of a Party Ideology* (Ithaca, N.Y., 1978).

[4] Robert E. Shalhope, "Toward a Republican Synthesis: The Emergence of an Understanding of Republicanism in American Historiography," *William and Mary Quarterly*, 3d Ser., XXIX (1972), 49-80.

[5] Bailyn, ed., *Pamphlets of the American Revolution, 1750-1776* (Cambridge, Mass., 1965).

between the colonies and Britain was henceforth to be explained primarily by understanding the circumstances as the participants perceived them. In this introduction and in subsequent publications Bailyn contended that patriot leaders consistently displayed a world view characterized by libertarian republicanism. They adhered to this ideology because the actions of Britain and the structure of colonial politics gave it peculiar persuasiveness. A volatile political situation arising from "a presumptuous prerogative and an overgreat democracy" led colonial publicists to see in actions taken by the British following the French and Indian War a deliberate design to destroy liberty.[6] For Bailyn, "the outbreak of the Revolution was not the result of social discontent, or of economic disturbances, or of rising misery, or of those mysterious social strains that seem to beguile the imaginations of historians straining to find peculiar predispositions to upheaval." Rather, "American resistance in the 1760s and 1770s was a response to acts of power deemed arbitrary, degrading, and uncontrollable—a response, in itself objectively reasonable, that was inflamed to the point of explosion by ideological currents generating fears everywhere in America that irresponsible and self-seeking adventurers— what the twentieth century would call political gangsters—had gained the power of the English government and were turning first, for reasons that were variously explained, to that Rhineland of their aggressions, the colonies."[7]

Since 1965 many scholars dealing with the Revolution have worked within Bailyn's paradigm. That is, they have continued to analyze the period in terms of the participants' view of the world. At the same time, Bailyn's interpretation of the patriots' world view has stimulated spirited controversy. Criticism has focused on several themes. It is contended that (a) Bailyn's analysis rests on a misleading view of a homogeneous colonial America that slights internal diversity and conflict; (b) ideologies other than the one outlined by Bailyn governed the way participants in the Revolution saw and responded to their world; (c) there are alternative explanations of the appeal of libertarian republicanism; (d) Bailyn's studies treat ideology abstractly, without sufficient grounding in circumstances, environment, and experience, and thus seem to imply ideational autonomy; and (e) Bailyn's analysis is one-dimensional, causing republican ideology to appear centrally, even exclusively, political and constitutional.[8]

Recent examinations of republican thought have fragmented the intellectual consensus portrayed by Bailyn and others. These inquiries reveal a

[6] Bailyn, *Origins of American Politics*, 106.

[7] Bailyn, "The Central Themes of the American Revolution: An Interpretation," in Stephen G. Kurtz and James H. Hutson, eds., *Essays on the American Revolution* (Chapel Hill, N.C., 1973), 3-31 (quotation on pp. 12-13).

[8] There is a tremendous amount of crosscutting and interlocking among these themes in the recent literature. Therefore, this essay makes every attempt to integrate rather than to isolate these ideas.

major weakness of most early studies of republicanism—the failure to deal with the dynamic interrelationships between ideological perceptions and the environment in which they occur. The new studies also take critical note of a tendency to emphasize perceptions held in common by Americans rather than to analyze local circumstances that may have created distinctive variations in thought. Scholars whose approach is essentially socioeconomic believe that Bailyn's emphasis (and that of many others) on the commonwealth ideology as the dominant moving force behind the Revolution has resulted in a simplistic, consensus view of colonial behavior.[9] These critics do not see colonial Americans as an undifferentiated mass joined by belief in a single ideology. They consider Bailyn and his "neo-Whig" followers "idealists" who view thought as an autonomous construct divorced from specific time and place. In addition, they take issue with Bailyn's contention that the material conditions of life in America were so generally favorable that social and economic factors deserve little consideration in explaining the origins of the Revolution. For their part, these historians find in colonial America diverse and often conflicting political beliefs, personal and group motives, class views, and economic interests. The colonies, in their eyes, experienced political, social, and economic changes that produced serious distress and tension. The Revolution, they conclude, was rooted in this complex substructure, rather than in a narrowly focused political and constitutional ideology. They do not deny the validity of ideological interpretation, but they recognize the possibility of alternatives to commonwealth doctrine and suggest that distinctive situations or local circumstances shaped the predisposition of people to accept certain ideas and to reject others.

Though the substantive research that supports this broad point of view is scattered through a great many books and essays, its central themes are clearly manifested in *The American Revolution,* a collection of essays edited by Alfred F. Young.[10] Basic to many of the contributions is the belief that the economic substructure of eighteenth-century British America—with

[9] Representative examples include Joseph Albert Ernst, *Money and Politics in America, 1755-1775: A Study in the Currency Act of 1764 and the Political Economy of Revolution* (Chapel Hill, N.C., 1973), and "Ideology and the Political Economy of Revolution," *Canadian Review of American Studies,* IV (1973), 137-148; Jackson Turner Main, *The Sovereign States, 1775-1783* (New York, 1973); Ronald Hoffman, *A Spirit of Dissension: Economics, Politics, and the Revolution in Maryland* (Baltimore, 1973); Stephen E. Patterson, *Political Parties in Revolutionary Massachusetts* (Madison, Wis., 1973); James Kirby Martin, *Men in Rebellion: Higher Governmental Leaders and the Coming of the American Revolution* (New Brunswick, N.J., 1973); Dirk Hoerder, *Crowd Action in Revolutionary Massachusetts, 1765-1780* (New York, 1977); Gary B. Nash, "Radicalism and the American Revolution," *Reviews in American History,* I (1973), 75-81; Staughton Lynd, "Tories and Neo-Whigs," *ibid.,* 201-208; and Jesse Lemisch, "Bailyn Besieged in His Bunker," *Radical History Review,* VII (1977), 72-83.

[10] Young, ed., *The American Revolution: Explorations in the History of American Radicalism* (DeKalb, Ill., 1976).

its tensions and antagonisms—is central to any understanding of the Revolution.[11] Joseph Ernst makes this clear in an essay that contends that specific events, issues, and interests must be interpreted in light of the economic transformation of the colonies after 1720.[12] Conditions in this period pitted local elites against politically awakened middle and lower classes. In Ernst's view, rational and self-conscious links existed between the rhetoric of the various groups and their social experience. Only by understanding the relations between specific groups and the ideology each espoused can one understand the complexity of the Revolution. Belief in the motivational power of a single, all-inclusive ideology obscures such understanding.

Marvin L. Michael Kay, Ronald Hoffman, and Edward Countryman focus on another characteristic theme of this perspective: the severe social tension and unrest that, they believe, characterized colonial American society. Kay finds class antagonism at the base of the Regulator movement in North Carolina, where class-conscious farmers attempted to alleviate economic and social distress by democratizing their local governments.[13] Hoffman contends that the entire South suffered serious social discontent and internal tensions simultaneously with the war against Britain. Unpopular whig elites survived only by channeling popular unrest into the creation of the new republic.[14] Countryman finds the land riots in the northern colonies to be class-based rather than ethnocultural in origin, and he connects them with the domination of land and with the political and social power that accompanied it. The success or failure of the outbreaks varied according to circumstances: rural radicals in New York remained divorced from power, but their counterparts in Vermont wrote a constitution that represented the high point of radical republicanism.[15]

The essays by Eric Foner, Dirk Hoerder, and Gary B. Nash (like Ernst's) suggest that more than a single ideology may have been instrumental in bringing about the Revolution. Foner's analysis of Philadelphia

---

[11] The spring 1976 issue of the *Journal of Interdisciplinary History* includes a number of pertinent essays: Gary B. Nash, "Urban Wealth and Poverty in Pre-Revolutionary America"; G. B. Warden, "Inequality and Instability in Eighteenth-Century Boston: A Reappraisal"; Duane E. Ball, "Dynamics of Population and Wealth in Eighteenth-Century Chester County, Pennsylvania"; Edward Countryman, "Consolidating Power in Revolutionary America: The Case of New York, 1775-1783"; and Robert M. Weir, "Who Shall Rule at Home: The American Revolution as a Crisis of Legitimacy for the Colonial Elite."

[12] Ernst, " 'Ideology' and an Economic Interpretation of the Revolution," in Young, ed., *American Revolution*, 160-185. This essay expands on an earlier one which Ernst coauthored with Marc Egnal, "An Economic Interpretation of the American Revolution," *WMQ*, 3d Ser., XXIX (1972), 3-32.

[13] Kay, "The North Carolina Regulation, 1766-1776: A Class Conflict," in Young, ed., *American Revolution*, 71-123.

[14] Hoffman, "The 'Disaffected' in the Revolutionary South," *ibid.*, 273-316.

[15] Countryman, " 'Out of Bounds of the Law': Northern Land Rioters in the Eighteenth Century," *ibid.*, 37-69.

and Tom Paine reveals a politically alert lower class activated by an egalitarian, evangelical strain of thought that espoused traditional values of community and emphasized the existence of a uniform general interest. Opposed to this was the whig ideology of the merchant class centering on the conviction that the competing ambitions of self-interested individuals would produce the greatest public benefit.[16] Hoerder, too, sees a struggle that pitted lower-class radicals captivated by an ideology based on Protestant and common-law traditions against upper-class whigs who employed the rhetoric of the commonwealthmen.[17] Both Hoerder and Foner believe that class-consciousness remained rudimentary, even though lower-class radicals managed to force cautious merchant leaders to become outspoken politicans in opposition to England. In the end, however, the republican ideology of the gentry was able to absorb the radical thrust.

Nash also hints that a popular ideology emerged from the material conditions of port cities, where an inequitable distribution of wealth and economic insecurity created severe distress and tension. Under these circumstances, the upper classes remained wedded to the whig ideology and its defense of property lodged in constitutional rights and political liberties.[18] Such an ideology did not, however, speak to the changing economic and social environment of the cities. New conditions called forth a popular rhetoric that transcended constitutional rights and advocated a more equitable arrangement of wealth and power. The artisan and laboring classes, buttressed by this rhetoric, became highly politicized and assumed a dynamic role in urban politics. Nash, however, does not believe that their ideas ever developed into a fully articulated ideology. Like Hoerder and Foner, he discovers within the lower ranks of society restive elements who, though politically self-conscious, could not fully conceptualize their purpose in such a way as to separate themselves from the ideas and goals of the gentry leadership.

In *The Urban Crucible* Nash skillfully weaves the themes of *The American Revolution*—disparate, tentative, and occasionally strident—into a thoughtful and provocative study essential to a fuller understanding of the Revolution and republicanism.[19] Nash's intensive examination of

---

[16] Foner, "Tom Paine's Republic: Radical Ideology and Social Change," *ibid.*, 187-232.

[17] Hoerder, "Boston Leaders and Boston Crowds, 1765-1776," *ibid.*, 233-271.

[18] Nash, "Social Change and the Growth of Prerevolutionary Urban Radicalism," *ibid.*, 3-36.

[19] The authors of a number of essays in *American Revolution* made a distinct effort to meet the expectations raised by that volume's subtitle. As a consequence, their desire to find a viable base of American radicalism and, perhaps, to attack Bailyn led them to overstatements regarding popular or radical activity. For example, the broad hints of class-based ideologies appearing in the essays by Hoerder and Nash are much more subtly stated and carefully circumscribed in their books, *Crowd Action in Revolutionary Massachusetts* and *The Urban Crucible: Social Change, Political Consciousness, and the Origins of the American Revolution* (Cambridge, Mass., 1979).

eighteenth-century Boston, New York, and Philadelphia reveals the dynamic interdependence of economic shifts, social changes, and political consciousness. He describes how these seaport towns became caught up in the changes affecting the entire Atlantic community. Impersonal market forces disrupted traditional social and economic relationships, led to an increasingly unequal distribution of wealth, and restructured urban society along rigid class lines. As Americans adjusted to these changes, two conceptions of economic life vied for ascendancy. One clung to traditional communal norms. The other encouraged a nascent system of values that emphasized private profit seeking, accepted the demise of traditional controls designed to promote the good of all, and claimed that the free pursuit of individual self-interest would foster the common good. As time passed, more and more successful merchants, shopkeepers, and land speculators came to accept this "modern" economic thought. At the same time, the older corporate ideology of an indivisible public good would not die. The severe economic crisis brought on by the colonial wars prompted the lower orders of society to assert a traditional value system that stressed communal obligations rather than free enterprise. While the lower orders looked to the past for guidance regarding proper economic relationships, they supported a more modern participatory form of politics in order to secure economic justice. In addition, they felt that their social superiors employed the rhetoric of the commonwealth ideology merely to mask their own avarice. Gradually the feeling arose that the rich became richer because the poor became poorer. The Great Awakening exacerbated such feelings, as Old Lights pragmatically accepted the new capitalist ethic while radical Awakeners expressed alarm over the urban elite's acquisitiveness. Thus by the time of the Revolution the dialogue over American constitutional rights took place in urban locales marked by poverty at the bottom, economic uncertainty in the middle, and opulence among the upper ranks. Nash believes that, as a result, American urban areas entered the Revolution facing severe crises in class relations.

Nash's discussion of the political consciousness of various groups provides excellent insight into the competing ideologies of the period and their relationship to republicanism. He identifies two broad ideologies—whig and evangelical—that overlap at a number of points, as well as several groups of ideas that were not yet fully articulated. In his view, whig ideology, with its emphasis on balanced government, a popularly elected legislature, and support of free speech and press, constituted the dominant perception of the age. In America, the whigs split into conservative and liberal groups. The conservatives—wealthy merchants, Anglican clergymen, and placeholders—valued social stability, fostered capitalistic economic relations, and believed in their own political stewardship. They were economic modernizers with a profoundly conservative social philosophy. The liberal whigs—some wealthy traders, ship captains, non-Anglican clergymen, small manufacturers, and craftsmen—also eagerly espoused the new spirit of commercial life, but they embraced more egalitarian social and political ideas, including equality of opportunity.

The other major perception Nash identifies—the evangelical ideology—overlapped with that of the whigs in that its adherents advocated balanced government, electoral institutions, and freedom of speech and press. However, the evangelicals had a different vision for America. They, too, divided into two groups: the radicals and the social reformers. The radicals—drawn from the lower orders—favored the traditional ideas of a moral economy rather than capitalistic enterprise. They were egalitarian and communalistic in spirit. Considering the merchant elite their oppressors, they hoped that the Revolution would establish basic political rights and social justice for all, rather than simply protect the private property and constitutional liberties of the wealthy. The social reformers—clergymen, middle-class doctors, lawyers, tradesmen, and teachers—shared a highly moralistic temperament. These were the people who espoused most clearly the classical republicanism and "civic humanism" that recent scholars have emphasized. They, too, decried the new capitalistic spirit as the cause of decadence in their society.

The whig and evangelical casts of mind clashed at some points while blending at others. The evangelical espousal of basic republican principles—that virtue was incompatible with the pursuit of private interests, that commerce corrupted, and that social inequality led to oligarchy—grated on most urban whigs. The essentially antirational and antibourgeois spirit of the evangelicals conflicted, moreover, with the emerging economic liberalism that would soon be articulated by Adam Smith. For their part, the whigs, while rejecting the evangelical bias against commercial enterprise, accepted the moral strictures of the reformers, who concentrated on defects in the American character rather than on structural inequalities. Virtually all of the Revolutionaries perceived England as corrupt and responded positively to republicanism's call for regeneration through virtuous conduct. Thus republicanism's emphasis on virtue and sound character became the ground on which men of differing persuasions could unite against a common enemy.

It becomes clear from Nash's analysis that different groups approached the Revolution from different perceptions of what America was and should become. These divergent views were rooted in experience and values. Everyone desired some reformation from the Revolution, but, depending on an individual's position in society, each drew on republican theory selectively. While all saw England as a threat, Americans ranged from radical to conservative in their views about how to confront that threat and in their hopes for the future. Clearly, no single ideology could serve them all.

Research by Foner and Robert Kelley supports Nash's suggestion that republicanism did not exist as a monolithic entity. Through a study of Tom Paine and his working-class followers in Philadelphia, Foner reveals an urban variant of republicanism that fostered egalitarianism as well as economic enterprise.[20] Paine outlined a society in which republican

---

[20] Foner, *Tom Paine and Revolutionary America* (New York, 1976).

government, together with economic progress, would produce social harmony, equality, and abundance. Kelley broadens this focus to include the entire nation, within which he identifies four distinct varieties of republicanism, each tied closely to the social circumstances in which it originated and each offering a vision for America.[21] Kelley considers New England republicanism moralistic with an emphasis on an organic community bound together by a strong government that promoted a shared way of life. Such a government and society were anathema to southerners, whose republicanism remained basically libertarian. They desired a relatively weak central government that would allow a nation of white men to live as they saw fit. Kelley believes that the Middle Atlantic states offered opposing perceptions of republicanism. One, supported by Scotch-Irish Presbyterians and their working-class allies, fostered egalitarianism and individualism. The other, nationalistic republicanism, was favored by an anglicized and cosmopolitan mercantile elite who advocated a highly centralized government, an active commercial life, and a deferential social order. Kelley concludes that republicanism offered Americans a universe of discourse, not a prescriptive faith. It established a framework for discussion; certain generally accepted ideas and goals existed, and a special language was shared. What those goals meant and how they were to be reached, however, remained quite unsettled.

Joyce Appleby, too, suggests the need to go beyond a narrow definition of republicanism. Drawing on the work of social historians such as Kenneth A. Lockridge, Richard L. Bushman, and Philip J. Greven, Jr., and pursuing her own explorations into seventeenth-century English economic thought, Appleby seeks the origins of the liberalism she believes characterized post-Revolutionary America.[22] She contends that colonial America underwent a modernizing process that gave rise to "the aggressive individualism, the optimistic materialism, and the pragmatic interest-group politics that became so salient so early in the life of the new nation."[23] Synthesizing this perception with ideas found in essays by Nash,

[21] Kelley, "Ideology and Political Culture from Jefferson to Nixon," *American Historical Review*, LXXXII (1977), 531-562, and *The Cultural Pattern in American Politics: The First Century* (New York, 1979).

[22] Representative of a great bulk of research by a good many scholars are Bushman, *From Puritan to Yankee: Character and the Social Order in Connecticut, 1690-1765* (Cambridge, Mass., 1967); Lockridge, *A New England Town, the First Hundred Years: Dedham, Massachusetts, 1636-1736* (New York, 1970); and Greven, *Four Generations: Population, Land, and Family in Colonial Andover, Massachusetts* (Ithaca, N.Y., 1970). Appleby's work includes *Economic Thought and Ideology in Seventeenth-Century England* (Princeton, N.J., 1978), "Liberalism and the American Revolution," *New England Quarterly*, XLIX (1976), 3-26, "The Social Origins of American Revolutionary Ideology," *Journal of American History*, LXIV (1978), 935-958, "Ideology and Theory: The Tension between Political and Economic Liberalism in Seventeenth-Century England," *AHR*, LXXXI (1976), 499-515, and "The New Republican Synthesis and the Changing Political Ideas of John Adams," *American Quarterly*, XXV (1973), 578-595.

[23] Appleby, "Social Origins," *JAH*, LXIV (1978), 937.

Countryman, and Hoerder, Appleby maintains that restive lower and middle orders in colonial America, imbued with aggressive modern characteristics, drew on a body of seventeenth-century English economic literature quite distinct from classical republicanism in order to advance their opportunities. Thus the upwardly mobile, advocating "liberal republicanism"—an ideology that "elevated their goals to a universal law of self-interest"—turned the resistance movement into a revolution that gave birth to modern liberalism.[24] From Appleby's perspective, this historical process has been obfuscated by historians' insistence on the preeminence of classical republicanism as the driving force of the Revolution. She believes that if historians infer a premodern social order from this premodern ideology, they will create a colonial past ill-suited to provide the foundations of nineteenth-century American society. Worse yet, the ideological historians threaten to sink the social historians' careful reconstruction of the past in a "quagmire of explanations which rely more upon theories of social psychology than evidence supporting a connection between presumptive cause and discernible effect."[25]

Appleby's work reveals a noteworthy characteristic of historical research over the last decade. Historians interested in the ideological impact of republicanism have concentrated on the literate elite, whereas scholars with a socioeconomic perspective have focused on the lower classes and hinted at the presence of a rudimentary popular ideology. These approaches, by and large, remained separate enterprises until the publication of several essays by Rhys Isaac on colonial Virginia that perceptively analyze the relationship between the whig gentry and the evangelical elements of the populace.[26]

Virginia has been commonly viewed as the classic example of a colony

---

[24] Ibid., 954. Here Appleby draws on Bernard Friedman, "The Shaping of the Radical Consciousness in Provincial New York," JAH, LVI (1970), 781-801. She also depends on Nash's essay "The Transformation of Urban Politics, 1700-1765," ibid., LX (1973), 605-632, as well as the one in American Revolution. Like a number of authors in American Revolution, Appleby assumes that a popular ideology must have existed because the socioeconomic conditions were ripe for one. Therefore she grafts her own findings on economic liberal thought to the groups she assumed must have or should have espoused these ideas. However, Nash and others, drawing heavily on Alfred Young's unpublished manuscript, "The Crowd and the Coming of the Revolution: From Ritual to Rebellion in Boston," have subsequently concluded that the lower and lower-middle class elements espoused the traditional communal ideology rather than the liberal one of Appleby.

[25] Appleby, "Liberalism and the American Revolution," NEQ, XLIX (1976), 25.

[26] Isaac, "Preachers and Patriots: Popular Culture and the Revolution in Virginia," in Young, ed., American Revolution, 125-156, "Religion and Authority: Problems of the Anglican Establishment in Virginia in the Era of the Great Awakening and the Parsons' Cause," WMQ, 3d Ser., XXX (1973), 3-36, "Evangelical Revolt: The Nature of the Baptists' Challenge to the Traditional Order in Virginia, 1765 to 1775," ibid., XXXI (1974), 345-368, and "Dramatizing the Ideology of Revolution: Popular Mobilization in Virginia, 1774 to 1776," ibid., XXXIII (1976), 357-385.

united behind its gentry against the British.[27] It has seemed a perfect fit for the Bailyn thesis, which minimizes internal disorder and emphasizes ideology as the primary explanation for the timing and focus of revolt. Isaac's research, however, indicates that although there may have been an eventual common front against the British, it was accomplished only after the rapprochement of two violently antagonistic cultural forces: the gentry and their Baptist opponents. The conflict resulted from the confrontation between a courthouse culture reflecting the interests and rivalries of proud gentlemen and a communalistic order in which God-humbled men sought fellowship in the deep emotions of a religious faith that stressed equality. Baptists attempted through preaching and good works to create a new and more popular structure for the maintenance of social order. Their attacks on traditional authority, which led to physical retaliation by the gentry, constituted a revolt indicative of serious strains in Virginia society.

The British actions of the 1760s intruded on this scene of conflict and provoked a more general form of excitement in Virginia: the patriot movement. This movement, which subsumed the internal contest, reveals republicanism as the element that united the gentry and the evangelicals. The message imparted by patriot leaders emphasized republican concepts of liberty, virtue, and frugality. It drew meaning from a nagging source of anxiety for a broad range of Virginians: how could they denounce British corruption if their own virtue was questionable? This uneasiness resonated with the gentry's growing concern over luxury, idleness, indebtedness, and slavery, as well as with the evangelical resistance to the dominant culture. Thus, even though striking contrasts and sharp tensions existed between the evangelicals and the gentry, at a deeper level, where the need for psychic relief from oppressive feelings of guilt and anxiety was rooted, republican ideas struck a single responsive chord.

Isaac contends that the manner in which patriot leaders communicated their message to the people tells us a great deal about the dramaturgical needs of an oral culture. Employing the spoken word and communal rituals—voting, militia musters, and economic associations—the gentry, closely integrated in rural society, responded heartily to preaching and good works whenever these tended to secure their cause rather than condemn their way of life. The Baptists, too, gained the more orderly moral authority they sought. Both sides found relief from anxieties by participating in symbolic communal activities. Such public behavior and communication created a collective conscience that affirmed membership in a virtuous community aroused in common defense of its most cherished rights. Thus republicanism gave force and expression to a movement that concealed a deep split in Virginia culture.

[27] The clearest and most recent statement of this position is Jack P. Greene's essay, "Society, Ideology, and Politics: An Analysis of the Political Culture of Mid-Eighteenth-Century Virginia," in Richard M. Jellison, ed., *Society, Freedom, and Conscience: The American Revolution in Virginia, Massachusetts, and New York* (New York, 1976), 14-76.

While the work of Isaac, Nash, Kelley, and others reveals the vulnerability of the supposition of an ideological consensus in colonial society, another major weakness of earlier analyses of republicanism has also become apparent; namely, a focus on political and constitutional issues to the detriment of economic analysis. Two authors, J. E. Crowley and Drew R. McCoy, address this problem and offer major contributions to an understanding of the political economy of republicanism.[28] In his analysis of the manner in which eighteenth-century Americans conceptualized their economic life, Crowley notes the concern they showed for industry and frugality. These terms helped define one's relationship with society long before the libertarian rhetoric of the Revolution flourished. Crowley's observation is important because it reveals the ways in which these ideas contributed to a pervasive "moral economy" that transcended any divisions among the various ranks of society. In addition, it suggests the possibility that republican thought may have helped synthesize the popular evangelical beliefs noted by Nash, Young, and others with the whig ideas of the gentry. Such a possibility gains credence from the fact that, like Isaac, Crowley recognizes that visible and ritualized behavior, such as the enforcement of nonimportation pacts, was vital in gaining community support for resistance to Britain. Republican ideas may have provided the catalyst for uniting behind the patriot cause the conflicting groups identified by the socioeconomic historians. In addition, Crowley's epilogue, "Republicans as Economic Men," is suggestive in another direction: republicanism accommodated the requirement of the American situation that commerce be embraced, rather than restrained or even eliminated in accordance with classical strictures against it. While some Americans retained anticommercial feelings, the vast majority of those who gave public expression to their thought integrated the ideas of Adam Smith and other economic liberals into their own republicanism.

McCoy's work provides the most cogent analysis of American attempts to reduce the tension between the economic "liberalism" of Smith and "classical" American republicanism.[29] McCoy acknowledges the admiration many Americans felt for the precommercial social values of classical

[28] Crowley, *"This Sheba, Self": The Conceptualization of Economic Life in Eighteenth-Century America*, Johns Hopkins University Studies in Historical and Political Science, XCII (Baltimore, 1974); McCoy, "Republicanism and American Foreign Policy: James Madison and the Political Economy of Commercial Discrimination, 1789 to 1794," *WMQ*, 3d Ser., XXXI (1974), 633-646, "Benjamin Franklin's Vision of a Republican Political Economy for America," *ibid.*, XXXV (1978), 605-628, and *The Elusive Republic: Political Economy in Jeffersonian America* (Chapel Hill, N.C., 1980).

[29] Pocock clearly identified these strains in "Virtue and Commerce in the Eighteenth Century," *JIH*, III (1972), 119-134. Donald Winch's *Adam Smith's Politics: An Essay in Historiographic Revision* (New York, 1978) indicates that Smith was more influenced by libertarian thought than previously imagined. Smith, too, was affected by the strains created by the commercial changes of the era.

republicanism, but he also notes their commitment to an expansive commercial society. This ambivalence necessitated some kind of synthesis, which Americans accomplished primarily by integrating the ideas of Smith—whose sociological view of English corruption blended nicely with that of the libertarians—into their republican social perspective. Smith's analysis of the aging process of nations assumed great relevance for Americans. They acknowledged that societies aged naturally through the inexorable pressure of population growth but could also be forced into premature decay by the machinations of a corrupt, mercantilist government that sacrificed the public good to special interests. Convinced that republican government and a healthy society depended on the expansion of agriculture and the export trade, Americans saw the oportunity to forestall the evils of Old World decadence. The virility of their nation could be sustained by a republican economy of moderately prosperous, self-reliant producers. America would remain in this ideal middle state of civilization (thus escaping the curses of overpopulation, inequality, and poverty) only if it secured a republican political economy that combined orderly expansion across the continent and a vigorous foreign commerce fostered by free trade. American republicanism was thus not anticommercial or anticapitalistic. Nor was it a static, premodern libertarian ideology transferred intact from its English context. Instead, McCoy portrays republicanism as an ideology in transition, one that accommodated change in an effort to reconcile classical republican virtues and an expansive commercial economy.

The research of the last ten years, then, makes clear that it is no longer possible to see a single, monolithic political ideology characterizing American thought on the eve of the Revolution. While the new complexity adds depth to our understanding of republicanism, it also raises two important questions. First, what became of republican thought in the half century after the Revolution? Second, in light of the welter of new interpretations, how are historians to make sense of the role and function of republicanism in early American history?

II

The first question directs our attention to current scholarship dealing with the early nineteenth century, where a stark contrast with colonial and Revolutionary research becomes apparent. James M. Banner, Jr., Lance Banning, Gerald Stourzh, and McCoy, among others, offer insights into the relationship between republican thought and the political partisanship of the 1790s and early 1800s, but their work exists in comparative isolation.[30] For the half century following the Revolution we lack the

---

[30] Banner, *To the Hartford Convention: The Federalists and the Origins of Party Politics in Massachusetts, 1789-1815* (New York, 1970); Banning, *Jeffersonian Persuasion*; Stourzh, *Alexander Hamilton and the Idea of Republican Government* (Stanford, Calif., 1970).

careful re-creation of social and economic life typified by the colonial studies of Nash, Greven, Lockridge, Bushman, Jack P. Greene, and Edmund S. Morgan. Without such an understanding of the fabric of life in the early national period, it is difficult to deal fruitfully with republicanism or with concepts like laissez-faire and liberalism in the nineteenth century.[31]

Two essays by Rowland Berthoff and John M. Murrin offer a provocative hypothesis that may serve as a starting point.[32] By focusing on two of republicanism's central themes, the independent citizen and equality of condition, these scholars suggest some consequences of republican thought for nineteenth-century America. Basic to both essays is the belief that the American colonies were modernizing rapidly during the eighteenth century and, had not the imperial crisis intervened, might well have developed a system of thought that could deal realistically with modernity. Instead, classical republicanism, already anachronistic when the Revolution erupted, captured the minds of a great many Americans with far-reaching effects on post-Revolutionary society.

The republican ideal of the selfless independent citizen as the basis of social harmony was embraced by the Revolutionaries even though that image represented a reaction against, rather than a fulfillment of, dominant tendencies in colonial society. In actuality, late eighteenth-century America already exemplified the aggressive, individualistic, entrepreneurial spirit described by Appleby and others. Murrin and Berthoff's contribution is to show that as the gap widened between classical ideals and social realities in the nineteenth century, Americans grasped more urgently the republican view of themselves that obscured the actual ramifications

---

[31] Some scattered beginnings have been made. Ronald P. Formisano's "Deferential-Participant Politics: The Early Republic's Political Culture, 1789-1840," *American Political Science Review*, LXVIII (1974), 473-487, provides an outstanding analysis of the relationship between cultural transformations and political change. Howard B. Rock offers insights into the artisan's social and political roles in a marketplace in transition from a preindustrial to an industrial economy (*Artisans of the New Republic: The Tradesmen of New York City in the Age of Jefferson* [New York, 1979]). Paul A. Gilje's "The Baltimore Riots of 1812 and the Breakdown of the Anglo-American Mob Tradition," *Journal of Social History*, XIII (1980), 547-564, suggests basic societal alterations through a study of changing mob behavior in the nineteenth century. Studies such as Paul E. Johnson's *A Shopkeeper's Millennium: Society and Revivals in Rochester, New York, 1815-1837* (New York, 1978), and Stuart M. Blumin's *The Urban Threshold: Growth and Change in a Nineteenth-Century American Community* (Chicago, 1976), are excellent examples of the kind of work that needs to be done for the Jeffersonian years.

[32] Berthoff, "Independence and Attachment, Virtue and Interest: From Republican Citizen to Free Enterpriser, 1787-1837," in Richard L. Bushman *et al.*, *Uprooted Americans: Essays to Honor Oscar Handlin* (Boston, 1979), 97-124; Berthoff and Murrin, "Feudalism, Communalism, and the Yeoman Freeholder: The American Revolution Considered as a Social Accident," in Kurtz and Hutson, eds., *Essays on the Revolution*, 256-288.

of accelerated economic development.[33] As time passed, the republican image of the virtuous citizen became ambiguous. Civic virtue came, ironically, to be measured in terms of personal ambition and devotion to the acquisition of wealth, as the spirit of free enterprise, entirely detached from its eighteenth-century context, emerged as the essence of the republican ethic. "Long before the United States reached its centennial celebrations," Berthoff asserts, "the 'equally free and independent' citizen of 1776 had indeed been corrupted into what in 1876 was just beginning to be recognized as the modern embodiment of both those classical specters: the entrepreneur set free, by the American dream of virtuous independence, to dominate a society grown so narrowly acquisitive that it could only admire his success."[34]

Republican emphasis on equality of condition—idealized in the figure of the yeoman freeholder—raised an even more complex difficulty. The commitment of nineteenth-century Americans to social equality and political democracy evolved from a Revolutionary ideology that drew on an already anachronistic image of agrarian simplicity. This persistent and misleading perception of the United States as a nation of independent freeholders hamstrung post-Revolutionary reforms and shaped the direction that "egalitarian" change would take.[35] Berthoff and Murrin maintain that even though American society became increasingly stratified during the half century after 1775, Americans continued to honor egalitarian social and political rhetoric. This detachment of rhetoric from reality contributed to the banality of Jacksonian thought, which idealized the image of a golden age of republican equality in a society of yeomen freeholders while American society was in fact moving rapidly toward greater complexity and inequality. It is true that Americans in this period assaulted many artificial barriers to equality—suffrage restrictions, legal privileges, monopolistic advantages, and the like. But such reforms did not actually promote equality of material or social condition; rather, they enhanced the free individual's opportunity to compete with and surpass his neighbor. Post-Revolutionary reform rhetoric couched political liberties in egalitarian terms, but when Americans attacked social problems and pursued social opportunities they did so in an essentially libertarian cast of mind. "Partly because of their Revolutionary heritage Americans could not really face the possibility that their liberty—their freedom to com-

[33] Easing the tension resulting from the gap between the real and the ideal in any society is one of the prime functions of an ideology. See Erik H. Erikson, *Young Man Luther: A Study in Psychoanalysis and History* (New York, 1958), 22; Francis X. Sutton *et al.*, *The American Business Creed* (Cambridge, Mass., 1956); and Clifford Geertz, "Ideology as a Cultural System," in David E. Apter, ed., *Ideology and Discontent* (New York, 1964), 47-76.

[34] Berthoff, "Independence and Attachment," in Bushman *et al.*, *Uprooted Americans*, 120.

[35] Richard Bushman also suggests this in a penetrating essay, " 'This New Man': Dependence and Independence, 1776," in Bushman *et al.*, *Uprooted Americans*, 77-96.

pete—was undermining their equality."[36] Post-Revolutionary reforms that promised an equality patterned on an agrarian ideal actually freed Americans to become unequal on a scale that escalated with the economic development of the nineteenth century.

The republican view of America as a land of independent freeholders had its greatest impact on the role of government. Because government was largely irrelevant to the image, it was gradually divorced from society. In particular, the general welfare no longer seemed to require regulation of the economy. The emergence of the liberal principle of laissez-faire, which was designed to promote equality in a land of independent entrepreneurs, sanctioned the separation of government from the realm of economy and society. Thus the Jacksonians destroyed the federally chartered Bank of the United States to foster individual equality. In time, however, this action contributed to the formation of unrepublican concentrations of wealth and power. Similarly, Murrin and Berthoff observe that "the transportation revolution, after an initial stage of public capitalization and control, and the Industrial Revolution from its inception were allowed to proceed as though an unregulated modern economy would distribute the wealth it produced as satisfactorily as the simple agricultural and mercantile economy of the colonial past had done—or as parts of the contemporary but old-fashioned West were still doing."[37] On the contrary, the second half of the nineteenth century brought extremes of inequality that far exceeded the greatest fears of eighteenth-century republicans. The irony is that as modern Americans faithfully articulated an egalitarian dogma centered on the anachronistic figure of the yeoman freeholder, they were contributing to the demise, rather than the fulfillment, of the republican vision. Such disembodied republican language made it difficult to define, much more to resolve, the tensions between community needs and individual desires. In the opinion of Murrin and Berthoff, therefore, the ultimate effect of republican rhetoric may well have been to separate power from politics and the political world from social reality. The Revolution, with its idealization of classical republicanism, helped to prevent America from developing a social and political system that could recognize and deal realistically with the changes brought about by modernization.

The essays by Berthoff and Murrin draw together nicely several strands of inquiry. They fully incorporate the work of social historians who have explored social change in eighteenth-century America and have shown that opposing interests and social tensions characterized the late colonial and early national periods. Berthoff and Murrin also give full credit to the ideological historians, not for explaining the Revolution, but for elucidating republican thought. Unlike Appleby and others, they do not believe that the ideological historians have obfuscated early American history.

[36] Berthoff and Murrin, "Feudalism, Communalism, and the Yeoman Freeholder," in Kurtz and Hutson, eds., *Essays on the Revolution*, 283.
[37] *Ibid.*, 285.

Rather, these historians have uncovered the ideology that divorced political rhetoric from social and economic reality. For Berthoff and Murrin, classical republicanism provided the operative principles of nineteenth-century America, its "definitive ideas, as a lasting legacy of the American Revolution."[38]

III

The second issue raised by recent research—the role and function of republicanism in early America—leads in interesting new directions. Scholars are providing fresh perspectives that contribute greatly to a deeper understanding of that ideology. Their insights have transformed it from a narrow constitutional and political perspective to a far broader, more powerful force. This literature adds much-needed sophistication to our knowledge of republicanism and provides the substantive basis for a number of observations about its study—observations that may prove helpful in better understanding early America.

The work of McCoy and others, for example, reveals that republicanism was not a static, premodern concept but rather a dynamic one capable of synthesizing classical republican social thought and modern commercial ideas. This discovery, combined with the insights of Pocock, Appleby, Berthoff, Murrin, and Wood, demonstrates that America did not make a neat or smooth march into modernity. Instead, liberal and classical ideas existed in constant tension. They shaped and influenced each other until the end result was a bastardized form of each. Wood characterizes this aptly in his observation that by 1820 American culure was completely republicanized, but hardly in the manner most Revolutionaries had intended. Rather than embodying the best of ancient republics, America had developed into "a sprawling, materialistic, and licentious popular democracy unlike anything that had ever existed before."[39] Prosperity replaced austerity, and the meaning of virtue was subtly transformed. Instead of sacrificing their private desires in the interest of the community, nineteenth-century Americans relentlessly engaged in the individual pursuit of wealth and even justified such activity as the sole legitimate foundation for a free society. Yet, as Berthoff and Murrin convincingly suggest, this society also viewed itself largely in terms of classical republican simplicity and virtue. It seems, then, that post-Revolutionary America was an odd mixture of the archaic and the modern. While liberalism characterized Americans' economic and social behavior, classical republican rhetoric continued to influence their perceptions of themselves and helped shape the development of nineteenth-century society.

If many studies of republicanism have overlooked its economic content, so, too, have they slighted its religious element. The evangelical tradition, in particular, has appeared in recent work to be far more vibrant and long-

---

[38] Berthoff, "Independence and Attachment," in Bushman *et al.*, *Uprooted Americans*, 124, n. 96.

[39] Wood, ed., *The Rising Glory of America, 1760-1820* (New York, 1971), 8.

lasting than most early studies of republicanism recognized. Research by Morgan, Greven, and Alan Heimert demonstrates that eighteenth-century religious divisions contributed greatly to the political and social consciousness of the Revolutionary and early national periods.[40] These insights have been further developed by Nathan O. Hatch, James West Davidson, and William G. McLoughlin, who analyze the emergence of what Cushing Strout terms "political religion."[41] They believe that a "republican eschatology," resulting from a convergence of traditional millennial thought and republican political ideas, emerged in the 1760s. Congregational ministers projected the image of Antichrist in one breath and attacked the "Robinocracy" in the next. Indeed, McLoughlin presents the Revolution, which implemented the new republican ideology, as the secular fulfillment of the religious ideals of the Great Awakening.

Such findings have influenced the work of Hoerder, Young, Nash, Isaac, and others. These historians see Americans embracing deeply entrenched religious perspectives in an effort to find meaning in an age of confusion. Two authors in particular—Isaac and Crowley—attempt to show how the republican temperament that emerged during the Revolution drew on basic evangelical values (virtue, frugality, temperance) to forge a strong ideological force supportive of the Revolution. Such analyses indicate that republicanism offered a vehicle for synthesizing religious, political, economic, and social beliefs that provided Americans with a sense of identity and direction in their lives.

Republican ideology, therefore, was broad enough to incorporate diverse economic and religious ideas. It must also be recognized, however, that republicanism alone does not constitute a sufficient cause or motive to explain action. The mere presence of republican language cannot explain differences between groups or individuals. For example, men as diverse as John Taylor of Caroline, Elbridge Gerry, and Theodore Sedgwick considered themselves good republicans and employed similar language, yet each clearly believed in a different kind of society and envisioned a different kind of America. Their political actions sprang from distinctive perceptions of reality—perceptions that each chose to articulate in terms of republicanism.[42]

---

[40] Morgan, "The Puritan Ethic and the American Revolution," *WMQ*, 3d Ser., XXIV (1967), 3-43; Greven, *The Protestant Temperament: Patterns of Child-Rearing, Religious Experience, and the Self in Early America* (New York, 1977); Heimert, *Religion and the American Mind: From the Great Awakening to the Revolution* (Cambridge, Mass., 1966).

[41] Hatch, *The Sacred Cause of Liberty: Republican Thought and the Millennium in Revolutionary New England* (New Haven, Conn., 1977); Davidson, *The Logic of Millennial Thought: Eighteenth-Century New England* (New Haven, Conn., 1977); McLoughlin, *Revivals, Awakenings, and Reform: An Essay in Religion and Social Change in America, 1607-1977* (Chicago, 1978); Strout, *The New Heavens and New Earth: Political Religion in America* (New York, 1974).

[42] George Athan Billias, *Elbridge Gerry: Founding Father and Republican States-*

The research of Isaac, Hoffman, Richard Alan Ryerson, and others demonstrates that republican language was indeed capable of supporting different groups in different situations. An entrenched gentry in Virginia employed republican rhetoric to further the patriot cause, while the same language mobilized political outsiders in Philadelphia to bring pressure on the established order when the latter resisted the Revolutionary effort.[43] Focusing on the fact that the Revolution influenced and was influenced by many local tensions, Edward Countryman observes that " 'to make the revolution' conjugated differently in Portsmouth, Dedham, Albany, Annapolis and Ninety-Six."[44] Though similar language was employed in each of these areas, it certainly did not carry the same meanings for all involved. Clearly, then, the identification of an individual or group as "republican" is insufficient to explain behavior. Here the work of such scholars as Kelley, Foner, and Nash is valuable, precisely because it helps clarify the republican views held in different regions of the nation and even by different groups within those regions. *Why* a person or group chose one version of republicanism rather than another, or even chose to support republicanism at all, however, remains problematic.

Research by historians interested in the dialogue between "Court" and "Country," as well as Greven's work on "temperament," may offer suggestive hypotheses. The concepts Court and Country, long associated with the English Revolution, have also been employed in an effort to understand America's Revolutionary era.[45] These ideas are central, for example, to Pocock's discussion of civic humanism, Banning's treatment of the division between Hamiltonians and Jeffersonians, and Murrin's analysis of late eighteenth-century American society.[46] These authors perceive Americans arranged along an ideological spectrum. The Country position on the left, made up of "virtuous farmers strugg[ling] desperately to protect their land and hence their independence against a darkly

---

man (New York, 1976); Banner, *To the Hartford Convention*; Robert E. Shalhope, *John Taylor of Caroline: Pastoral Republican* (Columbia, S.C., 1980).

[43] Ryerson, "Political Mobilization and the American Revolution: The Resistance Movement in Philadelphia, 1765 to 1776," *WMQ*, 3d Ser., XXXI (1974), 564-588, and *The Revolution Is Now Begun: The Radical Committees of Philadelphia, 1765-1776* (Philadelphia, 1978).

[44] Edward Countryman, "A Review Article: The Problem of the Early American Crowd," *Journal of American Studies*, VII (1973), 77-90 (quotation on p. 89).

[45] Perez Zagorin's *The Court and the Country: The Beginning of the English Revolution* (London, 1969), is essential for understanding the background and meaning of these terms.

[46] Pocock, *Machiavellian Moment;* Banning, *Jeffersonian Persuasion*; Murrin, "The Great Inversion, or Court versus Country: A Comparison of the Revolution Settlements in England (1688-1721) and America (1776-1816)," in Pocock, ed., *Three British Revolutions: 1641, 1688, 1776* (Princeton, N.J., 1980), 368-453. James H. Hutson interprets the Antifederalists from a Country perspective in "Country, Court, and Constitution: Antifederalism and the Historians," *WMQ*, 3d Ser., XXXVIII (1981), 337-368.

corrupt, grasping, anonymous, pervasive, and mysterious money power, which did indeed threaten their autonomy," contrasted with the Court stance on the right, where "the disciples of public order were merely rallying to defend property and protect the 'worthy' against the 'licentious.' "[47] Advocates of the Country position, usually rural, employed republican language to express their suspicion of governmental corruption and sinister conspiracies against liberty, while Court advocates, most often urban dwellers with commercial interests, emphasized republican aversion to disorder and anarchy.

This analytic framework of Court and Country is capable of incorporating insights from a broad range of research. For instance, Jackson Turner Main's identification of the division between "cosmopolitans" (wealthy, educated individuals who had extensive experience beyond their own cities and states) and "localists" (individuals lacking these characteristics who remained closely identified with their home communities) provides excellent insight into why a group or individual would accept Court or Country ideas.[48] David Szatmary's analysis of Shays's Rebellion as a clash between a traditional way of life and an ever-encroaching commercial society provides another thoughtful treatment of cultural differences and their potential for generating diverse perspectives.[49] Such work, combined with that of Pocock, Banning, Murrin, and others who emphasize the Court-Country dialogue, indicates that cultural forces—rooted in the region and type of community involved—heavily influenced an individual's or group's gravitation toward the Court or Country strains of republicanism.

The question remains: why did individuals within similar environments choose differently? Here Greven's analysis of temperaments provides a challenging starting point.[50] In an effort to link the inner lives of Americans, their feelings and pieties, with their outer behavior, Greven suggests that child-rearing practices produced in colonial America three distinctive temperaments—evangelical, moderate, and genteel—that shaped perceptions of the self and world in vastly different ways, with significant ideological consequences. Greven identifies at least three patterns of ideology—moderate, evangelical, and "non-Whig"—which correspond with the temperaments he discusses. He makes clear that different groups defined liberty and authority in different ways and that these definitions were linked to intimate familial experiences. Such research contributes greatly to an understanding of the importance of experience and values as determinants of ideological stances.

Equally important is the need to learn how ideology was employed to motivate public action. Here the work of Isaac is exemplary. He shows

[47] Murrin, "Great Inversion," in Pocock, ed., *Three British Revolutions,* 401.
[48] Main, *Political Parties before the Constitution* (Chapel Hill, N.C., 1973).
[49] Szatmary, *Shays' Rebellion: The Making of an Agrarian Insurrection* (Amherst, Mass., 1980).
[50] Greven, *Protestant Temperament.*

how the ideological language of the Virginia gentry was communicated to the lower orders. In addition, he has begun the process of analyzing how ideological commitment could support a popular movement. His skillful treatment of Virginia demonstrates that analyses of regional subcultures are needed to understand fully responses to the imperial crisis of the 1760s and 1770s.[51]

Isaac's observation that scholars must avoid the false assumption of a simple, single American society is of substantial importance. The American Revolution created a single political nation but certainly did not fashion a cohesive national community. Rather, during the Revolution and for some time thereafter, America was composed of regional subcultures. This perception is vital to any attempt to assess the role of republicanism in early America. It may well be that republicanism, in its local variant forms, constituted a hegemonic consensus within particular regions.[52] That is, the diffusion of republican ideas was so complete within each subculture as to form a hegemony or consensus that shaped social relations and political principles as well as morality and customs. This helps to explain the phenomenon that appears in the work of Ryerson, Nash, Hoerder, and others: they have discovered, for a number of different regions, active groups among the lower ranks who, although politically united, could not articulate their purpose in a manner distinct from the dominant republican language of their superiors. In the end, class or popular ideologies remained stillborn. This does not mean that the various egalitarian or radical strains identified by Countryman and Nash did not exist or were unimportant. Rather, they may prove to be limiting cases that tested the boundaries of the local consensus, thus allowing the historian to investigate the mechanism whereby men in authority secured their ideological hegemony.[53] In any event, it is clear from recent research that republican ideas, broadly defined, predominated in the local areas that have been carefully investigated.

IV

The extraordinary promise of recent research on republicanism for furthering our understanding of early America has not been fully realized. By exaggerating differences and obscuring potentially common ground, constant bickering between "ideological" historians and "social" historians

[51] Robert A. Gross does just this in his excellent *The Minutemen and Their World* (New York, 1976), which reveals how republican ideas healed a serious division among the inhabitants of Concord and united them against the British. See esp. chap. 3, "A Well-ordered Revolution."

[52] For a discussion of hegemonic consensus see Eugene D. Genovese, *In Red and Black: Marxian Explanations in Southern and Afro-American History* (New York, 1971), 136-153.

[53] Aileen S. Kraditor offers a provocative discussion of the "limiting case" in "American Radical Historians on Their Heritage," *Past and Present*, No. 56 (1972), 136-153.

has proved counterproductive. In its present form, the discussion finds intellectual historians contending for the causative power of ideas, while the "new" social historians and others by and large consider ideas to be epiphenomenal or merely rationalizations of social and economic needs. Constant sniping between the two camps has prevented useful questions regarding republicanism's role in early American society from being asked, much less being answered.[54]

The suggestions of a number of social scientists offer historians a potential escape from the conundrum. The research of Clifford Geertz, Kenneth Burke, Erik Erikson, and others attempts to understand ideologies as cultural systems as well as to analyze the meaning of their language. These scholars suggest that the sociopsychological dimension of ideology—perhaps best defined as the "unconscious tendency underlying religious and scientific as well as political thought: the tendency at a given time to make facts amenable to ideas, and ideas to facts, in order to create a world image convincing enough to support the collective and the individual sense of identity"—arises from individual or group efforts to escape strain rather than to pursue interests.[55] In addition, these scholars demonstrate that ideologies operate as cognitive and expressive symbol systems that provide a pattern or guide for organizing social and psychological processes. Being extrinsic sources of information, cultural symbol systems become crucial in situations "where institutionalized guides for behavior, thought, or feeling are weak or absent." Just as one needs a map when traveling through strange territory, so, too, one requires a sociopsychological guide at times. Ideology functions in such a way as to make possible a clearly defined political movement by providing "the authoritative concepts that render it meaningful, the suasive images by means of which it can be sensibly grasped." When a society's general cultural orientation and its pragmatic answers prove inadequate, ideologies become crucial in giving meaning to life. "It is a confluence of sociopsychological strain and an absence of cultural resources by means of which to make (political, moral, or economic) sense of that strain, each exacerbating the other, that sets the stage for the rise of systematic (political, moral, or economic) ideologies." Thus, in the final analysis, ideologies constitute "maps of problematic social reality and matrices for the creation of collective conscience."[56]

Similarly, the language of ideologies, often considered excessive or

---

[54] Throughout this essay a conscious effort has been made to avoid classifying individual scholars or points of view as representative of a "school" of thought in order to be able to deal effectively with ideas common to differing approaches.

[55] The quotation is from Erikson, *Young Man Luther*, 22. The fullest discussion of the sociopsychological determinants of ideology are found in Sutton *et al.*, *American Business Creed*, and Geertz, "Ideology as a Cultural System," in Apter, ed., *Ideology and Discontent*.

[56] The foregoing discussion of ideologies is drawn from Geertz, "Ideology as a Cultural System," in Apter, ed., *Ideology and Discontent* (quotations on pp. 62-64).

simplistic, is best interpreted in light of the research of Burke. For him, words hold the key to understanding the dramatic encounter between the internal world of images and meaning and the external one of circumstances and experience. Ideas are the result of mind's encounter with the world, and language represents our attempt to order that encounter. Consequently, language becomes action. More precisely, it becomes "symbolic action." It represents the individual's strategic response to the selectively perceived situation in which he finds himself. Burke is primarily concerned with what an idea or word suggests, and he reaches outward from the word not to find what "causes" it but rather to discover what it is in the world to which the idea responds. He wishes, above all, to discern the dialogic encounter between "subjective mind" and "objective world." Burke's important insight here is the recognition that words hold a key to understanding the encounter between mind and environment.[57]

Historical research attuned to the ideas of scholars such as Burke and Geertz might, in fact, dissolve the familiar idealist-materialist dichotomy between thought and action. Such a perspective would consider ideas or beliefs to be neither causes nor effects of social forces; instead, they become functional and instrumental. Recognizing this, Wood contends that "ideas thus influence behavior, not by being motives for action, but by giving meanings to action and thus publicly prescribing and circumscribing what behavior is legitimate and permissible, indeed, possible."[58]

An understanding of republicanism that comprehends the origins, functions, and language of ideology offers immense potential for the study of early America. Once it is recognized that the presence of an ideology with the depth and strength of republicanism is indicative of serious strains in American society, an analytic framework emerges that permits the drawing together of disparate or even contradictory strands of historical inquiry. Nash's urban tensions, Isaac's cultural clash between gentry and evangelicals, and Appleby's belief that qualitative changes taking place in pre-Revolutionary America placed great strain on the free individual all become integral elements of (in Geertz's phrase) a "problematic social reality" defined in republican terms. As a consequence, scholars should not be content with merely discovering and analyzing the content of republican language; they must consider it as a clue or symptom. They must follow Burke's lead, in short, and probe the dynamic interaction between life and language.

For historians willing to transcend the rather narrow focus of the various "schools" of thought or thematic subgroupings in their discipline, the recent literature of the colonial and Revolutionary era has a great deal to offer. And republicanism, considered as a cultural system, may well provide the most stimulating means of integrating the many insights of separate approaches into a useful reappraisal of early American society.

[57] Burke, *The Philosophy of Literary Form: Studies in Symbolic Action* (Baton Rouge, La., 1941), 1-137 *passim*.

[58] Gordon S. Wood, "Intellectual History and the Social Sciences," in John Higham and Paul Conkin, eds., *New Directions in American Intellectual History* (Baltimore, 1979), 27-41 (quotation on p. 36).

THE REPUBLICAN IDEOLOGY OF
THE REVOLUTIONARY GENERATION

LINDA K. KERBER

University of Iowa

> Fraud lurks in generals. There is not a more unintelligible
> word in the English language than republicanism.
> —John Adams to Mercy Otis Warren, 8 August 1807

NOT SO LONG AGO, AS WE RECKON ACADEMIC STYLES, AMERICAN HISTORIANS used the ungainly term "early national period" to describe the years between the adoption of the Constitution and the inauguration of Andrew Jackson. The phrase was so vague as to be of little use except to underline a general sense that nationalism was central to American life. A new label has been devised in the last decade; the modest phrase "early republic" is not much more descriptive, but it is richer in nuance. Aggressive nationalism has come to seem somewhat less important to an understanding of the early American political system than does the widely shared sense that Americans were engaged in a republican experiment. Substitution of "republican" for "national" in the historians' lexicon may have had some relationship to a growing distaste, among people writing in the midst of the Vietnam conflict, for nationalism as a nonpejorative explanatory device. But it also owes much to an enlarged sensitivity to and respect for words as carriers of culture, and to a respect for ideology as an authentic expression of political situation and cultural condition. It also represents historians' response to a growing body of work that seeks to place the concepts of republicanism in a practical political context, a context large enough, in the hands of Bernard Bailyn and his students: to include the opposition politics of eighteenth-century Britain; and stretching even further back, in the hands of J. G. A. Pocock, to the Florentine Renaissance.

As more and more historians swelled the crowd who came to recognize the achievement of a republic as a legitimate goal of the Revolutionary generation, Robert Shalhope thoughtfully provided an umbrella for them in his essay, "Toward a Republican Synthesis." Like Moliere's gentleman who was delighted to discover he was speaking prose, thanks to Shalhope a collection of rather disparate historians have discovered that they were part of a school.

90

Shalhope's use of the tentative "toward" in his title suggests that agreement on the use of the concept of republicanism in explaining American political culture had not yet been reached in 1972, as indeed it still is not. But it is certainly possible to identify some of its main features and to suggest some of the ways in which our understanding of early American society and culture is being reshaped.[1]

*   *   *

Republicanism was once thought to be a simple, even self-evident, matter. It does not appear at all in Randolph G. Adams' magisterial *Political Ideas of the American Revolution*, nor did Carl Becker need it to explain *The Declaration of Independence*. The only place where the word republican appears in the Constitution is Article IV, section 4: "The United States shall guarantee to every state in this union a Republican form of government, and shall protect each of them against invasion; and, on application of the legislature, or of the executive, (when the legislature can not be convened), against domestic violence."[2]

Usually republicanism was simply what monarchism was not; the usage was vague, and in *The Federalist* no. 39, James Madison kept it general: "we may define a republic to be, or at least may bestow that name on, a government which derives all its powers directly or indirectly from the body of the people; and is administered by persons holding their offices during pleasure, for an unlimited period, or during good behavior." Often, the argument between Federalist and Anti-Federalist had to do with the sort of republic each had in mind, rather than whether to have a republic at all. Madison was at some pains to assure his readers that all existing state constitutions fit the broad definition of "republican form" in the federal constitution. Each state had a wide range of options, and the federal government did not need to take a position on each one. For example, in the Constitutional Convention Gouverneur Morris could be reassured that the guarantee of a republican form of government would not require the federal government to guarantee the paper money laws of Rhode Island. (Madison

---

[1]Robert Shalhope, "Toward a Republican Synthesis: The Emergence of an Understanding of Republicanism in American Historiography," *William and Mary Quarterly*, (hereafter cited as *WMQ*), 3rd ser., 29 (1972), 49-80, and idem, "Republicanism and Early American Historiography," ibid. 39 (1982), 334-56. The latter historiographical article deals with the work that appeared in the intervening decade. Other recent historiographical essays include J.G.A. Pocock, "*The Machiavellian Moment* Revisited: A Study in History and Ideology," *Journal of World History*, 53 (1981), 49-72; Isaac Kramnick, "Republican Revisionism Revisited," *American Historical Review*, 87 (1982), 629-64. Other important essays include Gordon W. Wood, "Conspiracy and the Paranoid Style: Causality and Deceit in the Eighteenth Century," *WMQ*, 39 (1982), 401-41; and Rowland Berthoff, "Peasants and Artisans, Puritans and Republicans: Personal Liberty and Communal Equality in American History," *Journal of American History*, 69 (1982), 579-98.

[2]Randolph G. Adams, *Political Ideas of the American Revolution* (Durham: Trinity College Press, 1922); Carl Becker, *The Declaration of Independence* (New York: Knopf, 1922, 1942).

should be pardoned if he could not foresee that the issue would be raised again in the debates over the admission of Utah to the Union, when it would be alleged that a community that countenanced polygamy could not possibly have a republican form of government.)[3]

In *The Federalist*, Madison also separated the matter of guaranteeing republican forms from the assurance that rebellior. would be put down. He assumed that rebellion would come from antirepublicans, seeking "aristocratic or monarchical innovations." Despite Shays' Rebellion, which he regarded as "commotions" rather than a coherent challenge to the principles of republicanism, he did not in *The Federalist* explore alternative responses to future rebellions which might seek to increase the degree of republicanism. The states had the right to expect "that the forms of government under which the compact was entered into, should be substantially maintained."[4]

As it turned out, little recourse has been had to the constitutional clause guaranteeing a republican form of government. It was not used to settle the issues in Rhode Island's Dorr War in 1841, even though the popular tumult was explicitly about whether the state's government was authentically republican. In *Luther v. Borden* (1849) the Supreme Court left it to the President to decide which of two contending governors was the lawful executive rather than rule on the proper degree of republicanism.[5] In the antebellum years there was no attempt to force the judiciary to any determination that slavery was unrepublican; indeed after the Dred Scott case the Court surely would have said that slavery was republican, just as it told Virginia Minor in 1875 that it was republican to exclude women from the suffrage. The definition was an operational one even if it risked being circular; what had been acceptable in 1789 was in good faith to be respected subsequently as authentically republican.

But critics of the Court—abolitionists and suffragists—complained that the Court's definition was too narrow, a choice of form over substance. "The will

---

[3]*The Federalist* no. 39. See also *The Federalist* no. 14 and *The Federalist* no. 10: "a Government in which the scheme of representation takes place." [Also implied is majority rule and an absence of hereditary office.] Herbert Storing makes the point that the word *democracy* "is ambiguous, containing a range of ideas from simple, direct popular rule to a regulated, checked, mitigated rule of the people. Generally, especially when aiming at precision of expression, both the Federalists and the Anti-Federalists used the term 'popular government' to contain this whole range of ideas, reserving 'democracy' for the former end of the scale and 'republic' for the latter." See "What the Anti-Federalists Were *For*," in *The Complete Anti-Federalist* (Chicago: Univ. of Chicago Press, 1981), 1:90, n. 19. For polygamy, see Frederick Merk, *The History of the Westward Movement* (New York: Knopf, 1978), 111. I am grateful to Lewis Perry for providing this reference.

[4]*The Federalist* no. 43. Madison's reluctance to define Shays' as a rebellion challenging the foundations of the republic may be due to the fact that his criticism of the Shaysites was balanced by his reluctance to use excessive force to silence a majority. He was particularly troubled by efforts to disguise anti-Shaysite recruiting by the fiction that enlistments were needed to put down a nonexistent Indian uprising. See Irving Brant, *James Madison: The Nationalist* (Indianapolis: Bobbs-Merrill Co., 1948), 391, 401.

[5]Arthur E. Bonfield, "The Guarantee Clause of Article IV, Section 4: A Study in Constitutional Desuetude," *Minnesota Law Review*, 46 (1962), 533-34.

of the entire people is the true basis of republican government," asserted Victoria Woodhull in 1871.[6] To insist on the "essence" of republicanism had the effect of driving the term *republican* into the realm of metaphor and uncertainty, making it vulnerable to a host of alternate and conflicting definitions. It would be available to signify almost anything so long as it was nonmonarchical. It would become rich in overtones, useable in alternate contexts; we find ourselves speaking of republican religion, republican children, republican motherhood.

I suspect these varying definitions may help to explain why so little attention was paid to republicanism as ideology by otherwise sensitive and intelligent historians for so long. They naturally expected to find a political term accompanied by political analysis; instead "republicanism" was more likely, when it appeared, to be accompanied by hyperbole. A political term not used in a disciplined way was naturally taken to be a screen for self-interest, probably economic; the task of the historical analyst seemed to be to penetrate behind the metaphor to economic and political reality. When historians of the Progressive generation—who were already inclined to expect reality to lurk behind a screen of self-interest—came upon politicians arguing about the qualities of a republic they hastily concluded that the argument must *really* be about something else.

In the 1950s, however, there was a fresh sense of the importance of metaphor. J. H. Hexter has ascribed this interest simply to "a common sense, accessible to everybody in the craft, of the impropriety of anachronism."[7] Common sense surely did have something to do with renewed respect for rhetoric and willingness to take words and their overtones seriously. But so too did the reaction of a generation of historians, for whom Edmund Morgan spoke in his 1957 essay "The American Revolution: Revisions in Need of Revising," who admired the Progressive historians but began to suspect that the case had been overstated and oversimplified. "In the study of history," Morgan would write a few years later, "it is always dangerous to assume that men do not mean what they say, that words are a facade which must be penetrated in order to arrive at some fundamental but hidden reality."[8]

---

[6]Ibid., 537, 548; Victoria Woodhull, "Address to the Judiciary Committee of the House of Representatives," 11 January 1871, reprinted in Anne Firor Scott and Andrew McKay Scott, *One Half the People: The Fight for Woman Suffrage* (Urbana: Univ. of Illinois Press, 1982), 78. See also Arthur E. Bonfield, "*Baker v. Carr*: New Light on the Constitutional Guarantee of Republican Government," *California Law Review*, 50 (1962), 245-63; J. R. Pole, *The Pursuit of Equality in American History* (Berkeley: Univ. of California Press, 1978), 113ff; William M. Wiecek, *The Guarantee Clause of the United States Constitution* (Ithaca: Cornell Univ. Press, 1972).

[7]J. H. Hexter, "Republic, Virtue, Liberty, and the Political Universe of J.G.A. Pocock," in J. H. Hexter, ed., *On Historians: Reappraisals of Some of the Makers of Modern History* (Cambridge: Harvard Univ. Press, 1974), 267, n. 5. See also the chapter entitled, "Languages and their Implications," in J.G.A. Pocock, *Politics, Language and Time* (New York: Atheneum, 1971), 3-41.

[8]Edmund S. Morgan, "The Revolution Considered as an Intellectual Movement," originally published in 1963, reprinted in *The Challenge of the American Revolution* (New York: Norton, 1976), 60. For Morgan's comments on his generation of historians, see his introductory notes to "Revisions in Need of Revising," originally published 1957, in *Challenge*, 43-59.

This shift was contemporaneous with the development of studies of culture in
the 1950s, the establishment of programs that were then called American
Civilization, and the popularity of books like Henry Nash Smith's *Virgin Land*
or John William Ward's *Andrew Jackson: Symbol for an Age*, which
demonstrated how profitable it could be to read second- and third-rate literature
and political pamphlets with the critical care usually given to literary texts. This
development in turn was also dependent on a technological revolution in the
accessibility of research materials. Thanks to microfilm and Readex microprint,
every major university library could hold virtually every item in standard
bibliographies of rare books and pamphlets. From the late 1950s on, graduate
students had ready access to resources which an older generation of senior
scholars had sought out at substantial expense.[9] As a result, historians began to
argue, with Marshall Smelser, that the Federalist period had been "an Age of
Passion." John Howe linked the passion to republicanism, and, from the 1960s
on, historians were apt to pay careful attention to the revolutionary generation's
choice of words—especially when that generation appeared to be saying that
republicanism was at the core of their actions.[10]

"Republicanism," wrote Gordon Wood, "meant more for Americans than
simply the elimination of a king and the institution of an elective system. It added
a moral dimension, a utopian depth, to the political separation from England—a
depth that involved the very character of their society." The major themes of
republicanism, as Wood outlined them, included the inspiration of classical
antiquity, self-disciplined civic virtue, and equality of opportunity. In this
context, Montesquieu was particularly useful; indeed he had been cited in the
Constitutional Convention more than Locke. One way or another, Montesquieu
had said, all governments rested on their subjects; what makes the law effective
in despotic governments is fear; what makes law effective in a republic is virtue.
When post-Revolutionary Americans worried whether a virtuous citizenry
would continue to sustain the republic, their words were less likely to be seen by
historians as hyperbole and more likely to be understood as expressions of
concern rooted in their culture and their education.[11]

Meanwhile, historians of Britain were doing their own variety of listening
with care. The answers to the old question—why did the least-taxed people in the
western world make a revolution about taxes?—seemed to be found in an ever
more complex British-American social and political interaction. Setting the
American Revolution in its eighteenth-century context, hearing the language of
British political rivalry transplanted to America, we understand better the

[9]Henry Nash Smith, *Virgin Land* (Cambridge: Harvard Univ. Press, 1950); John William Ward,
Andrew Jackson: Symbol for an Age (New York: Oxford Univ. Press, 1955).
[10]Marshall Smelser, "The Federalist Period as an Age of Passion," *American Quarterly*,
(hereafter cited as *AQ*), 10 (1958), 391-419; John R. Howe, "Republican Thought and the Political
Violence of the 1790's," ibid., 19 (1967), 147-65.
[11]Gordon S. Wood, *The Creation of the American Republic 1776-1787* (Chapel Hill: Univ. of
North Carolina Press, 1969), 47-53; see also Linda K. Kerber, *Federalists in Dissent: Imagery and
Ideology in Jeffersonian America* (Ithaca: Cornell Univ. Press, 1970), ch. 7.

sources of the complaint that British policies were infected by hypocrisy and corruption. Indeed, thanks to J.G.A. Pocock's *The Machiavellian Moment*, we now understand the legacy of early modern republican theory to be a far more complex and ambivalent inheritance than we once thought it to be. In the antique balance between "the one, the few, and the many," the cards were stacked in favor of the few. In the Venetian Republic, even the Great Council, ostensibly the forum of "the many," was strictly confined to representatives of a severely limited list of old aristocratic families; in Florence its counterpart was more accessible but still closed to the *hoi polloi*. Republicanism could be comfortably congruent with aristocracy; it certainly was expected that the citizen had enough property to free himself to find his fulfillment in serving the public good. Republicanism was, in Pocock's words, "a civic and patriot ideal" which did not necessarily imply that all people, or even all men, were part of the political scheme. The ideal *did* imply that male citizens were made independent by their control of property. Moreover, it was understood that the integrity of republicans was perpetually threatened by corruption.[12]

Republicanism in America thus claimed a complex political heritage. It had traveled from Renaissance Italy and early modern France into the the political language of the eighteenth-century British Opposition, located solidly among country gentry who looked with suspicion on the patronage and the commercialism of metropolitan politics in London. Following Pocock's suggestion, John Murrin, Lance Banning and A. G. Roeber have traced Country habits of thought as carriers of civic republicanism into the American eighteenth and nineteenth centuries. They have shown that it is often easier to line up Americans of the Revolutionary era in terms of their congruity with British Court and Country political alignments than in terms of how well they anticipated nineteenth-century categories of Left and Right. Murrin observed astutely:

> The Court-Country paradigm heavily colored nearly all participants' perceptions of the issues and personalities of the era. The political rhetoric of the age implicitly assumed a spectrum of possibilities from an extreme Court position on the right, through Hamiltonism, then various stages of moderation in the middle, then a pure Country position on the left, and on to radical jacobinism. . . . Wherever one stood in this spectrum, he was likely to suspect anyone to his right of sinister conspiracies against liberty. . . . Conversely, everybody to one's left had to be flirting with disorder and anarchy.[13]

[12]J.G.A. Pocock, *The Machiavellian Moment: Florentine Political Thought and the Atlantic Republican Tradition* (Princeton: Princeton Univ. Press, 1975), 507. For an important and fresh reading of the theme of corruption, see Gordon S. Wood, "Conspiracy and the Paranoid Style: Causality and Deceit in the Eighteenth Century," *WMQ*, 39 (1982), 401-41.

[13]John G. Murrin, "The Great Inversion, or Court versus Country: A Comparison of the Revolution Settlements in England (1688-1721) and America (1776-1816)," in J.G.A. Pocock, ed., *Three British Revolutions: 1641, 1688, 1776* (Princeton: Princeton Univ. Press, 1980), 421. A related argument, to the effect that Court-Country polarity emerges in Federalist-Anti-Federalist debate of the 1780s, is found in James H. Hutson, "Country, Court and Constitution: Antifederalism and the Historians," *WMQ*, 38 (1981), 337-68.

Court and Country are not neatly analogous to our modern Left and Right, because both were variants of elite politics, and because Country was itself a complex political amalgam which included Tory gentry as well as radical Whigs; Bolingbroke as well as Trenchard and Gordon. Banning has found an uncanny persistence of Country habits of thought in post-Revolutionary America, encouraging ambivalence about any policy which seemed to have elements of patronage (understood to be corruption) and forceful exercise of national power. Roeber has carefully traced the way in which leading patriot lawyers in revolutionary Virginia successfully fended off charges that they had deferred to Court interests. Although men like Jefferson, Madison and George Mason, in their desire for a more sophisticated legal system which would also be responsive to the needs of a commercial society, had something in common with Court habits, they positioned themselves as republicans and discredited the old-line Country gentry (whose spokesmen in the years of the early republic were John Taylor of Caroline and John Randolph of Roanoke). J. G. A. Pocock, Dorothy Ross, and Robert Kelley have in various ways been impressed by the persistence of classical republican patterns of reasoning long after the early republic had receded into history, and have suggested that utopian thought in nineteenth-century America ought to be understood as an effort to cling to a Country vision which in Ross's words, "would counter the corrupting effects of industrial growth with the moral strength of an agrarian yeomanry and fend off the decadence of increasing civilization with the dynamic energies bred in the conquest of nature." The old dream of the pure republic had a static quality; fear for the survival of the republic encouraged the skepticism about partisanship for which the postwar years were famous. This skepticism was also inherited from the Whig Opposition. Reading American political polemic from the other side of the ocean enormously enlarges our perspective; in this context the American was, as the title of a recent collection of essays has it, the third in a triad of *British* revolutions.[14]

But as republicanism has widened greatly in usage it is in danger of coming to signify too much and therefore to mean too little. Rowland Berthoff has recently used it to stand for the communal values of traditional peasantry; following Pocock, it has also often been taken to imply the presence of urban humanism. "Republicanism" has become so all-embracing as to absorb comfortably its own contradictions.

---

[14]Lance Banning, *The Jeffersonian Persuasion: Evolution of a Party Ideology* (Ithaca: Cornell Univ. Press, 1978); A.G. Roeber, *Faithful Magistrates and Republican Lawyers: Creators of Virginia Legal Culture, 1680-1810* (Chapel Hill: Univ. of North Carolina Press, 1981), ch. 7. Dorothy Ross, "The Liberal Tradition Revisited and the Republican Tradition Addressed," in John Higham and Paul K. Conkin, eds., *New Directions in American Intellectual History* (Baltimore: Johns Hopkins Univ. Press, 1979), 118. See also Robert Kelley, "Ideology and Political Culture from Jefferson to Nixon," *American Historical Review*, 82 (1977), 531-62, and J.G.A. Pocock, "Virtue and Commerce in the Eighteenth Century," *Journal of Interdisciplinary History*, 3 (1972), 119-34.

*   *   *

Yet the overtones of the term *republicanism* have not been fully identified; its possibilities as a guide—and also as a cautionary signal—for the historian are not fully played out. If it is in danger of becoming merely trendy, it has not yet become so. Historians continue to find it of use for complex purposes. But if they are to continue to use it, they will need to display increased precision in identifying its nuances. Paul Conkin has recently complained that just as the founders "had no accepted semantic convention governing their use of the word *republic*, so contemporary historians do not have a firm convention for either *republican* or ideology."[15] Perhaps it is enough to say that the appearance of "republican" is a market signifying that there is, somewhere, a political dimension to what is to be read; a warning that the critic will have to deal with metaphoric prose, will be drawn into what has been called the "hermeneutics of suspicion." As Gerald Bruns explains, "what appears to go on, whether in a mind or in any of its cognates (a text, language, society, and so on), is taken to be a problematic that needs to be penetrated by analysis in order to lay bare the structures or dynamic principles, the forces or illusions, the ideologies or systematic dispositions of desire that form the content of what *really* goes on."[16] Thus drawn in, we are perhaps not so far removed from the Progressive historians who were also sure that reality stalked somewhere *behind* the text.

Historians of the United States have displayed relatively little taste for complex theoretical analysis of how best to treat ideological terms; recently they have relied heavily on Clifford Geertz's essay "Ideology as a Cultural System." A double definition of ideology is offered there. Geertz speaks of ideology in the sense of system imposed on reality; system against received tradition. He calls attention to Edmund Burke's famous contrast between unexamined tradition and systematic ideological formulations: "The function of ideology is to make an autonomous politics possible by providing the authoritative concepts that render it meaningful." But Geertz also offers the contrasting definition that ideology is *embedded* in every culture, where it provides "maps of problematic social reality." If republicanism is thought of as the first sort of ideology then it did indeed make "autonomous politics possible" by providing the justification for revolution; but if it is of the second sort, an ideology embedded in the psychosocial map of its culture, then the American Revolution and subsequent political behavior will seem more emergent and less clearly intentional.[17] Ronald Walters has warned, "Geertz's semiotics, so exciting a tool of

---

[15]Paul Conkin, review of Drew R. McCoy, *The Elusive Republic, WMQ*, 38 (1981), 301-05, quotation 304.
[16]Gerald L. Bruns, *Inventions: Writing, Textuality, and Understanding in Literary History* (New Haven: Yale Univ. Press, 1982), x, xiii.
[17]Clifford Geertz, "Ideology as a Cultural System," in *The Interpretation of Cultures* (New York: Basic Books, 1973), 218, 220.

explication, can . . . tend to freeze theory at a middle level [and] . . . ironically, has the potential to divorce itself from the gritty experiences of the common folk it intends to study . . . by elevating them to literature."[18]

Geertz has written another essay, "Ideology as a System of Common Sense," which strengthens the case for the second of his two definitions, and which argues that ideology is to be located in those ideas people take so for granted that they assume no definition is needed. "In short," Geertz writes, "given the given, not everything else follows. Common sense is not what the mind cleared of cant spontaneously apprehends; it is what the mind filled with presuppositions . . . concludes."[19] For example, as Dorothy Ross, following Pocock, argues, the civic humanist legacy of republicanism "stimulated its adherents to begin to think analytically about historical conditions that could maintain virtue and about the historical changes that bred corruption; in effect, they began to develop a 'sociology of virtue.' "[20] Not only in Renaissance Florence, but in Revolutionary America, it became the common sense of the matter that social change can be controlled and directed. In fact, history itself, which had been thought to be composed of ceaselessly recurring cycles of advance, corruption, and decay, was by the late eighteenth century understood to be interruptible and vulnerable to direction toward improvement and progress. When the term *republican* creeps into Americans' discourse, especially when it is not associated with political forms, we do well to take it as a mark of an effort to systematize an understanding of the world—an effort to connect two concepts which are not obviously connected—and so to make sense of what is experienced.

Republicanism may therefore be used as a theme which helps us understand not only particular political arrangements, but the complexity of a culture. It has been used that way recently by many historians, among them John Kasson, who, in *Civilizing The Machine*, has described early nineteenth-century efforts to justify industrial change in the hope that it would strengthen republicanism. In "Raising the Republican Child," Jacqueline Reimer has linked child-rearing advice to the hope of sustaining subsequent virtuous generations.[21] Treating republicanism as a *cultural* as well as political phenomenon opens the way to evaluating the extent to which the experience of republicanism varied by gender. Montesquieu had, as in so much else else, led the way. Explicitly, in *The Spirit of the Laws* and implicitly, in *The Persian Letters*, he had argued forcefully that

---

[18]Ronald G. Walters, "Signs of the Times: Clifford Geertz and Historians," *Social Research*, 47 (1980), 537-56. See also Joyce Appleby, "Ideology and the History of Political Thought," *Intellectual History Group Newsletter*, No. 2 (1980), 10-18.

[19]Clifford Geertz, *Local Knowledge: Further Essays in Interpretative Anthropology* (New York: Basic Books, 1982), 84.

[20]Ross, "Liberal Tradition Revisited," 117. See also Dorothy Ross, "Historical Consciousness in Nineteenth Century America," *American Historical Review*, 89 (1984), 911.

[21]John E. Kasson, *Civilizing the Machine* (New York: Penguin Books, 1977); Jacqueline Reiner, "Rearing the Republican Child: Attitudes and Practices in Post-Revolutionary Philadelphia," *WMQ*, 3rd. ser., 39 (1982).

it made a substantial difference to women whether or not they lived under a republican form of government. Despotic societies normally reduce women to a state of servitude: "In a government which requires, above all things, that a particular regard be paid to its tranquillity . . . it is absolutely necessary to shut up the women." Monarchies were apt to deflect elite women into vapid conspicuous consumption in the service of courtiers; women are better served by republics, where he assumed they are "free by the laws and [only] constrained by manners." In republics, Montesquieu suggested, women might have at least a modest degree of ability to forge their own political identities.[22]

Lester Cohen's recent subtle reading of Mercy Otis Warren provides a good example of how one woman reshaped the concept of republicanism to fit her own distinctive needs. Cohen argues that when Warren became disillusioned with Federalists, she drew on traditional political analysis and blamed Federalist failures on corruption. In an effort to forge her own personal identity as a republican and in an attempt to integrate public and private roles for herself, she subsequently developed, in Cohen's words, an analysis which identified "the role of mother with republican principles." Warren's answer to the question of how virtue can be preserved is that women would sustain civic virtue by subordinating their own self-fulfillment to the needs of the republic. They would raise their sons to be active citizens committed to the good of the republic; they would monitor their relations with their husbands and other men so as to reinforce and reward displays of civic virtue. The irony, as Cohen sees it, is that Warren was prepared to sacrifice her autonomy to republicanism at the moment when her male counterparts, though also committed Anti-Federalists, were drifting away from civic republicanism and were slowly being co-opted into positions of self-aggrandizement and of national power where they tested their principles and compromised on issues, participating in the complex development of postwar republicanism. Excluded from this experience, female republicanism became, Cohen concludes, an exercise in nostalgia.[23]

Although the language usually used gender-neutral terms, republicanism did indeed have different variants for men and for women. It could hardly be otherwise in a culture which had not begun seriously to question the inherited assumption that men and women have distinctive relationships and responsibilities to the state. Indeed the political incompatibility of men and women was embedded in the language of early modern political discourse. Virtue was understood to be a male attribute, not only because of its obvious derivation from the Latin root *vir* but also because it was steadily contrasted with its opposite, *Fortuna*—understood to be a feminine attribute. *Fortuna* was

[22]Charles Louis de Secondat, Baron de Montesquieu, *The Spirit of the Laws*, trans. Thomas Nugent (New York: Hafner Publishing Co., 1949), I, 101-04.
[23]Lester Cohen, "Explaining the Revolution: Ideology and Ethics in Mercy Otis Warren's Historical Theory," *WMQ*, 37 (1980), 200-18, and idem, "Mercy Otis Warren: The Politics of Language and the Aesthetics of Self," *AQ*, 35 (1983), 481-98.

feminine not only because of its etymology, but also because it was personified as an eccentric, changeable, female quality, symbolized by her wheel, emblem of insecurity and chance. "This opposition," writes Pocock, "was frequently expressed in the image of a sexual relation: a masculine active intelligence was seeking to dominate a feminine passive unpredictability which would submissively reward him for his strength or vindictively betray him for his weakness." In a new, insightful study of Machiavelli's thought, Hanna Fenichel Pitkin takes her theme from a famous passage in *The Prince*, in which the distrust of women is explicit: "it is better to be impetuous than cautious, because Fortune is a woman and it is necessary to keep her under, to cuff and maul her."[24]

A political language fully composed of civic republican terms could not effectively describe an active role for women in the republic. Indeed, it was absolutely frozen at a standstill by the element in Florentine republicanism, derived directly from Roman republicanism, which assumed that the *sine qua non* of citizenship is the ability to bear arms in defense of the republic. Since Americans found the notion of the woman in arms outrageous, the Woman Question was enthralled in a circular argument: man is a political being; his virtue and reason can flourish only in political associations (the test of his commitment being has willingness and ability to risk his life for the republic); women are not part of political associations nor do they guarantee the security of the republic by their valor; therefore their virtue and reason do not flourish and they can not be considered political beings. Early modern political discourse virtually ensured that a republicanism which derived from it would be most comfortable in a political culture in which the common sense of the matter was that women could only be counted on to muck things up.

Understanding that the concept which I have elsewhere named "the republican mother" emerged from the older variant of republicanism helps us locate it with precision on the political spectrum. It is Janus-faced. Because it was framed in the language of civic humanism it could lend itself, as Cohen shows in Warren's case, to a politics of nostalgia. (As Montesquieu suspected, even that hesitant politicization represented a major departure from the ancient tradition that women were not political creatures. Dedicated to raising virtuous citizens for the republic, a mother's traditional private duty took on a new element of public obligation.) In a society in which deference was fast eroding, republican mothers played a conservative, stabilizing role, deflecting the radical potential of the revolutionary experience. In effect, republican mothers were an

---

[24]Pocock, *Machiavellian Moment*, 37. Hanna Fenichel Pitkin, *Fortune Is A Woman: Gender and Politics in the Thought of Niccolo Machiavelli* (Berkeley: Univ. of California Press, 1984), 152. The passage continues: "She more often lets herself be overcome by men using such methods than by those who proceed coldly; therefore always, like a woman, she is the friend of young men, because they are less cautious, more spirited, and with more boldness master her." See also chs. 5, 6, 11, 12.

important mechanism by which the memory of the standards of civic humanism were preserved long after they had faded elsewhere. Nostalgia was one face of republican motherhood. But consciousness of their civic obligation also meant that old boundaries on women's lives were stretched, making room for the questioning of hierarchies within the family and outside it, in the public world. In this way, republican motherhood could also sustain a major step in the direction of a liberal individualism which recognized the political potential of women.[25]

*   *   *

While we extend widely the scope of republicanism as a theme which helps us understand a complex culture, we must also be sensitive to issues which republicanism *cannot* explain and did not solve. In his new book, *The Lost Soul of American Politics*, John Diggins argues that issues like labor, sectionalism, and equality do not lend themselves to formulation in terms of classical thought. Theories of mixed government which stressed reciprocal relations among the three orders of monarchy, aristocracy, and the people did not offer much advice to those who wanted to reduce the gaps between the orders. There were in fact "two languages of politics . . . that had 'liberty' as the key word in their vocabulary throughout the time span of the Machiavellian moment, c. 1500 - c. 1800," explained J. H. Hexter. The Florentine language stressed participation as the foundation of civic virtue; its key words were participation, virtue and corruption. The other language was defensive, a "freedom *against* intrusion," whose key words were limited government, due process, and fundamental law.[26] As Isaac Kramnick has recently argued, we should take care lest we fall into assuming that the "republican tradition emphasizing citizenship and public participation" is sufficient to understand eighteenth-century politics

---

[25]Linda K. Kerber, "The Republican Mother—Women and the Enlightenment: An American Perspective," *AQ*, 28 (1976), 187-205; idem, *Women of the Republic: Intellect and Ideology in Revolutionary America* (Chapel Hill: Univ. of North Carolina, 1980), ch. 9. Mary Beth Norton's characterization of my position in "The Evolution of White Women's Experience in Early America," *American Historical Review*, 89 (1984), 615, should be used with caution. I have not "contended that the postwar changes decreased . . . women's autonomy" except in certain specific cases, like the erosion of dower protection in Massachusetts. Rather I have argued that revolutionary claims by women for autonomy, initiative and independence were one side of an inherently paradoxical ideology of republican motherhood that legitimized political sophistication and activity while at the same time deflected political energy into domestic life.

[26]J.H. Hexter, *On Historians*, 293-94, 301. "Citizen liberty available only to the members of the Consiglio Maggiore or to the electorate of the unreformed House of Commons leaves an awful lot of people out. The other idea of liberty is more ecumenical in its embrace. It does not profess, however, to give much to those it embraces. Mainly, it offers them some fairly clear constraints on the extent to which they can be rightfully booted about by current controllers of the machinery of political coercion." (302).

without "the liberal individualist heritage preoccupied with private rights" and largely associated with Locke.[27]

This distinction has some elements of the arbitrary. In some hands Locke would not be contrasted so sharply with Bolingbroke. Henry F. May, for example, links them together as exemplars of what he called "The Moderate Enlightenment."[28] But it does remind us that the American situation was not static, and that we should not be content when we have traced out the persistence of civic republicanism or Country habits of thought. Country politics provided a rhetoric, and even a general sort of political guidance, but it could not provide all political solutions; indeed it should not be expected to provide a context for thinking creatively about new issues that could not be said to mimic old ones. Targeted as it was at specifics of Walpolean politics, Country ideology had no need to raise basic questions about the relationship between the individual and authority, or between church and state.

Traditional republicanism, for example, had assumed that deference was the glue of society. Aristocrats were defined primarily by their property, but also by their manners and by the recognition that humble folks freely vouchsafed to them.[29] In this sense deference is not a passive, but an "active virtue"; it is for the masses what leadership is for the elite. Although the deference of the many to the elite was clearly evident in colonial society, it was a self-conscious sort of deference which eroded erratically but nonetheless rapidly in the Revolution. The shrill calls by the High Federalists to have it back after the war suggest it had disappeared. Republicanism of the older variety did not offer guidance about what to do with a society without deference, and, according to Pocock, "soon after the end of the War of Independence, the Revolution faced a crisis of confidence born of the realization that the naturally differentiated people, presupposed by every republican theorist from Aristotle to Machiavelli, had simply failed to appear."[30] The post-Revolutionary generation had to construct a republic without the mortar of deference; it would have to co-opt those whose deference could not be taken for granted. It is not by accident that the story of Andrew Jackson's inaugural, with the famous muddying of White House carpets and furniture, has become a staple of American political mythology. The story represents the co-optation of the nondeferential; it is the triumphant counterpart to the tale of the destruction of Governor Thomas Hutchinson's home by the revolutionary mob sixty-three years before. In the task of understanding how

---

[27]Kramnick, "Republican Revisionism Revisited," 629. See also John P. Diggins, *The Lost Soul of American Politics: Virtue, Self-Interest, and the Foundations of Liberalism* (New York: Basic Books, 1984), 12.

[28]Henry F. May, *The Enlightenment in America* (New York: Oxford Univ. Press, 1979).

[29]Pocock, *Machiavellian Moment*, 395, 485. See also J.G.A. Pocock, "The Classical Theory of Deference," *American Historical Review*, 81 (1976), 516-23.

[30]Pocock, *Machiavellian Moment*, 516; 98, restating Giovanni Cavalcanti.

Americans moved from the one to the other, inherited civic republicanism would be only of marginal and rhetorical help.

Republicanism of the civic humanist tradition circumvented the problem of slavery by confining itself to the relations between men who were already free. It did not offer clear solutions to the problem of representation and balance in an expanding territory. Indeed, as Gordon Wood has deftly shown, Florentine concepts of republicanism, tightly linked as they were to the idea that the "orders" of society were the one, the few and the many, had to be jettisoned before Americans could begin to think in an original way about the relationship of state and society. Nor did civic republicanism appeal to those who felt the need for, as Robert Calhoun phrases it, "absorption into the sublime." It left the task of making political language congruent with religious language to the new evangelicals, who, in turn, led a religious revival that was complementary to the political revolution but not at all the same thing. As Rhys Isaac has argued, "the language and terms of classical republicanism that underlay the literate gentry's conception of the struggle could not readily arouse a populace whose limited experience of higher culture was of the Bible rather than the classics. More effective than the imagery of Roman republicanism was the Anglo-Virginian sense of identity as a Protestant people."[31]

Nor, finally, did traditional republican theory help either Jeffersonians or Federalists think creatively about the place of women in republican society. As we have seen, Mercy Otis Warren found the effect of traditional theory was to separate her from her male contemporaries. Lockean and radical Enlightenment ideas were needed for the development of new ideas about the role of women in political society, as the French showed in the Jacobin stages of their revolution. To deal with the woman question would require a political language derived not from the Moderate but from the Skeptical or Revolutionary Enlightenment (to use Henry May's categories). It would mean recourse back through time to Locke or forward in time to the liberal individualism of John Stuart Mill. It would require recognition of the female restiveness and social problematic that Gary Nash points to when he recognizes that widows' poverty had become a significant social problem in northeastern cities on the eve of the Revolution.[32]

---

[31]Wood, *Creation of the Republic*, 589. Robert Calhoun in letter to author, 1983; Rhys Isaac, *The Transformation of Virginia, 1740-1790* (Chapel Hill: Univ. of North Carolina Press, 1982), 246. Gordon Wood writes, "The new millenialism of many post-Revolutionary Americans represented both a rationalizing of revelation and a Christianizing of the Enlightenment belief in secular progress." Wood, "Evangelical America and Early Mormonism," *New York History*, 61 (1980), 359-86.

[32]On the important connection between citizenship and military obligation, see Pocock, *Machiavellian Moment*, 88-90, 390. In classical as well as early modern republican thought, Pocock points out, arms were understood to be the "*ultimo ratio*" whereby the citizen exposes his life in defense of the state and at the same time ensures that the decision to expose it cannot be taken without him; it is the possession of arms which makes a man a full citizen, capable of, and required to

Happily, American political discourse was not fully dependent on civic humanist categories. Republican motherhood was a conceptualization which grafted the language of liberal individualism onto the inherited discourse of civic humanism. Because republican motherhood assumed that women's lives were shaped primarily by family obligations, it offered a politics congruent with the world as most women experienced it. Buttressed by Enlightenment commentary on natural rights, republican motherhood could be used effectively, as it was by Judith Sargent Murray and many others, to claim for women the independence and self-sufficiency that *Common Sense* had made a commonplace for adult men. Anyone who wants to start with the proposition that all are "by nature free, equal, and independent of one another," whether they be British radical artisans in the London Corresponding Society or Elizabeth Cady Stanton before the New York State Legislature in 1854, will need Locke, not Machiavelli.[33]

* * *

Our understanding of republicanism is now being greatly enriched by a major exploration of the interaction of the political revolution and economic development, particularly the Industrial Revolution. The juxtaposition of the two in time has long been noted, but especially in America it has been hard to see how they interacted.[34]

Now, haltingly, the narratives of political and economic development are being brought together by historians who recognize that actual political and economic development is necessarily synergistic. Isaac Kramnick describes the main elements in the sequence as it developed in England:

---

display, the multiple versatility and self-development which is the crown (and the prerequisite) of citizenship." (90). I deal with this issue at greater length in " 'May All Our Citizens Be Soldiers and All Our Soldiers Citizens': The Ambiguities of Female Citizenship in the New Nation," in Robert Beisner and Joan Challinor, eds., *The Work of Peace* (Westport, Conn.: Greenwood Press, forthcoming). See also Lois G. Schwoerer, *"No Standing Armies": The Antiarmy Ideology in Seventeenth Century England* (Baltimore: Johns Hopkins Univ. Press, 1974). On widows' poverty, see Gary B. Nash, *The Urban Crucible: Social Change, Political Consciousness and the Origins of the American Revolution* (Cambridge: Harvard Univ. Press, 1979), 126-27, 182-89.

[33]Kramnick, "Republicanism Revisionism Revisited," 648-48; Elizabeth Cady Stanton, "Address to the Legislature of New York 1854," in Ellen DuBois, ed., *Elizabeth Cady Stanton/Susan B. Anthony—Correspondence, Writings, Speeches* (New York: Schocken Books), 45, 51.

[34]Gerald Stourzh, *Alexander Hamilton and the Idea of Republican Government* (Stanford: Stanford Univ. Press, 1970). For Hamilton's correspondence, which suggested how closely early industrial manufacturing was tied to women's work at home, see Harold C. Syrett, et al., eds., *The Papers of Alexander Hamilton* (New York: Columbia Univ. Press, 1965), Volume 9, especially Nathanial Gorham to AH, 13 October 1790 (371); James Davenport to John Chester, 16 Sept. 1791 (340) and Peter Colt to John Chester, 21 July 1791 (320-23). The Report itself appears in Volume 10. For a summary of the process of home manufacture and its gradual transformation into factory work, see J. Bruce Sinclair, "The Merrimack Valley Textile Museum," *Publications of the Colonial Society of Massachusetts*, 18 (1966), 406-16. For a recent social history of the early stages of industrialization, see Gary Kulik, "The Beginnings of the Industrial Revolution in America: Pawtucket, Rhode Island, 1672-1829," Diss. Brown Univ. 1980.

America and the crisis over taxation introduced new noncountry issues into politics. The taxation controversy raised to the center of debate the issue of representation, which in its trail brought to the fore basic concerns about the origins of government and authority in general . . . It transcended the paradigms of country ideology to more class-based categories.

At the same time, the Industrial Revolution politicized an emerging middle class, "owners of small and moveable property" who resented their exclusion from the political process at the same time that their financial support of the state was demanded. "In Locke far more than in Bolingbroke and his ilk, the unenfranchised middle class and especially the Protestant dissenters found intellectual authority and legitimacy for their radical demands." Kramnick concludes, "The transformation . . . involved a changed emphasis on the nature of public behavior. The moral and virtuous man was no longer defined by his civic activity but by his economic activity. . . ." Adam Smith provided a different language for explaining how a stable and free social order could be maintained: not by disinterested and unspecialized citizenship, but by "economic productivity and hard work." It was understood that selfish private behavior in the marketplace could ultimately redound to the public good. "The world view of liberal individualism was fast pushing aside the older paradigms during the last three decades of the century. . . ."[35]

What Kramnick has done for England, Joyce Appleby has done, in more detail, for the United States in a series of essays which have appeared in scholarly journals in the course of the last ten years and, most recently, in *Capitalism and a New Social Order: The Republican Vision of the 1790's.* Appleby acknowledges that there were two vocabularies of republican discourse; like Kramnick, she views the liberal concept of liberty as fundamentally *incompatible* with the classical tradition. Drawing on her own extensive examinations of the debate on trade and the economy in seventeenth-century England, Appleby draws our attention to the fresh view of human psychology that accompanied the development of free market economics. The concept of liberty expressed by writers from Locke to Adam Smith was incompatible with the classical tradition because it treated *all* people—not just the gentry—as rational beings capable of making sensible decisions, first in the marketplace and, by extension, in political life as well.[36] The Jeffersonians, Appleby argues, continued this vein of argument. Far from being agrarian traditionalists or an American "country party," she maintains, the Jeffersonians

[35]Kramnick, "Republicanism Revisionism Revisited," 635, 637, 662-64.
[36]See Joyce Appleby, "Ideology and Theory: The Tension Between Political and Economic Liberalism in Seventeenth-Century England," *American Historical Review,* 81 (1976), 499-515; idem, "Locke, Liberalism, and the Natural Law of Money," *Past and Present,* (1976), 43-69; idem, *Capitalism and a New Social Order: The Republican Vision of the 1790's* (New York: Oxford Univ. Press, 1984), 21. This work retains the agreeably conversational tone that characterized it when originally delivered as the Anson G. Phelps Lectures at New York University.

embraced the international market enthusiastically. They welcomed the heightened European demand for American wheat and other agricultural products; they aggressively sought to enlarge America's share of the market by improvements in the quality of its produce.[37] For cosmopolitan, upwardly mobile people, whether they lived in cities or depended on urban markets to sell their produce, it was no longer natural to continue to function "within the old assumptions about a politically active elite and a deferential, compliant electorate. . . . The right of participation could not be extended to the many without changing the style and the substance of republican government." Thus the Jeffersonians transformed the traditional republicanism which they had inherited, developing its Lockean ingredients, adding to it "the liberal position on private property and economic freedom," and "banishing the political distinction between the few and the many."[38]

Appleby asks a rhetorical question which forces historians to make a choice. "If the Revolution was fought in a frenzy over corruption, out of fear of tyranny, and with hopes for redemption through civic virtue, where and when are scholars to find the sources for the aggressive individualism, the optimistic materialism, and the pragmatic interest-group politics that became so salient so early in the life of the new nation?" In his expansive forthcoming book, *The Republic Reborn*, Steven Watts finds those sources in the writing and experience of a group of strategically placed articulate republicans who, he believes, "took the lead in moving liberal capitalist values from their emergent position in colonial America to one of cultural dominance in early national America." Watts' work is distinctive in its sensitivity to the ways in which personal experience articulated with political trends and in his extensive effort to include consideration of psychological tensions and literary imagery as they shaped political analysis. In the hands of Appleby, Kramnick, Watts, and others including Jeffrey Barnouw and John Diggins, the old civic humanist politics fades, and is replaced by a dynamic set of behaviors more congruent with the demands of bourgeois society and a capitalist marketplace.[39]

It may remain, however, possible that sharp choices between distinct alternatives do not have to be made. Edwin Burrows works out in detail the

---

[37]Appleby, "Commercial Farming and the Agrarian Myth in the Early Republic," *Journal of American History*, 68 (1982), 845.

[38]Appleby, *Capitalism*, 48-49, 73, 99, 101. In Appleby's formulation, the Federalists display a politics of nostalgia and unambivalent elitism. She provides little room for the distinctions between high and moderate Federalism made, for example, by David Hackett Fisher and most students of party politics in the early republic, except insofar as the two branches of the party echo Court-Country polarization. See David Hackett Fisher, *The Revolution of American Conservatism: The Federalist Party in the Era of Jeffersonian Democracy* (New York: Harper and Row, 1965). See note 46 below.

[39]Appleby, "The Social Origins of American Revolutionary Ideology," *Journal of American History*, 64 (1978), 937; Steven Watts, *The Republic Reborn: The War of 1812 and the Making of Liberal America* (Baltimore: Johns Hopkins Univ. Press, forthcoming). See also Jeffrey Barnouw, "The Pursuit of Happiness in Jefferson and Its background in Bacon and Hobbes," *Interpretation: A Journal of Political Philosophy*, 11 (1983), 225.

elements in the English Opposition tradition—especially the fear of a national debt—to which aspiring entrepreneurs like Albert Gallatin could resonate. In a very practical way, Gallatin was convinced that Hamiltonian finance would usher in economic privilege, encourage speculation, and underwrite patronage. He and his colleagues were all too sure that these had been the same policies which had once forced the British to the taxation which in turn had engendered the American Revolution. They thought Hamilton was set on course to replay the same drama. In many respects Gallatin—always in debt, always drowning in some land speculation or mercantile venture, a man, in Burrows's phrase, "on the make"—fits Appleby's characterization of American republicans as people who made their careers by taking advantage of new economic opportunities. Gallatin would have agreed with Appleby that Hamilton represented a reincarnation of Court politics. But Burrows's Gallatin would see no contradiction between embracing entrepreneurship on the one hand and acting to ensure that traditional sources of corruption could not operate. In employing Country principles for contemporary ends, he would have denied that he was operating from a politics of nostalgia.[40]

Thus an alternate interpretation is available, offered by historians who believe that the major concepts of the older republicanism retained their vitality longer than Appleby or Kramnick would concede and doubt that socio-psychological change occurred as sharply as the former group suspect. In *The Elusive Republic*, Drew McCoy describes a "hybrid republican vision," characteristic of American thinking as early as the 1770s, in which the "moral and social imperatives of classical republicanism" were adapted "to modern commercial society." Realistic republicans like Franklin sought to integrate "commerce and its consequences" into republican patterns of analysis; indeed, McCoy suggests that Poor Richard's maxims should be read as an effort to blend the "virtue" of traditional republicanism with the self-aggrandizement of assertive commercialism. By the time the decision for war to protect free trade was made in 1812, older definitions of virtue had given way to emphasis on individual industriousness; free trade meant that the state relied on the market to provide the social stability previously thought guaranteed only by self-restrained choices made by virtuous citizens. Although McCoy conceded that that decision might be reguarded as a new departure, he emphasizes the ambivalence with which it was made: "Most Jeffersonians continued . . . to interpret the interdependent realm of polity, economy and society in the light of the same fears and concerns that had informed Franklin's outlook on the eve of the Revolution."[41]

---

[40] The phrase is Kramnick's; in full it is "the politics of nostalgia untainted by bourgeois liberal or individualist ideals," in "Republicanism Revisionism Revisited," 634. See Edwin Burrows, "Albert Gallatin and the Political Economy of Republicanism, 1761-1800," Diss. Columbia Univ. 1974.

[41] Drew McCoy, *The Elusive Republic: Political Economy in Jeffersonian America* (Chapel Hill: Univ of North Carolina Press, 1980), 236-39. In E. James Ferguson, "Political Economy, Public Liberty, and the Formation of the Constitution," *WMQ*, 40 (1983), 389-412, the argument is made that currency finance strategies are in the Country political tradition.

In *Chants Democratic*, his subtle discussion of the political and economic transformation of the later years of the early republic, Sean Wilentz is less impressed by national prosperity than he is by "the subordination of wage labor to capital." The international industrial revolution and capitalist development altered the "locus and texture" of human relations "across the shifting barriers of trade, region, race, sex or ethnicity." In this transformed political economy, in which the middle-class entrepreneurs focused on by Kramnick and Appleby found the language of liberal individualism a close fit to the reality of their own experience, the independent artisans and craft workers who are the subjects of Wilentz's attention found themselves losing their options and pushed, in an inexorable cycle of downward mobility, into the sweated trades and the status of dependent wage earners. For them, the language of the individual freely contracting in a free market became less and less descriptive of a reality they welcomed; as they came ever nearer to the status of working class, the old dream of a commonwealth of cooperation and civic virtue became more attractive. Wilentz finds them apt to use the older language of traditional republicanism.[42]

Impressed by the persistence of the rhetoric, Wilentz insists—he has Gordon Wood in mind—that it is "premature to claim that classical politics died in 1787," or, for that matter, in 1812. There remained a resilient republican language which had absorbed, or fused with, major liberal ingredients and which continued to be central to American political discourse. Americans used this modern variant with no sense that they had created an oxymoron. "Early nineteenth century politicians and party spokesmen thought primarily not in straightforward liberal terms but in classical republican terms leavened by egalitarian notions of natural political rights—of a polity of independent virtuous citizens, working to build and maintain a commonwealth of political equality," writes Wilentz. He reads the Jacksonian party system as energized by "a specific conception of republican politics, one that *combined* republican rhetoric with a post-Madisonian liberalism." Daniel Walker Howe firmly makes the point that the pervasive vocabulary of Whig-Democratic debate—virtue, balance, luxury, degeneration, restoration—reveals the continued influence of long-familiar patterns of classical and Renaissance political thought. That Whigs and Democrats were both using this language helps explain why their debate was so bitter; "if they had not had such terms in common, they might not have understood each others' terms so well." Howe finds that "the staple of Whig political culture [in the 1840s] remained the Anglo-American 'country-party' tradition"; their intellectual ancestor was James Madison and his moderate Republican colleagues. The doubled concept of republican motherhood was a similar alloy.[43]

---

[42]Sean Wilentz, *Chants Democratic: New York City and the Rise of the American Working Class, 1788-1850* (New York: Oxford Univ. Press, 1984), 18-19, and ch. 3.
[43]Sean Wilentz, "On Class and Politics in Jacksonian America," *Reviews in American History*, 10 (1982), 54, 56. Italics mine. Daniel Walker Howe, *The Political Culture of the American Whigs* (Chicago: Univ. of Chicago Press, 1979), 78, 87, 90-91.

Whomever we choose as our guide, we arrive at the same place: the liberal individualism of the antebellum years and the capitalist free market economy. The distinctions made between the substitution of Court for Country, replacement of both by liberalism, or fusion of classical republicanism with liberalism, are not merely semantic. Appleby finds in the shift to liberalism a major social-psychological change which made democratic politics possible. "Instrumental, utilitarian, individualistic, egalitarian, abstract, and rational, the liberal concept of liberty was everything that the classical republican concept was not." Arguing for the persistence of classical republican thinking in post-Revolutionary America, Murrin suggests that because Americans have thought that their nation contined to be ruled by descendents of an anti-Court party, (that is, by authentic dissidents and revolutionaries), incipient dissent may well have been inhibited and the sense of alienation kept to a minimum. "In America, except for the generation of older Federalists after 1800 and Southerners after 1850, alienation has been directed at the society rather than the polity, until our own Vietnam-Watergate era."[44] Wilentz and Howe give credit to an amalgam of classical and liberal ideology for deflecting class tensions in an industrializing society. Political elites were enabled to divert working-class hostility away from themselves and toward speculators, monopolists, and other people whom classical rhetoric had long since defined as enemies to the republic. One ingredient to the answer to the old question about why American political parties did not divide neatly along class lines may therefore be the continuing vitality of classical republicanism in American political discourse. Moreover, the old organic vision of community never fully disappeared, and was available for social critics to draw on as an authentic alternative throughout the nineteenth and into the twentieth centuries when an expanding economy had not made good on its promise to end major class distinctions, and capitalism and free trade no longer seemed quite as promising as they had appeared in the halcyon days of the early republic.

*   *   *

We may now be persuaded that Jeffersonians saw in their Federalist opponents the reincarnation of their British opponents of the prewar days. But even if this is not simply a matter of perspective, even if the Republicans were right in seeing the Federalists as a revival or continuation of the Court interest, I think we should also recognize that the Federalists had their own mythology. Federalists *also* believed themselves to be heirs of an authentic republican revolution, inheritors of the traditional understanding that republics were frail and required protection. Federalists would understand their role to be that they build a wall of

[44]Appleby, *Capitalism and the Social Order,* 23; idem, "Social Origins," 955-58; Murrin, "Great Inversion," 428-30.

protection around the republic. Their emphasis on the vulnerability of republics to both foreign and domestic enemies was also an authentic part of their inheritance from Florentine civic humanism. In seeking to understand the tensions of the post-Revolutionary years, we must concede that there was authenticity of belief on both sides of the partisan split.[45]

Federalists were captives of the belief that the good citizen was a political amateur, not a political technician. Observing their opponents professionalizing pqlitics, Federalists concluded that it was the opposition which demeaned the integrity of citizenship. When Federalists said that Republicans aimed at subversion and were desperate men, they meant to certify that Republicans had become Court politicians, who would use all available means, with much energy and few scruples, and who were comfortable with the prospect of an open-ended, unpredictable future. This is a goal Federalists associated with Court and with connivance. They imagined, especially after the transfer of power in 1800, that the Republicans were heirs of Court politics.[46]

With both Federalists and Republicans racing as fast as they could to connect with and control the market economy of the Industrial Revolution, Jefferson's phrase of his First Inaugural, "We are all Federalists, we are all Republicans," takes on new vibrancy and new irony. The two parties shared a heritage of antique republicanism transformed by the political rivalries of Stuart and Hanoverian England. They shared a political language which had attached complex penumbra of meaning to certain words—among them *virtue*, *corruption*, and *liberty*. Useful though that language had been in helping them articulate their political resistance, it had never been sufficient; it had always been accompanied by an alternate liberal language that embraced competition and ambition as means to economic prosperity and political balance. During the years of the early republic, both parties groped toward economic modernization and a liberal politics. In the process, the very meaning of the code words shifted even as they continued in use. *Virtue* referred increasingly to individual choice, with perhaps religious overtones; *balance*, which had once referred to the relationship between "the one, the few, and the many," or King, Lords, and Commons, came to refer to the balancing of powers within the government as organized by the Federal Constitution. The sounds of civic republicanism persisted longer than the fact of it.

It may be that in a long perspective, historians of this generation will be seen

---

[45]I have made this point in a different context in *Federalists in Dissent: Imagery and Ideology in Jeffersonian America* (Ithaca: Cornell Univ. Press, 1970).

[46]In "What is Still American in the Political Philosophy of Thomas Jefferson?" Appleby argues that the Court-Country dichotomy was played out within the Federalist party: "the archetypal Country leader, Adams, found his prefigured enemy in the classical Court political, Hamilton." *WMQ*, 39 (1982), 307. This view contrasts sharply with the interpretations of Murrin and of Banning.

to have devised yet another variant of consensus history, stressing the assumptions which Americans shared rather than the distinctions which divided them. Yet in their defense it should be recognized that historians who identified a republican consensus moved almost immediately to make distinctions within it, and to show that it in turn contained the possibility of contradictions. The language of early American politics reflected the absorption of Enlightenment ideas as well as Oppositionist ones, and was reshaped by real people, who had to make real judgments, as they moved toward the liberal, individualist, capitalist compromise which we have come to know.*

*I am grateful for the careful readings Dorothy Ross, Lewis Perry, John Murrin, Sydney V. James and Richard Beeman gave to earlier drafts of this essay. The usual reminders that they are not responsible for my failures apply with special force.

Federalism in the Foundation and Preservation of the American Republic

Jean Yarbrough*
University of Connecticut, Groton
for Peter

For students of the republic, it usually comes as a surprise to learn that federalism, the uniquely American contribution to the theory and practice of free government, was considered by many of the Framers to be one of its most serious defects. Far from praising this novel arrangement of power—which resulted in neither a consolidation nor a confederation, but in the creation of two constitutionally protected governments, each sovereign in its own sphere, many of the Framers viewed the powers reserved to the states with suspicion and hostility. As far as they were concerned, the safety and happiness of the American people required not a balance between the federal and state governments, but a preponderance of power in the national government. Seen in this light, the relevance of the Framers' views of federalism is obvious: they anticipated and approved the steady expansion of the national government into state and local affairs as essential to the preservation of liberty. Then as now, federalism appears to some to be antithetical to the rights of the citizens and to the common good.

The purpose of this paper is to examine the role of federalism in the political thought of two leading founders, James Madison and Alexander Hamilton, and to challenge the assumptions upon which it rests. I will try to show that their rejection of federalism is based upon too narrow a view of the problems of preserving republican government. The preservation of the republic requires additional checks to safeguard liberty from abuse by the national government,

*The author gratefully acknowledges the generous support of the University of Connecticut Research Foundation and the cheerful assistance of Mrs. Helen Petty, research librarian, University of Connecticut, Groton.

and more importantly, the promotion of civic virtue. The *principle* of federalism contributes to this end and, hence, is vital to the maintenance of the republic. Seen in this light, the relevance of the Framers' view of federalism is more complicated: an understanding of why they failed to appreciate the federal principle may shed some light on certain contemporary problems whose roots lie in the defects of the foundation.

I

The Constitution of the extended republic was chiefly a response to the problem of liberty. The presumed failure of the states to guard against the evils of faction led Madison and other supporters of free government to urge that the confederation of sovereign states be replaced by a vigorous national government in which the states would be retained, but in a clearly subordinate role. This is not, however, the origin of modern federalism. For Madison's initial hostility to the states, based on his belief that as independent political associations they endangered liberty, caused him to propose a government which was not only national—by which he meant empowered to act directly upon the citizens[1] —but far more consolidated than the principle of federalism allows.

Not only were the states to lose their representation as political bodies, but they were to be deprived of the bulk of their powers as well. The principal justification for these proposals was that the people are the source of all political power, and their happiness and safety are the sole objects of government. Since the states' contribution to these ends was minimal, they should be stripped of their power and independence. Accordingly, Madison proposed that the national government be equipped with an absolute veto over all state acts.[2] Nothing short of this "defensive" power would protect the citizens against encroachments by the state governments.

Had Madison's original proposals succeeded, the Constitution would have established a basically consolidated, rather than federal, republic. For the principal characteristic of American federalism is the recognition that within their limited but proper sphere the states

---

[1] James Madison to N. P. Trist, December 1831, in *The Records of the Federal Convention*, ed. Max Farrand, 4 vols. (New Haven and London: Yale University Press, 1937), III:517.

[2] James Madison to George Washington, 16 April 1787, in *The Forging of American Federalism*, ed. Saul K. Padover (New York: Harper and Row Publishers, 1953), p. 185; and *Federal Convention*, 1:27, 165.

are free to govern themselves, subject only to constitutional restraints.[3] What Madison and the other radical nationalists at the federal convention sought, then, was not a federal system, but the reduction of the states to something resembling administrative agencies. As such, their existence would have depended upon the will of the general government and that government's estimation of their ability to be "subordinately useful." This is the relation which the towns bear to the states, and Madison recommends it as the model for relations between the states and the national government. As "corporations dependent upon the General Legislature,"[4] the states could continue to perform "beneficial" tasks, but they would lack the power to act unjustly.

The difference between these two positions is profound, for it stems from opposing views of how liberty and the general good are best secured. Federalism rests on the assumption that a large consolidated government is itself a danger to liberty, since it must necessarily degenerate into monarchy—if not in name, at least in principle. Dividing power between the state and federal governments lessens this danger, but even then, abuses are likely since power is of an encroaching nature. Federalism further assumes that such invasions of rights may be carried out by the national government as well as the states;[5] consequently, it provides constitutional protection to the states as political bodies so that both governments may act as barriers against the undue accumulation and abuse of power by the other.

Administrative decentralization, on the other hand, assumes that the states as political associations are the primary threat to liberty. Consequently, it seeks to reduce them to local corporations, whose purpose is merely to administer those objects to which the general government cannot conveniently extend. So unnecessary are the states as political bodies to the protection of liberty that, were it possible for the general government to "extend its care to all the minute objects which fall under the cognizance of local jurisdiction,"[6] there would be no need to retain the states at all. Their function is purely administrative.

---

[3] Although the states also retain their constituent power, the new federalism depends much less upon the participation of the states in the national government, especially since there is no recall or bloc voting in the Senate.

[4] *Federal Convention*, I:357-358; also Hamilton, I:287.

[5] See, for example, George Mason's speeches of 7 June and 20 June in *Federal Convention*, I:115-116 and 340.

[6] *Federal Convention*, I:357-358.

According to this view, liberty is secured not by a balance of power between the state and federal governments, but by a preponderance of power in the national government whose powers are properly distributed and whose officers are duly dependent upon the people. This was the view of Madison and Hamilton at the federal convention. Consequently, they opposed the compromises which resulted in the modern federal republic; their support for the Constitution was given in spite of its federal aspects.

II

However surprising it is to discover the antipathy of many of the leading Framers toward the federal principle at the secret debates of the convention, it is even more surprising to discover that these views are subtly reiterated in the *Federalist Papers*. For not only does the title seem to support this principle, but the papers themselves appear to be sympathetic to the states. Yet beneath the apparent praise of the states as bulwarks of liberty, there is the constant reminder that one reason why a vigorous national government is necessary is because the states have failed to protect public and private rights.

These views are not openly stated, however, because one of the tasks of the *Federalist* was to persuade citizens that the Constitution establishes a republic which is sufficiently "federal" in the older meaning of the word, i.e. confederal. Accordingly, they addressed themselves to the objection that the national government possessed too many powers and the states too few to preserve liberty. The main tack of the *Federalist* was to emphasize the present power and authority of the states, while at the same time implying that in the future the national government would be supreme. The argument for national supremacy the *Federalist* wisely leaves to experience.

Against the objection that the Constitution gives too many powers to the national government, Madison argues that the specific powers vested in the general government are consistent with the objects of government and, hence, are both necessary and proper. The *Federalist* then turns to the more difficult issue of implied powers. For even more than enumerated powers, critics feared that these provisions and rules of constitutional interpretation—by which the general government could exercise any power consistent with the great aims for which the Constitution was established, even if that power was not expressly granted—would serve as the "pernicious engines by which

... local governments ... (would) be destroyed and ... liberties exterminated."[7]

Against the abuse of these powers in particular, and the totality of powers vested in the national government in general, the *Federalist* offers three safeguards. The first is psychological. The national government will have no incentive to absorb the objects of the states because these ends are so puny. Men in high office are ambitious: "the regulation of the mere domestic police of a state appears to men to hold out slender allurements to ambition." Thus, the states are safe from encroachments "because the attempt to exercise those powers would be as troublesome as it would be nugatory."[8] This, however, is a curious defense.

The second check is institutional. Should the national legislature overleap its bounds, the executive and judiciary will restrain it because they possess the "constitutional means and personal motives" to do so. If this fails, the people can in the last resort elect new representatives. Here, Madison, recurring to the federal principle, suggests that the states may play a part. Sensitive to national encroachments, they will sound the alarm and awaken the citizens to the necessity of changing the federal representatives. Even then, Madison manages to turn this federal argument to national advantage. The great benefit of vesting power in the national government is that there are states to restrain it.

> There being no such intermediary body between the state legislatures and the people, interested in watching the former, violations of the state constitutions are likely to remain unnoticed and unredressed.[9]

Nevertheless, Madison does not believe that resort to the state governments will be necessary to preserve liberty; the proper distribution of power among the three branches of the national government and a due dependence of these officers upon the people will be sufficient in most cases to restrain national encroachments.

The third check against abuse by the national government is constitutional. Implied powers extend only to those objects which the Constitution entrusts to the national government. In these areas, it is true, the power of the national government is subject only to the limitations which the Constitution imposes. But the Constitution does not give the national government power over all objects.

---

[7] *Federalist* No. 33, in *The Federalist*, ed. Jacob E. Cooke (Middletown, Conn.: Wesleyan University Press, 1961), p. 204.

[8] *Federalist* No. 17, pp. 105–106.

[9] *Federlaist* No. 44, p. 305.

It was not, however, sufficient to show that the Constitution vested in the general government only those powers which were necessary and proper, that these powers were adequately checked, and that all other powers remained with the states. The *Federalist* had also to satisfy its critics that the powers reserved to the states were adequate to protect their rights, and the rights of their citizens. This meant that the authors had to persuade their opponents that the states did retain sufficient power to predominate, since they believed that it was only by the states remaining supreme that liberty would be secured. Although Madison and Hamilton had fought to prevent just this, and supported the Constitution precisely because it promised to reverse this tendency of "confederations," they could (putting their own opinion of such measures aside) nevertheless point out the considerable powers reserved to the states, and their probable effects.

Not only did the states participate in the conduct of national affairs, but their powers were "numerous and indefinite." It is true that Hamilton had termed these powers "tedious" and "uninteresting," but this is only from the perspective of men with great ambition. Matters of local legislation might not attract men who aspired to national fame and glory; but as far as the citizens were concerned, they were matters of the highest importance, for they touched on "all those objects which, in the ordinary course of affairs, concerned the lives, liberties, and properties of the people." [10] Consequently, it seemed likely that the citizens would be more attached to the states. Their confidence and loyalty—together with the powers remaining in the states—made it probable that these local governments would not only check national encroachments, but that they would actually predominate.

This then is the surface argument of the *Federalist*—an argument which Madison and Hamilton could make in part *in spite of* their private opinions and in part *because* of their genuine fear that the states were still too powerful. For the *Federalist* does not doubt the combined power of the states to act, or for that matter, even a single great state; what it doubts is that the states will act in the interests of the general good. More likely the states would continue to protect their own privileges and powers by executing the wishes of a factious majority.

In spite of those dangerous centrifugal tendencies, Madison and Hamilton supported the Constitution because they expected these

[10] *Federalist* No. 45, p. 313.

tendencies to subside in the future. The *Federalist* suggests that, as the people became more familiar with the general government and experienced the benefits of its superior administration, they would welcome its extention "to what are called matters of internal concern."[11] For they would recognize that their rights are better protected by the national government than by the states. Consequently, the people would overcome their natural tendency to love best what is near, and would think of themselves as citizens of the United States. The decline of the states, therefore, seemed inevitable—not because of usurpation, but ironically because "in republics strength is on the side of the people."[12] And in the future the people were more likely to support the national government because it provided greater security for their rights.

Still, Madison sought to assure the states that even if the citizens do grow more attached to the national government, the states need not fear annihilation: there are limits to how far the federal powers can be advantageously administered.[13] Thus, Madison returned to his arguments at the federal convention. As the national government established itself at the center of American life, the proper role of the states would be to administer those objects to which it was inconvenient for the national government to extend.

Thus, in spite of its seeming defense of the states as a barrier against encroachments by the national government, the *Federalist* suggests that the proper relationship between the states and the federal government should be administrative rather than political because it believes that the states endanger liberty. Accordingly, liberty will be better secured in the future when the national government is supreme: the states will be less able to meddle in national affairs and the federal government will be restrained from abuses by the internal arrangement of its powers[14] and the dependence of its officers on the people.[15] For the *Federalist*, representation and the proper distribution of power provide the keys to republican liberty. To Madison and Hamilton federalism was important in the foundation of the American republic only in a negative way: it allowed for the removal of matters concerning the general good from the states to the national government and, in so doing, insured greater dignity and justice for the rights and interests of all.

[11] *Federalist* No. 27, p. 174; and *Federalist* No. 46, p. 317.
[12] *Federalist* No. 31, p. 198.
[13] *Federalist* No. 46, p. 317.
[14] *Federalist* No. 31, p. 197; and *Federalist* No. 44, p. 305.
[15] *Federalist* No. 28, p. 178; and *Federalist* No. 46, p. 322.

III

Still the question remains: what role does federalism play in the preservation of the American republic? [16] To be precise, were Madison and Hamilton correct in assuming that the principal danger to republican liberty was the failure of the states to control the effects of majority faction? In the following pages I will suggest that this understanding of the problems of preserving republican government was inadequate. First, because as Madison shortly discovered, liberty can also be endangered by the national government. And second, because even when the national government is able to resolve domestic disputes more impartially than the states, republican government requires more than superior administration. Enlightened and public spirited citizens are essential, and this requirement clashes with the removal of public affairs to a distant and disinterested national government. To the extent that the federal principle satisfies these requirements, it is necessary for the preservation of the republic.

In his defense of the necessary and proper clause in *Federalist* No. 44, Madison sought to assure the citizens that if the national legislature overstepped its bounds, it would be restrained by the executive and judicial branches. Although Madison acknowledged that the states might also play a role, it was only in the last resort. In general, the proper distribution of power among the three branches of the national government, each of which represents the people, would secure liberty.

It was not long, however, before this thesis was tested and found wanting. The failure of the federal and federalist courts to strike down the Alien and Sedition Acts as unconstitutional usurpations of power by the national government changed Madison from an ardent nationalist to a supporter of the federal principle. The Virginia Resolutions reflect this change in Madison's political thought: for here the states are cast as defenders of the constitutional system against encroachments by the national government.

The point of the Virginia Resolutions is that the Constitution creates a government of specific and enumerated powers. When the national government overleaps these bounds by construing its powers too broadly, it is the proper function of the states to restrain it. In such cases, the states

---

[16] For a somewhat different interpretation, see Martin Diamond, "The *Federalist's* View of Federalism," in *Essays in Federalism*, ed. George C. S. Benson (Claremont, California: Institute for Studies on Federalism, 1962), pp. 21-64.

have the right and are in duty bound to interpose for arresting the progress
of the evil, and for maintaining in their respective limits the authorities,
rights and liberties appertaining to them. [17]

The failure to resist these encroachments will result in a "speedy
consolidation," because as the states grow weaker, they will lose the
affections of the citizens and become objects of contempt. [18] Whereas Madison saw nothing objectionable in such a development in 1787
when the general government seemed in need of all the help it could
get against the centrifugal tendency of the states, the rapid success of
the national government in establishing itself, due in part to the early
triumphs of the Federalist Party, made Madison see consolidation in
an altogether different light. The man who once defended a veto over
all state acts, and who announced that if the national government
could conveniently administer all local objects, "no fatal consequence" could result from the abolition of the states, now recognizes
that there are dangers in consolidation. Consolidation would increase
the power and patronage of the executive—it being impossible for the
deliberative branch to extend its care to the ever increasing objects of
legislation. This strengthening of the executive branch at the expense
of the legislature would obviously and inevitably "transform the
present republican system of the United States into an absolute, or,
at best, a mixed monarchy." [19]

Thus, it was Madison's recognition that, despite internal checks,
the national government was also capable of encroaching upon the
rights of the citizens and dangerously consolidating political power,
which led him to defend the legitimate power and authority of the
states. This revised view of the dangers to republican liberty was
what caused Madison to change his earlier opinion of the states as
useful administrative agencies of the national government and to
defend them as political bodies necessary for the preservation of
liberty. It was precisely because the Constitution recognized the
states as political associations that they were able to safeguard the
rights of the citizens and to resist the tendency toward consolidation.

That Madison later supported the federal principle does not, however, mean that he became an advocate of states' rights. States' rights
insists that the Constitution is a compact among the sovereign states
and, consequently, that in all disputes arising under the Constitution,

---

[17] James Madison, *The Writings of James Madison*, ed. Gaillard Hunt, 9 vols. (New York
and London: G. P. Putnam's Sons, 1906), VI:326.
[18] Ibid., p. 333.
[19] Ibid., p. 327.

the states, as parties to the compact, must judge the issue for themselves. Federalism, on the other hand, acknowledges the constitutional division of power between the national and state governments, but it recognizes the supremacy of the Constitution over the governments, and the people over the Constitution. Accordingly, it is not the states as political units which are supreme, but the people in those states, for whose happiness both the state and national governments exist. Under the federal principle, then, the states contribute to the defense of the constitutional system by maintaining the distribution of power essential to the happiness of the people.

Taking the Resolutions by themselves, it is easy to see why Madison has been accused of advocating states' rights. For the Resolutions maintain that the powers of the federal government result from a "compact to which the states are parties," and that "in case of a deliberate, palpable, and dangerous exercise of other powers not granted by the compact," the states have a right and duty to interpose. Appeal was then made to the other states to concur with Virginia in declaring the Alien and Sedition Acts unconstitutional and to take the necessary and proper measures for cooperating to maintain their rights and authorities.

But when we consider the Report of 1800, written to clarify his position in the Resolutions, it is clear that Madison was supporting federalism and not states' rights. For the Report removed the ambiguity surrounding the word "states" and defended the necessity and propriety of the measures proposed in a manner consistent with the principles of the Constitution. Although Madison conceded that the term "states" is vague and ambiguous, he maintained that in the Resolutions it meant "the people composing those political societies in their highest sovereign capacity." This is the sense in which the Constitution was submitted to the "states," in which it was ratified by the "states," and consequently, in which the "states" are parties to the compact under which the federal powers arise. [20] Accordingly, whenever the federal government exceeds its rightful limits by exercising powers not granted to it, it is the right and duty of the *people* in the states to interpose to restrain these violations. Madison rejected the authority of the state governments to judge in these cases because it was the people in the states who were the parties to the compact.

This means, however, that the judiciary is also not competent to resolve such disputes since it too has only delegated authority. In

[20] Ibid., p. 348.

these "great and extraordinary cases" only the parties to the compact, that is the people in the states, can determine when the Constitution has been breached.[21] Still, there is nothing improper in these measures. Although the people are the final judges of the constitutionality of the laws, their decisions, as embodied in the declarations of their state legislatures, are only "expressions of opinion."[22] They were not intended to substitute for the judgment of the courts, but rather to arouse the citizens to "promote a remedy according to the rules of the Constitution." As such, the Virginia Resolutions are not only consistent with the Constitution, but they tend to preserve it by returning to first principles in speech. As a "declaratory recurrence to the principles of the Revolution,"[23] the Resolutions alert the citizens to dangerous encroachments upon their rights in time to avoid an actual return to first principles.

What the Virginia Resolutions signify, then, is Madison's recognition that the states can play a positive role in maintaining liberty. As constitutionally protected political societies, they can resist the tendency toward consolidation and check invasions upon the rights of the people. Although ultimately it is the people in the states who are supreme, the states contribute to their safety and happiness by preserving the constitutional balance necessary for republican liberty.

IV

However important federalism is to the protection of liberty, its first function, according to the republican tradition, was to foster civic virtue, for no republic could be preserved without virtuous citizens. According to the tradition, civic virtue meant a willingness to put aside private interest for the sake of the common good. This personal sacrifice was achieved, in part, by the citizens sharing in public affairs; participation taught them to care for what they held in common. Federalism made participation possible by allowing the republic to remain small enough for the citizens to enter the public realm. Consequently, federalism was essential to the preservation of the republic since it provided a way to promote civic virtue without sacrificing protection against external dangers.

This aspect of the tradition the Framers emphatically rejected. Direct participation by all the citizens would require the subdivision of the states into city-sized republics. Not only was such a proposal

[21] Ibid., p. 349.
[22] Ibid., p. 402.
[23] Ibid., p. 352.

incompatible with the greatness of America, but it was incompatible with the protection of liberty. In general, the mass of people are incompetent to conduct public affairs in person. A small territory compounds this difficulty, since it provides no protection against majority faction. Moreover, the Framers gradually came to realize that the requirements of disinterested virtue clashed with their commitment to civil liberty. For civic virtue, as the tradition understood it, not only required participation, but depended upon harsh laws which suppress individual interest and opinions.

That the Framers of the American republic sought primarily to safeguard civil liberty does not, however, mean that they abandoned the traditional concern with virtue. For they did not believe that republican government could be sustained without regard to the character of the citizens. As Madison remarked at the Virginia Ratifying Convention:

> if there be ... (no virtue among us), we are in a wretched situation. No theoretical checks, no form of government, can render us secure. To suppose that any form of government will secure liberty or happiness without any virtue in the people is a chimerical idea. [24]

Nevertheless, because their paramount commitment was to individual liberty, the virtue required to sustain the republic could not be of "heroic" [25] proportions. In other words, civic virtue cannot rest upon either the government's compelling a homogeneity of interests, passions, and opinions, or upon the participation of the citizens in public affairs via the federal principle. Both these methods are incompatible with liberty.

Instead, the Framers sought to encourage virtue primarily through social means. Although lacking the power and right to legally suppress individual differences, these institutions—the chief of which were education and religion—could instruct the citizens in their public duties by appealing to social mores and individual conscience. Thus, one way in which the Framers sought to circumvent the dilemma of the liberal republic—a dilemma which rested on the fact that the government was prevented by its commitment to private rights from entering into those concerns which were necessary to its preservation—was by relying upon the institutions of society to do what it could not.

---

[24] Jonathon Eliot, ed., *Debates on the Adoption of the Federal Constitution*, 5 vols. (Philadelphia: J. B. Lippincott Company, 1901), III:536-537. For a different view, see Paul Eidelberg, *A Discourse on Statesmanship* (Urbana: University of Illinois Press, 1974).

[25] Perhaps nowhere is this shift away from "heroic" virtue more obvious than in the political thought of John Adams, though the term itself is taken from *Cato's Letters*, by John Trenchard and Thomas Gordon.

Nevertheless, the Framers also recognized that moral and religious motives are not sufficient to direct the citizens toward the public good. Consequently, additional safeguards were necessary. The solution they proposed was to multiply the interests and sects in society by the extension of the republic, and to arrange the internal structure of government so that interest checks interest, and power checks power, thereby preventing the triumph of faction.

There is, however, a difference between these two mechanisms. Social pluralism discourages the formation of majority faction, but it does little to improve the political character of the people as citizens. Indeed, the largely economic nature of this diversity tends to strengthen the habits and attitudes which undermine civic virtue.

The proper distribution of political power, on the other hand, does more than discourage the formation of faction in the absence of "wise and virtuous rulers." For it seeks to instill a certain amount of civic virtue in those who do not already possess it. By designing offices in which the interest of the man coincides with his duty, and which are further restrained by the interests and powers of the representatives in other branches, the Framers sought to compel lesser men to moderate their interests in the direction of the public good. The point here is that even if a man's motives are selfish, the gradual moderation of interest toward duty will eventually teach him to care for the common good. The Framers' reliance upon institutional devices was not a substitute for civic virtue, but another means of promoting it among men who are not virtuous. It is true that this virtue never reaches the level of pure disinterestedness, but it does improve the character of public men to some extent, and in a manner which is consistent with the Framers' commitment to civil liberty.

Moreover, the proper distribution of political power seeks to encourage the best men to enter public office. For it provides them with the opportunity to fulfill their own interests, interests which in this case coincide with the good of the republic. [26] Even with the best men, then, virtue is not heroic, but depends upon the mutual fulfillment of interest and duty, which public responsiblity can provide.

Thus, the difference between the Framers' solution to the problem of virtue in the citizens and in their representatives was that for the citizens, the solution takes place almost entirely outside the public

[26] *Federalist* No. 72, p. 488; and Gerald Stourzh, *Alexander Hamilton and the Idea of Republican Government* (Stanford: Stanford University Press, 1970), pp. 101-106.

realm. The citizens were to be educated in political and moral principles, but for the most part, the only public activity in which the citizens would "participate" would be in the selection of their representatives. The Framers of the Constitution made no provision for institutions in which ordinary citizens could publicly appear to have their various interests and passions moderated or their opinions refined by deliberation with their fellow citizens. Yet since civic virtue requires participation, the virtue that the Framers tried to foster was insufficient for the preservation of the republic. Upon reflection, it appears to be concerned more with private morality than with public virtue.

What makes this absence of public virtue dangerous to the preservation of the republic is that, even though the citizens no longer participate in public affairs, they remain the fountain of all political power. For it is inevitable that when citizens retain political power but are deprived of any opportunity to exercise it, except for the solitary act of electing their representatives every few years, they will misuse or abuse their power. [27] Without experience in political affairs, they will not recognize that the public realm is governed by standards which are independent of, and sometimes in conflict with, the requirements of the private domain. [28] Thus, the failure to provide institutions in which the citizens can participate creates an entirely novel problem for the preservation: it corrupts the republic at the grass roots, for it reserves power to the people without teaching them how to use it.

V

Since civic virtue requires participation in political affairs and not simply "closeness" to government, federalism, as we know it, cannot meet the requirements of civic virtue. For federalism refers to the constitutional distribution of power between the general government and the states; it does not include constitutional guarantees for the municipalities, the one place where, indeed, because of their smallness, citizens would have the greatest opportunity to participate.

---

[27] Alexis de Tocqueville, *Democracy in America*, ed. Phillips Bradley, 2 vols. (New York: Alfred A. Knopf, 1966), II:320-321.

[28] Hans Morgenthau, *The Purpose of American Politics* (New York: Vintage Books, 1964), pp. 197-215; and Hannah Arendt, *On Revolution* (London: Faber and Faber, 1963), pp. 279-285.

These local units are actually creatures of the states;[29] as such, they lack the constitutional powers to defend themselves against state encroachments. Yet if civic virtue is essential to the preservation of the republic, and if local units are the most likely area where citizens can participate, the question arises: why didn't the Framers try to promote civic virtue by extending protection to these local governments?

One answer is the federal system itself, for it is precisely the constitutional recognition of the autonomy of the states over their domestic affairs which precludes intervention in local affairs. Thus, the irony of the federal solution is that the measures required to preserve the political independence of the states, i.e. the non-interference in the relations between the states and their local governments, leaves the Constitution powerless to prevent the state governments— which governments, to add to the irony, the Framers so heartily mistrusted when it came to the protection of private rights—from sapping the foundation of the republic by depriving the citizens of their public rights.

Yet I do not mean to imply that the Framers would have incorporated these self-governing communities into the structure of the federal republic had they not been caught in this dilemma. This seems unlikely for several reasons. First, the Framers did not maintain that it was participation simply which fosters a concern for the common good, but participation in a particular set of institutions designed to promote such care. Yet the factors which compelled this concern for the common good depended upon conditions of largeness; hence, they were necessarily absent in local governments, and to some extent, even in the states. Thus, the first reason why the Framers were unenthusiastic about local self-government was because they feared that without a multiplicity of interests, the proper distribution of powers and nobility of purpose, political activity would degenerate into faction.[30]

Second, the Framers generally assumed that what most men want is a secure and comfortable life. This being the case, not only was participation in political affairs unnecessary for men to be happy, but by taking them away from the pursuit of gain and the enjoyment

[29]I wish to thank Professor Daniel J. Elazar for having pointed out to me that during the revolutionary period the question of the relationship of local governments to the states had not yet been definitively resolved. Especially in the North, and more particularly in New England, there was considerable support for the doctrine of the inherent right to local self-government. This doctrine existed side by side with the opposite interpretation that the local governments are the creatures of the states. Only later was the dispute resolved in favor of the latter interpretation, which came to be known as Dillon's Rule.

[30]Madison, in *Adoption of the Federal Constitution*, III:256.

of the fruits of their labor, it may actually make them unhappy. As for the few who are motivated by political ambition and the love of fame, the objects of local government are too puny. Thus, the implication is that the Constitution of the extended republic satisfies the desires of most men: it provides political men with a space in which to win honor and glory and it frees ordinary citizens from politics so that they may pursue their private happiness without interference.

Yet, since prior to the foundation of the republic, Americans did to some extent associate freedom and happiness with the citizen's right to participate in political affairs, even if the public realm extended no further than the town hall. Why, then, did the Framers understand happiness and freedom almost exclusively in terms of the protection of private rights and the promotion of moral virtue? Ironically, it was precisely the participation of the citizens in public affairs during and after the war for independence which accounts for the third reason why the Framers were unsympathetic to local self-government. For the activities of independence unleashed a destructiveness which the Framers properly recognized could not continue once the republic was established. Thus, the problem of the foundation was not how to preserve the power and spirit of the towns and voluntary associations but, on the contrary, how to defuse them.

It is true that during the revolutionary era widespread participation by the people had all too frequently ended in violent majority faction and mob rule;[31] indeed, the Constitution is largely a response to this problem. But, although the Framers correctly recognized that once the republic was founded it could not continue to tolerate acts of violence by the citizens, they did not recognize to what extent this violence was characteristic of the foundation, rather than of political activity in general. Nor can the glory of the foundation—understood as the opportunity to lay the foundation for freedom—counteract this view. Although the Framers considered constitution-making one of the highest human activities, it nevertheless remains unique to the foundation. It cannot, as Madison properly recognized in *Federalist* No. 49, provide a model for the politics of the preservation.

This means, however, that the Framers' solution is flawed, for their failure to recognize that not all political activity by the citizens is either destructive or unique to the foundation (such as the delib-

---

[31] Gordon Wood, *The Creation of the American Republic 1776-1787* (Chapel Hill: University of North Carolina Press, 1969), pp. 319-328.

eration and debate surrounding the framing and ratification of the Constitution), leads them to channel the entire energy of the revolution into private enterprises, rather than seek to direct some of this energy toward activities which promote civic virtue and, hence, contribute to the preservation of the republic. [32]

In other words, because they mistakenly assumed that the foundation provided a model for all political activity, they necessarily failed to understand what the preservation of the republic required. Their emphasis upon violence, and if not violence, their belief that once the republic is established there will be nothing for the citizens to do, makes the larger question of the preservation appear to be the same as stability. Yet since the Framers promoted stability by encouraging the citizens to devote themselves to the pursuit of wealth, the requirements of stability actually undermine the political virtues necessary to the preservation of the republic. [33] Ironically, then, the defect of the Framers' solution is that it succeeds too well, for not only does it discourage later generations of citizens from acting violently but it discourages them from acting at all. [34]

VI

The Framers' failure to protect the local institutions, which allow the citizens to participate in public affairs, cannot be understood as a repudiation of the need for civic virtue to sustain the republic. Rather, it is a failure to understand what civic virtue requires. Given the tremendous activity of the citizens during the revolution, they thought it was sufficient to speak of civic virtue in terms of moral and political education. It is a testimony to the vitality of the towns that they did not believe it was necessary to provide constitutional protection for these local units. Indeed, they feared that these political associations would encourage too much spirit.

The towns were—and to some extent, continue to be—schools for civic virtue. By providing ordinary citizens with the opportunity to share in the activities of the republic according to their competence, they mitigate the worst effects of materialism and individualism. Moreover, these self-governing communities put teeth into the claim that the people are the source of all political power, for alone among the institutions of the republic, these governments provide the citi-

[32] Hannah Arendt, *On Revolution*, pp. 234-242.

[33] George Anastoplo, *The Constitutionalist: Notes on the First Amendment* (Dallas: Southern Methodist University Press, 1971), pp. 214-216.

[34] Wilson Carey McWilliams, *The Idea of Fraternity in America* (Berkeley: University of California Press, 1973), p. 173.

zens with a space in which to exercise their political power jointly with their fellow citizens. Consequently, it is these elementary republics which make citizenship in the extended republic meaningful—and in a manner consistent with liberal democracy—for these local institutions are all that the citizens in our heterogeneous society have in common politically.

Despite their role in promoting civic virtue, the Framers did not seek to incorporate these local institutions into the Constitution by extending the federal principle to include them because they feared that too much participation would endanger liberty. According to the Framers, the purpose of federalism is to protect civil liberty, not civic virtue; consequently, it applies only to the relations between the states and the general government.

It is true that increasing the opportunities for political activities involves certain risks: the people may act unjustly; they may seek political power for their own ends; they may be incompetent. But without political activity, there is lethargy, and lethargy also endangers the republic. The problem of republican government, then, is that it requires more than stable and wise administration; it requires active and alert citizens who understand the meaning and enjoy the exercise of their liberty. This means that the preservation of the republic is precarious, since it requires balancing the conflicting claims of civil liberty and civic virtue. [35] Although there can never be a perfect solution to this problem, I have tried to suggest that the Framers' efforts are flawed because they place too much emphasis upon protecting civil liberty against faction, with the result that they then endanger it by lethargy.

Ironically, the way out of this dilemma lies, in part, in the expanded use of the principle they so much distrusted at the foundation: federalism. The principle of federalism, understood as the constitutional recognition and protection of independent spheres of political activity—and hence capable not only of expansion as Madison suggested, but of division—serves the needs of both civil liberty and civic virtue. By preventing the consolidation of political power and by creating centers of power capable of checking each other, it protects liberty. By bringing the republic within reach of the citizens on matters within their competence, it promotes virtue. Seen from this perspective, the principle of federalism is both conservative and revolutionary: it provides a means of conserving the spirit of the revolution in a manner consistent with the Framers' commitment to civil liberty and, hence, is vital to the preservation of the republic.

[35] Michael Walzer, "Civility and Civic Virtue in Contemporary America," *Social Research* 41, no. 4 (Winter 1974):593-611.

The Virtues of Liberalism: Christianity, Republicanism, and Ethics in Early American Political Discourse

James T. Kloppenberg

Historians sometimes forget that Dante reserved a special place in the Inferno for sowers of discord. Having spent their lives tearing apart families, communities, and religions, such lost souls spend eternity with a demon who slices their bodies in two. Their wounds do slowly heal, Dante tells us, but no sooner has "the gashed flesh reunited its grain" than their bodies are again split by the fiend's sharp sword. So it goes forever. A visitor from outside the circles of American colonial and early national history, observing the polemics in which partisans of competing interpretations carve each other up, might well wonder what students of American political culture have done to deserve a fate similar to the one Dante prescribed for schismatics. These disputes have continued to heat up in recent years, as the exchanges between John Diggins and Paul Conkin and between Lance Banning and Joyce Appleby illustrate.[1]

Readers who relish such controversies may be disappointed, but I do not intend in this essay to audition for the role of Dante's demon. Instead I hope to suggest a way out of our historiographical inferno by mapping what may appear to be a singularly unpromising escape route, a rediscovery of the virtues of liberalism. By examining the diverse sources of liberalism in the eighteenth century, I hope to demonstrate how and why liberal ideas could be joined with ideas from the different

James T. Kloppenberg is assistant professor of history at Brandeis University.

For comments offered on an earlier version of this essay, which was read at the meeting of the Organization of American Historians in New York on April 11, 1986, I am grateful to Joyce Appleby, Lance Banning, Hendrik Hartog, James Henretta, James Hoopes, Richard L. McCormick, Drew McCoy, J. R. Pole, David Thelen, and Gordon Wood. They bear a share of the responsibility for whatever virtues the essay may have; I take credit for any vices that remain.

[1] Dante Alighieri, *The Divine Comedy*, Cantica I: *Hell (L'Inferno)*, trans. Dorothy L. Sayers (Harmondsworth, 1949), Canto XXVIII, 246–50; John Patrick Diggins, "Comrades and Citizens: New Mythologies in American Historiography," *American Historical Review*, 90 (June 1985), 614–38; Paul Conkin, "Comment," *ibid.*, 639–43; John Patrick Diggins, "Reply," *ibid.*, 644–49; Lance Banning, "Jeffersonian Ideology Revisited: Liberal and Classical Ideas in the New American Republic," *William and Mary Quarterly*, 43 (Jan. 1986), 3–19; Joyce Appleby, "Republicanism in Old and New Contexts," *ibid.*, 20–34. See also the essays collected in the special issue "Republicanism in the History and Historiography of the United States," ed. Joyce Appleby, *American Quarterly*, 37 (Fall 1985), 461–598.

traditions of Protestant Christianity and classical republicanism at two decisive moments, when Americans were launching the Revolution and formulating the Constitution, and to suggest how and why the three streams almost immediately diverged. In my conclusion, I will discuss the two themes of individual autonomy and popular sovereignty that were at the center of the American vision of politics during those years.

The last three decades have yielded a wide variety of competing interpretations of the late eighteenth century. In the 1950s Louis Hartz and Daniel Boorstin offered two verdicts on a common version of America's liberal tradition. In the 1960s Bernard Bailyn and Gordon Wood explained why Americans were drawn to varieties of classical republicanism as they tried to separate from Britain and consolidate their revolution. In the 1970s Henry F. May and Morton White led a squadron of intellectual historians who emphasized the importance of Scottish common sense philosophy in the complex of ideas that constituted America's version of the Enlightenment. Finally, in the 1980s J. G. A. Pocock has reiterated and extended his earlier claims for the centrality of republicanism and the relative insignificance of John Locke's liberalism, while Diggins has countered by resurrecting Hartz's search for an abusable past in a passionate indictment of an American liberalism that has lost its soul.[2]

Is this a trajectory of accumulating knowledge or a downward spiral of increasingly futile circularity? Have we learned anything from these competing interpretations, or do they simply cancel each other out? In light of the work that has been done since the 1960s in social and political history, it is possible to argue that at least a few conclusions remain standing when the smoke of rhetoric clears. Some of the grander claims appear untenable, other arguments appear increasingly solid, and certain methodological guidelines for studying ideas appear helpful. I will discuss these topics in reverse order.

First, it is now uncontroversial to conclude that the nonhistorical study of ideas is dead. Contributions from hermeneutics, from linguistically sensitive versions of Marxism, and from analytic philosophy have combined to demonstrate the fruitfulness of contextualist analysis and the uselessness of studying ideas detached from their historical settings. Moreover, despite some nostaliga for the promised neatness of structuralism, intellectual historians now tend to agree that, although patterns of discourse do provide frameworks for thought, such frameworks are historical

[2] Louis Hartz, *The Liberal Tradition in America: An Interpretation of American Political Thought since the Revolution* (New York, 1955); Daniel Boorstin, *The Genius of American Politics* (Chicago, 1953); Bernard Bailyn, *The Ideological Origins of the American Revolution* (Cambridge, Mass., 1967); Gordon Wood, *The Creation of the American Republic, 1776-1787* (New York, 1969); Henry F. May, *The Enlightenment in America* (New York, 1976); Morton White, *The Philosophy of the American Revolution* (New York, 1978); Garry Wills, *Inventing America: Jefferson's Declaration of Independence* (Garden City, 1978); D. H. Meyer, *The Democratic Enlightenment*," ed. Joseph Ellis, *American Quarterly*, 28 (Summer 1976), 147-293; J. G. A. Pocock, *The Machiavellian Moment: Florentine Political Thought and the Atlantic Republican Tradition* (Princeton, 1975); J. G. A. Pocock, *Virtue, Commerce, and History* (Cambridge, Eng., 1985), see esp. 48, 79, for particularly sharp formulations of this argument; and cf. John Patrick Diggins, *The Lost Soul of American Politics: Virtue, Self-Interest, and the Foundations of Liberalism* (New York, 1984), see esp. 3-145, 345.

rather than eternal. Discourse, in other words, shifts, often slowly, sometimes rapidly, but always unevenly, in response to the imaginative manipulation of language by creative thinkers confronting unprecedented problems. Prevailing theories of rationality suggest that individuals interpret the meaning of experience only slowly and imperfectly, because experience is always culturally mediated by the systems of symbols that render ideas and behavior significant. The meaning of the past emerges for historians in the same way, as we attempt to uncover progressively clearer understandings of what experience meant for earlier generations. Intellectual historians who insist on viewing the past from the angle of those who lived it tend to be equally impatient with the claims of Marxists and Whigs to understand grand patterns of development, because such patterns may distort our understanding by imposing meanings different from those that ideas had historically. Just as social historians have turned increasingly to the project of reconstructing the past as it was lived, so intellectual historians have tried to reconstruct ideas as they were thought, by trying to uncover what thinkers believed themselves to be doing—what they meant to be doing—when they wrote what they did.[3] This hermeneutical approach to historical inquiry does not rule out the attempt to find larger patterns of change. Indeed, that is precisely what I will try to do in this essay, as I sort through the various interpretations of early American political culture in search of a new perspective on some familiar problems. The hermeneutical approach merely requires that such interpretations be seen in terms of the meanings available in the past. These meanings are then examined critically in light of later developments, rather than through some lens designed to broaden or deepen perspectives in order to fit events to a preconceived pattern.

Shifting from method to content, it is possible to identify an emerging consensus among historians concerning the persistence of diversity in American patterns of thought and behavior during the colonial and early national periods. Partisans of both the republican and the liberal interpretations have identified strands of American political culture whose presence can no longer be convincingly denied. When Pocock all but dismisses liberalism, for example, or when Diggins dismisses republicanism, they ignore an increasingly impressive body of scholarship not merely suggesting, but showing, evidence of contrast and diversity. In this essay, after examining three different sources of colonial American ideas about virtue—religious,

    [3] Recent discussions include Richard J. Bernstein, *Beyond Objectivism and Relativism: Science, Hermeneutics, and Praxis* (Philadelphia, 1983); Richard Rorty, J. B. Schneewind, and Quentin Skinner, eds., *Philosophy in History* (Cambridge, Eng., 1984); Quentin Skinner, ed., *The Return of Grand Theory in the Human Sciences* (Cambridge, Eng., 1985); Pocock, *Virtue, Commerce, and History*, 1–34; James A. Henretta, "Social History As Lived and Written," *American Historical Review*, 84 (Dec. 1979), 1293–1322. For a critique of such ideas, see John Patrick Diggins, "The Oyster and the Pearl: The Problem of Contextualism in Intellectual History," *History and Theory*, 23 (1984), 151–69; and Diggins, *Lost Soul of American Politics*, 347–65. Two collections of essays that not only discuss methodology, but also provide splendid examples of how the methodology works are Dominick LaCapra and Steven L. Kaplan, eds., *Modern European Intellectual History: Reappraisals and New Perspectives* (Ithaca, 1982); and David A. Hollinger, *In the American Province: Studies in the History and Historiography of Ideas* (Bloomington, 1985). For more detailed discussion of these issues, see James T. Kloppenberg, "Deconstruction and Hermeneutics as Strategies for Intellectual History: The Recent Work of Dominick LaCapra and David Hollinnger," *Intellectual History Newsletter*, 9 (April 1987), forthcoming.

republican, and liberal—and suggesting inconsistencies within each source, I will indicate how their evident incompatibilities and quite different regional strengths could be muted precisely because of the tensions that persisted within each tradition.

Virtue in various forms lay at the heart of Christian doctrine. Between the discussion of the virtues in the *Summa theologica* of Thomas Aquinas and *The Nature of True Virtue* of Jonathan Edwards ran a string of less carefully constructed, but nonetheless powerfully influential, meditations on universal benevolence as the ideal of Christian ethical doctrine. Several of these meditations have recently attracted renewed attention through the work of Norman Fiering.[4] Outside New England, which is at the center of Fiering's vision, it seems likely that Christian concepts of virtue flowed through colonial American culture principally in the form of mainstream Anglicanism and a complementary secular literature. Other historians, again looking primarily at New England, have emphasized the importance of evangelicalism as a source of social and political unrest in eighteenth-century America. After a period in which both European and American historians tended to downplay the religious dimensions of eighteenth-century thought and presented it as a celebration of science and skepticism, recent work has concentrated on the persistence of either explicit or implicit religious ideals in the Enlightenment on both sides of the Atlantic, and especially on the corrosive effect of religious enthusiasm on prevailing patterns of deference. The "irrepressibly democratic dynamic in Protestant theology," to use Perry Miller's exuberant phrase for it, remained all too repressible in most American denominations until social tensions brought it bubbling to the surface in a variety of forms. The idea of the covenant, central to Puritan theology from the outset, contained a doctrine of participation that threatened hierarchical stability. Several recent studies have refined earlier hypotheses concerning the connection between the Great Awakening and the American Revolution. Although the pattern and timing varied by region and denomination, it seems clear that the dissenting tradition, which originally flourished in the eroding soil of community, was transplanted into a republican environment in which it continued to grow.[5]

---

[4] Norman Fiering, *Moral Philosophy at Seventeenth-Century Harvard: A Discipline in Transition* (Chapel Hill, 1981); Norman Fiering, *Jonathan Edwards's Moral Thought and Its British Context* (Chapel Hill, 1981). See also Bruce Kuklick, *Churchmen and Philosophers: From Jonathan Edwards to John Dewey* (New Haven, 1985), 5–111; and Elizabeth Flower and Murray G. Murphey, *A History of Philosophy in America* (2 vols., New York, 1977), I, 3–361.

[5] For emphasis on the "paganism" of the Enlightenment, see Peter Gay, *The Enlightenment: An Interpretation* (2 vols., New York, 1966–1969). On the American side, see esp. May, *Enlightenment in America*. Recent discussions of the Enlightenment emphasizing its multidimensionality include Lester Crocker, "Interpreting the Enlightenment: A Political Approach," *Journal of the History of Ideas*, 46 (April–June 1985), 211–30; and Roy Porter and Mikuláš Teich, eds., *The Enlightenment in National Context* (Cambridge, Eng., 1981).

For a seminal discussion of Puritanism and politics, see Perry Miller, *Errand into the Wilderness* (Cambridge, Mass., 1956), 16–47, esp. 47. The overly ambitious claims of Alan Heimert, *Religion and the American Mind: From the Great Awakening to the Revolution* (Cambridge, Mass., 1966), have been moderated, and the role of religion carefully assessed, in several recent studies. See Richard L. Bushman, *From Puritan to Yankee: Character and the Social Order in Connecticut, 1690–1765* (Cambridge, Mass., 1967); William G. McLoughlin, "The Role of Religion in the Revolution: Liberty of Conscience and Cultural Cohesion in the New Nation," in *Essays on the American Revolution*, ed. Stephen G. Kurtz and James H. Hutson (Chapel Hill, 1973), 197–255; William G.

New Englanders hold a town meeting in a Congregational church.
From the sometimes chaotic practice of self-government, Americans
developed the principle of popular sovereignty.
Courtesy Library of Congress.

Religion continued to contribute to the shaping of American culture in the eighteenth century, but the Christian notion of virtue was sufficiently expansive to contain contradictory ideas. Did the challenge to authority represented by the
awakening involve the abrogation of all rules, or did New Light communities merely
seek to reconstitute order on a purified foundation? Did the renewed emphasis on
man's depravity signal the distance America had fallen from its lofty mission, or

McLoughlin, *Revivals, Awakenings, and Reform: An Essay on Religion and Social Change in America, 1607–1977*
(Chicago, 1978), 24–97; Nathan O. Hatch, *The Sacred Cause of Liberty: Republican Thought and the Millennium
in Revolutionary New England* (New Haven, 1977); Patricia U. Bonomi, " 'A Just Opposition': The Great
Awakening as a Radical Model," in *The Origins of Anglo-American Radicalism*, ed. Margaret Jacob and James Jacob
(London, 1984), 243–56; Rhys Isaac, "Radicalised Religion and Changing Lifestyles: Virginia in the Period of the
American Revolution," *ibid.*, 257–67; and David D. Hall, "Religion and Society: Problems and Reconsiderations,"
in *Colonial British America: Essays in the New History of the Early Modern Era*, ed. Jack P. Greene and J. R. Pole
(Baltimore, 1984), 317–44 On declension and the jeremiad, cf. Gene Wise, "Implicit Irony in Perry Miller's *New
England Mind*," *Journal of the History of Ideas*, 29 (Oct.–Dec. 1968), 579–600; Robert G. Pope, "New England
versus the New England Mind: The Myth of Declension," *Journal of Social History*, 3 (Winter 1969–1970), 95–108;
and Sacvan Bercovitch, *The American Jeremiad* (Madison, 1978).

did it testify to the community's faithfulness to its original ideals? Did the commitment to God, "whom to serve is perfect freedom," require selfless obedience — or rather the individual's liberation from all merely earthly forms of authority? Different communities answered those questions in different ways, and their recognition of those disagreements only made their competing claims to Christian virtue more strident.

The presence of classical republicanism as a second tradition in American political discourse during the latter half of the eighteenth century is no longer in doubt. Reasonable people certainly will continue to disagree about the centrality or the pervasiveness of these ideas and to question who articulated republican arguments for what reasons and for how long. These are serious questions to which I will return. Classical republicans called for independent citizens to protect fragile civic virtue against the threat of corruption represented by the extension of executive power. Their ideal of a community, in which individuals define their interests in terms of the common good, figured prominently in the political literature produced in America, particularly between the end of the Seven Years' War and the ratification of the Constitution. A successful challenge to the work of Caroline Robbins, Bailyn, Wood, and others would not merely have to deny the legitimacy of their understanding of the role of ideas in historical change, it would also have to destroy the formidable mountain of evidence on which their arguments rest. Although republicanism was not the only vocabulary of virtue available to Americans concerned with political questions, it surely was one of the several vocabularies available to them.[6]

Yet just as the Christian ideal of virtue was both central and ambiguous, so the republican ideal of the virtuous citizen was fuzzy. Did classical republicans fear change and distrust popular government? Did they tolerate hierarchy, embrace Spartan simplicity, and encourage militarism? It would be a caricature of republicanism in Britain or America to identify those characteristics as essential to the classical tradition in all its many "court" and "country" forms. Yet one need look no further than Machiavelli to discover the problematical nature of an ideal inspired by the Renaissance fascination with *virtù*. Neither Montesquieu nor James Madison nor John Adams subscribed to a version of republican virtue that elevated the will to combat fortune above the individual's responsibility to adhere to the moral law. The powerful, although brief, appeal of republicanism as a weapon to be wielded against corruption seems clear enough. But its meaning for a nation attempting to establish itself on a foundation of natural rights, equality, and the pursuit of happiness proved a good deal murkier.[7]

[6] Caroline Robbins, *The Eighteenth-Century Commonwealthman: Studies in the Transmission, Development, and Circumstances of English Liberal Thought from the Restoration of Charles II until the War with the Thirteen Colonies* (Cambridge, Mass., 1959); Bailyn, *Ideological Origins*; Bernard Bailyn, ed., *Pamphlets of the American Revolution, 1750–1776* (Cambridge, Mass., 1965); Wood, *Creation*; Robert E. Shalhope, "Toward a Republican Synthesis: The Emergence of an Understanding of Republicanism in American Historiography," *William and Mary Quarterly*, 29 (Jan. 1972), 49–80; Pocock, *Machiavellian Moment*; and J. G. A. Pocock, "*The Machiavellian Moment* Revisited: A Study in History and Ideology," *Journal of Modern History*, 53 (March 1981), 49–72.
[7] A recent study of Machiavelli that challenges Pocock's view is Mark Hulliung, *Citizen Machiavelli* (Princeton,

The individual, Locke counseled, must master his inclinations
"for the sake of what is fit to be donne."
Reproduced from the *London Magazine*, 21 (Oct. 1752), 468.

The third tradition I want to consider is liberalism. Since the false trail left by
Hartz has distracted us from the meanings of liberal virtue, Appleby's work has been
especially valuable. As she has pointed out, liberalism first took shape in the battle
against both the inherited patterns of social hierarchy and the economic ideas of
mercantilism that together served as props for privilege in the seventeenth and
eighteenth centuries. Diggins has quite properly insisted that unless we restore
liberalism to our vision of American politics, the republican perception may become
as static and one-dimensional as the Hartzian view it set out to replace. But which
liberalism should we recover? There is a liberal tradition that originated with

---

1983). See also Robert Shackleton, *Montesquieu: A Critical Biography* (Oxford, 1961); Mark Hulliung, *Montesquieu and the Old Regime* (Berkeley, 1976); Marvin Meyers, ed., *The Mind of the Founder: Sources of the Political Thought of James Madison* (Hanover, 1981), xi–xli; John R. Howe, Jr., *The Changing Political Thought of John
Adams* (Princeton, 1966); and Alasdair MacIntyre, *After Virtue* (Notre Dame, 1981), 210–21.

Thomas Hobbes's hardheaded cynicism and developed into the market liberalism examined by Appleby and excoriated in C. B. Macpherson's study of possessive individualism. That liberalism failed to make rapid progress either in England or in America precisely because, in Appleby's words, it "rested upon a moral base so shallow as to threaten the whole complex of conventional religious precepts." Although such liberalism promised freedom, it "delivered most of the propertyless into the hands of a new master—the market." Given the persistence of both religious and republican ideas running directly counter to the "radical reductionism" of personality required for the acceptance of behavior motivated solely by economic considerations, the resistance this version of liberalism encountered in eighteenth-century England and America should occasion little surprise.[8]

But there was another liberal tradition, whose roots stretched to the sober Puritanism of Locke rather than the stark individualism of Hobbes. Largely through the work of John Dunn, we now have a portrait that rescues the historical Locke from Macpherson's cartoon. The persuasiveness of Dunn's argument derives largely from his insistence that we take Locke on his own terms, instead of imposing on him meanings gathered from the social consequences of capitalism. His concept of individual liberty dissolves if it is removed from the context of divinely established natural law, which encumbers the freedom of individuals at every turn with the powerful commands of duty. Locke's belief in a natural law discernible by reason led him to condemn the unregulated pursuit of self-interest that Hobbes considered natural and that later writers who celebrated a market economy sanctioned. "He that has not a mastery over his inclinations," Locke wrote in 1687, "he that knows not how to resist the importunity of present pleasure, or pain, for the sake of what, reason tells him, is fit to be donne, wants the true principle of Vertue, and industry; and is in danger never to be good for anything."[9]

[8] C. B. Macpherson, *The Political Theory of Possessive Individualism* (Oxford, 1962); Joyce Appleby, "Ideology and Theory: The Tension between Political and Economic Liberalism in Seventeenth-Century England," *American Historical Review*, 81 (June 1976), 512, 515. For an especially pointed formulation of her critique of Pocock, see Joyce Appleby, "Response to J. G. A. Pocock," *Intellectual History Newsletter*, 4 (Spring, 1982), 20–22.

[9] Locke quoted in John Dunn, *Rethinking Modern Political Theory: Essays, 1979–83* (Cambridge, Eng., 1985), 194n43. Cf. this passage: "In January 1698, in a letter to his friend William Molyneux, Locke summed up the convictions of a lifetime: 'If I could think that discourses and arguments to the understanding were like the several sorts of cates [foodstuffs] to different palates and stomachs, some nauseous and destructive to one, which are pleasant and restorative to another; I should no more think of books and study, and should think my time better imploy'd at push-pin than in reading or writing. But I am convinc'd of the contrary: I know there is truth opposite to falsehood, that it may be found if people will, and is worth the seeking, and is not only the most valuable, but the pleasantest thing in the world'"; John Dunn, *Locke* (Oxford, 1984), 87. See also John Dunn, *The Political Thought of John Locke: An Historical Account of the "Two Treatises of Government"* (Cambridge, Eng., 1969). In his most recent work Dunn has continued to emphasize the necessity of understanding Locke's conception of rights in the context of his religious belief. In John Dunn, "What is Living and What is Dead in the Political Theory of John Locke?" paper delivered in Cambridge, Mass., in 1986 (in the possession of James T. Kloppenberg), 10–11, he wrote, "For Locke all the rights human beings have (and which they certainly do possess prior to and independently of all human political authority) derive from, depend upon and are rigidly constrained by a framework of objective duty: God's requirements for human agents. Within this setting, but as he supposed only within this setting; the claims of right are indeed decisive and all human beings have a duty to observe them and to enforce them." Dunn's interpretation relies in important respects on Peter Laslett's brilliant essay on Locke: Peter Laslett, "Introduction," in John Locke, *Two Treatises of Government*, ed. Peter Laslett (Cambridge, Eng., 1960), 15–168; this interpretation has been extended in James Tully, *A Discourse on Property: John Locke and His Adversaries*

The recent emphasis on the pervasiveness of Scottish common sense philosophy in the American Enlightenment has been as important as the recognition that natural law provided the screen on which Locke projected his political ideas. Locke's Christianity may have shielded him from the unsettling implications of his empiricist epistemology, but those implications became apparent in David Hume's skepticism. The attractiveness of such thinkers as Francis Hutcheson, Adam Ferguson, Thomas Reid, and Dugald Stewart for Americans can be explained by their ability to reassure anxious religious sensibilities. Different Scots appealed to different Americans, as Henry May and others have shown. Despite their disagreements, the Scottish philosophers did share a commitment to the accountability of the individual to the community, and that commitment appealed to Americans as much as did their comforting theories of knowledge. Even Hume, whose social ideas betrayed no trace of sentimentality, conceded that "a tendency to public good, and to the promoting of peace, harmony, and order in society does, always, by affecting the benevolent principles of our frame, engage us on the side of the social virtues." Hume derived this argument from imagination and custom rather than reason; thus his approach differed from those of writers who grounded moral sense on feelings, with Hutcheson, or on rational intuition, with Reid.[10]

The Scottish Enlightenment was dedicated to discovering methods by which a provincial culture could create forms of social virtue without having to rely on republican political institutions unavailable to a province that was, like America, uncomfortable with its status. Thus the Scots turned to local, cultural, and, most notably, economic forms of association as potential fields for the cultivation of virtuous community life. The most influential of their efforts, of course, identified the mysterious workings of an invisible hand capable of transforming even the activity of the least virtuous into socially constructive behavior. As students of Adam Smith, including Jacob Viner, Donald Winch, and Richard Teichgraeber, have emphasized, Smith did not seek to establish the workability of a market economy to make possible the unchecked exercise of self-interest in the pursuit of wealth. Smith aimed

(Cambridge, Eng., 1980). Morton White incorporated this view of Locke in his analysis of Jefferson; see White, *Philosophy of the American Revolution*, 57–60. The possibility that Locke himself provided the best arsenal of arguments against C. B. Macpherson's critique is explored in Patrick Riley, *Will and Political Legitimacy: A Critical Exposition of Social Contract Theory in Hobbes, Locke, Rousseau, Kant, and Hegel* (Cambridge, Mass., 1982), 61–97.

10 David Hume, *An Enquiry concerning the Principles of Morals* (La Salle, 1938), 67; see also the discussion of this passage in Gertrude Himmelfarb, *The Idea of Poverty: England in the Early Industrial Age* (New York, 1984), 35. The critical literature on the Scottish moral philosophers is vast and growing rapidly. A thoughtful review of recent work is Nicholas Phillipson, "The Scottish Enlightenment," in *The Enlightenment in National Context*, ed. Porter and Teich, 19–40. An early exploration of the similarities between Scotland and the American colonies was John Clive and Bernard Bailyn, "England's Cultural Provinces: Scotland and America," *William and Mary Quarterly*, 11 (April 1954), 200–213; more extensive investigations of Scottish ideas in America include May, *Enlightenment in America*; White, *Philosophy of the American Revolution*; Wills, *Inventing America*; D. H. Meyer, *The Instructed Conscience: The Shaping of the American National Ethic* (Philadelphia, 1972); Meyer, *Democratic Enlightenment*; and Terence Martin, *The Instructed Vision: Scottish Common Sense Philosophy and the Origins of American Fiction* (Bloomington, 1961). For a balanced assessment of the impact of Scottish common sense on American thought, see J. R. Pole, "Enlightenment and the Politics of American Nature," in *The Enlightenment in National Context*, ed. Porter and Teich, 209.

instead to make possible, through ingeniously anti-utopian methods, a world of both plenty and justice. Barriers restricting freedom and insuring poverty would yield to market mechanisms facilitating general prosperity. Smith worked within two contexts, the tradition of natural law articulated by Grotius and Pufendorf and reworked by Smith's mentor Hutcheson and the tradition of political economy established in late seventeenth-century England by the critics of mercantilism. The cold comfort enjoyed by later generations liberated from what E. P. Thompson and others have called the "moral economy" of precapitalist England has caused us to lose sight of Smith's intent. Just as Locke's enterprise is misunderstood when his liberalism serves as the midwife of possessive individualism, so Smith's purpose is distorted when the market mechanism he envisioned as a means to a moral end is presented as itself the goal of political economy. This interpretation of the *Wealth of Nations* resolves the thorniest part of the Adam Smith problem by suggesting that Smith expected a market economy to make possible the virtue he examined in *The Theory of Moral Sentiments*: "How selfish soever man may be supposed, there are evidently some principles in his nature, which interest him in the fortune of others, and render their happiness necessary to him, though he derives nothing from it, except the pleasure of seeing it." This concept of benevolence, flowing from the springs of natural law that fed Locke's liberalism as well as various streams of Protestantism in America, thus played as large a part in Smith's philosophy as it did in those versions of Scottish common sense that figured more directly in eighteenth-century American thought.[11]

Yet just as religious and republican ideas contained ambiguities blurring implicit inconsistencies, so tension remained latent even in versions of liberalism oriented

---

[11] Adam Smith, *The Theory of Moral Sentiments* (Indianapolis, 1969), 47. Cf. the following passage: "There can be no proper motive for hurting our neighbor, there can be no incitement to do evil to another which mankind will go along with, except just indignation for evil which that other has done to us. To disturb his happiness merely because it stands in the way of our own, to take from him what is of real use to him merely because it may be of equal or of more use to us, or to indulge, in this manner, at the expense of other people, the natural preference which every man has for his own happiness above that of other people, is what no impartial spectator can go along with"; *ibid.*, 160. For a splendid discussion of Smith's attempt to integrate his political economy with the philosophy of moral sense he derived from his mentor Francis Hutcheson, who had tried to unify the competing strands of natural law represented by Grotius's radical individualism and Pufendorf's responsible communitarianism, see Richard Teichgraeber III, *'Free Trade' and Moral Philosophy: Rethinking the Sources of Adam Smith's* Wealth of Nations (Durham, 1986); and "Introduction," in Adam Smith, *An Inquiry into the Nature and Causes of the Wealth of Nations,* ed. Richard Teichgraeber III (New York, 1985), ix–xlviii. Teichgraeber also emphasizes Smith's debts to the seventeenth-century British economists who were impatient both with mercantilism and with what E. P. Thompson and others have called the tradition of "moral economy." See E. P. Thompson, "The Moral Economy of the Crowd in Eighteenth-Century England," *Past and Present*, 50 (Feb. 1971), 76–136. Cf. the following passage: "For Smith political economy was not an end in itself but a means to an end, that end being the wealth and well-being, moral and material, of the 'people,' of whom the 'laboring poor' were the largest part. And the poor themselves had a moral status in that economy—not the special moral status they enjoyed in a fixed, hierarchic order, but that which adhered to them as individuals in a free society sharing a common human, which is to say, moral, nature"; Himmelfarb, *Idea of Poverty*, 63. This interpretation of Adam Smith, first advanced by Jacob Viner in the 1920s, has since become less revisionist than orthodox. See Jacob Viner, "Adam Smith and Laissez-Faire," in *The Long View and the Short: Studies in Economic Theory and Policy* (Glencoe, Ill., 1958), 213–45. An influential presentation of this view is Donald Winch, *Adam Smith's Politics: An Essay in Historiographic Revision* (Cambridge, Eng., 1978); see also the range of perspectives in Istvan Hont and Michael Ignatieff, eds., *Wealth and Virtue: The Shaping of Political Economy in the Scottish Enlightenment* (Cambridge, Eng., 1983). On the roots of liberal political economy in the tradition of natural law, see Richard Tuck, *Natural Rights Theories: Their Origin and Development* (Cambridge, Eng., 1979).

more toward ideals of virtue than toward simple acquisitiveness. Could Locke's theory of money as the symbol of tacit consent, for example, justify forms of property holding that threatened the natural right of the poor to survive? Were Locke's strictures against extravagant accumulation incompatible with the legitimacy he accorded any social arrangements that earned popular assent? Did the Scottish philosophers expect man's innate moral sense to provide a standard that would rule out any social order resting on exploitation, or did they suppose instead that the impulse toward benevolence would suffice as a brake on oppression regardless of the form of economic organization? Finally, by identifying the inadvertently beneficial effects of consumption, did Smith encourage the prodigality scorned by earlier generations devoted to the Protestant ethic? In every case it seems clear that a gap separated the intentions of liberal thinkers from the world of possessive individualism that eventually emerged. Nevertheless, the inversion of means and ends that accompanied the process Max Weber described as the replacement of substantive rationality by instrumental rationality did lead to the rise of a mentality giving priority to consuming over producing, and to wealth over virtue. Istvan Hont and Michael Ignatieff have shown how the development of the concept of property in the transformation of natural jurisprudence from Aquinas to Grotius, and then from Locke to Smith, steadily attenuated the legitimate claims of the poor on the rich. Ironically, only when widespread prosperity seemed at last a possibility did recognition of the residual rights of the poor disappear.[12]

Thus the ideas that sailed to America during the seventeenth and eighteenth centuries were rich in diversity and in ambiguity. Montesquieu was only confirming what contemporaries already knew when he distinguished, in *The Spirit of the Laws*, between three sorts of virtue — Christian, political, and moral. With neatness of a sort that usually makes historians uneasy, they conform to the ideas of virtue in the traditions of religious, republican, and Scottish common sense philosophy. Not only were those conceptions of virtue not clearly compatible, as Montesquieu pointed out, there were inconsistencies within each of the three traditions as well, as I have tried to make clear. When Americans feverishly debated their future in the second half of the eighteenth century, they had available to them three distinguishable, if not altogether discrete, vocabularies of virtue. Each was unsteady enough by itself, but when combined they became unpredictably explosive. In America, moreover, an "inadvertent pluralism" emerged from the interaction of diverse cultures and the experimentation encouraged by the existence of opportunity. Because the roots of recently transplanted traditons were comparatively shallow, testing new alternatives was an attractive option in the colonies. Perhaps for that reason different intellectual and cultural patterns tended to rearrange themselves, or even to merge, rather than remaining altogether separate.

---

[12] See Dunn, *Locke*, 36–44, for a brief discussion of this problem, and Tully, *Discourse on Property*, for a more extended treatment. On Adam Smith and the consequences of political economy, cf. Istvan Hont and Michael Ignatieff, "Needs and Justice in the *Wealth of Nations*: An Introductory Essay," in *Wealth and Virtue*, ed. Hont and Ignatieff, 1–44; and Nicholas Phillipson, "Adam Smith as Civic Moralist," *ibid.*, 179–202. Max Weber's most straightforward discussion of the varieties of rational action appears in Max Weber, *Economy and Society*, ed. Guenther Roth and Claus Wittich, trans. Ephraim Fischoll et al. (2 vols., Berkeley, 1978), I, 24–26.

Regional differentiation further enriched the blend of diverse ideas and experience. Although not without exceptions, the first settlers of New England embraced ideals of social cohesion and patterns of precommercial agriculture. The Middle Colonies, culturally and intellectually more heterogeneous, were from the beginning less stable socially, and they more rapidly developed economic diversification and commercial farming. The southern colonies, founded by adventurers and called to order by a planter oligarchy, lacked both the restraints imposed by piety and community in New England and the experience of flexibility and fragmentation in the Middle Colonies. Further complicating this already-crazy quilt is the increasing emphasis social historians have placed on change and on religious, political, and socioeconomic diversity in colonial America. The explosion of research since the 1960s has demolished simple pictures of a stable prerevolutionary America, and it is now apparent not only how diverse were the patterns of experience in different regions, but also how complicated were the processes of development. Established forms of behavior persisted uneasily alongside innovations, as experience altered the cultures the colonists brought with them from Europe. Ideas have different meanings in different contexts, and as various religious, political, and ethical assumptions encountered the social and economic realities of life in a new and rapidly changing world, the potential meanings of virtue grew exponentially.[13]

It was precisely this variety of ideas that enabled the colonists to converge in the 1760s in opposition to British efforts to reassert the Crown's authority. Because of the ambiguities of the traditions from which they drew, and because of the unsteadiness and the inconsistencies of the arguments they advanced, they were able to join together behind a banner of ideas stitched together from three different sources: religious, republican, and liberal. I will be able to suggest only briefly how these traditions figured in revolutionary thinking. While the most ambitious claims for a tight causal connection between religious enthusiasm and political rebellion have not survived careful scrutiny, historians have shown how Puritan millennialism in the North, and Baptist evangelicalism in the South, could join forces with more secular forms of radicalism. Through participation in symbolic communal activities, colonists were able to put aside their differences and unite — however briefly — against the British. The galvanizing effect on American thinking of the second set of ideas I have isolated, classical republicanism, needs little discussion. The pamphlets of the revolution spoke the language of civic humanism as clearly as they spoke the language of dissenting Protestantism, and the evidence that the two languages coexisted in revolutionary political discourse is incontrovertible. As for Locke

---

[13] Two collections of essays provide extremely helpful overviews of recent work in American colonial social history, and both are transatlantic in focus. The phrase "inadvertent pluralism" appears in an essay in the first collection; see Joyce Appleby, James Jacob, and Margaret Jacob, "Introduction," in *Origins of Anglo-American Radicalism*, ed. Jacob and Jacob, 11. The other collection is *Colonial British America*, ed. Greene and Pole. Comparative analyses of Europe and America have transformed the study of colonial intellectual life. Discussions of recent work reflecting that influence include Daniel Walker Howe, "European Sources of Political Ideas in Jeffersonian America," *Reviews in American History*, 10 (Dec. 1982), 28–44; Robert E. Shalhope, "Republicanism and Early American Historiography," *William and Mary Quarterly*, 39 (April 1982), 334–56; and Pole, "Enlightenment and the Politics of American Nature," 192–214.

Thomas Jefferson, Richard Henry Lee, Patrick Henry, and
Francis Lightfoot Lee in the Raleigh Tavern, May 1774.
Reproduced from *Harper's New Monthly Magazine*, 92 (May 1896), 948.

and Scottish moral philosophy, it seems clear both that these ideas were not the entire story, as used to be argued, and that they were not irrelevant, as it was popular
to contend in the 1970s. It should not surprise us that the intricacies of philosophers'
arguments rarely surfaced in broadsides designed to arouse patriots to war. For those
gentry who traveled the road to independence via what May called the Moderate
Enlightenment, however, such ideas made a decisive difference. Moreover, understanding that central document of the Revolution, the Declaration of Independence, as Morton White has demonstrated more persuasively than Garry Wills, requires seeing it against the background of natural rights philosophy and Scottish
common sense.[14]

[14] See John Dunn, "The Politics of Locke in England and America in the Eighteenth Century," in *John Locke:
Problems and Perspectives*, ed. John W. Yolton (Cambridge, Eng., 1969), 45–80; May, *Enlightenment in America*,
3–101, 153–304; White, *Philosophy of the American Revolution*; and Wills, *Inventing America*.

In articles published over the last two decades, Appleby has given a distinctive twist to the argument for the importance of liberalism in American revolutionary ideology. She concedes that a "regenerative republicanism" was part of the ferment leading to rebellion, but she insists that "deliverance from the strictures of classical republicanism came from the ideology of liberalism, from a belief in a natural harmony of benignly striving individuals saved from chaos by the stability worked into nature's own design." This liberalism, she concludes, "not only justified a revolution against an intrusive sovereign, it also offered ordinary people an escape from the self-denying virtue of their superiors." These passages, from her essay "The Social Origins of American Revolutionary Ideology," illustrate that at times Appleby has carefully qualified the nature of the liberalism she imputes to American revolutionaries. Theirs was a liberalism rooted in the natural law tradition and informed by Scottish moral sense philosophy, precisely the liberalism White discovered in *The Philosophy of the American Revolution*.[15]

Thomas Jefferson was optimistic about the harmonious interaction of self-interested individuals only because he believed their inner moral gyroscopes would prevent them from oppressing one another. Jefferson was a liberal who defined self-interest as Locke's virtue rather than Hobbes's possessive individualism. In his meditation on the "foundation of morality in man," Jefferson distinguished benevolence from egoism. "Self-love, therefore, is no part of morality. . . . It is the sole antagonist of virtue, leading us constantly by our propensities to self-gratification in violation of our moral duties to others. . . . nature hath implanted in our breasts a love of others, a sense of duty to them, a moral instinct, in short, which prompts us irresistably to feel and to succor their distresses." Jefferson went on to describe the utility of this moral sense, but he defined utility in terms of benevolence rather than vice versa, and his ethics was thus unrelated to the utilitarianism of eighteenth-century philosophers such as Jeremy Bentham. Jefferson believed that his theories of moral sense and natural rights were consistent with the available empirical evidence about man, but they were grounded more solidly in Hutcheson's intuitionism than in the behavior of Virginia planters. Indeed, the contrast between those theories and actual politics illustrates what Diggins has called the "pathos of the Enlightenment," the distance separating principles from practice that explains the failure of such American revolutionaries as Jefferson to repudiate slavery.[16]

---

[15] Joyce Appleby, "The Social Origins of American Revolutionary Ideology," *Journal of American History*, 64 (March 1978), 939–58, esp. 955–56. See also Joyce Appleby, "Liberalism and the American Revolution," *New England Quarterly*, 49 (March 1976), 3–26; Joyce Appleby, "What Is Still American in the Political Philosophy of Thomas Jefferson?" *William and Mary Quarterly*, 39 (April 1982), 287–304; Joyce Appleby, "Commercial Farming and the 'Agrarian Myth' in the Early Republic," *Journal of American History*, 68 (March 1982), 833–49; Joyce Appleby, "The Radical *Double-Entendre* in the Right to Self-Government," in *Origins of Anglo-American Radicalism*, ed. Jacob and Jacob, 275–83; and Joyce Appleby, *Capitalism and a New Social Order: The Republican Vision of the 1790s* (New York, 1984).

[16] Thomas Jefferson, *Writings*, ed. Merrill D. Peterson (New York, 1984), 1335–39. Cf. the similar discussion in Thomas Paine, *The Rights of Man*, ed. Eric Foner (New York, 1984), 163. On Jefferson, see John P. Diggins, "Slavery, Race, and Equality: Jefferson and the Pathos of the Enlightenment," *American Quarterly*, 28 (Summer 1976), 206–28; and Pole, "Enlightenment and the Politics of American Nature," 200–203. On the anti-utilitarian thrust of Jefferson's ethics, see White, *Philosophy of the American Revolution*, 97–141. His account is more persuasive than that of Adrienne Koch, *The Philosophy of Thomas Jefferson* (New York, 1943), 15–43.

Jefferson was hardly the only American to embrace this conception of liberalism. The constraints it included, the characteristics that distinguished it from the laissez-faire liberalism that developed in the nineteenth century, must be kept in mind. As John E. Crowley has emphasized, economic life in America was generally discussed within a religious framework. Even Benjamin Franklin, that notoriously calculating embodiment of the spirit of capitalism, sought only the degree of comfort midway between destitution and extravagance, and he too offered religious rather than economic reasons for his activities. Also jostling alongside the natural rights liberalism that informed much economic argument were competing ideas drawn from the older English idea of "moral economy" and the new egalitarianism of Tom Paine, both of which figured prominently in the writings of urban artisans in the revolutionary years. Finally, Forrest McDonald has demonstrated in his recent study *Novus Ordo Seclorum* the presence of a wide range of additional limits, including the natural jurisprudential tradition, the English common law, and various colonial American legal practices, that further held in check the appearance of an unrestrained market capitalism. For all these reasons, it would be a mistake to exaggerate the attractiveness of purely individualistic, proto-capitalist behavior during the 1770s.[17]

Reflecting on the ideas present and absent in those years, I believe we ought to think of autonomy rather than freedom as the aim of the American Revolution, autonomy not only for the nation, but for individuals as well. The concept of autonomy, in its everyday as well as its Kantian sense, is inseparable from the concept of self-government, and inseparable from the nuances of restraint, law, and moral responsibility that may be missed in the ambiguity of freedom as an idea divisible into negative as well as positive forms. Americans sought independence as a nation to secure autonomy as individuals.[18]

The unity achieved during the Revolution dissolved quickly during the 1780s— almost as quickly as historical syntheses of the period have tended to dissolve. I will not attempt to bring order to the chaos of the critical period, because that chaos reflected the persistence of the disagreements present in colonial America and suppressed, but hardly resolved, during the war for independence. Before examining the persistence of diversity and the intensification of ideological and regional disputes in the 1790s, however, I want to discuss one idea Americans could agree upon

[17] John E. Crowley, *"This Sheba, Self": The Conceptualization of Economic Life in Eighteenth-Century America* (Baltimore, 1974), 84. For evidence of the diverse ideas animating Americans from different backgrounds during the Revolution, see Alfred F. Young, ed., *The American Revolution: Explorations in the History of American Radicalism* (DeKalb, 1976); Eric Foner, *Tom Paine and Revolutionary America* (New York, 1976); and Gary B. Nash, "Artisans and Politics in Eighteenth-Century Philadelphia," in *Origins of Anglo-American Radicalism*, ed. Jacob and Jacob, 162–82. The contrast between these ideas and the interpretation Appleby has advanced in her essays on the Revolution is discussed by Shalhope, "Republicanism and Early American Historiography," 343n24. Although it finally dissolves into a polemical division of the American political world between heroic "nationalists" and dastardly "ideologues," there is a wealth of valuable material, particularly on American and English law, in Forrest McDonald, *Novus Ordo Seclorum: The Intellectual Origins of the Constitution* (Lawrence, 1985).

[18] The concept of autonomy, most carefully formulated by Immanuel Kant but also crucial for John Locke and Jean Jacques Rousseau, filtered into American thought largely through the influence of Francis Hutcheson and Thomas Reid, the Scottish philosophers whose ideas most nearly resembled Kant's.

after securing autonomy through successful revolution. That idea was popular sovereignty, the location in the people themselves of the ultimate decision-making authority for the new nation. The American decision to appeal beyond the traditional rights of Englishmen to the rights of men, their decision to reject the definition of government as the sovereignty of an executive in a legislature, has been described by Pocock as "the most profound breach ever to have occurred in an anglophone political practice." Robert R. Palmer, J. R. Pole, Gordon Wood, and Forrest McDonald have all identified the doctrine of popular sovereignty as the decisive achievement of the American political imagination.[19]

It is clear that the idea of popular sovereignty grew from the colonial experience of self-government. It is sobering to realize, as Michael Kammen has pointed out, how poorly we understand what the colonists thought they were doing when they embarked on that venture by establishing representative institutions. Again regional variations must be acknowledged. Timothy H. Breen has shown how New England Puritans held the electorate responsible for the quality of government and demanded from citizens more than mere obedience. Even when political questions became increasingly secularized in the eighteenth century, arguments in New England continued to reflect a mixture of concerns about property and concerns about piety and responsibility. In Pennsylvania, the assembly claimed powers more extensive than those of any other colonial legislature; it resisted temptations to compare itself to the House of Commons because that might mean reducing its powers vis-à-vis the executive. Yet according to John M. Murrin, this swaggering legislature was probably less active in exercising its elaborate powers than any other colonial representative assembly. Finally, in Virginia, the activities of the assembly consolidated citizens' rights while stabilizing a system of exploitation. Even if, to follow Pole's revision of Edmund S. Morgan's formulation, American freedom served as a means of guaranteeing American slavery, it also served as a means of guaranteeing the survival of republicanism in practice as well as theory. Despite differences in regional political habits, it was above all the experience of self-government that enabled the colonists to fight the war for independence, to survive the critical period, and to create the federal republic. Yet the growth of representative institutions in America was as accidental as the fragmented form national political authority finally assumed as the new nation sought to accommodate the competing demands of the states. The triumph of popular sovereignty represented a watershed in the theory as well as the practice of politics. As Martyn P. Thompson has recently pointed out, the tension between competing efforts to establish fundamental law on the basis of either history or reason dissolved once the foundation of governmental authority was located in the people. Instead of grounding law on either ancient custom, on

---

[19] J. G. A. Pocock, "Radical Criticisms of the Whig Order in the Age between Revolutions," in *Origins of Anglo-American Radicalism*, ed. Jacob and Jacob, 44; Robert R. Palmer, *The World of the French Revolution* (New York, 1971), 269–70; J. R. Pole, *Political Representation in England and the Origins of the American Republic* (London, 1966), 503–39; Wood, *Creation*, 344–89, 605–15; and McDonald, *Novus Ordo Seclorum*, 260, 280–93. For the contention that the idea of popular sovereignty can be traced to Locke's writings, see Julian Franklin, *John Locke and the Theory of Sovereignty* (Cambridge, Eng., 1978), 97, 104, 123–26.

the one hand, or the logical fiction of a contract, on the other, American proponents of popular sovereignty followed the lead of Montesquieu and Rousseau by replacing the idea of fundamental law with the idea of the public will as the legitimating principle of the republic. Its haphazard development notwithstanding, the idea of popular sovereignty, rooted firmly in experience, had a universal appeal. It seemed to represent at once the fulfillment of the Puritan concept of the covenant, the republican idea of a public-spirited citizenry, and the liberal idea of responsibly self-interested individuals exercising their right to self-government.[20]

All three of the traditions apparent in colonial American political thought persisted into the 1790s, but the relations among them altered as the tensions within each tradition changed. The ideal of austere Christian virtue that had inspired and haunted Edwards lingered in the form of the jeremiad. Increasingly, though, as the nineteenth century dawned, American Protestantism accommodated itself to a comfortable position as guardian of a new, privatized virtue characterized above all by propriety, the centerpiece of what would become the genteel tradition. Evangelicals bemoaned the smug worldliness of Americans, and at least some of their enthusiasm assumed a militaristic form that enabled them to reenact, in style if hardly in substance, the glorious struggle of God's chosen people against the popish plots of King George and Archbishop Laud.

If religious divisions during the 1790s did not fit neatly into the emerging pattern of party alignments, neither did the divisions among those who remained drawn toward varieties of classical republicanism. Although John Adams and Alexander Hamilton continued to use the republican vocabulary, the bitterness of their rivalry makes it apparent that they did not always speak the same language or see the same future for Federalism.[21]

The Jeffersonians were no less contentious. In a review of Appleby's provocative *Capitalism and a New Social Order*, John Ashworth pointed out that many of the disputes concerning Jeffersonian ideology turn on questions of definition and selection. What is to count as republicanism? Which republicans were Jeffersonians, and

[20] Michael Kammen, *Deputyes & Libertyes: The Origins of Representative Government in Colonial America* (New York, 1969); Timothy H. Breen, *The Character of the Good Ruler: Puritan Political Ideas in New England, 1630–1730* (New York, 1970); John M. Murrin, "Political Development," in *Colonial British America*, ed. Greene and Pole, 439–40; Edmund S. Morgan, *American Slavery—American Freedom: The Ordeal of Colonial Virginia* (New York, 1975); J. R. Pole, *Paths to the American Past* (New York, 1979), 55–74; Jack P. Greene, *The Quest for Power: The Lower Houses of Assembly in the Southern Royal Colonies, 1689–1776* (New York, 1972); Jack P. Greene, "An Uneasy Connection: An Analysis of the Preconditions of the American Revolution," in *Essays on the American Revolution*, ed. Kurtz and Hutson, 32–80; Pole, *Political Representation*, 508–13; Martyn P. Thompson, "The History of Fundamental Law in Political Thought from the French Wars of Religion to the American Revolution," *American Historical Review*, 91 (Dec. 1986), 1103–28.

[21] McLoughlin, *Revivals, Awakenings, and Reform*, 98–140; Bercovitch, *American Jeremiad*, 132–75. My understanding of the recreation of revolutionary fervor in the revivals of the Second Great Awakening rests on conversations with Christine Heyrman, who is exploring the process as it occurred in the Carolinas. On the formation of the genteel tradition, see May, *Enlightenment in America*, 307–62. On the Federalists, see James M. Banner, *To the Hartford Convention* (New York, 1970); Linda Kerber, *Federalists in Dissent* (Ithaca, 1970); and Gerald Stourzh, *Alexander Hamilton and the Idea of Republican Government* (Stanford, 1970). For the suggestion that in the early nineteenth century party loyalty emerged as yet another (mutant) species of civic virtue, see David Hackett Fischer, *The Revolution of American Conservatism: The Federalist Party in the Era of Jeffersonian Democracy* (New York, 1965).

vice versa? For Drew McCoy, James Madison serves as the archetypal Jeffersonian Republican. For Lance Banning, John Taylor's pamphlets are "probably the most important source for an understanding of Republican thought in the middle 1790s." For Appleby, Taylor, a classical republican from the "country" mold, is not a Jeffersonian Republican at all.[22]

If republicanism is defined as backward-looking elitism opposed to commerce and economic growth, then clearly many Jeffersonians were not republicans. As Banning concedes in a recent essay, any attempt to depict the "thought of Americans in the 1790s as encapsulated in the conceptual world of Montesquieu's civic humanism" would be a serious error. Proponents of the republican hypothesis, Banning protests, specifically deny "that either English oppositionists or Jeffersonian Republicans identified their enemies as those involved in manufacturing or commerce." McCoy's *The Elusive Republic*, as Banning accurately points out, emphasizes again and again the transformation of the republican tradition in the 1790s. Madison and his allies repudiated the ideal of a "Christian Sparta" and embraced commercial agriculture and economic growth as the salvation of the American republic. Although worried about the consequences of that growth, they worked diligently to make it happen. "Recent scholarship," Banning concludes, "often actually *insists* on American departures from received ideas, most especially on American hostility to privilege and American rejection of 'the distinctions of class and rank whose balancing played so central a role in classical republicanism.' This scholarship should not be condemned as though the authors claimed that an entire, unchanging, civic-humanist tradition persisted into the new republic. Such criticism charges it with errors never made." I suspect that partisans of the liberal hypothesis such as Appleby have derived a measure of satisfaction from such remarks, since their challenges to the more extreme formulations of the republican argument—for example, those Pocock continues to make on occasion—have now elicited such a useful clarification.[23]

Yet the ideal of civic virtue, although transformed by the experiences of fighting the Revolution, writing the Constitution, and facilitating the expansion of commercial agriculture, did persist in Jeffersonian discourse. A crucial passage from Madison's speech before the Virginia ratifying convention, June 20, 1788, underscores this point.

> I have observed, that gentlemen suppose, that the general legislature will do every mischief they possibly can, and that they will omit to do every thing good which they are authorised to do. If this were a reasonable supposition, their objections would be good. I consider it reasonable to conclude, that they will as readily do

---

[22] John Ashworth, "The Jeffersonians: Classical Republicans or Liberal Capitalists?" *Journal of American Studies*, 18 (Dec. 1984), 425–35. Cf. Drew McCoy, *The Elusive Republic: Political Economy in Jeffersonian America* (Chapel Hill, 1980), 10; Lance Banning, *The Jeffersonian Persuasion: Evolution of a Party Ideology* (Ithaca, 1978), 193; and Appleby, *Capitalism and a New Social Order*, 80.

[23] Banning, "Jeffersonian Ideology Revisited," 6–8; see also McCoy, *Elusive Republic*, esp. 49, 61, 90–100. Pocock has hammered this theme repeatedly; for a particularly sharp statement of his position, see Pocock, *Virtue, Commerce, and History*, 66–67, 69–71.

their duty, as deviate from it: Nor do I go on the grounds mentioned by gentlemen on the other side—that we are to place unlimited confidence in them, and expect nothing but the most exalted integrity and sublime virtue. But I go on this great republican principle, that the people will have virtue and intelligence to select men of virtue and wisdom. Is there no virtue among us? If there be not, we are in a wretched situation. No theoretical checks—no form of government can render us secure. To suppose that any form of government will secure liberty or happiness without any virtue in the people, is a chimerical idea. If there be sufficient virtue and intelligence in the community, it will be exercised in the selection of these men. So that we do not depend on their virtue, or put confidence in our rulers, but in the people who are to choose them.

Madison's argument illuminates his ideas on the relation between the structure of the federal republic and the necessity of a virtuous citizenry. As this passage indicates, Madison was a realist but not a cynic. *The Federalist* No. 10 and No. 57 likewise suggest that Madison considered the separation of powers a necessary, but not sufficient, condition to insure what he called "the common good of the society."[24]

This idea of civic virtue did not die with the ratification of the Constitution, as Ralph Ketcham demonstrates in his study of presidential leadership in the early republic. Ketcham emphasizes the classical sources of the idea of the president as a nonpartisan patriot king, exercising leadership by appealing to citizens' moral sensibilities rather than pandering to narrow conceptions of self-interest. Of course something was gained when the chaotic democracy of Andrew Jackson replaced that more refined conception of what politics ought to be about, but something, namely the republican ideal of civic virtue, was also lost.[25]

If the idea of a common good continued to animate the republicanism of at least some Jeffersonians—and some Federalists—during the last decade of the eighteenth century, did the third tradition, the tradition of liberalism based on responsibility rather than cupidity, also survive? At least for a short time, for what might be called a Jeffersonian moment, it did, and its memory has lingered into the present. This liberalism is not to be confused with the liberal tradition that served as Hartz's whipping boy or with Macpherson's possessive individualism, and it also seems somewhat different from the economic individualism to which Appleby has directed our attention. Recovering the virtues of this liberalism is important if we wish to understand the peculiar vitality of American democratic theory. As Appleby argued persuasively in *Capitalism and a New Social Order*, Jeffersonians in the 1790s sought to effect two related revolutions, both premised on the idea of equality. The first was economic. It was to be accomplished by an expansion of commercial farming that would bring greater prosperity and equality of opportunity. The second was political. It was to be accomplished by dismantling the politics of defer-

---

[24] Madison's speech is in *The Papers of James Madison*, vol. XI: *7 March 1788–1 March 1789*, ed. Robert A. Rutland and Charles F. Hobson (Charlottesville, 1977), 163. See also James Madison, Alexander Hamilton, and John Jay, *The Federalist*, ed. Jacob E. Cooke (Middletown, 1961), 56–65, 384–90.

[25] Ralph Ketcham, *Presidents above Party: The First American Presidency, 1789–1829* (Chapel Hill, 1984). See also the insightful review by Gordon Wood, "Politics without Party," *New York Review of Books*, Oct. 11, 1984, pp. 18–21.

ence and encouraging the active political participation of all men. The surprising congruence between these two aims and the aims of McCoy's Madisonian republicans should be clear enough. As he wrote in *The Elusive Republic,*

> American republicans valued property in land primarily because it provided personal independence. The individual with direct access to the productive resources of nature need not rely on other men, or any man, for the basic means of existence. The Revolutionaries believed that every man had a natural right to this form of property, in the sense that he was entitled to autonomous control of the resources that were absolutely necessary for his subsistence. The personal independence that resulted from the ownership of land permitted a citizen to participate responsibly in the political process, for it allowed him to pursue spontaneously the common or public good, rather than the narrow interest of the men—or the government— on whom he depended for his support. Thus the Revolutionaries did not intend to provide men with property so that they might flee from public responsibility into a selfish privatism; property was rather the necessary basis for a committed republican citizenry.[26]

If McCoy is right, and I think he is, and if Appleby is right, and I think she is, then McCoy's republicans and Appleby's liberals were all struggling to achieve autonomy as economic individuals and the right to equal political participation as citizens. When this revised republicanism is viewed in its postrevolutionary American context, and when this restrained liberalism is appreciated in its ethical and political as well as economic depth, as a way of thinking rooted in the natural jurisprudential tradition inherited by Locke and the Scottish moral philosophers, then at least the potential coexistence of the two traditions becomes apparent.

Liberal Republicans, in Appleby's words, "endowed American capitalism with the moral force of their vision of a social order of free and independent men. The vision itself was grounded in the particular promise of prosperity held out to Americans at the end of the eighteenth century." Banning's charge that Appleby has exaggerated her portrait of republicanism by presenting it as backward-looking and antiegalitarian may be correct, but his own portrait of liberalism as a celebration of the "unrestrained pursuit of private interests" is also one-sided. His portrait depends, as Banning notes, on Macpherson's analysis of possessive individualism. That is certainly one face of liberal capitalism, the Hobbesian face that becomes more familiar as the nineteenth century progresses. But it is not the only face liberalism has worn. Appreciating the role earlier liberals played in a world breaking free from feudal hierarchies and mercantilist economic assumptions may help us understand why they considered themselves rebels with a moral cause.[27]

---

[26] McCoy, *Elusive Republic,* 68.

[27] Appleby, *Capitalism and a New Social Order,* 104. Even Pocock now concedes that he has underestimated the importance of the tradition of natural jurisprudence as a factor shaping—and perhaps ultimately combining with—classical republicanism. See Pocock, *"The Machiavellian Moment Revisited,"* 54. The impulse to identify *the* Jeffersonians, unfortunately, appears to be as irresistible to Banning as to Appleby: "The presence of such variety, however, does not exclude the possibility of identifying a core of belief that held Jeffersonians together, and I remain willing to argue both that the Republicans were bound together by the concepts explored in *The Jeffersonian Persuasion* and *The Elusive Republic* and that the thought of the great party leaders should be placed some-

Unfortunately for this vision of historical harmony, time did not stand still with the election of Jefferson to the presidency in 1800. Instead Dante's demon appeared, sword in hand. The continuing development of the contradictory religious, political, and economic tendencies apparent in the 1790s gradually destroyed the bonds that might have linked an optimistic and egalitarian republicanism to an ethically attuned and democratically alert liberalism. The latent inconsistencies between Locke's theory of rights and his theory of money, for example, and between Smith's moral philosophy and his political economy, became manifest when social and economic change upset their unsteady equilibrium. The masters and journeymen who had flocked to Jefferson's republicanism divided into capitalists and industrial workers, the Second Great Awakening challenged the notion of a self-regulating secular order driven by calculating but benevolent individuals, and Southern Jeffersonians gradually retreated into the stronghold of interest politics to defend their peculiar institution.

Franklin wrote that "only a virtuous people are capable of freedom." The American record in the early nineteenth century suggests that a free people may be incapable of virtue. During those years the meaning of virtue lost its earlier religious, civic, and ethical significance and became a label for bourgeois propriety or feminine purity. When independence lost its identification with benevolence, when self-interest was no longer conceived in relation to the egalitarian standard Jefferson upheld—in his theory if not in his practice—then freedom itself, especially the freedom to compete in the race for riches without the restraint of natural law, became an obstacle in the way of justice. That process is, of course, the story of the nineteenth century, and the growing dissatisfaction with the societies spawned by such freedom fueled the reform movements that appeared on both sides of the Atlantic. But it is important to appreciate the sequence of these developments in order to understand the cunning of freedom. Laissez-faire liberalism was not present at the creation of the American republic but emerged over the course of the nation's first hundred years.[28]

---

where toward the middle of the party's spectrum"; Banning, "Jeffersonian Ideology Revisited," 19n46, 12–13, 16, 33. The realization of diversity has rendered this sort of argument unhelpful and unnecessarily contentious, as several historians have pointed out. See, for example, Shalhope, "Republicanism and Early American Historiography," 350; John Zvesper, *Political Philosophy and Rhetoric: A Study of the Origins of American Party Politics* (Cambridge, Eng., 1977), 39–44, 87–131; and Richard Twomey, "Jacobins and Jeffersonians: Anglo-American Radical Ideology, 1790–1810," in *Origins of Anglo-American Radicalism*, ed. Jacob and Jacob, 291–97. See especially the conclusion drawn by John Ashworth: "As far as virtue and self-interest are concerned, then, neither party was wholly classical—and neither was unambiguously liberal. The labels cannot be made to stick." Ashworth, "The Jeffersonians," 430. This is not to say that all of these competing interpretations are equally correct; instead they seem to me almost equally incomplete. Perhaps historians of the early Republic should follow the lead of historians of the American Progressive period, who have abandoned the search for the quintessential Progressives and now examine the various elements that cooperated to form various progressive coalitions. See, for example, John Buenker's essay in John Buenker, John Burnham, and Robert Crunden, *Progressivism* (Cambridge, Mass., 1977), 31–69; and Daniel T. Rodgers, "In Search of Progressivism," *Reviews in American History*, 10 (Dec. 1982), 113–32.

[28] Albert H. Smyth, ed., *The Writings of Benjamin Franklin* (10 vols., New York, 1905–1907), IX, 80. See also Pole, *Political Representation*, 531–32; Rowland Berthoff, "Independence and Attachment, Virtue and Interest: From Republican Citizen to Free Enterprise, 1787–1837," in *Uprooted Americans: Essays to Honor Oscar Handlin*, ed. Richard L. Bushman et al. (Boston, 1979), 97–124. Berthoff's essay elaborates on a theme suggested by Rowland

The significance of ideas can change dramatically over time. The ideas of autonomy and popular sovereignty had explosive force in a world emerging from the assumptions and institutions of early modern European culture, but their meaning proved to be quite different when used to legitimate conditions in urban industrial America. We must avoid reading back into the struggles of the eighteenth century contending forces that did not appear until later.

My interpretation of the intermingling of religious, republican, and liberal themes in the political culture of America in the late eighteenth century, which emphasizes the distance between the ethical thrust of such ideas and the flattened discourse of nineteenth-century individualism and democracy, rests primarily on my reading of the meaning of the ideas of autonomy and popular sovereignty. Autonomy meant the combination of personal independence and moral responsibility that was central to the ideas of John Locke and Adam Smith, James Madison and Thomas Jefferson. It was autonomy that Samuel Harrison Smith, co-winner of the American Philosophical Society's prize for an essay on the sort of education appropriate to a republic, seems to have been seeking. The new nation, Smith wrote, required educational works "defining correctly political, moral, and religious duty." Only if American educators could instill such feelings of responsibility would "the radical ideas we have already established, and which are in great measure peculiar to us," be sufficient to secure "the virtue and happiness of the United States." In short, autonomy meant balancing the radical ideas of freedom and equality against the demands of duty.[29]

Popular sovereignty meant the commitment to representative government as a form uniquely attractive because of its open-endedness. Although few Americans seem to have echoed Jefferson's blithe endorsement of periodic revolutions to water liberty's tree, many did believe that the new nation should commit itself unwaveringly to the principle of change. The principle of popular sovereignty was consistent with that belief. In the words of James Wilson, "This revolution principle—that, the sovereign power residing in the people, they may change their constitution whenever they please—is . . . not a principle of discord, rancour, or war: it is a principle of melioration, contentment, and peace." That dimension of the doctrine of popular sovereignty in America comes into focus when the American conception of democracy as an endless series of provisional approximations of the public interest is contrasted with the ideas embodied in the French Revolution. In an essay pub-

Berthoff and John M. Murrin: "Other reforms of the post-Revolutionary half century also promised to make men more equal, on the model of the yeoman freeholder, but instead made them free to become unequal, and on a far grander scale than was possible through land speculation." Rowland Berthoff and John M. Murrin, "Feudalism, Communalism, and the Yeoman Freeholder: The American Revolution Considered as a Social Accident," in *Essays on the American Revolution*, ed. Kurtz and Hutson, 284.

[29] See Samuel Harrison Smith, "Remarks on Education: Illustrating the Close Connection between Virtue and Wisdom," in *Essays on Education in the Early Republic*, ed. Frederick Rudolph (Cambridge, Mass., 1965), esp. 216. See also David M. Post, "Jeffersonian Revisions of Locke: Education, Property Rights, and Liberty," *Journal of the History of Ideas*, 47 (Jan.–March 1986), 147–57. As Appleby writes, "The attribution of autonomy to the individual members of society also suggested a moral and material self-sufficiency, and this self-sufficiency conveyed new meaning to the idea of self-interest"; Appleby, "The Radical *Double-Entendre* in the Right to Self-Government," 276.

lished in 1971, Appleby recounted the strange career of unicameralism in France and America. She pointed out that the fear of perpetuating a hierarchical system prevented French revolutionaries from accepting the division of authority symbolized by a bicameral legislature. Americans were persuaded to accept that division, Wood has shown, not for the reasons advanced by John Adams—reasons reflecting long-standing assumptions about necessarily different social orders—but instead because both houses of the legislature, like the various levels of authority preserved in the federal structure, were grounded on the bedrock of popular sovereignty. The fragmentation of authority institutionalized by the United States Constitution reflected the reality and the ideals of a wildly diverse, pluralistic society.[30]

In France, by contrast, the violent twists and turns of the Revolution can best be understood as a search for unitary authority. The Terror was not a reflection of the ideas of Rousseau. Roger Masters has argued persuasively that the *Social Contract* should be read as a warrant for popular government in which the general will is nothing more ominous than the assertion of the people's sovereign authority embodied in a constitution expressing their fundamental purposes. Robespierre translated Rousseau's call for virtue into terror not because the *Social Contract* pointed in a direction different from Adams's *Thoughts on Government* or Jefferson's Declaration of Independence, but because in France the splintering of opinions that was a fact of life in America simply proved too great a threat to the Revolution. As François Furet has suggested, the legacy of the ancien régime imposed on the Revolution an unavoidable burden. The Republic had to establish a unitary and authoritative "opinion" in place of the chaos of "opinions" that bubbled up from the contradictory pressures of popular protest. Although many of Rousseau's later interpreters have doubted that he thought the conflict between private virtue and public virtue could be ended through politics, Robespierre was confident that the French republic could accomplish precisely that. "Man is good, as he comes from the hands of nature," Robespierre proclaimed; "if he is corrupt, the responsibility lies with vicious social institutions." If constructing new institutions that would not merely make possible, but require, both private and public virtue was indeed the goal of the Revolution, then the Terror represents not an aberration but a logical extension of the desire to reconstitute absolute authority on the basis of the public will.[31]

[30] James Wilson quoted in Wood, *Creation*, 614. For a complementary discussion of Wilson and the idea of popular sovereignty, see Pole, "Enlightenment and the Politics of American Nature," 209–11. On bicameralism and popular sovereignty, see Appleby, "America as a Model for the Radical French Reformers of 1789," *William and Mary Quarterly*, 28 (April 1971), 267–86; Appleby, *Capitalism and a New Social Order*, 61–67; Wood, *Creation*, 576–615; Robert R. Palmer, *The Age of the Democratic Revolution* (2 vols., Princeton, 1959–1964), I, 282. Commentators from Tom Paine to Robert R. Palmer have noted the striking similarities between the Virginia Declaration of Rights, Jefferson's Declaration of Independence, and the French Declaration of the Rights of Man and Citizen. See Paine, *Rights of Man*, ed. Foner, 110–15; and Palmer, *Democratic Revolution*, I, 518–21.

[31] My reading of Rousseau has been influenced primarily by the writings of Roger Masters. See Roger Masters, *The Political Philosophy of Rousseau* (Princeton, 1968); Roger Masters, "Introduction," in Jean Jacques Rousseau, *The First and Second Discourses* (New York, 1964); and Roger Masters, "Introduction," in Jean Jacques Rousseau, *On the Social Contract* (New York, 1978). For a detailed examination of Rousseau's debts to the tradition of natural law, see Robert Derathé, *Jean-Jacques Rousseau et la science politique de son temps* (Paris, 1979). For a contrasting view, see Judith Shklar, *Men and Citizens: A Study of Rousseau's Social Theory* (Cambridge, Eng., 1969). Recent

The genius of Rousseau and Madison lay in their realization that the public spirit they sought was in tension with—Rousseau may even have considered it antithetical to—the personal independence of democratic man. Rousseau, in the *Social Contract*, and Madison, in his writings and speeches on the Constitution, were looking for different ways to ease that tension.[32] Both republics failed to find the solution these theorists sought. In France, as Robespierre's life and death showed, that tension was resolved in ways that threatened the survival of democratic individuals and elevated the power of public authority. In America, as Alexis de Tocqueville understood, that tension was resolved in ways that elevated the power of democratic individuals and threatened the survival of public authority.

In conclusion, American revolutionaries committed themselves to a pair of principles that held out a formidable challenge to the new nation. Gordon Wood is surely right that American political debate narrowed in the nineteenth century, and Joyce Appleby is also right that the Jeffersonian moment of an equal commitment to material and moral progress was short lived. But the principles of autonomy and popular sovereignty had been enshrined, and they exerted a powerful hold on the American imagination. When the challenge of socialism emerged in the nineteenth century, it was not so much co-opted by a liberal consensus as it was preempted by the nation's own prior commitment to liberty and equality. While debate may have narrowed, the breadth and depth of the ideas of autonomy and popular sovereignty enabled American radicals for the next two centuries to expand it again by appealing to the stated ideals of the Republic.[33].

studies concentrating on the tension between the tradition of absolute authority and the assertion of individual rights include Nannerl O. Keohane, *Philosophy and the State in France: The Renaissance to the Enlightenment* (Princeton, 1980); and Stephen Holmes, *Benjamin Constant and the Making of Modern Liberalism* (New Haven, 1984). See also François Furet, *Interpreting the French Revolution*, trans. Elborg Forster (Cambridge, Eng., 1981), 28–79. Cf. the discussions of Furet in Keith Michael Baker, "Enlightenment and Revolution in France: Old Problems, Renewed Approaches," *Journal of Modern History*, 53 (June 1981), 281–303; and Lynn Hunt, *Politics, Culture, and Class in the French Revolution* (Berkeley, 1984). The passage from Gustave Laurent, ed., *Oeuvres complètes de Robespierre*, vol. V (Paris, 1961), 207, is discussed in Norman Hamson, "The Enlightenment in France," in *The Enlightenment in National Context*, ed. Porter and Teich, 49. For a provocative consideration of Rousseau's relation to the other *philosophes* and to the Revolution, which emphasizes the revolutionaries' need to legitimate a *droit public* for the Republic, see Keith Michael Baker, "On the Problem of the Ideological Origins of the French Revolution," in *Modern European Intellectual History*, ed. LaCapra and Kaplan, 197–219.

[32] In the larger study of democracy in America and Europe since 1680 that I am preparing, I will emphasize the extent to which certain ideas in American political thought parallel Rousseau's—and perhaps even more controversially, Kant's—and distinguish between those ideas and the utilitarianism developed by British radicals in the late eighteenth and early nineteenth centuries. For a discussion of the contrast between the ideas of natural law and utilitarianism, see the comparison of Jonathan Edwards's Augustinianism and Benjamin Franklin's utilitarianism in Norman Fiering, "Benjamin Franklin and the Way to Virtue," *American Quarterly*, 30 (Summer 1978), 199–223; and Fiering, *Jonathan Edwards's Moral Thought*, 346–61. On the rise of an ethically flattened political economy in Britain, see Isaac Kramnick, "Republican Revisionism Revisited," *American Historical Review*, 87 (June 1982), 629–64. On the ideological and moral conflicts such as an amoral political economy provoked in Britain, see Himmelfarb, *Idea of Poverty*, 101. The conflict was different in Britain and America, but it is important to remember that the idea of laissez-faire encountered resistance in both political cultures.

[33] Appleby, *Capitalism and a New Social Order*, ix–x; Wood, *Creation*, 562–64. See also Martin Diamond, "Ethics and Politics: The American Way," in *The Moral Foundations of the American Republic*, ed. Robert H. Horwitz (Charlottesville, 1979), esp. 68–72; Marvin Meyers, "Liberty, Equality, and Constitutional Self-Government," in *Liberty and Equality under the Constitution*, ed. John Agresto (Washington, 1983); and Marvin Meyers, *Revolutionary Thoughts in the Founding* (Claremont, Calif., 1984). The persistence of the religious, republican, and liberal vocabularies of virtue in nineteenth-century America can be seen by comparing the following: Herbert G.

Taken together, and understood in all of their ethical and political dimensions, the ideas of autonomy and popular sovereignty were the virtues of liberal republicanism. It is one of the most familiar maxims of La Rochefoucauld that "our virtues are frequently but vices in disguise." In American politics, our vices have instead been virtues in disguise, because it was only by securing liberty and democracy in the eighteenth century that Americans became capable of developing the irresponsible individualism and the erosive factionalism of the nineteenth and twentieth centuries. Emphasizing the original meaning of these ideas may help explain the perennial appeal of Jefferson and Madison for Americans puzzled by the disjunction between the world we experience, a world of dependency and inequality, and the promise of autonomy and popular sovereignty. In sum, recovering these ideas may help us understand, even if it cannot help us recapture, the brief moment of alliance between the virtues of republicanism and the virtues of liberalism.

Gutman, "Protestantism and American Labor," *Work, Culture, and Society in Industrializing America* (New York, 1977), 79–117; Marvin Meyers, *The Jacksonian Persuasion: Politics and Belief* (Stanford, 1960); Daniel Walker Howe, *The Political Culture of the American Whigs* (Chicago, 1979); Dorothy Ross, "The Liberal Tradition Revisited and the Republican Tradition Addressed," in *New Directions in American Intellectual History*, ed. John Higham and Paul K. Conkin (Baltimore, 1979), 116–31; and Sean Wilentz, "On Class and Politics in Jacksonian America," *Reviews in American History*, 10 (Dec. 1982), 45–63. For a thoughtful overview, see Dorothy Ross, "Liberalism," in *The Encyclopedia of American Political History*, ed. Jack P. Greene (3 vols., New York, 1984), II, 750–63. On the transformation of these ideas in the late nineteenth and early twentieth centuries, see James T. Kloppenberg, *Uncertain Victory: Social Democracy and Progressivism in European and American Thought, 1870–1920* (New York, 1986).

J. G. A. Pocock

Virtue and Commerce in the Eighteenth Century

The Creation of the American Republic, 1776–1787. By Gordon S. Wood (Chapel Hill, University of North Carolina Press, 1969) 653 pp. $15.00

Alexander Hamilton and the Idea of Republican Government. By Gerald Stourzh (Stanford, Stanford University Press, 1970) 278 pp. $8.50

These two books form the latest statements in a process of re-evaluating the character and role of ideology in the American Revolution. Rossiter's *Seedtime of the Republic* may be said to have initiated it by his attack on the belief that eighteenth-century political thought consisted of *Locke et praeterea nihil.* Robbins" *The Eighteenth-Century Commonwealthman* revolutionized accepted concepts of oppositional theory relevant between 1688 and 1776. But the central occurrence in this process remains the series of works published by Bailyn, in particular *The Ideological Origins of the American Revolution.*[1] We are now living with the consequences of a major upheaval in historiography and attempting to assess a changed landscape.

It is now apparent that the Revolution employed—and in some measure was occasioned by—an oppositional ideology that had been nurtured in British politics for nearly a century.[2] Late in the reign of Charles II the idea developed that the main threat to parliamentary liberty lay in the crown's effective employment of an enlarged patronage power. During the reigns of William III and Anne, England–Great Britain had emerged as a major European and Atlantic war-making power, fortified by an expanding professional army and a system of

---

J. G. A. Pocock is Professor of History and Political Science at Washington University, St. Louis. He is the author of *The Ancient Constitution and the Feudal Law* (New York, 1967) and *Politics, Language and Time* (New York, 1971). He is working on a study of Florentine, English, and American republican thought (1494–1789) and preparing an edition of the works of James Harrington (1611–76).

1 Clinton Rossiter, *Seedtime of the Republic: The Origin of the American Tradition of Political Liberty* (New York, 1953); Caroline Robbins, *The Eighteenth-Century Commonwealthman: Studies in the Transmission, Development and Circumstances of English Liberal Thought from the Restoration of Charles II until the War with the Thirteen Colonies* (Cambridge, Mass., 1959); Bernard Bailyn, *Political Pamphlets of the American Revolution* (Cambridge, Mass., 1965), I; idem., *The Ideological Origins of the American Revolution* (Cambridge, Mass., 1967); idem., *The Origins of American Politics* (New York, 1968).

2 See J. G. A. Pocock, *Politics, Language and Time* (New York, 1971), Chs. 3 and 4.

public credit and national debt. Both of these phenomena were seen by their adversaries as not only increasing the crown's patronage powers, but also multiplying the incidence in society of individuals whose modes of social and political existence entailed a dependence upon government that made them a menace to their neighbors.

Consequently, an ideology opposing all of these things arose, variously known to historians as "Old Whig," "Commonwealth," or (the term to be used here) "Country." It stressed the independence of the organs of mixed government (King, Lords, and Commons; executive, judiciary, and legislature) from one another, as against the supposed attempts of patronage manipulators to bring the second and third branches into dependence on the first; and it stressed the role of the independent proprietor (ideally the landowner, although merchants were not excluded) as against the rentier, officer, placeman, pensioner, and (lowest of all in the scale of humanity) stock-jobber or speculator in public funds.

In this interweaving of the themes of mixed government and personal independence, the Country ideology—as a study of its vocabulary and its transmission clearly shows—belonged to a tradition of classical republicanism and civic humanism,[3] anchored in the Florentine Renaissance, Anglicized by James Harrington, Algernon Sidney, and Henry St. John, Viscount Bolingbroke, but looking unmistakably back to antiquity and to Aristotle, Polybius, and Cicero. Its wide dissemination and acceptance account for much of the classicism of the eighteenth century, whose character is civic and patriotic rather than leisured or Arcadian.

An effect of the recent research has been to display the American Revolution less as the first political act of revolutionary enlightenment than as the last great act of the Renaissance.[4] In a variety of ways, we are now to see the Founding Fathers as the culminating generation of civic humanists and classical republicans; but it is the intention of Wood and Stourzh to display their thought both in the hour of victory and,

3 The former term is especially associated with Zera S. Fink, *The Classical Republicans: An Essay in the Recovery of a Pattern of Thought in Seventeenth-Century England* (Evanston, 1945), the latter with Hans Baron, *The Crisis of the Early Italian Renaissance* (Princeton, 1966; rev. ed.).

4 Howard Mumford Jones, *O Strange New World* (New York, 1964); H. Trevor Colbourn, *The Lamp of Experience: Whig History and the Intellectual Origins of the American Revolution* (Chapel Hill, 1965); Richard M. Gummere, *The American Colonial Mind and the Classical Tradition: Essays in Comparative Culture* (Cambridge, Mass., 1963).

simultaneously, in the agony of crisis and transformation—a theme anticipated by Bailyn and now being further exploited.[5]

Among the classicist characteristics which the Country ideology carried into the eighteenth century was a Renaissance pessimism concerning the direction and reversibility of social and historical change. The health of the balanced constitution lay in the independence of its parts; should a change or disturbance bring one of these into dependence upon another, a degenerative trend would commence which would soon become almost impossible to remedy. Similarly—or indistinguishably—the moral health of the civic individual consisted in his independence from governmental or social superiors, the precondition of his ability to concern himself with the public good, res publica, or commonweal. Should he lose the economic foundations of this ability (i.e., independent property), or be demoralized by an exclusive concern with private or group satisfactions, a comparable imbalance or disturbance in the civic and social foundations of moral personality would set in which would also prove irreversible. The name most tellingly used for balance, health, and civic personality was "virtue"; the name of its loss was "corruption." Since the former was essentially a static ideal, any change was likely to threaten corruption, and degeneration was likely to prove uncheckable. Men could not be born in new natures; the concept was at once post-Christian and pre-historicist.

The classical view of politics was consequently a closed ideology. Bailyn—now followed by Wood—argued that its grip on the colonial mind was so absolute that the Americans of the 1760s and 1770s were compelled, first, to identify as "corruption" what seemed to be threats to their polities and, second, to conclude that the degeneration not merely of their liberties but also of their moral personalities would soon pass beyond redemption unless they reaffirmed the first uncorrupt principles of civic virtue. Their revolution was thus primarily a rivoluzione, ricorso, or ridurre ai principi—the terminology is appropriately Machiavellian—rather than a transformation; only in its consequences did it become the latter.[6]

But this argument has resurrected the old problem of ideological causation. Bailyn argued that the omnipresence of Old Whig or Country ideology—the conditioning and imprisoning effects of its conceptual

5 Bailyn, "The Transforming Radicalism of the American Revolution"—the title used in the introduction to Political Pamphlets of the American Revolution.
6 There are many stimulating remarks on this theme in Hannah Arendt, On Revolution (London, 1963).

system—offered a self-sustaining explanation of why Americans resorted to revolutionary action. Their vocabulary, conceptual framework, and entire mental set offered them no alternative.

Bailyn flung a most refreshing challenge at that historians' orthodoxy which insists that ideologies and concepts are purely epiphenomenal to other social phenomena—that they are always effect and never cause. But, looked at more narrowly, the argument of the Bailyn school appears far less causal than structural. A reevaluation of the historiography of political thought has been going on for a long time, and it seems less useful to consider conceptual systems as theories (which here includes "ideologies") and to mediate them back to "practice" than to treat them as elaborations, explorations, and unpackings of the conceptual languages used within society.[7] If language is not epiphenomenal but part of the structure of both personality and world, it is legitimate once more to study the languages men have used and to ask how far they could have done other, or been other, than their languages indicate. The Country ideology did not cause the Revolution; it characterized it. Men cannot do what they have no means of saying they have done; and what they do must in part be what they can say and conceive that it is.

But a sophisticated, institutionalized, and highly factional "language," such as the Country ideology, is unlikely to be the only language in use within a given society, and here we are on the way back to treating "language" as a dependent variable. It is not enough to show that the ideology was in itself a closed system; we also need to know whether and why no other ideology was available. More work might be done, for example, with the thesis that eighteenth-century England, Massachusetts, Pennsylvania, and Virginia were subcultures within a single Anglophone world whose disruption is a main theme of Revolutionary history.[8]

The Americans were using, or were enclosed by, an ideology that had originated in England and was still very much in use there. In the minds of James Burgh, John Cartwright, or Richard Price, it was as obsessive and terrifying as in any American mind. It formed the conceptual framework of all early- and middle-Georgian demands for parliamentary and franchise reform. Butterfield, describing it as part

7 For this, see "Language and their Implications: The Transformation of the Study of Political Thought," in Pocock, *Politics, Language and Time*, 3–41.
8 But see J. R. Pole, *Political Representation in England and the Origins of the American Republic* (New York, 1966).

of his study of the Yorkshire associations of 1780, was right at least to ask why a movement having such an ideology did not take on revolutionary characteristics.[9] Part of the answer, it seems, may be found in reflecting that in England the word "Country" possessed an opposite, namely "Court," and that "Court" and "Country" were highly interdependent terms.

In both England and America there existed an ideology which presented governmental "corruption" as a nearly total threat to society and personality. It was sparked into life in America by the first apparent encroachments.[10] In England, the threat was mitigated by long familiarity with the Court and means of countering its machinations, and the Court had its own ideology for which men had long been arguing in intimate dialogue with their adversaries.[11] The Country ideology ran riot in America, but in England its referents were better known and a more complex intellectual scheme existed for dealing with them. The scene grows more involved, however, when we discover the presence of alternative ideologies, already established in the eighteenth-century tradition, as part of the process of the post-Revolutionary transformation which both Wood and Stourzh study.

Wood restates Bailyn's thesis of "the transforming radicalism of the American Revolution" in a way that may be summarized as follows: The Revolution originated as a response to executive and parliamentary encroachment; Americans found at hand, and their thinking was dominated by, an ideology which developed the concept of "corruption" as both the cause and the effect of such encroachment, to the point where it could be asserted that the people's representatives, whether in the colonial assemblies or at Westminster, were themselves corrupt. At this point, the only way for the people to avoid becoming corrupt themselves was to assert their "virtue" in autonomous, popular, civic action, which at this stage of the ideology's articulation should ideally take the form of a reaffirmation of the basic "principles" of

9 Herbert Butterfield, *George III, Lord North and the People, 1779–80* (London, 1949).
10 Burke may have had this in mind when he remarked during the Second Speech on Conciliation: " . . . they snuff the approach of tyranny in every tainted breeze" (Wood, 5).
11 The best study of this is Isaac F. Kramnick, *Bolingbroke and His Circle: The Politics of Nostalgia in the Age of Walpole* (Cambridge, Mass., 1968). Since this article was written, a valuable and suggestive comment has appeared on the interdependence of Court and Country attitudes in England as opposed to the colonies: Paul Lucas, "A Note on the Comparative Study of the Structure of Politics in Mid-Eighteenth-Century Britain and its American Colonies," *William and Mary Quarterly*, XXVIII (1971), 301–309.

constitutional and social life, in which virtue itself was defined. The idea of appeal from a corrupt representative to a virtuous "country" or "people" can be found in English oppositional ideology at intervals during the preceding century;[12] but in America the thing actually took a variety of revolutionary forms during the middle 1770s, whereas in England it was talked about by a few, repressed by the authorities, and seriously attempted by no one.

The idea of power reverting to the people can, of course, be stated in the language of Locke's *Second Treatise*, but it is overwhelmingly important to realize that the predominant language in which it was expressed by eighteenth-century radicals was one of virtue, corruption, and reform, which is Machiavellian, classical, and Aristotelian, and in which Locke himself did not figure. But—to resume the summarization of Wood—the "people" conceived as so acting were defined, in John Adams' terms, as a "trinity in unity" (577), divisible into a one, few, and many, constituted as modes of action called monarchy, aristocracy, and democracy, and, in a special sense, distinguishable into a "natural aristocracy" or elite capable of political initiative, and a "many" or "democracy" capable of judgment but not of initiative, who might be said (but the word should be used with caution) to have "deferred" to the former category. And in a doctrine of "balanced government" as old as Polybius, the balance was defined as a relationship between "virtues" no less than between classes or powers, so that "virtue" consisted not merely in the exercise of one's own virtue—the mode of intelligence and action proper to membership in the one, the few, or the many—but also in respect for the virtues of the two categories to which one did not belong, and in maintenance of the constitutional structure in which the balance of virtues was institutionalized. "Deference," therefore, was part of the "virtue" of the many, often inaccurately termed the "people"; but it was far from being the whole of it.

It is Wood's thesis (and has been that of others) that this aristodemocratic differentiation of the people broke down under the stresses of revolution, and with it the whole classical conception of politics. Not merely was the American patriciate insufficiently entrenched to maintain its social ascendancy; it was discovered that a "constituent people" (to borrow the phrase of Robert R. Palmer), under the conditions which Locke had defined as "dissolution of government," simply

12 Such as the demand for frequently-elected parliaments as a remedy against corruption—from 1675; or the far more dangerous idea of a convention or anti-parliament—hardly before George III's reign.

did not differentiate itself along trinitarian lines. The one, few, and many, as Aristotle himself had emphasized, might be distinguished by the application of many criteria besides that of number, such as birth, wealth, education, leisure, talent, and intelligence; these might be employed in many combinations, and the results might vary from relatively aristocratic to relatively democratic. But the self-constituent Americans discovered, in a series of constitutional experiments described by Wood (those in Massachusetts and Pennsylvania being the most interesting), that no attempt to restructure the people along any of the lines of distinction derived from Aristotle produced viable results, while the bold Pennsylvania experiment of assembling a unicameral legislature and leaving an aristocracy of talent to assert itself proved no more satisfactory.

It might be that the undifferentiated people were not the "mob" or "great beast" of classical fears; but what were they? Here the conceptual framework of antique and Renaissance ideology, within whose confines the Americans had begun their revolution, imposed a frightening dilemma. If the people could not be differentiated into separately-characterized groups, there could be no ascribing to them that higher virtue of respecting (or, if you like, deferring to) the virtues of others who in their turn defer, which is at the root of both the Polybian concept of mixed government and the Aristotelian concept of citizenship. The entire classical tradition of man the political animal seemed at the point of breaking down. An undifferentiated people could not be a virtuous people—and so, not a political people.

The masters of Federalist theory proposed an escape from this dilemma, which involved ceasing to regard the "people" as trinitarian and regarding them instead as an undifferentiated unity which elected to be represented in many ways, by a complex of assemblies, legislative, judicial, and executive bodies, entrusted by them with a diversity of powers. To a doctrine which defined the people as sovereign rather than as simply constituent, they added the one transforming originality of their contribution to political thought. This is the proposition that each mode of exercising political power constituted a separate "representation" of the people, who chose to be represented in a diversity of ways, and to entrust diverse organs with a diversity of powers, and that the classical "checks and balances" continued to exist between these powers when the classical mode of conceiving "the people" had passed away. The hard core of Wood's book lies in those chapters that trace the emergence and deployment of this new vocabulary, and that indicate the ways in which it seemed better adapted than its predecessor to deal with the political experience of the 1780s. It is, however, with the long-term consequences of the values articulated and implied in Federalist theory that this essay is concerned; and here emphasis must fall on certain ambiguities which Wood detects in the Federalist attitude to the concept of virtue, which is basic to the whole ideology and to the whole argument.

In the first place, he contends, it was a Federalist purpose to restore a patrician "natural aristocracy" to their proper role in politics, and in so doing to restore threatened elements of the classical concept of virtue. This was in the sense of restoring the leadership of a leisured elite that was supposed to look further and attend more effectively to the public good than were lesser men, and in the sense of restoring that dualism of political capacity between whose poles—symbolized as "few" and "many"—there could be that mutual respect and mutual deference in which "virtue" so largely consisted. But at a deeper level this purpose must be frustrated, for in supposing a people which was merely represented by the differing political capacities instead of being embodied in them—one is almost driven to the language of Christology—they had denied that it could be differentiated into parts and a whole, and so that the individuals and groups composing it could exercise or display virtue in the classical sense at all. It was, he shows, an output of Federalist politics that theorists appeared who denied that the health of the republic depended on the virtue of its members (610–612).[13] Interest groups and interested individuals, who need not be thought of as looking beyond the realization of their separate (or "selfish") interests, could be induced to relate themselves to a government composed of checked-and-balanced powers in such a way that private interests were satisfied and public authority maintained. Since the interested party need no longer be so constituted as to possess a built-in regard for the good of others ("virtue"), it was now possible to replace a classical and organic with a romantic and kinetic theory of politics; the interest groups could change rapidly as the society grew, yet the structure of government could persist unchanged (612–614).

Wood's interpretation thus falls into line with—although it is not its main intention to assert—the view that the Revolution and the

---

13 See also Melvin Richter, "The Uses of Theory: Tocqueville's Adaptation of Montesquieu," in *idem.* (ed.), *Essays in Theory and History: An Approach to the Social Sciences* (Cambridge, Mass., 1970), 74–102.

Constitution marked the establishment of American politics on the basis of an interest-group theory of politics, a theory and practice of pluralism and consensus which has characterized the national life ever since. Such a conception of politics is under strong attack from the intellectual dissenters of the present moment, and—as often happens—the vigor of their critique tends to reinforce the view, originally put forward by those more favorably disposed to a pluralist ideology, that it has dominated the national history since the latter's beginnings. It is still the conventional wisdom to term American pluralist ideology "the Lockean-liberal consensus." Wood, more cautiously, speaks of "that encompassing liberal tradition which has mitigated and often obscured the real social antagonisms of American politics" (562), and either phrase is liable to recall the doctrine, put forward by Hartz, that American thinking was, for good historical reasons, dominated from its outset by Lockean ideas to the point where no other theory of politics ever became viable.[14] But the time has perhaps arrived for a reevaluation of this orthodoxy. Locke is a visible but hardly a dominating figure in Wood's enormously detailed survey of Revolutionary, Federalist, and Anti-Federalist thinking. Dunn has boldly argued that it is a myth that Locke was an especially authoritative political thinker—as philosopher it is another matter—in eighteenth-century America or England.[15]

The time for a reassessment of Locke's reputation and authority in the age between the Revolutions may be at hand, for at any rate it is clear that the image of a monolithically Lockean eighteenth century has gone forever. The rejection of virtue as (in Montesquieu's phrase) the principle of republics emerged slowly and painfully from an intellectual scene dominated to the point of obsessiveness by concepts of virtue, patriotism, and corruption, in whose making and transmission Locke played little part. Aristotle, Polybius, Machiavelli, Harrington, Sidney, John Trenchard, Thomas Gordon, Bolingbroke, and Burgh were its lineage; and the extent to which our thought is dominated by a fiction of Locke is shown by our uncertainty whether the later figures in this tradition were Lockeans under the skin or that they found in Locke their chief dialectical adversary. Was even the emergent interest-group theory of the Federalists significantly Lockean? We need to

14 Louis B. Hartz, *The Liberal Tradition in America* (New York, 1955).
15 John Dunn, "The Politics of Locke in England and America in the Eighteenth Century," in John W. Yolton (ed.), *John Locke: Problems and Perspectives* (Cambridge, 1969), 45–80.

know; and one line of investigation is to return to the circumstance, mentioned earlier, that in England the Country ideology had long had its adversaries, and that alternatives to virtue were known.

It is here that Stourzh's study of Alexander Hamilton is of value. What we call the Country ideology was a reaction—performed by men in opposition, though its strength was that it seemed to express and explain so many things that it dug itself into the fabric of social thinking at large—against the growth of banks and paper credit, professional armies and bureaucrats, and patronage and political machines. In opposition to these developing phenomena it stated the images of a return to an older, purer time, of society as founded on principles from which any departure must be decay, and of the individual whose virtue was rooted in an independence of governmental and social processes so complete that no form of property less autonomous than an inheritable freehold could truly guarantee it. The reply of the Court writers— which was at a peak about 1730, in the controversy between Bolingbroke and Sir Robert Walpole—denied both the historical and the social foundations of Country thought.[16] It asserted that commerce and professionalization had come to stay; that the older agrarian world of Country nostalgia had gone forever, and had, in any case, rested on feudal ties of dependence between man and man which were now being replaced by the new dependences created by patronage and credit. It denied that society was or ever had been founded upon a set of original principles—if such existed, they had been found out no earlier than 1689—and presented instead an image of the historical existence of individuals and societies which consisted of incessant pragmatic adjustments to changing emergencies and social conditions. This adjustment had to be carried out under the protection supplied by a government exercising sovereign authority, and it was the ideologues of the Court and the ruling Whigs who built up the doctrine of a sovereign and illimitable parliament for whose sake Englishmen went to war with Americans in the 1770s. The pluralist consensus, now subject to criticism under the none-too-appropriate name of "liberalism," was, in its origins as a doctrine, English rather than American, Court rather than Country.

There is not, at present, sufficient evidence that it was significantly Lockean. Locke was simply not a central figure in the Court-Country

16 Kramnick, *Bolingbroke and His Circle*, Ch. 5; Pocock, *Politics, Language and Time*, 141–144.

debates, though an ingenious analyst would no doubt have little difficulty in interpreting him so that he would rank on the Court side. It was the far more copious and diverse genius of David Hume that emerged from this controversy with an interpretation of English history as the interplay between agrarian and mercantile, Country and Court elements, although the connection between Hume's history and his political philosophy is still a matter of controversy.[17] The fact is that the key problems of Anglo–Scottish–American political thought in the eighteenth century were of a nascent historicism, of a perception of general historical change taking place in the contemporary world. Locke's thought is notoriously not organized around historical concepts at all. For the first time, eighteenth-century men were setting their conceptions of politics in a context of historical change, the transition from the agrarian world of the Middle Ages to the mercantile and specialized world of their own generations. The Country resisted this change and the Court welcomed it; the growth of public credit and professional armies, and the novelty of a conception of politics that went with these things, were the commonly-acknowledged facts around which they mustered their divergent value-judgments and philosophies of history; and the key concepts in organizing these latter were "virtue" and "commerce." "Virtue," the slogan of the Country, required an individual so independent of other men and their social structures that his dedication to the *res publica* could be wholly autonomous. It must be autonomous if he were not to be another man's creature, and so a source of illegitimate private, instead of public, power; therefore he must be master of his own family, property, and arms. "Commerce," the slogan of the Court, denoted a world in which "virtue" had become historically obsolete, since the growth of wealth had bred professional armies, the structures that maintained them, and the necessity of a politics that managed men no longer rendered independent by the private possession of arms. It is important to notice, first, that "commerce" stemmed from a perception of the rentier and salariate, rather than of the merchant and entrepreneur, as new historical phenomena; second, that "virtue" might be thought of as inhabiting a hierarchized world of separately-ordered capacities, but equally as inhabiting a fiercely egalitarian and amateur world of independent warrior-farmers. Some located it in the Great Chain of Being; others in the Highland clans.[18]

17 Giuseppe Giarrizzo, *Hume politico e storico* (Turin, 1962). See also the review by Duncan Forbes, *Historical Journal*, VI (1963), 280–294.
18 For hierarchical elements in Bolingbroke's thinking, see Adam Ferguson (ed.

Finally, the extent to which Court and Country used a shared language and premises is discoverable in the Court's willingness to admit that "commerce" was the antithesis of "virtue." In a commercialized and professionalized world, they conceded, men were not virtuous, and means must be found of governing them in the full knowledge that they were not. Historical pragmatism and egoistic philosophies of human nature enter and become ascendant in eighteenth-century political theory, largely in consequence of the Court's willingness to accept the Country's definition of virtue and of history as the movement away from it.[19]

It emerges from Stourzh's admirable study that Hamilton was a thinker in the direct Court tradition—although we do not seem to know whether he and his contemporaries were conscious or unconscious of his predecessors. He held that interest was a mainspring of government, that the establishment of a national government necessitated the establishment of a class of persons, in legislatures and out of them, directly interested in supporting it, and that patronage and the development of a system of governmental credit were appropriate ways of doing so. The issue was precisely that which had been debated at the time of the Bank of England's foundation in the 1690s and under the fully-fledged Walpolean system in the 1720s. Hamilton held that as societies became increasingly commercialized, specialization impelled them to maintain large professional armies by which their mercantile interests were protected and extended, so that commercial societies found themselves in military competition for wealth and looked upon themselves as empires rather than as republics. This is the same issue as that explored by John Toland and Charles Davenant, Jonathan Swift and Daniel Defoe, and again during the zenith of empire in the mid-eighteenth century. Hamilton held all of the views which Marlborough or Charles Montagu, John Somers or Robert Walpole had been attacked for holding—with the single major difference that he held them in a context of continental revolution and the creation of a new state[20]— and he was attacked in precisely the same language and on precisely

---

Duncan Forbes), *Essay on the History of Civil Society* (Edinburgh, 1966), and Forbes' introduction.

19 Montesquieu—much affected by the English debate—was a crucial figure here. For the exploitation by Hamilton of his concessions to commerce, see Stourzh, 140–146, 154–161.

20 If this is indeed so different from the situation of Anne's reign, when England became Great Britain and a great power in transforming the European states-system.

the same ground as they had been attacked. To a quite remarkable degree, the great debate on his policies in the 1790s was a replay of Court-Country debates seventy and a hundred years earlier.[21]

But it is further apparent that he accepted a dichotomy of value and history, and agreed that "commerce" involved a departure from values which "virtue" quite truly defined. Stourzh quotes him as saying in 1788: "As riches increase and accumulate in few hands; as luxury prevails in society; virtue will be in a greater degree considered as only a graceful appendage of wealth, and the tendency of things will be to depart from the republican standard. This is the real disposition of human nature. . . . It is a common misfortune, that awaits our state constitution as well as all others" (71). The passage from virtue to interest was not, in Hamilton's mind, a serene withdrawal into liberal complacency. He was opting for empire, not for free trade, and acknowledging that "the real disposition of human nature" was to outdistance its deepest values through economic growth and historical change. A vision of power and glory, not of adjustive pragmatism, lay at his furthest horizon, and the dynamic and demonic elements which contemporaries sensed in his personality are explicable in terms of perceived historical tensions. The ambivalence of his feelings about Caesar fall into this pattern of interpretation. Since Machiavelli, Caesar had figured as the agent who destroyed a republic, and substituted a principate, in consequence of the former's having acquired an empire; and Jefferson accused Hamilton of thinking Caesar the greatest of men. But what he wrote was: "It has been aptly observed that Cato was the Tory, Caesar the Whig, of his day. The former frequently resisted, the latter always flattered, the follies of the people. Yet the former perished with the republic, the latter destroyed it" (Stourzh, 99). The language is that of English party controversy, at any date since the advent of Old Whig ideologues, and replete with its ambivalences. If Hamilton ever saw himself as Caesar, he was accepting a role in a Machiavellian tragedy which he could see as the triumph of history over virtue (*sed victa Catoni*); and when he wished to denounce Aaron Burr, he called him an "embryo-Caesar" and a Catiline. Burr symbolized to Hamilton the dark forces which Hamilton symbolized to Thomas Jefferson—military ambition, the consequences of the replacement of virtue by commerce.

21 See Lance G. Banning, "The Quarrel with Federalism," unpub. Ph.D. thesis (Washington University, 1972), for a treatment of this subject.

What all of this should reveal to us is not that the "Lockean-liberal consensus," the pragmatic operation of interest-group politics, was from the beginning what Hamilton said it was, but that the idea of such a consensus had to emerge from travail and trauma, from an intense and occasionally tragic struggle between opposing ideals and against a sense of history's march. The trouble with the concept of Lockean consensus—apart from the very considerable historical misstatements which seem to be involved in this use of the word "Lockean" —is that it carries the idea of a prolonged ideological serenity.

American politics have often been complacent; but when were they serene? A study of the transition from a classical to an interest-group theory of politics in Revolutionary and Federalist thought reveals it to have been rooted in a tension between "virtue" and "commerce" sufficiently ancient by 1776 to dispel any idea that a "Lockean consensus" existed before that time. If one were subsequently established, it had to struggle for its existence and articulation; and it would be a proper question to ask whether the tensions out of which it may have emerged were overcome or whether they remained ingrained in the American value system.

Clearly, the simple republic–empire antithesis which Stourzh uncovers in Hamiltonian rhetoric will carry us only into a limited area of our inquiry. If a pragmatic–consensus theory of politics emerged out of the American Revolution, it should have been able to articulate its social values by means of a simple bourgeois ideology: an image of economic man, tranquilly pursuing his interests and maximizing his satisfactions, certain that by doing no more he was automatically serving the general good. Such an ideology can no doubt be discovered at appropriate times, but it is remarkable how little it has met the eyes of those who have analyzed the thinking behind the transition to interest-group constitutionalism; and where it has appeared, as in a recent article by Edmund S. Morgan on "The Puritan Ethic and the American Revolution," one reader at least has been struck by the extent to which much of it was lightly–disguised classicism.[22] No inconsiderable part of the emphasis which fell on the "frugality" and "self-denial" of acquisitive man, it can be suggested, was occasioned by a need to explain how he could resist the temptations of luxury, respect the good of others, and generally remain virtuous in a commercial society. Is there a solution to our problem here? It is curious that so little work

22 *William and Mary Quarterly*, XXIV (1967), 3–43.

appears to have been done on the reception into America of the ideas of Adam Smith and the Scottish economists, who are credited with developing the concept of "economic man," and certainly retained a deep concern with the ancient problem of corruption at the very point where this was about to become the modern problem of alienation.[23]

It might also be valuable to know more about the decline of the Country ideology in the Atlantic subculture that gave it birth. Georgian radicals, in the era of the Revolutionary War and its aftermath, used a language indistinguishable from that of their American peers, and we are getting a picture of what the latter subsequently did with it; but, especially if we decide that the Federalist-Republican debate was so largely a Court-Country replay that we must postpone the demise of the Country style in America to (say) the end of the First Party System, then we shall observe that in the contemporaneous era of Edmund Burke and Jeremy Bentham, Adam Smith and David Ricardo, Samuel Taylor Coleridge and Thomas Arnold, and the emergence of an industrial working-class consciousness, English political thought departed from eighteenth-century classicism more decisively—it can be argued— and certainly along other lines than was the case in America. To know what took place on one shore of the now sundered Atlantic culture may illuminate what developed upon the other.

Wood may slightly overstate his insistence that the classical theory of politics was overthrown and abandoned at the point where the Federal Constitution emerged as something other than a balanced republic of one, few, and many. "Virtue" consisted as much of the civic independence of the arms-bearing freeholder from private patron or governmental interest, as of his membership in one of a hierarchy of orders who respected and deferred to one another; and it is only from one aspect, though a very real one, that republican theory can be described as hierarchical.

Wood's argument is valid, important, and not to be minimized: the inadequacies of the classical theory of balance do explain how John Adams came to be left behind by the very constitution that he hastened to defend (Ch. XVI). But there was more to the classical theory than balance and its legion of accompanying ideas; there was the inveterate opposition between the agrarian man of independent virtue and the professionalized man of government and commerce; and John Taylor of Caroline, who exposed the obsolete character of Adams's *Defence*,

23 Pocock, *Politics, Language and Time*, 188–190.

also wrote anti-Hamiltonian polemic in which the spirit of Bolingbroke stalked on every page.

Deeply entrenched in eighteenth-century agrarian classicism was an image of the human personality, at once intensely autonomous and intensely participatory, entailing a *vita activa* and *vivere civile* which carry us back to the beginnings of humanism. In the essays collected in the book referred to above,[24] I have tried to show that there are messianic and apocalyptic overtones to this image, and that it possessed important affinities with the image of the Puritan saint. The present intellectual mood, of suspicion toward a privatized pluralism and "liberalism," and a willingness to see this replaced by something more dynamic, civic, and participatory, is tending to warp and foreshorten our image of the past.

It is the whole strength of the historiographical movement to which Bailyn, Kramnick, Wood, and Stourzh all belong that they have demonstrated the existence, throughout the eighteenth century, of a line of thought which staked everything on a positive and civic concept of the individual's virtue. This, I have argued, carried on through Jefferson into the whole tradition of American agrarian and populist messianism. There is no hurry to adopt a neo-Beardian interpretation whereby the founders shall be seen to have sold out from a civic to a merely liberal ideal in the moment of triumph; but should this come to be adopted, it will need to be expressed in the form of a continuing tension between working institutions and underlying values. To a newcomer during the 1960s, the American psyche, if not the governing structure, suggested less a nation of pragmatic Lockeans than one of tormented saints. The clamor of jeremiads, sick jokes, and enquiries as to what became of the dream at times became deafening and obsessive. And it seemed evident that the eighteenth-century quarrel between virtue and commerce, citizen and government, republic and empire was still going on in the twentieth century, and that historiography and political philosophy were still much involved in it. For this reason, it may be important to get the historical story straight. It may be that parts of the eighteenth-century debate can be interpreted as a dialogue between privatization and patriotism in the civic consciousness; but a good deal will have to be done before what was a straightforward thesis that a liberal consensus obtained dominance at the beginning of United States history can be restated in a form satisfactory to historians. That is why these two books are so valuable.

24 See fn. 2, above.

Commerce and Character:
The Anglo-American as New-Model Man

Ralph Lerner

> The hope of glory, and the ambition
> of princes, are not subject to arith-
> metical calculation. — Franklin
>
> In democracies nothing has brighter
> luster than commerce. — Tocqueville

BETWEEN them, Adam Smith and Alexis de Tocqueville have provided us with a detailed, fully realized portrait of the new man of
commerce. Their psychological analysis—both of the universal type
and of its American democratic exemplar—is by now familiar and persuasive. We not longer startle at the strange blend of limitless aspiration,
quasi-heroic effort, and sensible calculation that characterizes their model
man of the future. And, of course, we rarely wonder at how much domestic
tranquillity owes to the influence of commerce upon men's tastes, thoughts,
and manners. In the eighteenth century, however, when this model of civil
behavior was being formulated, all this stood in need of explication and
argument. A case had to be made, and then won. The advocates—men as
diverse as Montesquieu and John Adams, Adam Smith and Benjamin
Franklin, David Hume and Benjamin Rush—were united at least in this:
they saw in commercial republicanism a more sensible and realizable alternative to earlier notions of civic virtue and a more just alternative to the
theological-political regime that had so long ruled Europe and its colonial
periphery. However much these advocates differed—in their philosophic
insight, in their perception of the implications of their proposal for the
organization of economic life, even in the degree of their acceptance of the
very commercial republic they were promoting—for all this, they may be
considered a band of brethren in arms.[1]

Mr. Lerner is a member of the Collegiate Division of the Social Sciences at the
University of Chicago. He wishes to thank especially Marvin Meyers and Thomas S.
Schrock for criticism and suggestions.

[1] In proposing to treat the advocates of commercial republicanism as a conscious
collectivity I run the risk of asserting what cannot be proved for the sake of

The language of campaign and contention is no empty figure, for in many respects the commercial republic is defined best by what it rejects:[2] constraints and preoccupations based on visions of perfection beyond the reach of all or most; disdain for the common, useful, and mundane; judgments founded on a man's inherited status rather than on his acts. These were characteristics of an order or orders that the advocates of the commercial republic might still (in a limited way) admire but could not recommend. They saw fit, rather, to promote a new ordering of political, economic, and social life. Further, they perceived in the Anglo-American people and setting both the matter and the fitting occasion for their great project's success.

My intention here is not to trace the philosophic reasoning that led these men to reject the foundations of the older orders. That would lead us back to Locke and Spinoza, to Hobbes and Descartes, to Bacon and Machiavelli. Consider, rather, the public speech by which eighteenth-century thinkers—European and American—sought to persuade their contemporaries to adopt maxims, conclusions, and rules of action so much at odds with the certitudes of the day before yesterday. They had first to show their audience that the old preoccupations entailed unacceptable costs and consequences. Then—a much larger task—they had to propose a new model of political and social life, sketch its leading features in some detail, develop a case for preferring it, and defend it as sufficient to cope with the shortcomings of the existing order. In all these undertakings the advocates of the commercial republic show

---

emphasizing what tends to be neglected. It was their shared commitment to ordered liberty and their desire to promote it by emancipating men from many of the modes of thought of the past that led these thinkers to commend the commercial republic in the first place. What was a republic might, in this sense, be ascertained better by regarding the sphere of liberty rather than the formal organization of a state. Thus, for Montesquieu, England was a republic masquerading as a monarchy; for Smith, the trading world as a whole was a mercantile republic. Compare Albert O. Hirschman, *The Passions and the Interests: Political Arguments for Capitalism before Its Triumph* (Princeton, N.J., 1977), esp. 100–112, for an argument that differs from the one offered here by (among other things) seeing greater significance in Smith's divergences from his predecessors and less significance in Smith's political intentions and expectations.

[2] For a recent analysis of the economic category as presupposing an emancipation from the political domain and the general run of morality, "only at the price of assuming a normative character of its own," see Louis Dumont, *From Mandeville to Marx: The Genesis and Triumph of Economic Ideology* (Chicago, 1977), esp. 26, 36, 61, 67, 106–108. A parallel treatment of this "isolation of the economic impulse" traces the Anglo-Americans' break with traditional morality but, unlike my analysis in this essay, views the result as simply amoral or morally neutral. See J. E. Crowley, *This Sheba, Self: The Conceptualization of Economic Life in Eighteenth-Century America*, Johns Hopkins University Studies in Historical and Political Science, 92d Ser., No. 2 (Baltimore, 1974), 34-49, 123-124.

---

themselves to have been uncommon men, exceptionally clear- and sharp-sighted moderns who knew what they were rejecting and why.

Prideful Pretensions Detected

The old order was preoccupied with intangible goods to an extent we now hardly ever see. The king had his glory, the nobles their honor, the Christians their salvation, the citizens of pagan antiquity their ambition to outdo others in serving the public good. However much men vied for a fine field, a good herd, a large purse, it was not by these alone that they would make their mark. So at least they said. A latter-day man might be inclined to discount these pretensions but could not dismiss them out of hand. Like Tocqueville, he might doubt "whether men were better in times of aristocracy than at other times," and he might ponder why those earlier men "talked continually about the beauties of virtue" while studying its utility "only in secret."[3] The sense of shame or pride that kept that study secret was itself a revealing social fact. To thinkers like Montesquieu, Hume, and Smith, those earlier pretensions evinced a state of mind in some respects admirable, in other respects astonishing, in most respects consequential, but at bottom absurd. A good part of the political program of these commercial republicans was getting other men to judge likewise.

Eighteenth-century men had to be brought to see how fanciful those noncommercial notions were. To the commercial republicans, aristocratic imagination and pretension were not totally devoid of social value. Honor could be specious and yet politically useful; pride could engender politesse and delicacy of taste, graces that make life easy. The weightier truth, however, was that concern with these fancies skewed public policy and public budgets, sacrificing the real needs of the people to the petty desires of their governors. As Montesquieu put it, these "imaginary needs are what the passions and foibles of those who govern ask for: the charm of an extraordinary project, the sick desire for a vain glory, and a certain impotence of mind against fantasies."[4]

It was not only the few who labored under such delusions. An entire populace might be so taken up with its peculiar vision of what was most important as almost to cease being recognizably human. As little as Rousseau could imagine a nation of true Christians, could Hume imagine a nation of latter-day Spartans consumed with a passion for the public good. Though the "positive and circumstantial" testimony of history kept Hume from dismissing the original Spartan regime as "a mere philosophical whim or

[3] Alexis de Tocqueville, *Democracy in America*, ed. J. P. Mayer and Max Lerner (New York, 1966), 497, hereafter cited as Tocqueville, *Democracy in America*.

[4] Montesquieu, *De l'Esprit des lois*, III, 7, IV, 2, XIII, 1.

fiction," it did not compel him to say much, if anything, good about "a people addicted to arms, who fight for honour and revenge more than pay, and are unacquainted with gain and industry, as well as pleasure."[5] If men would only recognize what is genuinely human, they would see these distorting preoccupations for the grotesques they truly were.

Disabusing the many was no small task. Those whom Smith pleased to call "the great mob of mankind" were the awe-struck admirers of wealth and greatness, of success, however well or ill deserved. Such popular presumption in favor of the powerful had its good side, too, making more bearable the obedience that the weak dared not withhold. But that was hardly the whole story, according to Smith, for men came to perceive heroic magnanimity where there was only "extravagant rashness and folly"; "the splendour of prosperity" kept them from seeing "the blackness of . . . avidity and injustice" in the acts of those in high places. Smith pointed to an escape from these conventional delusions. We have within us, he maintained, a means of distinguishing the admirable from the meretricious, the genuine from the fanciful—a means of more truly assessing both our own worth and "the real merit" of others. How, he asked, would a particular act appear to an "impartial spectator," the vicarious conscience of mankind within everyone's breast? From this uncommon vantage of common humanity, we could see what "the most successful warriors, the greatest statesmen and legislators, the eloquent founders and leaders of the most numerous and most successful sects and parties" rarely were able to see: how much of their success and splendor was owing to their excessive presumption and self-admiration. If such excess was useful and necessary—for the instigators to undertake what "a more sober mind would never have thought of," and for the rest of mankind to acquiesce and follow them—it was, nonetheless, excess bordering on insane vanity. Hardly anything Smith taught was more subversive of the older order than his cool deflation of the proud man's "self-sufficiency and absurd conceit of his own superiority."[6] He did not seek to have his readers deny or sneer at the real differences between men but rather to discount the claims of all who presumed on those differences, real or imagined.

These presumptuous men imposed terrible costs on the whole of society—political costs that were insupportable, economic costs that were irrational. Hume believed that to some extent ambitious pretensions were

[5] Jean-Jacques Rousseau, *Du contrat social*, IV, 8; "Of Commerce," in David Hume, *Essays Moral, Political and Literary* (Oxford, 1963), 264-266, 268-269.
[6] Adam Smith, *The Theory of Moral Sentiments* (Indianapolis, 1976), 127, 235, 405-409, 416, 420-421. See also D. D. Raphael, "The Impartial Spectator," in Andrew S. Skinner and Thomas Wilson, eds., *Essays on Adam Smith* (Oxford, 1975), 86-94; Arthur O. Lovejoy, *Reflections on Human Nature* (Baltimore, 1961), 247-264; and Joseph Cropsey, *Polity and Economy: An Interpretation of the Principles of Adam Smith* (The Hague, 1957), 18-19.

self-correcting: enormous monarchies overextend themselves, condemned to repeat the chain of causes and effects that led to the ruin of Rome. In this way "human nature checks itself in its airy elevation." But another kind of preoccupation with intangible goods was less surely or easily deflected. Though Hume found no counterpart in modern times to the factional rage of ancient oligarchs and democrats, another type unknown to the pagans still persisted. It was the effect of what Hume called "parties from principle, especially abstract speculative principle." That men should divide over distinct interests was intelligible, over affection for persons and families only somewhat less so. But that they should divide, with mad and fatal consequence, in "controversy about an article of faith, which is utterly absurd and unintelligible, is not a difference in sentiment, but in a few phrases and expressions, which one party accepts of without understanding them, and the other refuses in the same manner"—that they should so divide was even more absurd than the behavior of those Moroccans who waged civil war "merely on account of their complexion." For a variety of reasons Christianity had fostered a persecuting spirit "more furious and enraged than the most cruel factions that ever arose from interest and ambition."[7] On this point Hume and the commercial republicans generally could agree with the ancients: fanaticism prompted by principle was incompatible with civility, reason, and government.

The economic costs of pursuing imaginary preoccupations might be less bloody than the political costs, but they were no less real; for proof consider the colonies in the New World. The frugal, simple, yet decent civil and ecclesiastical establishments of the English colonies were, for Smith, "an ever-memorable example at how small an expence three millions of people may not only be governed, but well governed." They also were an indictment of contrasting pretensions and practices, most notably in the Spanish and Portuguese colonies where both rich and poor suffered the oppressive consequences. A plundering horde of mendicant friars "most carefully" taught the poor "that it is a duty to give, and a very great sin to refuse them their charity"; this licensed, consecrated beggary "is a most grievous tax upon the poor people." The rich, too, were ill instructed: the elaborate ceremonials in those colonies habituated the rich to vanity and expense, thereby perpetuating "the ruinous taxes of private luxury and extravagance."[8] Though vanity (as with the French) might be productive of refinement, tastefulness

[7] "Of the Balance of Power," in Hume, Essays, 347-348; "Of the Populousness of Ancient Nations," ibid., 405; "Of Parties in General," ibid., 57-61; "Of the Coalition of Parties," ibid., 484-485.

[8] Adam Smith, An Inquiry into the Nature and Causes of the Wealth of Nations, ed. Edwin Cannan (New York, 1937), 541, 742, hereafter cited as Smith, Wealth of Nations. See Cropsey, Polity and Economy, 33-34, on the luxury of benevolence.

and luxury, as well as industry, pride (as with the Spanish) generally produced nothing but laziness, poverty, and ruin.[9] Aristocratic pride, in particular, was singled out by the commercial republicans for censure. Whatever slight sense feudal institutions might once have made, they had become atavisms, sustained by bizarre notions of honor and shame. Family pride, absorption with honor and glory, habitual indulgence of one's fancy for ornament and elegance: all these unfitted a man to perceive, let alone tend to, his "real interest." "Nothing," Smith asserted, "could be more completely absurd" than adhering to a system of entails and, by extension, to the system of thought that made entails seem sensible. Clearly, no mode of thought was less likely to render a man inclined and able to pay "an exact attention to small savings and small gains."[10] In recommending an alternative mode, the commercial republicans thought they were returning to simple reason.

Utility Resplendent

That alternative was what we today would call the market model, what Smith called "the natural system of perfect liberty and justice." This way of getting rid of a kind of unreason did not presuppose that men at large would use their reason more. Far from seconding the proud aspirations of Reason to grasp the whole of society and to direct its complex workings in detail, the commercial republicans counseled humility. They thought human behavior was adequately accounted for by dwelling upon the wants by which men are driven—wants that are largely, though not exclusively, physical; wants that are part and parcel of the self-regarding passions; wants that cannot in most cases be satisfied. Butchers and bakers, prelates and professors—all could be understood in more or less the same way. Once the similitude of our passions was recognized (however much the objects of those passions varied from man to man), our common neediness and vulnerability became apparent. This Hobbesian truth was axiomatic for the commercial republicans. Their reason told them that a surer guide to sane behavior could be found in the operations of a nonrational mechanism, the aggregate of small, anonymous

[9] The distinction between these forms of excessive self-esteem is critical for Montesquieu's analysis, but the reader is left to define them for himself (*Esprit des lois*, XIX, 9-11, XX, 22). Lovejoy's attempt to impose terminological order on 18th-century discussions of the passions (*Reflections on Human Nature*, 87-117) was in the end frustrated by his many authors' "exceedingly variable and confused" usage (p. 129). Here I follow Smith in treating vanity as a man's ostentatious display undertaken in the hope that others would regard him as more splendid than he really is at the moment; and pride as the self-satisfied and severely independent behavior of a man sincerely convinced of his own superiority (*Theory of Moral Sentiments*, 410-421). See the cogent analysis of Smith's doctrine concerning pride in Cropsey, *Polity and Economy*, 49-53.
[10] Smith, *Wealth of Nations*, 362-364.

calculations of things immediately known and felt by all. It was more reasonable to rely on the impersonal concourse of buyers and sellers than on the older standard of reasoned governance for proper hints and directions precisely because the market could better reckon with the ordinary passions of ordinary men. Indeed, where the ancient polity, Christianity, and the feudal aristocracy, each in its own fashion, sought to conceal, deny, or thwart most of the common passions for private gratification and physical comfort, the commercial republic built on those passions. Seen in this light, the market, and the state that secured its preconditions, were impersonal arenas where men could sort out their wants and tend to them.[11] The openness of these institutions to attempts at satisfying all kinds of wants would especially commend them to all kinds of men.

In seeking satisfaction under the new dispensation a man needed to be at once warm and cool, impassioned and calculating, driven yet sober. Eschewing brilliance and grandeur, the new-model man of prudence followed a way of life designed to secure for himself a small but continual profit. As Smith noted, he avoided whatever "might too often interfere with the regularity of his temperance, might interrupt the steadiness of his industry, or break in upon the strictness of his frugality." He deferred present ease for greater enjoyment later; he did his duty, but beyond that minded his own business. He was, in short, a private man whose behavior "commands a certain cold esteem but seems not entitled to any very ardent love or admiration."[12] Notwithstanding these reservations, preoccupation with incremental gains made sense to Smith the political economist. The energies set in motion would bring forth an array of small comforts and conveniences beyond the reach or imagining of serf or savage, relieving miseries once thought fated. As men looked more to their economic interest, that interest would loom larger in their eyes and thoughts. Other concerns would matter less— sometimes because the accumulation of wealth was seen as the key to satisfying all desires, sometimes because a conflicting noneconomic interest (family feeling, attachment to a landed estate) was seen as only sentimental, illusory. It was but a short step from this awakening to the adoption of what Tocqueville called "standards of prudent and conscious mediocrity," the adjustment of production and of products to satisfy ordinary men's demands for the gratification of their wants. In the end "there is no sovereign will or national prejudice that can fight for long against cheapness."[13]

The implications of all this for how and what men think were not lost

[11] Ibid., 572, 14, 717; Smith, Theory of Moral Sentiments, 487-494, 417; "Of the Dignity or Meanness of Human Nature," in Hume, Essays, 87-88; Thomas Hobbes, Leviathan; or the Matter, Forms and Power of a Commonwealth, Ecclesiasticall and Civil, ed. Michael Oakeshott (Oxford, 1946), 6, 98, 138-139.

[12] Smith, Theory of Moral Sentiments, 350-353. See also Montesquieu, Esprit des lois, XX, 4.

[13] Tocqueville, Democracy in America, 45-46, 372, 433-434. 591.

upon Montesquieu and Smith. But it remained for Tocqueville—with a commercial, if barely industrialized, Jacksonian America before him—to make the full depiction. Wherever he turned, he saw men calculating and weighing and computing. Everything had more or less utility and hence could be hefted and judged with a trader's savvy. Because knowledge was seen to be a source of power, because knowledge paid, men sought it. The market mentality shrugged off that "inconsiderate contempt for practice" typical of aristocratic ages; the *use* to which the discoveries of the mind could be put became the leading question. Tocqueville traced the modern predilection for generalizations to a "lively yet indolent" democratic ambition: generalizations yielded large returns for very small investments of thought. Among commercial republicans even religion was brought down to earth: "in the very midst of their zeal one generally sees something so quiet, so methodical, so calculated that it would seem that the head rather than the heart leads them to the foot of the altar."[14] Where the central concern was with utility, there could be little room for the play of the imagination, for poetry; men not only spoke prose but thought prose, all the days of their lives.[15]

Quiet and prosaic though such men might be, they could be passionate, energetic, and willing to run risks. Just as Montesquieu saw these qualities in England, his model commercial republic,[16] so Tocqueville saw them in America, *his* model commercial republic. Again and again he remarked on "the soaring spirit of enterprise"—a product in part of peculiarly American conditions, to be sure, but at a deeper level a natural consequence of man's freedom to indulge in "a kind of decent materialism." Restlessness goaded men on, and the prospect of happiness, like the horizon, beckoned and receded before them. Life itself became a thrilling gamble as greed and ever-changing desires elicited efforts of heroic proportions from unheroic men for unheroic objectives.[17]

No sketch of the commercial republic should neglect to stress that, as a model both for a national polity and for the entire trading world, it tended to ignore or transcend the conventional divisions within nations and among them. Its eighteenth-century proponents could realistically urge men to consider their larger interdependence without expecting (or even desiring) the neglect of national interest and identity, for commerce, properly understood and reasonably conducted, would serve both man and citizen. Commerce inclined men to consider one another primarily as demanders and

[14] *Ibid.*, 405, 424-425, 428-429, 501.
[15] *Ibid.*, 573, 585. See especially his fine contrast of the effects of slavery's presence or absence on the mores of southerners and northerners. *Ibid.*, 344-345.
[16] Montesquieu, *Esprit des lois,* XIX, 27, XX, 4.
[17] Tocqueville, *Democracy in America,* 148, 225, 260-262, 319, 504-505, 633, 707. See also Marvin Meyers, *The Jacksonian Persuasion: Politics and Belief* (Stanford, Calif., 1957), 31-41.

suppliers, to consider the world as constituting "but a single state, of which all the [particular] societies are members."[18] Commerce was preeminently traffic in movables—things that have little if any identification with a particular state of the kind real property necessarily has. In what Adam Smith called "the great mercantile republic"—by which he meant all producers and traders of movables—the owners and employers of capital stock were properly citizens of the world and "not necessarily attached to any particular country."[19] What began as a simple recognition of our separate and common needs would end in a complex, ever-changing interdependence. Even as each labored intently to satisfy his own wants, men would become commercial cousins, cool fellow-citizens of a universal republic.

A More Human Alternative

This was the world—part vision, part fact—that these eighteenth-century advocates pronounced good. If others were to judge likewise, they had to understand *why* the commercial republicans preferred the market regime: they had to see that, better than any of its predecessors and alternatives, this regime suited human nature because, more than any of its predecessors and alternatives, it could be realized taking men as they are.

The contrast with and opposition to the Christian and Greek worlds could hardly have been greater. In Montesquieu's analysis it was the Christian Schoolmen—and not the commercial practices they condemned—that deserved the label criminal. In condemning something "naturally permitted or necessary," the doctrinaire and unworldly Scholastics set in train a series of misfortunes, most immediately for the Jews, more generally for Europe. Gradually, however, princes had learned to be more politic; experience taught them that toleration paid. "Happy is it for men to be in a situation in which, while their passions inspire in them the thought of being wicked, it is, nevertheless, to their interest not to be." The calculation prompted by nature or necessity overpowered the passion prompted by religion and corrected the enthusiastic excesses of those professing it.

For Montesquieu, the reliance of Greek thinkers on virtue as the support of popular government displayed an equal disregard for how men are. Political thinkers of his own time, in contrast, "speak to us only of manufac-

---

[18] Montesquieu, *Esprit des lois*, XX, 23. See the interpretation of this attenuation of parochial passions in J. G. A. Pocock, *The Machiavellian Moment: Florentine Political Thought and the Atlantic Republican Tradition* (Princeton, N.J., 1975), 492-493.

[19] Smith, *Wealth of Nations*, 412, 800; see also 345-346, 395, 858, 880. The point is nicely illustrated by the political neutrality or indifference of late 18th-century Nantucket whalemen. See the editorial discussion and Jefferson's echoing of Smith's characterization of merchants in Julian P. Boyd *et al.*, eds., *The Papers of Thomas Jefferson*, XIV (Princeton, N.J., 1958), 220-221.

ture, commerce, finance, opulence, and even of luxury." This was not a change that Montesquieu regretted.[20] According to the commercial republicans, the ancient polity rested on a distortion of almost every quality of human nature. Nowhere was this seen more clearly than in the case of Sparta. The Spartan's heroic virtue and his indifference to his own well-being were almost perfectly antithetical to the cast of the commercial republican. John Adams's characterization could serve as the verdict of all the commercial republicans: "Separated from the rest of mankind, [the Spartans] lived together, destitute of all business, pleasure, and amusement, but war and politics, pride and ambition; . . . as if fighting and intriguing, and not life and happiness, were the end of man and society. . . . Human nature perished under this frigid system of national and family pride."[21] This attack on Sparta (an extreme case if ever there was one) may be seen as a rejection of that primary reliance on virtue placed not only by the ancients but by latter-day men who drew their inspiration from classical models. Commercial republicans could reject the ancient premises even while admiring some ancient accomplishments.[22] In so doing, some may have been unaware or perplexed, and others torn between zealous wishes and sober doubts, but the foremost of them were, for these purposes, concerned less with the rare excellence of a rare individual than with what might ordinarily be expected of the generality of men.

Sparta, and the ancient world generally, accomplished astonishing feats, astonishing because they defied "the more natural and usual course of things." For Hume and his fellows, Sparta was a "prodigy," less a model than a freak. The ancient policy of preferring the greatness of the state to the happiness of the subject was "violent"; recurrence to that policy in modern times was "almost impossible." But beyond that, what sense did such a policy make? The sovereign who heeded Hume's counsel would know that "it is his best policy to comply with the common bent of mankind, and give it all the improvements of which it is susceptible. Now, according to the most natural course of things, industry, and arts, and trade, increase the power of the sovereign, as well as the happiness of the subjects." Far from being tempted to deal harshly with his subject to compel him to produce a surplus, the modern sovereign would take care to "furnish him with manufactures and

[20] Montesquieu, Esprit des lois, XXI, 20, III, 3.

[21] Charles Francis Adams, ed., The Works of John Adams, Second President of the United States, with a Life of the Author, Notes and Illustrations (Boston, 1850-1856), IV, 554.

[22] See the pithy analysis in Gerald Stourzh, Alexander Hamilton and the Idea of Republican Government (Stanford, Calif., 1970), 63-75; and the extensive documentation in Pocock, Machiavellian Moment, chaps. 14-15. Whether "the founders of Federalism were not fully aware of the extent to which their thinking involved an abandonment of the paradigm of virtue" (ibid., 525) is a question that cannot be answered while dealing with aggregates.

commodities, [so that] he will do it of himself." This sovereign would take to heart Hume's lesson that "our passions are the only causes of labour"; he would appreciate and use the mighty engine of covetousness. And let it even be granted that the ancient policy of infusing each citizen-soldier with a passion for the public good might not be *utterly* futile, for it is at least conceivable that a community might be converted temporarily into a camp of lean and dedicated citizens. "But as these principles [of ancient citizenship] are too disinterested, and too difficult to support, it is requisite to govern men by other passions, and animate them with a spirit of avarice and industry, art and luxury."[23] With less pain—and less nobility—commercial republican principles could lead to a strong, secure polity.

American commercial republicans did not promote this new policy with quite the breezy equanimity of Hume. The groping, hesitation, and even anguish catalogued by Gordon Wood amply document that fact.[24] But neither did the leading Americans reject Hume's premises. In the long run, perhaps, the corruption of the republic was inevitable. Precautions might be taken to postpone that day, but the foundations were not themselves in question.[25] Again, we find in Tocqueville a distillation of what most Americans were not yet able or willing to state for themselves. The generalized expression of the commercial republican view of man and of human association was what Tocqueville called "the doctrine of self-interest properly understood," the fusing of public interest and private profit to the point where "a sort of selfishness makes [the individual] care for the state." The result was a kind of patriotism in no way to be confused with the ardent love of the ancient citizen for his city; it was less a public passion than a private conviction, a conviction arising out of private passions. Each man would come to recognize his need for involvement with others; he might even learn to temper his selfishness. Whatever else might be said of his frame of mind, there was no denying that it sustained and was sustained by commercial activity. Even as commerce reminded men of their common needs and made them more like one another and more aware of that likeness, the doctrine of self-interest properly understood taught them simply and plainly to give the dictates of "nature and necessity" their due. Human nature stood stripped of the pretensions that had kept earlier men from satisfying their natural wants.[26]

[23] "Of Commerce," in Hume, *Essays*, 262-269.

[24] Gordon S. Wood, *The Creation of the American Republic, 1776-1787* (Chapel Hill, N.C., 1969).

[25] Gerald Stourzh, "Die tugendhafte Republik—Montesquieus Begriff der 'vertu' und die Anfänge der Vereinigten Staaten von Amerika," in Heinrich Fichtenau and Hermann Peichl, eds., *Österreich und Europa* (Graz, Austria, 1965), 247-267, esp. 260-262.

[26] Tocqueville, *Democracy in America*, 85, 217, 481-482, 497-499, 524-525, 602. Compare Melvin Richter's interpretation in "The Uses of Theory: Tocqueville's

Mild Ambitions and Wild Ones

Though some might well prefer the commercial republic because it better suited men as they are, they had to look still further. Were the political ills that had beset men and nations from time out of mind less likely under the new dispensation? To what extent would the commercial republic ameliorate the self-induced miseries of political life? Its eighteenth-century proponents had high but not excessive hopes that men and nations would live in greater security as more of mankind adopted the market model. They believed that, on the whole, men would find it easier to be less cruel toward one another as they came to care more about their own safety and comfort.

Montesquieu clearly expected this to be the case in relations among the nations. "Commerce cures destructive prejudices"; it "polishes and softens barbaric morals." In making men more aware of both human variety and sameness, commerce made them less provincial and in a sense more humane. "The spirit of commerce unites nations." Driven by their mutual needs, trading partners entered into a symbiosis they could ill afford to wreck by war. They would learn how to subordinate disruptive political interests to those of commerce. Such nations, devoting themselves to a "commerce of economy," had, so to speak, a necessity to be faithful; since their object was gain, not conquest, they would be "pacific from principle."[27]

American variations on these themes were both more and less sober than the Montesquieuan original. Writing in the nonage of the American nation, Thomas Paine noted with seeming indifference that the preoccupation with commerce "diminishes the spirit both of patriotism and military defence." He could accept this diminution (once the times that tried men's souls were past) because "our plan is commerce," not "setting the world at defiance."[28] For John Jay and Alexander Hamilton, however, a reliance on the presumed pacific genius of commercial republics would be "visionary." If anything, commerce—especially when conducted in the forward American manner— would create its own occasions for aggrandizement and warfare.[29] Thus, according to Hamilton, the proposition that the *people* of a commercial republic, under the influence of the new prevailing modes of thought, had to

---

Adaptation of Montesquieu," in Richter, ed., *Essays in Theory and History: An Approach to the Social Sciences* (Cambridge, Mass., 1970), 95-97.

[27] Montesquieu, *Esprit de lois*, XX, 1, 2, 7, 8. See Thomas L. Pangle, *Montesquieu's Philosophy of Liberalism: A Commentary on "The Spirit of the Laws"* (Chicago, 1973), 203-209. See also "Of the Jealousy of Trade," in Hume, *Essays*, 338, and the discussion by Paul E. Chamley, "The Conflict between Montesquieu and Hume," in Skinner and Wilson, eds., *Essays on Adam Smith*, 303-304.

[28] Thomas Paine, "Common Sense," in Philip S. Foner, ed., *The Life and Major Writings of Thomas Paine* (New York, 1961), 36, 20.

[29] Jacob E. Cooke, ed., *The Federalist* (Middleton, Conn., 1961), No. 4, 19-20, No. 6, 31-32, No. 11, 66, hereafter cited as *Federalist*. See Stourzh, *Hamilton and the Idea of Republican Government*, 140-150.

grow less martial would not, even if true, entail a belief in an end to war. It was more likely that where the business of the people was business, the economic objections to a citizen army would be "conclusive" and war would be left to the professionals.[30] Generally, however, European and American commercial republicans believed that commerce gave promise of influencing international relations for the better. Like Benjamin Rush, they viewed commerce as "the means of uniting the different nations of the world together by the ties of mutual wants and obligations," as an instrument for "humanizing mankind."[31] Hamilton was the outstanding demurrer.

Even greater than these transnational benefits was the anticipated dividend in increased domestic security.[32] For Hume, the simultaneous indulgence and tempering of men's passions was almost a matter of course. Men would continue to be instructed in "the advantages of human[e] maxims above rigour and severity." Relieved of the distortions imposed by ignorance and superstition, political life would come more and more to wear a human face. "Factions are then less inveterate, revolutions less tragical, authority less severe, and seditions less frequent." Free to pursue happiness as each individual saw it, men would be able to continue to rise above their ancestors' ferocity and brutishness. Furthermore, the development of commerce and industry drew "authority and consideration to that middling rank of men, who are the best and firmest basis of public liberty."[33] Smith seconded Hume's observation, pronouncing this effect the most important of all those stemming from commerce and manufacturing. Where before men had "lived almost in a continual state of war with their neighbours, and of servile dependency upon their superiors," now they increasingly had "order and good government, and, with them, the liberty and security of individuals." The self-regarding actions of a part had led to the gradual elevation of the whole.[34]

The turmoils and revolutions of the seventeenth and eighteenth centuries demonstrated that the monopoly of public service enjoyed by the great could be broken. They also suggested how even the humblest man, by adopting and acting on commercial maxims, might serve himself and thereby the public good.[35] These lessons were not lost upon a newly emancipated order of men, whose typical member (in Smith's sketch) was an impatient "man of spirit

[30] *Federalist*, No. 24, 156-157, No. 25, 162, No. 29, 183-184.
[31] Benjamin Rush, "Of the Mode of Education Proper in a Republic," in Dagobert D. Runes, ed., *The Selected Writings of Benjamin Rush* (New York, 1947), 94.
[32] Pangle, *Montesquieu's Philosophy of Liberalism*, 114-117, 125-130, 147-150, 197-199.
[33] "Of Refinement in the Arts," in Hume, *Essays*, 280-281, 283-284.
[34] Smith, *Wealth of Nations*, 385.
[35] Harvey C. Mansfield, Jr., "Party Government and the Settlement of 1688," *American Political Science Review*, LVIII (1964), 933-946, esp. 936, 944-945.

and ambition, who is depressed by his situation." For him and his kind, escape from the mediocrity of one's station was the first order of business.[36] In principle he would stick at nothing to accomplish this. "He even looks forward with satisfaction to the prospect of foreign war or civil dissension," the attendant confusion and bloodshed creating opportunities for him to cut a figure. In the old regime such a frustrated man would have been ridiculous and might have been dangerous, but in the commercial republic he came into his own—and without having to take to the barricades. For it was above all in the world of commerce and in the polity devoted to commerce that this new man enjoyed a comparative advantage over the conventional aristocrat, over "the man of rank and distinction." The latter "shudders with horror at the thought of any situation which demands the continual and long exertion of patience, industry, fortitude, and application of thought." For the new man, however, such humdrum exertions afforded the likeliest escape from detested obscurity and insignificance. His prudence consisted of a blend of foresight and self-command with a view to private advantage. His road to fame and fortune was straight and narrow; he respected the conventions of society "with an almost religious scrupulosity," of which Smith deemed him a much better example than that frequently set by "men of much more splendid talents and virtues." His virtues, indeed, were closer to the virtues of "the inferior ranks of people" than to those of the great. They were emphatically private virtues. Needless to say, they would have been altogether unfashionable in the reign of Charles II.[37]

Where such burghers were preponderant, civil life took on a distinctive coloration. The private preoccupations, the quiet virtues, the insistent passions of commercial individuals became the core of an entire system of honor. When Tocqueville looked at the Americans more than half a century later, he thought he saw a people who carried the "patient, supple, and insinuating" habits of traders into political life. He was struck by their love of order, regard for conventional morality, distrust of genius, and preference for the practical over the theoretical. He offered what he thought a sufficient explanation: "Violent political passions have little hold on men whose whole thoughts are bent on the pursuit of well-being. Their excitement about small matters makes them calm about great ones."[38] It would not be hard to regard this broad characterization of American life as at best fanciful and tendentious. But any such quick dismissal probably says more about differing understandings of "great" and "small" than about the validity of Tocqueville's explanation.

[36] See Harold C. Syrett and Jacob E. Cooke, eds., *The Papers of Alexander Hamilton*, I (New York, 1961), 4.
[37] Smith, *Theory of Moral Sentiments*, 52-53, 167, 188-191, 177-178.
[38] Tocqueville, *Democracy in America*, 262-263, 612-613, 617.

Whatever else it is, this prosaic, politically cautious people was anything but sluggish. Its tastes and feelings were intense but well channeled. Thus the natural taste for comfort became an all-consuming passion, filling the imaginations and thoughts of all ranks of the people with middling expectations. "It is as hard for vices as for virtues to slip through the net of common standards." Tocqueville saw democratic ambition as "both eager and constant," but generally confined to "coveting small prizes within reach." Self-made men found it hard to shake off the prudent habits of a lifetime: "a mind cannot be gradually enlarged, like a house." Courage and heroism, too, were present, but again with a difference. Trade and navigation and colonization were with the Americans a surrogate for war. The ordeals they endured, the dangers they braved, the defeats they shrugged off were astonishing, not least because the coveted laurel was, more often than not, something comparable to being able to "sell tea a farthing cheaper than an English merchant can." From such a man of commerce, who treated all of life "like a game of chance, a time of revolution, or the day of a battle," much was to be expected and little feared.[39]

American experience confirmed Hamilton's observation that "the love of wealth [is] as domineering and enterprising a passion as that of power or glory." But it also showed that the effects of that passion could go beyond avaricious accumulation. John Adams maintained that "there is no people on earth so ambitious as the people of America." Whereas in other lands, he thought, "ambition and all its hopes are extinct," in America, where competition was free, where every office—even the highest—seemed within one's grasp, the ardor for distinction was stimulated and became general. In America "the lowest can aspire as freely as the highest." The farmer and tradesman pursued their dream of happiness as intensely as any man. Most revealing, however, were the objects of those dreams. "The post of clerk, sergeant, corporal, and even drummer and fifer, is coveted as earnestly as the best gift of major-general." No man was so humble but a passion for distinction was aroused; no object so small but it excited somebody's emulation. In Adams's Arcadian vision the general emulation taking place in a properly constituted, balanced government "makes the common people brave and enterprising" and—thanks to their ambition—"sober, industrious, and frugal. You will find among them some elegance, perhaps, but more solidity; a little pleasure, but a great deal of business."[40] The commercial republicans could, in good conscience, recommend the unleashing of men's ambition because they saw how, in the case of the Many (even including most of the traditional Few), that ambition would be tame. Political checks, powerfully

---

[39] *Ibid.*, 502-505, 598, 604-605, 368-370.
[40] *Federalist*, No. 6, 32; Adams, ed., *Works of John Adams*, IX, 633-634, IV, 199-200.

supported by new social and economic aspirations, would keep men busy, wary, and safe.

What, though, of the problem posed by the others, those whom James Madison in *The Federalist* noted as "a few aspiring characters"? A philosopher or statesman concerned with promoting and sustaining a commercial republic had to be mindful of the political threat likely to arise from such individuals. What, Hamilton asked, was to be done about men whose aspirations fell only sometimes within the ordinary system of rewards held out by a republic—men of "irregular ambition," intent on seizing or even creating chances for self-promotion?[41] To this challenge the commercial republicans responded with counsel and modest hopes, but no sure solution. The limits of the market model were in sight.

John Adams's lifetime of rumination on this theme testifies to its importance—and its intractability. There was, he thought at age twenty-six, no "source of greater Evils, than the Tendency of great Parts and Genius, to imprudent sallies and a Wrong Biass." It was to "the giddy Rashness and Extravagance of the sublimest Minds" that man's bloody and tumultuous past was owed. Popular government, far from being immune, was more vulnerable to this danger than any other form. The proper course to follow was not "the general Method in Use among Persons in Power of treating such spirits." Experience indicated, rather, that "unskilfull and rough Usage" only succeeded in making genius more desperate and troublesome. Treated differently, "with a wise and delicate Management," such minds might be made into "ornaments and Blessings."[42]

Would an example of a beneficent management be Smith's proposal, in *The Wealth of Nations,* for dealing with the "ambitious and high-spirited men" of British America? Smith's premise was that free government could endure, and endure well, only if "the greater part of the leading men, the natural aristocracy of every country," had it within their power to gratify their sense of self-importance. He went on to make a suggestion that seemed to him "obvious." Present those colonial worthies with "a new and more dazzling object of ambition"; raise their sights from "piddling for the little prizes" offered by "the paltry raffle of colony faction" to "the great prizes which sometimes come from the wheel of the great state lottery of British politics"; direct their hopes and abilities to the imperial seat of "the great scramble."[43] Smith's was a more politic proposal than those brought forward by successive ministries and privy councils after 1763. But was it enough? A wearier and less sanguine Adams might doubt that. Among men of spirit,

[41] *Federalist,* No. 57, 386, No. 59, 402, No. 72, 491-492.
[42] L. H. Butterfield *et al.,* eds., *Diary and Autobiography of John Adams,* I (Cambridge, Mass., 1961), 221-222.
[43] Smith, *Wealth of Nations,* 586-588, 898.

whose private interest could be enlisted chiefly or only through non-commercial appeals, he knew there were some few—the extreme and practically most important cases—who insisted on engrossing all the coin of pride. "This . . . is the tribe out of which proceed your patriots and heroes, and most of the great benefactors to mankind." As he confided to his old comrade, Benjamin Rush, "there is in some souls a principle of absolute levity that buoys them irresistibly into the clouds."[44] Just as prudential investments held little charm for the likes of these, so would honors shared with others not satisfy. The threat and the problem remained. In the last analysis, the only safeguard against a dangerously overreaching ambition was what Hume called the "watchful *jealousy*" of the people.[45]

Consider this modestly elevated multitude on whom the shapers of the commercial republic placed their hopes.[46] At the end, they soberly expected, ordinary farmers, mechanics, and tradesmen would remain just that—and voters as well—busy with their own affairs, forever preoccupied with the economic side of life and without more vaulting ambition. But that did not exhaust the matter. Though the ordinary work of society remained to be done by ordinary men, the commercial republic promised these citizens literally a new birth of freedom and invested them with a new sense of self-esteem. For now, as these men collectively and for the first time assumed decisive political and social significance, they found their aspirations raised, their energies stirred and directed, their capacities enlarged.[47] They would

[44] Adams, ed., *Works of John Adams*, VI, 248-249; John Adams to Benjamin Rush, Apr. 12, 1807, in John A. Schutz and Douglass Adair, eds., *The Spur of Fame: Dialogues of John Adams and Benjamin Rush, 1805-1813* (San Marino, Calif., 1966), 78.

[45] "Of the Liberty of the Press," in Hume, *Essays*, 10-11. This was a common theme in the period under discussion, and one on which many changes were rung. In a class apart, though, is the profound—and profoundly disquieting—discussion in Lincoln's "Young Men's Lyceum Address," Jan. 27, 1838, in Roy P. Basler *et al.*, eds., *The Collected Works of Abraham Lincoln*, I (New Brunswick, N.J., 1953), 108-115. See the interpretations by Gerald Stourzh, "Alexander Hamilton: The Theory of Empire Building" (paper delivered at the American Historical Association meeting, New York, Dec. 30, 1957); Stourzh, *Hamilton and the Idea of Republican Government*, 204-205; and Harry V. Jaffa, *Crisis of the House Divided: An Interpretation of the Issues in the Lincoln-Douglas Debates* (Garden City, N.Y., 1959), 182-232.

[46] With these commercial republicans we ought to include even Jefferson while he was extolling the chosen people of God who labor in the earth. The commercial character of agriculture in the Jeffersonian vision deserves emphasis. The rising nation spreading over a wide and fruitful land, which he contemplated, was not an agglomeration of peasants eking out a living, indifferent to the economic implications of the latest discoveries of scientific husbandry. For all his urging of household self-sufficiency, cottage industry, and the like, Jefferson thought of American agriculture clearly as a business and as a part of a world economy.

[47] In reading the history of the life of "the youngest Son of the youngest Son for

move forward with confidence, believing that "one Man of tolerable Abilities may work great Changes, and accomplish great Affairs among Mankind" if only he brought the proper method and diligence to his task. They would move forward with no apology to those who might view their concerns as "trifling Matters not worth minding or relating," for a "seemingly low" or trivial matter, when recurring frequently, gained "Weight and Consequence." They would act on the belief that "Human Felicity is produc'd not so much by great Pieces of good Fortune that seldom happen, as by little Advantages that occur every Day."[48] Thus, in promoting their private affairs and tending to their public business—however slight or narrow—they could look forward to physical gratification, enhanced social standing, and the satisfaction of performing an acknowledged public service. Even their notions of what *is* their business grew; they would come to take a selfish interest in the public weal. This, then, was the electorate that, freed of the benighting miseries of the past, might yet be alert enough in their own interests to keep the threatening natural aristocracy in check. Given a properly contrived constitution, they might even employ that aristocracy's talents to advantage.

The commercial republicans were cautiously hopeful that the emancipation promised by their new regime would not be self-destructive. Tocqueville, taking in the scene at a later date and from a different perspective, was somewhat less hopeful. Looking beyond the jarring wishes and fears of Jacksonian America,[49] he thought he saw how a preoccupied electorate might turn into an indifferent crowd, how a "people passionately bent on physical pleasures" might come to regard the exercise of their political rights as "a tiresome inconvenience," a trivial distraction from "the serious business of life." He thought he saw how, with their anxieties fueled by a self-contradictory hedonism, such a people might readily hand over their liberties to whatever able and ambitious man promised them the untroubled enjoyment of their private pursuits.[50] Alternatively, they might slide—quietly, mindlessly—into a bondage altogether new, where "not a person, or a class . . . , but society itself holds the end of the chain." Either way they would lose their liberty and their very character as men and citizens.[51] It was in

---

5 Generations back" of an "obscure Family," they would learn how little ashamed he was of having no distinguished ancestry; they would have a vivid demonstration of "how little necessary all origin is to happiness, virtue, or greatness" (Leonard W. Labaree *et al.*, eds., *The Autobiography of Benjamin Franklin* [New Haven, Conn., 1964], 46, 50, 137). In the details of this individual's career they might easily glimpse their own career, "the manners and situation of *a rising* people" (*ibid.*, 135). The last two quotations are from a letter by Benjamin Vaughan, Jan. 31, 1783, which Franklin intended to insert in his autobiography.

[48] *Ibid.*, 163, 207.
[49] Meyers, *Jacksonian Persuasion*, 4-23, 92-107.
[50] Tocqueville, *Democracy in America*, 503, 508-509, 511-512, 613.
[51] *Ibid.*, 667-668; and see 641-680, *passim.*

anticipation of this Tocquevillean nightmare that Rousseau inveighed against those who would rather hire a representative than spare the time to govern themselves, and rather pay taxes than serve the community with their bodies. Absorbed in their ledgers and accounts, they stood to lose all. "The word 'finance,'" Rousseau wrote, "is slave language; it has no place in the city's lexicon."[52]

Assessing Benefits and Costs

Although the founding fathers of commercial republicanism were neither money-grubbers nor philistines nor indifferent citizens, Rousseau's statement could not be farther from their conclusion. In the last analysis, commerce commended itself to them because it promised a cure for destructive prejudices and irrational enthusiasms, many of them clerically inspired. Commerce was an engine that would assault and level the remaining outposts of pride in all its forms: family pride, aristocratic pride, pride that concealed from "mankind that they were children of the same father, and members of one great family," pride in "learning" (which Rush distinguished sharply from "useful knowledge"), pride in whatever led men to believe that they could rise above the workaday world. Commerce, like the plain teachings of the Gospels, like useful knowledge, would humble the mind, soften the heart, help bring "the ancient citizen to a level with the men of [only] yesterday," and assimilate all men everywhere to one another.[53] If, in a sense, commerce imposed a ceiling upon some men's aspirations, it more significantly also supplied most men with a floor to stand on. Commercial men would come at last to regard themselves and their societies as members of a single universal state, a brotherhood of demanders and suppliers.

That this triumph of commerce would entail significant human losses was a foregone conclusion for these commercial republicans. Nonetheless, they were prepared to accept those losses, even as they sought ways to mitigate them. For Montesquieu, a regime dedicated to commerce partook less of a union of fellow citizens, bound together by ties of friendship, than of an alliance of contracting parties, intent on maximizing their freedom of choice through a confederation of convenience. It was in this character of an alliance that men found themselves cut off from one another or, rather, linked to one another principally through a market mechanism. It was a world in which everything had its price—and, accordingly, its sellers and

---

[52] Rousseau, *Contrat social*, III, 15.
[53] Rush, "Of the Mode of Education," in Runes, ed., *Selected Writings of Rush*, 94; "Observations upon the Study of the Latin and Greek Languages," in Benjamin Rush, *Essays, Literary, Moral and Philosophical*, 2d ed. (Philadelphia, 1806), 43; "Leonidas" [Benjamin Rush], "The subject of an American Navy," *Pennsylvania Gazette*, July 31, 1782.

buyers. Not surprisingly, the habits of close calculation and "exact justice" appropriate to one kind of activity were extended to all kinds, and political community was replaced by a marketplace of arm's-length transactions.[54]

Smith was even more explicit and detailed than Montesquieu in assessing "the disadvantages of a commercial spirit." He saw it as bringing about a narrowing and demeaning of men's souls, with the "heroic spirit" being "almost entirely extinguished." As in his discussion of the effects of the division of labor upon "the great body of the people," Smith squarely faced the debasement implicit in his scheme of civilization. Whether his proposals for public education would forfend the predicted "mental mutilation," "gross ignorance and stupidity," and corruption of "all the nobler parts of the human character," is not my present question. I note here only that Smith recognized the need that civilized society had for civilized men, a kind that his society normally would not nurture.[55]

The American commercial republicans who struggled with this problem sought a solution in some passion or pride that might vie with the love of wealth. For them, America's dedication to commerce was both fitting and frightening. On the one hand, it would take commerce and all the energies it could command to exploit the opportunities offered by the new land.[56] Modern statesmen, such as Hamilton, were mindful of how effectively commerce moved men. "By multiplying the means of gratification, by promoting the introduction and circulation of the precious metals, those darling objects of human avarice and enterprise, it [that is, commercial prosperity] serves to vivify and invigorate the channels of industry, and to make them flow with greater activity and copiousness. The assiduous merchant, the laborious husbandman, the active mechanic, and the industrious manufacturer, all orders of men look forward with eager expectation and growing alacrity to this pleasing reward of their toils."[57] Discerning statesmen, such as Adams, also understood how, in certain European lands, it was

[54] Montesquieu, *Esprit des lois*, XIX, 27, XX, 2; Aristotle, *Politics*, 3. 9. 1280b, 6-11. See also Richard Jackson to Benjamin Franklin, June 17, 1755, in Leonard W. Labaree *et al.*, eds., *The Papers of Benjamin Franklin*, VI (New Haven, Conn., 1963), 81.

[55] Edwin Cannan, ed., *Lectures on Justice, Police, Revenue and Arms, Delivered at the University of Glasgow by Adam Smith, Reported by a Student in 1763* (Oxford, 1896), 259; Smith, *Wealth of Nations*, 734-740, 744-748. See Cropsey, *Polity and Economy*, 88-95.

[56] "We occupy a new country. Our principal business should be to explore and apply its resources, all of which press us to enterprise and haste. Under these circumstances, to spend four or five years in learning two dead languages, is to turn our backs upon a gold mine, in order to amuse ourselves in catching butterflies" ("Observations upon the Study of the Latin and Greek Languages," in Rush, *Essays*, 39).

[57] *Federalist*, No. 12, 73-74.

in the general interest for the nobility to affect "that kind of pride, which looks down on commerce and manufactures as degrading." Reinforced by "the pompous trumpery of ensigns, armorials, and escutcheons," "the proud frivolities of heraldry," aristocratic prejudice might retard "the whole nation from being entirely delivered up to the spirit of avarice." Though these particular pretensions could only be considered mischievous and ridiculous in America,[58] the need for some countermeasures persisted. For in this respect America was no exception: an unrestrained indulgence in the passion for wealth would lead only to "cowardice, and a selfish, unsocial meanness," "a sordid scramble for money." To save "our bedollared country" from "the universal gangrene of avarice," Adams suggested making republican use of the rivals of ambition and pride of birth, thereby employing "one prejudice to counteract another."[59] All this befitted a man who knew something of himself and had hopes for his son. Individuals and indeed families might reasonably cherish qualities that set them apart and above—for example, a deserved reputation for public service in war and peace.[60] In a commercial republic such pretensions would be manageable, even indispensable. The solution, however, remained an uneasy one, and Adams himself wavered between hope and despair for his country.

Benjamin Rush's ambivalence toward commercialism is especially revealing. Though he did not think commercial wealth was necessarily fatal to republican liberty, he hastened to add parenthetically, "provided that commerce is not in the souls of men." For commerce, "when pursued closely, sinks the man into a machine."[61] And yet when considering the mode of education proper in a republic, he exalted commerce as right for America and for mankind. However much his taste as a private man was offended by a merchant class who "have little relish for the 'feast of reason and the flow of soul,'"[62] as a public man Rush could only be pleased by the promotion and triumph of the commercial mode of thought. "I consider commerce in a much higher light [than as a means of promoting public prosperity] when I

[58] Adams, ed., *Works of John Adams*, IV, 395. See also John Adams to James Warren, July 4, 1786, in Worthington C. Ford, ed., *Warren-Adams Letters: Being Chiefly a Correspondence among John Adams, Samuel Adams, and James Warren*, II (Massachusetts Historical Society, *Collections*, LXXIII [Boston, 1925]), 277.

[59] Adams, ed., *Works of John Adams*, VI, 270-271; Adams to Rush, June 20, 1808, in Schutz and Adair, eds., *Spur of Fame*, 110-111. See Mercy Warren, *History of the Rise, Progress and Termination of the American Revolution, Interspersed with Biographical, Political and Moral Observations*, III (Boston, 1804), 415.

[60] Peter Shaw, *The Character of John Adams* (Chapel Hill, N.C., 1976), 198-199, 232-235, 241, 315-316.

[61] L. H. Butterfield, ed., *Letters of Benjamin Rush*, I (Princeton, N.J., 1951), 285, 85. See also Crowley, *This Sheba, Self*, 99, 152.

[62] Butterfield, ed., *Letters of Rush*, I, 85. Rush was quoting from Pope's *Imitations of Horace: Satires*, Bk. 2, sat. 1, line 127.

recommend the study of it in republican seminaries. I view it as the best security against the influence of hereditary monopolies of land, and therefore, the surest protection against aristocracy."[63] In this perspective, the costs of commerce could be borne gladly.

The American Terminus

In the beginning, Locke asserted, all the world was America. In the end, Tocqueville predicted, all the world would be American. To speak of America, then, was to speak of man's fate, perhaps even of a divine decree. This country's rapid passage from a Lockean state of nature to a Tocquevillean democracy instructively telescoped the creation or emergence of the new man of commerce. The American democrat was the man of the future, an exemplar for humanity. He had adopted habits of mind and action that could not fail to be intelligible and attractive to most men everywhere. So, at any rate, Tocqueville thought; and in this he was not alone. In setting forth the American commercial republican as the new-model man, Tocqueville was simultaneously predicting and prescribing. In each case, however, he was beset by foreseeable certainties and by a sense that "the spirit of man walks through the night."[64] If we draw back from the margin of the providentially predestined circle and confine our speculations to things we can see with our own eyes, the reasons for his prescription emerge clearly enough.

Consider the spectacle of a united people spreading relentlessly over the land, a people who for all their present or future diversities and divisions were made one and kept one by their social state and by their habits, manners, and opinions. Whatever the future might bring, "the great Anglo-American family" would remain kinsmen by virtue of their equality of social condition, their taste for physical well-being, and their single-minded enterprise in seeking to gratify that taste. That much, at least, would remain both common and constant; "all else is doubtful, but that is sure."[65] Lifting our gaze above the fortuitous and peculiarly American features of this scene, we can detect what Tocqueville deemed fundamental for all men and all places in the new world aborning. As "the great bond of humanity is drawn tighter," men would become more equal, more comfortable, and more alike in conforming to some middling standard. Much of what set people against people and country against country would loosen its grip; all men, in a sense, would become votaries at the same shrine.[66] To this extent, the realm of freedom would be constricted. But though we are fated to live our lives as

[63] Rush, "Of the Mode of Education," in Runes, ed., Selected Writings of Rush, 94.
[64] Tocqueville, Democracy in America, 677.
[65] Ibid., 376-378.
[66] Ibid., 678-679.

members of the new egalitarian cosmopolitan regime, we are not without choices, choices that tax to the limit our strength, our will, and our art.[67] The province of statesmanship or of political science is preserved with Tocqueville's assurance (at the end of the second volume of *Democracy in America*) that it is up to us "whether equality is to lead to servitude or freedom, knowledge or barbarism, prosperity or wretchedness."[68] It is in the light of *that* choice that Tocqueville's recommendations are to be understood: a recommendation of the commercial republic, and a recommendation of those means consistent with the regime that are most likely to foster freedom, knowledge, and prosperity.

There was much in the commercial republic that Tocqueville found distasteful: its discreet sensualism, the counting-house character of its politics, the stifling of public spirit by the petty concerns of private life. But beyond the commercial republic, beyond "America," was the alternative: not Greece or Rome, not "China,"[69] but "Russia." The grand and awesome alternatives with which Tocqueville ended *Democracy in America* were prefigured (at the conclusion of the first volume) by the contrast between "Russia" and "America." He insisted that the servitude and centralization of the one were as compatible with egalitarianism as were the freedom and individualism of the other.[70] Indeed, that equality of condition which Tocqueville would have us regard as a providential fact, a fated certainty, might more easily be manifest in servitude than in the kind of independence that crumbles into anarchy.[71] If, in one sense, "Russia" is literally Russia—a harsh, barbarous despotism, an atavism totally apart from the modern egalitarian tendency—in another sense it may be Tocqueville's relevant cautionary example of the vast and terrible power that can be generated by uniformity and concentration. The saving grace of "America," then, and of the commercial republic for which it stands, is the way in which it "relies on personal interest and gives free scope to the unguided strength and common sense of individuals."[72] "Trade makes men independent of one another and gives them a high idea of their personal importance; it leads them to want to manage their own affairs and teaches them how to succeed therein."[73] But for all its utility, even necessity, commerce may not be sufficient. For though commerce was part of Tocqueville's solution, it also was part of Tocqueville's

[67] *Ibid.*, 679-680, 649, and cf. 55.
[68] *Ibid.*, 680.
[69] A code-word for the limp, prosperous barbarism that a civilized people can impose on itself. *Ibid.*, 82, n. 50, 431, 512, 605-606.
[70] Consider an analogous kind of equality of condition that Tocqueville saw as having prevailed in the Roman empire at the time of Christianity's origin. *Ibid.*, 411.
[71] *Ibid.*, 643.
[72] *Ibid.*, 378-379.
[73] *Ibid.*, 612.

problem. To counter the forces that press in on modern men and narrow their souls, Tocqueville looked to the commercial man's predisposition to liberty. Yet commerce may also predispose men to acquiesce in a new type of oppression—not the naked personal power of a Muscovite czar, but the gloved and masked impersonal power of a modern "sovereign, whatever its origin or constitution or name." Faced with an alternative that would degrade men into "a flock of timid and hard-working animals,"[74] Tocqueville searched for the highest grounds on which he could justify men's "strongest remaining guarantee against themselves."[75]

That search led him to "the doctrine of self-interest as preached in America." Most generally stated, men are more preoccupied with wants they feel than with needs they must reason about. And oddly enough, a system that frees men to try to satisfy their physical wants is more apt than any likely alternative to lead them to see their need for liberty. More apt, that is, if their egoism were enlightened, if each (as with the Americans) "has the sense to sacrifice some of his private interests to save the rest." But where a political system failed to instruct and encourage men in this calculated self-restraint and failed to show them that what is right may also be useful, there could be neither freedom nor public peace nor social stability. Where each (as with the Europeans) insisted on keeping the lot for himself, he often ended up losing the lot.[76] Tocqueville, like some predecessors of his, could praise and recommend the commercial republican way of life because it can go beyond accommodating itself to our weaknesses. It also invites us to "try to attain that form of greatness and of happiness which is proper to ourselves."[77] Tocqueville, like a successor of his, might well have called this the last, best hope of earth.

[74] *Ibid.*, 666-668, 675.
[75] *Ibid.*, 499.
[76] *Ibid.*
[77] *Ibid.*, 679.

Republican Revisionism Revisited

ISAAC KRAMNICK

FOR OVER A HUNDRED YEARS the world of scholarship agreed that Locke was the patron saint of Anglo-American ideology in the eighteenth century and that liberalism with its stress on individuality and private rights was the dominant ideal in that enlightened and revolutionary era. For the Victorian Leslie Stephen, it was self-evident that "Locke expounded the Principles of the Revolution of 1688 and his writings became the political bible of the following century." For the more recent Harold Laski, it was equally clear that Lockean liberalism dominated English political thought in the eighteenth century. Colonial Americans, it was assumed, were also schooled on Locke and became, in fact, his most self-conscious disciples. Thus, for Carl Becker, "the lineage is direct, Jefferson copied Locke," and, for Merle Curti, the "Great Mr. Locke" was "America's philosopher." Louis Hartz has summarized this scholarly consensus. "Locke," he wrote in 1955, "dominates American political thought as no thinker anywhere dominates the political thought of a nation."[1]

As it comes to all orthodoxies, revisionism has set in, and this received wisdom has been assaulted with a vengeance. Over the last twenty years a fundamental reinterpretation of Anglo-American eighteenth-century social and political thought has occurred. The liberal individualist heritage preoccupied with private rights has, to a great extent, been replaced by a republican tradition emphasizing citizenship and public participation, a tradition with roots deep in the classical and Renaissance worlds. Fundamental to this republican revisionism has been rethinking the hegemony of Locke. As Stanley N. Katz has noted,

This essay was written at the Center for Advanced Study in the Behavioral Sciences during academic year 1979–80. Many thanks go to its splendid, hospitable staff as well as to the National Endowment for the Humanities, whose grant to the center allowed me to be there. I should also thank Professor Philip Siegelman of San Francisco State, who once again was the catalyst for my work. His invitation to participate in the Western Political Science Association's Spring 1980 meetings was the prod to get some of this on paper in its original form. Professors Jack Greene and Joyce Appleby both read and criticized the completed essay. I am in their debt for their constructive comments. Final acknowledgment is due Professor J. G. A. Pocock, part of whose seminal scholarship I depart from here. That he has set the terms of discourse within which we may debate should be self-evident.
[1] Stephen, *A History of English Thought in the Eighteenth Century*, Harbinger edn., 2 (New York, 1962): 114; Laski, *The Rise of European Liberalism* (New York, 1936), and *Political Thought in England from Locke to Bentham* (New York, 1920); Becker, *The Declaration of Independence: A Study in the History of Political Ideas* (New York, 1922), 79; Curti, "The Great Mr. Locke, America's Philosopher, 1783–1861," *Huntington Library Bulletin*, no. 11 (1939): 107–51; and Hartz, *The Liberal Tradition in America* (New York, 1955), 140.

Locke et praetera nihil, it now appears, will no longer do as a motto for the study of eighteenth century Anglo-American political thought. The state of nature, doctrine of consent, and theory of natural rights were not as important before 1776 as the ideas of mixed government, separation of powers and a balanced constitution. We are only in the opening phases of a major reassessment of our constitutional heritage.[2]

Replacing Locke as the vital center of political discourse in the century is the country, opposition ideology of the Walpole years. In turn, these ideas are themselves read as part of a larger tradition—the civic humanist, or republican, tradition.

The revisionist school makes two distinct claims. The first de-emphasizes the role of Lockean ideas in the early eighteenth century. The second questions Locke's influence on the entire century, including the radicalism of post-Wilkes England and the ideology of the American founding. In its first claim, revisionism is on solid ground. Locke deserves the de-emphasis he has received for the early part of the century. In its second claim, however, the revisionist position is much more dubious; here it has gone too far.

THE REPUBLICAN, REVISIONIST READING has replaced Lockean liberalism with civic humanism. Part Aristotle, part Cicero, part Machiavelli, civic humanism conceives of man as a political being whose realization of self occurs only through participation in public life, through active citizenship in a republic. The virtuous man is concerned primarily with the public good, *res publica*, or commonweal, not with private or selfish ends. Seventeenth-century writers like James Harrington and Algernon Sidney adapted this tradition, especially under the influence of Machiavelli (according to J. G. A. Pocock),[3] to a specifically English context. This significantly English variant of civic humanism, "neo-Machiavellianism" or "neo-Harringtonianism," became, through the writings of early eighteenth-century English Augustans like Davenant, Trenchard, Gordon, and especially Henry St. John, Viscount Bolingbroke, the ideological core of the "country" ideology that confronted Walpole and his "court" faction. Bolingbroke provided a crucial link in this intellectual chain by associating corruption with social and political themes,[4] a critical concept in the language of eighteenth-century politics. Much richer than simple venality or fraud, the concept is enveloped by the Machiavellian image of historical change: corruption is the absence of civic virtue. Corrupt man is preoccupied with self and oblivious to the public good. Such failures of moral personality, such degeneration from the fundamental commitment to public life,

---

[2] Katz, "The Origins of American Constitutional Thought," *Perspectives in American History*, 3 (1969): 474. Also see Robert E. Shalhope, "Toward a Republican Synthesis: The Emergence of an Understanding of Republicanism in American Historiography," *William and Mary Quarterly*, 29 (1972): 49–80.

[3] For J. G. A. Pocock's arguments, see his *The Machiavellian Moment: Florentine Political Thought and the Atlantic Republican Tradition* (Princeton, 1975), "Virtue and Commerce in the Eighteenth Century," *Journal of Interdisciplinary History*, 3 (1972): 119–34, *Politics, Language, and Time: Essays on Political Thought and History* (New York, 1971), and "Early Modern Capitalism—The Augustan Perception," in Eugene Kamenka and R. S. Neale, eds., *Feudalism, Capitalism, and Beyond* (Canberra, 1975).

[4] See my *Bolingbroke and His Circle: The Politics of Nostalgia in the Age of Walpole* (Cambridge, Mass., 1968).

fuel the decline of states and can be remedied only through periodic revitalization by returning to the original and pristine commitment to civic virtue. Calls for such renewals, for *ridurre ai principii* (Machiavelli's phrase), form the response to corruption.

Bolingbroke's achievement was to appropriate this republican and Machiavellian language for the social and economic tensions developing in Augustan England over the rise of government credit, public debt, and central banking as well as for political issues, such as Walpole's control of Parliament through patronage or concern over standing armies. Themes of independence and dependence, so critical to the republican tradition (the former essential to any commitment to the public good), were deployed by Bolingbroke into a social map of independent country proprietors opposing placemen and stock jobbers and a political map of a free Parliament opposing a despotic court. In addition, Bolingbroke stamped this eighteenth-century republican-country tradition with its socially conservative and nostalgic quality, in terms of not only its anticommercialism but also its antiegalitarianism. But this court-country reading eschews class analysis, at least in terms of the conventional dichotomy of progressive bourgeoisie and reactionary aristocracy. Its categories and frames of reference are older and more complicated.

To a great extent, the innovative scholarship of J. G. A. Pocock has shaped this new way of looking at English political thought. His writings on Harrington and his magisterial *Machiavellian Moment* (1975) have made the concept of civic humanism a strikingly useful tool with which to understand the political mind of late seventeenth- and early eighteenth-century England. The more ambitious extension of civic humanism's reign, however, is questionable. In the hands of Pocock and others, like John Murrin and Lance Banning, this insightful reading of early eighteenth-century politics through Bolingbroke's dichotomy of virtuous country and corrupt court does not stop with Augustan England. It becomes the organizing paradigm for the language of political thought in England as well as America throughout the entire century.[5] As a result, revisionism in this second claim also insists on the irrelevance of class in political discourse, which in conventional progressive or liberal scholarship has been linked to the later decades of the century via the emergence of the Industrial Revolution. Analyses of the late eighteenth-century that refer to class consciousness or conflicting class ideologies or that use concepts such as aristocracy, capitalist, feudal, or bourgeois are thus dismissed by republican scholarship as simplistic and proleptic. Challenges to the "primacy" or "omnipresence" of "civic ideology," of "Aristotelian and civic humanist values," derived throughout the century not from "simple bourgeois ideology" or from visions of "economic" or "capitalist man" but from a court ideology, part commercial and part elite, that was not representative of a class in any conventional sense. There is no dialectical tension between middle and upper classes. To claim it existed is to engage in "much distortion of history." There is for Pocock only one

---

[5] For Murrin, see his "The Great Inversion, or Court versus Country: A Comparison of the Revolution Settlements in England (1688–1721) and America (1776–1816)," in J. G. A. Pocock, ed., *Three British Revolutions: 1641, 1688, 1776* (Princeton, 1980), 368–455; and, for Banning, see his *The Jeffersonian Persuasion: Evolution of a Party Ideology* (Ithaca, N.Y., 1978).

proper dialectical reading, which sees everywhere "the dialectic of virtue and commerce." All of Anglo-American political thought in the eighteenth century involves, then, "a continuation, larger and more irreconcilable of that Augustan debate."[6]

Locke and possessive individualism in this scheme have obviously had to go.[7] And a chorus of distinguished scholars have joined John Dunn in de-emphasizing the importance of Locke throughout eighteenth-century Anglo-American thought. "Eighteenth century English political thought," according to Gordon Wood, "perhaps owed more to Machiavelli and Montesquieu than it did to Locke." Indeed, Bernard Bailyn has persuasively argued that "the effective triggering convictions that lay behind the [American] Revolution were derived not from common Lockean generalities but from the specific fears and formulations of the radical publicists and opposition politicians of early eighteenth century England."[8]

J. G. A. Pocock has been the most insistent in repudiating Locke's influence on the entire century. He has seen the history of political thought "dominated by a fiction of Locke," whose importance "has been wildly distorted." He and others are engaged in what he has called "a shattering demolition of [Locke's] myth." Their concern is to prove that the predominant language of politics for the eighteenth century, even for its radicals, "is one of virtue, corruption and reform, which is Machiavellian, classical and Aristotelian, and in which Locke himself did not figure." What we have come to, Pocock has insisted, is the end of "the image of a monolithically Lockean eighteenth century," the end of "a convention of writing as if Locke dominated the thought of the eighteenth century, and imposed on it a pattern of liberal individualism." Indeed, he concluded, to understand the debates of eighteenth-century politics does "not necessitate reference to Locke at all."[9]

Pocock has applied this revisionist verdict about Locke to an alternative reading of America and its founding. American political culture has been haunted by myths, the most mistaken of which is the role of Locke as "the patron saint of American values." The proper interpretation "stresses Machiavelli at the expense of Locke." The Revolution was, Pocock wrote, "the last great act of the Renaissance . . . emerging from a line of thought which staked everything on a positive and civic concept of the individual's virtue." The Revolution was a Machiavellian *rinnovazionne* in a new world, "a republican commitment to the renovation of virtue." America was born in a "dread of modernity," according to Pocock. In its early years "the country ideology ran riot." The debate over Hamilton's economic policies in the 1790s "was a replay of court-country debates seventy and a hundred years earlier." In Jefferson's polemics, however, "the spirit of Bolingbroke stalked

[6] Pocock, "Virtue and Commerce in the Eighteenth Century," 130–34.

[7] The term "possessive individualism" is, of course, C. B. Macpherson's from *The Political Theory of Possessive Individualism: From Hobbes to Locke* (Oxford, 1962), and his reading of Locke significantly informs mine.

[8] Dunn, "The Politics of Locke in England and America in the Eighteenth Century," in John W. Yolton, ed., *John Locke: Problems and Perspectives* (Cambridge, 1969), 45–80; Wood, *The Creation of the American Republic* (New York, 1972), 29; and Bailyn, *The Origins of American Politics* (New York, 1972), ix–x, 56–58. Also see Bailyn's *The Ideological Origins of the American Revolution* (Cambridge, Mass., 1976).

[9] Pocock, *The Machiavellian Moment*, 424, "Virtue and Commerce in the Eighteenth Century," 124, 127, 129, and *Politics, Language, and Time*, 144.

on every page." John Murrin concurred. The Jeffersonians, he wrote, "like an English country opposition . . . idealized the past more than the future and feared significant change, especially major economic change, as corruption and degeneration."[10] Welcome from this perspective, then, is Gary Wills's recent book on Jefferson's Declaration of Independence. Wills, too, got rid of Locke, but, behind Jefferson, he saw not Locke but Hutcheson and the Scottish Enlightenment.[11]

Perhaps the best summary of this more ambitious school of revisionist scholarship in making the claim for both the early and late eighteenth century can be found in Donald Winch's recent work on Adam Smith. Winch set out to rescue Smith from those who have misread him as a theorist of individualism and liberal capitalism, from what Winch has labeled as Marxist and Whig scholarship—"Those who come to bury capitalism as well as those who come to praise it." To so read Smith is to disregard "the remarkable body of revisionist literature" that depicts the entire eighteenth century free of Locke and free of the bourgeoisie:

Those political theorists and historians who are committed,. for one present-minded reason or another, to the enterprise of constructing a genealogy of liberal or bourgeois individualism which is continuous from Locke to the nineteenth century and beyond have suffered a major casualty as a result of recent research on eighteenth century political thought and ideology. That casualty is no less a figure than Locke himself, the "founder" of liberal constitutionalism.

Winch then described "the remarkable historiographic upheaval . . . which converges on the conclusion that Locke's *Two Treatises* [*sic*] was of strictly limited significance to many of the most lively as well as profound developments which took place in Anglo-American political thought during the eighteenth century." Nor were the traditional issues of liberalism important. Political thought in the period, Winch concluded, "owed far less to Locke's concern with questions of obligation, original contract, and natural rights than was originally thought to be the case."[12]

It has, indeed, been a "remarkable historiographic upheaval." Republican revisionism has sharpened our perceptions of the ideological currents operating in the eighteenth century, but its two claims must remain distinct. Revisionism has informed us of the continuity and hold of older political and cultural ideals, competing with a Lockean emphasis on natural rights and individualism, on the early eighteenth-century mind. But, in seeking to free the entire eighteenth century of Locke, of socioeconomic radicalism, and of bourgeois liberalism, this new broom has also swept away much that is truth.

There are serious difficulties in applying to Anglo-American politics after 1760 the model of court and country or the dialectic of virtue and commerce. These difficulties derive from the basic revisionist assumption of a continuous meaning throughout the century of concepts like corruption and virtue. The nostalgia,

---

[10] Pocock, *The Machiavellian Moment*, 469, 529, 548, and "Virtue and Commerce in the Eighteenth Century," 130–31, 134; and Murrin, "The Great Inversion, or Court versus Country," 406.

[11] Wills, *Inventing America: Jefferson's Declaration of Independence* (New York, 1978).

[12] Winch, *Adam Smith's Politics: An Essay in Historiographic Revision* (Cambridge, 1978), 28, 36, 41, 54, 180.

hierarchialism, and anticommercialism of the earlier part of the century cannot be that easily read into the later years of the century. A study of the writings and politics of British reformers from 1760 to 1800 illustrates the problematic nature of such a reading. Is Locke irrelevant to the reformers' radicalism? Are their ideological paradigms republicanism and civic humanism? Is theirs the politics of nostalgia untainted by bourgeois liberal or individualist ideals?

THE VERDICT OF RECENT REPUBLICAN SCHOLARSHIP is that Locke and progressive liberal ideals were, in fact, unimportant in the agitation for parliamentary reform in Britain from the 1760s through the French Revolution. Relying heavily on the work of British historians like Herbert Butterfield and Ian Christie, the revisionists emphasize the nostalgic and even reactionary quality of the reform movement.[13] What were being sought were lost historical rights, Anglo-Saxon rights. Alternatively, the reformers were country ideologues concerned only with mixed government and an independent House of Commons. Republican scholarship denies that any social or economic motives or grievances were at work among the reformers, either democratic or bourgeois. Continuity and nostalgia are the key, not radical appeals to abstractions like the rights of man or nature. In such a configuration of ideas, Locke is seldom to be found.

For Pocock, the reform movement was simply civic humanism and country rage. "Georgian radicals in the era of the Revolutionary War and its aftermath used a language indistinguishable from that of their American peers." That same language of corruption and virtue was being used "against the ministries of George III," by the foes of Bute "and the friends of Wilkes." This was no casual flirtation with the language of civic humanism by the radicals. Pocock has noted that the country ideology of republican virtue that the Americans adopted "had originated in England and was still very much in use there. In the minds of James Burgh, John Cartwright, or Richard Price, it was as obsessive and terrifying as in any American mind." It was "the conceptual framework" behind "radical demands for parliamentary and franchise reform." In *The Machiavellian Moment*, Wyvill, Price, and Cartwright are described as using "a vocabulary of corruption and renovation little different from that of their American contemporaries." In an earlier article, Pocock placed Burgh, Wilkes, the Yorkshire movement, the Society for Constitutional Information, and, *miracula mirabilis*, John Thelwell in the tradition of country and civic humanism. They are "key points in the long continuous history of a political language and its concepts." The terminology and ideas of country ideology, Pocock has concluded, "were extensively borrowed by the radical left when one began to appear in George III's reign."[14]

---

[13] See Butterfield, *George III, Lord North, and the People, 1779–80* (London, 1949), esp. 229–56, 337–52; and Christie, *Myth and Reality in Late Eighteenth-Century British Politics and Other Papers* (London, 1970), "Introduction" to G. S. Vetch, *The Genesis of Parliamentary Reform* (London, 1964), and *Wilkes, Wyvill, and Reform* (London, 1962).

[14] Pocock, "Virtue and Commerce in the Eighteenth Century," 133, 122, *The Machiavellian Moment*, 507, 547, and *Politics, Language, and Time*, 133, 145–46. Also see Ian Hampshire-Monk, "Civic Humanism and Parliamentary Reform: The Case of the Society of the Friends of the People," *Journal of British Studies*, 18

This backward-looking reading of British reform is shared by Gordon Wood, who has also described Price, Burgh, and even Paine as members of this camp of virtue-obsessed republicans.[15] Bernard Bailyn has agreed:

The leaders of the [American] Revolutionary movement were radicals—but they were eighteenth century radicals concerned, like the eighteenth century English radicals, not with the need to recast the social order nor with the problems of economic inequality and the injustice of stratified societies but with the need to purify a corrupt constitution and fight off the apparent growth of prerogative power.[16]

But this essay offers a very different reading of these radicals and of British reform in general between 1760 and the French Revolution. Locke was very much alive and well in their arguments.

The radicals of the later eighteenth century, both English and American, were much more likely to base their arguments on natural rights than on historical rights; they were preoccupied less with nostalgic country concerns than with very modern socioeconomic grievances. They shared a deeply felt sense that the unreformed British constitution failed to serve the interests of the talented and hard-working middle class.[17] Locke was, indeed, unimportant to the earlier Augustan country ideology. Its basic hierarchical commitment, in fact, led Bolingbroke to repudiate all notions of the state of nature with its egalitarian overtones.[18] But two great historical developments operated to change the context of ideological discourse and most especially among the radicals. The 1760s represent the crucial turning point. The concerns of the earlier part of the century—the mixed constitution, annual Parliaments, the independent Commons, anti–place legislation, and the standing army controversy—were shunted aside. America and the crisis over taxation introduced new noncountry issues into politics. The taxation controversy raised to the center of debate the issue of representation, which in its trail brought to the fore basic concerns about the origins of government and authority in general. Taxation was the curse of all, yet few were enfranchised. Emphasizing taxation flew in the face of ideas of virtual representation and expanded the notion of property beyond landed wealth or freehold. What this emphasis on movable property did, as John Brewer has noted, was to enable radicals like Burgh and Cartwright to extend "the debate about parliamentary reform far beyond its previous confines."[19] It transcended the paradigms of country ideology to more class-based categories.

[15] Wood, The Creation of the American Republic, 21, 23, 36, 47, 56–57, 92, 100.

[16] Bailyn, The Ideological Origins of the American Revolution, 283.

[17] This is by no means to take the case as far as Staughton Lynd has in his Intellectual Origins of American Radicalism (New York, 1969). He was quite correct in stressing the social content of the English radicals read by Americans during the revolutionary era but quite wrong in reading this content as critical of private property.

[18] Kramnick, Bolingbroke and His Circle, 95–106. Also see my "An Augustan Reply to Locke: Bolingbroke on Natural Law and the Origin of Government," Political Science Quarterly, 82 (1967): 571–94.

[19] As should be clear, I share this point of view with John Brewer, who has argued it brilliantly in his Party Ideology and Popular Politics at the Accession of George III (Cambridge, 1977), 255. This essay does not address, except in passing, the question of Locke in America during these years. Others, like Joyce Appleby and Ronald Hamowy, are at work questioning republican revisionism on that score. It might be noted here, however, that, if Locke was indeed alive and well in the circles of British reform during these later eighteenth-century years, there must be a high presumption he thrived in America too, if only because writers like Burgh, Price, and

Figure 1: "The Friends of the People." In this Cruickshank caricature (1792), Thomas Paine and Dr. Priestley conspire under diabolical supervision. Note that Priestley sits on gunpowder; a famous speech in which he referred to toppling the religious establishment earned him the nickname "Gunpowder Joe." Reproduced courtesy of the British Library.

The American crisis coincided with a second crucial development, the early years of the Industrial Revolution and the emergence of a new middle-class radicalism. The first decades of industrialization in England saw, as D. E. C. Eversley has calculated, a greatly expanding middling level of English society, families with an income between £50 and £400. This "free, mobile, prudent section of the population" was turning to politics.[20] These owners of small and movable property, as well as the new entrepreneurs like Wedgwood and Wilkinson, felt excluded from a political process that affected them daily in their credit transactions, in their tax burden, and in the proliferation of intrusive statute law.[21]

Priestley were the staple reading of Americans in the revolutionary era. See Appleby, "The Social Origins of American Revolutionary Ideology," *Journal of American History*, 64 (1977–78): 935–58, and "Thomas Jefferson and the Interpreters of Nostalgia," *William and Mary Quarterly* (in press); and Hamowy, "Jefferson and Scottish Enlightenment: A Critique of Gary Wills' *Inventing America*," *ibid.*, 36 (1979): 503–23. Also see earlier investigations of the relation between English and American radical thought: Thad W. Tate, "The Social Contract in America, 1774–1787: Revolutionary Theory as a Conservative Instrument," *William and Mary Quarterly*, 22 (1965): 375–91; and Curti, "The Great Mr. Locke, America's Philosopher," 107–51. For the vogue of English radicals in America, see the writings of Bailyn and Wood. Also see Lynd, *Intellectual Origins of American Radicalism*; Jack P. Greene, "Political Mimesis: A Consideration of the Historical and Cultural Roots of Legislative Behavior in the British Colonies in the Eighteenth Century," *AHR*, 75 (1969–70): 337–60; Pauline Maier, *From Resistance to Revolution: Colonial Radicals and the Development of American Opposition to Britain, 1765–1776* (New York, 1972); Oscar Handlin and Mary Handlin, "James Burgh and American Revolutionary Theory," *Proceedings of the Massachusetts Historical Society*, 73 (1963): 38–57; Edward I. Morgan, "Slavery and Freedom: The American Paradox," *Journal of American History*, 59 (1972–73): 5–29; Nicholas Hans, "Franklin, Jefferson, and the English Radicals at the End of the Eighteenth Century," *Proceedings of the American Philosophical Society*, 98 (1954): 406–22; H. Trevor Colburn, *The Lamp of Experience: Whig History and the Intellectual Origins of the American Revolution* (Chapel Hill, 1965); and Colin Bonwick, *English Radicals and the American Revolution* (Chapel Hill, 1977).

[20] Eversley, "The Home Market and Economic Growth in England, 1750–1780," in E. C. Jones and G. E. Mingay, eds., *Land, Labour, and Population in the Industrial Revolution: Essays Presented to J. D. Chambers* (London, 1967), 206–59.

[21] See John Brewer, "English Radicalism in the Age of George III," in Pocock, *Three British Revolutions: 1641, 1688, 1776*, 334–36.

This is not to dismiss out of hand the existence of lingering country content in the radical ideology of Wilkes, Burgh, Cartwright, or Sawbridge. It had been, after all, the ideological reflex of the excluded for a century. Calls for frequent elections and a reformed suffrage along with attacks on placemen were often still uttered in the Machiavellian language of corruption, restoration of first principles, and historical analogies from Roman history. But beneath the familiar surface of the new radicalism that began to emerge during the 1760s were different themes. The new radicalism goes beyond the praise of wise and virtuous landed MPs independent of both the crown and constituent pressure. It goes beyond the Rockingham Whigs' sense that all was well with the political system and that only a change of leadership in which men of virtue replaced wicked men was needed to end "the present discontents." In the new radicalism, there is a new dimension, the conviction that those now excluded—the urban and commercial interests—wanted "in," wanted to be represented in Parliament and wanted their MPs to be their spokesmen, serving their interests, not serving as wise men independent of both court and those who elected them. Thus, in their anger, the new radicals turn on *both* the landed classes and the court-government.

Precisely in this context of a critical shift in the nature and aims of the opposition, Lockean ideas made a dramatic and decisive comeback in the 1760s and 1770s. In Locke far more than in Bolingbroke and his ilk, the unenfranchised middle class and especially the Protestant dissenters found intellectual authority and legitimacy for their radical demands. Locke's ideas reflecting the revolutionary upheavals of the previous century spoke more directly to a Burgh, a Paine, or a Priestley than did the nostalgia of a St. John, a Pope, or a Swift.

The revival of Lockean influence is apparent in the pamphlet that contained the first important call for the reform of Parliament. The anonymous *Reflexions on Representation in Parliament* was published in 1766. Although the pamphlet ostensibly provides a sympathetic reading of James Otis's arguments on taxation and representation, over its defense of the colonies and its plea for reform of the suffrage hovers the spirit of John Locke. The author expounded the principles of the British constitution, offering an idea "of what it was in its original purity." This could well have been the civic humanist quest for first principles or the search for lost Anglo-Saxon rights, but it was instead a search for "principles of truth and reason." At the heart of these principles is the "cession which every man, on entering into civil government makes of some of his natural rights, to enjoy the rest in greater security." On the principles of "equity," the author demanded an "equal representation in Commons." (The Saxon past is cited, but the justification for "equal" representation is the ahistorical "principle of equity.") Representation is "a question of right." The pamphlet ends with a direct invocation of "the celebrated assertions of Mr. Locke's . . . that there remains still inherent in the people a supreme power to remove or alter the legislature, when they find the legislative act contrary to the trust reposed in them; for when such trust is abused it is thereby forfeited and desolves to those who gave it."[22]

Locke, whose principles "so favour the natural rights of mankind," is central to

[22] *Reflexions on Representation in Parliament* (London, 1766), 4, 6–7.

this opening salvo in the campaign to reform Parliament, and his use here set the pattern for the next thirty years. His notion of contract, of governors as trustees, subject to dismissal if they forfeited this trust, was the intellectual weaponry used in the assault on the unreformed Commons. This is abundantly clear in Wilkes's agitation and its offshoot, the Society of the Supporters of the Bill of Rights. By 1771 the society, led by Horne Tooke, had moved from merely defending Wilkes's right to a seat in Commons to offering a comprehensive program for parliamentary reform. Central to that program was an oath to be required of all parliamentary candidates that they "endeavour to obtain a more fair and equal representation of the people." Echoes of the 1766 pamphlet are clear. Equitable and equal became "fair and equal." John Wilkes moved in the House of Commons on March 21, 1776, "that leave be given to bring in a bill, for a just and equal representation of the people of England in Parliament." In his speech he cited "the present unfair and inadequate state of the representation of the people in Parliament. It has now become so partial and unequal from the lapse of time."[23] The language used in Wilkes's bill is important. For the next thirty years the reform movement used the phrases "fair and equal representation" and "just and equal representation." This abstract language of reason and nature does not derive from specific calculations from the Saxon past, and the principal author of these abstract phrases is none other than John Locke.

In a most striking case of historical oversight, few who have written on this period have noted that this formulation, so central to reform politics and writing for the remainder of the eighteenth century, is lifted directly from Locke, who in paragraphs 157 and 158 of *The Second Treatise of Government* wrote,

> It often comes to pass that in government where part of the legislative consists of representatives chosen by the people that by tract of time this representation becomes very unequal and disproportionate to the reasons it was at first established. . . . For it being the interest as well as intention of the people to have a fair and equal representative, whoever brings it nearest to that is an undoubted friend to and establisher of the government and cannot miss the consent and approbation of the community.[24]

The key phrase of the reform movement was Locke's of nearly one hundred years earlier. Scholars' failure to note the textual derivation from Locke is all the more striking since most eighteenth-century users of the "fair and equal" demand cited Locke as their authority. So it was that Wilkes in his speech of March 21, 1776, noted that "this evil has been complained of by some of the wisest patriots our country has produced. I shall beg leave to give that close reasoner, Mr. Locke's ideas in his own words. . . . [He then read paragraphs 157 and 158.] After so great an authority as that of Mr. Locke, I shall not be treated on this occasion as a mere visionary."[25]

---

[23] Wilkes, as quoted in Society for Constitutional Information, *Minutes of a Meeting on Friday 29th of March 1782* (London, 1782), 11–12. For Wilkes, see Christie, *Wilkes, Wyvill, and Reform;* and Brewer, *Party Ideology and Popular Politics,* chap. 9.

[24] Locke, *The Second Treatise of Government,* Library of the Liberal Arts (New York, 1952), 89–90. This link between Locke and the reformers in the late eighteenth century is not developed by either J. R. Pole or John Cannon; see Pole's *Political Representation in England and the Origins of the American Republic* (London, 1966), and Cannon's *Parliamentary Reform, 1640–1832* (Cambridge, 1973).

[25] Society for Constitutional Information, *Minutes,* 14–15.

Even more important than this textual linkage between Locke and the reformers, however, is the far deeper theoretical bond the reformers constructed between themselves and such Lockean themes as contract, state of nature, and natural rights and government as a trust in all of their writing on taxation and representation. This becomes evident by shifting the focus from Wilkes to more respectable and learned reformers. But Wilkes and his supporters both in London and in the provinces—by and large merchants, manufacturers, and entrepreneurs—forged the link for the enduring character of reform agitation: its antiaristocratic, middle-class bias. Wilkes the fool, Wilkes the court jester, was a living repudiation of hierarchical piety and the due subordination of rank and degree.[26]

John Cartwright, the grand old man of British reform, illustrates how Lockean ideas, not the more hierarchical views of country ideology, were at the heart of the reform movement. In his *Take Your Choice*, written in 1776, he noted that "the all wise creator hath likewise made men by nature equal as well as free. . . . None are set above others prior to mutual agreement." Freedom implies choice and equality excludes degrees in freedom. "All the commons have a right to vote in the elections of those who are to be the guardians of their lives and liberties . . . , and no man shall be taxed but with his own consent, given either by himself or his representative in parliament." The antiaristocratic flavor of the reform movement is apparent in Cartwright, too: "What right has 1/7 of the people who wear laced coats and eat white bread to tell 6/7 who have plain coats and eat brown bread that they have no right to interfere in the election . . . because their want of riches deprived them of many other indulgences, enjoyed by the wearers of laced coats and eaters of white bread?" The source of his arguments is nature, not history. Cartwright insisted that "mankind universally have in all ages had the same unalienable rights to liberty. . . . No charters, exclusions, prescriptions can add to or diminish this right."[27]

The middle years of the 1770s saw an outpouring of radical texts in England. The crisis with the colonies did, indeed, raise fundamental questions of authority and obligation, which the civic humanist reading of the period sees as secondary to themes of corruption and virtue. In 1774, for example, there appeared James Burgh's three-volume *Political Disquisitions*. Burgh ran the influential dissenter academy at Newington Green from 1747 to 1771. There he taught legions of dissenter youth and wrote his huge tome, which schooled generations of British radicals and their American cousins. Samuel Parr, when asked if he had read *Political Disquisitions*, is alleged to have replied, "Have I read my bible, sir?" Much has been made of Burgh's writings in constructing a case for nostalgic, civic humanist, country ideology at the heart of the reform movement.[28] There is, indeed, good reason for this claim. In his three volumes, Burgh often cited Bolingbroke, *Cato's Letters*, and even Mach..avelli. He also wrote at great length about an independent Commons, placemen, corruption, standing armies, annual

---

[26] For this picture of Wilkes, see Brewer, *Party Ideology and Popular Politics*, 197–99.

[27] Cartwright, *The Legislative Rights of the Communality Vindicated: or, Take Your Choice* (London, 1776), 1–2, 31, 27, 116–17.

[28] See, in addition to the literature cited in note 19, above, Carla H. Hay, "The Making of a Radical: The Case of James Burgh," *Journal of British Studies*, 18 (1978–79): 90–118. For the Parr anecdote, see *The Dictionary of National Biography*, s.v. "Burgh, James."

Parliaments, and lost Saxon rights. But there is much more to Burgh than this simple dependence on mid-eighteenth-century arguments and formulas, and it has generally been overlooked. He is very much in the Lockean individualist tradition, and he injected into the reform movement not only a strong dose of Locke but also a good deal of the bitter, middle-class resentment of the aristocratic quality of the British constitution.

Burgh began and ended his massive work with Locke. At the outset he provided a declaration of his political beliefs that is pure Locke. Authority originates from the people, who, he suggested, receive that power back when their governors betray their trust. When Burgh turned to the inadequate state of representation in Britain early in volume 1, the first authority cited on "the monstrous inequality of parliamentary representation" is Locke. Three volumes later, in concluding his huge tome, Burgh called for a popular association movement to push Parliament to reform. Here he again quoted Locke. Those who accept the trust of governing are answerable to the people, who can refuse obedience and take back power into their own hands. Locke is made the theorist of a popular movement against a corrupt legislature.[29]

Burgh was no disciple of Bolingbroke, no nostalgic country ideologue defending a gentry-based polity. Parliamentary reform for him formed part of a general assault on aristocratic England:

The landed interest is too well represented, to the detriment of the mercantile and monied. This is an occasion of various evils. For many of our country gentlemen are but bad judges of the importance of the mercantile interest, and do not wisely consult it in their bills and acts. . . . It is the overbalance of the power in the hands of the landed men, that has produced the bounty on exportation of grain which increases the manufacturers' expense of living, and discourages the exportation of our manufactures.

Burgh's attack on placemen, a perennial country opposition issue from the days of Walpole, is very different, however, from Bolingbroke's. Burgh was less incensed with placemen as threats to an independent Commons than he was with them as nonmeritorious, untalented officeholders, who denied the talented middle class access to public positions: "All honours and powers ought to be personal only, and to be given to no individuals, but such as upon scrutiny, were found to be men of such distinguished worth, as to deserve to be raised to distinguished places, though sprung of mean parents."[30]

Although now overshadowed by Godwin, Priestley, Price, and Paine, James Burgh through his *Political Disquisitions* was literally the schoolmaster for a whole generation of middle-class radicals in England and America, and it bears repeating that his critique was in large part a self-conscious apology for the assertive middle class. He railed against a British government that parceled out its profitable and prestigious jobs to the nobility and gentry who dominated Parliament. Why has the nobleman, he asked, any more claim to this respect than the artisan or manufacturer? "If the nobility and gentry declined to serve their country in the great offices of

[29] Burgh, *Political Disquisitions: An Enquiry into Public Errors, Defects, and Abuses*, 3 vols. (London, 1774): 1: 3–4, 72–73, 2: 279, and 3: 449.
[30] *Ibid.* 1: 51–53, and 2: 89–90.

Figure 2: "Smelling Out a Rat." In this Gilray caricature (1790), Burke, bearing the symbols of church and king, reveals himself to a startled Richard Price. Price was, of course, a distinguished mathematician. Reproduced courtesy of the British Library.

the state, without sordid hire, let the honest bourgeoisie be employed. They will themselves be sufficiently regarded by the honour done them." Rather than "half our nobility . . . and over drenched court sponges . . . being upon the parish" (that is, having public jobs), these jobs, he suggested, should go to men of merit. Burgh proposed, in fact, that public jobs, like public contracts, be filled by "sealed proposals." The talented individual most capable of serving his country would then be selected. If men of the meritorious middle class took over public service and Parliament, then public expenditures, he predicted, would decline dramatically, for these new men would not demand great salaries, they would not dance "at Mrs. Conneley's masquerades." They would "rise up early and sit up late and fill up the whole day with severe labour."[31]

This bourgeois demand for careers open to the talented was a most critical element in British reform during this period. It is Figaro's lament to the great Count Almaviva, translated for Englishmen in 1784 by Godwin's close friend, Thomas Holcroft: "What did you do to deserve what you have—nothing but to be born." It is Tom Paine's suggestion that what "nobility" really means is "no-ability."[32] The dissenting schoolmaster James Burgh was neither country apologist nor classical republican. His was an individualist ideology of an insurgent middle class. In America and in Britain, he wrote, the dissenters have rejected the ways of the aristocracy and the poor. They have "bounded" their "riotous appetites" and their "lusts." They have turned their backs on gaming, drunkenness, lewdness, operas, cockfighting, and the theater. Dissenter "sobriety and temperate ways of living," "their thrift and regular manner of living," their awareness "that every

[31] *Ibid.*, 2: 97–98.
[32] Paine, *The Rights of Man*, ed. H. Collins, Penguin Books (London, 1969), 128.

moment of time ought to be put to its proper use," their "industriousness," and
their "order and regularity" have produced prosperity and wealth. But to what avail
is such talent and merit? What are the rewards in an aristocratic society for such
achievement, when "the people may be brought, by inveterate tyranny, to bear
patiently to see the most worthless part of mankind (for surely the great by mere
birth, in all ages and countries are commonly among the most worthless of
mankind) set up above them and themselves obliged to crouch"? Sometimes, of
course, such "tyranny" becomes too much to bear: "And if the people rouse to
vengeance, woe to those who stand in the way. Let merit only be honoured with
privilege and prerogative, and mankind will be contented."[33]

Richard Price's *Observations on the Nature of Civil Liberty*, another critical text in the
reform tradition, appeared in 1776. Price did not leave room for doubt about his
source, for in his preface he noted that "the principles on which I have argued form
the foundation of every state as far as it is free; and are the same with those taught
by Mr. Locke." Government for Price is a trust, in which the people set up
governors to serve particular ends. When the trust is betrayed, government is
dissolved. Price insisted that the rights of the Americans are the natural rights of all
free men, not the product of history, tradition, statute, charter, or precedent. The
enemies of the colonists, like Josiah Tucker, condemned the American colonists,
Price noted, by calling them "Mr. Locke's disciples." "What a glorious title," Price
replied.[34]

Price's praise of America provides an interesting insight into the Lockean world
view, which so prompted British reformers to excitement when they looked to
America. America was, as Locke himself had noted, as it was "in the beginning."
Price and others saw America as a land of individual freedom and equality, where
hierarchy and subordination were unknown. The colonies had no rich or poor, he
wrote, no beggars and no "haughty grandees." The Americans were strangers to
luxury, and they worked hard. There was no large government, and there were
few taxes. Most important of all, Price claimed, in America merit was the only path
to distinction.[35] To his dying day, Price repeated these themes: in his speech in 1789
and in his *Discourse on the Love of Country*, which so infuriated Burke that he
answered with his *Reflections on the Revolution in France*. In the sermon at Old Jewry
in 1789, Price alleged that the greatest defect of the British constitution was
representational inequality and that its remedy lay in a representational structure
that was "fair and equal"—Locke again.[36]

There are, to be sure, other strains in Richard Price's work. There is, for
example, a deeply pessimistic tone in much of his writings, especially in his repeated
fears over the national debt—fears that are also found in the writings of Horne

---

[33] Burgh, *Political Disquisitions*, 3: 30, 172, 425. Also see his *The Dignity of Human Nature* (London, 1754), 33.
[34] Price, *Observations on the Nature of Civil Liberty, the Principles of Government, and the Justice and Policy of the War with America* (London, 1776), ix, 16, 32, 93.
[35] Price, *Observations on the Importance of the American Revolution and the Means of Making It a Benefit to the World* (London, 1784), 68–70.
[36] Price, *A Discourse on the Love of Our Country Delivered November 4, 1789* (London, 1789), 39.

Tooke and James Burgh and, indeed, in the work of most of the radicals.[37] Given as well Price's fascination for the independent farmer in his writings on America, republican scholarship does seem to have a point in insisting that such as Price are not individualist liberals and optimistic modernizers who speak for an insurgent middle class but antimarket nostalgics steeped in civic humanism's "Renaissance pessimism" over the direction of social change and the inevitability of degeneration and decline. In short, the English radicals and their American counterpart Jefferson seem to be direct descendants of Bolingbroke.

There are, however, serious problems with this republican reading. Space here does not permit a full discussion of the rich symbolism of the national debt, and the credit system in general, in Anglo-American political discourse in the eighteenth century. Suffice it to note that by the end of the century criticisms of the debt, of paper money, and of banks and, in turn, praise of independent farmers could not automatically be translated into a politics of nostalgia or a repudiation of capitalism or even of urbanism. Fear of national ruin from an ever-growing national debt was as widespread in the entrepreneurial and manufacturing circles as it was among the middle-class intellectuals in the dissenting chapels and academies. Those who made money in the funds or through the manipulations of the credit system were seen as idle and unproductive. They were part of the immoral, nonindustrious camp that included the nobility, most landed gentlemen, and the nonworking poor. The talented men of the middle class were unknowingly revising the classical, Thomistic dichotomy between a natural and artificial economy. No longer was a subsistence economy "natural" and a market economy for profit "artificial." A natural economy was now characterized by productive hard work and industry, profit notwithstanding; the artificial economy was characterized by idleness and nonproductivity, and its practitioners were the useless aristocrats by birth and the equally useless parasites by profession, the money men who lived off the national debt. Protestant dissenters looked with little favor on the ill-gotten gains of gaming, whether at the table or in the funds.

More important still in accounting for middle-class and modernist sentiment against the debt was its symbolic role as the endless fountain of corruption, the source of jobs and patronage that not only corrupted Parliament but gave society's rewards to the untalented, those without merit. Critical here was the popular identification (well founded in fact) between the growth of the national debt and war. A vast military establishment generated the debt and left the impression in the virtuous, hard-working middle class of an immoral and unholy alliance. All of these came together in the debt. To wage useless wars, to pay for a useless court establishment, to provide jobs and pensions for useless men of no merit there existed a vast debt, which saddled the useful and productive manufacturers and

---

[37] See Price, *Observations on the Importance of the American Revolution,* 60–83, *An Appeal to the Public on the Subject of the National Debt* (London, 1771), *Observations on the Nature of Civil Liberty,* 70–85, 109–30, and *Additional Observations on the Nature and Value of Civil Liberty and the War with America* (London, 1777), 44–46; Tooke, *Causes and Effects of the National Debt and Paper Money on Real and Natural Property in the Present State of Civil Society* (London, 1795); and Burgh, *Political Disquisitions,* e.g., 1: 408, and 2: 298.

artisans with burdensome taxes and high prices. The natic.:al debt, moreover, drained capital from industry and raised interest rates and thus was the very symbol of unproductivity and uselessness. The apparent gloom and pessimism of Price and the other reformers has thus been misread. Although Price and Burgh shared a deep Calvinist appreciation of human depravity, they also shared a hatred of the idle. For them, the idle "monied interest" along with idle aristocrats posed a grave threat to the creation of a truly just and moral society in which hard work and productive enterprise are the central values.

It may well be that Price and Burgh were wrong and that those whom they considered immoral and idle funders and bankers would be essential in the creation of the very world they sought.[38] It is a mistake, however, to read their views in terms of later economic knowledge. Their opposition to the national debt, the funding system, and the system of paper credit was not reactionary; it went hand in hand with their vision of a moral, middle-class society. Indeed, the national debt enshrined for them much that their new order sought to replace.

It is also true that Price praised America as the home of the independent farmer, and in his writings he warned lest this noble species be overrun by cities, debts, and taxes.[39] But, as is the case with Jefferson, this agrarian bias must again not be automatically translated into nostalgia, antimodernism, and anticommercialism, for it is by no means clear that the city was perceived in the late eighteenth century as standing for modernity and capitalism and the countryside for reaction and agrarianism. Yeoman farmers operated very much in the capitalist marketplace and had highly developed commercial networks. The yeoman ideal of both Price and Jefferson was not, as Richard Hofstadter depicted it, "non-commercial, non-pecuniary, self-sufficient."[40] In defending American agriculture against the Hamiltonian system, Thomas Cooper recognized that encomia for farming did not necessitate a nostalgic repudiation of a commercial society. Although agriculture was a morally superior pursuit, its superiority did not lie in any more virtuous, precapitalist ideal. Commerce had less value only insofar as it drained away resources: "To foster every, or any other employment of capital at the expense of agriculture—by diminishing the savings of the farmer and forcing him to maintain the manufacturer—or by tempting the capitalist from agriculture into manufacture, is plainly contrary to our most undoubted policy."[41]

No less committed to a commercial society than others in this period, what distinguishes the economic vision of a Price, a Cooper, a Paine, or a Jefferson is its

[38] For an important discussion of the relationship between the entrepreneurial manufacturer and the banking and credit system, see the essays in François Crouzet's *Capital Formation in the Industrial Revolution* (London, 1972). Most manufacturers could decry the national debt and the banking system at this stage in the development of British capitalism because they, in fact, made little use of that system for their capital. Much more characteristic was the self-generation of capital. A good sense of industrial anger with the national debt can be found in Thomas Walker's *A Review of Some of the Political Events which Have Occurred in Manchester during the Last Five Years* (London, 1794). Walker, a wealthy cotton manufacturer and leading dissenter, concluded his book with an attack on the growth of the national debt and "the tremendous burden it makes of additional taxes on the manufacturers."
[39] Price, *Observations on the Importance of the American Revolution*, 69–77.
[40] Hofstadter, *The Age of Reform* (New York, 1955), 23–24.
[41] Cooper, ed., *Emporium of the Arts and Sciences*, new ser., vol. 1, no. 1 (1813): 8.

individualistic, decentralized, and nonhierarchical flavor. Thus, Jefferson preached the virtues of unrestrained free trade in terms of an idealized, individualistic marketplace. "Our interest will be to throw open the doors of commerce, and to knock off all its shackles," he wrote, "giving perfect freedom to all persons for the vent of whatever they may choose to bring into our ports, and asking the same in theirs." So, too, Price praised America because, unlike "older countries" where rural life was graduated into ranks of "gentry, yeomanry and peasant," America had just yeomen, "all independent and nearly upon a level."[42] The market was not the villain, hierarchy and dependence were. As Joyce Appleby has noted of Jefferson, "what was distinctive about the Republican's economic policy was not an anti-commercial bias, but a commitment to growth through the unimpeded exertions of individuals" with "access to economic opportunity."[43]

The rural-urban dichotomy and the preference for the rural is compatible with the emerging middle-class vision. The countryside (where, after all, in England the early manufacturing occurred) represented hard work, simplicity, frugality, industry, and productivity. The city represented courts, office holders, pensioners, luxury, waste, money, and funds. In the city congregated the idle, either the very rich or the very poor. In the city were gaming, opera, theater, and other useless, time-wasting activities. To label the city corrupt and the countryside virtuous need not, then, immediately connote a dread of modernity. The ideological thrust of such activities is never simply read. Who is virtuous and who is corrupt is not reducible to who is engaged in agriculture and who in commerce, who lives on the land or who on city streets. Hard work, talent, and productivity are what are really critical in the distribution of moral worth, and the secondary distinctions based on geography have to be read in light of these much more crucial, more primary issues.

Joseph Priestley is a case in point. He did, to be sure, become involved in the Pantisocracy, a scheme with Coleridge for a rural utopia in America, and he finally settled in the Pennsylvania back country, near Northumberland. Yet no more zealous a modernizer and liberal apologist for the middle class can be found in the ranks of British reform in these years. More than anyone else, he qualifies as the central intellectual figure among these middle-class radicals. Radical in politics, laissez faire theorist in economics, innovator in science and technology, founder of the modern Unitarian movement, Priestley schooled England's new men of

[42] Jefferson, *Notes on the State of Virginia*, ed. W. Peden (Chapel Hill, 1955), 174; and Price, *Observations on the Nature of Civil Liberty*, 70–71.

[43] Appleby, "Thomas Jefferson and the Interpreters of Nostalgia," *William and Mary Quarterly* (in press). Price's life was that of urban preacher and intellectual. He was intimately connected with the dissenter industrialist community, and as a mathematician his work in actuarial science became the basis of that most commercial of enterprises, the life insurance industry. Jefferson was not above having labor-saving machines and manufacturing mills at Monticello. Indeed, as Merrill Peterson has noted, "Here was no pastoral Eden but belching smoke and clanging hammers"; Peterson, *Thomas Jefferson and the New Nation: A Biography* (New York, 1970), 535–36. Industry and manufacture on a small scale were clearly compatible with a virtuous life of hard work and productivity. For a late-eighteenth-century argument that factories and manufacturing contribute "to paths of virtue, by restoring frugality and industry" while counteracting aristocratic corruption and luxury, see Trench Coxe, "An Address to an Assembly of the Friends of American Manufacturers," *American Museum*, 2 (1787): 251, 253–55.

business in the series of dissenting academies at which he taught, while personally serving as the critical link between virtually every aspect of the progressive liberal nexus. Brother-in-law to Wilkinson, friend of Price and Wollstonecraft, "guide, philosopher, and friend of Boulton, Watt, and Wedgwood at Birmingham," he was "gunpowder Joe" to Burke and the Church-and-King mob that burned his laboratory and home in 1791, sending him to finish his days in the reformer's paradise—America.[44]

Even more than Price, Joseph Priestley used Locke in the 1770s. *An Essay on the First Principle of Government* (1771) is virtually a gloss on *The Second Treatise*. Priestley began by describing a state of nature filled with people "living independent and unconnected," who "voluntarily resign some part of their natural liberty" to magistrates who then are the people's servants. These magistrates are accountable to the people, and, if they abuse the trust given them, they can be deposed. Punishing their governors is a natural right of the people. So keen on arguments from nature was Priestley that he dismissed out of hand those who cited historical rights, specifically lost Saxon rights. Saxon England, Priestley argued, was a time of idleness, treachery, cruelty, and insecurity of property. It was no golden age or moment of pure principle that should be reinstated.[45] In his economic thought, Priestley offered a vigorous defense of laissez faire and individualistic attacks on the poor laws. He also attacked the national debt. But, again, this was the politics not of nostalgia but of a modernizing middle class. He complained that, among other things, the growing debt raised prices. Particularly distressing was the rising price of bread, for, "by keeping bread at a reasonable price, workmen's wages are kept lower, and more fixed, a thing of the greatest consequence in manufactures."[46]

The spirit of John Locke hovers over Priestley's writings on religious individualism, which so influenced Jefferson and which are directly derivative of Locke's *Letters on Toleration* and, in turn, of Locke's views of government in *The Second Treatise*. Government, Priestley wrote, should not be involved in the religious beliefs of citizens:

The magistrate's concern is not with opinions and beliefs. His proper duty is to preserve the peace of society, or to see that no member of it injures another man in his person or his property.... How is any person injured in these respects by my holding religious opinions of which he disapproves? ... If you say it will endanger the salvation of others what does that matter to the magistrate whose business is with the things of this life only, who was not appointed to act any part in things of a spiritual but only in those of a temporal nature.[47]

Once again Locke lives, for it was clear in the late eighteenth century that behind such ideas as these stood, among others, Locke. In America a well-known cartoon

[44] Robert E. Schofield, *The Lunar Society of Birmingham* (Oxford, 1963), 353.

[45] Priestley, *An Essay on the First Principles of Government and on the Nature of Political, Civil, and Religious Liberty, Including Remarks on Dr. Brown's Code of Education* (London, 1771), 2–7, and *Lectures on History and General Policy* (London, 1788), 349.

[46] Priestley, *Lectures on History and General Policy*, 394. For his critical views of the poor and the poor laws, see *ibid.*, 295–305, and *An Account of a Society for Encouraging the Industrious Poor to which Are Prefixed Some Considerations on the State of the Poor in General* (Birmingham, 1787).

[47] Priestley, *Conduct to Be Observed by Dissenters in Order to Procure the Repeal of the Corporation and Test Acts* (Birmingham, 1789), 6–7.

Figure 3: Dr. Joseph Priestley, Unitarian minister, educator, distinguished scientist, and eminent disciple of John Locke. Priestley is buried in Northumberland, Pennsylvania. Portrait reproduced courtesy of the British Museum.

of 1769 labeled "An Attempt to Land a Bishop in America" shows the bishop hastily sailing back to England. At the departing cleric, the angry crowd is throwing epithets labeled "Calvin's Works," "liberty and freedom of conscience," and "Locke."[48]

Locke also flourished in the two major organizational expressions of British reform in these years, the Society for Constitutional Information (SCI) of the 1780s and the London Corresponding Society (LCS) of the 1790s. Founded in the early 1780s, the SCI circulated to its members excerpts from books, speeches, and

[48] For a full description of this cartoon, see Herbert D. Foster, "International Calvinism through Locke and the Revolution of 1688," *AHR*, 32 (1926–27): 476.

pamphlets that the society's leaders—Horne Tooke, Capel Lofft, Christopher
Wyvill, John Jebb, and John Cartwright—felt argued for reform of Parliament or
more generally praised freedom. Here, as in Burgh's *Political Disquisitions*, much use
was indeed made of Bolingbroke, *Cato's Letters*, and the whole arsenal of country
opposition to Walpole. There is even occasional talk of Machiavellian "ritorno ai
principii," signifying a return to the lost rights and purer principles of Saxon times.
The SCI leader most likely to use this older country language was Christopher
Wyvill. His letters and political papers are full of pleas to the other reformers to
back Pitt's more moderate reform bills, to avoid plans of "theoretical perfection" or
schemes "to form a government on a perfect theory." He spoke less of natural than
of Saxon rights, and he spent a good deal of energy in the 1790s criticizing the
abstractions and ahistorical arguments of Thomas Paine.[49]

But alongside Wyvill's country ideology and civic humanism spoke another and
more dominant voice in the SCI, the voice of Locke, of natural rights, of compact,
of government as trust, of natural equality, and of the people's power to change
governments. John Jebb, the Peterhouse Anglican who converted to Priestley's
Unitarianism, rejected Wyvill's expectation that Parliament would reform itself. It
was too subject to the will of the prime minister. Better for the people themselves in
public association and assembly to reassert their natural right to change governments. This was their residual right from the original compact. Only by popular
pressure outside Parliament, Jebb insisted, could the fair and equal representation
that Wilkes sought be realized.[50]

Capel Lofft, another major figure in the SCI leadership, offered a gloss on Locke
in 1779, applying the principles of natural law and the social compact to the reform
of Parliament. All men were equal "by the law of nature," and the power of
governors derives "only from consent and contract." Neither Saxon nor seventeenth-century commonwealth history are the sources of Lofft's radicalism: "As to
our liberty, we derived it not, if we mean the right from our forefathers or from the
Revolution; we had it from God, from the nature of man, and the nature and ends
of society. We respect human authority so far as it is founded in public consent and
directed by that principle to public utility." In the 1790s Lofft repeated the superior
claim of natural rights over historical rights. The former "is of date far higher, and
of origin transcendentally more venerable. It is an inheritance coeval with the
commencement of humanity." In general, Lofft defended the dissenters from
Burke's wrath, and he invoked the familiar cry that no longer should "those of
useful industry" be barred from "public counsel." It was time, he urged, to break
down the barrier "separating the useful from the honored classes in the Community." The "temples of honour" were open only to the "mere presumptions of merit."
Reformers meant, he wrote, to "expand the gates and enlarge the avenues" to these
temples.[51]

[49] Wyvill, *Political Papers*, 4 vols. (London, 1794), 2: 605, 3: Appendix, 154, and 4: 75–90.
[50] Jebb, *The Works of John Jebb*, 3 (London, 1787): 180, 455–84. Also see Jebb to Wyvill, August 7, 1781, in
Wyvill's *Political Papers*, 4: 497–521.
[51] Lofft, *Elements of Universal Law and Particularly of the Laws of England* (London, 1779), 10–15, *Observations on
Mr. Wesley's Second Calm Address* (London, 1777), 55, and *Remarks on the Letter of the Rt. Honourable Edmund Burke
concerning the Revolution in France* (London, 1790), 3, 31, 35.

The Butterfield-Christie reading of English reform in the late eighteenth century, so crucial for republican scholarship, needs rethinking. Far from being principally backward-looking seekers of lost Saxon rights, uninterested in socioeconomic themes, those who called for the reform of Parliament in the late eighteenth century were, in fact, very much preoccupied with the social question. Moreover, in the SCI documents, lost Saxon rights were read as natural rights. The purpose of the Saxon constitution, according to the SCI leadership, was to preserve natural rights. To re-establish the Saxon constitution, then, was seen as recapturing inalienable natural rights of free men. This is a very different emphasis from that found in Bolingbroke and his circle. Most of the pamphlets circulated by the SCI affirm that reason and nature, not custom and history, are the points of reference. The dictates of reason and nature have all men free, possessing absolute rights, from the "immutable laws of nature." Among these rights are the right to be taxed only through consent and the right to "fair and equal representation." Here, too, in the SCI America was held up as the beacon for a corrupt Britain, and not because it represented a repudiation of modernity but because it stood behind the rights of nature, of equity, and of reason.[52]

Locke is quoted extensively in SCI documents on the people's responsiblity when their natural rights are violated. The SCI's pamphlets never tire of describing governors as trustees who may be turned out when they have violated the people's trust. He was the source of the judgment that the people could remove legislators who violated that trust. The people have a recourse for a corrupt, despotic House of Commons. They have "a just and natural control" and a right "to a just resistance . . . to an invasion of their natural and inalienable rights."[53] In the SCI pamphlet of 1780, *The Letter of Lord Carysfort on Parliamentary Reform*, this Lockean theory is called down to the world of practice:

Mr. Locke is of the opinion, that "there remains inherent in the people a power to remove or alter the legislative, when they find the legislative act contrary to the trust reposed in them; for when such a trust is abused, it is thereby forfeited, and dissolves to those who gave it." If this conclusion is just in theory, it must be just in practice; and . . . may be adopted and argued from under the present dispensation of Government.[54]

This translation of Locke from theory to practice was even more apparent in the London Corresponding Society. This artisan-based, more radical group of the 1790s also shows the unmistakable stamp of John Locke. The call to establish the LCS in 1792 describes how men voluntarily give up some of their rights better to secure the possession of others. Among the rights an individual retains is "the right to share in the government of that society of which he is a member." To insure that right, Thomas Hardy, the secretary of the society, advocated "a fair, equal and

[52] Society for Constitutional Information, *Minutes of the Meetings . . . Held at No. 2 in New-Inn* (London, 1782), 1–30.

[53] *Ibid.*, 37. Also see Society for Constitutional Information, *An Address to the Public . . .* (London, 1780), 1–8, and *A Second Address to the Public . . .* (London, 1780), 1–15.

[54] Society for Constitutional Information, *A Letter from the Rt. Honourable Lord Carysfort to the Huntingdonshire Committee* (London, 1780), 4–5.

impartial representation." Like the SCI, the LCS was able to cite as the source of these rights both "our Saxon inheritance" and "our inheritance from nature and the immutable principles of justice." But much more typical of these friends of liberty and ideological kinsmen of Tom Paine was the invocation of nature.[55]

It is important to note the imprint of Locke on the LCS, for much has been made of the LCS recently by E. P. Thompson as an example of early working-class ideology in action.[56] Radical the members of the society were, granted, but radical petty bourgeoisie. Their *Declaration of Principles* is a fascinating document, very much influenced by the spirit of Locke. Principle Number One proclaims "that all men are by nature free, equal and independent of each other." No reference is made to Locke, but this passage is, of course, taken verbatim from the opening of paragraph 95 of *The Second Treatise*. Principle Number Two states that, "to enjoy all the advantages of civil society, individuals ought not to relinquish any more of their natural independence than is necessary to preserve the weak against the strong, and to enable the whole body to act with union." The LCS *Declaration of Principles* also includes a listing of the civil rights of every individual. At the top is "equality of protection for his liberty, life and property." Further down another important civic right is claimed, one that is by now familiar as a critical issue for these reformers. It is "equality of encouragement for the exercise of his talents, and consequently the free enjoyment of the advantages thereby obtained."[57]

The LCS pamphlets and manifestoes abound with references to the membership as "taxpaying, industrious and useful inhabitants" or "industrious and worthy citizenry." The society's world view, like that of the reform movement in general, saw two classes in British society, the useful and the useless:

We take pride in acknowledging ourselves a part of that useful class of citizens which placemen (pensioned with the extorted produce of our daily labour) and proud nobility wallowing in riches (acquired somehow) affect to treat with a contempt too degrading for human nature to bear, unless reconciled to it by the reflection that though their inferiors in rank and fortune, we equal them in talents and excel them in Honesty.

The LCS was by no means an enemy of private property. It acknowledged "that differences of strength, of talents, and of industry, ought to afford proportional distinctions of property which when acquired and confirmed by the laws, is sacred and inviolable."[58]

When these talented and industrious citizens convened in a huge open-air meeting at Chalk Farm on April 14, 1794, they knew full well the mood of Pitt's government and the growing evidence of repression. Their unanimous resolution, critical of the government, was a paraphrase of Locke. It was sound constitutional doctrine, to be sure, but in the context of the mid-1790s even the spirit of Locke was suspect. The LCS resolved

[55] London Corresponding Society, *The. . . Society to the Nation at Large* (London, 1792), 1–2, 6, and *An Account of the Proceedings of the British Convention Held in Edinburgh, the 19th of November 1793* (London, n.d.), 10–12.
[56] Thompson, *The Making of the English Working Class* (New York, 1963), esp. 152–57.
[57] London Corresponding Society, *Report of the Committee Appointed to Revise and Abridge a Former Report of the Constitution of the . . . Society* (London, n.d.), 1, 2.
[58] London Corresponding Society, *Addresses and Resolutions* (London, n.d.), 1, *Address of the . . . Society to Other Societies of Great Britain United for Obtaining a Reform in Parliament* (London, 1793), 8, and *Address from the . . . Society to the Inhabitants of Great Britain on the Subject of a Parliamentary Reform* (London, 1792), 2–3.

that any attempt to violate those yet remaining laws, which were intended for the Security of Englishmen against the Corruption of dependent judges ought to be considered as dissolving entirely the social compact between the English nation and their Governors, and driving them to that incontrovertible maxim of eternal Justice, that the safety of the people is the supreme, and in cases of necessity, the only law.[59]

WHAT BETTER PROOF COULD THERE BE of Locke's importance in the late eighteenth century than a crusade to root out his ideas waged by the opponents of reform? So common was the reformers' use of Locke's "close reasoning" that their Tory and clerical opponents often singled out Locke as the sinister influence behind radical agitation. Richard Hey and Bishop William Paley ridiculed the reformers'—that is, Lockean—notions of contract, the state of nature, and natural rights.[60] The *Anti-Jacobin* lamented that "Price, Priestley, Rousseau, Paine could justify on the principles of Locke, their own visionary doctrines, pregnant with consequences so mischievous to society and so different from what Locke himself intended."[61]

George Horne, the bishop of Norwich and chaplain to George III, criticized Locke's notion of natural equality and independence in the state of nature, "since from the beginning, some were born subject to others." Samuel Horsley, bishop successively of St. David, Rochester, and St. Asaph, chimed in that Locke's description of an original compact and an independent state of nature were "absurd and unphilosophical creations of something out of nothing." In his annual sermon marking the anniversary of the decollation of Charles I, Horsley linked together in unholy alliance Lockean doctrine, Protestant dissenters, and French Jacobins. "Contractual ideas of popular sovereignty inflamed the phrensy of that fanatical banditti," and the "dissemination of those infernal maxims that kings are the servants of the people, punishable by their masters" has led now to the murder of Louis XVI. Behind it all, Horsley lamented, is English seventeenth-century doctrine.[62]

The most vocal denouncers of Locke in this period, however, were Josiah Tucker, the dean of Gloucester, and Edward Tatham, an Anglican divine from Oxford. Tucker's *Treatise Concerning Civil Government* (1781) is one long diatribe against Locke and those whom Tucker called his "eminent disciples"—Priestley and Price. What particularly upset Tucker about Locke, Price, and Priestley was their conviction "that government is a work of art, and that nature has no share in forming it, in predisposing or inclining mankind to it." He repudiated their notion that men were ever "independent and unconnected beings" who voluntarily chose to set up governments. He also rejected what he described as their conviction that "civil government is a necessary evil, rather than a positive good." What folly, he

---

[59] *The Annual Register* (London, 1794), 264.

[60] See Hey, *Happiness and Rights: A Dissertation upon Several Subjects Relative to the Rights of Man and His Happiness* (York, 1792); and Paley, "Elements of Political Knowledge," in *The Collected Works of William Paley*, 3 (London, 1838): bk. 6.

[61] *Anti-Jacobin*, as quoted in Anthony Lincoln, *Some Political and Social Ideas of English Dissent, 1763–1800* (Cambridge, 1938), 114.

[62] Horne, *Discourses on the Origins of Civil Government* (London, 1800), 271; and Horsley, *A Sermon Preached before the Lords Spiritual and Temporal . . . , January 30, 1793* (London, 1793), 4, 22–23.

DOCTOR PHLOGISTON,
The PRIESTLEY politician or the
Political Priest.

Figure 4: "Dr. Phlogiston" (1791), unattributed. This anti-Priestley cartoon was published in the same year that his laboratory and home were burned in Birmingham by a Church and King mob. Note the titles of his manuscripts: "Political Sermon," "Essay on Government," "Essays on Matter and Spirit," "Gunpowder," and "Revolution Trusts." Reproduced courtesy of the Birmingham Public Library.

wrote, to describe men as "all equal, all free, and independent, all masters of self." Against Locke and his late eighteenth-century radical disciples Tucker invoked Aristotle, who, Tucker insisted, had correctly described the inherent sociability of human beings and the naturalness of the political community. Tucker was particularly angered by the use of Locke in America, for the Americans had taken to heart his pernicious doctrines and would create a "Lockean Republic, where all taxes are to be free gifts! and every man is to obey no further, and no otherwise, than he himself chooses to obey."[63]

Edward Tatham in 1791 continued the assault on Locke and those he called "the two captains" of his teachings in England, Price and Priestley. And Tatham had the same alternative to Locke. Priestley should have read more Aristotle and less Locke, Tatham suggested. The Aristotle Tatham invoked is not, however, Aristotle the theorist of citizenship and the *zōon politikon* so dear to twentieth-century republican scholarship but Aristotle the theorist of hierarchy and privilege. Aristotle, Tatham wrote, "took men as he found them and as history informed him they have been always found, connected in society, subordinate and dependent on each other." Against Locke, Price, and Priestley, Tatham preferred an Aristotle who taught "that men are made by their Creator different and unequal, some formed for authority, and others for subjection." Locke and his eighteenth-century captains, Tatham insisted, would "throw down all ranks and distinctions of man."[64]

Late-eighteenth-century observers thus made a clear link from Locke to British reform and socioeconomic change, a link that has been denied by the "Republican School." The real threat of Locke and his "eminent disciples" was their leveling tendencies, their assault on traditional aristocratic society. In *The True Basis of Civil Government in Opposition to the System of Mr. Locke and His Followers*, Tucker criticized the reformers for denying what he saw as basic in human nature: "a certain ascendancy in some, a kind of submissive acquiescence in others." There are, Tucker insisted, certain natural "ranks in society" and "stations in life," which contract theory undermines in its subversive preoccupation with natural freedom and equality. These critics perceptively understood the intentions of the "eminent disciples" of Locke. The praise of achievement and talent, the ideology of equal opportunity, and the cult of industry and productivity, all wrapped in doctrines of natural equality and independence, were in fact self-consciously directed at "the age of chivalry." The true nostalgics were the likes of Burke, Tucker, and Tatham. Theirs was the defense of a world with "Kings, princes, nobles and gentlemen. . . . For in the whole scale of beings, and in the nature of things, there must be regular gradations and regular distinctions."[65]

Less concerned with nostalgia than with repression, Pitt's government brought numerous leaders of the reform movement to trial for treason. Even above the trials hovered the spirit of John Locke. So subversive were his ideas considered that

---

[63] Tucker, *Selections from His Economic and Political Writings*, ed. R. L. Schuyler (New York, 1931), 407–553 *passim*, esp. 464.

[64] Tatham, *Letters to Edmund Burke on Politics* (Oxford, 1791), 7, 12, 22, 26.

[65] Tucker, *Economic and Political Writings*, 477; and Matthew Goodenough, *Plain Thoughts by a Plain Citizen of London* (London, 1792), 11.

to be thought a Lockean in the 1790s was itself grounds for suspicion. According to Priestley, "any sentiment in favour of liberty that is at all bold and manly, such as till of late, was deemed becoming Englishmen and the disciples of Mr. Locke, is now reprobated as seditious."[66] No surprise, then, that sympathy with Locke's ideas was raised as an issue in the trials of Hardy, Gerald, and Paine.[67]

Despite these attacks, Locke had his proud defenders. Thomas Erskine, the eloquent defense attorney for so many of Pitt's victims, still invoked Locke as a warning to the government. "It is justly observed by Locke," he declared, that "after much neglect and provocation the people will be roused to a reasonable and justifiable resistance." Robert Hall, the dissenting minister, was unafraid to praise Locke in his published reply to Bishop Horsley's anniversary sermon. Hall proudly proclaimed that the doctrine of Locke and his followers "is founded on the natural equality of mankind; for as no man can have any natural or inherent right to rule any more than another, it necessarily follows, that a claim to dominion, wherever it is lodged, must be ultimately referred back to the explicit or implied consent of the people." The "immortal Locke" is, indeed, the patron of English reform.[68]

Joseph Towers, the dissenting minister in Highgate and a friend of Price and Priestley, wrote *A Vindication of the Political Principles of Mr. Locke*, in which he praised the reformers' use of Locke, describing him as "an ornament and an honour to the country which gave him birth." Towers met the historical objections to Locke head on, insisting that the "great excellence of his maxims" is that they are based not "upon the iniquities of a dark and intricate and disputable nature" but upon the more indisputable "principles of reason and justice . . . apparent at all times." As for objections to Locke's doctrine of changing governors who act "contrary to the trust given them," Towers responded, "You might as well say, honest men may not oppose robbers or pirates, because it may occasion disorder or bloodshed." Towers even wrapped himself in Locke when demanding the suffrage for Birmingham, Manchester, and Leeds. Had Locke not begun it all, Towers asked, with the passage on "bringing Parliament to a fair and equal representation"? Far from denying Locke's role, the Presbyterian Towers praised it: "It may be readily admitted, that Mr. Locke and his followers wish to extend the present partial representation of the people, and to make it more agreeable to reason and to justice . . . , but this is not one of the defects of Mr. Locke's system, but one of its principal excellencies."[69]

Even more telling than Towers's *Vindication* was the pamphlet of 1794, *The Spirit of John Locke*, written by Henry Yorke of Sheffield, who in that same year was tried for treason.[70] The pamphlet, widely distributed to all radical associations by the

[66] Priestley, *An Appeal to the Public on the Subject of the Riots in Birmingham* (Birmingham, 1792), 113–14.

[67] Thompson, *The Making of the English Working Class*, 88–89, 128–29; F. D. Cartwright, ed., *The Life and Correspondence of Major Cartwright*, 1 (London, 1826): 214–17; and Lloyd Paul Stryker, *For the Defense—Thomas Erskine* (Garden City, N.Y., 1947), 224.

[68] Erskine, *A View of the Causes and Consequences of the Present War with France* (London, 1797), 22; and Hall, *An Apology for the Freedom of the Press and for General Liberty, to Which Are Prefixed Remarks on Bishop Horsley's Sermon* (London, 1793), 40, 72, 62.

[69] Towers, *A Vindication of the Political Principles of Mr. Locke* (London, 1782), 13, 16, 40, 65.

[70] For Yorke's fascinating career, see J. Taylor, "The Sheffield Constitutional Society," *Transactions of the Hunter Archaeological Society* (Sheffield), 5 (1943): 133–46; and G. P. Jones, "The Political Reform Movement in Sheffield," *ibid.*, 4 (1937): 57–68. Later in his career (after a long prison term), Yorke moved to the right and published an attack on his former radical colleagues.

Constitutional Society of Sheffield, was a popular abridgment of *The Second Treatise of Government* designed to bring Locke's ideas more readily to "that part of the community who have not leisure to employ themselves in perusing the whole of the work." The abridged Locke, Yorke wrote, was

applicable to the present times.—It may serve to open the eyes of our deluded Countrymen, who are persecuting and hating us, because we are vindicating the ancient Liberties of our Country. It will expose the fallacious reasoning of those who would persuade the People that they have no other rights but what their rulers please to give them. It will prove passive obedience to be folly, and RESISTANCE AGAINST OPPRESSION to be the duty of the people.

Locke's credentials were good, Yorke informed the reader, and his ideas had served well in the recent American "cause" so sacred to the dissenters and the reformers:

While America was gloriously struggling to throw off the yoke of British oppression, the name of John Locke resounded even in the British Senate, and was echoed in Congress. The principles, which he had so admirably digested from amidst the crude volumes of remoter times, were, to oppressed Humanity, the alarum of Liberty. They taught the criteria of good and bad Government, and instructed the injured how, and when, to trample Despotism under foot.

Locke's writings might be dull, Yorke conceded, but Locke was relevant and his spirit alive. Speaking for his reforming colleagues in Sheffield, he commended Locke to readers who were less familiar with the "close reasoner" than they:

We commit to your wisdom and prudential reflection, the following Abstract from a book, difficult to be purchased, and, throughout the greatest part, uninteresting even when purchased. We have declined making any notes to the body of the work. But he who runs may read, and the Man who cannot take a broad hint from the *last* century, must not expect one from the *present*.

In trying to make the strongest case he could for knowledge of Locke, Yorke noted that Edmund Burke, "Knight Errant of Feudality," had claimed on the floor of the House of Commons that "Locke's Treatise on Civil Government, was the worst book ever written." Yorke was therefore "certain it needs no farther recommendation."[71]

To PARAPHRASE MARK TWAIN, the scholarly consensus on Locke's death in the late eighteenth century is greatly exaggerated. Late eighteenth-century English reformers dramatically worked Lockean themes into the heart of their critique of traditional England, turning to Locke because *The Second Treatise of Government* was uniquely appropriate to their peculiar problem. Parliament, the representative body, was itself the barrier to reform. Locke's belief in the residual power of the people against their governors legitimized the reformers' campaign against the unreformed House of Commons. Locke's political theory legitimated their demands, both substantive and procedural, for a reform of the suffrage and of

---

[71] Yorke, *The Spirit of John Locke on Civil Government* (Sheffield, 1794), iii–iv, viii.

Figure 5: "The Contrast" (1792), unattributed. The critics of the radicals were quite specific about what horrors Jacobinism would bring to England. Reproduced from the author's collection.

parliamentary representation. His concept of a limited secular magistrate legitimated their demand for the separation of church and state.

The reformers also turned to Locke because their ideological concerns were similar. These spokesmen for an insurgent middle-class radicalism were drawn to this liberal theorist of possessive individualism. No one had better expressed their economic and social convictions than Locke had. His socioeconomic vision was perfectly compatible with—indeed, had helped shape—their image of a world peopled by hard-working, industrious property owners. Locke had often written on the themes of industry and talent and was perceived as a crucial part of the Protestant tradition that so informed much of this reform movement. In the libraries of the dissenting academies, Locke's works were standard references, not only for psychology and education but also for politics and commerce.[72] Had not, in fact, *The Second Treatise* contended that God had set some men to be more industrious than others and thus to acquire more property? Locke's conviction that God "gave the world to the use of the industrious and Rational . . . , not to the Fancy or the Covetousness of the Quarrelsome and Contentious," was critical to his thought; it symbolized a central tension in his work: the struggle between the industrious and the idle—a struggle at the core of the world view of those late eighteenth-century dissenting reformers who read Locke in the libraries of their academies.[73]

The praise of industry, of what the seventeenth and eighteenth centuries considered "skill, assiduity, perseverance and diligence," and the denunciation of idleness were, of course, by no means unique to Locke.[74] Protestant writers, especially Puritans like Baxter, had long made them a crucial part of their notions of work, of the obligation to labor, and of the importance of one's calling. What Locke did was wed these earlier views to a political theory of private rights and individualism with his argument that property was an extension of self, the injection of personality into nature through work.[75] Less apparent, however, is the extent to which other Lockean texts read in these dissenting academy libraries spoke to the themes of industry, idleness, and the glory of work. Indeed, so concerned with these themes was Locke that it is little exaggeration to suggest that he saw industriousness as the central characteristic of the human personality, of personal behavior, and of social and personal activity.

In his *Essay Concerning Human Understanding*, Locke linked activity to anxiety, a connection not unfamiliar to later readers of Weber and Tawney. "The chief, if not the only spur to human industry and action is," he wrote, "uneasiness." This feeling of uneasiness, a desire for "some absent good," drove men to enterprise and unrelenting activity. Once motivated, they were permanently active, for they had a

[72] Lincoln, *Some Political and Social Ideas of English Dissent, 1763–1800*, 87.

[73] Locke, *The Second Treatise of Government*, chap. 5, secs. 48, 35.

[74] For a discussion of the word "industry," see Raymond Williams, *Culture and Society, 1780–1950* (London, 1958), 13.

[75] The following argument owes a good deal to the interesting work of E. J. Hundert. See his "The Making of *Homo Faber*: John Locke—Between Ideology and History," *Journal of the History of Ideas*, 33 (1972): 3–22, and "Market Society and Meaning in Locke's Political Philosophy," *Journal of the History of Philosophy*, 15 (1977): 33–44.

never-ending "itch after honour, power and riches," which in turn unleashed more "fantastical uneasiness."[76]

Activity and industry, according to Locke, also characterized childhood. His widely read *Thoughts Concerning Education* is a veritable diatribe against idleness. Children were the model for the species. They "generally hate to be idle. All they care then is, that their busy humour should be constantly employ'd in something of use to them." All life is industrious activity, Locke wrote; even in recreation human beings are never idle. "For *Recreation* is not being idle (as every one may observe) but easing the wearied Part by Change of Business: and he that thinks *Diversion* may not lie in hard and painful Labour, forgets the early Rising, hard Riding, Heat, Cold and Hunger of Huntsmen, which is yet known to be the constant Recreation of Men of the greatest Condition." Recreation should not just delight and provide ease, it should refresh one for "regular business" and "produce what will afterwards be profitable." Uneasiness again preoccupied Locke, as he prescribed that parents keep their children busy and fight "the dead weight of unemployed Time lying upon their hands," since "the uneasiness it is to do nothing at all."[77]

Children should be taught to keep account books, according to Locke, which not only would keep them busy but would also teach them frugality. Such practices would contribute to the habitual and orderly management of their lives. Industriousness required that children also learn to postpone immediate gratification: "He that has not a mastery over his Inclinations, he that knows not how to *resist* the Importunity of *present Pleasure* or *Pain*, for the sake of what Reason tells him is fit to be done, wants the true Principle of Virtue and Industry."[78]

Two groups in the community—some aristocrats and all of the poor—were not, however, active and industrious. According to Locke, they provided the "fancy or the covetousness of the Quarrelsome and contentious." As Burgh, Price, Priestley, and all dissenting middle-class reformers eventually did, Locke divided society into an industrious, enterprising middle beset by two idle extremes. In his essay of 1691 on lowering the interest rate, Locke criticized the profligate aristocrat, whose plight was produced by "debauchery and luxury beyond means." He was not criticizing the "industrious and rational" among the aristocracy, only the "covetous" and "contentious," who "will have and by his example make it fashionable to have more claret, spice and silk." Such men would soon lose their power and authority to "men of lower condition who surpass them in knowledge."[79]

While only some of the aristocracy were lazy and "debauched," Locke presumed that most of the poor were idle and inactive, and his harshness toward them knew no bounds. He urged that the provisions of the poor law be made stricter so that the poor could be taught industry, hard work, and frugality. One way to break them of their wasteful idleness was through the establishment of what Locke called

[76] Locke, *An Essay Concerning Human Understanding*, ed. A. C. Fraser, 2 (Oxford, 1894): bk. 20, sec. 6.

[77] Locke, *Some Thoughts Concerning Education* (Cambridge, 1892), 110–11, 180–81.

[78] *Ibid.*, 183, 29.

[79] Locke, *Some Considerations on the Consequences of Lowering the Interest and Raising the Value of Money* (1691), in *The Works of John Locke*, ed. J. Law, 5 (London, 1801): 53, 60.

"working schools." A full century before Bentham and his charity schools, Locke proposed that all children of the poor "shall be obliged to come" at the age of three to live in "schools" where the only subjects taught would be spinning and knitting. This would cure them of idleness, for they would then "from infancy be inured to work, which is of no small consequence to the making of them sober and industrious all their lives after." Rounding up the children of the poor and incarcerating them in order to teach them industry and hard work would, Locke conceded, cost the parishes dearly; but it would ultimately prove profitable in the account books of the spinning and knitting managers, for "the earnings of the children [would] abat[e] the charge of their maintenance, and as much work [would] be required of each of them as they are reasonably able to perform," so that "it will quickly pay its own charges with an overplus."[80]

From such Lockean schemes and the values they embody there is a direct link not only to Bentham but to the middle-class Protestant reformers of the late eighteenth century. Priestley's proposal for *A Society for Encouraging the Industrious Poor*, submitted to Wilkinson the ironmaster in 1787, contains similar sentiments. But the clearest link is in the equally repressive plan offered by James Burgh to eliminate idleness and encourage industry. He proposed in his *Political Disquisitions* that the police and press gangs "seize all idle and disorderly persons, who have been three times complained of before a magistrate, and to set them to work during a certain time, for the benefit of great trading or manufacturing companies."[81] These are expressions neither of nostalgic country ideology nor of republicanism but of an ideology of hard work and industry. Middle-class reformers in the late eighteenth century were more likely to read the world and assess its institutions—economic, social, and political—in terms of the dialectic of industry and idleness than "virtue and commerce." Here, too, they bore the indelible imprint of "that close reasoner, Mr. Locke."

Chapter 5 of *The Second Treatise*, "On Property," became the received wisdom in advanced radical circles in the late eighteenth century. Priestley described "a difference in industry" as introducing and legitimating inequalities of property, "so that in time some will become rich and others poor." In turn, those with property are led to create civil society by "the desire of securing the undisturbed enjoyment of their possessions."[82] The philologist and radical Horne Tooke is a less likely spokesman for these views, but he, too, felt the impact of Locke's economic ideas. His essay on the nature of property and wealth, published in 1795, begins by proclaiming that "Industry, the bodily labour of the human being is the foundation of all property." The idle, however, "according to the original and natural constitution of things have no right or property in anything." But, by his reckoning,

---

[80] Locke, *Some Thoughts Concerning Education*, 189–90. For Bentham, see Gertrude Himmelfarb, "Bentham's Utopia: The National Charity Company," *Journal of British Studies*, 10 (1970): 80–125.

[81] James Burgh, *Political Disquisitions*, 3: 220–21. It should be noted that Francis Hutcheson, so favored by Gary Wills as the intellectual grey eminence behind Thomas Jefferson, went even further. Although Hutcheson opposed slavery of Africans, he insisted that slavery should be "the ordinary punishment of such idle vagrants, as, after proper admonitions and tryals of temporary servitude, cannot be engaged to support themselves and their families by any useful means"; Hutcheson, *A System of Moral Philosophy*, 2 (London, 1755): 202.

[82] Priestley, *Lectures on History and General Policy*, 303, 297.

this was by no means the case in Tooke's England. With the exaggerated flair of the middle-class apologist, he asked, "Though it may be easily conceived that this was the case originally when men lived in a state of nature . . . , how is it that [today] the most industrious and laborious are scarcely able to procure even the common necessities of life" at the same time that "the idle, those who never work at all are rolling in luxury, and possess all the property in the kingdom, an inversion of the laws of nature"?[83]

Middle-class reformers in the late eighteenth century used the older language of civic humanism and corruption, to be sure. They and their American friends, like Jefferson and Franklin, complained often of the corruption that hung heavy over Britain.[84] But corruption was a very different notion for these reformers from what it had been for the earlier Bolingbroke and his country ideology. A corrupt man for Burgh, Price, and Priestley was idle, profligate, unproductive, and lacking in talent and merit. A corrupt system was one in which such drones held important public offices, one in which privilege, not merit, distributed the prizes in the race of life, and one in which patronage insured the rule of unproductive—that is, corrupt— men of no ability instead of that of deserving men of talent. When Francis Place complained that "the whole system of our Government is essentially corrupt," he was not invoking a court-country equation with commerce and modernity, he was using a new public language that saw government as a reserve for privileged parasites. It was the same language used by the Sheffield reformer, Henry Yorke, in linking corruption to the aristocratic system:

From the privileged orders where birth supplies the lack of ability, virtue, knowledge and experience the executive officers of the nation are selected. . . . They preclude the industrious citizen from all honourable enterprise and patriotic exertion. . . . Intrigue and corruption are the only trades of the aristocracy. In these they excell. By these they enrich themselves. By such criminal means they monopolise all the offices of the church, the law and the army . . . ; they first corrupt you, and then they intrigue against you; they purchase you, in order to sell themselves. . . . The aristocracy desire to be distinguished from you, not to be distinguished by you. In a government where such a system is prevalent what is to be expected, but the extension of that corrupt influence by which it is upheld.[85]

These useless idlers presided over a system that denied careers to the talented. The real nation was, as earlier in the century, seen as outside that corrupt government, but that nation was not a warmed-over Augustan country. Now it was the virtuous, hard-working, and frugal middle class and artisanry, who were as uninterested in a republican order of civic virtue as they were in an aristocratic order of deference and privilege. What they wanted was a meritocracy of talent. Had not Locke written, after all, that God "gave the world to the use of the Industrious and the Rational"?

---

[83] Tooke, *Causes and Effects of the National Debt and Paper Money on Real and Natural Property in the Present State of Civil Society* (London, 1795), 2–4.

[84] See Drew R. McCoy, "Benjamin Franklin's Vision of a Republican Political Economy for America," *William and Mary Quarterly*, 25 (1978): 605–28.

[85] Place, as quoted in Graham Wallas, *The Life of Francis Place, 1771–1854* (New York, 1919), 256; and Yorke, *Thoughts on Civil Government Addressed to the Disenfranchised Citizens of Sheffield* (London, 1794), 55–59.

These radical dissenters were the first fully developed theorists of the liberal ideal of equal opportunity. James Burgh, in attacking the Test and Corporation Acts, which denied religious dissenters important civil and military positions, demanded that England "give all an equal chance for rising to honours in the state according to merit." Priestley described the reformers' vision as one of "free access to honour and employments to every member of the state and free scope . . . given the exertion of every man's ability."[86] Anna L. Barbauld, a member of Priestley's circle, made the same point in 1790. The natural equality of Lockean theory had by then become a natural right to equal opportunity. In opposition to aristocracy, these individualist liberals offered meritocracy. Barbauld did not ask for a favor but for "a natural and inalienable right," which she claimed was hers and every dissenter's.

To exclude us from jobs is no more reasonable than to exclude all those above five feet high or those whose birthdays are before the summer solstice. These are arbitrary and whimsical distinctions. . . . We want civil offices. And why should citizens not aspire to civil offices? Why should not the fair field of generous competition be freely opened to every one?[87]

The issue was "power, place, and influence."

Pocock and other revisionists have been quite right to see the court-commerce connection earlier in the century. But, by the late eighteenth century, the country reform tradition came to terms with the market and, indeed, in the hands of middle-class industrial dissent turned that reform tradition into a wholehearted ideology of the market. The court, while bound to the market and commerce from Walpole on, was enmeshed in the principle of patronage, which ultimately flew in the face of market notions of careers neutrally open to talent and hard work. It is here that the conflict emerges. Patronage and privilege are principles that pitted the court against the bourgeois reformers. Middle-class radicals inveighed against corrupt patronage, but it was a new sense of corruption, the corruption of jobs and places going to undeserving, untalented men of birth. It was the privileged court that in this period responded with a nostalgic defense of the ancient constitution, hierarchy, and paternalism. Its defenders ridiculed the leveling ideas of monied men and provincial bumpkins.

A court-country reading of the later eighteenth century becomes too confusing to be useful, because, with the emergence and eventual supremacy within the country "outs" of a class-conscious bourgeoisie, the court-commerce linkage becomes obsolete. In the eyes of the middle-class radical "outs," the earlier equation was reversed. The "ins," the court and all it stood for, were identified not with the market and commerce but with idle, unproductive privilege. The commercial and financial revolution stood behind the court-country split of the Augustan era. Its relevance receded, however, with the early years of the Industrial Revolution, when new dichotomous distinctions captured the fancy of reformers, not the least of which was virtuous commerce versus corrupt privilege. The marriage of

---

[86] Burgh, *Crito: or, Essays on Various Subjects* (London, 1767), 68; and Priestley, *Lectures on History and General Policy*, 320.

[87] Barbauld, *Address to Opposers of the Repeal of the Corporation and Test Acts* (London, 1790), 17–18.

industrial England with dissenter reform doomed court-country politics and
introduced class politics.

What emerged in the course of the late eighteenth century—and most vividly in
the writings of the middle-class radicals—was a new notion of virtue, one that
dramatically rejects the assumptions of civic humanism. Citizenship and the public
quest for the common good were replaced by economic productivity and hard work
as the criteria of virtue. It is a mistake, however, to see this simply as a withdrawal
from public activity to a private, self-centered realm. The transformation also
involved a changed emphasis on the nature of public behavior. The moral and
virtuous man was no longer defined by his civic activity but by his economic activity.
One's duty was still to contribute to the public good, but this was best done through
economic activity, which actually aimed at private gain. Self-centered economic
productivity, not public citizenship, became the badge of the virtuous man.

A new cultural ideal was taking shape in the work and writings of these radicals.
Homo civicus was being replaced by *homo oeconomicus*. In his letters, Josiah Wedgwood, Priestley's patron, described how he had "fallen in love" with and "made a
mistress" of his pottery business. His productivity was merely to abide by the will of
God. Wedgwood obeyed what he called the "eleventh commandment—Thou shalt
not be idle." His friend, the dissenting cotton manufacturer Jedediah Strutt, was
convinced, "whatever some Divines would teach to the contrary," that the "main
business of the life of man was the getting of money."[88] The early classics of
children's literature produced in England from 1760 to 1800 by these very same
middle-class radicals in Priestley's circle contain few lectures or parables extolling
civic responsibility (unlike *Émile*), but they continually praise productive hard
work.[89] In Anna Barbauld's children's tale "True Heroism," she wrote that great
men were no longer those who devote themselves to public life—"Kings, lords,
generals, and prime ministers." There were new heroes, men who instead "invent
useful arts, or discover important truths which may promote the comfort and
happiness of unborn generations in the distant parts of the world. They act still an
important part, and their claim to merit is generally more undoubted, than that of
the former, because what they do is more certainly their own."[90] A pamphleteer of
1780 spelled out even more clearly who these new heroes were: "Consider the
gradual steps of civilization from barbarism to refinement and you will not fail to
discover that the progress of society from its lowest and worst to its highest and
most perfect state, has been uniformly accompanied and chiefly promoted by the
happy exertions of man in the character of a mechanic or engineer!"[91]

The middle-class radical praise of economic man no longer shares what Pocock

---

[88] [Wedgwood] *The Selected Letters of Josiah Wedgwood*, ed. A. Finer and G. Savage (London, 1965), 46, 247;
and Strutt, as quoted in R. S. Fitton and A. P. Wadsworth, *The Strutts and the Arkwrights: A Study of the Early
Factory System* (Manchester, 1972), 109–10.

[89] See my "Children's Literature and Bourgeois Ideology: Observations on Cultural and Industrial
Capitalism in the Later Eighteenth Century," in Perez Zagorin, ed., *Culture and Politics: From Puritanism to the
Enlightenment* (Berkeley and Los Angeles, 1980), 203–40.

[90] Barbauld, *Evenings at Home: or, The Juvenile Budget Opened*, 6 (Philadelphia, 1796): 223.

[91] *Letters on the Utility and Policy of Employing Machines to Shorten Labour* (London, 1780), 3.

described as the republican dread of Aristotle's banausic men, who are "less than citizens because they specialised in the development of one's capacity."[92] Specialization for the radicals, far from a sign of corruption, was a characteristic of virtuous man. It did not render economic man dependent on government or make him the servant of others, like priests, lawyers, rentiers, or soldiers. The specialist, like the entrepreneur, the scientist, the engineer, the inventor, or any man of talent, was the true social hero, who through his ingenious productivity and private pursuits shaped the public good. The older praise of the public citizen as a nonspecialized amateur smacked too much of the aristocratic rule of idle and untalented privilege. A self-conscious glorification of specialization against Aristotle's "ethos of *zöon politikon*" is implicit in an ideology that extols talent, merit, and skill. Hence, not just Adam Smith but a chorus of writers in the last decades of the eighteenth century sang the praises of specialization and the division of labor. The very heart of civic humanism was repudiated and its values reversed by the radical middle-class crusade to professionalize and specialize, to replace what it saw as corrupt political man with virtuous and productive economic man.

Josiah Wedgwood approached civic life as a specialist in industry and commerce. "Sunk again I find into politicks" was how he described himself, reluctantly having to leave his business for citizenship. Not "fame" but "money getting" was his concern. When his friend, the great engineer Brindley, died, Wedgwood noted that it was talents like his that truly benefited mankind. The public good done by such men of genius, the contribution to the commonweal by such men of "ingenuity and industry," far surpassed the contribution of political men, of "many noble lords." The economic benefactors "will be remembered with gratitude and respect" when the others "are totally forgotten." For Thomas Cooper, the industrialist and scientist who like Priestley eventually settled in America, virtue and privilege were incompatible. Only those with "insatiable ambition" could be able, wise, or virtuous.[93]

THE MIDDLE CLASS WRAPPED ITSELF in this new notion of virtue. They were "not adorn'd, it's true with coats of arms and a long Parchment Pedigree of useless members of society, but deck'd with virtue and frugality." When Jedediah Strutt in composing his own epitaph wrote that "he had led a life of honesty and virtue," thoughts of country purity and citizenship could not have been further from his mind.[94] His life was virtuous compared to the corruption of the idle nobility and the wretched poor, for he had worked harder and contributed more with his talent, ingenuity, and industry to the increased productivity and wealth of his nation than they had. He was typical of a new species of self-centered virtuous men—men like

---

[92] Pocock, *Politics, Language, and Time*, 92, and *The Machiavellian Moment*, 499.
[93] [Wedgwood] *Selected Letters*, 233, 81, 136, 182; and Cooper, *A Reply to Mr. Burke's Invective against Mr. Cooper and Mr. Watt* (London, 1792), 16.
[94] J. Stit, *A Sequel to the Friendly Advice to the Poor* (Manche..er, 1756), 17; and Strutt, as quoted in Fitton and Wadsworth, *The Strutts and the Arkwrights*, 108.

those seen in Birmingham by an eighteenth-century chronicler of the middle class:

I was surprised at the place, but more so at the people: they were a species I had never seen: they possessed a vivacity I had never beheld: I had been among dreamers, but now I saw men awake: their very step along the street showed alacrity: Everyman seemed to know and prosecute his own affairs: the town was large, and full of inhabitants and those inhabitants full of industry.[95]

When such self-centered, virtuous men addressed themselves to public issues, they did so less and less in terms of the paradigms and language of civic humanism or classical republicanism and more and more with the conceptual framework they knew best, the market. Joel Barlow—financial speculator, international entrepreneur, radical friend of Jefferson, Paine, Price, Wollstonecraft, Godwin, and Priestley—wrote of the French Revolution in his *Advice to the Privileged Orders in the Several States of Europe* in the language and the paradigms he knew best. He began, "It must be of vast importance to all classes of society . . . to calculate before hand what they are to gain or to lose by the approaching change; that like prudent stock jobbers, they may buy in or sell out, according as this great event shall effect them."[96]

Barlow and his friends, British and American, knew their Aristotle, their Machiavelli, and their Montesquieu. But they also knew their Locke. The world view of liberal individualism was fast pushing aside older paradigms during the last three decades of the century in the wake of the American crisis and the inventions of Watt and Arkwright. Two hundred years later, republican revisionism depicts these late eighteenth-century figures as preoccupied with public virtue and civic humanism and as uninterested in Lockean liberal ideals. When allowed to speak for themselves, however, these radicals seem to tell a different story.

[95] W. Hutton, *An History of Birmingham to the End of the Year 1780* (Birmingham, 1781), 63.
[96] Barlow, *Advice to the Privileged Orders in the Several States of Europe* (London, 1792), 3.

Just War, Holy War, and Millennialism in Revolutionary America

Melvin B. Endy, Jr.

MILLENNIALISM and the attendant understanding of America as a New Israel have become prominent topics in the recent historiography of the American Revolution. Historians have long been aware of the strong support that New England clergymen lent to the political and military struggle for Independence. In 1966 Alan Heimert, in *Religion and the American Mind,* presented a new understanding of the sources and rationale for that support. Finding among the proponents of New Light evangelicalism the staunchest spokesmen for American autonomy, Heimert argued that the Great Awakening had begun a process by which the Puritans' "errand into the wilderness" was recast in a millennial framework that accommodated the thrust toward Independence. Influenced by Heimert, many students of the eighteenth century have argued that the New Englanders' conviction that they were a latter-day Israel with a central role in salvation history produced a postmillennialism that spread throughout the colonies.[1] It has come to be generally agreed that by the 1770s religious leaders were incorporating political developments into their salvation history and urging their people to regard the Revolution as a holy war between the forces of Christ and Antichrist to bring about the millennium.

The thesis of this article is that the large majority of ministers who published sermons during the Revolutionary era justified the war effort by a rationale that was more political than religious. They believed that the war deserved the support of true Protestants, and they assumed responsi-

Mr. Endy is Dean of the College at Hamilton College, where he is a member of the Department of Religion. This article is a product of his continuing inquiry into the history of American religious thought on war.

[1] Heimert, *Religion and the American Mind: From the Great Awakening to the Revolution* (Cambridge, Mass., 1966). "Postmillennialism" denotes the belief that the 1000-year reign of Christ predicted in the book of Revelation will come after developments in history preparing the way for Christ's return, such as the universal spread of the true Gospel and the increasing hegemony of Christian nations. Although postmillennialists understood the millennium as a long prelude to the end of history, the conviction was in certain respects the religious counterpart to the secular belief in progress. By "salvation history" I mean the working out of the Christian God's plan to redeem the saints and to establish in power the divine kingdom.

bility for motivating their congregations to help achieve victory. But in so doing they provided less a distinctively religious millennial justification than arguments harmonizing religion with the Real Whig legitimations of the Revolution and with warnings of the adverse consequences that a British victory would have for religious liberty. The clergy liberally applied biblical imagery to the conflict, as in their reference to the American Israel, but for the most part did not thereby intend to elevate the struggle to the plane of sacred history. Their understanding of legitimate authority for the war, its justifying causes, and the mood and motives of its participants more often fit the just war tradition of the Christian church than the interpretation of the Revolution as a holy war— an interpretation to which many recent scholars have contributed and subscribed.

These scholars have traced the development of the holy war perspective on the Revolution along a number of intersecting but diverse routes. Perhaps the longest path is that described by Sacvan Bercovitch in *The Puritan Origins of the American Self* and *The American Jeremiad*. Stressing the continuity of colonial history, Bercovitch argues that the Massachusetts Bay Puritans believed that they were fusing secular and sacred events in a manner unique in early modern times.[2] In their estimation, the founding of Boston was the *telos* and point of convergence of the whole of history, especially of salvation history. Bercovitch claims that from the beginning the Puritans were certain that they as a people had been assigned a central role in the progress of salvation like that of ancient Israel, whose antitype they were. Their own history had then unfolded in such a manner as to make the parallels even more striking to their descendants. With this conviction firmly entrenched, it remained only for Jonathan Edwards, interpreting the Great Awakening, to assert a continuity between present history and the millennium and to extend the New Israel identity to the colonies generally. Preachers of the 1760s and 1770s then recast the mythic view of history into the progressive, libertarian political language of the Enlightenment. Under the sway of their clerical leaders, many Americans became convinced that the Revolution, in the words of Ezra Stiles, marked the full and final "accomplishment of the *magnalia dei*,—the great events . . . designed from eternal ages to be displayed in these ends of the earth."[3] For the Puritans, according to Bercovitch, a new era had begun with the founding of the New World, and the Revolution brought that holy history to its culmination and marked the decisive development in the spiral of events leading to the millennium.

[2] Bercovitch develops his thesis regarding the uniqueness of the Puritan myth of the New Israel in *The Puritan Origins of the American Self* (New Haven, Conn., 1975). For his understanding of the continuity of the theme in colonial history see *The American Jeremiad* (Madison, Wis., 1978), and "New England's Errand Reappraised," in John Higham and Paul K. Conkin, eds., *New Directions in American Intellectual History* (Baltimore, 1979), 85-104.

[3] Stiles, *The United States Elevated to Glory and Honour* . . . (New Haven, Conn., 1783), 41. Unless otherwise noted, the authors cited were Congregationalists.

Other students of the religious significance of the Revolution focus, like Heimert, more directly on the Great Awakening. J. F. Maclear, Cedric B. Cowing, William G. McLoughlin, and Charles Royster, among others, have found an evangelical, crusading frame of mind prominent in Revolutionary America and have traced it to the religious unification of the colonies brought about by the Awakening and to the optimistic postmillennialism first clearly put forward by Edwards. These developments supposedly prepared Americans to expect revolutions in public affairs corresponding to those they experienced in their own hearts.[4] This scholarship attributes the religious thrust of the Revolution less to a specifically American salvation history than to the "enthusiastic" state of mind of a self-consciously Christian people. Americans saw the Revolution as a divine test which demanded a general conversion that was a counterpart to their own individual awakenings. According to Royster, "a millennium-like vision of peace, love, and ease shaped the expectations of many revolutionaries" and "made political striving a means to the redemption of the world from age-old politics, a means to the achievement of happiness based on righteousness." In this view, "the criterion against which the revolutionary had to measure his service on behalf of the promised future was not a relative, expedient, political one, but an absolute call for the attainment of permanent happiness. The continent, like the individual Christian, would be saved or it would not."[5] The military effort to secure liberty thus became an urgent test of righteousness and a crusade for the salvation of the world.

A third route to the understanding of the Revolution as a holy war is taken by Nathan O. Hatch in *The Sacred Cause of Liberty*. Convinced that the postmillennial optimism of Edwards in the early 1740s was not sustained either by Edwards himself or by his New Light successors, Hatch holds that the belief in progress prevalent among ministers of the Revolutionary era can be explained only by reference to the power of Real Whig ideology and to the merging of that ideology with the millennialism of the ministers beginning with the French and Indian War. The lesson of the war was that the pope was no longer Satan's primary agent in the struggle against God's plan of history. The main arena of the conflict between good and evil shifted from the ecclesiastical to the political realm; the ultimate battle was between the forces of liberty and those of tyranny. When England replaced France as the perpetrator of a tyrannical assault on

[4] Maclear, "The Republic and the Millennium," in Elwyn A. Smith, ed., *The Religion of the Republic* (Philadelphia, 1971), 183-194; Cowing, *The Great Awakening and the American Revolution: Colonial Thought in the 18th Century* (Chicago, 1971); McLoughlin, " 'Enthusiasm for Liberty': The Great Awakening as the Key to the Revolution," American Antiquarian Society, *Proceedings*, LXXXVII, Pt. i (1977), 69-95, and "The Role of Religion in the Revolution: Liberty of Conscience and Cultural Cohesion in the New Nation," in Stephen G. Kurtz and James H. Hutson, eds., *Essays on the American Revolution* (Chapel Hill, N.C., 1973), 197-255; Royster, *A Revolutionary People at War: The Continental Army and American Character, 1775-1783* (Chapel Hill, N.C., 1979), esp. chap. 4.

[5] Royster, *Revolutionary People at War*, 156, 154.

the colonies, the ministers responded by granting a millennial role to Real Whig ideology and its political program. The victory of spiritual and political liberty over spiritual and political tyranny now came to be seen as essential to the accomplishment of God's purposes in history. This gave renewed significance to the New England covenantal self-understanding as a chosen people uniquely parallel in significance to ancient Israel. "And because the future of liberty, the cause of God, depended entirely upon the war's outcome, the conflict assumed all the emotional intensity of a crusade of heaven against hell. Americans were not fighting for themselves, but for the well-being of the whole world."⁶

⁶ Hatch, *The Sacred Cause of Liberty: Republican Thought and the Millennium in Revolutionary New England* (New Haven, Conn., 1977), 88, 17, 36, 59-60. See also Mark A. Noll, *Christians in the American Revolution* (Washington, D.C., 1977), a nuanced study with interesting insights about the diversity of clerical views of the war, the affinities between Real Whig and Puritan thought, and the relationship between religious and political ideology in the Revolutionary era. Its major problem is Noll's claim that most of the patriot preachers merged their religious and political views in such a way as to preach the war as a crusade. Other studies making a similar assertion include George Marsden, "The American Revolution: Partisanship, 'Just Wars,' and Crusades," in Ronald A. Wells, ed., *The Wars of America: Christian Views* (Grand Rapids, Mich., 1981), 11-24; Jon T. Alexander, "Christian Attitudes toward War in Colonial America," *Church and Society*, LXIV (1974), 16-24; Leonard J. Kramer, "Muskets in the Pulpit: 1776-1783," Presbyterian Historical Society, *Journal*, XXXI (1953), 229-244, XXXII (1954), 37-51; and John F. Berens, *Providence and Patriotism in Early America, 1640-1815* (Charlottesville, Va., 1978), esp. chap. 4. Berens quotes from a wide variety of sources to show that most Americans of the Revolutionary era regarded the nation that was coming to birth as a New Israel whose God fought their battles by means of providential interventions to push forward his cosmic mission. That loyalists and the largely deistic Founding Fathers, as well as more evangelical New England clergy, "discerned the hand of God in each specific military development during the American Revolution" does not alert Berens to the need to consider the specific contexts of the constant references to the "American Israel" and "the interposing Hand of Heaven," the rhetorical practices of the period, or the differing understandings of providence and its relationship to natural causality (see pp. 88-89, 108-109).

A fourth interpretation of the Revolution as a crusade may be seen in Catherine L. Albanese, *Sons of the Fathers: The Civil Religion of the American Revolution* (Philadelphia, 1976). While Albanese strongly emphasizes the "enthusiastic spirit" and "revivalistic ardor" of the Americans in a manner similar to Heimert and his followers, she takes a distinctive line in arguing that the war started as a zealous millennial struggle under God's direction but gradually became an authentic ideological crusade. Reference to and reliance on God faded, and the nation-state itself became an object of awesome and transcendent power. The agent of that process was the war, which became the center of a ritual cult of sacrifice. The Revolution was seen in retrospect as the sacred mythic time of the creation of the nation, and all later American wars came to be viewed as sacralizing events. Despite the similarities of her interpretation to those that emphasize the significance of the Great Awakening for the development of the Revolutionary mentality, Albanese's views are probably most appropriately linked with those of

However the ideological roots may be traced, these interpreters agree that for most New England clergymen the Revolution became a religious event and that they "rallied to the American Revolutionary cause as a veritable crusade."[7] The Americans are pictured as fighting a holy war under the ideological leadership of the "black regiment." It is noteworthy, however, that none of the scholars mentioned discusses the ethical principles used by the ministers to justify war and their application of these principles to the American rebellion. Because of this lacuna and because of their recognition of the importance to colonial leaders of Real Whig political thought with its secularizing, natural rights approach to politics, the historians cited are occasionally unclear whether their theme is the sacralization of politics or the secularization of religion.

Seeking the ideological roots of the progressive, dynamic worldliness of modern middle-class American society, Bercovitch describes the translation of the Puritan jeremiad into the secular terms of an enlightened liberalism that appealed less to the authority of Scripture than to the history of the American colonial experiment. Royster recognizes at times that much of the so-called millennial language of the Revolutionary era was rather worldly and bore little relation to schemes of salvation history. Similarly, Hatch sometimes seems to be describing not so much a process by which the political realm took on ultimate significance as one in which the ministers aided the Revolutionary cause by making available "religious values, imagery, and emotional force to legitimate secular political ideals and institutions."[8]

Did the ministers who preached the cause of the Revolution view the event essentially as a holy war or as a just war? The question can be made precise by definition and differentiation of the categories originally developed by Christian theologians and canon lawyers.

As Christian pacifism declined with the Christianization of the Roman Empire in the fourth century, theologians, facing the necessity of coming to terms with war, turned both to the holy war tradition of the Hebrew scriptures and to the more secular justification for war developed in

---

Hatch because of her focus on the birth of an American civil religion (see esp. pp. 40-42, 101-108, 142, 194-195).

[7] Hatch, Sacred Cause of Liberty, 13.

[8] Bercovitch, American Jeremiad, 23, 125-127; Royster, Revolutionary People at War, 154, 156, 164; Hatch, Sacred Cause of Liberty, 12n. Hatch describes his topic as "the systems of meaning that helped New England ministers legitimate their needs and interests in terms of their religious ideals" (p. 9). Legitimation of a government by sacralizing it was a cultural necessity in 18th-century America and may be a universal condition of social order, especially in a new society. But it need not entail a self-regard as what Abraham Lincoln was to call "the last best, hope of earth" and hence a crusading mentality (Annual Message to Congress, Dec. 1, 1862, in Roy P. Basler, ed., The Collected Works of Abraham Lincoln, V [New Brunswick, N.J., 1953], 537).

Greek and Roman thought, particularly by Aristotle and Cicero. According to the former, Israel fought as a chosen nation or holy people under divine command to further God's saving purposes in history. According to the latter, political bodies contravening the jus gentium may be opposed by legitimate political authorities to defend the rights of those attacked and bring about a return to the status quo ante. The just war tradition, normally attributed to Augustine, has been portrayed by Roland H. Bainton and others as the normative Christian tradition since the early Middle Ages, with the Crusades and the religious wars of the Reformation being seen as aberrations. In fact, it was not until the movement of thought from Gratian and Aquinas of the twelfth and thirteenth centuries to the Spanish theorists Francisco Vitoria and Francisco Suarez of the sixteenth century that a truly political or secular just war model came into being. Although the holy war tradition was reinterpreted by Protestants—especially Calvinists—and by Catholics to justify their struggles during the Reformation, the advance of religious pluralism and other secularizing political influences in the early modern era led to the development of a distinctly political and secular understanding of war in the seventeenth and eighteenth centuries.[9]

Holy war and just war differ in three ways relevant to the issue under consideration here. (1) In a holy war the authorization comes from a religious authority (pope or church) or from God himself by a special revelation commanding the political authorities to fight. In a just war the authorization comes from the political authorities, who act on their own political and ethical knowledge in light of their understanding of God's will. (2) A holy war is fought for religious causes rather than in defense of political or natural rights. In the early modern era this commonly meant war between Roman Catholic and Protestant forces for hegemony in Europe or the New World; on the Protestant side such war was often justified on the ground that history had entered its climactic era with the Reformation and was moving toward the millennium. (3) A holy war is conceived by the warriors as a struggle between a "justified" or saintly army engaged in acts of piety against a demonic and damned enemy committing sacrilege, rather than as a battle between political agents of just and unjust causes. The mood of a holy war is one of righteous enthusiasm on the part of warriors of the Lord fighting for God's honor and their own salvation. The mood of the just war is sobered by the

---

[9] On the development of Christian justifications for war see Bainton, *Christian Attitudes toward War and Peace: A Historical Survey and Critical Re-evaluation* (New York, 1960); Frederick H. Russell, *The Just War in the Middle Ages* (Cambridge, 1975); Leroy Brandt Walters, Jr., "Five Classic Just-War Theories: A Study in the Thought of Thomas Aquinas, Vitoria, Suarez, Gentili, and Grotius" (Ph.D. diss., Yale University, 1971); and James Turner Johnson, *Ideology, Reason, and the Limitation of War: Religious and Secular Concepts, 1200-1740* (Princeton, N.J., 1975), and *Just War Tradition and the Restraint of War* (Princeton, N.J., 1981).

realization that warfare is at best a lesser evil demanded by the need to minimize injustice in relations between peoples.[10]

Elements of all three holy war criteria are found in the interpretations represented by Bercovitch, Hatch, and Royster, but each of these historians seems to focus on one of them as the compelling reason for seeing the Revolution as a holy war. Bercovitch stresses the Puritans' conception of sacred *authority*. The Puritans saw themselves making a "leap from secular into sacred history," which they explained by a typological exegesis that placed them prophetically in Scripture and on a level with ancient Israel.[11] Their history was a revelation of God's will, and their civil rulers possessed sacred authority in a theocracy preparing for the millennium. Their unique sense of national election led them to believe that their battles were commanded by God: divinity infused their history and demanded victory at any cost and by any means.[12]

Hatch's concern is with the holy *cause* of the war and the way in which the political cause stressed by the Real Whigs became suffused with religious significance and crusading zeal. What happened when the religious symbols of the millennium and the New Israel were translated into the secular grammar of Real Whig ideology was not a secularizing of the images but a renewal of their plausibility for understanding salvation history. In this "politics of religious conviction" there developed "a fundamental reordering of values that gave a profoundly new religious significance to the function of man as citizen."[13] The just cause was not simply given religious meaning for the pious; it was made into a sacred cause, and the war became the central development in the redemption of humanity.

Royster is less concerned with millennial and New Israel visions as part of salvation history than with the evangelical cast of mind that made the Revolution a struggle between saints and devils requiring righteous *zeal*. Whether or not "most revolutionary spokesmen" had faith that God's will would soon be done on earth as it already was in heaven, they "believed that service in the Continental Army had a clear religious meaning for the soldier. A recruit could enlist in two armies at once—the Continental Army for the salvation of his country and Christ's army for the salvation of

---

[10] The criterion of just means of warfare, or *jus in bello*, has often been cited as an additional distinguishing factor. By this criterion combatants are to observe the principle of discrimination between military and civilian targets and the principle of proportionality between the importance of the military objective of a campaign and the level of destructiveness to be tolerated in achieving it. Since I am discussing primarily the ideology by which the American Revolution was justified, rather than the way it was fought, and since the ministers said little about means of warfare, I ignore this criterion.

[11] Foreword to Charles Segal and David Stineback, eds., *Puritans, Indians, and Manifest Destiny* (New York, 1977), 17.

[12] See esp. *Puritan Origins*, chap. 3.

[13] Hatch, *Sacred Cause of Liberty*, 4, 11.

his soul." Because tyranny was sinful, by "stopping the British and the tories from enslaving America, he would also escape the bondage of his soul to sin." According to Royster, participation in the war was viewed as a zealous religious act against a demonic enemy.[14]

These interpretations can be assessed by analyzing the ethical thought of the Revolutionary clergy in relation to the war. The sources for such an analysis include nearly two hundred sermons and tracts published from late 1774 to early 1784. These were written by ministers of English descent, about two-thirds of whom were Congregationalists, while most of the remainder were Presbyterian.[15] It is among these English Calvinists, rather than among Anglicans, sectarian Baptists, and two-kingdom Lutherans and Dutch Reformed, that one is most likely to find a crusading spirit. It is therefore especially significant that, when the just war and holy war criteria are applied to these sources, one discerns that a large majority of the documents fit the just war model. While it is true that holy war themes are marked in the writings of about one-fifth of the ministers, including a number of prominent men, the Revolutionary clergy for the most part presented themselves not as priests of a holy people but as the religious and moral leaders of a body politic fighting what they perceived to be a just war.[16]

[14] Royster, *Revolutionary People at War*, 16.

[15] About 130 ministers produced a total of 190 publications dealing at least briefly with public affairs from late 1774, when rebellion began to appear a distinct possibility requiring justification, to early 1784, shortly after the signing of the peace treaty. Eighty-seven of the ministers were Congregationalists, with seventeen Presbyterians, thirteen Anglicans, and six Baptists. The rest I have been unable to identify by denomination. About 170 of the publications are sermons, including 38 thanksgiving sermons (including some for military events and the peace treaty), 24 sermons to soldiers, 21 fast sermons, 22 election sermons, 16 commemorating military events, and 9 commemorating political events. Half of the remaining 20 documents are treatises on political or military events, with the rest made up of apocalyptic treatises, histories, and prayers.

[16] Despite the popularity over the past 15 years of the interpretation of the war as a crusade, many historians have recognized that the ministers placed themselves at the service of an essentially secular ideology. Perhaps the most felicitous statement of the relationship between the Revolutionary ideology and the clergy is that of Bernard Bailyn, "Religion and Revolution: Three Biographical Studies," *Perspectives in American History*, IV (1970), 83-169. Although it does not comprehensively discuss ministerial views, a recent study that stresses the "limited war" mentality of the Revolutionary era is Reginald C. Stuart, *War and American Thought: From the Revolution to the Monroe Doctrine* (Kent, Ohio, 1982). Stuart argues that American political and religious leaders shared the 18th-century European view that war was an inevitable part of human affairs and that it was the duty of Christians to make it as restrained and civilized a possible. His argument seems considerably more persuasive than the studies claiming that the Americans' wilderness experience left them more eager for, and unrestrained in, war than their European counterparts, and that the American Revolution was the first modern ideological war. See, for example, John E. Ferling, *A Wilderness of Miseries: War and Warriors in Early America* (Westport, Conn., 1980).

Disagreements over the interpretation of this literature may be attributed in part to differences of judgment about the influence of certain
notable sources. Sermons of Samuel Sherwood, Ezra Stiles, Ebenezer
Baldwin, Abraham Keteltas, and a few others are quoted endlessly and
furnish a large part of the platform for overgeneralized interpretation. The
millennial enthusiasm, literal linking of Israel and America, and crusading
tone of such regularly cited sermons need to be considered with greater
sensitivity to rhetoric and context, but in any case these characteristics are
either muted in, or absent from, the large majority of the documents.
Although most of the ministers espoused a just war position and saw the
conflict in essentially political terms, they also believed that Americans
had in hand the work of forming a more truly Christian nation than
England had become. For this reason, and because even those who
regarded the war as a primarily religious phenomenon did not openly
break with the just war tradition and explicitly take a crusading approach
linked in their minds with the papacy, it is difficult in some contexts to
draw a clear distinction between a holy war and a just war outlook.
Nevertheless, it is usually possible to determine when the myth of a New
Israel, millennial hopes, and crusading mood so modify the just war
categories as to make plain that the preacher saw the war as a sacred
concern. The essential characteristic of a holy war is the belligerents'
conviction that they are playing an indispensable role in a struggle that
must be won if the ultimate goal of history is to be achieved. Only a
minority of the American clerics had such a grandiose regard for their
provincial outposts, and most of those who did entertain such thoughts
were hesitating and tentative.

On the issue of legitimating authority, the clergy who left a record of
their views were clear and consistent. A people whose natural rights were
threatened had the obligation to defend themselves. Although the right of
revolution did not enter the Christian just war tradition until the
seventeenth century, the Real Whig justifications of the Puritan and
Glorious revolutions were incorporated into the ministers' ethical
thought. The preachers rarely paused to counter the loyalist use of
Romans 13:2—"Whosoever therefore resisteth the power, resisteth the
ordinance of God"—and I Peter 2:13—"Submit yourselves to every
ordinance of man for the Lord's sake." To most ministers it was axiomatic
that society was a compact among people who possessed inalienable rights,
so that, as Ebenezer Baldwin said, it is as just for the people to oppose
tyrants "as 'tis to oppose a Robber that makes an Attempt upon my Life or
my Property."[17]

[17] Baldwin, *The Duty of Rejoicing under Calamities and Afflictions* ... (New
York, 1776), 29-30. See also [Samuel Mather], *The Dying Legacy of an Aged
Minister of the Everlasting Gospel* ... (Boston, 1783), 9; Dan Foster, *A Short Essay
on Civil Government. The Substance of Six Sermons* ... (Hartford, Conn., 1775), 59-
67; Nathan Perkins, *A Sermon, Preached to the Soldiers* ... (Hartford, Conn.,
[1775]), 9; Ezra Sam[p]son, *A Sermon Preached at Roxbury-Camp, before Col. Cotton's
Regiment* ... (Watertown, Mass., 1775).

Such a justification of the authority to make war depends on a belief in universal natural rights known by reason and conscience. It precludes the faith that God rules by means of revelation either directly from heaven or indirectly through his ministers. Several clerical writers combined a whig understanding of political authority with a strong conviction that legitimate political authority exists only where the lordship of Christ is recognized in Reformed Protestant fashion. When they claimed, in the words of Peter Powers, that "we, of all people in the world, have cause to own and acknowledge the prince of peace to be our sovereign," they implied that the justification for the Revolutionary War stemmed from adherence to Reformed beliefs and practices and was not limited by the jus gentium.[18] But only a small minority in this manner came close to seeing the colonies as a crusading theocracy like ancient Israel.

Although the ministers did not generally regard themselves as inspired authorizers of the war or sources of a peculiarly religious legitimation, they did take seriously their obligation to inspire their listeners and readers to contribute to an eminently just and therefore divinely favored cause. One way of doing so was to convince them that the political struggle had implications for religion. To the clergymen it was not accidental that liberty flourished in the colonies. The true Protestant, accustomed to verifying by study and experience the theological directives of religious leaders and given to exercising personal judgment in calling and dismissing ministers and in setting standards for congregational life, quite naturally demanded a similar role in civic life. If tyranny were allowed its victories in the latter realm, before long the Protestant way would lose out to hierarchy and superstition in religion. In John Murray's words, "Between civil liberties and those of religion there is a near and necessary connexion; when the one expires, the other cannot long survive."[19]

The clergy also contributed to the legitimacy of the struggle against England by setting the issues, personages, and events in the context of history, especially biblical history. A majority of the sermons published in the Revolutionary era were based on Old Testament texts, and the constant reference to the biblical world magnified the American cause by associating it with the epic of God's people. Historians who believe that the clergy justified the war primarily by reference to America's divine calling or sacred status tend to regard all references to biblical history and all assertions of similarity between Israel and America as signifying an

[18] Powers, *Jesus Christ the True King and Head of Government* . . . (Newburyport, Mass., 1778), 29. See also Samuel West, *A Sermon Preached before the Honorable Council* . . . (Boston, 1776); Henry Cumings, *A Sermon Preached in Billerica* . . . (Worcester, Mass., [1776]); and Elijah Fitch, *A Discourse, the Substance of Which Was Delivered at Hopkinton* . . . (Boston, 1776).

[19] Murray (Presbyterian), *Nehemiah: Or the Struggle for Liberty Never in Vain* . . . (Newbury, Mass., 1779), 21. See also Joseph Lyman, *A Sermon Preached at Hatfield* . . . (Boston, 1775); William Foster (Presbyterian), *True Fortitude Delineated* . . . (Philadelphia, 1776); and James Dana, *A Sermon, Preached before the General Assembly of* . . . *Connecticut* (Hartford, Conn., 1779).

intention to sacralize the American experience. The evidence suggests, however, that the Bible provided primarily a set of sagas and heroes that served to reinforce and legitimate the Real Whig ideology and its application to the war but without granting it the status of revealed truth.

The clergy saw the whole of political history as the story of the rise and demise of tyranny. Although they found the pattern in classical and Continental history, they focused above all on the Bible as a historical text on tyranny and opposition to it. As Bernard Bailyn and Pauline Maier have observed, the Real Whigs reconciled their emphasis on readiness for resistance with their conservative instincts by studying history assiduously on the assumption that tyrants' techniques are as systematic as the movement of the tides.[20] The ministers scoured the Old Testament as the most convincing textbook for teaching Americans the justice, seriousness, and necessity of their struggle. Biblical knowledge of God's *general* providence enabled them to justify opposition to tyrants and to predict their fate. Knowledge of God's *particular* providence facilitated understanding of the pattern of his interventions on behalf of liberty, especially in wars.[21]

It was in the context of this whig interpretation of history that the clergy turned to the Bible as a source of models for patriots, soldiers, and rulers. When the Continental Congress became a Sanhedrin and Washington a Joshua, their authority was indeed being legitimated by association with Scripture.[22] But regular allusions to the "inspired" leadership and biblical counterparts of the political and military leaders, especially the encomia to Washington, need not be understood as going so far as to signify that, for the preachers, America was God's new holy land. Postcolonial nations normally gain a measure of legitimacy by elevating a charismatic leader. Whatever their propensities for speaking in awed terms of the leaders of the new American nation, the largely Congregational and Presbyterian clergy who preached up the war found it difficult in reflective moments to

[20] Bailyn, "Religion and Revolution," *Perspectives Am. Hist.*, IV (1970), 137; Maier, *From Resistance to Revolution: Colonial Radicals and the Development of American Opposition to Britain, 1765-1776* (New York, 1972), esp. chap. 2. See Elijah Fitch, *A Discourse, . . . Being the Next Sabbath Following the Precipitate Flight of the British Troops from Boston* (Boston, 1776); Henry Cumings, *A Sermon Preached at Lexington . . .* (Boston, 1781); Jonas Clark[e], *A Sermon Preached before His Excellency John Hancock . . .* (Boston, [1781]); and Oliver Noble, *Some Strictures upon the Sacred Story . . .* (Newburyport, Mass., 1775).

[21] Robert Breck, *Past Dispensations of Providence Called to Mind . . .* (Hartford, Conn., 1784), 6; Samuel Cooke, *The Violent Destroyed: And Oppressed Delivered . . .* (Boston, 1777), 6; William Linn (Presbyterian), *A Military Discourse, Delivered in Carlisle . . .* (Philadelphia, 1776); John Devotion, *The Duty and Interest of a People to Sanctify the Lord of Hosts . . .* (Hartford, Conn., 1777), 26.

[22] See, for example, Josiah Meigs, *An Oration Pronounced before a Public Assembly in New-Haven . . .* (New Haven, Conn., 1782), 11; Thomas Brockway, *America Saved, or Divine Glory Displayed . . .* (Hartford, Conn., 1784), 17-18; Eliphalet Porter, *A Sermon, Delivered to the First Religious Society in Roxbury . . .* (Boston, 1784), 22-23.

place at the head of a holy nation, as heirs of Winthrop and Cromwell, let alone Moses and Joshua, the collection of Anglicans, proto-Unitarians, deists, and Masons who formed the nucleus of the Revolutionary leadership.

As Bercovitch says in reference to English and other "elect nation" traditions, the parallels between Israel and one's own nation were made "deuteronomically: as analogy, precedent, and moral *exemplum*." Bercovitch's insistence that the ministers related Israel and America as type and antitype rather than precedent and moral exemplum, and that many of them raised America from profane to sacred history, is not borne out by close analysis of the Revolutionary sources.[23] Some exegetes did see unique parallels between Israel and the colonies, but even in the midst of their holy war rhetoric most of them lacked the temerity to suggest that America was a true counterpart of Israel and that the people or their leaders enjoyed, like Israel and the apostolic church, immediate direction from God. Some, such as Israel Evans, a chaplain, spoke of their day as an era "when time was most dignified, and boasted an unrivalled glory," but most zealous holy nation spokesmen had to admit in their less rhetorical moments that the age of miracles in the true sense had ended.[24] The Revolutionary clergy believed that enough strange occurrences had become evident in the course of the war to warrant the conviction that God was in some special sense involved, but the large majority knew that God worked for the American cause by means of storms and similar events that could be seen in terms of the special providential use of natural law. Few seriously claimed divine intervention comparable to the dividing of the waters that enabled the Israelites to escape Egypt or the epiphany that constituted Isaiah's call to prophesy. Even Israel had heard God's voice and seen his miraculous power only at special times, namely, those high points when God was manifestly pushing forward his plan of salvation, as in the Exodus, the calling of the prophets, and the Christ events. For most of its life as a nation, Israel had to make do with God's

[23] Bercovitch, *Puritan Origins*, 80. According to Bercovitch, although the history of Israel could provide any nation with instruction in God's general providence and Christian nations with exemplary situations illustrating God's special providential interventions for his peoples, American exegetes believed that Israel was a type in the sense that persons, objects, and events in its life were prophetic of precisely parallel developments in later salvation history that fulfilled them. America was Israel's antitype in the sense that it was a uniquely chosen nation that could expect to play the indispensable role in the latter days of the Christian dispensation that Israel had played in the old dispensation. Moreover, specific events in Israel's life, such as the Exodus, foreshadowed similar events in America's life that would fulfill and surpass in significance the original events. Typology, according to Bercovitch, thus placed America at the center of the biblical revelation. See esp. *ibid.*, chaps. 2, 3, and *American Jeremiad*, chap. 4.

[24] Evans (Presbyterian), *A Discourse, Delivered in New-York, before a Brigade of Continental Troops* . . . (New York, [1784]), 10. See also Levi Frisbie, *An Oration . . . on Account of the Happy Restoration of Peace* (Boston, 1783), 6-7.

providential guidance by means of secondary causes. Possibly God would intervene directly once again to turn the wheel of salvation history in the eschatological era proper, but most of the clergymen of the Revolutionary period saw themselves as living at best in the prelude to that time.

According to the ministers, in postbiblical times God sometimes gave certain nations special responsibilities, and a prayerful observer might discern a peculiar concatenation of developments implying God's providential intervention on behalf of a Christian people. Nevertheless, neither typological exegesis, nor emphasis on parallels between Israel and America, nor the conviction that God was aiding the cause induced even the most zealous ministers to place America truly on a par with Israel. With Samuel Webster, they believed that "as God does not now direct his voice immediately to us, we must not counterfeit it, and say—*the Lord saith*—when the Lord hath not spoken. But yet, in similar circumstances, we may, by analogy, take the ancient voice of God, as directed to us. This is the use we are to make of a great part of the old testament."[25] This use of Scripture was available to all Christian peoples, and the Revolutionary clergy themselves drew parallels between Israel and other modern peoples as well as between Israel and America.

They knew that since biblical times there was no longer a uniquely chosen national people. In the words of John Lathrop, "the Jewish nation was formerly the peculiar people,—the chosen nation and elect of God. But after the death of Jesus Christ, all former distinctions between nations and families, in a religious view, were done away. The separating wall was broken down. The company of disciples—the followers of Jesus Christ—sincere Christians of all nations and languages under heaven, from the death of Jesus Christ, and ever after, are to be considered as the *elect*, the *peculiar people* of God." New England was simply one of several "professing peoples" in the Christian dispensation.[26] The clergy believed that the struggle of liberty against tyranny was God's cause and that their conflict was center stage in God's providential rule, but only a few held forth the American people as the peculiar antitype of Israel.

In regard to the second criterion for distinguishing a holy war from a just war—justifiable cause—the clerics were as whiggish as in their understanding of legitimating authority. Having emphasized the role of consent in all important human relationships and the need to hem in human depravity by limiting all power, the Calvinist clergy in particular readily supported the whig commitment to political rights and contracts. When defending the legitimacy of the American rebellion, they cited political writers who denounced the British attacks on property and self-

[25] Webster, *A Sermon Preached before the Honorable Council, . . . of the State of the Massachusetts-Bay* . . . (Boston, 1777), 7.
[26] See Lathrop, *A Sermon, Preached at the Ordination of William Bentley* . . . (Salem, Mass., 1783), n. pag.; Brockway, *America Saved*, 7; and Joseph Willard, *A Thanksgiving Sermon* . . . (Boston, 1784).

government by measures imposing taxation without representation. The ministers believed that the colonists were defending their natural rights to life, liberty, and property in a defensive war, although they maintained that a people subjected to a systematic threat to their fundamental rights were justified in taking the offensive to defend themselves.[27]

The argument of historians that the clergy turned the political cause into a holy one emphasizes the extent to which the ministers set it in the context of a millennial scheme, thereby subordinating the political conflict to the salvific ends God was achieving by means of the conflict. Hatch is surely right about the widespread tendency among the ministers to stress the religious significance of the political cause and, in particular, to make the struggle for religious and civil liberty central to God's historical purposes. Nonetheless, his melding of religious and political elements is problematic in certain respects.

From 1775 to at least 1780, the large majority of the clergy who published sermons and tracts lacked the boldness to suggest that there was anything especially important about the colonies' place in either world or salvation history. The prominent millennialists of those years, in addition, were much more tentative than is granted by historians who understand millennialism as the progenitor of a holy war mentality. Ebenezer Baldwin, who claimed in 1776 that America might become both "a great and mighty Empire" founded on principles of civil and religious liberty such as the world had never seen, and "the principal Seat of that glorious Kingdom, which Christ shall erect upon earth in the latter days," thought of suppressing the millennial "Conjecture" when his sermon was printed, "lest it should appear whimsical and Enthusiastical." Samuel Sherwood, whose sermon of 1776 is the most widely quoted as the typical millennial jeremiad, backed into his millennialism hoping that he might "conjecture ... without a spirit of vanity and enthusiasm, that some of those prophecies of St. John may, not unaptly, be applied to our case."[28]

In the course of the war great claims began to be made about what Seymour Martin Lipset has called "the first new nation," and by the time victory was imminent clergymen were envisioning an extraordinary future prominence for the American people.[29] Ezra Stiles, who recognized that

[27] Peter Whitney, *The Transgression of a Land Punished by a Multitude of Rulers* (Boston, 1774), 18; Sam[p]son, *Sermon Preached at Roxbury-Camp*, 19; [Moses Mather], *America's Appeal to the Impartial World* ... (Hartford, Conn., 1775), 10–20, 22, 34, 37. On the affinity of the clergy for radical whig views see Cushing Strout, *The New Heavens and New Earth: Political Religion in America* (New York, 1974), chap. 4.

[28] Baldwin, *Duty of Rejoicing*, 38, 38n; Sherwood, *The Church's Flight into the Wilderness* ... (New York, 1776), 18.

[29] It is nevertheless instructive that of twenty-five sermons published in 1783 and early 1784, only eight have any significant millennial content, including five of twelve sermons commemorating the national day of thanksgiving after the peace. The quoted phrase comes from Lipset, *The First New Nation: The United States in Historical and Comparative Perspective* (New York, 1963).

even in the flush of victory many Americans would find his view of history "utopian" and "visionary," was not unique in suggesting that this American Israel would be raised high above the nations as it fulfilled its historical role on the way to the millennium. Some of the ministers did not apply the term "millennial" to their grandiose visions of the future; those who did sometimes fused imperial and millennial predictions uncritically. Such sources, which are millennial in only the loosest sense, are usually cited by scholars who have stressed the prominence of millennialism in the Revolutionary climate of opinion.[30]

Millennialism can be seen as widespread or normative only if it is defined so broadly that it loses any necessary correlation with traditional salvation history. Much of the supposed evidence is primarily composed of visions of a grand future for Americans, and through them for all people, because of the New World's natural abundance and the energy of its inhabitants. If, in Royster's words, "the wealth, harmony, creativity, and ease Americans anticipated for their continent in worldly terms appeared in visionary eloquence that hardly differed from and sometimes led to anticipations of the millennium," this rhetoric also had what he calls "a broad strain of worldly ambition [that] did not necessarily arise from a revolutionary's religious beliefs."[31] Much of this language appears to be mainly a product of an Enlightened nationalism predicated on the myth of progress and includes neither explicit eschatological hopes nor any clear salvific role for the Americans. Possibly one-sixth of the documents dealing with public events published in Revolutionary America by ministers placed the nation in the context of millennial history, and this estimate includes sermons with only very brief millennial suggestions in the rhetorical flourish at the end, as well as short apocalyptical treatises prompted by such occurrences as earthquakes and fires.[32]

Many writers who did relate their millennialism to a plan of salvation history did not grant particular millennial significance to the war. Others gave to the war a fairly precise millennial role but insisted that events that might be part of God's cosmic plan should be regarded by the human participants as a struggle among human beings who see "through a glass, darkly."[33] Such participants are bound by the political and moral restraints

[30] Stiles, United States Elevated, 23.

[31] Royster, Revolutionary People at War, 157, 154. It is perhaps the realization that millennialism in the proper sense was not as widespread as sometimes portrayed that leads interpreters such as Royster to focus on the Revolutionary cast of mind rather than on holy history in the millennial sense.

[32] See, for example, Nathan Williams, A Sermon Preached in the Audience of the General Assembly ... (Hartford, 1780), 25-26; David Osgood, Reflections on the Goodness of God ... (Boston, 1784), 31; and Phillips Payson, A Memorial of Lexington Battle ... (Boston, 1782), 10.

[33] Millennialists who did not sacralize the war included Ebenezer Baldwin, Thomas Brockway, Thomas Bray, Benjamin Trumbull, and Chauncey Whittelsey of Connecticut; Sylvanus Conant, Joseph Roby, Isaac Story, David Tappan, and Charles Turner of Massachusetts; and Joseph Buckminster of New Hampshire.

people have devised to keep wars as civilized and limited as possible. In the words of Thomas Bray, in his *Dissertation on the Sixth Vial*, although the war is part of God's purpose in these latter days,

> we may not infer from hence, that we are to adopt, or pursue any undue measures, to accomplish this great and benevolent end [that is, the salvation of mankind]. Not in this general sense, *do evil that good may come;* such as being the aggressors in any quarrel; attempting to kindle the flames of war in the world in an unjustifiable manner; where we have no call to plead the cause of the oppressed, or seek assistance in our own defence. We have no call of God to do this, under any pretence of fulfilling his will, and accomplishing the designs of his providence. Jehovah will accomplish his own work in its season, and in a way most for his own glory. In this sense, to begin the horrors of war where we had no just call, would be a very different thing from that of defending our injured country, and endeavouring to break the oppressor's arm.[34]

Though such an explicit repudiation of a holy war perspective is unusual in a millennial treatise in which the Revolution has a place, Bray's *Dissertation* is nonetheless representative of most of the writings of the period that treat the millennium without developing a crusading approach to the war.

Because of the dichotomy drawn by many ministers between the divine use of the war on the plane of sacred history and the human perspective on it, Hatch's "civil millennialism" did not exert the formative sacralizing role that he attributes to it. The millennialism that might have turned the war into a crusade by no means consistently played that role and was not as widespread as he infers. Moreover, the sermons were often too "civil" to be millennial in any proper sense and to have the effects that Hatch imputes to them. The melding of millennialism and Real Whig thought did as much to secularize the former as to sacralize the latter, as Hatch's own references to the secularizing currents of the era imply. Hatch is correct in arguing that for the clergy the cause of God had come to include a particular definition of political liberty. In fact, however, this very definition encompassed a view of religious liberty that inevitably led toward secularization of the state and denied it much of its aura of sacred authority. Moreover, this view included a conception of universal rights that precluded the kind of subordination of human rights to divine causes of which holy wars are made. If all human beings have certain *inalienable*

---

[34] Bray, *Dissertation* . . . (Hartford, Conn., 1780), 102-103. The reasons for this lack of correlation between millennialism and attitudes toward the Revolution are discussed insightfully by James West Davidson in *The Logic of Millennial Thought: Eighteenth-Century New England* (New Haven, Conn., 1977), esp. chap. 6. Davidson concludes that the millennial thought of the Revolutionary period was essentially unchanged from that of 20 years earlier, that it was apolitical, and that it played no significant role in causing or shaping the Revolution.

rights, one cannot use a religious rationale to justify forfeiture of those rights. This did not prevent the later paradoxical development by which this very political ideology became for some Americans an object of ultimate, crusading allegiance, but in the Revolutionary era reliance on natural rights served as a brake on the crusading mentality. There is little evidence that large numbers of the Revolutionary clergy era idolized their cause to a significant extent.

The third criterion, the mood of the participants and their attitudes toward the fighting, when applied to the Revolution, places the ministers even more clearly in the just war tradition. Only a minority exhibited crusading zeal. The Real Whig belief in the moral and military superiority of citizen armies over standing armies of professionals was strongly reinforced by the contrast some ministers drew between the "hardy and bold, persevering and patient . . . valorous sons of New-England, tempered in these northern climes, and braced by these frigid north-westerly blasts," and the cutthroats and social outcasts sent from England in red coats.[35] For a few preachers this contrast became one between sacred and profane, as when Samuel Mather, deploring the presence of Britain's "profane" legions, claimed that God had "sanctified [the American soldiers] or set them apart."[36] But the "innocence" of the American soldiers, after the decline of what Royster calls the "rage militaire" of 1775-1776, turned out to be a kind of prelapsarian innocence of rural sons unaccustomed to the freedom and allurements of life away from home in city or camp. Soldiering did not preclude, but in fact encouraged, a plunge into what were for many young men "original" forms of sin. Whatever similarities the clergy may have envisioned between the military congregations of ancient Israel or Cromwell's army of saints, on the one hand, and the colonial camps on the other, were not destined to become realities. It is not surprising to find the clergy devoting many of their camp sermons to the moral and spiritual dangers of military service.

In referring to the profane influences of army life, the ministers were not for the most part holding soldiers to standards appropriate only for a holy army and thereby indulging in the paradoxical damning that presupposes salvation. They knew full well that soldiering was a secular, though certainly honorable and necessary, vocation. Admittedly, war, because it killed, could be a religious prod. Moreover, for some of the liberal or arminian clergy a courageous death in a just and divinely favored cause might be the "work" that earned a soldier entrance to heaven. But the ministers were thoroughly imbued with the Real Whig association of militarism with tyranny. War was far from glorified in the clerical

[35] Zabdiel Adams, *The Grounds of Confidence and Success in War* . . . (Boston, 1775), 30. See also the Presbyterian George Duffield, *A Sermon Preached in the Third Presbyterian Church in the City of Philadelphia* . . . (Philadelphia, 1784), 8-9.
[36] [Mather], *Dying Legacy*, 21, 29.

literature. It was generally regarded as a product of human lusts and as an unmitigated disaster for all involved. Defense against the murderous designs of tyrants was noble and even, for the New Lights, a sustained act of benevolence toward victims of the ravages of aggression. It was, however, to be approached mournfully.[37]

Fighting was only rarely seen as a religious vocation that earned spiritual rewards. Most sermons to the soldiers discussed moral issues relating to their duties and climaxed by calling them to enlist under the banner of Christ, the great captain of their salvation. Martial acts, mundane enemies, and struggles for liberty put ministers in mind of religious counterparts, namely, zeal for truth, spiritual enemies, and liberation from sin. Preachers made liberal and appropriate use of military images and metaphors to enlist the zeal of the troops, but the analogy between spiritual and temporal warfare served, for the most part, not to mix the modes of combat but to place them in separate realms—the one sacred, the other secular. Lest the two become confused, Joseph Willard, speaking for many chaplains, stated bluntly that, contrary to what some soldiers might believe, one who acquitted himself well in battle and died therein did not necessarily win salvation because he had given his life in "a good cause." Soldiers who hoped for a heavenly rest were warned that the spiritual battle had to be won before the military engagement was undertaken.[38]

---

[37] The perspective of innumerable sermons is well put by Zabdiel Adams in his Massachusetts election sermon of 1782: "What judgment is there greater than this? How are the civil establishments of former times subverted by war, and confusion introduced into the world?" "What benevolent heart can contemplate the ravages of war without pain? There are none but the *fierce* and *savage* who can delight in scenes of carnage. But, though the horrors of *war* are great; yet, when we come to contrast them with *slavery*, we find the darkness of the *night-piece* immediately lessens" (A *Sermon Preached before ... John Hancock ...* [(Boston, 1782)], 45). Josiah Stearns of Epping, N.H., who provided the most careful and sustained elaboration of the just war tradition in the literature of the period, went so far as to suggest that it was difficult to speak of true justice in war, since the victims of aggression, sinful creatures that they are, are thrown off their moral equilibrium by the wrong done to them and rarely respond in a guiltless manner. See *Two Sermons, Preached at Epping ... on a Public Fast* (Newburyport, Mass., 1777), 8-9, 24. On the necessity of a sober approach to war see also Thaddeus Maccarty, *Praise to God, a Duty of Continual Obligation* (Worcester, Mass. [1776]), 16; Cooke, *Violent Destroyed*, 13; and the Presbyterian John Witherspoon, *The Dominion of Providence over the Passions of Men ...* (Philadelphia, 1776), 10-11.

[38] Willard, *The Duty of the Good and Faithful Soldier ...* (Boston, 1781), 8. See also Payson, *Memorial of Lexington Battle*, 10, 21-24; Isaac Morrill, *Faith in Divine Providence, the Great Support of God's People in Perilous Times ...* (Boston, 1780), 28; and Cumings, *Sermon Preached at Lexington*, 38. Despite his major thesis, Royster provides evidence showing that the military leaders found most of the chaplains less than inspiring, in part because they did not relate their religion clearly enough to politics and warfare (*Revolutionary People at War*, 161-168).

If it was difficult for Congregational and Presbyterian ministers to see themselves as allies of the likes of Washington, Franklin, and Jefferson, it was even harder for most of them to conceive of Englishmen as allies of Antichrist. Abraham Keteltas could turn "the cause of justice and integrity, against bribery, venality, and corruption" into "the cause of heaven against hell," but this kind of imagery was foreign to most of the clergy.[39] They had begun with a horror of English corruption and tyranny precisely because they viewed the English as "flesh of our flesh" and England not only as "the wisest nation on earth" but as the leader of the Protestant struggle against Rome.[40] Although this veritable English civil religion collapsed during the war, most clergy were unable to regard Protestant England as the agent of the traditionally Catholic Antichrist. Some perceived the former parent state as an unwitting dupe of the devil, but ingenious millennialists maneuvered around that by making political rather than religious tyranny the devil's main strategy in *this* chapter of the cosmic struggle. Here, too, however, it was difficult for clergymen to see England as more than a temporary base of tyranny, and such politicizing of the devil and his works served less to sacralize the war than to secularize the devil.[41] When the new nation became allied with a Catholic state whose absolute monarch was regarded as "the Defender of the Rights of Mankind" and which one minister called "the most enlightened, civilized nation on earth," whatever tendency there had been to make the struggle a cosmic one against a demonic enemy was muted. With the pope's main military supporter on their side, most of the ministers were content to leave the old imagery in the closet.[42]

It is not easy to account for the discrepancies between the conclusions drawn here and those of other recent interpreters of the Revolution simply in terms of historical methodology. The crusading emphasis and

---

[39] Keteltas, *God Arising and Pleading His People's Cause* ... (Newburyport, Mass., 1777), 30. See also Sherwood, *Church's Flight into the Wilderness,* although Sherwood was not sure whether the beast of tyranny in his day was France or Great Britain (p. 15).

[40] Adams, *Grounds of Confidence,* 34; Jonathan Bascom, *A Sermon Preached at Eastham on Thanksgiving-Day* (Boston, 1775), 18. See also [Mather], *America's Appeal to the Impartial World,* 3; Joseph Montgomery (Presbyterian), *A Sermon, Preached at Christiana Bridge and Newcastle* ... (Philadelphia, 1775), 10; and Maccarty, *Praise to God,* 26.

[41] This changing view of England is seen in Cooke, *Violent Destroyed,* 23-24; John Rodgers (Presbyterian), *The Divine Goodness Displayed, in the American Revolution* ... (New York, 1784), 10; Stiles, *United States Elevated,* 33-34; and Benjamin Trumbull, *God Is to Be Praised for the Glory of His Majesty* ... (New Haven, Conn., 1784), 35.

[42] Israel Evans, *A Discourse Delivered Near York in Virginia* ... (Philadelphia, 1782), 42; Duffield, *Sermon Preached in the Third Presbyterian Church,* 11.

the millennial interpretation came to the fore in historical writing at a time
when, stimulated by the Vietnam War and preoccupied with American
civil religion, students of American culture set about finding the roots of
what Robert Jewett has called the "Captain America Complex."[43] No
doubt this interest in the origins of the American sense of destiny was
itself at least in part a product of the search for an American identity and
for social cohesion in the wake of the disunity that became evident in the
late 1960s. And the historiographical emphasis on the formative power of
the Great Awakening and its influence during the period of our national
birth was understandable at a time when evangelical Christianity was
becoming recognized once again as part of the mainstream of religious
America.

Those who turned to the colonial and Revolutionary periods to find the
roots of the "Captain America Complex" or sense of national destiny had
reason to seek it among the Puritans and especially in that period of our
history that Americans have regarded as the sacred time of national
origins. Since the 1930s most interpreters of American colonial culture
have accepted Perry Miller's idea that the Puritans came to the New
World on what they believed to be a divine mission and that Revolutionary Americans saw themselves as renewing and reinterpreting the mission.
As heirs of Reformed Protestantism who adapted its dynamic view of
history to their national experience, Puritans could hope to participate in
the eschatological accomplishment of the kingdom of God. But with some
exceptions, such as Edward Johnson's *Wonder-Working Providence,* such
thoughts served mainly to allow colonists to suggest that their exodus
from England had not been caused simply by failure of nerve. Rumina-
tions about their role in God's historical scheme belonged in the category
of pious hopes and were usually too conjectural, hesitant, and at times
defensive to serve as a basis for political and military policy.

The aspect of their "errand" about which New England's Puritan
founders had been most firmly convinced was that, in the words of John
Winthrop in "A Modell of Christian Charity," "the end is to improve our
lives to doe more service to the Lord the comforte and encrease of the
body of christe whereof wee are members that our selves and posterity
may be the better preserved from the Common corrupcions of this evill
world to serve the Lord and worke out our Salvation under the power and
purity of his holy Ordinances."[44] Sunk in sin like the rest of humanity, all
that most Puritans dared claim was that the relative purity of their worship
redounded to God's glory more adequately than the idolatrous ordinances
of less reformed Christians and might preserve them more effectively

---

[43] Jewett, *The Captain America Complex: The Dilemma of Zealous Nationalism*
(Philadelphia, 1973). The discussion of American civil religion was sparked by
Robert N. Bellah's article, "Civil Religion in America," *Daedalus,* XCVI (1967), 1-
21.

[44] Massachusetts Historical Society, *Winthrop Papers,* II (Boston, 1931), 293.

from God's wrath. Throughout the seventeenth and eighteenth centuries, almost all published New England sermons alluding to the goal of the original crossing to the New World followed Winthrop in placing primary emphasis on the themes of preservation from corruption and the purity of ordinances. If this meant that those who attacked the Puritans, whether heathen Indians or idolatrous Romanists, were seen as enemies of God, it also meant that the colonists were too preoccupied with their own purification from sin and preparation for the next world, and too attentive to the glory of God, to focus consistently on their historical success as the key to God's ultimate purposes in history.

Although he has found its sources much earlier, Bercovitch has written that a millennial crusading zeal took wings in the course of the eighteenth century when the Puritan myths, emptied of their specificity and scriptural substance, became filled with American content. "During the eighteenth century, the meaning of Protestant identity became increasingly vague; typology took on the hazy significance of metaphor, image, and symbol; what passed for the divine plan lost its strict grounding in Scripture; 'providence' itself was shaken loose from its religious framework to become part of the belief in human progress."[45] The general process described by Bercovitch is surely important to the drawing out of the crusading implications of the New Israel theme in America in the nineteenth and twentieth centuries. But Bercovitch and other recent scholars have predated that development. What is striking about the clerical literature of the Revolutionary era, relative to that of the nineteenth century, is its otherworldliness and its dissociation of private faith from public events.

The political and military struggle against England was not accorded a prominent place in the sermons in the Revolutionary era, even when they were delivered in the military camp. Appropriate enough for special days of commemoration, the war and associated worldly subjects were usually introduced on other occasions with apologies for an intrusion justified only by the extraordinary nature of the times. John Witherspoon claimed not to have discussed the struggle against English tyranny from the pulpit until 1776. The pastoral letter of the Presbyterian Synod of New York and Philadelphia in 1775 said that "perhaps no instance can be given on so interesting a subject, in which political sentiments have been so long and so fully kept from the pulpit."[46] Many ministers were not so self-restrained during the next few years, but an analysis of the general, ordination, and funeral sermons of the Revolutionary period—including funeral sermons for military and political figures—indicates that the primary concern of ministers on such occasions was eternal life gained through either redemption by Christ or moral behavior (depending on the

---

[45] Bercovitch, *American Jeremiad*, 93.
[46] *Records of the Presbyterian Church in the United States of America* (Philadelphia, 1841), 467.

theology of the speaker) and that even in July 1776 and December 1783 the joys or torments of the next world were seen as infinitely more important than the passing pleasures or trials of this one. Many of the clergy perceived a need to warn their parishioners against preoccupation with the lively events of the day and against the delusive hope that after the Revolution a temporal paradise would replace this world of trouble.[47]

Ironic as it may seem in view of the propensity of many historians to find in the Great Awakening the origins of the Revolutionary cast of mind, the major problem with the recent emphasis on the Revolution as a religious event may be a failure to recognize the *full* significance of the evangelical mind-set of eighteenth-century Americans. Americans of the Revolutionary era—including those of a liberal or even deist persuasion, as the constitutional debates were soon to attest—knew the universal extent and the power of sin in the world. They found sin above all in their own hearts, and when they were tempted in times of national danger to shift the burden to the enemy, ministers reminded them that it was all too easy in war to drape damnable corruption in a mantle of righteousness. The point was eloquently made by David Tappan in May 1783 in an attempt to counter the enthusiasm of the hour. "Is human nature essentially different in this new world, from what it ever has been and still is in the old? Or are we more strongly fortified against the insinuating, bewitching charms of a prosperous condition? Are we a people of more established virtue than all others that have lived before us? Alas, Sirs, such self-flattering ideas are equally false and vain—our national character . . . is perhaps as degenerate as that of any people in the world."[48] Since true righteousness was in short supply in America as elsewhere, it ill behooved the colonists to identify their cause with God's in the crusading sense, even when they suspected that they were, in spite of themselves, God's agents in a decisive chapter of history. Moreover, for the true evangelicals, the supply of righteousness was more dependent on the grace of God's forgiveness than on activity even in a divine cause.

Crusading zeal would come to the fore on many occasions among religious leaders in the nineteenth and twentieth centuries, especially in time of war. It was present in the Revolution as well, but only fitfully among more than a minority of the clergy. Only after American leaders had diminished the sense of distance between themselves and God could Lincoln regard the Civil War as a crusade to preserve "the last best, hope of earth" and Wilson call the American doughboys "disinterested champions of right" who "were recognized as crusaders, and as their thousands

---

[47] For example, Brockway, *America Saved*, 21. Ordination sermons enumerating pastoral duties rarely mentioned ministers' public or civic duties and seldom referred to current events.

[48] Tappan, *The Question Answered, Watchman, What of the Night?* . . . (Salem, Mass., 1783), 14.

swelled to millions their strength was seen to mean salvation."[49] In both cases ministers fleshed out the crusading rationale. History became for Americans the scene of salvation only when the myth of New World regeneration had sapped the sense of sinfulness. That revolution in American religious thought had hardly begun by the time the revolution for Independence ended in 1783.

[49] Lincoln, Message to Congress, Dec. 1, 1862, in Basler, ed., *Works of Lincoln*, V, 537; Wilson, Address to the Senate, July 10, 1919, in Conrad Cherry, ed., *God's New Israel: Religious Interpretations of American Destiny* (Englewood Cliffs, N.J., 1971), 285-286.

THE GENDERED MEANINGS OF VIRTUE IN REVOLUTIONARY AMERICA

RUTH H. BLOCH

In its contemporary colloquial usage, "virtue" is usually a term for female sexual prudence and benevolent activity with old-fashioned connotations. It evokes traits like chastity and altruism and, in a cynical post-sexual-revolution world, prudery and hypocritical do-goodism.

On the one hand, these connotations are very old in Western culture. The sexual meaning of the word dates back to medieval and ancient times when the virtues were symbolized as virgins.[1] The Catholic ideals of celibacy and charity also reinforced the association of Christian virtue with sexual purity and personal sacrifice. On the other hand, the Protestant Reformation placed less emphasis on these qualities, criticizing the monastic ideal of celibacy and denying the spiritual efficacy of church offerings. It stressed other individual virtues—piety, temperance, frugality, and work in a useful calling.

Earlier versions of this paper were presented to the 1985–86 Gender Seminar at the Institute for Advanced Study in Princeton and to the Faculty Research Seminar on Women at the University of California, Los Angeles. Many members of these seminars provided useful criticisms. I am especially grateful to the anonymous readers for *Signs* and to Joyce Appleby, Daniel Walker Howe, Jan Lewis, Phyllis Mack, Debora Silverman, and Kathryn Kish Sklar for their helpful suggestions.

[1] Morton W. Bloomfield, *The Seven Deadly Sins* (East Lansing: Michigan State University Press, 1952), 64, 137.

[*Signs: Journal of Women in Culture and Society* 1987, vol. 13, no. 1]

37

The view that women were capable of greater sexual self-control and generosity than men arose later, in the eighteenth and nineteenth centuries, at different times and to different degrees in different places and social groups. This transformation was, at most, only indirectly a consequence of the cultural changes brought on by the Reformation. In middle-class America, where both Calvinism and early evangelical Protestantism were particularly strong, it was not until the end of the eighteenth century that women were commonly idealized as selfless and pure. According to the quintessentially Victorian view, intrinsically feminine traits—traits eventually satirized as "motherhood and apple pie"—lay at the base of the American nation. It is the echo of this nineteenth-century culture that we hear in the colloquial use of the word virtue today.

Among historians identified with the recent interpretation of the American Revolution known as the "Republican synthesis," the word "virtue" has, however, been invested with an older political meaning.[1] Resurrected in its classical and early modern republican forms, the term refers not to female private morality but to male public spirit, that is, to the willingness of citizens to engage actively in civic life and to sacrifice individual interests for the common good. Is virtue, then, to be understood as a word with two different meanings—one personal and female, the other political and male? Or is there a deeper historical and symbolic connection between the two definitions?

An appreciation of the eighteenth-century political use of the term is essential to an understanding of the American Revolution, but it is becoming increasingly clear that such an appreciation must also take into account the history of masculine and feminine symbolism. Conceptions of politics and of gender were tied together in late eighteenth-century America in ways that historians have only begun to unravel. The transition toward the personal and feminine definition of "virtue" was a development already occurring during the Revolutionary period, partly in response to political events and partly in response to changes in gender-based symbols that had already begun.

The experiences and perceptions of women during the American Revolution have attracted considerable scholarly attention from historians of women. So far, most studies point to the importance of women's activity during the Revolution and to the ways in which their social status was

---

[1] For a useful review of this literature, see Robert Shalhope, "Republicanism and Early American Historiography," *William and Mary Quarterly* 39 (1982): 334–56. The classical republican idea of virtue has also been invoked outside the historical discipline. See, e.g., Sheldon Wolin, *Politics and Vision: Continuity and Innovation in Western Political Thought* (Boston: Little, Brown & Co., 1960); Robert N. Bellah, *The Broken Covenant: American Civil Religion in a Time of Trial* (New York: Seabury Press, 1975); Alasdair MacIntyre, *After Virtue: A Study in Moral Theory* (Notre Dame, Ind.: University of Notre Dame Press, 1981).

affected, for good or ill.[3] Here the relationship of women to the Revolution will be approached from a somewhat different angle. Pursuing insights contained in a few recent writings, I would suggest that conceptions of sexual difference—views that were at once deeply held (often only implicitly) and highly unstable—underlay some of the most basic premises of the Revolution and shaped important ideological changes in the early Republic.[4] However much the meaning of virtue changed over the course of this period, it remained a word laden with assumptions about gender.

The focus of this essay, in other words, is less on the Revolution's impact on women and more on the influence of gender-based symbols in the formation of Revolutionary thought. To trace the late eighteenth-century changes in this symbolism contributes to our understanding of gender as a cultural—and, therefore, historical—construct. The connections between the constructions of gender and politics point to the importance of women's history in exploring the conventional questions of political history.[5]

Some of the most influential recent intellectual historians of Anglo-American political thought have considered individual words—liberty, tyranny, corruption, and especially virtue—as keys that unlock the meaning of the broadly consensual historical "discourse" of classical republicanism.[6] A few others have only just begun to challenge the overly static

---

[3] See esp. Linda K. Kerber, *Women of the Republic: Intellect and Ideology in Revolutionary America* (Chapel Hill: University of North Carolina Press, 1980); Mary Beth Norton, *Liberty's Daughters: The Revolutionary Experience of American Women, 1750–1800* (Boston: Little, Brown & Co., 1980); Joan Hoff-Wilson, "The Illusion of Change: Women and the American Revolution," in *The American Revolution: Explorations in the History of American Radicalism*, ed. Alfred F. Young (Dekalb: Northern Illinois University Press, 1976), 383–445.

[4] A few studies that partly address this question and helped to stimulate this article are: Kerber, *Women of the Republic*, 269–88, and "The Republican Ideology of the Revolutionary Generation," *American Quarterly* 37 (1985): 474–95; Paula Baker, "The Domestication of Politics: Women and American Political Society, 1780–1920," *American Historical Review* 89 (1984): 620–47; Jan Lewis, "The Republican Wife," *William and Mary Quarterly*, 3d ser., vol. 44 (October 1987); J. G. A. Pocock, "Modes of Political and Historical Time in Early Eighteenth-Century England," in his *Virtue, Commerce, and History* (New York: Cambridge University Press, 1985), 98–100; Hanna Fenichel Pitkin, *Fortune Is a Woman* (Berkeley: University of California Press, 1984).

[5] Joan W. Scott calls for this in her "Gender: A Useful Category of Analysis," *American Historical Review* 91 (December 1986): 1053–75.

[6] See esp. J. G. A. Pocock, *The Machiavellian Moment: Florentine Political Thought and the Atlantic Republican Tradition* (Princeton, N.J.: Princeton University Press, 1975), and *Virtue, Commerce, and History*; Bernard Bailyn, *The Ideological Origins of the American Revolution* (Cambridge, Mass.: Harvard University Press, 1967); Caroline Robbins, *The Eighteenth-Century English Commonwealthmen* (Cambridge, Mass.: Harvard University Press, 1959); Gordon S. Wood, *The Creation of the American Republic, 1776–1787* (Chapel Hill: University of North Carolina Press, 1969); Lance Banning, *The Jeffersonian Persuasion: Evolution of a Party Ideology* (Ithaca, N.Y.: Cornell University Press, 1978); Drew R. McCoy,

39

and holistic conception of culture that this "republican synthesis" implies.[7] I argue here that an examination of the multivalent meanings embedded in the term virtue leads to a more complex and dynamic understanding not only of gender but also of Revolutionary ideology itself.

The work of Caroline Robbins, Bernard Bailyn, Gordon Wood, and J. G. A. Pocock outlines the extent to which American patriots conceptualized the American Revolution within the intellectual framework of classical republicanism. As we now understand this intellectual background, the revival of ancient republican theories—first in the city-states of the Italian Renaissance, then in seventeenth-century England—was kept alive into the eighteenth century by a small, disunified, yet vociferous group of political dissidents in England. The distinctive structural conditions of politics in the colonies, in combination with the values of American Protestantism, led the colonists of the mid-eighteenth century to embrace many of the tenets of classical republicanism.

According to the basic constitutional theory of classical republicanism, the preservation of liberty depended on a mixed and balanced government. Such a government consisted essentially of three parts, each representative of a different social order: the king in the monarchy, the aristocracy in the House of Lords (or the colonial Councils), and the property-holding populace in the elected legislature. The hallmark of a free republic, according to this theory, was the autonomy of a legislature with institutionalized power to tax. The social base necessary to sustain this arrangement, described most fully by James Harrington in the seventeenth century,[8] was a large class of arms-bearing freeholders—fairly equal and independent property owners, able to defend themselves, and sharing a regard for the public good—whose common voice would be expressed in their elected legislature. When in the 1760s and 1770s the British imperial government challenged powers traditionally exercised by the elected colonial legislatures, including the power to tax, colonists interpreted the new policy in the terms of republican theory—as a fundamental assault on their liberty.

Even then, however, the political ideas espoused by the American Revolutionaries were a hybrid mixture. Some of these derived not from the classical republican tradition of Machiavelli and Harrington but from con-

---

The Elusive Republic: Political Economy in Jeffersonian America (Chapel Hill: University of North Carolina Press, 1980).

[7] For example, from the perspective of liberalism, Joyce Appleby, *Capitalism and a New Social Order: The Republic Vision of the 1790s* (New York: New York University Press, 1984); from the perspective of American Protestantism, Ruth H. Bloch, *Visionary Republic: Millennial Themes in American Thought* (New York: Cambridge University Press, 1985).

[8] The key text is James Harrington, *Oceana*, ed. S. B. Liljegren (Heidelberg: Carl Winters Universitätsbuchlung, 1924).

stitutional ideas about individual rights and from Protestant theories about
the providential purpose of government. For American Revolutionaries, as
for those English opposition writers, such as John Trenchard and William
Gordon, who were most widely read in the colonies, the ideas of egalitarian
individualism and Nonconforming Protestantism were blended with classical republican notions about the sovereignty of the popular legislature.

Throughout the Revolutionary period, virtue was the most valued
quality defining individual commitment to the American republican cause.
One reason for its salience was that both the classical republican and the
Protestant traditions emphasized the value of public virtue. According to
both, virtue reconciled otherwise contradictory commitments to both
individual political freedom and the greater public good because virtue
would prompt otherwise selfish individuals to actions on behalf of a just and
harmonious social order. The main difference between these traditions lay
in their assumptions about the source of virtue: within orthodox Protestantism, it was bestowed by Providence or faith; within classical republicanism,
it was obtained through independent property holding and mixed government. Each tradition, moreover, had its own way of describing the relation
of virtuous citizens, high and low, to the body politic. Within orthodox
Protestantism political virtue was primarily a trait of good rulers who, with
God, tended the political order. Ordinary members of the covenanted
community assumed the more limited responsibility of obeying good rulers
and living according to the moral code. Within classical republicanism,
also, the few and the many exercised their virtue in dissimilar ways: the
titled and the propertied were to rule; the people were to rise against
threats of foreign invasion and political corruption. Yet according to each of
these traditions, the virtue of both the rulers and the populace was indispensable to preserving the good health of the polity.

The orthodox Protestant and classical republican traditions also fundamentally agreed that public virtue was an inherently masculine trait.
Patriarchal analogies pervaded seventeenth-century English and American Protestant political thought, which drew heavily on Old Testament
models: a good leader, like a good father, was wise, caring, and firm.[9] In
1637, the New England Puritan governor John Winthrop defended the
power of the Massachusetts magistrates against Henry Vane, a supporter of
Anne Hutchinson, by insisting on the superior judgment of the "fathers of
the commonwealth." The Aristotelian notion of virtue as always "united
with a rational principle"—a notion that continued to dominate American

[9] Gordon Schochet, *Patriarchalism in Political Thought* (Oxford: Basil Blackwell, 1975).
The patriarchal familial imagery within New England Puritan writings about political lead-
ership is well known. For a recent explication, see Melvin Yazawa, *From Colonies to
Commonwealth: Familial Ideology and the Beginnings of the American Republic* (Baltimore:
Johns Hopkins University Press, 1985).

41

Puritan ethical theory until the late seventeenth century—by definition favored men since men were deemed more rational than women.[10]

Not that women were ever regarded as incapable of all kinds of virtue. Women were thought to be as rational as men in exercising the private, Christian virtues—temperance, prudence, faith, charity. It was specifically public virtue—active, self-sacrificial service to the state on behalf of the common g(d—that was an essentially male attribute. While there were a few exceptional early American women who won recognition for their heroic defense of the wider community, these were the kind of exceptions that proved the rule. Public virtue was indeed possible for exceptional women, but it was never an inherently feminine characteristic.

Among the most renowned examples of exceptional women were the New Englanders Hannah Dustin and Mary Rowlandson who bravely withstood Indian attacks.[11] Hannah Dustin, who won her fame by brutally scalping her assailants, demonstrated qualities of physical courage and strength that conformed to a typically male model of virtue. What distinguished her as a heroine was precisely her ability to step out of her femininity. Mary Rowlandson, to the contrary, never overtly violated the Puritan conception of a virtuous woman. Her heroism consisted in her pious adherence to Puritan faith and in her shrewd use of domestic skills to earn the protection of her enemies. Yet it was the very fact that she was an *exceptional* woman—a woman who kept her faith and maintained her wits amid heathens—that largely accounts for the sensational popularity of her captivity narrative. Despite the striking differences between them, Hannah Dustin and Mary Rowlandson won public acclaim precisely because they, as women, went so far beyond typical expectations: they proved themselves neither weaker nor less capable of absorbing and retaining the standards of civilization than men.

In the classical republican tradition, the masculine attributes embedded in the concept of public virtue are even more pronounced than those in American Puritanism. The ancient origins of this highly gendered concept can be traced as far back as the Homeric idea of *aretê* or human excellence

---

[10] John Winthrop, as quoted in Thomas Hutchinson, ed., *A Collection of Original Papers Relative to the History of the Colony of Massachusetts Bay* (Boston: Thomas & John Fleet, 1769), reprinted in Joyce O. Appleby, ed., *Materialism and Morality in the American Past: Themes and Sources* (Reading, Mass.: Addison-Wesley Publishing Co., 1974), 34, 38. For the Aristotelian notion of virtue, see Norman Fiering, *Moral Philosophy at Seventeenth-Century Harvard* (Chapel Hill: University of North Carolina Press, 1981), 72. The abundant literature documenting the negative cultural evaluation of female reason is summarized briefly in Ruth H. Bloch, "Untangling the Roots of Modern Sex Roles: A Survey of Four Centuries of Change," *Signs: Journal of Women in Culture and Society* 4, no. 2 (Winter 1978): 237–52.

[11] These cases are described in more detail in Laurel Thatcher Ulrich, *Good Wives* (New York: Oxford University Press, 1982), 184–201; Nancy Woloch, *Women and the American Experience* (New York: Alfred A. Knopf, 1984), 1–15.

42

(later translated as "virtue"), which stressed the physical strength and bravery displayed in athletic contests and in battles. This emphasis on courage remained a basic component of the classical tradition and later fused with Greek and Roman ideas about the intellectual and cooperative virtues (such as judgment, justice, and friendship) that bind men in citizenship within the polis.[12] According to the revitalized Renaissance republicanism of Machiavelli, virtue was, again, best displayed in acts of military heroism and civic activism. Exemplary citizens were above all daring soldiers and inspired orators—those who risked danger and won glory in valiant defense of liberty. As Pocock has defined it, the Machiavellian *virtù* that proved so influential in America consisted in "the skill and courage by which men are enabled to dominate events and fortune."[13] Hannah Pitkin examined the gender implications of the word in her book on Machiavelli's political theory: "Though it can sometimes mean [Christian] virtue, *virtù* tends mostly to connote energy, effectiveness, virtuosity. . . . The word derives from the Latin *virtus*, and thus from *vir*, which means 'man.' *Virtù* is thus manliness, those qualities found in a 'real man.'"[14] The political realm was constituted by the actions of fathers and sons—patriarchal founders and fraternal citizens. Typically, women appeared in this symbolic matrix as the dangerous, unreliable force of *fortuna* (or, later, according to Pocock, public credit), threatening to sabotage the endeavor of virtuous men.[15]

On the face of it, the masculinity embedded in ideas of public virtue appears trivial, the simple reflection of the male domination of political institutions. In fact, property requirements guaranteed that statesmen, soldiers, and enfranchised citizens would be, by definition, men. The intrinsic maleness of the term virtue could be seen, then, as the logical,

---

[12] For examples of the specialized debate over the various classical meanings of these terms, see MacIntyre (n. 2 above), 114–53; Arthur Madigan, "Plato, Aristotle and Professor MacIntyre," and A. A. Long, "Greek Ethics after MacIntyre and the Stoic Community of Reason," both in *Ancient Philosophy* 3 (1983): 171–83, 184–97. That *virtù* was a fundamentally male quality, associated with courage and involvement in civic life, is a common theme. For the purposes of this essay, what is important is that these elements were revived by Machiavelli and other Renaissance republicans and then transmitted to America.

[13] Pocock, *The Machiavellian Moment*, 92. The traditional idea of virtue as glory is also explicated in Albert O. Hirschman, *The Passions and the Interests: Political Arguments for Capitalism before Its Triumph* (Princeton, N.J.: Princeton University Press, 1977), 7–66.

[14] Pitkin (n. 4 above), 25.

[15] Ibid.; Pocock, "Modes of Political and Historical Time" (n. 4 above), 98–100. Quentin Skinner has taken issue with Pitkin's exclusive emphasis on the negative feminine symbolism in Machiavelli, pointing out that he used feminine Italian nouns (including *virtù* itself) to describe the abstract goals and ideals of the republic. Yet Pitkin herself questions the value of this kind of narrow linguistic analysis (n. 4 above, 131), and even Skinner agrees that Machiavelli's words to describe "the active and shaping features of public life" are masculine (Skinner, "Ms. Machiavelli," *New York Review of Books* [March 14, 1985], 29–30).

even automatic, cultural consequence of male political hegemony. But there is more to it.

These notions of masculinity were fundamental to the concept of public virtue in a way that would change in Revolutionary America without corresponding changes in military recruitments, property holding, or franchise requirements. As ideas about the political order underwent a profound transformation during the Revolutionary period, so did the understanding of virtue. Even as political institutions continued to be essentially male, underlying shifts in the gendered meaning of virtue expressed (even, perhaps, helped to make possible) a new understanding of republican politics.

* * *

In the mid-1770s, with the outbreak of revolution and war, the specifically masculine qualities embedded in conceptions of public virtue received, if anything, still more emphasis. The model patriot was frequently described according to classical republican ideals as a heroic orator or citizen-soldier.[16] In a widely distributed 1775 oration commemorating the Boston Massacre, Joseph Warren envisioned "fathers / looking / . . . with smiling approbation on their sons who boldly stand forth in the cause of virtue."[17] Virtue was above all the mark of "the uncorrupted patriot, the useful citizen, and the invincible soldier."[18] Even as military enthusiasm began to flag in subsequent years, calls to "virtuous Americans" to give "firm and manly support" to the war effort continued.[19] According to a minister preaching before Virginia troops in New Jersey in 1777, virtue was inextricably associated with glory and fame: "Glory is the reward of honourable toils, and public fame is the just retribution for public service; the love of which is so connected to virtue, that it seems scarcely possible to be possessed of the latter without some degree of the former."[20]

If the virtues of heroic courage, glory, and fame were inherently male, the opposites—cowardice, idleness, luxury, dependence—were, not sur-

[16] Isaac Story, *The Love of our Country Recommended and Enforced* (Boston: John Boyle, 1774), 13–16. The association of virtue with military courage during the *"rage militaire"* of 1775 is described in Charles Royster, *A Revolutionary People at War* (Chapel Hill: University of North Carolina Press, 1979), 25–53.

[17] Joseph Warren, *An Oration Delivered March Sixth 1775* (Boston: Edes & Gill, 1775), 21.

[18] John Witherspoon, *The Dominion of Providence over the Passions of Men* (Philadelphia: Aitken, 1776), 60.

[19] Phillips Payson, *A Sermon Preached before the Honourable Council . . . of the State of Massachusetts Bay* (Boston: John Gill, 1778), 32.

[20] John Hurt, *The Love of Our Country* (Philadelphia: Styner & Cist, 1777), 17. Also, see Richard Henry Lee as quoted in Pauline Maier, *The Old Revolutionaries: Political Lives in the Age of Samuel Adams* (New York: Vintage Trade Books, 1980), 198.

44

prisingly, castigated as the "effeminate" weaknesses of unpatriotic men. Whereas the Americans were "a hardy virtuous set of men," proclaimed a patriot orator in 1776, their corrupt British enemies had succumbed to "that luxury which effeminates the mind and body."[21] But what about women themselves? Was there any model of female public virtue consistent with the glorification of male heroism in the Revolution? The most famous examples were the legendary "Molly Pitcher" of the Battle of Monmouth and Deborah Sampson Gannett, a young woman subsequently glorified for disguising herself as a man in order to enlist in the Revolutionary army.[22] More typical were the women gathered in such organizations as the Daughters of Liberty and the Ladies Association, who abstained from tea drinking, boycotted loyalist shops, made homespun clothing, and raised money in support of the Revolutionary cause.[23] Neither the courage of Gannett nor these women's less heroic—Protestant as well as republican—virtues of industriousness, abstention, charity, and frugality differed markedly from what was expected of patriotic men. Essentially the only distinctively feminine images of Revolutionary virtue during the 1770s were those of a mother passively donating her sons to the struggle or of a helpless virgin physically abused by the enemy.[24]

[21] Peter Thacher, *Oration Delivered March 5, 1776*, as quoted in Wood (n. 6 above), 100. Morally deficient American as well as British men were frequently depicted as feminine. See, e.g., John Witherspoon, *Dominion of Providence*, 57; [Royall Tyler], *The Contrast* (Philadelphia: Prichard & Hall, 1790); Kerber, *Women of the Republic* (n. 3 above), 31; Wood, 110. Within the classical republican tradition, such rhetoric goes back to Machiavelli and beyond (see Pitkin [n. 4 above], 109–10).

[22] Such rare if dramatic examples of female heroism are recounted in Sally Smith Booth, *The Women of '76* (New York: Hastings House, 1973), 173–74, 266–70.

[23] For a full account and analysis of these activities, see Mary Beth Norton (n. 3 above).

[24] Kerber, *Women of the Republic*, 106. For more examples of the maternal imagery, see Royster (n. 16 above), 30, 90; Story (n. 16 above), 16–17. For examples of women physically abused by the enemy, see Jay Fliegelman, *Prodigals and Pilgrims* (New York: Cambridge University Press, 1982), 117, 137–44. A similar religious image was that of America as the woman in the wilderness of the book of Revelation, pursued by minions of Satan: see, e.g., William Foster, *True Fortitude Delineated* (Philadelphia: John Dunlap, 1776), 17; [Wheeler Case], *Poems, Occasioned by Several Circumstances and Occurrencies* (New Haven, Conn.: Thomas & Green, 1778), 21. This theme of women as innocent, passively virtuous victims of male vice—tyranny and lust—was an extension of the themes of popular fiction into political discourse. Jan Lewis explores this association in "The Republican Wife" (n. 4 above). For the opposite image of Great Britain as a bad mother, see Edwin G. Burrows and Michael Wallace, "The American Revolution: The Ideology and Psychology of National Liberation," *Perspectives in American History* 6 (1972): 190–214. This theme also had its analogues in fiction about bad mothers (see Fliegelman, 51–52, 118). For examples of the biblical scarlet whore image, see Henry Cumings, *A Sermon Preached in Billerica on the 3rd of November, 1775* (Worcester, Mass.: L. Thomas, 1775), 12; Enoch Huntington, *A Sermon, Delivered at Middletown, July 20th, A.D. 1775* (Hartford, Conn.: Ebenezer Watson, 1775), 21. The rebellious implications of unmasking ignoble political origins are explored in Judith N. Shklar, "Subversive Genealogies," in *Myth, Symbol, and Culture*, ed. Clifford Geertz (New York: W. W. Norton & Co., 1971), 129–53.

45

It was later, in the 1780s and 1790s, when a significantly separate image of female public spirit began to appear. During the period in which the exigencies of warfare gave way to the politics of state, women were increasingly presented as indispensable and active promoters of patriotism in men. As mothers, young social companions, and wives, women came to be idealized as the source not only of domestic morality but also of civic virtue itself.

Historian Linda Kerber has already drawn attention to the emerging idea of the "republican mother" in the late eighteenth century.[25] It was already a cliché of the age that mothers, not fathers, were particularly responsible for inculcating children with the piety, benevolence, and self-discipline that compose virtue.[26] By the turn of the century, several patriotic commentators had extended this responsibility to include the public virtue deemed necessary to sustain the republic. Women, according to this view, would serve the new nation by making good citizens of their sons despite formal exclusion from institutional political life. A few even justified the education of women on these grounds as a patriotic necessity. A young female graduate of Susanna Rowson's Academy foresaw the day when "future heroes and statesmen," having learned "the love of virtue" as children, "shall exaltingly declare, it is to my mother I owe this elevation."[27] In the words of one minister preaching in 1802, "How should it enflame the desire of the mothers and daughters of our land to be the occasion of so much good to themselves and others! —You will easily see that here is laid the basis of public virtue; of union, peace and happiness in society. . . . Mothers do, in a sense, hold the reins of government and sway the ensigns of national prosperity and glory."[28]

Though they held this responsibility as mothers, women were to instill public virtue in men through courtship and marriage perhaps even more.[29] It was repeatedly claimed, by American and English moralists both, that women's influence over men gave them the power to reform the manners

---

[25] Kerber, *Women of the Republic*, 265–88.

[26] See Ruth Bloch, "American Feminine Ideals in Transition: The Rise of the Moral Mother," *Feminist Studies* 4 (June 1978): 101–26.

[27] As quoted in Kerber (n. 3 above), 229. Also see Benjamin Rush, "Thoughts upon Female Education" (originally published in 1787), in *Essays on Education in the Early Republic*, ed. Frederick Rudolph (Cambridge, Mass.: Harvard University Press, 1965), 25–40; "Oration upon Female Education, Pronounced . . . in Boston, September, 1791," in *The American Preceptor*, ed. Caleb Bingham, 44th ed. (Boston: Manning & Loring, 1813), 47–51.

[28] William Lyman, *A Virtuous Woman the Bond of Domestic Union* (New-London, Conn.: S. Green, 1802), 22.

[29] In this period there was still far more literature on courtship, marriage, and the social utility of female education than on motherhood per se. In her forthcoming article, Jan Lewis (n. 4 above) argues that the image of the "republican wife" was more prevalent than that of the "republican mother."

46

and morals of society.[30] In the writings of American patriots, this notion took on a distinctively republican coloring. "Love and courtship, it is universally allowed, invest a lady with more authority than in any other situation that falls to the lot of human beings," declared a Columbia College orator in 1795. Describing American women as "patriots and philanthropists," he insisted that it was up to them to withstand "the deluge of vice and luxury, which has well nigh overwhelmed Europe, . . . [and] to save, to aggrandize your country! . . . The solidity and stability of the liberties of your country rest with you; since Liberty is never sure, 'till Virtue reigns triumphant."[31] Another writer similarly insisted that "female virtue," by which he essentially meant chastity, was the key to "national prosperity and the honour and happiness of posterity," because "the profoundest politicians, wisest statesmen, most invincible champions, greatest generals, ingenious artists, and even pulpit orators" spent so much of their time with women.[32] American men were advised that good republican citizenship, as well as personal happiness, would follow ineluctably from true love and marriage.[33]

* * *

To understand the origins of this transformation of ideas about public virtue, it is necessary to look not only at Revolutionary political discourse but also at the seemingly nonpolitical ideas about human psychology, education, and women that were current in the eighteenth century. In this broader intellectual history one finds the origins of a long-term redefinition of gender distinctions already well underway by the 1770s and intimately connected to changes in the nonpolitical understanding of virtue. Over the course of the Revolutionary period, particularly as debates surrounding the Constitution formulated a new conception of republican government, these nonpolitical ideas about virtue came to assume political significance. Changes in the gender-based meaning of public virtue in the late eighteenth century owed as much to these earlier intellectual developments as to the influences of Revolutionary politics.

[30] For example, Rush; Jane West, *Letters to a Young Lady* (Troy, N.Y.: O. Penniman, 1806), 27; "Scheme for Encreasing the Power of the Fair Sex," *Baltimore Weekly Magazine* 1 (April 1801): 241–42; *Advice to the Fair Sex; in a Series of Letters on Various Subjects: Chiefly Describing the Graceful Virtues* (Philadelphia: Robert Cochran, 1803), 3–4; Samuel Kennedy Jennings, *The Married Lady's Companion, or Poor Man's Friend* (Richmond, Va.: T. Nicholson, 1804), 5.

[31] "Female Influence," *New York Magazine* (May 1795), 299–305.

[32] Thomas Branagan, *The Excellency of the Female Character Vindicated* (New York: Samuel Wood, 1807), xii.

[33] "Panegyrick on Marriage," *Columbia Magazine and Universal Advertiser* (October 1786), 74; "On Love," *New York Magazine* (June 1791), 311.

47

It is possible to identify at least three understandings of virtue that emerged in the American colonies during the eighteenth century—not one of which was derived from traditional Protestant or classical republican ideas of public virtue. The first, most pronounced in New England, was essentially religious. It concerned, above all, the relationship between virtue and grace. American Puritans, like Reform theologians in general, had long sought to balance the Calvinist belief in faith as the free gift of God with the view that individuals could voluntarily take certain steps to prepare for salvation. Acts of virtue themselves, the offspring of the human will and the intellect, could never lead to redemption. Yet at the same time a life of virtue would be the likely consequence of a predisposition toward grace.

Recent scholarship emphasizing the emotional, experiential aspects of Puritan piety has pointed to the continuities between developments within seventeenth-century Puritanism and the new forms of eighteenth-century evangelical Protestantism.[34] Even among seventeenth-century Harvard students of moral philosophy, the idea of virtue gradually became inseparable from a positive evaluation of the emotions.[35] In the middle of the eighteenth century, Jonathan Edwards used his formidable intellectual talent to reconcile this increasingly naturalistic conception of virtue with an uncompromising Calvinist belief in the sovereignty of God. An articulate proponent of religious revivalism, Edwards preached that only saving grace, experienced through the affections, could give rise to the real virtue of "disinterested benevolence." Unregenerate self-love could, he acknowledged, give rise to behavior in conformity with a narrowly utilitarian moral law. But "true virtue," as he defined it, consisted in a selfless "love to Being in general."[36]

When Edwards distinguished between sinful self-love and the virtue of "public benevolence," he did not mean public virtue in the classical republican sense.[37] He measured virtue by the disposition of the will and heart rather than by the performance of civic duty. Yet, for all his denial of the importance of external behavior, his ideal individual, like the classical republican one, would disregard narrow self-interest when it conflicted

[34] See, e.g., Robert Middlekauff, *The Mathers: Three Generations of Puritan Intellectuals* (New York: Oxford University Press, 1971); Norman Pettit, *The Heart Prepared: Grace and Conversion in Puritan Spiritual Life* (New Haven, Conn.: Yale University Press, 1966); Charles Hambrick-Stowe, *The Practice of Piety* (Chapel Hill: University of North Carolina Press, 1982); Charles Lloyd Cohen, *God's Caress: The Psychology of Puritan Religious Experience* (New York: Oxford University Press, 1986).

[35] Norman Fiering, *Moral Philosophy at Seventeenth-Century Harvard* (n. 10 above), and *Jonathan Edwards's Moral Thought in Its British Context* (Chapel Hill: University of North Carolina Press, 1981).

[36] Jonathan Edwards, "The Nature of True Virtue," in *Jonathan Edwards*, ed. Clarence H. Faust and Thomas H. Johnson, rev. ed. (New York: Hill & Wang, 1962), 351.

[37] Ibid., 365.

with the common good. Not surprisingly, during the American Revolution individuals combined elements of his nonpolitical conception of virtue with classical republicanism. In 1774 a Marblehead minister defined patriotism as "the grand law of love," explaining that "disinterested benevolence" led to "the support of virtue; the controul of vice, and the advancement of the best interests of [the] country." For many Revolutionary clergymen, the words virtue, piety, and righteousness were basically interchangeable.[38]

This type of religious virtue was not, of course, regarded as distinctively feminine. Yet there is, beginning in the late seventeenth century, a steady climb in the number of sermons that celebrate models of female virtue and piety. Women, long regarded as morally encumbered by their supposedly excessive emotionalism, were beginning to be regarded as particularly receptive to grace. The first vigorous proponent of this view was the third generation Puritan pietist Cotton Mather. He explained that the greater tendency of women to experience religious conversion was a response to the distinctively female "difficulties both of *Subjection* and of *Child bearing*."[39] Over the course of the eighteenth century, evangelical and liberal Protestant ministers alike increasingly preached on the theme of female piety.[40]

A second, though related, conception of virtue that emerged in eighteenth-century America came from the psychological theories of John Locke and the Scottish moral philosophers. Medieval faculty psychology, which had survived even the Protestant Reformation, became a subject of controversy in the late seventeenth and in the eighteenth century. Among the many points at issue was the status of the "moral sense": Was it a rational or an emotional faculty? Some figures of the British Enlightenment, including John Locke and Thomas Reid, agreed with the older scholastic position that it was rational. Virtue was the chief object of Locke's educational theory and was, for him, still an essentially masculine trait. He wrote above all for the fathers of sons, emphasizing not only reason, but other qualities culturally associated with men as well: stoicism, self-sufficiency, and physical hardiness.[41]

---

[38] Story (n. 16 above), 7, 10. This religious use of the word virtue in revolutionary literature is discussed in Bloch, *Visionary Republic* (n. 7 above), esp. 109; Royster (n. 16 above), 17–25.

[39] Cotton Mather, *Ornaments for the Daughters of Zion* (Cambridge: Samuel Phillips, 1692), 45. Also see Cotton Mather, *Elizabeth on Her Holy Retirement* (Boston: B. Green, 1710).

[40] For a few examples of this literature, see Benjamin Colman, *The Honour and Happiness of the Vertuous Woman* (Boston: B. Green, 1716); Chauncy Whittelsey, *A Discourse . . . Mary Clapp* (New Haven, Conn.: Thomas & Samuel Green, 1769); Deborah Prince, *Dying Exercises of Mrs. Deborah Prince; and Devout Meditations of Mrs. Sarah Gill* (Newbury-port, Mass.: John Mycall, 1789); George Strebeck, *A Sermon on the Character of the Virtuous Woman* (New York: n.p., 1800); Samuel Worcester, *Female Love to Christ* (Salem, Mass.: Pool & Palfray, 1809).

[41] Despite one perfunctory remark to a female friend on how the education of the sexes

Another wave of Enlightenment opinion, represented in Scotland by Francis Hutcheson and in England by Lord Shaftesbury, claimed morality for the emotions.[42] It was, argued Hutcheson, not the offspring of reason but an inborn principle of sociability, "an instinct toward happiness."[43] If innate, however, moral sense was dependent, especially in infancy and early childhood, on parental nurturance. In their emphasis on education, if not in their epistemology, Locke and the Scots agreed: they all stressed noncoercive child rearing, saw children as corruptible but not corrupt, and posited innate qualities—whether reason or moral sense—which, if cultivated, would lead to virtue.[44] Although these particular philosophers envisioned men as the principal educators, their ideas about the importance of early childhood education gradually led to a greater emphasis on the motherhood role in didactic and medical literature.[45]

The question of whether reason or emotion was the more important source of virtue was never, of course, fully answered, but it is clear that the eighteenth century was a time of particular confusion and conflict over these basic epistemological issues.[46] Albert O. Hirschman has argued, for example, that avarice, previously regarded as a sinful "passion," was elevated to the status of a rational "interest" in this period.[47] This realignment coincided, more or less explicitly, with a revision of binary gender distinctions: rationality, long associated with men, was linked to interest; the emotions, long associated with women, to morality. Scottish philosophy and evangelical Protestantism, each occupying a kind of middle ground between the atomistic individualism of Locke and Hobbes and the communitarian ethos of classical republicanism, were particularly important in establishing these new connections.

---

should be largely the same, at least "in their younger years," Locke explicitly focused *Some Thoughts concerning Education*—including key passages on virtue—on the upbringing of "young Gentlemen." When women do appear, as mothers, they tend (by their excessive "Fondness") to be an obstacle to good education (*The Educational Writings of John Locke*, ed. James L. Axtell [London: Cambridge University Press, 1968], 117, 117n., 123, 125, 166–67, 170, 344–46).

[42] On differences among Scottish moral philosophers, see Daniel W. Howe, "European Sources of Political Ideas in Jeffersonian America," *Reviews in American History* 10 (1982): 28–44.

[43] As quoted in Fliegelman (n. 24 above), 24.

[44] Fliegelman (23–26) points to this underlying similarity in contrast to the sharp separation drawn between Locke and the Scots by Garry Wills in his *Inventing America: Jefferson's Declaration of Independence* (Garden City, N.Y.: Doubleday & Co., 1978), and *Explaining America: The Federalist* (Garden City, N.Y.: Doubleday & Co., 1981).

[45] Bloch, "American Feminine Ideals in Transition" (n. 26 above).

[46] Fiering, *Moral Philosophy at Seventeenth-Century Harvard* (n. 10 above), and *Jonathan Edwards's Moral Thought in Its British Context* (n. 35 above).

[47] Hirschman (n. 13 above).

Yet a third cultural movement—literary sentimentalism—contributed to this eighteenth-century reassessment of emotional life. Indeed, the intellectual boundaries between British moral philosophy, evangelical Protestantism, and sentimental fiction are impossible to draw clearly. As Norman Fiering has recently emphasized, the new moral philosophy of Hutcheson and Shaftesbury owed its origins to Puritan piety.[48] Edwards, determined to discourage a belief in a natural moral sense, nonetheless shared many of the ideas of the new moral philosophy. Edwards read sentimental fiction, and the Scottish moralists, also known as "sentimental philosophers," influenced those works through the writings of popularizers like Lord Kames.[49]

Yet, despite these historical interconnections, literary sentimentalism had a different orientation, style, and audience than either evangelicalism or moral philosophy. It concentrated on neither salvation nor epistemology, but on the quest for personal happiness through domestic relationships. Like exhortatory evangelical writings, but unlike moral philosophy, sentimental fiction was a relatively popular literary form in America (though largely imported from Britain). And, of all three movements, it was clearly literary sentimentalism that had the most to say specifically to and about women.

According to literary sentimentalism, virtue was above all a feminine quality. In the chain of being, women were the link between men and angels; they "ennoble human nature" by being not only "the fair" but also the "cherishing," "pious," "pacific," "sympathetic," and "reverential" sex.[50] The chief female virtues were "modesty," "tenderness," "delicacy," and "sensibility."[51] Women have a "superior sensibility of their souls," read one piece that appeared in several late eighteenth-century American magazines. "Their feelings are more exquisite than those of men; and their sentiments greater and more refined."[52] Others summed up this idealized impression of women by stressing the female "qualities of the heart."[53]

[48] Fiering, *Moral Philosophy at Seventeenth-Century Harvard*, 147–206, 239–94, and *Jonathan Edwards's Moral Thought in Its British Context*, 106.

[49] For example, Henry Home, Lord Kames, *Loose Hints upon Education, Chiefly concerning the Heart* (Edinburgh: John Bell, 1782). See n. 53 below for an example of its use.

[50] "On Woman," *Pennsylvania Magazine* (November 1775), 527; Thomas Branagan (n. 32 above), 111–12.

[51] Marchioness de Lambert, "Reflections on Female Virtues," *Royal American Magazine* (June 1774), 220; "Qualifications Required in a Wife," *American Museum* (December 1788), 578; [Noah Webster], "Address to Ladies," *American Museum* (March 1788), 244; "On Sensibility," *Pennsylvania Magazine* (April 1774), 176.

[52] "Comparison of the Sexes," *American Museum* (January 1789), 59. This piece was reprinted at least twice, in the *Christian Scholar's and Farmer's Magazine* (April and May 1789), 85–87; and in *Lady's Magazine* (August 1792), 111–13.

[53] For example, John Gregory, *A Father's Legacy to His Daughters* (Boston: J. Douglass M'Dougall, 1779), 35; John Bennet, *Letters to a Young Lady* (New York: John Buel, 1796), 68.

51

According to one American work of didactic fiction, women were best equipped to teach what Lord Kames had taught was "the chief branch" of learning, "the culture of the heart."[34]

If women were idealized for these supposedly innate qualities of emotionalism, tenderness, and delicacy, so too were they valued for a kind of self-discipline. The sentimental conception of female virtue was closely linked to chastity and to the maintenance of simple tastes and manners. Often the word virtue was used simply to mean chastity, and in the didactic literature of the period women were repeatedly enjoined to protect their sexual purity.[35] In the midst of the early Revolutionary fervor a patriot magazine instructed its readers, "What Bravery is in man, Chastity is in Woman." Among the dominant themes in the popular fiction of the period, best exemplified in such works as Samuel Richardson's *Clarissa* and Susanna Rowson's *Charlotte Temple*, was that of the innocent virgin ruined by male lust. Another variation on this theme of seduction was that of the adulterous husband redeemed by his faithful and forgiving wife—also a plot developed by Richardson in *Pamela*.[36]

As Ian Watt stressed many years ago in his *Rise of the Novel*, this literature conveyed a specifically middle-class version of personal morality. Typically, the lustful men were aristocratic rakes, and the women were wholesome commoners. In America, especially after the Revolution, such plots took on an additional patriotic significance. The villains could be seen as representing not only aristocratic but European decadence as well. While the idea that women should abstain from sexual temptations and ornamental refinements was scarcely new in this period—American Protestant teachings had traditionally instructed housewives to be sexually self-restrained, frugal, and industrious—the equation of female virtue with chastity, modest dress, and useful knowledge became more pronounced in the late eighteenth century as women were increasingly deemed the moral instructors of men.[37] The numerous proponents of a practical education for women repeatedly made this point.[38] No longer were the traditional ascetic and self-sacrificial virtues regarded as more easily achieved by men. The older view of women as more closely tied to base physical nature than men

[34] Enos Hitchcock, *Memoirs of the Bloomsgrove Family* (Boston: Thomas & Andrews, 1790), 47–48.

[35] For example, [William Kenrick], *The Whole Duty of Woman . . . Sixth Ed.* (Boston: Hall, 1790), 46; Gregory, 12, 16, 18, 22, 41; "A Letter," *Lady's Magazine* (November 1782), 281; Branagan.

[36] "Reflections on Chastity," *Royal American Magazine* (February 1775), 61. For the popularity of the forgiving-wife plot, see Lewis (n. 4 above).

[37] Lewis; Bloch, "American Feminine Ideals in Transition" (n. 26 above).

[38] For example: Rush (n. 27 above); Thomas Dawes, "Resolves Respecting the Education of Poor Female Children," *American Museum* 6 (September 1789): 213; John Bennet, *Strictures on Female Education* (Philadelphia: W. Spotswood & H. P. Rice, 1793).

52

had been gradually displaced by an image of women as particularly receptive to moral education. On the one hand, female virtues were themselves regarded as essentially natural. On the other hand, such virtues in women needed cultivation, and still more important, women were needed to cultivate virtue in men. In these respects, the late eighteenth century can be seen as a time in Western history when the nearly universal association of women with nature, and men with culture, was disrupted.[59]

* * *

Each in a different way, then, American Protestantism, Scottish moral philosophy, and literary sentimentalism opened the way for the feminization of ideas about public virtue. During the course of the Revolutionary period, these seemingly nonpolitical ideas began to displace the earlier idea of public virtue as military courage and civic glory. Royall Tyler's *The Contrast*, a popular play of the late 1780s, publicized as the first dramatic work by a "Citizen of the United States," conveniently marks the transition. The hero, appropriately named Colonel Manly, combines the new and old ideals of virtue. On the one hand, he is depicted as an old-fashioned New Englander and former Revolutionary War officer, who believes, in classical republican fashion, that the reason for the decline of ancient Greece was that "the common good was lost in the pursuit of private interest." His heroic manliness stands in contrast to the foppish and self-indulgent effeminacy of the English villain. Yet, the virtuous Manly himself, like the woman he loves, exudes "tenderness" and speaks "the language of sentiment."[60]

The changing meaning of virtue at once facilitated and reflected a transformation within American political thought. Several historians of political culture have noted that American Revolutionaries gradually revised their conceptions of public virtue. Earlier classical republican ideas increasingly competed with a more instrumental theory of government in which virtue played a much less conspicuous part.[61] Already in 1776 Thomas Paine's *Common Sense* argued that human cooperation and happiness were rooted in "society," not "government." Far from being the arena for the expression of virtue, a minimal state was necessary only because of

---

[59] For the argument that this female-nature/male-culture dichotomy is universal, see esp. Sherry Ortner, "Is Female to Male as Nature Is to Culture?" in *Women, Culture, and Society,* ed. Michelle Rosaldo and Louise Lamphere (Stanford, Calif.: Stanford University Press, 1974), 67–88. For another work on the eighteenth century that qualifies this perspective, see L. J. Jordanova, "Natural Facts: A Historical Perspective on Science and Sexuality," in *Nature, Culture, and Gender,* ed. C. MacCormack and M. Strathern (New York: Cambridge University Press, 1980).

[60] [Tyler] (n. 21 above), 48–49, 55.

[61] For example, Wood (n. 6 above); most recently, Yazawa (n. 9 above).

53

the "inability of moral virtue to govern the world."[62] By the late 1780s, in the argument for the U.S. Constitution in the *Federalist Papers*, the maintenance of the Republic no longer depended on a conception of goodness within collective social life. Instead, the most realistic and necessary conditions of liberty were the competition of conflicting factional interests and the balance of governmental powers. Such conditions ideally would encourage the rise of a "virtuous" elite of political representatives, but the conception of virtue implied here was not the classical republican one.[63] The word virtue itself scarcely appeared in the *Federalist Papers*. Instead of being based in a self-sacrificial public spirit, the moral underpinnings of good government were reason, justice, and enlightenment—all qualities presumably embodied in the "natural aristocracy" that would emerge to lead the Republic. Good leadership was in this view fully compatible with "true" or "enlightened" self-interest.[64]

Not that the republican belief in disinterested public virtue altogether vanished with the creation and ratification of the Constitution. This classical idea continued to find expression in opposition movements well into the nineteenth century.[65] Moreover, even in the late eighteenth-century ideological mainstream, a revised notion of republican virtue remained very much alive on the periphery of political debate. The demise of classical conceptions of virtue did not simply give rise to purely individual and utilitarian standards of morality devoid of reference to the common good.[66] Unlike the early Revolutionary virtue, the public virtue that remained was for the most part located outside rather than inside the state—the virtue of a diffuse, patriotic public whose allegiance was not to particular rulers or to the common interest of a homogeneous property-holding social order but to a large and impersonal republican nation. The

[62] Thomas Paine, *Common Sense*, ed. Isaac Kramnick (New York: Viking Penguin, Inc., 1976), 68.

[63] For example, [James Madison], "Federalist Paper Number 57," in *The Federalist Papers*, ed. Clinton Rossiter (New York: New American Library, 1961), 350. On virtue in the *Federalist Papers*, see Wood (n. 6 above), 610; and Garry Wills, *Explaining America* (n. 44 above). The distinction between these meanings of virtue is clarified in Daniel W. Howe, "The Political Psychology of *The Federalist*," *William and Mary Quarterly*, 3d ser., vol. 4 (1987).

[64] Howe, "The Political Psychology of *The Federalist*."

[65] Lance Banning, *The Jeffersonian Persuasion: Evolution of a Party* (Ithaca, N.Y.: Cornell University Press, 1978); Drew R. McCoy, *The Elusive Republic: Political Economy in Jeffersonian America* (Chapel Hill: University of North Carolina Press, 1980); Sean Wilentz, *Chants Democratic: New York City and the Rise of the American Working Class* (New York: Oxford University Press, 1984); Dorothy Ross, "The Liberal Tradition Revisited and the Republican Tradition Addressed," in *New Directions in American Intellectual History*, ed. John Higham and Paul K. Conkin (Baltimore: Johns Hopkins University Press, 1979); and a special issue on republicanism, ed. Joyce Appleby, *American Quarterly*, vol. 37 (Fall 1985).

[66] Compare MacIntyre (n. 2 above).

institutional basis of this collective identification was to be found not in the military or in participatory government but in churches, schools, and families. Women—as social companions, wives, and mothers—assumed a major role in instructing men to be virtuous.

This transition can be seen in part as a response to political events between the 1770s and 1790s. By the late 1780s, Revolutionaries had generally given up the quest for heroic mastery associated with the early war effort and had taken on the task of political reform involved in the process of state building. The early ethic of public service called on the presumably voluntary participation of free and independent (male) individuals. It was, at bottom, deeply anti-institutional—hostile to established churches, to government bureaucracy, to standing armies, to banks. The movement toward a more personal, domestic, and feminized definition of morality in the 1780s and 1790s was linked to a greater acceptance of institutionalized public order. A similar transformation, also expressed in the substitution of female for male Revolutionary symbolism, has been recently traced in the French Revolution by historian Lynn Hunt.[67] In America, this transitional phase in the Revolution coincided with the creation and establishment of the American Constitution in the late 1780s.

The *Federalist Papers* insisted on strengthening national government—giving it, in Alexander Hamilton's words, the "energy" the decentralized Confederation had previously lacked—while at the same time denying that the government had the power to interfere with natural rights or to eliminate inevitable factional conflict. Gone was the assumption that citizens would unite around a common conception of the public good. This false hope had only given rise to the specter of "majority tyranny" under the state constitutions of the 1770s and 1780s. In the words of an especially hard-bitten Federalist newspaper polemicist, "*virtue*, patriotism, or love of country, never was nor never will be till men's natures are changed, a fixed, permanent principle and support of government."[68]

The political order produced by the Constitution was designed more to protect private virtue than to be the arena for the expression of manly *virtù*. Despite the increased power of the national government in relation to that of the states, a continuing hostility to formal political institutions remained a major theme in American reform efforts well into the nineteenth century. The Constitution's provision of stable, limited government opened the way for the proliferation of voluntary associations that enlisted significant numbers of women as well as men. These associations,

---

[67] In France, however, prior to the ascendency of the conservative images of Marianne and Liberty in the late 1790s, a militant version of Marianne competed with that of the male radical symbol Hercules (see Lynn Hunt, *Politics, Culture, and Class in the French Revolution* [Berkeley and Los Angeles: University of California Press, 1984], 87–119).

[68] *Providence Gazette*, December 29, 1787, as quoted in Wood (n. 6 above), 610.

often formed for the "benevolent" purposes of moral and social reform, were repeatedly justified on patriotic grounds as vital to the preservation of the liberty and harmony of the American nation.

The Revolution had in effect accelerated a long-term cultural process that began well before the outbreak of the imperial conflicts with Britain. A transition in the meanings of virtue associated with changes in ideas about sex difference meant that women and the emotions became increasingly associated with moral activity, while men and reason became more exclusively associated with the utilitarian pursuit of self-interest. By the end of the eighteenth century, most people were beginning to believe that these were complementary contributions to the common good.[69]

These changes in themselves owed little to the American Revolution or to republican thought. The underlying cultural transformation was already underway by the 1770s, and it was, from the beginning, transatlantic in scope. What did change as a specific consequence of the American Revolutionary experience was that the feminine notion of virtue took on a political significance it had previously lacked. Americans never altogether abandoned the idea that the populace of the republic should be virtuous. Instead, they relegated the production and maintenance of public virtue to a new realm, one presided over largely by women. Women, as Lester Cohen and Linda Kerber have observed about the Revolutionary writer Mercy Otis Warren, continued to embody the collectivist values of classical republicanism after they had ceased to resonate in national politics.[70] The transformation in conceptions of femininity and masculinity, the emotions, and self-interest that had occurred in the eighteenth century made it possible to preserve the notion of public virtue while at the same time divesting it of its former constitutional significance. Virtue, if still regarded as essential to the public good in a republican state, became ever more difficult to distinguish from private benevolence, personal manners, and female sexual propriety.[71]

Subsequent developments among the early nineteenth-century middle and upper classes deepened these symbolic associations.[72] The declining

[69] Hirschman (n. 13 above); Appleby (n. 7 above); Howe, "The Political Psychology of *The Federalist*"; Michael Zuckerman, "A Different Thermidor: The Revolution beyond the American Revolution" (paper presented to the Philadelphia Center for Early American Studies, May 1986).

[70] Lester Cohen, "Explaining the Revolution: Ideology and Ethics in Mercy Otis Warren's Historical Theory," *William and Mary Quarterly*, 3d ser., 37 (1980): 200–218, and "Mercy Otis Warren: The Politics of Language and the Aesthetics of Self," *American Quarterly* 35 (1983): 481–98; Kerber, "The Republican Ideology of the Revolutionary Generation" (n. 4 above), 483.

[71] Pocock has pointed similarly to a shift from virtue to manners, although he misses the gender symbolism involved in this change and associates it only with elite English culture (Pocock, *Virtue, Commerce, and History* [n. 4 above], 49–50).

[72] This historical overview is especially indebted to the interpretation in Nancy F. Cott,

birth rate in the nineteenth century may have been a result of the growing ability of women to discipline male sexuality.[73] As the American polity became more democratic and expansionist, women, as teachers in the school system, played an increasingly important role in service to the republican nation—a role often seen as an extension of the practice of maternal virtue.[74] The fervent religious revivalism of the Second Great Awakening along with the birth of romantic literature furthered the connections between morality and the emotions already perceived by evangelicals, moral philosophers, and sentimental writers in the previous century. As eager supporters and occasional leaders, women were active participants in both the revivalist and the romantic cultural movements.[75]

From the late eighteenth century onward, the conflation of the virtuous with the feminine produced tensions. Looking back over the Revolutionary period with characteristic pessimism, John Adams once commented, "The people are Clarissa."[76] Public virtue had, for him, become associated with the passive virtues of female chastity—destined to be deceived and violated by unscrupulous men in power. Indeed, the representation of public virtue as a feminine trait hinged on the exclusion of women from institutional public life. If virtue was regarded as outside politics, what better way to conceive of it than as feminine? In an increasingly competitive male political system, the distinction faded between virtuous men committed to public service and unvirtuous men pursuing narrow self-interest. The new distinction between feminine virtue and masculine self-interest eased the process by which all white men (whether rich or

---

The Bonds of Womanhood: Woman's Sphere in New England, 1780–1835 (New Haven, Conn.: Yale University Press, 1977).

[73] Daniel Scott Smith, "Family Limitation, Sexual Control, and Domestic Feminism in Victorian America," *Feminist Studies* 1 (Winter–Spring 1973): 40–57; Carl Degler, *At Odds: Women and the Family in America from the Revolution to the Present* (New York: Oxford University Press, 1980), 144–278.

[74] Katherine Kish Sklar, *Catherine Beecher: A Study in American Domesticity* (New Haven, Conn: Yale University Press, 1973); Keith Melder, "Woman's High Calling: The Teaching Profession in America, 1830–1860," *American Studies* 13 (Fall 1972): 19–32; Nancy Hoffman, *Women's 'True' Profession* (Old Westbury, N.Y.: Feminist Press, 1981); Anne Firor Scott, "What, Then, Is This American: This New Woman?" *Journal of American History* 65 (December 1978): 679–703.

[75] Keith Melder, *The Beginnings of Sisterhood: The American Women's Rights Movement, 1800–1850* (New York: Schocken Books, 1977); Barbara Leslie Epstein, *The Power of Domesticity: Women, Evangelism, and Temperance in Nineteenth-Century America* (Middletown, Conn.: Wesleyan University Press, 1981); Mary P. Ryan, "The Power of Women's Networks: A Case Study of Female Moral Reform in Antebellum America," *Feminist Studies* 5 (Spring 1979): 66–86; Ann Douglas, *The Feminization of American Culture* (New York: Alfred A. Knopf, 1977); Susan P. Conrad, *Perish the Thought: Intellectual Women in Romantic America, 1830–1860* (New York: Oxford University Press, 1976).

[76] As quoted in Fliegelman (n. 24 above), 89.

57

poor, individually "virtuous" or not) could become political actors and all women could not.[77] That the ideal of female virtue was typically extended to upper- and middle-class women but not to poor women—who, as Christine Stansell has shown, continued to be characterized in the new nation in blatantly misogynist terms—reveals the extent to which the older republican emphasis on both virtue and social rank remained particularly strong within conceptions about women.[78]

The transformation in the meaning of virtue during the Revolutionary period sharpened the social boundaries between the sexes in ways that continue to deny power to all classes of women. The deep cultural connections between American patriotism and female middle-class domesticity persist to the present day, most conspicuously among conservative evangelical groups. Yet the increasing participation of early nineteenth-century women in the teaching profession, religious benevolent associations, and voluntary reform societies—activities that led directly to the early women's rights movement—suggests another side to the story. Virtue, even if domesticated, still contained residues of *virtù*, which for a long time helped to legitimate women's activities in American public life.

Department of History
University of California, Los Angeles

[77] This sexual asymmetry is stressed in Gerda Lerner, "The Lady and the Mill Girl: Changes in the Status of Women in the Age of Jackson, 1800–1840," in *A Heritage of Her Own*, ed. Nancy F. Cott and Elizabeth H. Pleck (New York: Simon & Schuster, 1979), 182–96.

[78] Christine Stansell, *City of Women: Sex and Class in New York, 1789–1860* (New York: Alfred A. Knopf, 1986), 19–37.

Familial Politics:
Thomas Paine and the Killing of the King, 1776

WINTHROP D. JORDAN

T HIS exploratory paper attempts a probe into the problem of who killed George III and why. It seeks as well to inquire into the subliminal sources of popular political influence. It also raises indirectly the problem of how and indeed whether historians should explore such arcane instances of homicide. Granted, any reports concerning the death of George III in 1776 may be said in one sense to be greatly exaggerated. Nonetheless one can propose that in 1776 George III was killed in his American provinces vicariously but very effectively by an anonymous hand and that this act of murder constitutes a legitimate subject for historical inquiry. The American Revolution has been occasionally placed upon the couch for a brisk session of psychiatric analysis; the resulting diagnoses of American independence as a rejection of the British father have not been difficult.[1] But they have also apparently not been wholly persuasive to the rather large number of historians who think that generalizations about a major historical event ought somehow to be tied to what "facts" are known about it.

If one looks at these "facts," and particularly at the public discussion during 1775 and during the first six months of 1776 about separation from Britain, one becomes impressed by the way Americans strummed persistently upon certain themes: that there was the utmost necessity for union among the colonies, that the British government had mounted a conspiracy to deprive American colonials of their rights, that Americans were threatened with outright enslavement, that Great Britain and especially the British government was steeped in corruption and degeneracy. These are familiar. Yet one theme which one might reasonably expect to find usually arose only implicitly: American patriots simply assumed that an independent America would be republican, that monarchy would come to an end in

Winthrop D. Jordan is professor of history in the University of California, Berkeley.

[1] For example, see Geoffrey Gorer, *The American People: A Study in National Character* (New York, 1948).

294

America once independence was declared. Perhaps this assumption is unsurprising, though historians do need some explanation as to why such an age-old, traditional institution as monarchy did not receive much discussion, pro or con.[2] What is more arresting is that the one piece of political writing which everyone at the time acknowledged to have by far the greatest influence on the public mind contained a forthright attack upon monarchy itself. There were not many such attacks, and Thomas Paine's *Common Sense* was easily the most extended and the most vehement.[3]

Taking American history as a whole, one can make a very good case for the proposition that, with the possible exception of *Uncle Tom's Cabin*, *Common Sense* was demonstrably the most immediately influential political or social tract ever published in this country. Its impact was noted by numerous contemporaries. In a famous comment, George Washington observed that "by private letters, which I have lately received from Virginia, I find 'Common Sense' is working a powerful change there in the minds of many men."[4] Abigail Adams, in thanking her husband for sending a copy, wrote: "tis highly prized here and carries conviction wherever it is read."[5] A contributor to the *Connecticut Gazette* lavished extravagant praise upon the still anonymous author: "you have declared the sentiments of Millions. Your production may justly be compared to a land-flood that sweeps all before it. We were blind, but on reading these enlightening works the scales have fallen from our eyes; even deep-rooted prejudices take to themselves wings and flee away. . . . The doctrine of Independence hath been in times past, greatly disgustful; we abhorred the principle—it is now become our delightful theme, and commands our purest affections."[6] One of the earliest historians of the Revolution, a participant himself, explained that the pamphlet "produced surprising effects. Many thousands were convinced, and were led to approve and long for a separation from the Mother

[2] Gordon S. Wood remarks that the "ease of transition into republicanism remains remarkable and puzzling even today," and he quotes in a footnote to a statement by Cecelia M. Kenyon: "What is puzzling is the reason for the sudden and virtually complete revolution in attitude." Gordon S. Wood, *The Creation of the American Republic, 1776-1787* (Chapel Hill, 1969), 93.

[3] The most notable of the few precursors is in the *Pennsylvania Packet*, Nov. 14, 1774, reprinted in Merrill Jensen, ed., *American Colonial Documents to 1776* (New York, 1955), 816-18. A search by the author disclosed no piece rivaling this after fighting began until the publication of *Common Sense*. See William David Liddle, "A Patriot King, or None: American Public Attitudes towards George III and the British Monarchy, 1754-1776" (doctoral dissertation, Claremont Graduate School, 1970).

[4] John C. Fitzpatrick, ed., *The Writings of George Washington from the Original Manuscript Sources, 1745-1799* (39 vols., Washington, 1931-1944), IV, 455.

[5] Lyman H. Butterfield, ed., *Adams Family Correspondence* (2 vols., Cambridge, Mass., 1963), I, 350.

[6] *Connecticut Gazette*, March 22, 1776.

Country. Though that measure, a few months before, was not only foreign from their wishes, but the object of their abhorrence, the current suddenly became so strong in its favour, that it bore down all opposition. The multitude was hurried down the stream. . . ."[7] It is certain, moreover, that *Common Sense* was widely read: some 120,000 copies were sold in the three months following publication in January 1776.[8] To match this figure for the American population today, the press run of a brief book would have to reach ten million.

It ought to be inquired, then, why *Common Sense* was so influential when it advanced a line of argument which American patriots did not seem interested in pursuing. Indeed it might be asked, more broadly, why this rambling, disorganized, and at times rather dull pamphlet was so popular and effective in disposing Americans to accept a final separation from the mother country. Part of the answer lies in Paine's racy, epigrammatic phraseology, in his discovering to Americans that "Government, like dress is the badge of lost innocence," that "there is something very absurd, in supposing a Continent to be perpetually governed by an island," that George III is "the Royal Brute of Great Britain."[9] It is difficult, however, to accept these zesty phrases as being altogether responsible for breaking the logjam of continued public attachment to the mother country. *Common Sense* was not the first public plea for independence, nor was it the only vigorous one. Historians need to look further, or rather more deeply, for some of the sources of its appeal.

A more analytic reading of *Common Sense* suggests how much of that appeal was essentially subliminal. To take one example before looking at Paine's assault upon monarchy, the opening discussion of the origin of government describes the state of nature in terms which implicitly but with the utmost clarity identify the beginnings of human society and government with the early settlement of America; in describing mankind living long ago in a state of nature Paine several times refers casually to those first people as "emigrants" without, of course, saying where these first people had emigrated from![10] At one level of logic this makes very little sense; at another, it makes a great deal.

[7] David Ramsay, *The History of the American Revolution* (2 vols., Philadelphia, 1789), I, 338-39.
[8] Merrill Jensen, *The Founding of a Nation: A History of the American Revolution, 1763-1776* (New York, 1968), 668-69.
[9] [Thomas Paine,] *Common Sense; Addressed To The Inhabitants of America, On the following interesting Subjects: I. Of the Origin and Design of Government in general, with concise Remarks on the English Constitution. II. Of Monarchy and Hereditary Succession. III. Thoughts on the present State of American Affairs. IV. Of the present Ability of America, with some miscellaneous Reflections* (Philadelphia: R. Bell, 1776), 2, 45, 57.
[10] *Ibid.*, 3.

Paine's discussion of monarchy and hereditary succession is even more heavily freighted with appeals to the unarticulated half-thoughts of his audience. For example, he rested a considerable portion of his case against monarchy on scripture, contending that "Government by Kings was first introduced into the World by the Heathens," that it was not until 3000 years after the creation that the Jews, who had been living in "a kind of Republic," "under a national delusion requested a King"; that God warned them of the evils of kings before he permitted them to establish a monarchy; in short, that "Monarchy is ranked in scripture as one of the sins of the Jews."[11] It scarcely needs to be pointed out that there were in America many who would sense in Paine's remarks the force not merely of explicit scriptural injunction but of the analagous experiences of God's chosen peoples.[12]

A similar utilization of the American experience may be found in some of Paine's more prosaic though no less aggressive attacks upon monarchy. As one would expect, Paine played his fire upon the luxury, extravagance, and dissipation which were natural to kingship. What is more impressive, Paine possessed a superb capacity for saying two things at the same time, for striking two blows in one sentence, one above and one below the probable threshold of consciousness of most of his readers. In some countries, Paine wrote, kings have no real "business" to conduct and they were always "sauntering away their lives"; in countries where kings are not absolute monarchs, Paine went on, "as in England, a man would be puzzled to know what *is* his business." Having thus described the king of England as possessed of no legitimate calling, Paine strikes his double blow: "The nearer any government approaches to a Republic," he declared in what was a not inaccurate description of the American colonies before 1763, "the less business there is for a King."[13] In this single sentence Paine had not only rendered monarchy antithetical to the Protestant ethic but also suggested that in America there existed no *need* for a king. With a single stroke he had rendered monarchy both reprehensible and superfluous.[14]

---

[11] *Ibid.*, 13-15.

[12] Thomas Paine's idea was not, of course, original. Jonathan Mayhew, for example, gave Samuel, I: 8 as authority for his contention that "*absolute* monarchy" was introduced by God as a punishment on the Jews. Jonathan Mayhew, *A Discourse Concerning Unlimited Submission and Non-Resistance to the Higher Powers: With Some Reflections on the Resistance made to King Charles I. And on the Anniversary of his Death: In which the Mysterious Doctrine of that Prince's Saintship and Martyrdom is Unriddled: The Substance of which was delivered in a Sermon preached in the West Meeting-House in Boston the Lord's-Day after the 30th of January, 1749/50* (Boston, 1750), 32n.

[13] [Paine,] *Common Sense*, 27-28.

[14] John Adams found that his contemporaries had an opinion of *Common Sense* remarkably congruent with that of this paper. "You ask, what is thought of Common sense. Sensible

Much the most striking instance of Paine's ability to play upon hidden chords of feeling was his proposal for the symbolic transfer of sovereign power from the king to the people of the American republic. This passage in *Common Sense* is of critical importance and deserves to be read carefully. "But where," Paine asks, ". . . is the King of America? I'll tell you Friend, he reigns above, and doth not make havoc of mankind like the Royal Brute of Great Britain. . . . let a day be solemnly set apart for proclaiming the Charter [of the new republic]; let it [the charter] be brought forth placed on the Divine Law, the Word of God; let a crown be placed thereon, by which the World may know, that . . . in America THE LAW IS KING. . . . But lest any ill use should afterwards arise, let the Crown at the conclusion of the ceremony be demolished, and scattered among the People whose right it is."[15]

We need to listen to the inner meaning of this extraordinary passage. Placement of a crown, the emblem of kingship, upon the charter of fundamental law imparts to the charter the king's power, his sovereignty. But this transfer is, as Paine says, dangerously insufficient. The crown, the king, must be "demolished." How? By breaking the crown, the king, into pieces —pieces which must be distributed among the people in order that they may acquire his power. The king is dead; his power is in the people.

It is scarcely possible to ignore the similarity of this ceremony to one which was and is traditionally performed in Christian churches. But one could for a moment be a good deal more outrageous than merely to suggest that Paine had fashioned a political eucharist. This ceremony was rooted in the prehistoric human past, in the days when men sometimes not only killed their father, the leader of the horde, but ate him in order magically to acquire his power. Admittedly, there seems to be a certain lack of hard data on this point, and no historian can properly feel altogether comfortable with such a lack. Yet a crucial and often overlooked distinction needs to be borne in mind: it is far less important whether one thinks such activities actually transpired than whether or not one thinks that men now and in the historical past act *as if* such prehistoric events took place. Given this distinction, it is possible to say a good many things about prehistoric man

Men think there are some Whims, some Sophisms, some artfull Addresses to superstitious Notions, some keen attempts upon the Passions, in this Pamphlet. But all agree there is a great deal of good sense, delivered in a clear, simple, concise and nervous Style. His Sentiments of the Abilities of America, and of the Difficulty of a Reconciliation with G. B. are generally approved. But his Notions, and Plans of a Continental Government are not much applauded. Indeed this Writer has a better Hand at pulling down than building." Butterfield, ed., *Adams Family Correspondence*, I, 363.
[15] [Paine,] *Common Sense*, 57-58.

but it is not possible to say just any old thing, not if one has any notions about the nature of modern man. With these precautions in mind it is possible to advance quite seriously the following propositions: that human beings have worshipped the spirit of their father in the form of a tree, or, more commonly nowadays, in the form of a tree-like cross, and furthermore, that the story of the original sin of man as recorded in the third chapter of Genesis expresses man's sense of guilt for having eaten his fathers, his gods, by recapitulating these long forgotten crimes in the apparently innocent act of eating part of an apple tree.[16]

Having made these suggestions, it will be well to turn again to Paine's aggressive assault upon monarchy and hereditary succession. The only historical evidence adduced to support the claim that Paine was killing the king has been derived from the internal content of his great pamphlet. Yet there are other kinds of evidence available, other ways of ascertaining the subliminal import of this, or any other important historical document.

There seem to be at least three additional ways of getting at the inner meaning of any popular political tract. One is to inquire what needs the tract seems to have met in the people reading it. In the case of *Common Sense* one of these needs is obvious and well known: by January 1776, after nine months of warfare, after being told by Britain that they were aiming at independence, after the American Prohibitory Act stopped their commerce, the colonists were surely ready for a plea for separation.

It is a good deal less obvious that Americans needed to have their king killed. There are in fact a great many indications that as late as 1776 there persisted within Americans a vague feeling that their king was somehow, in some measure, the legitimate father of his subjects. It is well known, of course, that Americans thought of their relationship with the king as being primarily contractual; they said outright that all political authority, including a king's, was based on compact. Nonetheless, when one attends to the imagery rather than to the explicit logic of American political writing in the Revolutionary era, it becomes clear that the age-old notion that a king stood in a paternal relationship with his people was not altogether dead.

Which may explain, indeed, why Paine called George III a "wretch . . . with the pretended title of FATHER OF HIS PEOPLE."[17] It has been con-

---

[16] See Theodor Reik, *Myth and Guilt: The Crime and Punishment of Mankind* (New York, 1957); Sigmund Freud, *Totem and Taboo: Some Points of Agreement between the Mental Lives of Savages and Neurotics*, James Strachey, trans. (New York, 1950); Sigmund Freud, *Moses and Monotheism*, Katherine Jones, trans. (London, 1939). It will occur to most readers, more perhaps than a few years ago, that *man* displaced his guilt onto *woman*.

[17] [Paine,] *Common Sense*, 47.

vincingly established that this notion existed in England in the late seventeenth century when John Locke spent so much effort attempting to demolish Sir Robert Filmer's contention that the basis of kingly authority was the paternal power which kings had inherited from the first father of mankind, Adam.[18] In 1775 the loyalist Jonathan Boucher actually attempted to resuscitate Filmer.[19] In the same year another loyalist called the king "the provident father of all his people."[20] Such sentiments were not confined to those who remained loyal to the king, for in the years before the Revolution the colonial assemblies were referring to the "paternal Care"[21] of the king, to his "paternal regard,"[22] his "paternal Care and Tenderness,"[23] and were addressing him as "our most gracious Sovereign and Father"[24] and as "the father of all his people."[25] These and similar expressions were proffered by various churches, ministers, mayors, merchants, college presidents, and chambers of commerce.[26] Nor were these terms simply pro forma: many addresses to or about the king did not employ them. Moreover, the analogy with parenthood was used in much more extended discussions of monarchy. Jonathan Mayhew, preaching on the anniversary of the execution of Charles I, argued that subjects ought to obey "when their prince exercises an equitable and paternal authority over them"; but that "when from a prince and common father, he exalts himself into a tyrant—when from subjects and children he degrades them into the class of slaves," then they ought to overthrow him.[27]

Utilization of this paternal analogy was by no means confined to rationalist clergymen like Mayhew. At the death of George II in 1760, for example, evangelical ministers like Gilbert Tennant eulogized him as "the

[18] Peter Laslett, ed., *Patriarcha and Other Political Works of Sir Robert Filmer* (Oxford, 1949).

[19] Jonathan Boucher, *A View of the Causes and Consequences of the American Revolution; in Thirteen Discourses, Preached in North America between the Years 1763 and 1775: With An Historical Preface* (London, 1797), 522-33.

[20] John Adams and Jonathan Sewall [i.e., Daniel Leonard], *Novanglus, and Massachusettensis; or Political Essays, Published in the Years 1774 and 1775. On the Principle Points of Controversy, Between Great Britain and Her Colonies. The Former by John Adams, Late President of the United States; The Latter by Jonathan Sewall, Then King's Attorney General of the Province of Massachusetts Bay. To Which Are Added A Number of Letters, Lately Written by President Adams, to The Honourable William Tudor; Some of Which Were Never Before Published* (Boston, 1819), 167.

[21] *South-Carolina and American General Gazette*, June 20, 1766.

[22] *South-Carolina Gazette*, Jan. 23, 1755.

[23] New York *Gazette, or the Weekly Post-Boy*, Dec. 5, 1765.

[24] Boston *News-Letter*, Aug. 21, 1760.

[25] *Virginia Gazette* (Purdie and Dixon), May 18, 1769.

[26] For example, see *Pennsylvania Gazette*, March 10, Nov. 17, 24, 1763; *New-Hampshire Gazette*, July 3, 1767; New York *Gazette, or the Weekly Post-Boy*, Dec. 5, 12, 19, 1765, Oct. 29, Nov. 5, 12, 19, 1770, July 15, 22, 29, 1771.

[27] Mayhew, *Discourse*, 39n.

Father of his People"[28] and urged Americans "to drop your filial Tears over the sacred Dust of your Common Father."[29] And when relations with Great Britain had reached nearly the breaking point in 1774, the Continental Congress solemnly petitioned George III "as the loving father of your whole people."[30] Finally, in the winter and spring of 1776 Americans began to call for independence because, as the freeholders of Charlotte County, Virginia, declared, "King George the Third . . . under the character of a parent, persists in behaving as a tyrant."[31] In light of these expressions there is a special meaning and poignancy in Abigail Adams' comment, made in January 1776, just after her husband had departed to serve in the Continental Congress, that "Our Country is as it were a Secondary God, and the first and greatest parent." Like her husband, she was among those Americans who had decided well before publication of *Common Sense* that there was to be no "reconciliation betwen our, no longer parent State, but tyrant State, and these Colonies."[32]

The reasons for the persistence of this imagery are so complex and so tightly interwoven with centuries of political and social change that they cannot be even briefly summarized. The point to be made is that Paine's pamphlet helped meet the need of Americans—a need of which they were not fully aware—to deny their king as their sovereign father. At first their undeclared war against Great Britain seemed to them, as it was so incessantly denominated, "unnatural,"—like any violence between those who stood in the "natural" relation of parent and child. Here again, Paine struck precisely the right chord by calling George III a "brute," that is to say, as existing outside the legitimate arena of human relationships. Paine was able to help Americans to feel less filial and more, as it were, fraternal among themselves.

[28] Gilbert Tennent, *A Sermon, On I Chronicles xxix. 28. Occasioned by the Death of King George the Second, Of happy Memory, who departed this Life on the 25th Day of* OCTOBER, *ir the Year of our Lord, 1760, in the 77th Year of his Age, and the 34th of his Reign; beloved and honored by his Subjects, for his Eminent-Royal-Virtues.* TOGETHER, *With some brief Hints, of the amiable* CHARACTER *of His Majesty King George the Third, Now seated on the British* THRONE, *and the auspicious* OMENS, *that attend his Infant* REIGN (Philadelphia, 1761), 12.

[29] Samuel Davies, *A Sermon delivered at Nassau-hall, January 14, 1761. On the death of His Late Majesty, King George II* (New York, 1761), 19.

[30] *Pennsylvania Magazine,* I (Jan. 1775), 51.

[31] Peter Force, ed., *American Archives: Consisting of a Collection of Authentick Records, State Papers, Debates, and Letters and other Notices of Publick Affairs, the Whole Forming a Documentary History of the Origin and Progress of the North American Colonies; of the Causes and Accomplishment of the American Revolution; and of the Constitution of Government for the United States, to the Final Ratification Thereof* (6 vols., Washington, 1837-1846), V, 1035.

[32] Butterfield, ed., *Adams Family Correspondence,* I, 422, 324.

In addition to examination of the needs of his readers, there is a second obvious avenue for approaching the meaning of Paine's message. The circumstances of Paine's own life dovetail in a rough way with what has been suggested rather bluntly to be his patricidal accomplishments. His father was a Quaker and poor; his mother was an Anglican and the daughter of an attorney; his father was eleven years younger than his mother, and apparently they were not very happily married. Paine's extant references to his parents consist of affectionate ones concerning his father and none at all about his mother. Paine himself was married, rapidly widowed; remarried and soon legally separated; he never had children.[33]

The lower status of his father may well have angered Paine, and his affectionate remarks may have masked a hostility he could not admit. His own inability to get along with women may have been owing to an inability to identify with his masculine parent. Armed with these facts it is possible to stretch Paine out on the couch and have at him. It seems, though, that because these data are so susceptible of various interpretations and because so many attempts at this sort of analysis have been so patently disastrous, that one ought to shun speculation and turn to evidence concerning Paine's thought which can be interpreted without constant necessity of making completely unverifiable suppositions about what must, psycho- and historiologically, have happened in Paine's past.

For one thing, it is virtually certain that Paine borrowed from another writer most of the ideas he advanced concerning God's scriptural disapprobation of monarchy. If John Adams' memory was correct, Paine had told him that he got his ideas on this subject from John Milton; certainly two of Milton's political tracts contain the same arguments as Paine's.[34] What is particularly interesting in this circumstance is that Milton's tracts were written in defense of the killing of an English king. In defending the execution of Charles I by Puritan revolutionaries, Milton had insisted that "Fathers and kings are very different things"; Milton's own attempt to "distinguish," as he said, "the rights of a father from those of a king"

[33] Moncure D. Conway, The Life of Thomas Paine (2 vols., New York, 1892), I, especially chapters 1 and 2.

[34] Lyman H. Butterfield, ed., Diary and Autobiography of John Adams (4 vols., Cambridge, Mass., 1961-1962), III, 330-35. The more probable of the two tracts is John Milton, Pro Populo Anglicano Defensio (1651), which was first published in English in 1692 (after another revolution), but conceivably Paine may have read only John Milton, The Tenure of Kings and Magistrates (1650). The latter is available in Don M. Wolfe and others, eds., Complete Prose Works of John Milton (4 vols., New Haven, 1953-1966), III, 190-258. But see especially the passages in the Pro Populo, ibid., IV, 344, 346-47, 370, 376-77. Paine quoted from Paradise Lost in Common Sense.

demonstrated that he rightly sensed that regicide and patricide were felt by many people to be equivalent.[35]

This circumstantial derivation acquires greater force when considered in the context of what Paine himself was writing during the year prior to publication of *Common Sense*. As editor of the *Pennsylvania Magazine* Paine wrote numerous anonymous articles, some of them straightforward essays, such as those in which he attacked duelling and Negro slavery, and defended (with arguments which have a very modern ring) defensive wars. More striking is that Paine wrote repeatedly, in various modes, about two subjects: marriage and the downfall of powerful men. A link between these two themes may be found in his "Occasional Letter on the Female Sex" where he cries: "Man, with regard to them, in all climates, and in all ages, has been either an insensible husband, or an oppressor."[36] A similar link, and just possibly some of Paine's own background, can be discerned in Paine's fanciful tale about Cupid's prevention of a marriage between a rich old lord of a manor and a shepherdess whose heart belongs to a young village swain. As they walk in the marriage procession Cupid casts the lord and the maiden into a strange sleep during which the two separately experience the unhappiness of living in their mismatched marriage. Finally they break out into unwitting soliloquies, "He exclaiming, she rejoicing; he imploring death to relieve him, and she preparing to bury him."[37]

Even more revelatory of Paine's thinking are his metaphors and fancies concerning men of worldly rank and power. In an essay assailing titles of nobility and official station Paine refers to "the possessors of undue honours" and says that "when their repeated guilt render[s] their persons unsafe, they disown their rank, and, like glow-worms, extinguish themselves into common reptiles, to avoid discovery."[38] Paine similarly applauds the enforced self-destruction of great men in his "*Reflections on the Life and Death of Lord* CLIVE," where he describes the lordly conqueror of India spreading war, rapine, and devastation before returning to England with glory and riches. Upon his second return, however, Clive is hounded by censure and finally laid low by disgrace and poverty; he sinks into "melancholy" and is "found dead at last."[39] Paine did not have to inform his readers that Lord Clive died by his own hand.

It seems reasonable to suppose that Paine's delight in fancying that men

[35] Wolfe, ed., *Works of Milton*, IV, 326-27.
[36] *Pennsylvania Magazine*, I (Aug. 1775), 362-64.
[37] *Ibid.*, I (April 1775), 158-61.
[38] *Ibid.*, I (May 1775), 209-10.
[39] *Ibid.*, I (March 1775), 107-11.

of power could be pressured into destroying themselves constituted a displacement of his desire to do the murderous work himself, a desire which
was of course not consciously admissible. This displacement of aggressive
hostility wears only the thinnest possible disguise in Paine's astonishing
fantasy about Alexander the Great. Paine begins by saying that while he
was walking near the Schuylkill River his mind fancifully crossed the Styx
to see how the great conqueror was faring in the "Plutonian world." There
he spies the approach of a splendid chariot and inquires which of the richly
dressed riders is Alexander. He is told neither, that Alexander is one of the
horses, but *"not always"* a horse, *"for when he is apprehensive that a good
licking is intended for him, he watches his opportunity to roll out of the
stable in the shape of a piece of dung, or in any other disguise he can escape
by."* Later, as Paine is about to leave, he sees a bug on his clothes; he is
about to kill it when it screams out, *"Spare Alexander the* GREAT." There-
upon, Paine continues—and his words need to be read with care—"holding
up the Emperor between my finger and thumb, he exhibited a most con-
temptible figure of the downfall of tyrant greatness. Affected with a mixture of concern and compassion (*which he was always a stranger to*) I suffered him to nibble on a pimple that was newly risen on my hand, in order
to refresh him; after which, I placed him on a tree to hide him, but a Tom
Tit coming by, chopped him up with as little mercy as he put whole kingdoms to the sword."[40] Thus ended Alexander the Great: eaten off a tree.

It seems not unreasonable to conclude that Paine was a person who delighted in the destruction of tyrants and that he protected his own self-im-
age by compassionately nursing a tyrant whom he wished to destroy,
thereby denying that he, Paine, could harbor murderous passion. And it
also seems likely that a person who dwelt upon such fantasies could very
easily undertake, without of course fully knowing it, to kill a living king.

Having dealt as cautiously as possible with the personality of the author
of *Common Sense*, it is time to explore briefly a third way of getting at its
inner meaning. Since the pamphlet operated partly at an affective, symbolic
level, it ought to be helpful to look at the symbolic content of Revolutionary
thought and action. To what extent did such content dovetail with the suggestions already advanced concerning *Common Sense?* In many ways there
seems to be little connection, as for instance, with the patriots' penchant for
numerology and nocturnal illuminations. There would appear to be more
possibilities in the fact that Americans thought of the colonies as being children of the "mother" or "parent" (never "father") country and employed

[40] *Ibid.*, I (Feb. 1775), 61-62.

imagery of nurture and maturation. Paine himself used this image. Far more pertinent, however, was the common and revealing utilization of—of all things—the tree.

It is well known that liberty trees and poles served as rallying points for both the destructive and ritualistic activities of Revolutionary crowds. Precisely *why* is less certain. To gain some insight into the meaning, the psychic content, of these symbols, scholars can turn cautiously to the trees which appear in the political literature of the Revolution. One commentator, for example, ridiculed American patriots for *"Assembling in the open Air,* and performing *idolatrous* and *vociferous* Acts of Worship, *to a Stick of Wood."*[41] Perhaps there was a grain of truth in the charge. Paine himself wrote a poem about the Liberty Tree which the Goddess of Liberty had planted in America. "The fame of its fruit drew the nations around,/To seek out this peaceable shore./Unmindful of names or distinctions they came,/For freemen like brothers agree,/With one spirit endued, they one friendship pursued,/And their temple was *Liberty tree."*[42] While these lines reveal that Paine was a better pamphleteer than poet, they also make clear that it was the *brother*hood of the worshippers which mattered. Who indeed actually assembled about those trees in America but the *Sons* of Liberty, sons who presumably could not have two fathers. In England similar opponents of the government were called not the "Sons" but the "Friends of Liberty."

This suggestion that the tree of liberty in America constituted a new sovereign is perhaps not so tenuous or gratuitous as it may at first appear. The trees which one finds in the political writing of the Revolutionary era were used, more or less explicitly, to represent government. In *Common Sense* Paine explained that when men first abandoned the state of nature to form a "government," "some convenient Tree will afford them a State-House."[43] More metaphorically he linked the future development of America's "Continental union" to the growth of an oak tree.[44] A similar association forms the entire basis for a fanciful political tract written by Francis Hopkinson in April 1776. Through the mouth of a seer living in the remote past Hopkinson describes the peopling of America and then explains: "And it shall be that the king of islands shall send over and plant in the midst of them a certain tree. . . . And the people shall cultivate this tree with all possible

[41] Quoted in Arthur M. Schlesinger, *Prelude to Independence: The Newspaper War on Britain, 1764-1766* (New York, 1965), 29.

[42] *Pennsylvania Magazine*, I (July 1775), 328.

[43] [Paine,] *Common Sense*, 4.

[44] *Ibid.*, 30-31.

care, and they shall live under the shadow of its branches, and shall worship it as a God. But in process of time shall arise a *North* wind, and shall
blast the tree, so that . . . it shall become rotten at the heart." Then Hopkinson has a "prophet" with "spectacles upon his nose" (already Franklin
was a sage) "cry aloud and say—'Seeing that this tree . . . is become rotten
. . . behold now, let us cut it down and remove it from us: And in its place
we will plant another tree, young and vigorous; and we will water it, and it
shall grow. . . .' " After carrying on in this vein Hopkinson concludes that
"the people shall dwell under the shadow of its branches, and shall become
an exceeding great, powerful, and happy nation."[45]

What is even more arresting than these analogies is the protest of loyalists against the prospect of independence. Boucher objected that "We were
not lopped off the parent trunk as useless or noxious limbs, *to be hewn
down, or cast into the fire*; but carefully transplanted here."[46] In a somewhat different vein, Boucher and John Dickinson described
"independency" as "forbidden fruit"[47] and as "a tree of forbidden and ac-
cursed fruit."[48] Peter Van Schaack lamented that "the people of this country seem determined to lop off every excrescence from the body politic.
Happy if they can stop at the true point, and in order to obtain the fruit . . .
do not cut down the tree."[49] In short, opponents of independence were metaphorically equating the overthrow of the crown's authority with destruction
of a tree or with consumption of a portion of a tree.

A climax in the symbolic destruction of royal authority—and also the
acting out of Paine's proposed public ceremony—may be detected in the
days following the formal public readings of the Declaration of Independence. In Savannah, Georgia, a large crowd attended "a very solemn fu-

[45] *A Prophecy*, in Francis Hopkinson, *The Miscellaneous Essays and Occasional Writings
of Francis Hopkinson, Esq.* (3 vols., Philadelphia, 1792), I, 92-97. See also Matthew, 3:10:
"And now also the axe is laid unto the root of the trees: therefore every tree which bringeth
not forth good fruit is hewn down, and cast into the fire." The same language is in Luke.
3:9.
[46] Boucher, *A View of the Causes and Consequences of the American Revolution*, 475.
[47] *Ibid.*, 349.
[48] Paul Leicester Ford, ed., *The Writings of John Dickinson*. Vol. I: *Political Writings.
1764-1774* (Philadelphia, 1895), 491.
[49] Henry C. Van Schaack, *The Life of Peter Van Schaack, LL.D., Embracing Selections
from His Correspondence and Other Writings, during the American Revolution, and His
Exile in England* (New York, 1842), 25. For liberty trees in the French Revolution, see
Clarence Crane Brinton, *The Jacobins: An Essay in the New History* (New York, 1930),
185-86, 197-98. This imagery has also been used by modern historians. John C. Miller wrote
of *Common Sense*: "Paine did more than smash the oversized statue of George III: he ripped
up monarchy root and branch by pronouncing it to be a form of government condemned by
the Almighty and by right reason." John C. Miller, *Origins of the American Revolution*
(Boston, 1943), 469.

neral procession" in recognition of the demise of King George III; the crowd included "a greater number of people than ever appeared on any occasion before in this province."[50] In New York City, during the evening after proclamation of the Declaration in the presence of Washington and his troops, a crowd led by the Sons of Liberty gathered around the gilded equestrian statue of George III and, as a contemporary described what followed, the statue "was taken down, broken into pieces, and its honor levelled with the dust,"[51] or, as another observer said, "was by the sons of freedom laid prostrate in the dirt."[52] Elsewhere in the city, and indeed in most or all the thirteen colonies, the king's arms (usually made of carved and painted wood) where taken down and in most cases destroyed.[53] The royal arms in churches and painted on tavern signs were cut down. In Boston even such royal emblems as shop signs decorated with crowns and royal lions were thrown into a bonfire in King Street.[54] In Providence the king's arms were taken from the Colony House and from the Crown Coffee House and burned before a crowd.[55] Patriots in Baltimore carried an effigy of the king through the town and then threw it into a fire.[56] In Worcester it was reported that "the Arms of that Tyrant in Britain, George III" which hung on the court house "were committed to the flames and consumed to ashes."[57] From New York City came a similar report: "the coat of arms of his majesty George III was torn to pieces and burnt, in the presence of the spectators."[58] It is difficult to see how much more effectively, while still safely, Americans could kill their king than to gather about a fire while the emblem of his authority was, as the Worcester report said, "consumed." Yet an observer in Boston described a scene which recapitulated even more vividly the political eucharist which Paine had described: "In the afternoon

[50] *Connecticut Gazette*, Oct. 25, 1776. This citation was called to the author's attention by Michael Hindus.

[51] *New-England Chronicle*, July 18, 1776.

[52] *Maryland Gazette*, July 25, 1776. *Virginia Gazette*, July 29, 1776, reported, "A Gentleman, who was present at this ominous fall of leaden Majesty, looking back to the original's hopeful beginning, pertinently exclaimed, in the language of the angel Lucifer, 'If thou be'st he! But ah, how fallen! How chang'd!' " The lines are from *Paradise Lost*, where Satan is addressing the fallen Beelzebub, his chief lieutenant. The opening lines of the epic are, of course, familiar: "Of Man's First Disobedience, and the fruit/Of that Forbidden Tree, whose mortal taste/Brought Death into the World, and all our woe."

[53] Edmund F. Slafter, "Royal Memorials and Emblems in Use in the Colonies before the Revolution," *Proceedings of the Massachusetts Historical Society*, IV (1889), 239-64, and the additional information by Robert Walcott, 291-98.

[54] *Freeman's Journal or New-Hampshire Gazette*, July 27, 1776.

[55] Providence *Gazette*, July 27, 1776.

[56] New York *Gazette and the Weekly Mercury*, Aug. 12, 1776.

[57] Quoted in Slafter, "Royal Memorials and Emblems in Use in the Colonies before the Revolution," 240n.

[58] *Maryland Gazette*, Aug. 1, 1776.

the King's Arms were taken down and broken to pieces in the street, and carried off by the people."[59] The American people had not only declared their independence but had taken to themselves the power of their king.

This is to say that what our textbooks call the idea of "popular sovereignty" contained within it a substratum of psychic meaning which needs to be considered as both a part of that idea and as having provided a portion of the energy which went into its implementation. To claim more is to claim too much, but to claim less is to ignore an aspect of historical reality.

As for Paine, it can be claimed that he performed a vital service to Americans—but a momentary one: the sons of the Revolution soon lapsed into acclaiming their staunchest leader as the Father of His Country.

[59] Quoted in Slafter, "Royal Memorials and Emblems in Use in the Colonies before the Revolution," 253n.

REASON AND POWER IN BENJAMIN FRANKLIN'S POLITICAL THOUGHT

GERALD STOURZH

University of Chicago

Perhaps no period of modern history has been more a victim of generalization than the Age of Enlightenment. The worship of reason and progress and belief in the essential goodness and perfectibility of human nature are most commonly associated with the 18th century climate of opinion. Many of the stereotypes which have been applied to it have automatically been transferred to Benjamin Franklin. Already to contemporaries of his old age, Franklin seemed the very personification of the Age of Reason. Condorcet, who had known Franklin personally, summed up his description of Franklin's political career as follows: "In a word, his politics were those of a man who believed in the power of reason and the reality of virtue."[1] In Germany, an admirer was even more enthusiastic: "Reason and virtue, made possible through reason alone, consequently again reason and nothing but reason, is the magic with which Benjamin Franklin conquered heaven and earth."[2] This is also the judgment of posterity. F. L. Mott and Chester E. Jorgensen, who have so far presented the most acute analysis of Franklin's thought and its relationship to the intellectual history of his time, do not hesitate to call him "the completest colonial representative" of the Age of Enlightenment.[3] Unanimous agreement seems to exist that Franklin was "in tune with his time."[4]

This essay will attempt to show that these generalizations, instead of illuminating the essence of Franklin's moral and political philosophy, tend rather to obscure some of the mainsprings of his thought and action. Our investigation rests upon the assumption that man's understanding of politics is inseparable from his conception of human nature. Consequently, this reappraisal of Franklin's political thought will subject his views on human nature to close scrutiny; it is hoped that this procedure may lead to a rejection of some of the cliches to which he has fallen victim.

[1] *Oeuvres du Marquis de Condorcet,* eds. A. Condorcet O'Connor and M. F. Arago, 2nd ed., 12 vols. (Paris, 1847–49), Vol. 3, p. 420.

[2] Georg Forster, "Erinnerungen aus dem Jahre 1790," in "Kleine Schriften," *Georg Forsters saemmtliche Schriften,* ed. by his daughter, 9 vols. (Leipzig, 1843), Vol. 6, p. 207.

[3] *Benjamin Franklin, Representative Selections with Introduction, Bibliography, and Notes,* eds. F. L. Mott and Chester E. Jorgenson (New York, 1936), p. xiii.

[4] Carl Becker, review of the Franklin Institute's *Meet Dr. Franklin,* in *American Historical Review,* Vol. 50, p. 142 (Oct., 1944). Cf. Henry Steele Commager's statement that it was the faith in reason which gave unity to Franklin's life. "Franklin, the American," review of Carl Van Doren's *Benjamin Franklin,* in *New York Times Book Review,* Oct. 9, 1938, p. 1. Charles A. Beard explicitly referred to Franklin as an outstanding example of American writers on progress. Introduction to J. B. Bury, *The Idea of Progress* (New York, 1932), p. xxxvii.

I. THE "GREAT CHAIN OF BEING"

Many of the notions which are commonly applied to the 18th century, such as the belief in progress and in the perfectibility of human nature, are significant chiefly with respect to the currents of thought and action related to the American and French Revolutions, and do little to deepen our understanding of earlier developments. So it is to the first half of the 18th century that we must now turn. We are prone to overlook the extraordinary difference in age which separated Franklin from the other Founding Fathers of the Republic. Franklin was born in 1706, twenty-six years before Washington, twenty-nine years before John Adams, thirty-seven years before Jefferson, thirty-nine years before John Jay, forty-five years before James Madison, and fifty-one years before Alexander Hamilton.

Franklin's fame as a social and natural philosopher rests mainly on the achievements of his middle and late years. One needs to remember, however, that he was a moral philosopher long before he became a natural philosopher and before he advised his fellowmen how to acquire wealth.[5] At the age of twenty-two, he formed a "club for mutual improvement,"[6] the Junto, where great emphasis was laid on moral or political problems. Whether self-interest was the root of human action, whether man could attain perfection, whether "encroachments on the just liberties of the people"[7] had taken place—all these things were matters of discussion at Franklin's club. Already at the age of nineteen, during his first stay in London, he had printed his first independent opus, *A Dissertation on Liberty and Necessity, Pleasure and Pain.*[8] This piece

---

[5] Even after having achieved world-wide fame as a natural philosopher, he observed that we deserve reprehension if "we neglect the Knowledge and Practice of essential Duties" in order to attain eminence in the knowledge of nature. *The Writings of Benjamin Franklin*, ed. Henry Albert Smyth, 10 vols. (New York, 1905–7), Vol. 4, p. 22. (Hereafter cited as *Writings*.)

[6] *Autobiography, Writings*, Vol. I, p. 22.

[7] James Parton, *Life and Times of Benjamin Franklin*, 2d ed., 2 vols. (Boston, 1897), Vol. I, p. 160. See also *Writings*, Vol. 2, p. 89. The authors who so far have most closely scrutinized Franklin's political thought do not see the relevance of many of the younger Franklin's remarks on human nature, arbitrary government, or the nature of political dispute to his concept of politics. See M. R. Eiselen, *Franklin's Political Theories* (Garden City, N. Y., 1928), p. 13; R. D. Miles, "The Political Philosophy of Benjamin Franklin," unpub. diss. (Univ. of Michigan, 1949), p. 36; *Benjamin Franklin, Representative Selections* (cited in note 3), p. lxxxii. The most recent work in this field, Clinton Rossiter's "The Political Theory of Benjamin Franklin," *Pennsylvania Magazine of History and Biography*, Vol. 76, pp. 259–93 (July, 1952), pays no attention to Franklin's conception of human nature and his attitude towards the problem of power and the ends of political life. Rossiter's contention (p. 268) is that Franklin "limited his own thought process to the one devastating question: *Does it work?*, or more exactly, *Does it work well?*" Franklin, however, like everybody else, had certain ends and goals in view, and the question "Does it work?" is meaningless without the context of certain basic desiderata.

[8] This little work has been omitted in the Smyth edition of Franklin's writings, because "the work has no value, and it would be an injury and an offence to the memory of Franklin to republish it." *Writings*, Vol. 2, p. vi. It is, however, reprinted as an appendix to Parton, *op. cit.*, Vol. 1, and has since been republished independently with a bibliographical note by Lawrence C. Wroth (New York, 1930).

showed that no trace was left of his Presbyterian family background. The secularization of his thought had been completed.[9] Gone were the Puritan belief in revelation and the Christian conception of human nature which, paradoxically, included the notion of the depravity of man, as well as of his uniqueness among all created beings.[10] Franklin's *Dissertation* shows that he was thoroughly acquainted with the leading ideas of his time. The early decades of the 18th century were characterized by the climate of opinion which has been aptly called "cosmic Toryism."[11] Pope's *Essay on Man* and many pages of Addison's *Spectator*—both of which Franklin admired—most perfectly set forth the creed of a new age. Overshadowing everything else, there was joy about the discoveries of the human mind, which had solved the enigma of creation:

> Nature and Nature's Laws lay hid in Night:
> GOD said, *Let Newton be!* and all was Light.[12]

The perfection of that Great Machine, the Newtonian universe, filling humanity with admiration for the Divine Watchmaker, seemed to suggest that this world was indeed the best of all possible worlds. Everything was necessary, was good. Pope's "Whatever is, is right," is the key phrase of this period. The goodness of the Creator revealed itself in His giving existence to all possible creatures. The universe "presented the spectacle of a continuous scale or ladder of creatures, extending without a break from the worm to the seraph."[13] Somewhere in this "Great Chain of Being," to use a favorite phrase of the

[9] See Herbert Schneider, "The Significance of Benjamin Franklin's Moral Philosophy," *Columbia University Studies in the History of Ideas*, Vol. 2, p. 298 (1918).

[10] In his *Autobiography*, Franklin acknowledges his debt to Shaftesbury and Collins for becoming "a real doubter in many points of our religious doctrine." *Writings*, Vol. 1, p. 244. The question of Franklin's attitude toward the great moral philosophers and of their influence upon him is considerably more difficult to determine than the same question with regard to John Adams or Thomas Jefferson. With the exception of authors named in the *Autobiography*, comments on books Franklin read are extremely rare. His library has not been preserved; there is, however, a list of books known to have been in Franklin's library at the time of his death (compiled by Dr. George Simpson Eddy in Princeton University; photostat in the library of the American Philosophical Society in Philadelphia). See also Mr. Eddy's article, "Dr. Benjamin Franklin's Library," *Proceedings of the American Antiquarian Society*, new series, Vol. 34, pp. 206–26 (Oct., 1924). Except for comments in some English pamphlets, there exist nothing like the voluminous marginal notes of John Adams and Jefferson. Also he was not able to keep up a correspondence like Adams' or Jefferson's, discussing great problems from the perspective of a long life in retirement after the great events of their lives had taken place. Immersed in public business almost until his death, Franklin does not seem to have had much time left over for reading. Benjamin Rush told John Adams that "Dr. Franklin thought a great deal, wrote occasionally, but read during the middle and later years of his life very little." October 31, 1807, in Benjamin Rush, *The Letters of Benjamin Rush*, ed. L. H. Butterfield, 2 vols. (Princeton, 1951), Vol. 2, p. 953. For a compilation of the authors with whom Franklin was acquainted, see Lois Margaret MacLaurin, *Franklin's Vocabulary* (Garden City, N.Y., 1928), Ch. 1, and *Benjamin Franklin, Representative Selections* (cited in note 3), p. lv.

[11] Basil Willey, *The Eighteenth Century Background* (London, 1940), Ch. 3, *passim*.

[12] Pope's epitaph intended for Newton's tomb.

[13] Willey, *op. cit.*, pp. 47–48.

period,[14] there must be a place for Man. Man, as it were, formed the "middle link" between lower and higher creatures. No wonder, then, that Franklin chose as a motto for his *Dissertation* the following lines of Dryden:

> Whatever is, is in its Causes just,
> Since all Things are by Fate; but purblind Man
> Sees but a part o' th' Chain, the nearest Link,
> His Eyes not carrying to the equal Beam
> That poises all above.[15]

The consequences of the conception of the universe as a "Great Chain of Being" for Franklin's understanding of human nature are highly significant. To be sure, man had liberated himself from the oppression of Original Sin, and in his newly established innocence he hailed the Creator and praised the Creation. But if the depravity of human nature had been banished, so had man's striving for redemption, man's aspiration for perfection. There was nothing left which ought to be redeemed. Indeed, in the new rational order of the universe, it would not seem proper to long for a higher place in the hierarchy of beings. Man's release from the anguish of Original Sin was accompanied by a lowering of the goals of human life. "The imperfection of man is indispensable to the fullness of the hierarchy of being." Man had, so to speak, already attained the grade of perfection which belonged to his station. From the point of view of mortality, then, what this amounted to was a "counsel of imperfection—an ethics of prudent mediocrity."[16]

Quiet contentment with, and enjoyment of, one's place in the Great Chain of Being must have been a comforting creed for the wealthy and educated classes of the Augustan Age:

> Order is Heav'n's first law; and this confest,
> Some are, and must be, greater than the rest,
> More rich, more wise.[17]

This was not the optimism of progress, which we usually associate with the eighteenth century. It was an optimism of acceptance;[18] for the rich and complacent, the real and the good seemed indeed to coincide.

Not so for Benjamin Franklin. Late in his life, in 1771, he referred to "the poverty and obscurity in which I was born and bred." His innate desire for

[14] See A. O. Lovejoy, *The Great Chain of Being* (Cambridge, Mass., 1936). This brilliant analysis of that complex of ideas has been applied to Franklin only once, although it offers important clues for an understanding of Franklin's conception of human nature. Arthur Stuart Pitt in "The Sources, Significance, and Date of Franklin's 'An Arabian Tale,'" *Publications of the Modern Language Association*, Vol. 57, pp. 155–68 (March, 1942), applies Lovejoy's analysis to one piece of Franklin's and does not refer to relevant writings of Franklin's youth in which this idea may also be found. Pitt's article is valuable in pointing out the sources from which Franklin could have accepted the idea directly, namely Locke, Milton, Addison, and Pope.

[15] Parton, *Life and Times of Benjamin Franklin* (cited in note 7), Vol. 1, p. 605.

[16] Lovejoy, *op. cit.*, pp. 199, 200.

[17] Alexander Pope, "An Essay on Man," Epistle 4, in *Selected Works*, Modern Library ed. (New York, 1948), p. 127.

[18] Willey, *op. cit.*, p. 56.

justice and equality, his keen awareness of existing conditions of injustice and inequality, finally his own experience of things which he could not possibly call just or good—for instance, he tells us that his brother's "harsh and tyrannical treatment of me might be a means of impressing me with that aversion to arbitrary power that has stuck to me through my whole life"[19]—all this contravened the facile optimism of the Augustan Age.

Franklin, indeed, accepted the cosmological premises of his age (as witness the above quoted motto of the *Dissertation*). But his conclusions make the edifice of "Cosmic Toryism"—so imposing in Pope's magnificent language—appear a mockery and an absurdity. Franklin's argumentation was simple enough: God being all-powerful and good, man could have no free will, and the distinction between good and evil had to be abolished. He also argued that pain or uneasiness was the mainspring of all our actions, and that pleasure was produced by the removal of this uneasiness. If followed that "*No State of Life can be happier than the present, because Pleasure and Pain are inseparable.*" The unintentional irony of this brand of optimism cannot be better expressed than in young Franklin's conclusion:

I am sensible that the Doctrine here advanc'd, if it were to be publish'd, would meet with but an indifferent Reception. Mankind naturally and generally love to be flatter'd: Whatever sooths our Pride, and tends to exalt our Species above the rest of the Creation, we are pleas'd with and easily believe, when ungrateful Truths shall be with the utmost Indignation rejected. "What! bring ourselves down to an Equality with the Beasts of the Field! With the *meanest* part of the Creation! 'Tis insufferable!" But, (to use a Piece of *common* Sense) our *Geese* are but *Geese* tho' we may think 'em *Swans;* and Truth will be Truth tho' it sometimes prove mortifying and distasteful.[20]

The dilemma which confronted him at the age of nineteen is characteristic of most eighteenth-century philosophy: "If nature is good, then there is no evil in the world; if there is evil in the world, then nature so far is not good."[21]

Franklin cut this Gordian knot by sacrificing "Reason" to "Experience." He turned away from metaphysics for the quite pragmatic reason that his denial of good and evil did not provide him with a basis for the attainment of social and individual happiness:

Revelation had indeed no weight with me, as such; but I entertain'd an opinion that, though certain actions might not be bad *because* they were forbidden by it, or good *because* it commanded them, yet probably these actions might be forbidden *because* they were bad for us, or commanded *because* they were beneficial to us. . . . [22]

To achieve useful things rather than indulge in doubtful metaphysical speculations, to become a doer of good—these, then, became the principal aims of Franklin's thought and action.[23]

This fundamental change from the earlier to the later Enlightenment—from

[19] *Autobiography, Writings,* Vol. 1, pp. 226, 247 (n.1).

[20] Parton, *op. cit.*, Vol. 1, p. 617.

[21] Carl Becker, *The Heavenly City of the Eighteenth Century Philosophers* (New Haven, 1932), p. 69.

[22] *Autobiography, Writings,* Vol. 1, p. 296. See also *Writings,* Vol. 7, p. 412.

[23] See *Writings,* Vol. 1, p. 341; Vol. 2, p. 215; Vol. 3, p. 145; Vol. 9, p. 208; Vol. 10, p. 38.

passive contemplation to improvement, from a static to a dynamic conception of human affairs—did contribute to the substitution of the idea of human perfectibility for the idea of human perfection—a very limited kind of perfection, as we have seen; but it was by no means sufficient to bring about the faith in the perfectibility of human nature. Something else was needed: proof that "social evils were due neither to innate and incorrigible disabilities of the human being nor the nature of things, but simply to ignorance and prejudices."[24] The associationist psychology, elaborating Locke's theory of the malleability of human nature, provided the basis for the expansion of the idea of progress and perfectibility from the purely intellectual domain into the realm of moral and social life in general. The Age of Reason, then, presents us with a more perplexing picture than we might have supposed.

Reason, after all, may mean three different things: reason as a faculty of man; reason as a quality of the universe; and reason as a temper in the conduct of human affairs.[25] We might venture the generalization that the earlier Enlightenment stressed reason as the quality of the Newtonian universe, whereas the later Enlightenment, in spite of important exceptions, exalted the power of human reason to mold the moral and social life of mankind.[26] Franklin's "reason," as we shall see presently, is above all a temper in the conduct of human affairs.

This discussion is important for a correct understanding of Franklin's position in the center of the cross-currents of the Age of Enlightenment. The fact that the roots of his thought are to be found in the early Enlightenment is not always realized, or, if realized, not always sufficiently explained. Julian P. Boyd, in his introduction to Carl Becker's biographical sketch of Franklin, states that Franklin and Jefferson believed "that men would be amenable to rational persuasion, that they would thereby be induced to promote their own and their fellows' best interests, and that, in the end, perfect felicity for man and society would be achieved."[27] These ideas are certainly suggestive of the later Enlightenment, and appear to be more applicable to Jefferson than to Franklin. Carl Becker himself asserts, somewhat ambiguously and with undue generalization, that Franklin "was a true child of the Enlightenment, not indeed of the school of Rousseau, but of Defoe and Pope and Swift, of Fontenelle and Montesquieu and Voltaire."[28] There is little evidence that this school prophesied the achievement of perfect felicity for man and society.

Bernard Mandeville, a personal acquaintance of Franklin, joined the chorus of those who proclaimed the compatibility of human imperfection and the

[24] Bury, *The Idea of Progress* (cited in note 4), p. 128.

[25] This distinction is Roland Bainton's. See his "The Appeal to Reason and the American Revolution," in *The Constitution Reconsidered*, ed. Conyers Read (New York, 1938), p. 121.

[26] Cf. A. O. Lovejoy's statement: "The authors who were perhaps the most influential and the most representative in the early and mid-eighteenth century, made a great point of reducing man's claims to 'reason' to a minimum." " 'Pride' in Eighteenth Century Thought," in *Essays in the History of Ideas* (Baltimore, 1948), p. 68.

[27] Carl Becker, *Benjamin Franklin* (Ithaca, 1946), p. ix.

[28] *Ibid.*, p. 31.

general harmony. "Private Vices, Public Benefits" was the subtitle of his famous *Fable of the Bees*, which Franklin owned and probably read. Mandeville's paradoxical doctrines must have been a powerful challenge to Franklin's young mind. "The Moral Virtues," Mandeville asserted in terms reminiscent of Machiavelli, "are the Political Offspring which Flattery begot upon Pride." While arguing that men are actuated by self-interest and that this self-interest promotes the prosperity of society as a whole, Mandeville maintains a rigorous standard of virtue, declaring those acts alone to be virtuous "by which Man, contrary to the impulse of Nature, should endeavour the Benefit of others, or the Conquest of his own Passions out of a Rational Ambition of being good."[29]

By making ethical standards so excessively rigorous, Mandeville rendered them impossible of observance, and indirectly (though intentionally) pointed out their irrelevance for practical life. The very rigor of his ethical demands in contrast to his practical devices suggests that Mandeville lacked "idealism." This was not the case with Franklin. The consciously paradoxical Mandeville could offer no salvation for the young Franklin caught on the horns of his own dilemma. Shaftesbury, Mandeville's *bête noire*—whose works were already familiar to Franklin—had a more promising solution. In his *Inquiry Concerning Virtue or Merit* (1699), Shaftesbury had asserted that man by nature possesses a faculty to distinguish and to prefer what is right—the famous "moral sense."

Franklin's option for Shaftesbury was made clear from his reprinting two dialogues "Between Philocles and Horatio, . . . concerning Virtue and Pleasure" from the *London Journal* of 1729 in the *Pennsylvania Gazette* of 1730. In the second dialogue, reason was described as the chief faculty of man, and reasonable and morally good actions were defined as actions preservative of the human kind and naturally tending to produce real and unmixed happiness. These dialogues until recently have been held to be Franklin's own work; however, a reference in the *Autobiography* to a "Socratic dialogue" and "a discourse on self-denial," traditionally interpreted as concerning the two dialogues between Philocles and Horatio, recently has been shown to concern two pieces published in the *Pennsylvania Gazette* of 1735. The first piece is a dialogue between Crito and Socrates, never before correctly attributed to Franklin, in which he asserted that the "SCIENCE OF VIRTUE" was "of more worth, and of more consequence" to one's happiness than all other knowledge put together; in the second piece, a discourse on self-denial, Franklin combated the (Mandevillean) idea that "the greater the *Self-Denial* the greater the Virtue." Thirty-three years later, Franklin was still following Shaftesbury when he exhorted: "Be in general virtuous, and you will be happy." However, we shall see later that Franklin, in the last analysis, was not as far removed from Mandeville's pessimism as these cheerful views would suggest. His was a sort of middle position between Mandeville's "realism" and Shaftesbury's "idealism."[30]

[29] Bernard Mandeville, *The Fable of the Bees*, ed. F. B. Kaye, 2 vols. (Oxford, 1924), Vol. 1, pp. 48–49, 51. Franklin owned Mandeville's work, according to a list in the Mason-Franklin Collection of the Yale University Library. He was introduced to Mandeville during his first stay in London. *Writings*, Vol. 1, p. 278.

[30] The proof that the two dialogues between Philocles and Horatio were not written

II. THE IDEA OF PROGRESS

The restraining influence of the idea of the Great Chain of Being retained its hold on Franklin after his return to a more conventional recognition of good and evil. In his "Articles of Belief" of 1728 he said that "Man is not the most perfect Being but one, rather as there are many Degrees of Beings his Inferiors, so there are many Degrees of Beings superior to him."[31] Franklin presented the following question and answers to the discussions in the Junto:

Can a man arrive at perfection in his life, as some believe; or is it impossible, as others believe?

Answer. Perhaps they differ in the meaning of the word *perfection.* I suppose the perfection of any thing to be only the greatest the nature of the thing is capable of. . . .

If they mean a man cannot in this life be so perfect as an angel, it may be true; for an angel, by being incorporeal, is allowed some perfections we are at present incapable of, and less liable to some imperfections than we are liable to. If they mean a man is not capable of being perfect here as he is capable of being in heaven, that may be true likewise. But that a man is not capable of being so perfect here, is not sense. . . . In the above sense, there may be a perfect oyster, a perfect horse, a perfect ship; why not a perfect man? That is, as perfect as his present nature and circumstance admit.[32]

We note here the acknowledgment of man's necessarily "imperfect" state of perfection. However, it is striking to see that Franklin refused to employ this theory as a justification of the status quo. Within certain bounds, change, or progress for the better, was possible. Many years later, Franklin was to use exactly the same argument in the debate on the status of America within the British Empire. A pro-English writer had presented the familiar argument of "Cosmic Toryism" (and of conservatism in general, of course): "To expect perfection in human institutions is absurd." Franklin retorted indignantly: "Does this justify any and every Imperfection that can be invented or added to our Constitution?"[33]

This attitude differs from the belief in moral progress and perfectibility. There are, however, some passages in Franklin's later writings, better known than the preceding ones, which seem to suggest his agreement with the creed of moral progress and perfectibility. Two years before his death, looking with considerable satisfaction upon the achievements of his country and his own life, he explained to a Boston clergyman his belief in "the growing felicity of mankind, from the improvements in philosophy, morals, politics"; he also stressed "the invention and acquisition of new and useful utensils and instru-

by Franklin and the identification of the two other pieces have been furnished by Alfred O. Aldridge, "Franklin's 'Shaftesburian' Dialogues Not Franklin's: A Revision of the Franklin Canon," *American Literature,* Vol. 21, pp. 151–59 (May, 1949). See also *Writings,* Vol. 1, p. 343; Vol. 2, pp. 168–69. The discourse on self-denial is printed in *The Complete Works of Benjamin Franklin,* ed. John Bigelow, 10 vols. (New York, 1887–88), Vol. 1, pp. 414–17. The last quote, written in 1768, is in *Writings,* Vol. 5, p. 159.

[31] *Writings,* Vol. 2, p. 92; see also Vol. 10, p. 124 and note 14, above.

[32] *The Works of Benjamin Franklin,* ed. Jared Sparks, 10 vols. (Boston, 1836–40), Vol. 2, p. 554.

[33] Franklin's marginal notes in [Matthew C. Wheelock], *Reflections Moral and Political on Great Britain and the Colonies* (London, 1770), p. 48. Franklin's copy in the Jefferson Collection of the Library of Congress.

ments" and concluded that "invention and improvement are prolific. . . . The present progress is rapid." However, he immediately added: "I see a little absurdity in what I have just written, but it is to a friend, who will wink and let it pass."[24]

There remains, then, a wide gulf between this qualified view of human progress and the exuberant joy over the progress of man's rational and moral faculties so perfectly expressed in the lines of a good friend of Franklin's, the British non-conformist clergyman and philosopher, Joseph Priestley:

Whatever was the beginning of this world, the end will be glorious and paradisiacal beyond what our imaginations can now conceive. Extravagant as some people may suppose these views to be, I think I could show them to be fairly suggested by the true theory of human nature and to arise from the natural course of human affairs.[25]

Franklin himself was well aware of this gulf. He distinguished sharply between man's intellectual progress and the steadily increasing power of man over matter, on the one hand, and the permanency of moral imperfection, on the other. He wrote to Priestley in 1782:

I should rejoice much, if I could once more recover the Leisure to search with you into the works of Nature; I mean the *inanimate*, not the *animate* or moral part of them, the more I discover'd of the former, the more I admir'd them; the more I know of the latter, the more I am disgusted with them. Men I find to be a Sort of Beings very badly constructed, as they are generally more easily provok'd than reconcil'd, more disposed to do Mischief to each other than to make Reparation, much more easily deceiv'd than undeceiv'd, and having more Pride and even Pleasure in killing than in begetting one another.

He had begun to doubt, he continued, whether "the Species were really worth producing or preserving. . . . I know, you have no such Doubts because, in your zeal for their welfare, you are taking a great deal of pains to save their Souls. Perhaps, as you grow older, you may look upon this as a hopeless Project."[26]

One is struck by the remarkable constancy of Franklin's views on human nature. In 1787 he tried to dissuade the author of a work on natural religion from publishing it. In this famous letter, we may find the quintessence of Franklin's concept of human nature. There is little of the trust in human reason which is so generally supposed to be a mark of his moral teachings:

You yourself may find it easy to live a virtuous Life, without the Assistance afforded by Religion; you having a clear perception of the Advantages of Virtue, and the Disadvantages of Vice, and possessing a Strength of Resolution sufficient to enable you to resist common Temptations. But think how great a Proportion of Mankind consists of weak and ignorant Men and Women, and of inexperienc'd, and inconsiderate Youth of both Sexes, who have need of the Motives of Religion to restrain them from Vice, and support their Virtue, and retain them in the Practice of it till it becomes *habitual*, which is the Great Point for its Security. . . . If men are so wicked as we now see them *with religion*, what would they be *if without it?*[27]

[24] *Writings*, Vol. 9, p. 651. See also Vol. 9, pp. 489, 530; Vol. 1, p. 226.
[25] Quoted by Bury, *The Idea of Progress* (cited in note 4), pp. 221–22.
[26] *Writings*, Vol. 8, pp. 451–52.
[27] *Writings*, Vol. 9, pp. 521–22. See also Vol. 2, pp. 203, 393, and Vol. 9, pp. 600–1.

One is reminded of Gibbon's approval of conditions in the Rome of the Antonines, where all religions were considered equally false by the wise, equally true by the people, and equally useful by the magistrates.

III. THE BELIEF IN "REASON"

Reason as a temper in the conduct of human affairs counted much with Franklin, as we shall see later. However, reason as a faculty of the human mind, stronger than our desires or passions, counted far less. Often Franklin candidly and smilingly referred to the weakness of reason. In his *Autobiography*, he tells us of his struggle "between principle and inclination" when, on his first voyage to Philadelphia, his vegetarian principles came into conflict with his love of eating fish. Remembering that greater fish ate the smaller ones, he did not see any reason why he should not eat fish: "So convenient a thing it is to be a *reasonable creature*, since it enables one to find or make a reason for every thing one has a mind to do."[38]

Reason as a guide to human happiness was recognized by Franklin only to a limited degree.

Our Reason would still be of more Use to us, if it could enable us to *prevent* the Evils it can hardly enable us to *bear*.—But in that it is so deficient, and in other things so often misleads us, that I have sometimes been almost tempted to wish we had been furnished with a good sensible Instinct instead of it.[39]

Trial and error appeared to him more useful to this end than abstract reasoning. "We are, I think, in the right Road of Improvement, for we are making Experiments. I do not oppose all that seem wrong, for the Multitude are more effectually set right by Experience, than kept from going wrong by Reasoning with them." Another time he put it even more bluntly: "What assurance of the *Future* can be better founded than that which is built on Experience of the *Past?*"[40] His scepticism about the efficacy of "reason" also appears in his opinion that "happiness in this life rather depends on internals than externals; and that, besides the natural effects of wisdom and virtue, vice and folly, there is such a thing as a happy or an unhappy constitution."[41]

There remains one problem with regard to Franklin's rather modest view of the power of human reason in moral matters: his serenity—some might call it complacency—in spite of his awareness of the disorder and imperfection of human life. Sometimes, it is true, he was uneasy:

[38] *Writings*, Vol. 1, p. 267. See also Vol. 5, p. 225, and Vol. 9, p. 512.

[39] *The Letters of Benjamin Franklin & Jane Mecom*, ed. Carl Van Doren (Princeton, 1950), p. 112.

[40] *Writings*, Vol. 9, p. 489, and Vol. 4, p. 250. On another occasion Franklin acknowledged the weakness of reason by the use of a pungent folk saying: "An Answer now occurs to me, for that Question of Robinson Crusoe's Man Friday, which I once thought unanswerable, *Why God no kill the Devil?* It is to be found in the Scottish Proverb, 'Ye'd do little for God an the Dell' were dead.'" To John Whitehurst, New York, June 27, 1763. Unpub. letter in the Mason-Franklin Collection of the Yale University Library. Cf. also Vol. 3, pp. 16-17, Vol. 4, p. 120, and Vol. 6, p. 424.

[41] *Writings*, Vol. 3, p. 457. See also Vol. 9, p. 548.

I rather suspect, from certain circumstances, that though the general government of the universe is well administered, our particular little affairs are perhaps below notice, and left to take the chance of human prudence or imprudence, as either may happen to be uppermost. It is, however, an uncomfortable thought, and I leave it.[42]

But on another occasion Franklin felt obliged to quiet the anxieties of his sister, who had been upset by his remark that men "are devils to one another":

I meant no more by saying Mankind were Devils to one another, than that being in general superior to the Malice of the other Creatures, they were not so much tormented by them as by themselves. Upon the whole I am much disposed to like the World as I find it, & to doubt my own Judgment as to what would mend it. I see so much Wisdom in what I understand of its Creation and Government, that I suspect equal Wisdom may be in what I do not understand: And thence have perhaps as much Trust in God as the most pious Christian.[43]

Indeed, Franklin's pessimism does not contain that quality of the tragic sense of life which inevitably presents itself wherever a recognition of the discrepancy between man's actual depravity and the loftiness of his aspirations exists. We suggest a threefold explanation for this phenomenon: first of all, as we have pointed out, the complex of ideas associated with the concept of the "Great Chain of Being," predominant at the time of Franklin's youth, worked in favor of bridging this gulf by lowering the goals of human endeavor. Secondly, the success story of his own life taught him that certain valuable things in human life can be achieved. Thirdly, we cannot help thinking that Franklin himself was endowed with that "happy constitution" which he deemed a requisite for true happiness in this life.

IV. THE PASSION OF PRIDE

Having discovered that Franklin acknowledged the imperfection of human reason and consequently the existence and importance of the passions to a greater degree than one might have supposed, let us specify in greater detail his insight into the nature of the two outstanding passions of social life, the desire for wealth and the desire for power—avarice and ambition. "That I may avoid Avarice and Ambition . . . —Help me, O Father," was Franklin's prayer in the "Articles of Belief" of 1728.[44]

The universal fame of Poor Richard and the description of Franklin's own "way to wealth" in his *Autobiography* (Franklin's account of his life ends with his arrival in London in 1757 for the first of his three great public missions in Europe) have led many people to see in Franklin only the ingenious businessman pursuing thrift for thrift's sake and money for money's sake. Nothing could be further from the truth than this conception. To be sure, he recognized the existence and the nature of avarice in unequivocal terms: "The Love of

[42] Rev. L. Tyerman, *Life of the Rev. George Whitefield*, 2 vols. (London, 1876), Vol. 2, pp. 540–41, quoted in *Benjamin Franklin, Representative Selections* (cited in note 3), p. cxxxvi.

[43] *The Letters of Benjamin Franklin & Jane Mecom* (cited in note 39), pp. 124, 125–26. See also *Writings*, Vol. 2, p. 61; Vol. 4, p. 388; Vol. 9, p. 247.

[44] *Writings*, Vol. 2, p. 99.

Money is not a Thing of certain Measure, so as that it may be easily filled and satisfied. Avarice is infinite; and where there is not good Oeconomy, no Salary, however large, will prevent Necessity."[45] He denied, however, that desire for more wealth actuated his work. His early retirement from business (1748) to devote himself to the higher things of life—chiefly to public service and scientific research—seems to prove this point.

Franklin considered wealth essentially as means to an end. He knew that it was not easy "for an empty sack to stand upright." He looked upon his fortune as an essential factor in his not having succumbed to corruption.[46] In a famous and often quoted letter to his mother, Franklin said that at the end of his life he "would rather have it said, *He lived usefully* than *He died Rich.*" At about the same time (two years after his retirement) he wrote to his printer friend William Strahan in England: "London citizens, they say, are ambitious of what they call *dying worth* a great sum. The very notion seems to me absurd."[47]

On the other hand, the motive of power and prestige found much earlier recognition in Franklin's writings; he even confessed candidly that he himself was not free from this desire and from the feeling of being superior to his fellowmen. At the age of sixteen, in his first secret contributions to his brother's *New-England Courant* (he wrote under the pseudonym Mrs. Dogood), he gave a satisfactory definition of what we nowadays would call lust for power, and what was in the eighteenth century called Pride:

Among the many reigning Vices of the Town which may at any Time come under my Consideration and Reprehension, there is none which I am more inclin'd to expose than that of *Pride*. It is acknowledged by all to be a Vice the most hateful to God and Man. Even those who nourish it themselves, hate to see it in others. The proud Man aspires after Nothing less than an unlimited Superiority over his Fellow-Creatures.[48]

As Arthur O. Lovejoy has pointed out, the idea of Pride was frequently contemplated during the earlier half of the eighteenth century.[49] There are two different, though not unrelated, conceptions of Pride. First of all, it means "the most powerful and pervasive of all passions," which manifests itself in two forms: self-esteem and desire for the admiration of others. The second conception is closely connected with the idea of the Scale of Being; it means the generic Pride of man as such, the sin against the laws of order, of gradation, the revolt of man against the station which has been allotted to him by the Creator.

These different conceptions of Pride are indeed inseparable. In Franklin's own writings, the accent is on the first rather than on the second meaning.

[45] *Writings*, Vol. 5, p. 325.

[46] *The Letters of Benjamin Franklin & Jane Mecom* (cited in note 39), p. 123.

[47] *Writings*, Vol. 3, pp. 5, 6. Cf. Benjamin Rush to John Adams: "The Doctor was a rigid economist, but he was in every stage of his life charitable, hospitable, and generous." August 19, 1811, in *Letters of Benjamin Rush* (cited in note 10), Vol. 2, p. 1093.

[48] *Writings*, Vol. 2, pp. 18–19.

[49] Lovejoy, " 'Pride' in Eighteenth Century Thought," (cited in note 26), p. 62–68.

This topic runs through his work like a red thread. In 1729, at the age of 23, he wrote that "almost every Man has a strong natural Desire of being valu'd and esteem'd by the rest of his Species."[50] Observations in a letter written in 1751 testify to his keen psychological insight:

What you mention concerning the love of praise is indeed very true; it reigns more or less in every heart, though we are generally hypocrites, in that respect, and pretend to disregard praise. . . . Being forbid to praise themselves, they learn instead of it to censure others; which is only a roundabout way of praising themselves. . . . This fondness for ourselves, rather than malevolence to others, I take to be the general source of censure. . . .[51]

Quite revealing with regard to our discussion is Franklin's well-known account of his project of an "Art of Virtue." His list of virtues to be practiced contained at first only twelve: "But a Quaker friend having kindly informed me that I was generally thought proud . . . I added *Humility* to my list. . . . I cannot boast of much success in acquiring the *reality* of this virtue, but I had a good deal with regard to the *appearance* of it."[52] His account of his rise in Pennsylvania's public life and politics reflects his joy and pride about his career. In 1737 he was appointed Postmaster of Philadelphia and Justice of the Peace; in 1744 he established the American Philosophical Society; in 1748 he was chosen a member of the Council of Philadelphia; in 1749 he was appointed Provincial Grandmaster of the Colonial Masons; in 1750 he was appointed one of the commissioners to treat with the Indians in Carlisle; and in 1751 he became a member of the Assembly of Pennsylvania. He was particularly pleased with this last appointment, and he admitted candidly that his ambition was "flatter'd by all these promotions; it certainly was; for, considering my low beginning, they were great things to me."[53]

There is no change of emphasis with respect to Pride during his long life. The old man of 78 denounces the evil of Pride with no less fervor, though with more self-knowledge, than the boy of 16:

In reality, there is, perhaps, no one of our natural passions so hard to subdue as *pride*. Disguise it, struggle with it, beat it down, stifle it, mortify it as much as one pleases, it is still alive, and will every now and then peep out and show itself; you will see it, perhaps, often in this history; for even if I could conceive that I had compleatly overcome it, I should probably be proud of my humility.[54]

Furthermore, the experience of English political life which he acquired during his two protracted stays in England (from 1757 to 1762, and from 1765 to 1775) made an indelible impression on his mind. The corruption and venality in English politics and the disastrous blunders of English politicians which

[50] *Writings*, Vol. 2, p. 108.
[51] *Writings*, Vol. 3, pp. 54–55.
[52] *Writings*, Vol. 1, p. 337.
[53] *Writings*, Vol. 1, p. 374. For Franklin's acknowledgment of his own political ambition, see *Writings*, Vol. 5, pp. 148, 206, 357; Vol. 9, pp. 488, 621.
[54] *Autobiography* (end of the part written in Passy, France, 1784), *Writings*, Vol. 1, p. 339.

Franklin traced back to this cause[55] probably were the main reasons why he advocated at the Federal Convention of 1787 what he himself said some might regard as a "Utopian Idea": the abolition of salaries for the chief executive. The reason he gave for advocating such a step has hitherto not been appreciated as being of crucial importance for an understanding of his political thought:

There are two Passions which have a powerful Influence in the Affairs of Men. These are *Ambition* and *Avarice;* the Love of Power and the Love of Money. Separately, each of these has great Force in prompting Men to Action; but when united in View of the same Object, they have in many minds the most violent Effects. Place before the Eyes of such Men a Post of *Honour*, that shall at the same time be a Place of *Profit*, and they will move Heaven and Earth to obtain it.[56]

It has never been pointed out that this scheme of what might be called the "separation of passions" had been ripening in Franklin's mind for several years. The first expression of it is to be found early in 1783.[57] In 1784 he mentioned it several times, and it is in these statements that we find one of the few allusions to the concept of checks and balances in Franklin's thought. He recommended: "Make every place of *honour* a place of *burthen*. By that means the effect of one of the passions above-mentioned would be taken away and something would be added to counteract the other."[58]

V. THE NATURE OF POLITICS

Franklin's frequent praise of the general welfare did not blind him to the fact that most other people had a much narrower vision than his own. "Men will always be powerfully influenced in their Opinions and Actions by what appears to be their particular Interest," he wrote in his first tract on political economy, at the age of twenty-three.[59] Fortunately, one of the very few memoranda and notes dealing with the studies and discussions of young Franklin which have come to our knowledge directly concerns this problem. Franklin himself, in his *Autobiography*, gives us the text of *"Observations* on my reading history, in Library, May 19th, 1731" which, in his words, had been "accidentally preserv'd":

That the great affairs of the world, the wars, revolutions, etc., are carried on and affected by parties.

That the view of these parties is their present general interest, or what they take to be such.

That the different views of these different parties occasion all confusion.

That while a party is carrying on a general design, each man has his particular private interest in view.

That as soon as a party has gain'd its general point, each member becomes intent upon

[55] *Writings*, Vol. 10, p. 62. See also Vol. 5, pp. 100, 112, 117, 133. See also *Benjamin Franklin's Letters to the Press, 1758–1775*, ed. Verner W. Crane (Chapel Hill, 1950), pp. 59, 164, 232.

[56] *Writings*, Vol. 9, p. 591.

[57] *Writings*, Vol. 9, p. 23.

[58] *Writings*, Vol. 9, p. 170. See also *ibid.*, pp. 172 and 260.

[59] *Writings*, Vol. 2, p. 139.

his partcular interest; which, thwarting others, breaks that party into divisions, and occasions more confusion.

That few in public affairs act from a mere view of the good of their country, whatever they may pretend; and, tho' their actings bring real good to their country, yet men primarily considered that their own and their country's interest was united, and did not act from a principle of benevolence.

That fewer still, in public affairs, act with a view for the good of mankind. . . . [60]

These lines do not mirror Shaftesbury's benevolent altruism; Franklin's contention that men act primarily from their own interest "and . . . not . . . from a principle of benevolence," "tho' their actings bring real good to their country," strongly suggests the general theme of Mandeville's work: "Private vices, public benefits."

Many decades after the foregoing observations, the contrast between Franklin's views on politics and those of the enlightened rationalism of contemporary France is clearly expressed in a discussion with the French physiocrat Dupont de Nemours. Dupont had suggested that the Federal Convention be delayed until the separate constitutions of the member states were corrected —according to physiocratic principles, of course. Franklin mildly observed that "we must not expect that a new government may be formed, as a game of chess may be played." He stressed that in the game of politics there were so many players with so many strong and various prejudices, "and their particular interests, independent of the general, seeming so opposite," that "the play is more like *tric-trac* with a box of dice."[61] In public, and when he was propagandizing for America in Europe, Franklin played down the evils of party strife: after the end of the War of Independence he conceded somewhat apologetically that "it is true, in some of the States there are Parties and Discords." He contended now that parties "are the common lot of Humanity," and that they exist wherever there is liberty; they even, perhaps, help to preserve it. "By the Collision of different Sentiments, Sparks of Truth are struck out, and Political Light is obtained."[62]

In private, Franklin did not conceal his suspicion that "unity out of discord" was not as easily achieved as his just quoted method of obtaining "political light" might suggest. But he certainly did not believe that passions and prejudices always, or even usually, overrule enlightened self-interest. He held that "there is a vast variety of good and ill Events, that are in some degreee the Effects of Prudence or the want of it."[63] He believed that "reasonable sensible Men, can always make a reasonable scheme appear such to other reasonable Men, if they take Pains, and have Time and Opportunity for it. . ." However, this dictum is severely limited by the conclusion: ". . . unless from some Circumstance their Honesty and Good Intentions are suspected."[64] That Franklin thought those circumstances to exist frequently, we learn from a famous mes-

---

[60] *Writings*, Vol. 1, pp. 339–40. Cf. also Vol. 2, p. 196, and Vol. 4, p. 322.
[61] *Writings*, Vol. 9, p. 659; see also p. 241.
[62] *Writings*, Vol. 10, pp. 120–21. See also Vol. 4, p. 35.
[63] *Writings*, Vol. 7, p. 358.
[64] *Writings*, Vol. 3, pp. 41–42.

sage to George Washington, written in France in 1780. He told Washington how much·the latter would enjoy his reputation in France, "pure and free from those little Shades that the Jealousy and Envy of a Man's Countrymen and Cotemporaries are ever endeavouring to cast over living Merit."[65]

Although Franklin himself talked so much about "Common Interests," he could be impatient when others built their arguments on this point. He observed that "it is an Insult on common sense to affect an Appearance of Generosity in a Matter of obvious Interest."[66] This belief in self-interest as a moving force of politics appears with rare clarity in marginal notes in a pamphlet whose author argued that "if the Interests of Great Britain evidently raise and fall with those of the Colonies, then the Parliament of Great Britain will have the same regard for the Colonists as for her own People." Franklin retorted:

All this Argument of the Interest of Britain and the Colonies being the *same* is fallacious and unsatisfactory. Partners in Trade have a *common* Interest, which is the same, the Flourishing of the Partnership Business: But they may moreover have each a *separate* Interest; and in pursuit of that *separate* Interest, one of them may endeavour to impose on the other, may cheat him in the Accounts, may draw to himself more than his Share of the Profits, may put upon the other more than an equal Share of the Burthen. Their having a common Interest is no Security against such Injustice. . . . [67]

VI. DEMOCRACY

It is fair to ask how Franklin's views on the above matters square with his avowal of radically democratic notions after 1775. In view of the foregoing, Franklin would not, it seems, agree with the underlying assumptions of Jeffersonian democracy, stated by Jefferson himself: "Nature hath implanted in our breasts a love of others, a sense of duty to them, a moral instinct, in short, which prompts us irresistibly to feel and to succor their distresses . . ." It was also Jefferson who believed "that man was a rational animal, endowed by nature with rights, and with an innate sense of justice."[68] On this faith in the rationality and goodness of man, the theory of Jeffersonian democracy has been erected. Vernon L. Parrington said of Franklin that "he was a forerunner of Jefferson, like him firm in the conviction that government was good in the measure that it remained close to the people."[69] Charles A. Beard, discussing the members of the Federal Convention, tells us that Benjamin Franklin "seems to have entertained a more hopeful view of democracy than any other member of that

[65] *Writings*, Vol. 8, p. 28. Cf. the expression of the same idea 36 years earlier in *Writings*, Vol. 2, p. 242.

[66] *Benjamin Franklin's Letters to the Press* (cited in note 55), p. 183.

[67] Marginal comments in *Good Humour, or, A Way with the Colonies* (London, 1766), pp. 26–27. Franklin's copy is in the library of the Historical Society of Pennsylvania, Philadelphia. This comment is reprinted in *A Collection of the Familiar Letters and Miscellaneous Papers of Benjamin Franklin*, ed. Jared Sparks (Boston, 1833), p. 229.

[68] Jefferson to Thomas Law, June 13, 1814, and to Judge William Johnson, June 12, 1823, quoted by Adrienne Koch, *The Philosophy of Thomas Jefferson* (New York, 1943), pp. 19, 139.

[69] Vernon L. Parrington, *The Main Currents of American Thought*, 3 vols. (New York, 1930), Vol. 1, pp. 176–77.

famous group."[70] All this must seem rather strange in view of the none too optimistic conception of human nature which we have found in Franklin. His radically democratic views after 1775—before that time his outlook seemed essentially conservative—baffled contemporary observers as it has later students.

There is, as a matter of fact, plenty of evidence of Franklin's sincere devotion to monarchy during the greater part of his life. It was the most natural thing for him to assure his friend, the famous Methodist preacher George Whitefield, that a settlement of colonies on the Ohio would be blessed with success "if we undertook it with sincere Regard to . . . the Service of our gracious King, and (which is the same thing) the Publick Good."[71] Franklin loved to contrast the corruption of Parliament and the virtues of George III. To an American friend, he said that he could "scarcely conceive a King of better Dispositions, of more exemplary virtues, or more truly desirous of promoting the Welfare of all his Subjects."[72]

Another "conservative" aspect of Franklin which cannot be glossed over lightly is his acceptance of the Puritan and mercantilistic attitude towards the economic problems of the working class. Throughout his life he was critical of the English Poor Laws. He deplored "the proneness of human nature to a life of ease, of freedom from care and labour," and he considered that laws which *"compel the rich to maintain the poor"* might possibly be "fighting against the order of God and Nature, which perhaps has appointed want and misery as the proper punishments for, and cautions against, as well as necessary consequences of, idleness and extravagance."[73] This was written in 1753. But as late as 1789, long after he had come out for the political equality of the poor and for a radical theory of property, he still confirmed to an English correspondent that "I have long been of your opinion, that your legal provision for the poor is a very great evil, operating as it does to the encouragement of idlenesss."[74]

Franklin's endorsement of democracy is most emphatically revealed in his advocacy of a unicameral legislature for the Commonwealth of Pennsylvania, as well as for the federal government. The issue of unicameral versus bicameral legislative bodies—an issue much discussed in the latter decades of the eighteenth century—reflected faithfully, as a rule, the clash of views of two different theories of human nature and of politics. The bicameral system was based on the principle of checks and balances; a pessimistic view of human nature naturally would try to forestall the abuse of power in a single and all-powerful as-

[70] Charles A. Beard, *An Economic Interpretation of the Constitution* (New York, 1913), p. 197.

[71] *Writings*, Vol. 3, p. 339. See also Vol. 2, pp. 377–78; Vol. 4, pp. 94, 213.

[72] *Writings*, Vol. 5, p. 204. See also Vol. 5, p. 261. Another sign of Franklin's anti-radical attitude during his stay in England is his disgust with the Wilkes case. See *Writings*, Vol. 5, pp. 121, 133, 134, and 150. Also *Letters and Papers of Benjamin Franklin and Richard Jackson, 1753–1785*, ed. Carl Van Doren (Philadelphia, 1947), p. 139.

[73] *Letters and Papers of Benjamin Franklin and Richard Jackson, op. cit.*, pp. 34, 35.

[74] *Writings*, Vol. 10, p. 64. See for an elaboration of his arguments "On the Labouring Poor," *Writings*, Vol. 5, pp. 122–27, and "On the Price of Corn, and Management of the Poor," *Writings*, Vol. 5, pp. 534–39.

sembly. On the other hand, most of those who trusted in the faculties of human reason did not see the necessity for a second chamber to check and harass the activities of a body of reasonable men.

In the case of Franklin, however, this correspondence of political convictions with views on human nature is lacking. He was the president of the Pennsylvania Convention of 1776 which—almost uniquely among the American states—set up a unicameral system. This, of course, filled many of the French *philosophes* with great joy. Franklin, they supposed, had secured a triumph of enlightened principles in the new world. Condorcet, in his "Éloge de Franklin," had this to say:

Franklin's voice alone decided this last provision. He thought that as enlightenment would naturally make rapid progress, above all in a country to which the revolution had given a new system, one ought to encourage the devices of perfecting legislation, and not to surround them with extrinsic obstacles. . . . The opinion contrary to his stands for that discouraging philosophy which considers error and corruption as the habitual state of societies and the development of virtue and reason as a kind of miracle which one must not expect to make enduring. It was high time that a philosophy both nobler and truer should direct the destiny of mankind, and Franklin was worthy to give the first example of it.[75]

As a matter of fact, it has since been shown that Franklin, who at the time of the Pennsylvania Convention also served in the Continental Congress, played a minor role in the adoption of the unicameral system. The unicameral legislature was rooted in the historical structure of Pennsylvania's proprietary government.[76] This, however, is irrelevant from our point of view, since Franklin endorsed and defended the unicameral system in his "Queries and Remarks respecting Alterations in the Constitution of Pennsylvania," written in November, 1789.[77]

In the opposition to checks and balances and a second chamber, Franklin's most famous companion was Thomas Paine, author of *The Age of Reason*. This similarity of views between Franklin and one of the most vocal spokesmen of the creed of reason and the perfectibility of man perhaps contributes to the misinterpretation of Franklin's position among the eighteenth-century philosophers. Paine's arguments against the system of checks and balances and for a single house were characteristic of the later Enlightenment:

Freedom is the associate of innocence, not the companion of suspicion. She only requires to be cherished, not to be caged, and to be beloved is, to her, to be protected. Her residence is in the undistinguished multitude of rich and poor, and a partisan to neither is the patroness of all.[78]

This argument, of course, presupposes the rationality and goodness of human nature. We might perhaps agree with Paine that "no man was a better judge of

[75] *Oeuvres de Condorcet* (cited in note 1), Vol. 3, pp. 401–2.
[76] See J. Paul Selsam, *The Pennsylvania Constitution of 1776* (Philadelphia, 1926), and Charles M. Andrews, *The Colonial Period of American History*, 4 vols. (New Haven, 1934–38), Vol. 3, p. 320.
[77] *Writings*, Vol. 10, pp. 54–60.
[78] "A Serious Address to the People of Pennsylvania on the Present Situation of their Affairs" (Dec., 1778), in *The Complete Writings of Thomas Paine*, ed. Philip S. Foner, 2 vols. (New York, 1945), Vol. 2, p. 284.

human nature than Franklin,"[79] but Paine certainly did not have Franklin's conception of human nature.

The reasons for Franklin's almost radical attitude in 1776 and 1787 appear in his own writings. One thing seems certain: belief in the goodness and the wisdom of the people is *not* at the root of his democratic faith. This idea is quite foreign to Franklin. Discussing the Albany Plan of Union in 1754, he thought that "it is very possible, that this general government might be as well and faithfully administered without the people, as with them."[80] Nor did he fundamentally change his view in the last years of his life. "Popular favour is very precarious, being sometimes *lost* as well as *gained* by good actions." In 1788, he wrote publicly that "popular Opposition to a public Measure is no Proof of its Impropriety."[81] What a strange democrat it was who told the Federal Convention that "there is a natural Inclination in Mankind to kingly Government."[82] The most plausible and popular reason for belief in democracy, then, is eliminated.

On the other hand, Franklin did not believe in the intrinsic goodness of the wealthy or the wisdom of the powerful; he had no liking for aristocratic government, be it by an aristocracy of wealth or an aristocracy of birth. He was scornful of the House of Lords and thought "Hereditary Professors of Mathematicks" preferable to hereditary legislators because they could do less mischief.[83]

It is noteworthy that in the whole of Franklin's work only one reference to Montesquieu can be found; and that concerns his ideas on criminal law. Separation of powers, the role of the aristocracy in a healthy society—these are doctrines which never took possession of Franklin's mind.

The antithesis between Adams, under the influence of Harrington, and Franklin, chiefly influenced by his own experience, is remarkably complete. Adams wrote:

It must be remembered that the rich are *people* as well as the poor; that they have rights as well as others; they have as clear and as *sacred* a right to their large property as others have to theirs which is smaller; that oppression to them is as possible and wicked as to others. . . . [84]

Franklin mounts a formidable counterattack:

And why should the upper House, chosen by a Minority, have equal Power with the lower chosen by a majority? Is it supposed that Wisdom is the necessary concomitant of Riches . . . and why is Property to be represented at all? . . . The Combinations of Civil Society

[79] "Constitutional Reform" (1805), *ibid.*, pp. 998–99.

[80] *Writings*, Vol. 3, p. 231. See also p. 309.

[81] *Writings*, Vol. 9, pp. 564, 702. In 1788, Franklin repeatedly said that there was at present the "danger of too little obedience in the *governed*," although in general the opposite evil of "giving too much power to our *governors*" was more dreaded. *Writings*, Vol. 9, p. 638; and Vol. 10, p. 7.

[82] *Writings*, Vol. 9, p. 593.

[83] *Writings*, Vol. 6, pp. 370–71. For other attacks on the principle of hereditary honors and privileges, in connection with the Order of the Cincinnati see *Writings*, Vol. 9, pp. 162, 336.

[84] Quoted by Zoltán Haraszti, *John Adams and the Prophets of Progress* (Cambridge, Mass., 1952), p. 36.

are not like those of a Set of Merchants, who club their Property in different Proportions for Building and Freighting a Ship, and may therefore have some Right to Vote in the Disposition of the Voyage in a greater or less Degree according to their respective Contributions; but the important ends of Civil Society, and the personal Securities of Life and Liberty, these remain the same in every member of the Society; and the poorest continues to have an equal Claim to them with the most opulent. . . . [85]

It is this strong objection against the attempt to use—openly or covertly—a second chamber as a tool of class rule which seems to underlie Franklin's disapproval of the bicameral system. Franklin, it should be pointed out, was aware of the necessity and inevitability of poises and counter-poises. This is shown by his attempt, referred to above, to create a sort of balance of passions, checking avarice with ambition. There exist some, though quite rare, allusions to a balance of power concept in his utterances on imperial and international relations. The most pointed and direct reference to the idea of checks and balances, however, may be found in an unpublished letter to a well-known figure of Pennsylvania politics, Joseph Galloway, in 1767. Franklin discussed and welcomed a new Circuit Bill for the judges of Pennsylvania. He suggested and encouraged an increase in the salaries to be granted by the Assembly for the judges to offset the nominating and recalling powers of the Proprietor: "From you they should therefore receive a Salary equal in Influence upon their Minds, to be held during your Pleasure. For where the Beam *is moveable*, it is only by equal Weights in opposite scales that it can possibly be kept even."[86]

Consequently, the arguments of Thomas Paine or the French *philosophes*, which derive their validity from assumptions about the goodness or rationality of human nature, do not hold in the case of Franklin. In a brilliant recent essay it has been suggested that "despite the European flavor of a Jefferson or a Franklin, the Americans refused to join in the great Enlightenment enterprise of shattering the Christian concept of sin, replacing it with an unlimited humanism, and then emerging with an early enterprise as glittering as the heavenly one that had been destroyed."[87] As far as Franklin is concerned, however, the alternatives of Calvinist pessimism and the "unlimited humanism" of the European Enlightenment do not really clarify the essential quality of his political thought. His thought is rooted in a climate of opinion which combined the rejection of the doctrine of original sin with a rather modest view of human nature.

It seems, then, that the desire for equality, rather than any rationalistic concepts, offers the clue to an adequate understanding of those elements in Frank-

---

[85] "Queries and Remarks . . . , " *Writings*, Vol. 10, pp. 58–61. For Franklin's disagreement with the bicameral system of the United States Constitution, see *Writings*, Vol. 9, pp. 645, 674. The paradox of Franklin's attitude is thrown into relief if one considers that even Jefferson, in his *Notes on Virginia*, raised his voice against the dangers of an "elective despotism," and exalted "those benefits" which a "proper complication of principles" would produce. *The Works of Thomas Jefferson*, ed. Paul Leicester Ford (New York and London, 1904–5), Vol. 4, p. 19.

[86] April 14, 1767, in the William L. Clements Library, Ann Arbor, Michigan.

[87] Louis Hartz, "American Political Thought and the American Revolution," this REVIEW, Vol. 46, pp. 321–42, at p. 324 (June, 1952).

lin's political thought which at first sight appear inconsistent with his not too cheerful view of human goodness. His striving for equality also suggests a solution to the thorny problem of reconciling his democratic views after he had decided for American independence with his faithful loyalty to the Crown before that date. The American interest obliged him to fight against Parliament—an aristocratic body in those days—while remaining loyal to the King; in recognizing the King's sovereignty while denying the Parliament's rights over the Colonies, Franklin by necessity was driven into a position which—historically speaking—seemed to contradict his Whig principles. The complaining Americans spoke, as Lord North rightly said, the "language of Toryism."[88] During the decade before 1775 Franklin fought for the equal rights of England and the Colonies under the Crown. But his desire for equality went deeper than that. In his "Some good Whig Principles," while conceding that the government of Great Britain ought to be lodged "in the hands of King, Lords of Parliament, and Representatives of *the whole body* of the freemen of this realm," he took care to affirm that *"every man* of the commonalty (excepting infants, insane persons, and criminals) is, of common right, and by the laws of God, *a freeman"* and that "the poor man has an *equal* right, but *more* need, to have representatives in the legislature than the rich one."[89] It has not been widely known that Franklin, in a conversation with Benjamin Vaughan, his friend and at the same time emissary of the British Prime Minister Lord Shelburne during the peace negotiations of 1782, has confirmed this view. Vaughan reported to Shelburne that "Dr. Franklin's opinions about *parliaments* are, that people should not be rejected as electors because they are at *present* ignorant"; Franklin thought that "a statesman should meliorate his people," and Vaughan supposed that Franklin "would put this, among other reasons for extending the privilege of election, that it *would* meliorate them." It was Franklin's opinion, Vaughan thought, "that the lower people are as we see them, because oppressed; & then their situation in point of manners, becomes the reason for oppressing them."[90] The fact is that Franklin's overriding concern for equality foreshadows the attacks of the socialism of later generations on the absolute sanctity of private property:

All the Property that is necessary to a Man, for the Conservation of the Individual and the Propagation of the Species, is his natural Right, which none can justly deprive him of: But all Property superfluous to such purposes is the Property of the Publick, who, by their Laws, have created it, and who may therefore by other Laws dispose of it, whenever the Welfare of the Publick shall demand such Disposition.[91]

Franklin's previously quoted speech in the Federal Convention provides us with an essential insight: he expressed belief in "a natural Inclination in Mankind to kingly Government." His reasons are revealing: "It sometimes relieves

[88] Quoted by G. H. Guttridge, *English Whiggism and the American Revolution* (Berkeley, 1942), p. 62.

[89] *Writings*, Vol. 10, p. 130.

[90] Benjamin Vaughan to Lord Shelburne, November 24, 1782. Benjamin Vaughan Papers in the American Philosophical Society, Philadelphia. Photostat in the Benjamin Vaughan Collection in the William L. Clements Library, Ann Arbor, Michigan.

[91] *Writings*, Vol. 9, p. 138 (written in 1783). See also Vol. 10, p. 59.

them from Aristocratic Domination. They had rather one Tyrant than 500. It gives more of the Appearance of Equality among Citizens; and that they like."[92] Equality, then, is not incompatible with monarchy.

From all this a significant conclusion may be drawn. It is an oversimplification to speak of Franklin's "conservatism" before 1775 and of his "radicalism" after 1775. Professor MacIver illustrates the conservative character of the first stage of American political thought preceding the appeal to natural rights by reference to Franklin, who, in spite of his later attacks on the Order of the Cincinnati, "nevertheless clung to the principle of a hereditary, though constitutional monarchy, until the tide of revolution rendered it untenable."[93] The term "conservative" does not do justice to the possibility of paying faithful allegiance to a monarchy and still disliking aristocracies of heredity or wealth. Because of his innate desire for equality, as well as his defense of the American cause against the encroachments of Parliament, Franklin found it much easier to be a monarchist. Monarchy, rather than aristocracy, was compatible with those elements of his thought which after 1775 made him a democrat.

Another of the factors which, while not incompatible with monarchical feelings, contributed greatly to Franklin's acceptance of democracy, is the belief which he shared with Hume that power, in the last analysis, is founded on opinion. "I wish some good Angel would forever whisper in the Ears of your great Men, that Dominion is founded in Opinion, and that if you would preserve your Authority among us, you must preserve the Opinion we us'd to have of your Justice."[94] He thought that "Government must depend for it's Efficiency either on Force or Opinion." Force, however, is not as efficient as Opinion: "Alexander and Caesar. . .received more faithful service, and performed greater actions, by means of the love their soldiers bore them, than they could possibly have done, if, instead of being beloved and respected, they had been hated and feared by those they commanded." Efficiency, then, became an argument for democracy. "Popular elections have their inconvenience in some cases; but in establishing new forms of government, we cannot always obtain what we may think the best; for the prejudices of those concerned, if they cannot be removed, must be in some degree complied with."[95]

It has rarely been noticed how detached Franklin, the greatest champion of democracy in the Federal Convention, was from the problem of the best government. His speech at the conclusion of the deliberations of the Constitutional Convention may give us a clue to the perplexing problem of why he gave comparatively little attention to the theoretical questions of political philosophy and devoted almost all his time to the solution of concrete issues. He stated his disagreement with several points of the Constitution, nevertheless urging general allegiance and loyalty to its principles. Asking his colleagues to doubt a

[92] *Writings*, Vol. 9, p. 539.

[93] R. M. MacIver, "European Doctrines and the Constitution," in *The Constitution Reconsidered* (cited in note 25), p. 55.

[94] *Letters and Papers of Benjamin Franklin and Richard Jackson* (cited in note 72), p. 145 (written in 1764). See also *Writings*, Vol. 6, p. 129; Vol. 9, p. 608.

[95] *Benjamin Franklin's Letters to the Press* (cited in note 55), p. 193; *Writings*, Vol. 2, p. 56; Vol. 3, p. 228. See also Vol. 3, 231; Vol. 5, p. 79.

little their feeling of infallibility, Franklin summed up the experience of his life: "I think a general Government necessary for us, and there is no *form* of government but what may be a blessing to the people, if well administered."[96] Perhaps in speaking these words he was thinking of one of the favorite writers of his younger days, Alexander Pope:

> For Forms of Government let fools contest;
> Whate'er is best administer'd is best.[97]

VII. THE DUALITY OF FRANKLIN'S POLITICAL THOUGHT

There are two outstanding and sometimes contradictory factors in Franklin's political thought. On the one hand, we find an acute comprehension of the power factor in human nature, and, consequently, in politics. On the other hand, Franklin always during his long life revolted in the name of equality against the imperfections of the existing order. He himself stated the basic antithesis of his political thought: Power versus Equality.

Fortunately, Franklin's notes on the problem at hand have been preserved; they are to be found in his marginal comments to Allen Ramsay's pamphlet, *Thoughts on the Origin and Nature of Government*, which presents the straight view of power politics. Franklin rebelled against the rationalization and justification of the power factor. "The natural weakness of man in a solitary State," Ramsay proclaimed, "prompts him to fly for protection to whoever is able to afford it, that is to some one more powerful, than himself; while the more powerful standing equally in need of his service, readily receives it in return for the protection he gives." Franklin's answer is unequivocal: *"May not Equals unite with Equals for common Purposes?"*[98]

In the last analysis, Franklin looked upon government as the trustee of the people. He had stated this Whig principle in his very first publication as a sixteen-year-old boy[99] and he never deviated from it. So in opposition to Ramsay's doctrine, according to which the governed have no right of control whatsoever, once they have agreed to submit themselves to the sovereign, Franklin declared the accountability of the rulers:

If I appoint a Representative for the express purpose of doing a business for me that is for *my Service* and that of others, & to consider what I am to pay as my Proportion of the Expense necessary for accomplishing that Business, I am then tax'd by my own Consent.— A Number of Persons unite to form a Company for Trade, Expences are necessary, Directors are chosen to do the Business & proportion those Expences. They are paid a Reasonable Consideration for their Trouble. Here is nothing of weak & Strong. Protection on one hand, & Service on the other. The Directors are the Servants, not the Masters; their Duty is prescrib'd, the Powers they have is from the members & returns to them. The Directors are also accountable.[100]

[96] *Writings*, Vol. 9, p. 607.
[97] Pope, "Essay on Man," Epistle 3, *Selected Works* (cited in note 17), p. 124.
[98] [Allen Ramsay], *Thoughts on the Origin and Nature of Government* (London, 1769), p. 10. Franklin's copy in the Jefferson Collection of the Library of Congress. (My italics.)
[99] "Dogood Papers," *Writings*, Vol. 2, p. 26. Cf. *Benjamin Franklin's Letters to the Press* (cited in note 55), p. 140.
[100] Marginal notes to Ramsay, *op. cit.*, pp. 33–34.

Franklin refused to recognize that power alone could create right. When Ramsay declared that according to nature's laws every man "in Society shall rank himself amongst the Ruling or the Ruled, . . . all Equality and Independence being by the Law of Nature strictly forbidden . . . , " Franklin rejoined indignantly, "I do not find this Strange Law among those of Nature. I doubt it is forged. . . . " He summarized Ramsay's doctrine as meaning that "He that is strongest may do what he pleases with those that are weaker," and commented angrily: "A most Equitable Law of Nature indeed."[101]

On the other hand, Franklin's grasp of the realities of power inevitably involved him in moral and logical ambiguities of political decision. At times he expressed the tragic conflict of ethics and politics. Characteristic of the peculiar contradiction within his political thought was this statement three years before the Declaration of Independence on England's prospects in the Anglo-American conflict: *"Power does not infer Right; and, as the Right is nothing, and the Power (by our Increase) continually diminishing, the one will soon be as insignificant as the other."*[102] In this instance, obviously, he was trying to make the best of both worlds. But there were times when he was only too well aware of the conflict of these two worlds. In a passage which seems to have escaped the notice of most students of his political thought, Franklin observed that *"moral and political Rights sometimes differ, and sometimes are both subdu'd by Might."*[103]

The measured terms of Franklin's political thinking present a striking contrast to the optimism and rationalism which we usually associate with the Age of Enlightenment. Franklin's insight into the passions of pride and power prevented him from applying the expectation of man's scientific and intellectual progress to the realm of moral matters. To be sure, he would not deny the influence of scientific insights upon politics, and he thought that a great deal of good would result from introducing the enlightened doctrines of free trade and physiocracy into international politics. But Franklin, unlike many of his friends in France, was never inclined to consider these and other ideas as panaceas. The mutual adjustment of interests would always remain the chief remedy of political evils. It was in this domain that reason, as a temper in the conduct of human affairs, made its greatest contribution to his political thought. Moderation and equity, so he had been taught by his experience (rather than by abstract reasoning) were true political wisdom. His belief that the rulers ought to be accountable, together with his more pragmatic conviction that force alone, in the long run, could not solve the great problems of politics, brought forth his declaration of faith that "Government is not establish'd merely by *Power;* there must be maintain'd a general Opinion of its *Wisdom* and *Justice* to make it firm and durable."[104]

[101] *Ibid.*, pp. 12, 13.
[102] *Writings*, Vol. 6, p. 87.
[103] *Writings*, Vol. 8, p. 304. (My italics.)
[104] *Benjamin Franklin's Autobiographical Writings*, ed. Carl Van Doren (New York, 1945), pp. 184–85. Cf. *Writings*, Vol. 4, p. 269; Vol. 7, p. 390.

REASON AND REVOLUTION: THE RADICALISM OF DR. THOMAS YOUNG

PAULINE MAIER
University of Massachusetts, Boston

MORE THAN A DESIRE TO RECALL OBSCURE REVOLUTIONARY LEADERS prompts reexamination of the life and politics of Dr. Thomas Young. Historians are shifting their interests from founding fathers toward humbler revolutionary partisans as they seek to understand the relationship between socioeconomic and ideological factors in precipitating the Revolution and to explain the nature of preindustrial radicalism more generally. On both these counts Young demands an attention he has rarely received in the 199 years since his death.[1]

Neither an elite American nor a "winner" in the Revolution (for he was as much a loser as any Loyalist, even though he opted for the winning side), Young served the colonial cause in Albany (1765–66), Boston (1766–74), Newport (1774–75), and Philadelphia (1775–77). He was a devoted committee man for the Sons of Liberty, for Boston's North End Caucus, for the Boston Town Meeting. During his earliest years in Boston, he publicly justified the use of violence against the opponents of freedom. Later he organized crowds to enforce nonimportation and participated in the Boston Tea Party. But he was also known to mollify insurgents—standing in Boston's streets on the night of the "Massacre," telling rioters to go home; defending consignee Francis Rotch before a "Tea Meeting" in late 1773; urging patriots to call off their pursuit of customs commissioner Benjamin Hallowell in September 1774.[2] His role as peacemaker seems to have had little effect upon those op-

---

[1] For a recent study of Young see David Hawke, "Dr. Thomas Young—'Eternal Fisher in Troubled Waters'; Notes for a Biography," *New-York Historical Society Quarterly*, 54 (1970), 6–29. See also Henry H. Edes, "Memoir of Dr. Thomas Young, 1731–1777," *Publications of the Colonial Society of Massachusetts, Transactions 1906–1907* (Boston, 1910), 2–54.

[2] Committee work: Young to John Wilkes, Boston, September 6, 1769, in *Proceedings of the Massachusetts Historical Society* for 1913–1914, XLVII (Boston, 1914), 209; "Proceedings of the North End Caucus" in Elbridge H. Goss, *The Life of Paul Revere* (Boston: J. G. Cupples, 1891), II, esp. 636, 637, 638, 642–43, 644; *A Report of the Record Commissioners of the City of*

ponents who everywhere described him in almost identical terms—as a "flaming zealot," one of the "incendiaries of the lower order"; "a firebrand, ... an eternal Fisher in Troubled Waters, ... a Scourge, a Pestilence, a Judgment"; a paragon of "inaccuracy, malevolence, bad grammar, and nonsense," of "self-conceit, vain-baiting, and invincible impudence," of "quackery, ignorance, ... boorishness and impertinent loquacity"; a "bawling New England Man ... of noisy fame." Young was nonetheless an important contributor to the revolutionary movement, even, as Royal Tyler said in defending him to the more conservative Timothy Ruggles, a "necessary Man." "I was yesterday in a watchmaker's shop," Tyler said, invoking an earthy metaphor to make his point:

> and [I] looked over his shoulder, while he put a watch together. The Springs and Wheels were all clean and in good order, every one in its Place as far as I could see, but the Watch would not go. The Artist at length with his Thumb and forefinger groping in the Dust upon his shopboard, took up a little dirty Pin, scarcely visible to my naked sight, blew off the Dust and screwed it into a particular Part of the Wheelwork. The watch then clicked in an instant, and went very well.

"This little dirty Screw," Tyler told Ruggles, "are you in the Legislature and Dr. Young in the Town of Boston."[3]

An outspoken partisan of resistance to Britain, Young went on to become an ardent advocate of democratic reform in the new republic. On the issues that divided Americans both before and after 1776, then, Young qualified as radical. What accounts for his politics? He was poor. On the often-studied but problematic Boston tax assessment of 1771, Young was listed as having

Boston, XVI (Boston: Rockwell and Churchill, 1886), 253–55, and XVIII (1887), 47, 51, 53–54, 169, 183. See also "constitution" of the Albany Sons of Liberty in *The American Historian and Quarterly Genealogical Record,* I (Schenectady: The Historical Society, April 1876), 146–47. Violence: Young in *Boston Evening Post,* September 11, 1769, and note 44 below. Nonimportation: Hiller Zobel, *The Boston Massacre* (New York: Norton, 1970), 2–3; Anne Rowe Cunningham, ed., *Letters and Diary of John Rowe, Boston Merchant* (Boston: W. B. Clarke, 1903), 205; Thomas Hutchinson to Gov. Francis Bernard, August 20, 1770, in William V. Wells, *The Life and Public Services of Samuel Adams* (Boston: Little, Brown, & Co., 1865), I, 366; Christian Barnes to Elizabeth Smith, Marlborough, Mass., July 6, 1770, Christian Barnes Letterbook, Library of Congress. I am thankful to Prof. Mary Beth Norton of Cornell University for the last reference. Also Simon Pease to Joshua Winslow, Newport, November 3, 1774, Winslow Papers, Massachusetts Historical Society, Boston (henceforth MHS). Massacre: L. Kinvin Wroth and Hiller B. Zobel, eds., *Legal Papers of John Adams* (Cambridge: Harvard, 1965), II, 114, 142. Tea: Francis S. Drake, *Tea Leaves* (Boston: A. O. Crane, 1884), xci, and Benjamin W. Labaree, *The Boston Tea Party* (New York: Oxford, 1964), esp. 141. Hallowell: *Massachusetts Spy,* September 8, 1774.

[3]Thomas Hutchinson letter of January 1771 cited in Wells, *Samuel Adams,* I, 379, and see also 366; comments by Timothy Ruggles and Royal Tyler as recalled by John Adams in a letter to Benjamin Rush, Braintree, February 8, 1789, in *Old Family Letters: Copied from the Originals for Alexander Biddle,* Series A (Philadelphia: J. B. Lippincott, 1892), 30; Dr. Joseph Warren as "Philo Physic" in *Boston Gazette,* July 6, 1767, and Edward Shippen, Jr., to Jasper Yeates, Philadelphia, May 23, 1776, Balch Papers, Historical Society of Pennsylvania, Philadelphia (henceforth HSP).

no taxable property, which suggests that he was within the lower third of potentially taxable Bostonians in terms of wealth. He soon acquired a house but nonetheless his situation failed to improve substantially. Upon his death in 1777 he left "a sickly widow and six children wholly unprovided for." It is tempting to stop here, to assume—as Carl Becker did in his classic study of revolutionary New York—that poverty alone can explain radicalism.[4] But a far more complex network of factors fitted Young for the role he played during the 1760s and 1770s.

Born in Ulster County, New York, in 1731, the son of recent Irish immigrants, able, ambitious, and restless, Young resented the impediment that entrenched privilege offered to his advancement and, by extension, to that of others like him. Convinced the world was in need of improvement, he was attracted to an idiosyncratic strain of Deism; given to questioning, to reasoning, to bettering himself as well as his fellow men, and ill-prepared for more honorable alternatives, he took up medicine as an occupation. Young lived and worked for over thirty years in the rural Hudson Valley before moving to more cosmopolitan colonial cities. Yet he knew that his age was one of reason and science, understood their liberating force, and infused them into his religion and his medicine, which themselves shaped the politics that absorbed him during the final third of his relatively short life. As a result Young's career illustrates at once how social antagonisms, local in origin, fed into the American Revolution, and how that event participated in a far larger revolutionary culture indebted less directly to enlightened political thinkers than to the Enlightenment in science.

* * *

Young's hostility toward landed wealth may have been a family tradition. Did discontent over the maldistribution of property in Ireland inspire Young's parents to emigrate? His brother Joseph, who left a useful "Memoir of Thomas Young," recorded only that his relatives had grown "more and more dissatisfied with the government" of their homeland until they, with a group of neighbors, chose to emigrate to America. They came to Ulster County, an enclave of small farmers of Scotch-Irish, English, Dutch, Huguenot, and Palatinate origin, near the great neofeudal baronies of Dutchess, Westchester, and Albany Counties. There any earlier reservations about inherited privilege were reinforced and crystallized into political convictions. "Such a region was almost certain to be democratic in its

[4] "Boston Tax Lists, 1771," from Massachusetts Archives, vol. 132, State House, Boston, on microfilm at Harvard Univ. Library, and James A. Henretta, "Economic Development and Social Structure in Colonial Boston," *William and Mary Quarterly*, 3d Ser., XXII (1965), 85. Carl Lotus Becker, *The History of Political Parties in the Province of New York, 1760–1776* (1909; rpt. Madison: Univ. of Wisconsin Press, 1960), 50. Death notice from *Independent Chronicle* (Boston), July 17, 1777, in Frothingham Correspondence, MHS.

politics," the historian E. Wilder Spaulding wrote; and with time democracy became a matter of Young family pride. The descendants of his father "derived a double portion of Clinton blood, from their grandmothers," Joseph Young noted, "which they prize much more than to have been related to the assuming family of Livingston." Thomas Young's first personal confrontation with the haughtiness of the rich came when he was a schoolboy. A "pompous young man" upbraided him for making mischief, saying "since Providence has denied you the capacity or talents to acquire any useful knowledge, you should not interrupt those who have both the inclination and capacity to learn; besides I shall have a great estate to manage, which will require all the knowledge I can gain to manage it, and support my rank. But if you can gain a knowledge of pounds, shillings and pence, it is all you will ever have occasion for." Little Tommy answered that "before the end of six weeks I will be qualified to teach you," and, his brother claimed, made good his promise: ". . . from that hour he quit wild pranks and commenced the attentive student."[5]

As an adult, Young was always involved in conflicts with the landed rich on the side of the unprivileged. That concern seemed, in fact, to define his associates and his causes. He married into a family of Palatinates, a people who had been driven from their German homeland and were then sent to America through the beneficence of Queen Anne, only to be cruelly exploited by the great landlords of New York. He lived and practiced medicine in western Connecticut and nearby sections of New York during the 1750s, when the first rumblings occurred there of what became major land uprisings in the 1760s. Young in fact named the town of Amenia in southern Dutchess County, an area that became, according to Staughton Lynd, the center of tenant rioting.[6] In these years of Young's early adulthood he became a friend of the like-minded Ethan Allen and, equally important, supported, and perhaps invested in, the claims of Col. John Henry Lydius to lands in what is today Vermont. Lydius' title depended upon a grant from the Indians and had been confirmed, his partisans claimed—with questionable accuracy—by Massachusetts' governor William Shirley on the authority of the Crown. From about 1760 Lydius granted several townships on what Thomas Young described as very moderate terms—five shillings sterling rent per hundred acres of improvable land, first payable twenty years from the date of lease—in an effort to settle the land; but the government of

---

[5]Dr. Joseph Young in Edes, "Young," 11–13; E. Wilder Spaulding, *His Excellency George Clinton, Critic of the Constitution* (New York: Macmillan, 1938), 10.

[6]Newton Reed, *Early History of Amenia* (Amenia, N.Y.: DeLacey & Wiley, 1875), 16–18; Edes, "Young," 14–15; Lynd, "The Tenant Rising of 1766," in Lynd, *Anti-Federalism in Dutchess County, New York: A Study of Democracy and Class Conflict in the Revolutionary Era* (Chicago: Loyola Univ. Press, 1962), esp. 44–45. Also Matt Bushnell Jones, *Vermont in the Making, 1750–1777* (Cambridge: Harvard, 1939), 281–82; and Irving Mark, *Agrarian Conflicts in Colonial New York* (New York: Columbia Univ. Press, 1940), 107–15.

New York contested his title, inspired by "the great land-jobbers in New York" who wanted to "share in the profits."[7]

Young's colleagues in defending Lydius were, Young's brother claimed, "wealthy men," which suggests he may originally have been more interested in joining than fighting the rich. But in a pamphlet Young wrote in 1764—*Some Reflections on the Disputes between New York, New Hampshire, and Col. John Henry Lydius*—he defended the rights of humble settlers against Lydius' "envious monopolizing enemies" in New York. These avaricious land barons, Young charged, kept "thousands of acres of excellent soil in wilderness, waiting till the industry of others round them raise their lands to three, four, or more pounds per acre." Who, he asked, "that has the most superficial acquaintance with the country, can esteem the buyer of such lands any other than a slave during life?" That the low charges prescribed by Lydius and the state of New Hampshire, whose rights Young also supported, "should be disagreeable objects of such gentlemen's contemplation, we think nothing marvellous at all." "We, the common people," have freely lavished blood and treasure for liberty and property, the "Household Gods of Englishmen," Young argued in the rhetorical highpoint of his pamphlet and perhaps of his political writings in general, and now "want lands to exercise the arts of peace upon, at such rates as we can promise ourselves some recompense to our labours thereon," not as a reward for services, but as "undoubted rights." The foundations of government were at stake: only while "authority manifests a desire of equally protecting the rights and privileges of all His Majesty's liege subjects, indiscriminately," could it "justly expect to be loved and reverenced." All honest men should espouse Lydius' cause for "if we fall . . . they may very naturally expect to share the general ruin."[8]

Lydius lost his case; but Young's argument with privilege continued. He took the part of the insurgents in New York's tenant uprisings of 1766, although by then he lived in Boston. The suppression of insurgents was for him part of a long-term effort to expropriate the cultivator. "The Earth is the Lords, and the fullness thereof," Young wrote, "But N. York Gentlemen, have for about a Century pretty strong disputed his Title and seem resolved that neither he nor his Creatures shall have any share in the premises unless on the terms of being their servants forever." Soon, he suggested, even the sea would be "patented out to a Company," and how could a man make a living if "forbidden to trespass either on the Land or Water." Even the

---

[7] Thomas Young, as "Philodicaios," *Some Reflections on the Dispute between New York, New Hampshire, and Col. John Henry Lydius* (New Haven: Benjamin Mecom, 1764), 4; Edes, "Young," 15, 26 (Dr. Joseph Young). On Lydius, see Jones, *Vermont in the Making,* 142–48, and Mark, *Agrarian Conflicts,* 39.

[8] Dr. Joseph Young in Edes, "Young," 26; Thomas Young, *Some Reflections,* 4, 11, 12, 15, 17, 19.

rights of the Crown were involved: "A King was never designed more than a general Trustee of the Rights of the People," and so would be "very ill advised to ever grant extensive monopolies to any." If, for example, the fishery were restrained (as would be done a decade later), then "farewell forever to friendships with a Nation, of such infatuated Partiality!" Young sympathized, too, with those Connecticut people who attempted to settle the Wyoming valley of Pennsylvania, despite Pennsylvania's efforts to suppress them. In 1776, when he was deeply involved in Philadelphia radicalism, Young wrote that his opponents thought "liberty the *peculium* of Men of some rank." Their aim, he charged, was to "continue themselves and *favorites* in power, and make and execute what laws they please, frame new expeditions to Wyoming, and saddle *non electors* with all the expense." This, he argued, was "the system of Lord and Vassal, of *principal* and *dependent*," of private advantage and public loss that the new order should eliminate.[9]

Finally, he supported the efforts of his old friend Ethan Allen and the inhabitants of Vermont—a name Young invented—in, as he put it, their "struggle with the New York Monopolizers." Having "taken the minds of several leading Members in the Honourable the Continental Congress," he assured Vermonters in a circular of April 11, 1777, that independent statehood would be easily achieved. "You have nothing to do but send attested copies of the Recommendation to take up government to every township in your district," he wrote, "and invite all your freeholders and inhabitants to meet in their respective townships and choose members for a General Convention, . . . to choose Delegates for the General Congress, a Committee of Safety, and to form a Constitution for your State." Would Vermont delegates be admitted to Congress? Organize fairly and try, he urged, "and I will ensure you success at the risk of my reputation as a man of honour or common sense. Indeed, they can by no means refuse you! You have as good a right to choose how you will be governed, and by whom, as they had."[10]

Logic outran wisdom. New York was unwilling to countenance "this Attempt to dismember our State" on the part of its "revolted Subjects." And the Vermonters' argument that the Declaration of Independence dissolved all political obligations threatened to "destroy all Order, Stability and good Government," to "entail Disunion, Weakness, and Insecurity on the United

[9]Young to John Wendell, Boston, December 15, 1766, photostat, MHS; "An Elector," *Pennsylvania Gazette,* May 15, 1776. (Young is identified as "Elector" by Hawke in his "Young," 25, *n* 41.) Young may also have visited North Carolina during 1771, which would suggest an interest in the Regulators' uprisings. See Gov. Thomas Hutchinson's statement in Edes' "Young," 28, and Hawke's comment in his "Young," 17.
[10]"To the Inhabitants of Vermont," in Edes, "Young," 44–45.

States." And so the Continental Congress rejected the Vermonters' plea, explaining that Congress had been created to defend the separate states against Great Britain, not to "recommend or countenance any thing injurious" to their "rights and jurisdictions." Nor could Vermont's secession from New York "derive ... countenance or justification from the act of Congress declaring the United States to be independent of the Crown of Great Britain, nor from any other act or resolution of Congress." Congress' harshest words were reserved, however, for Young, whose circular was condemned as "derogatory to the honour of Congress" in its presumption to speak for its members. This personal censure alone met opposition, for six days earlier, on June 24, 1777, Young had died of a "virulent fever" while serving the American cause as senior surgeon in a military hospital.[11]

* * *

From childhood to death, then, Young was at odds with the men of land and power who controlled his world. Nor did his unorthodoxy stop there. In a society that took religious commitments seriously, Young was a Deist, which was tantamount to atheism in the eyes of many colonists. His religious iconoclasm was first announced in a characteristically flamboyant way, with a 1756 indictment in Dutchess County for blasphemy. Thomas Young, a "physician" and a previous resident of Crum Elbow precinct, the charge claimed, did "speak and publish these wicked false Blasphemious Words concerning the said Christian Religion (to wit) Jesus Christ was a knave and a fool ... and that he the said Thomas Young then and there declared"—lest there be any mistake—that "the said Jesus Christ of whom he then and there spoke was born of the Virgin Mary." Young at first pleaded "not guilty," but in 1758, for reasons unclear, confessed he had "abused the person and character, of Jesus Christ" and "said such things as were unworthy of him inadvertently and in Passion and fully clearly and absolutely renounce that opinion humbly begging the pardon of God Almighty the world of Mankind and the present Court of Sessions." Thirteen years later he would again profess "the most sincere attachment to the interest of the protestant religion," at least "in contradistinction" to Rome,[12] but his Christianity was at best radically unorthodox.

[11]New York Delegates to the President of the New York Convention, Philadelphia, April 22, 1777; James Duane to Robert R. Livingston, June 28, and July 1, 1777; and New York Delegates to the New York Council of Safety, Philadelphia, July 2, 1777, in Edmund C. Burnett, ed., *Letters of Members of the Continental Congress*, II (Washington: Carnegie Institution, 1923), 336, 389-90, 395, 396. Worthington C. Ford, ed., *Journals of the Continental Congress*, 8 (Washington: Library of Congress, 1907), 509-13. The Congressional Resolves of Monday, June 30, 1777, are also available in Edes, "Young," 47-48.

[12]Henry Noble MacCracken, *Old Dutchess Forever!* (New York: Hastings House 1956), 321-22, and Young in the *Boston Evening Post* (henceforth *BEP*), March 18, 1771.

In the 1750s he apparently worked closely with Ethan Allen in producing an early draft of *Reason, The Only Oracle of Man; Or A Compendious System of Natural Religion,* known more simply as *The Oracles of Reason* or *Ethan Allen's Bible,* which Allen finally published, without credit to Young, in 1784. One scholar concluded, in fact, that "Allen wrote less than one hundred of the four hundred and seventy-seven pages." Some ideas in *The Oracles* were affirmed publicly by Young during his years in Boston. Revelation, *The Oracles* argued, was seated in the natural world: "We learn from the works of nature an idea of the power and wisdom of God." In the *Boston Evening Post* Young similarly professed that "our beneficent Creator" had imprinted a "Revelation of his eternal wisdom, unlimited power, and unspeakable goodness, upon every atom of the Universe!" God's word was clear and consistent, "for infinite wisdom admits of no variation or shadow of turning, neither can a divine revelation admit of a doubt, ambiguity or obscurity." And the scriptures? The revelation of nature was open to the authors of the New and Old Testaments, Young wrote, and they denounced "many glorious things" from it. But certain doctrines derived from scripture he could not accept; they were inconsistent with his notion of a deity who was, in short, very republican in his attributes. God, Young wrote, was "no *respecter of persons,* ceremonies, or modes of worship," but looked "at the heart," accepting "worship which is afforded to him in spirit and truth." Acts of justice, humanity, and charity were, moreover, equally acceptable "whether performed by a Jew or a Samaritan" to a God who rewarded men not by rank, race, or other inherited distinction, but according to their works.[13]

Young was enthusiastic, even ebullient, over Alexander Pope's deistical *Essay on Man.* He claimed he had adopted perhaps every one of Pope's sentences and advised Abigail Dwight to read the *Essay on Man* "till you get every word by heart." Pope will "please and delight you when full of life and spirit," Young promised, and "smooth and support you when drooping or disconsolate." The *Essay* "will help you to make the best of life, and welcome death the grand response of weary nature." But his agreement with Pope, who had addressed his *Essay* to Lord Bolingbroke, was hardly total. Young sympathized, no doubt, with Pope's antagonism toward riches; he agreed with Pope's statement that "the science of human nature is, like all other sciences, reduced to a few clear Points: there are not many certain truths in this world." He obviously found both joy and consolation in Pope's assurance that all chance was but ". . . direction, which thou canst not see;/ All discord, harmony not understood;/ All partial evil, universal good."

[13]George Pomeroy Anderson, "Who Wrote 'Ethan Allen's Bible'?," *New England Quarterly,* 10 (1937), 685–96. *Reason, The Only Oracle of Man* (1784; rpt. New York: G. W. & A. J. Matsell, 1836), 9; Young in *BEP,* August 27, 1770, and March 18, 1771.

Though it seems unlikely, perhaps Young even condoned Pope's assurance that happiness was equal for all ranks in nature's order, that "Condition, circumstance is not the thing;/ Bliss is the same in subject or in king," that even among rich and poor "Heaven's just balance equal will appear,/ While those are placed in hope and these in fear." But the message of resignation Pope transmitted with the phrase "Whatever is, is right"—which Young specifically quoted—was never part of Young's creed.[14] Young's Deism was evangelical: there was, the *Oracles of Reason* announced, "an indispensible obligation on the philosophic friends of human nature, unanimously to exert themselves in every lawful, wise, and prudent met⸍od, to endeavour to reclaim mankind from . . . ignorance and delusion," enlightening men particularly as to God and morality, which would greatly serve "their happiness and well being." Here was Young's creed, which he professed in 1771. "God, delighting in the well being of all his creatures, requires of me the improvement of all the talents he has favored me with for the promotion of that great end," he wrote, "and . . . my neglect or refusal herein subjects me to his righteous displeasure."[15]

Young's Deism revealed, then, that he was not just an iconoclast but a revolutionary of sorts even before the Anglo-American conflict began, for the reordering of life to abolish ignorance and delusion, to promote the happiness and well-being of mankind, was a task of revolutionary magnitude. This God-given mission, moreover, had social implications, for Young once equated hierarchy with superstition, the ultimate form of ignorance and delusion.[16] Young's Deism also accentuated his position as an outsider and significantly restricted his political effectiveness, above all in Boston. He first migrated to the Bay Colony, it seems, with a desire of avoiding "every thing controversial," but repeatedly became the center of controversy. Even when disputes centered around unrelated issues, his religious beliefs were mentioned, suggesting the hostility and distrust they inspired. In 1767, for example, he was involved in a scurrilous newspaper debate over his medical practices, but a set of letters in the *Boston Evening Post* asked also whether "a Young Fellow, . . . a stranger" had censured and ridiculed the established religion of the country, or had only "vehemently enveighed" against its "*Superstitions*." In August 1770 an attack in the *Massachusetts Gazette* prompted Young to explain his views on revelation. The following March he

---

[14]Young to Dwight, Boston, February 13, 1767, Sedgwick II Papers, MHS; Pope, "An Essay on Man," "The Design," and Epistle I, lines 290–92, and Epistle IV, lines 57–58, 69–70. On Pope, see Isaac Kramnick, *Bolingbroke and His Circle* (Cambridge: Harvard Univ. Press, 1968), 217–23.

[15]*Reason, The Only Oracle of Man*, 1, and Young in *BEP*, March 18, 1771.

[16]Young as "Probus" in *BEP*, May 9, 1768. The identification here of newspaper essays signed "Probus," "Britano Americanus," or "Libermoriturus" as by Young is based upon his acknowledgment of those pseudonyms in a letter to Dr. Thomas Williams, 1768, in the Gratz Collection, HSP.

published a still fuller religious confession, denying charges that he was a person of "loose, profane and irreligious behavior," an atheist who denied man was accountable for his actions, and who had been banished from New York for blasphemy—even "publicly whipt out of Albany."[17]

Because of doubts concerning his character and beliefs, Young believed, several persons opposed his participation in a Boston town committee on the commemoration of the Boston Massacre. When he was appointed to the Committee of Correspondence twenty months later, controversy became open and serious. First Aaron Davis, Jr., of Roxbury refused to participate in any program led by Young: "Don't it look quite ridiculous," Davis explained, "for a Set of *Puritans,* deeply concerned for their religious as well as civil privileges," to set up "Atheists or Deists, men of profligate manners and profane tongues" as public leaders.[18] Then in March, 1773, an official in Barnstable charged that the Boston Committee of Correspondence included "men of no Principles, and infamous Characters" such as William Molineux, William Dennie, and Dr. Young, and so, it was said, produced "a great Disgust in the minds of the People against the Committee of Boston." Molineux and Dennie were defended since they were merchants long resident in Boston, but efforts were taken to gather testimonials in support of Young from individuals in widely separated places—from Solomon Williams of Lebanon, Connecticut, Eliphalet Williams of East Hartford, and even, strangely, Robert Livingston, "lord of the manor . . . in Albany county," New York.[19]

Religion was an inauspicious area in which to begin the work of revolution. Young's deistical radicalism was, moreover, distinct from that of "mainline" colonial Whigs, who spoke more of "virtue" than of human happiness, and condemned "corruption" more than ignorance and delusion. Young's identity as a physician may, in fact, have been a more immediate determinant of his politics before 1776 than his religion: his medical theories above all contributed to his willingness to advocate American independence. His practice of medicine, moreover, allowed Young to fulfill his God-given mission to promote the happiness and well-being of mankind, for fever—the leading killer of the eighteenth-century, which Young fought both as a prac-

[17]To Dwight, February 13, 1767, Sedgwick II Papers, MHS; "Socrates to the Athenians" and "St. Paul to the Athenians," *BEP,* May 18 and 25, 1767; Young in *BEP,* August 27, 1770, and March 18, 1771.

[18]On this occasion Samuel Adams came to Young's defense. See Davis letter, from the *Boston News Letter* for November 26, 1772; Adams reply, signed "Vindex," from *Boston Gazette,* November 30, 1772, and also Young's self-defense, from *BEP,* November 30, 1772, all available in Edes, "Young," 18–25.

[19]Correspondence file of the Boston Committee of Correspondence, photostats 41–50, MHS, esp. for letter from "an Inhabitant of Barnstable" to William Molineux, Barnstable, March 11, 1773, and an edited draft of the Boston Committee's response.

titioner and as a writer—was, he once wrote, a "general foe to human happiness."[20]

* * *

Young's interest in medicine, like his hostility toward landed privilege, went back into his childhood. If he could become emperor of the world on condition that he abandon the "study of physic," he told his brother, he would spurn the proposal. Medicine shaped his early education: he studied the relevant languages—Latin and Greek, Dutch and French—and developed an "indefatigable" interest in botany, learning the medicinal uses of all local plants. Finally, at age seventeen, Young began a two-year apprenticeship under a local doctor that concluded his formal education. Medicine was important because it provided an opportunity to serve mankind, but it also afforded him a means of serving his own insatiable curiosity: "I do not see what men of sense and just Taste can find fault with [in] a world so abounding with entertaining and interesting objects," he wrote in 1766.[21]

Medicine was, moreover, a logical career choice for the able children of immigrants who lacked position. Thomas Young's brother Joseph followed him into medical practice; and of the four surviving sons of his cousin Charles Clinton, who emigrated from Ireland with Young's father, two became doctors.[22] But medicine did not confer status: in fact it heightened concern for recognition, for medicine remained a relatively undeveloped occupation in prerevolutionary America. The conventions that in urban England and Scotland distinguished "physicians"—generally university men, gentlemen, and scholars—from the lesser surgeons and apothecaries had not survived the Atlantic crossing. Nor had the elaborate system of certification that regulated entrance into the English medical profession. In the colonies nothing prevented "unqualified" aspirants from claiming the title "doctor," reserved in London or Edinburgh for physicians alone. Some progress had been made: according to Richard Shryock, ". . . a dawning enlightenment in medicine paralleled the quite different Great Awakening in religion during the middle decades of the eighteenth century." But a 150-year struggle to define and upgrade the practice of medicine, to transform a marginal occupation into an established profession, was then only beginning. Local medical societies that sought to distinguish qualified personnel

[20] Young in *The Royal American Magazine*, April 1774, 129.
[21] Dr. Joseph Young in Edes, "Young," 13–14; Thomas Young to John Wendell, Boston, December 15, 1766, photostat, MHS.
[22] Of the two other sons of Charles Clinton, one, Gen. James Clinton, joined the army, and the fourth, George Clinton, made his way in life through politics, becoming a revolutionary governor of New York. See Spaulding, *His Excellency George Clinton*, ch. 1.

through licensing regulations and to impose harmony within the profession by voluntary regulation of competition began to proliferate only after the Revolutionary War.[23]

What would later be achieved through institutions was, as a result, done informally during the revolutionary era. Physicians characteristically engaged in public controversies with each other, no doubt in part due to a "competition for business and money," as Benjamin Rush argued. But the acrimony of medical disputes—opponents were called mountebanks, fools, madmen, "petulent Jackanapes," "cloaked murderers"—was at base social, part of a larger effort to distinguish an elite of "gentlemen," learned physicians, from others who were at best "pretenders to physic," "ignorant Empiricks," "quacks." The first of several attacks on Young's medical practice began, significantly, in the spring of 1767, only months after his arrival in Boston, but when he had already managed to attract, as he wrote a friend, "as much business as I can possibly attend," and centered on a patient he had taken from another local doctor. But the persistent abuse of Young also stemmed, one of his defenders suggested, from the fact that he was an outsider, an "exotic," and so had "no special connections."[24] In fact, his politics far more than his medicine may have finally won him acceptance by fellow doctors: in September, 1769, Young reported that Dr. Joseph Warren, a leading Boston patriot and former medical opponent, had waited upon him and assured him that "whatever may heretofore have happened I have now a real esteem of you and hearty friendship for you which I desire you may henceforth credit on the honor of a gentleman." Since Dr. Benjamin Church, another Son of Liberty, had already become "as faithful and agreeable a friend as ever man was blest with," Young felt himself then "as well settled respecting medical friendship as I can wish." But the carping continued: in June, 1771, with a tone of fatigue, and because "silence herein might be injurious to this Country," he answered the latest effort of his "despicable enemies" to impugn the treatment which, with the assistance of Warren, he administered to Royal Tyler during a terminal illness, and which involved "a strong infusion of milipedes in wine, crude sal armoniac in gruel, horseradish, &c."[25]

If acceptance by peers had to be gained through informal combat, public support for an elite medical profession had also to be won. The detailed medical essays Young published in the *Boston Evening Post* in late 1769 and

[23]Richard Shryock, *Medicine and Society in America, 1660-1860* (New York: New York Univ. Press, 1960), esp. 2-21, 31.

[24]Rush quoted in ibid., 32. Young to Abigail Dwight, Boston, February 13, 1767, Sedgwick II Papers, MHS. The newspaper controversy raged between April and June 1767 in the *BEP* and *Boston Gazette.*

[25]Young letter [Boston, September 1769] in Edes, "Thomas Young," 8, and Young in *BEP*, June 3, 1771.

early 1770 were addressed to this need: they sought to demonstrate to "every plain honest country gentleman and judicious citizen, that reading Culpeper's English Physician enlarged, or even Hutchins' Almanack improved, will not furnish a man with these articles of knowledge," that they needed, in short, trained doctors. His articles might serve, moreover, to win support for the founding of "a college of Physicians" at Boston and perhaps also "a competent library for the instruction of youth in the several branches of Anatomy, Surgery, Midwifery and Medicine; all to be under such regulations as to the wisdom of the legislature should seem meet." In summarizing the elements of medical learning, the nature of health and disease, the classification of disorders of "solids" and "humors," Young again awoke criticism. He had, an opponent charged, revived "the long and justly rejected corpuscularian, chymical and other fanatico philosophical systems, and blended them into one confused chaos."[26]

Despite his critics, however, Young's medicine was not fundamentally different from theirs, nor from that of eighteenth-century doctors more generally. The practice of "physic" was influenced by the previous century's advances in what is now called physics, or mechanics: "indeed," Young wrote, "natural philosophy seems more peculiarly a preliminary to physic than either of the other learned professions, the whole *theory* and *rational practice* of the art, being a continued exercise of its rules." Only after mastering the principles of natural philosophy, he argued, should the medical student turn toward anatomy, that is, "to a physiological enquiry into the structure, action and use of the parts in the living subjects, which he had examined in the dead one." The study was essentially that of a "material system, . . . subject to the laws of nature," of a machine whose "principles, powers, and laws of motion" must be known to workmen "charged with the care of keeping it in due order." Young once even referred to the human body as "a pneumatico hydraulic engine." Health and disease were understood above all in terms of the physical attributes of the body's component "solids" and liquids or "humors," their "principle of motion."[27]

Young was not, as his critics occasionally charged, an ignorant "Empirick," prescribing remedies from uninformed private observations of disease. He cited the authorities of eighteenth-century medicine, including Pitcairn, Sydenham, Haller, Whytt, Pringle, and above all the "great Boerhaave."[28] His learning was, however, imperfect: when accused in 1767

[26]Quotations from Young in *BEP*, December 25, 1769, and February 26, 1770. Other essays in the series were published in *BEP* for January 1, 8, 15, and 22, 1770: his critic, "Timetes," appeared in *BEP*, February 19, 1770.
[27]Young in *BEP*, December 25, 1769, and *Royal American Magazine* for February 1774, 47–48.
[28]See esp. Young essays in *BEP*, April 20, 1767, and December 25, 1769. For a general account of eighteenth-century medicine, see Lester S. King, *The Medical World of the Eighteenth-Century* (Chicago: Univ. of Chicago Press, 1958).

of quoting authorities he had not mastered, he responded ingenuously that he had perhaps neither the "ability nor inclination to read authors in whole or in part," and later opened himself to ridicule for a casual reference to Harvey's work on the circulation of the blood as that of a late author "whose name I have lost in much and multifarious reading." Nor did he have much confidence that the inherited "*Institutions* of Physic" which supposedly comprehended "the knowledge of every thing necessary for the preservation of health, and the cure of diseases" were in fact comprehensive. He advised the young physician "to add to them his own particular observations," that medical practice might be advanced in what Young called "this improving age."[29] Nor was practical success the only criterion behind his eclectic approach to medical authority. In explaining body heat—a crucial subject in an age of fevers—he yielded, for example, to the explanation in a medical essay from Edinburgh because it appeared "most simple, consonant to nature," as well as "beneficial in practice." Warmth depended upon, he believed, "the tendency of all substances to a separation of their component parts, when shut up in a close place and duly moistened." The body functioned much like a compost heap of fresh hay from which "a great heat arises," leading to "its near, or perhaps total putrefaction." From this precept followed logically Young's practice of medicine, his response to diseases as dissimilar as smallpox and rickets—and his politics as well.[30]

If the above theory of "animal heat" was correct, Young theorized, the body's temperature was determined by the speed of digestion: "the stronger it is, the more rapidly it proceeds, the more animal heat it produces." As such, "the greater part of the diseases we labour under may be deduced from an overweak or strong digestion." Foods putrified even in a healthy body, and unless "either assimilated to the living parts, or cast out of the system in a reasonable time they become violently noxious." Should the process for some reason be obstructed the "acrid matter" might make its way into the blood, but more often it remained in the digestive tract, requiring the administration of purgatives. Young's conclusions, he claimed, dated back to a "violent fever" he had suffered in 1758, from which he saved himself only by cathartics, concluding that "had all the ill conditioned matter resembling semiputrid gall, juice of the liver, &c. remained till it had acquired a much greater degree of putrefaction, it would soon have poisoned every drop of fluids, if not melted down the solid parts of the body." Long experience, involving even advanced cases, convinced him of the efficacy of bleeding, "puking," and above all the administration of purges—for which

[29] *BEP*, June 1, 1767, and December 25, 1769.
[30] *Royal American Magazine*, February 1774, 47, and, for his treatment of rickets, September 1774; 239–40. For his treatment of smallpox, see Young to Henry Ward, Philadelphia, March 27 [26], 1776, in Bernard Knollenberg, ed., *Correspondence of Governor Samuel Ward, May 1775–March 1776* (Princeton: Princeton Univ. Press, 1952), 201–04.

he favored the use of calomel, mercurous chloride, a remedy he passed on to Rush—followed finally by "a cooling and composing regime." Continually he argued the danger of hesitation: "a mistaken fear of weakening the patient by purging off humors running into the last stages of putrefaction," he claimed, "has deterred many from giving their patients some chance of recovery, when the neglect of it left none at all." The proven effectiveness of Young's technique supplanted older remedies such as the raising of a sweat, or the "still more cruel method of blistering from crown to ancle" on the assumption that disease could be terminated through the skin. These, he claimed, were continued only because of a pertinacious adherence to the "*tradition of the fathers.*"[31]

* * *

When Young first appeared among the Albany Sons of Liberty during the Stamp Act crisis, he was a man in his mid-30s with no political experience. He had never sat in a provincial assembly, or even held a position of authority within a local constabulary. He brought to politics, however, a dislike of privilege, a systematic if unorthodox religious creed, and a set of convictions about the practice of medicine that he would articulate with increased clarity in the next decade. He may have written more on medicine than politics between 1765 and his death twelve years later, but those subjects were closely connected. The term "constitution" in politics was, after all, drawn from its organic counterpart. Both the physical body and the body politic were described as machines, with principles of motion that must be understood. Both "bodies" were subject to dissolution from the abnormal extension of a trait present in the best of times, a runaway "putrefaction" in the physical body or, in the state, an unlimited expansion of power, or "corruption," founded upon the human depravity which Young, as much as any Calvinist, found a normal part of man's nature.[32] Even the cure was identical. Independence was a means of separating America from contagion, of purging her of British corruption—a "heroic" remedy perhaps, but a fitting one for Young to prescribe, since he had spent his medical career teaching that the greatest danger lay in hesitation, in delaying "heroic" remedies which alone could save the patient.

This relationship of politics and medicine was for Young real, not analogical. It was founded upon the assumption Young shared with other medical "systematists" throughout the western world—and which was articulated in the *Oracles of Man* and again in Pope's *Essay on Man*—that all natural truth could be reduced to a few basic principles. Among doctors,

[31]*Royal American Magazine* for February, March, and April 1774, pp. 47–48, 98–100, 129–31, and March 1775, 89–90. *Pennsylvania Gazette*, July 26, 1775.

[32]On human depravity, Young to Hughes, Boston, August 21, 1772, Miscellaneous Bound Manuscripts, MHS.

this meant that what are today recognized as fundamentally different diseases were considered similar disorders that could be treated in like ways. Moreover, as Pope made clear, the science of human nature, which was the basis of political science, was "like all other sciences" in this regard; truth was a unity. Colonists naturally used medical terms in political discourse. Ezra Stiles, for example, once likened England to a "hydropsical patient." Young's terminology fitted his own medical theories, with their emphasis upon putrefaction: "We long to hear of some thorough paroxisms among you that may forward a crisis of the lingering disease," he wrote John Wilkes on September 6, 1769; "such corrupt humors hanging so long on the vitals, threaten the utter extinction of the animal heat."[33] The revolutionaries' conclusion that Britain was beyond salvation was not an exercise of paranoia—a twentieth-century concept—but a triumph of scientific reason, a masterful diagnosis of the extent of corruption through its otherwise disparate symptoms. For Young, God's truth—whether in politics or in nature at large—was incompatible with "doubt, ambiguity, or obscurity," which manifested at best man's inability or unwillingness to perceive and accept truth. Thus, his stance as an enlightened man of science helped sustain him through the trials of a tumultuous world. His conviction that by reason and observation he had come to distinguish truth from error reinforced a personal tendency toward righteousness that others called impudence but also provided a "sternness of stuff" John Adams considered essential for a revolutionary leader.[34]

Young was no scholar of politics. He used authorities as eclectically in his political as in his medical treatises: he cited Locke's writings and a handful of other works, including Coke, a pamphlet by Anthony Ellys, Bishop of St. David's, an essay on the English constitution by Hill, even John Adams' "Thoughts on Government," but for isolated points, ignoring general disagreements between himself and his authorities.[35] His arguments were in part his own, derived from personal observations and logic more than reading, even when they repeated familiar notions of a larger culture. In medicine the result was an approach like that of other doctors; but in politics Young's emphases distinguished him from other revolutionaries. He understood, for example, the common conception of the British constitution,

---

[33]Pope, *Essay*, 1 ("The Design"); Stiles to Catharine Macaulay, December 6, 1773, Ezra Stiles Papers, Beinecke Library, Yale University, New Haven, Conn.; Young to Wilkes, *Proceedings of the Massachusetts Historical Society*, 47 (1913–14), 210.

[34]Young in *BEP*, August 27, 1770; John Adams to William Tudor Quincy, June 5, 1817, in Charles F. Adams ed., *The Writings of John Adams* (Boston: Little, Brown & Co., 1850–56), X, 262.

[35]His obliviousness to conflict is clear in his citation of Ellys for a discussion of the Saxons in *BEP*, November 9, 1767, where he wrote as "Libermoriturus." Ellys was a defender of High Church prerogative.

which, it was said, divided power between king, lords, and commons, creating a "political equilibrium where each was *checked* and neither destroyed." But he gave little heed to this complex balancing function. Instead, for him, the constitution served more simply to protect the common people from the rich and powerful. Where "the upper part of a nation . . . have the authority of government solely in their hands," he wrote, its members "will always be for keeping the low people under." Danger came above all from an "encrease of property" that made its possessors "haughty and imperious," "cruel and oppressive," considering themselves "above the law." For Young, then, it was essential that "people of the lower ranks" share in government. Even kings, he emphasized, were trustees of the rights of the people whose dependence upon their subjects could "never be too great."[36]

Because for him the problem of government was simply one of limiting the sway of the rich and powerful, he did not share his countrymen's enthusiasm for the Glorious Revolution of 1688/89, when, it was said, the power of king, lords, and commons were put in equilibrium. Young's golden age went back in time to the Saxons, who "considered every man alike as he came out of the hands of his maker—riches with them gave no power or authority over the poorest person in the state." Every householder who was "liable to pay his shot and bear his lot, might consent to every law that was made for his observence." Only then, he argued, was the "English constitution in its original purity," before Norman invaders destroyed "as many of the free customs of the people" as they could, and slowly introduced "that infernal system of ruling by a *few dependent favourites,* who would readily agree to divide the spoils of the lower class between the supreme robber and his banditti of feudal lords."[37]

Within the context of revolutionary politics Young was a democrat not just in theory but in practice. Soon after arriving in Boston, he expressed a wish that the town had a building large enough to allow "all that chose to attend" to witness the debates of their legislative assembly, and that the cost of lawsuits could be reduced so all might have the equal protection of law. His revolutionary politics also emphasized the "lower orders" of society: resistance, he understood, depended upon the common people, upon "those worthy members of society," the tradesmen, as well as "the yeomanry in our country towns," who would "form the revolution of the other ranks of Citizens."[38] He had no fear of the urban working people—who, it seems,

---

[36] Young as "An Elector," *Pennsylvania Gazette,* May 15, 1776, and in *BEP* as "Sobrius," September 15, 1767; "Britano-Americanus," September 23, 1767, and "Libermoriturus," November 9, 1767. Young is identified as "Elector" by Hawke in his "Young," 25, *n* 41.

[37] Young as "An Elector," *Pennsylvania Gazette,* May 15, 1776, and also as "Libermoriturus," *BEP,* November 9, 1967.

[38] Young to John Wendell, Boston, November 23, 1766, photostat, MHS; to John Lamb, June 19, 1774, Lamb papers, New-York Historical Society.

provided the bulk of his Boston patients[39]—nor of an insurgent backcountry: during 1774 he sent Samuel Adams a remarkably unfrightened, even approving account of western demands for governmental change. He was himself after all a westerner who, as a member of the Boston Committee of Correspondence, had helped instruct western Massachusetts in revolutionary politics, and he urged his New York City correspondents to take on the same function of "instructing the common people."[40] Later he supported an expansion of the franchise to all taxpayers and the enactment of Pennsylvania's democratic constitution of 1776, which he subsequently recommended that Vermonters take as their model of government. By rejecting the complex structure of the British constitution and reducing government to the people and their representatives, the Pennsylvania constitution satisfied not just Young's popular inclinations, but his preference, shared with Thomas Paine, for simple structures, which were, he noted in a different context, most consonant with nature.[41]

Yet Young was no leveller. He fought for acceptance as a doctor, and for the establishment of medicine as an elite profession. Though in the republican atmosphere of the mid-1770s he was willing to explain fevers and fluxes in terms of "common sense," he refused to abandon the technical terms of medicine. These were expressions of precision, the marks of learning. There could be no democracy there; until someone invented "a vocabulary of medical terms as concise and particular as the one in use," he wrote, "we must be indulged in writing *Hypochondria* in Physic as well as *Hypothenuse* in Mathematics." The social consciousness of his political writings lay not just in his emphasis upon the role of the people, but also in suggesting his own desire for acceptance and rank. "Slavery," he once wrote, ". . . is so vile . . . that it is hardly to be conceived an Englishman, *much less a Gentleman,* should plead for it."[42] Recognition and power in postrevolutionary America should be restricted to men of "capacity and integrity in public affairs," he wrote, although they would, of course, be obliged "to fall into the common mass of the people every year, and be sensi-

---

[39] His most outspoken opponent of 1767 charged that Young had descended "to the lowest arts of ingratiating him[self] with people, whose constant employment in other business renders it impossible that they should be judges of real merit," that he was "the great Apollo of the ignorant." See Dr. Miles Whitworth, *Boston Gazette,* April 27, 1767.

[40] Young to Adams, September 4, 1774, Frothingham Correspondence, MHS; to Hugh Hughes, December 21, 1772, Miscellaneous Bound Manuscripts, MHS. For the argument that there was tension between a more elitist, eastern revolutionary leadership and the democratic west, see, for example, Dirk Hoerder, *People and Mobs: Crowd Action in Massachusetts During the American Revolution, 1765-1780* (Dissertation, Free University of Berlin, 1971), and Stephen Patterson, *Political Parties in Revolutionary Massachusetts* (Madison: Univ. of Wisconsin Press, 1973).

[41] "An Elector," *Pennsylvania Gazette,* May 15, 1776, and Young, "To the Inhabitants of Vermont," in Edes, "Young," 44–46. *Royal American Magazine,* February 1774.

[42] Young to "Agricultor," *BEP,* March 28, 1774; as "Libermoriturus," *BEP,* November 9, 1767, my italics.

ble of their need of the popular good will to sustain their political importance."[43] Not all hierarchy, it seems, was superstitious. Privilege and authority would no longer be the automatic province of the rich, but rank would not be destroyed in postrevolutionary society. Instead it would be relocated in a republican meritocracy.

* * *

A first-generation American without claim to respectability by family or fortune, a persistent transient, but a man of quick wit, restless and ambitious, Thomas Young was forever an outsider, anxious for an acceptance he never received except among the cadres of the discontented. His revolutionary politics were influenced less by England's Radical Whig tradition than by the Enlightenment in science. In reason and nature he found alternative values to those that seemed to order his world; they were for him what virtue was for his sometime mentor, Samuel Adams, a standard upon which the old order was to be judged and the new constructed. But unlike the "virtue" of Adams, reason and nature were not attributes of earlier generations that the Revolution would recapture. Young had no roots in a provincial past. A self-conscious man of science, he found the legacies of the fathers sometimes irrational, even inhumane. He was as a result more naturally at ease with the prospect of a new order than even those New Englanders who served as fathers of the Revolution. In the years before independence, it seems, these distinctions were of little consequence. The resistance movement made fellows of men who came to oppose British "corruption" by widely separate paths. Within the circle of Boston revolutionary leaders, Young's impatience and his early arguments in defense of violence[44] caused more difficulty, it seems, than differences in the intellectual and social bases of a common commitment. But within a few years Young learned from Adams that "patience . . . is characteristick of the Patriot," that "ripeness for great enterprizes advances slowly," and, finally, that it was better to reduce mistaken enemies "to reason, and make them our friends," than to spill their blood.[45] Any divisions over the shape and policies

[43]Young, "To the Inhabitants of Vermont," in Edes, "Young," 45.

[44]During his earliest years in Boston, Young argued that the enemies of freedom could justly be put to death. He based his position upon a passage from John Locke's *Second Treatise of Government* (Ch. III, §17), which he cited in an essay signed "Libermoriturus" in the *BEP* for November 9, 1767, and again in a Boston Town Meeting of September 12, 1768, which had been called to discuss how the town should respond to the imminent arrival of British troops. See Young in *BEP*, September 11, 1769; and *A Report of the Record Commissioners of the City of Boston*, 18 (Boston, 1887), 259–64. Also "Journal of Transactions at Boston," Sparks mss. x, Papers Relating to New England, Vol. III, f. 56, Houghton Library, Harvard University, Cambridge, Mass.

[45]Samuel Adams to Young, Philadelphia, October [17,] 1774, in Harry Alonso Cushing, ed., *The Writings of Samuel Adams*, III (New York: G.P. Putnam's Sons, 1907), 163; Young to

of postrevolutionary America were postponed until a later day, when the abandonment of Britain became necessary and independence was declared.

If Young's views made him distinctive within the American revolutionary movement, he was hardly unique. There were other doctors prominent in the resistance to Britain—Benjamin Rush, Joseph Warren, Benjamin Church. Similarities between Young and Thomas Paine are, moreover, particularly compelling, even though Paine was only marginally interested in medicine. Both were men of humble origin who led lives of frustration before the Revolution; both were Deists; both harbored a deep hostility toward inherited privilege. In his later years Paine claimed that the "natural bent of his mind had always been to science," not politics, which he long considered a form of "Jockeyship"; but in fact his science and his politics were closely related. Paine's radicalism, Eric Foner argues, began well before he came to America, among those English "religious Dissenters and self-educated artisans and shopkeepers, many of whom leaned toward Deism," who frequented the lectures of itinerant popularizers of science. For such men, popular Newtonianism, with its suggestion that society as well as nature could be reduced to a science and that all human institutions must be judged against reason, easily bred conflict with an established system ordered not by logic but by precedent. And so Paine's interest in science introduced him to "articulate critics of English government" such as Benjamin Franklin, who was partly responsible for his migration to America. For Paine in England, then, as for Young in America, science proved "a breeding ground for radical politics."[46]

Young should not, however, be compared only to American revolutionaries. He had much in common, for example, with the hero of Beaumarchais's *Marriage of Figaro,* who was himself, as Crane Brinton recognized, a bellwether of revolution in France. Figaro, too, looked back upon a life of struggle without success; even an education in chemistry, pharmacy, and surgery allowed him to practice only veterinary medicine due to his low birth. His frustrations fed an absorbing hostility toward privilege: ". . . what have you done to deserve so many good things?" Figaro asked the Count Almaviva. "You took the trouble to get born!" The causes Young espoused were not, in any simple way, efforts to improve his status. Deism, for example, inhibited his chances for acceptance and respect. But on a more profound level he sought to reverse the priorities of a world in which, as Figaro complained, "savoir faire" was worth more than "savoir," or

---

Hugh Hughes at New York, Boston, August 21 and December 2, 1772, Miscellaneous Bound Manuscripts, MHS. Also Young to Samuel Adams, Boston, September 4, 1774, Frothingham Correspondence, MHS.

[46]Paine, "The Age of Reason," in Philip S. Foner, ed., *The Complete Writings of Thomas Paine* (New York: Citadel Press, 1969), II, 496. Eric Foner, *Tom Paine and Revolutionary America* (New York: Oxford, 1976), 6–7.

knowledge.[47] For such men, as for Marat and Brissot, who became leaders in the French Revolution, science had great appeal. In reason and scientific truth, as Robert Darnton has demonstrated, they found the basis of a deeply anti-establishment radicalism, of a plea for the reordering of society that it might better recognize ability and knowledge.[48] As such, the doctrine of reason reveals not just the confluence of social and ideological themes in the American Revolution, but the participation of Young, Paine, and others like them in a larger revolutionary world of the eighteenth century.*

[47]Crane Brinton, *The Anatomy of Revolution* (1952; rev. New York: Vintage, 1957), 67–68.
[48]Robert Darnton, *Mesmerism and the End of the Enlightenment in France* (Cambridge: Harvard Univ. Press, 1968), 91–95, 110–11, and passim.

*Research for this article was done at the Charles Warren Center for Studies in American History, Harvard University, under a grant from the National Endowment for the Humanities.

Explaining the Revolution:
Ideology and Ethics in Mercy Otis Warren's Historical Theory

Lester H. Cohen

THE American Revolution, like all major events, generated its own historical writings. At least fifteen patriot histories—not to mention loyalist works or historical "memoirs" and "retrospects"—were written between David Ramsay's *History of the Revolution of S.... ' Carolina from a British Province to an Independent State* (1785) and John Marshall's *Life of George Washington* (1804-1807). Philosophical statements about the nature of man, society, government, and history, the histories are also obvious efforts to justify the American separation from Britain. High-minded disquisitions on natural rights, they are also transparently partisan works that reveal their authors' opinions on a multitude of issues that arose in the 1780s and '90s. Ostensibly straightforward, unadorned descriptions of events in the Revolutionary era, they are also serious literary performances that challenge traditional conventions of narrative historical writing.[1]

In a crucial sense, the histories written in these decades demonstrate a greater concern for America's present and future than for its past. For they reveal their authors' anxiety, as William Gordon put it as early as 1777, that "a horrid corruption hath spread itself so rapidly thro' the American States; and that in the first year of our existence we should have adopted so many of the Old England vices." Two years later, David Ramsay

Mr. Cohen is a member of the Department of History at Purdue University. He wishes to thank two friends and colleagues, Linda Levy Peck and Cheryl Z. Oreovicz, for their insightful and valuable comments on earlier versions of this essay, and especially to thank Professor Oreovicz for instruction in Warren's poetry.

[1] See Arthur H. Shaffer, *The Politics of History: Writing the History of the American Revolution, 1783-1815* (Chicago, 1975), and William Raymond Smith, *History as Argument: Three Patriot Historians of the American Revolution* (The Hague, 1966). I have treated the histories as efforts to justify the Revolution in "The American Revolution and Natural Law Theory," *Journal of the History of Ideas*, XXXIX (1978), 491-502, and I have discussed some of the dominant conventions of narrative historical writing in "Narrating the Revolution: Ideology, Language, and Style," *Studies in Eighteenth-Century Culture*, IX (1979), 455-476. My forthcoming study, *The Revolutionary Histories: Philosophy, Ideology, Language* (Ithaca, N.Y., 1980), develops these and other themes in greater breadth and detail.

mourned that a "spirit of money-making has eaten up our patriotism. Our morals are more depreciated than our currency." By 1786 Ramsay feared that "we have neither honesty nor knowledge enough for republican governments."[2]

This fear of widespread corruption, which is especially emphatic in the historians' narratives of events from the late 1770s to (in most cases) the passage of the Constitution, is not surprising, for corruption had been a dominant patriot concern since the 1760s.[3] But the historians' persistent focus on corruption in history reveals more than patriotic zeal. The anxiety it reflects also gave rise to a theory of history that was designed to unite ideology and ethics in a single interpretive framework. The historians presupposed a dialectic between ideology and ethics, such that republican principles and institutions and the ethical practices of the people mutually affected one another. They assumed, moreover, that the dialectic gained its impetus from the ethical side, that principles and institutions were predicated upon the people's practice of republican virtue.

Thus, believing that the ethical foundation of society was weakening, they portrayed the years after independence as a period rife with the possibility of decline. At the same time that republican institutions were being shaped they were in danger of crumbling, and at the same time that republican principles were being voiced they were in danger of dissipating. From the monetary crisis of the late 1770s to the fraud and peculation they discerned in the early '80s, from the weaknesses most of them saw in society under the Articles of Confederation to Shays's Rebellion (1786) and the dangerous spirit of faction that arose in the early '90s, the historians tended to portray political events as ethical events, signs of the moral condition of the people.

Mercy Otis Warren's *History of the American Revolution* (1805) reveals the same concerns and the same attempt to fuse ideology and ethics in historical interpretation. She, too, believed that the nation was already in trouble. Instead of showing that independence would solidify the people's commitment to republican values, events of the 1780s and '90s, when her *History* was taking shape, seemed to confirm her worst apprehensions

---

[2] William Gordon to John Adams, June 5, 1777, "Letters of the Reverend William Gordon . . . 1770-1799," Massachusetts Historical Society, *Proceedings*, LXIII (1931), 340, hereafter cited as "Letters of Gordon"; Ramsay to William Henry Drayton, Sept. 1, 1779, and to Benjamin Rush, Aug. 6, 1786, in Robert L. Brunhouse, ed., *David Ramsay, 1749-1815: Selections from His Writings* (American Philosophical Society, *Transactions*, N.S., LV, Pt. 4 [1965]), 64, 105, hereafter cited as Brunhouse, ed., *Writings of Ramsay*.

[3] This essay, like all current studies of the concepts of virtue and corruption in Revolutionary America, is immeasurably indebted to Bernard Bailyn, *The Ideological Origins of the American Revolution* (Cambridge, Mass., 1967), and *The Origins of American Politics* (New York, 1970); Gordon S. Wood, *The Creation of the American Republic, 1776-1787* (Chapel Hill, N.C., 1969); and J. G. A. Pocock, *The Machiavellian Moment: Florentine Political Thought and the Atlantic Republican Tradition* (Princeton, N.J., 1975), esp. 462-552.

about human character and about the people's unwillingness to practice political self-discipline. She wrote her *History* in a mood of profound concern, explaining to John Adams in 1807 that many of her observations in it were prompted by her "cool reflections on the danger a young country was in, just relieved from a long war." She was anxious about the future of American republicanism because public virtue was yielding to private ambition, the rising generation "laying aside their simple habits, and . . . hankering after the modes, distinctions, and ranks of the servants of European despots." She added rhetorically: "Was it not obvious that dangers would thicken?"[4]

Warren's anxiety can be explained in part by her political attitudes and by events, particularly in the 1780s, that affected her personally. If, for example, Federalists like Ramsay and Marshall were comforted by the belief that the Constitution was likely to be an effective brake on corruption, the Antifederalist Warren had less sanguine expectations. Although for tactical purposes she softened her criticism of the Constitution in her *History*, in 1788 she feared that the Constitution represented a renunciation of popular sovereignty and that it might even prove to be a new way of enslaving the people.[5] Similarly, while William Gordon thought that the formation of the Society of the Cincinnati in May 1783 was ill-advised, and while John Marshall thought that public outrage warranted its disbanding (even though the society itself was innocuous), Warren roundly condemned it in the style of Aedanus Burke and of her husband, James, as a quest for "*a self-created rank*," "an order of military knighthood," and therefore a symptom of the pernicious doctrines of hereditary nobility.[6]

At the same time, Warren was frustrated by what she saw as the neglect of her family in the new political order. An Otis and a Warren, she had

---

[4] Mercy Otis Warren to John Adams, Aug. 15, 1807, in Charles Francis Adams, ed., "Correspondence between John Adams and Mercy Warren Relating to Her *History of the American Revolution*," Mass. Hist. Soc., *Collections*, 5th Ser., IV (1878), 453, hereafter cited as "Adams-Warren Letters."

[5] See David Ramsay, *History of the American Revolution* (Philadelphia, 1789), II, 339-356; John Marshall, *The Life of George Washington* . . . (Philadelphia, 1804-1807), V, 89-133; and Mercy Otis Warren, *Observations on the New Constitution, and on the Federal and State Conventions, By a Columbian Patriot* (Boston, 1788), in Paul Leicester Ford, ed., *Pamphlets on the Constitution of the United States* (New York, 1968 [orig. publ. Brooklyn, N.Y., 1888]), 2-23. Ford attributed the pamphlet to the Warrens' friend Elbridge Gerry, but recent studies show that Mercy Warren was the "Columbian Patriot." See Jackson Turner Main, *The Antifederalists: Critics of the Constitution, 1781-1788* (Chicago, 1964), 140, 287, and Cecelia M. Kenyon, ed., *The Antifederalists* (Indianapolis, 1966), xlix, n. 24.

[6] Gordon, *History of the Rise, Progress, and Establishment of the Independence of the United States of America* . . . , IV (London, 1788), 393-398; Marshall, *Life of Washington*, V, 24-30; Warren, *History of the Rise, Progress and Termination of the American Revolution. Interspersed with Biographical, Political and Moral Observations* (Boston, 1805), III, 280-297. See Wallace Evan Davies, "The Society of the Cincinnati in New England, 1783-1800," *William and Mary Quarterly*, 3d Ser., V (1948), 3-25.

actively supported the causes of resistance and revolution for four decades, establishing a reputation as a patriot. Daughter of James Otis and sister of James Otis, Jr., she was involved in radical Massachusetts politics from the opening rift between the Otises and Thomas Hutchinson in 1760-1761 through the struggle for independence; her home was a veritable salon for Sons of Liberty and various pre-Revolutionary committees. James Warren, whom she married in 1754, had also served the cause: a radical organizer in Plymouth County in the mid-1760s, he served Massachusetts in several positions, including Speaker of the House and president of the Provincial Congress. In Mercy Warren's view, however, James had been abandoned in the '80s, his virtuous pursuit of republican simplicity having become an embarrassment to those—like the Warrens' bête noire, John Hancock—who would use political power to foster their private ambitions. As she crafted her *History* in the '80s and '90s, she saw crumbling around her the values to which she had long been committed. Antifederalism had failed and Massachusetts politics was in shambles; her husband had been repudiated, three of the five Warren sons were tragically dead, and she and James were reduced to pleading for a minor government position for their son Henry. Warren's *History* may thus be seen as a mirror reflecting both its troubled time and its troubled author.[7]

Warren's personal and political convictions were strong, even strident, and they colored her interpretation of the era. But while events of the 1780s and '90s gave focus and direction to her historical theory, the theory was born much earlier and is reflected in her letters, poetry, and plays.[8] Moreover, though her concerns and the categories she used to interpret history were similar to those of the other historians, her *History* illustrates more clearly than theirs how a commitment to republican ideology and a concern for its future generated an ethical theory of history. For Warren had the most systematic understanding of the relationship between ideology and ethics, the best-developed interpretation of how corruption operated in history, and the clearest insight into the historian's role as a social and political critic. Thus her *History* is not merely a reflection of her personal concerns and convictions; it is also a work of moral art: a self-consciously created instrument of ideology and ethics that simultaneously

[7] See, for example, MOW to John Adams, Oct. 25, 1782, to Abigail Adams, Apr. 24, 1785, to John Adams, Dec. 1786, "The Letter-Book of Mercy Warren," MS, Mass. Hist. Soc., Boston, 185, 135, 197; and MOW to Elbridge Gerry, June 11, 1789, and May 24, 1790, in C. Harvey Gardiner, ed., *A Study in Dissent: The Warren-Gerry Correspondence, 1776-1792* (Carbondale, Ill., 1968), 227, 238-240. The most useful sources on Warren's life and political views are Maud Macdonald Hutcheson, "Mercy Warren, 1728-1814," *WMQ*, 3d Ser., X (1953), 378-402; Smith, *History as Argument*, 73-119, and "Mercy Otis Warren's Radical View of the American Revolution," in Lawrence H. Leder, ed., *The Colonial Legacy.* Vol. II: *Some Eighteenth-Century Commentators* (New York, 1971), 203-225; and Jean Fritz, *Cast for a Revolution: Some American Friends and Enemies, 1728-1814* (Boston, 1972).

[8] See Hutcheson, "Mercy Warren," *WMQ*, 3d Ser., X (1953), 382-389, 392-395.

expressed the Revolutionaries' commitment to republicanism and served as a beacon shining back upon the exemplary forebears.

Warren perceived herself as a writer "who wishes only to cultivate the sentiments of public and private virtue in whatsoever falls from her pen." She thought it her central duty as a playwright, poet, and historian "to form the minds, to fix the principles [and] to correct the errors" of "the young members of society," and to encourage them to tread the path of true virtue "instead of the hackneyed vulgar walks crowded with swarms of useless votaries, who worship at the pedestal of pleasure or bow before the shrine of wealth." As early as 1780 Warren called for "the steady influence of all the old republicans, to keep the principles of the revolution in view," already concerned that the spirit of the Revolution was eroding. For the "giddy multitude" was destroying all the gains of independence, rather than adhering to "the manners that would secure their freedom." With this end in mind, she presented her *History* as a work of partisan ideology that would "justify the principles of the defection and final separation from the parent state," and at the same time as a work of moral suasion, a manual of republican ethics designed to exhort future generations of Americans to engage in the uncompleted struggle.[9]

Although some contemporaries saw patriot history as polemics masquerading as objective narrative, Warren believed that she could both justify the Revolution and transcend partisan polemics.[10] By insisting on the priority of ethical categories in historical and political interpretation, she attempted to generate a vision of an American future that would fulfill the promise of the Revolution. Thus if her proximate aim was to justify the Revolution, she saw that aim subserving the greater principle of which it was a part: that, as Lord Bolingbroke put it, "history is philosophy teaching by examples," that it "inculcates images of virtue and vice," and that its proper task is to train people, particularly young people, in "public and private virtue." The fundamental requirement of this "exemplary theory" of history was that historical writing instruct in the principles of personal morality and public virtue; it enjoined the historian to suppress all personal biases in order to serve the higher end of providing models of virtue and deterrent images of vice.[11]

[9] MOW to Winslow Warren, Sept. 1785, and Nov. 20, 1780, to John Adams, Dec. 28, 1780, "Letter-Book," MS, 314-315, 256-257, 183; Warren, *American Revolution*, I, viii. Warren identified "the old patriots" with "the pure principles of republicanism" in a letter to Catharine Macaulay (Aug. 2, 1787, "Letter-Book," MS, 22).

[10] See Jonathan Boucher, *A View of the Causes and Consequences of the American Revolution* ... (London, 1797), i-vi, and John Adams to Thomas Jefferson, July 3, 1813, in Lester J. Cappon, ed., *The Adams-Jefferson Correspondence* ..., II (Chapel Hill, N.C., 1959), 349.

[11] Bolingbroke quoted in Isaac Kramnick, ed., *Lord Bolingbroke: Historical Writings* (Chicago, 1972), xvi. Warren evidently read Bolingbroke (or at least knew his work through conversation). See MOW to Winslow Warren, Dec. 24, 1779, "Letter-Book," MS, 242-243. The best short treatment of the exemplary theory is George H. Nadel, "Philosophy of History before Historicism," *History and Theo-*

Warren self-consciously wrote in this tradition of exemplary history both because she was convinced philosophically that historical models instructed youth and because the tradition provided a framework for developing her ideological commitments. In short, the exemplary theory was not only right but useful. As she wrote to the English historian Catharine Macaulay, British cruelties must be handed down "with redoubled infamy, when the tragic tale shall be faithfully transmitted to posterity." Indeed, "it requires the pen of a Macauley [sic] to trace the origins, to paint the prime actors, and give the true colouring to the source and prosecution of a war kindled by avarice, whetted by ambition, and blown up into a thirst of revenge by repeated disappointments."[12] Warren joyfully embraced the exemplary theory as the perfect vehicle for uniting her ethical and ideological concerns, for the theory required her to write what she longed to write: that the Revolution originated in British avarice, against which the colonists responded with moral outrage and political and military resistance. The Revolution epitomized the exemplary theory itself, pitting the forces of virtue against the forces of avarice. By grounding her ethical and ideological convictions, the exemplary theory accomplished two related aims: it provided Warren's historical theory with its explanatory categories, and it laid the foundation for her use of history as a mode of social and political criticism.

> Virtue turn'd pale, and freedom left the isle,
> When [Britain] stretch'd out her avaricious hand
> And show'd her sons her hostile bloody wand.[13]

In Warren's version of the exemplary theory, "virtue" and "avarice" were the fundamental categories of historical explanation, the terms in which historians properly interpreted and shaped events, because they were the leading principles of human character. Believing that the study of history "requires a just knowledge of character," Warren outlined the characterological terms that constituted history's ethical dynamic:

> The study of the human character opens at once a beautiful and deformed picture of the soul. We there find a noble principle implanted in the nature of man, that pants for distinction. This principle operates in every bosom, and when kept under the control of reason, and the influence of humanity, it produces the most benevolent effects. But when the checks of conscience are thrown aside, or the moral sense [is] weakened by the sudden acquisition of wealth or power,

ry, III (1964), 291-315. See also Kramnick, ed., *Bolingbroke*, xv-xxxix, and Dorothy A. Koch, "English Theories Concerning the Nature and Use of History, 1735-1791" (Ph.D. diss., Yale University, 1946).

[12] MOW to Macaulay, Feb. 21, 1777, "Letter-Book," MS, 10.

[13] Warren, "A Political Reverie," in *Poems, Dramatic and Miscellaneous* (Boston, 1790), 192.

humanity is obscured, and if a favorable coincidence of circumstances permits, this love of distinction often exhibits the most mortifying instances of profligacy, tyranny, and the wanton exercise of arbitrary sway.[14]

It is not clear here whether Warren believed that human character is fundamentally virtuous and that evil is introduced when certain social conditions (notably the acquisition of wealth and power) operate against the "noble principle," or whether she believed that virtue and avarice have equal status in character and that one or the other will be manifested to a greater degree given certain social conditions. Since she did not describe two "plants"—one virtuous, the other avaricious—she apparently believed that, while avarice is as manifest in conduct as is virtue, social conditions exert a preponderance of determining power.

This view squares with Warren's environmentalism. Although she refers here to "the nature of man," it is useful to distinguish her remarks on "human character" from whatever ideas about "human nature" we may wish to infer from them. For Warren was far less concerned with "human nature," understood as a set of fundamental passions or appetites that determine people's conduct, than she was with "human character," construed as the people's manifest social and political conduct itself. She was willing to generalize from time to time that man is "an absurd and ferocious, instead of a rational and humane being," and to confess that "I am more and more convinced of the propensity in human nature to tyrannize over their fellow men." But she argued more forcefully and consistently that "the character of man is never finished until the last act of the drama is closed," and that human action owes "*more* to the existing state or stage of *society*" than to the nature or disposition of mankind.[15]

It was clear to her, however, that avarice was unavoidable in history because man is a social being who craves distinction from his fellows. Virtue and reason were, for Warren, inseparable, and both rested on the principle of self-discipline. Bolingbroke saw virtue as "the moderation and

[14] Warren, *American Revolution*, I, 2. I have adopted the term "avarice" as the antithesis of "virtue" because Warren used the word so frequently in her private and published writings, and because it conveys more precisely than the traditional "vice" her sense of the lust for wealth, power, luxury, and distinction. "Vice" is too passive to capture her sense of a willful (even if blind) pursuit. At the same time, while Warren sees "corruption" as the product of avarice, both "corruption" and "commerce" (as J.G.A. Pocock has used the latter term) are essentially systemic concepts that go beyond her more limited usage of avarice. See Pocock, "Virtue and Commerce in the Eighteenth Century," *Journal of Interdisciplinary History*, III (1972), 120-134.

[15] Warren, *American Revolution*, III, 330; MOW to John Adams, Oct. 1775, "Letter-Book," MS, 157; to John Adams, July 16, 1807, "Adams-Warren Letters," 330; Warren, *American Revolution*, III, 83 (emphasis added). See Shaffer, *Politics of History*, chap. 4. An excellent discussion of the metaphysics of environmentalism is in Bernard Sheehan, *Seeds of Extinction: Jeffersonian Philanthropy and the American Indian* (Chapel Hill, N.C., 1973), 14-47.

government . . . of the appetites, desires and passions, according to the rules of reason, and therefore in opposition to their own blind impulses." And Warren wrote to her son James, in virtually the same language, that "the knowledge of ourselves . . . teaches [us] to resist the impulse of appetite, to check the sallies of passion, at the same time that it leads to certain permanent happiness, and renders us useful to society." Virtue was not, for Warren, preeminently a religious principle, although she believed that true religion always counseled the cultivation and practice of virtue.[16]

As a historian, Warren was less interested in virtue and avarice as traits of personal character than as principles of society and history. Unfortunately, in history avarice tended to get the better of virtue, for "ambition and avarice are the *leading springs* which generally actuate the restless mind. From these *primary sources of corruption* have arisen all the rapine and confusion, the depredation and ruin, that have spread distress over the face of the earth from the days of Nimrod to Cesar [*sic*], and from Cesar to an arbitrary prince of the house of Brunswick."[17] The historian had to recognize virtue when it appeared and applaud "the many signal instances of disinterested merit" among mankind. But the melancholy fact remained that "virtue in the sublimest sense, has an influence only on a chosen few," for "the guidance of reason . . . operates too little on the generality of mankind."[18]

Virtue and avarice were timeless and culturally universal because they were ontological facts of human character. But they were not, as Warren used them, vague abstractions like Good and Evil, for their observable manifestation in time constituted the ethical condition of people living in society. Since they were the basic terms of history's ethical dialectic, virtue and avarice provided Warren an explanatory schema for analyzing not only the American Revolution but all of human history. Like all the historians as well as others of their generation, she was preoccupied with the rise and fall of nations, particularly republics. Geneva represented "a striking portrait of the means by which most republics have been subverted." Subversion was accomplished not by the lone tyrant, but by "the pride of a few families, the ambition of individuals, and the supineness of the people." The few exerted such "an undue authority" over "the middling-class of mankind" that "the mass of the people" was rendered "abject and servile."[19] The "middling-class," of course, ought never to be supine and inattentive to their political condition, and it was the proper role of the republican historian to keep the people informed, to point out the danger of tyranny, and to call the people back to virtue and reason whenever their rights were threatened. But the problem persisted in history: in the face of

[16] Bolingbroke quoted in Koch, "English Theories," 25; MOW to James Warren, 1773, to George Warren, Feb. 17, 1793, "Letter-Book," MS, 217, 406. See MOW to James Warren, 1776, *ibid.*, 218.

[17] Warren, *American Revolution*, I, 2 (emphasis added).

[18] *Ibid.*, 3; MOW to John Adams, Dec. 1786, "Letter-Book," MS, 197; Warren, *American Revolution*, I, 216. See *ibid.*, 70, III, 309.

[19] Warren, *American Revolution*, III, 73-74.

an avaricious few, the people fall into a torpor of unconcern and irresponsibility, and their voice "seldom breathes universal murmur, but when the insolence or the oppression of their rulers extorts the bitter complaint."[20]

As she indicated by her reference to "an arbitrary prince of the house of Brunswick," Warren's immediate aim was to explain the Revolution, and she did so in ethical terms. Upsetting the general harmony that had prevailed for a century and a half, George III and his ministers began in the 1760s to tie imperial policy to trade objectives, thereby strengthening colonial subordination both to the English merchants and to the crown and Parliament (and, she strongly hinted, making the colonists virtual slaves of Britain). In addition, George and his ministers were not content to let the colonists raise their own taxes by the voluntary consent of the people's representatives. Instead, "grown giddy with the lustre of their own power, in the plenitude of human grandeur," they pursued "such weak, impolitic and unjust measures . . . as soon threw the whole empire into the most violent convulsions."[21]

The contrast between British avarice and American virtue grounded the theory that Britain (and Europe generally, until the French Revolution) was degenerating politically and culturally, whereas America was on the ascendant. As early as 1774 Warren wrote to Hannah Lincoln, who was unsympathetic to the patriot cause: "You ask why did we urge on this sudden display of ministerial power? In return let me ask by whose avarice and ambition the people were precipitated to take some rash and unjustifiable steps?" The answer was obvious, she pointed out a year later: Britain already was internally corrupt; its "venality and vice," "corruption and wickedness" were "nearly compleat." In the face of such corruption, Lexington and Concord were merely the signs of "the natural struggles which ensue when the genius of *liberty* arises to assert her rights in opposition to the ghost of Tyranny."[22]

Precisely as earlier republics had fallen—Greece, the Achaean League, the Amphyctions, Rome, Venice, Geneva—so England's "republican opinions and the freedom of the nation have been in the wane" since the accession of the first Stuart. England had become "an ungrateful, dissipated nation," fallen into "barbarism," her people "the ensigns of cruelty." Britain's degeneration was at no time more apparent than during the war. Hiring foreign mercenaries was the most obvious sign. Another was British treatment of the colonial citizenry. The Bostonians, wrote Warren in 1775, "are exposed to daily insults of a foe, who seem not only to have lost that sense of honour, freedom, and valour once the character-

---

[20] *Ibid.*, I, 40.

[21] *Ibid.*, 25.

[22] MOW to Hannah Lincoln, June 12, 1774, "Letter-Book," MS, 33; MOW to Mrs. E. Lothrop, 1775, *ibid.*, 97. To Mrs. Temple, Warren added in Aug. 1775: "It may be observed that when a nation has arrived at the plentitude of earthly grandeur, luxury and vice are the baneful attendants, which sap the foundation of its greatness, and the gazing world frequently behold its ruin ensue with much more rapidity than they rose to Empire" (*ibid.*, 92).

istic of the British nation—but that generosity, and humanity, which has [*sic*] long been the boast of the most civilized parts of the world." The employment of mercenaries, the many atrocities attributed to British soldiers, and Britain's cynical cruelties toward American citizens all served to prove that "pride, avarice, injustice, and ambition" were the emblems of British character.[23]

If avarice and corruption signalled Britain's political and moral decline, the question remained whether the Americans would, like the Genevans, lie supine in the face of tyranny or whether they would discover the spirit of virtue and resist. "I tremble for the events of the present commotion," Warren wrote in 1774; "there must be a noble struggle to recover the existing liberties of our injured country; we must repurchase them at the expense of blood, or tamely acquiesce, and embrace the hand that holds out the chain to us and our children." The prospect was hazardous, and Warren was uncertain "whether the patriots of the present day will be able to effect their laudable designs in our time."[24]

In retrospect, however, Warren argued that the Americans manifested the kind of virtue only rarely witnessed in history. Although a common maxim held that "a state of war has ever been deemed unfavourable to virtue," the Americans, at least until the late 1770s, displayed the virtues of patriotism, self-denial, industry, and prudence to an astonishing degree. On the civil front, virtue reigned supreme. The colonists answered British taxes and trade regulations with boycotts and encouragements to domestic manufactures, "wearing the stuffs fabricated in their own looms" as a badge of honor. In 1775, after the government of Massachusetts was dissolved, the people lived for more than a year "reduced nearly to a state of nature . . . without legal government, without law, and without any regular administration of justice, but what arose from the internal sense of moral obligation." Indeed, Warren found it almost incredible "that the principles of rectitude and common justice should have been so generally influential." Yet virtue did prevail and vice was abashed by exemplary "moderation, disinterestedness, and generosity." From the Stamp Act to the introduction of a standing army in Massachusetts, from the nonimportation agreements to the Coercive Acts, despite threats to the very fabric of society and law, "it must be ascribed to the virtue of the people, however reluctant some may be to acknowledge this truth, that they did not feel the effects of anarchy in the extreme."[25]

For Warren, then, the Revolution was properly to be explained in terms of virtue and avarice. Arising within the traditional exemplary theory of history, the categories accomplished more than could the mere citation of

---

[23] Warren, *American Revolution*, III, 399; MOW to Mrs. Janet Montgomery, Nov. 25, 1777, "Letter-Book," MS, 41-42; MOW to John Adams, Aug. 2, 1775, *ibid.*, 153; Warren, *American Revolution*, III, 330.

[24] MOW to Hannah Winthrop, 1774, "Letter-Book," MS, 70.

[25] MOW to John Adams, Oct. 15, 1778, *ibid.*, 167; Warren, *American Revolution*, I, 68, 226-227, 147.

heroic and ignoble figures in history, for she presented them as more than symbols of individual character. She used them to build a view of history as a vast morality play—strikingly similar in structure to the plays she wrote in the 1770s—in which the people's ideological commitments were measured by their ethical conduct. The American Revolution was one more example in the history of mankind of the lust for wealth and power subverting the principles of freedom. Unlike most such examples, however, in this one the oppressed resisted, manifesting an almost unparalleled virtue in opposition to a superior foe.

Warren's *History* thus easily explained the Revolution in terms of a simple moral opposition between American virtue and British avarice, an opposition that appears to subordinate ethical interpretation to ideological conviction. How else would a zealous patriot rationalize the Revolution in retrospect? That the ethical dimension of the *History* was more than a convenient rationale, however, is better understood by focusing on the anxiety the *History* betrays over two central and related issues: first, Warren's concern that America, too, was already showing signs of decline; second, the problem of distinguishing the American republic from all earlier ones, lest the logic of history hold true and America decline precisely as they had done. What was at stake in Warren's *History* was not British as much as American avarice and, therefore, the possibility of an American republican future. With respect to these issues, the historian of the Revolution asserted herself as a revolutionary historian, a writer who uses historical narrative as a tool of social and political criticism. For if the past was to be made comprehensible through the categories of virtue and avarice, the future still had to be lived in their terms—and the future was very much in doubt.

> Behold the schedule that unfolds the crimes
> And marks the manners of these modern times.
> [Freedom] sigh'd and wept—the folly of the age,
> The selfish passions, and the mad'ning rage
> For pleasure's soft debilitating charms,
> Running full riot in cold avarice' arms.[26]

Thomas Jefferson revealed the same anxiety and urgency as he concluded his discussion of religion in *Notes on the State of Virginia* (1786) with a prophecy of America's future. Religious liberty was temporarily safe, he argued, because "the spirit of the times" secured the people

---

[26] Warren, "The Genius of America, weeping the absurd Follies of the Day," in *Poems*, 246. Warren's footnote to this poem explains a good deal about her motives in writing her *History*: "This poem was written when a most deplorable depravity of manners pervaded the cities of the United States, in consequence of a state of war; a relaxation of government; the sudden acquisition of fortune; a depreciating currency; and a new intercourse with foreign nations" (*ibid.*, 249).

against pernicious legislation. But "the spirit of the times may alter, will alter," he predicted. "Our rulers will become corrupt, our people careless. A single zealot may commence persecutor, and better men be his victims." In short, he argued: "It can never be too often repeated, that the time for fixing every essential right on a legal basis is while our rulers are honest, and ourselves united. From the conclusion of this war we shall be going down hill." The very metaphor "down hill" presaged an American decline precisely as Warren had outlined it. At the same time that the rulers became corrupt, the people "will forget themselves, but in the sole faculty of making money, and will never think of uniting to effect a due respect for their rights."[27] Warren's attitude toward the likelihood of American decline was even gloomier than Jefferson's, for she believed that the attempt to institutionalize the future by "fixing every essential right on a legal basis" would prove fruitless without the precondition of a virtuous people. For more than thirty years her writings reveal an impelling concern about internal American corruption, born of avarice. It was clear to her that an American decline was virtually inevitable—if decline were the natural phenomenon that most theorists assumed it was.

"Corruption," "decay," "degeneration," the words most frequently used to describe the fall of republics, were borrowed from the language of nature and were freighted with connotations of necessity. Characteristically of those eighteenth-century theorists who viewed history cyclically, the anonymous author of "Thoughts on the Decline of States" argued in 1791 that all nations inevitably decline and die, and "he must think little of the order of nature who sees not that all of our efforts must be defeated at last, whether for the preservation of individuals, or the body politick."[28] The logic of nature presented difficulties to the historian who, like Warren, sought to distinguish the American republic from earlier ones. Thus, when she wrote in naturalistic terms at all, she tended to agree with such writers as Joseph Galloway who thought that, although the body politic is indeed "liable to disorders, which often terminate in death," *inevitable* decline could be avoided by performing "a radical cure."[29]

Warren went a step farther. She attempted to abandon the language of nature altogether by employing an ethical and social language to account for decline. While traditional theory held that corruption acted like a cancer, metastasizing through the state, eating at its vitals until the state died, Warren sought a non-naturalistic explanation for decline, and thus for a way of liberating America's future from the teleology of nature. She centered her analysis in virtue and avarice because they were fundamentally

[27] Thomas Jefferson, *Notes on the State of Virginia,* ed. William Peden (Chapel Hill, N.C., 1954), 161.
[28] *Massachusetts Magazine,* III (July 1791), 408. See Stow Persons, "The Cyclical Theory of History in Eighteenth-Century America," *American Quarterly,* VI (1954), 147-163.
[29] Galloway, *Historical and Political Reflections on the Rise and Progress of the American Rebellion* ... (London, 1780), 1.

societal, not natural, terms. Since avarice was the cause of corruption, the historian's proper task was to exhort her countrymen to virtue, even as she pointed to the pustulating signs of corruption and decay.

Warren, like the other historians, tended to emphasize the symptoms of decline in the decade after independence. The war, of course, played its insidious role in undermining American virtue, for war created opportunities for speculators and brought to America the influence of foreign manners. "[S]uch a total change of manners in so short a period I believe was never known in the history of man," she wrote to John Adams in 1778.[30] The problem was that avarice, once introduced, led to systemic corruption, infecting not only the manners of individuals but the society's ethical and political order as well. Burning with frustration, she wrote to Adams in 1786: "Emancipated from a foreign yoke, the blessings of peace just restored upon honourable terms, with the liberty of forming our own governments, framing our own laws, choosing our own magistrates, and adopting manners the most favourable to freedom and happiness, yet sorry I am to say I fear we have not virtue sufficient to avail ourselves of these superior advantages." Republicanism and independence "are nearly dwindled into theory," she wrote a few months later. Republicanism was "defaced by a spirit of anarchy," while independence was "almost annihilated by the views of private ambition and a rage for the accumulation of wealth by a kind of public gambling, instead of private industry."[31]

With nothing less at stake than independence and the possibility of an American republican order, David Ramsay called upon "the Press, the pulpit & all the powers of Eloquence" to counteract the ruinous avarice and "to excite us to the long neglected virtues of industry & frugality."[32] For Warren even more than for Ramsay, historical writing was just such an instrument of "Eloquence," and it was in this context that she expressed her anxiety over the rising generation and called for the vigor of "the old republicans." Indeed, apprehensive about the signs of imminent decline, Warren wrote of the social significance of the historian:

> It is an unpleasing part of history, when "corruption begins to prevail, when degeneracy marks the manners of the people, and weakens the sinews of the state." If this should ever become the deplorable situation of the United States, let some unborn historian, in a far distant day, detail the lapse, and hold up the contrast between a simple, virtuous, and free people, and a degenerate, servile race of beings, corrupted by wealth, effeminated by luxury, impoverished by licentiousness, and become the *automations* of intoxicated ambition.[33]

[30] MOW to James Otis, 1775, "Letter-Book," MS, 94; MOW to John Adams, Oct. 15, 1778, *ibid.*, 167.

[31] MOW to John Adams, Dec. 1786, to Macaulay, Aug. 2, 1787, *ibid.*, 195, 22.

[32] Ramsay to John Eliot, Aug. 6, 1785, in Brunhouse, ed., *Writings of Ramsay*, 91.

[33] Warren, *American Revolution*, III, 336-337.

That "far distant day," obviously, was now, and the "contrast" was clear, for the generation that had suffered English oppression, declared independence, and mobilized America's forces for war was being superseded by a younger generation that was sacrificing liberty and virtue at the shrine of private ambition. To this younger generation Warren addressed her *History*, mixing condemnation of their avarice with hope that moral suasion and the examples of the old republicans would turn their attention back to the virtues of their ancestors. Her *History* was thus a radically contemporary document, less concerned with the past for its own sake than with the bearing of the past on the present and future.

Motivating Warren's statements about American decline was the zeal of the revolutionary-as-historian who believes that narrative history is an instrument of social and political criticism. History could be instructive only if it exhorted future generations not to forget, for the problem with avarice was that it led to "forgetfulness," a denial of history's lessons. Thus the younger generation "cease to look back with due gratitude and respect on the fortitude and virtue of their ancestors, who, through difficulties almost insurmountable, planted them in a happy soil."[34]

There is no reason to think that Warren actually believed that the younger generation was altogether avaricious whereas her own had been filled with paragons of virtue. To think this is to depreciate her strategy of exhortation. Those who "lusted" for wealth, power, and distinction were always present in history, as apparent in America before the Declaration of Independence as afterwards. And, of course, Warren condemned the avaricious, like Thomas Hutchinson, and the timid, like those who capitulated to British policies rather than resisting them with "manly fortitude." But to portray a contrast between the generations was to rely on a theatrical convention, as useful to historical as to dramatic presentation, for creating among the characters a stark opposition that both simplified the moral drama and made its resolution more urgent. Indeed, she wrote of the rising generation more optimistically in her letters than in her *History*, and she wrote more optimistically of the Revolutionaries in her *History* than in her letters, revealing not so much a confusion in her beliefs as her notion that the creation of tense moral dichotomies was a valuable hortatory technique.[35]

The use of this technique also reveals more of Warren's motivation as a historian. She contrasted the rising generation with the seventeenth-cen-

[34] *Ibid.*, I, 4.
[35] See, for example, MOW to Winslow Warren, Jan. 18, 1781, and Dec. 18, 1782, to John Adams, Oct. 25, 1782, to Macaulay, [Sept.] 17, 1786, "Letter-Book," MS, 265, 280-281, 185, 18-20; and MOW to James Otis, 1775, to John Adams, Oct. 15, 1778, to Abigail Adams, Apr. 24, 1785, to Macaulay, July 1789, *ibid.*, 94, 167-168, 135-136, 28. Regarding Hutchinson, see Warren, *American Revolution*, I, chap. 4. Warren's character "Rapatio" in *The Adulateur* (1772) and in *The Defeat* (1773) was transparently Hutchinson. See Hutcheson, "Mercy Warren," *WMQ*, 3d Ser., X (1953), 382-384, and Bernard Bailyn, *The Ordeal of Thomas Hutchinson* (Cambridge, Mass., 1974), 202, 244, 50-62.

tury settlers and the Revolutionaries in order to establish hegemony over
the future. She sought not merely to influence how future Americans
would interpret the Revolution but, more important, to establish the very
categories in which interpretation was properly to be conducted. It was
bad enough that the younger generation was already acting avariciously; it
would be worse yet if they were permitted to abandon altogether the ethical terms in which Revolutionary history was to be understood. And they
were showing signs of doing just that, for they were adopting "new ideas"
that "from a rivalry of power and a thirst for wealth, had prepared the way
to corruption, and the awakened passions were hurried to new images of
happiness. The simpler paths which they had trodden in pursuit of competence and felicity, were left to follow the fantastic fopperies of foreign
nations, and to sigh for the distinctions acquired by titles, instead of that
real honor which is ever the result of virtue."[36] Future generations might
dispute this grim picture of American decline, but dispute would only
confirm Warren's major point: that the Revolution was properly to be
interpreted according to the ethical categories of virtue and avarice, in the
language of "simplicity," "competence," and "felicity," as against "rivalry,"
"corruption," and "passion." To write history was intrinsically, for Warren,
to exhort, for history was an ethical imperative of the Revolution itself.

> I look with rapture at the distant dawn,
> And view the glories of the opening morn,
> When justice holds his sceptre o'er the land,
> And rescues freedom from a tyrant's hand;
> When patriot states in laurel crowns may rise,
> And ancient kingdoms court them as allies;
> Glory and valour shall be here display'd,
> And virtue rear her long dejected head.[37]

Warren's persistent emphasis on avarice in history strongly suggests that
she refused to adopt the notions of historical progress then emerging in
Enlightenment Europe. The suggestion is strengthened by her version of
the exemplary theory, her view of her own ethical role as historian, and
her sense of the imminent possibility of catastrophe, for the "faith" in
historical progress, as J. B. Bury described it, was incompatible with her
ethical commitments. Bury argued that the idea of progress is a theory
"which involves a synthesis of the past and a prophecy of the future"; it is a
theory "which regards men as slowly advancing . . . in a definite and desirable direction, and infers that this progress will continue indefinitely."[38]

[36] Warren, *American Revolution*, III, 279-280. See Ramsay, *Revolution of South-Carolina*, II, 83-93, and William Gordon to "The Independent Chronicle," Feb. 26, 1778, "Letters of Gordon," 381.
[37] "A Political Reverie," in *Poems*, 189.
[38] Bury, *The Idea of Progress: An Inquiry into Its Origin and Growth* (New York, 1932), 4-7; quotations on p. 5.

Although several aspects of Warren's historical theory led logically toward an idea of progress, they were effectively undermined by her repudiation of any notion that mankind was "destined" to advance gradually "in a definite and desirable direction." If anything, she believed that the reverse was true, that history contained no interior principle conducive to man's betterment, for all past republics had been eaten away from within by corruption caused by avarice, and no subsequent republic seemed capable of building upon the failures of earlier ones. America, it appeared, would be no exception if the early signs of avarice were genuine presages.

Equally important, perhaps more so, Warren had no interest in showing abstractly that history was progressive. For it was precisely such comfortable conceptions that lulled people into a false sense of security or, worse yet, provided them with an excuse for avarice, as if civilization would progress regardless of what they did. She repudiated any principle—call it providence or progress—that guaranteed the shape of the future at the expense of wresting responsibility from man's hands.

Yet despite her repudiation of progressive history, Warren wrote optimistically. Even a jeremiad could not be a story of unrelieved gloom lest it inculcate despair; exhortation demanded at least the possibility of a desirable future. Thus at the same time that she depicted a younger generation declining from the ethical and ideological standards of the Revolutionaries, she held out the hope of a resurgence of American virtue, painting the future as opportunity. Consistent with her philosophical commitment to human efficacy in history, she wrote of the promise of the Revolution even as she condemned the rising generation for leaving the path of political and ethical propriety. To do this was to point simultaneously to the people's responsibility for what they wrought and to her sense of the value of her *History* as an exhortation. "[A] new century has dawned," she wrote in a typical aside clearly addressed to the generation of 1800: "From the revolutionary spirit of the times, the vast improvements in science, arts, and agriculture, the boldness of genius that marks the age, the investigation of new theories, and the changes in the political, civil, and religious characters of men, succeeding generations have reason to expect still more astonishing exhibitions in the next."[39]

Warren wrote this optimism back in time, attributing it to the Revolutionaries throughout their efforts to secure independence. But, at the same time, she sought to chasten optimism because the nation's virtue still required protection. "Notwithstanding the advantages that may be derived, and the safety that may be felt, under so happy a constitution," she wrote, muting her Antifederalism in the interest of making her *History* useful as exhortation, "yet it is necessary to guard at every point, against the intrigues of artful or ambitious men, who may subvert the system." The people of America had every reason to congratulate themselves on the success of their Revolution and on the spirit in which independence

[39] Warren, *American Revolution*, I, vi-vii.

had been won. But they had now to preserve their accomplishments "by a strict adherence to the principles of the revolution, and the practice of every public, social and domestic virtue."[40] These statements have the style of the secular jeremiad, presenting both a challenge and a hope.

To conclude, however, that Warren wrote with "guarded optimism" is to depreciate her sense of threat. For even after hostilities had ended, she wrote, "it was yet uncertain" whether the union could be consolidated "under wise, energetic, and free modes of government." Indeed, it remained uncertain whether such government, "if established, would be administered agreeable to laws founded on the beautiful theory of republicanism." For although "the name of *liberty* delights the ear, and tickles the fond pride of man, it is a jewel much oftener the play-thing of his imagination, than a possession of real stability." Liberty "may be acquired to-day in all the triumph of independent feelings," but, she added, scarcely veiling the challenge to her readers, "perhaps to-morrow the world may be convinced, that mankind know not how to make a proper use of the prize, generally bartered in a short time, as a useless bauble, to the first officious master that will take the burden from the mind, by laying another on the shoulders of ten-fold weight." This, as Warren repeatedly pointed out, was what generally happened in history—it was "the usual course of human conduct. . . . The game of deception is played over and over to mislead the judgment of men, and work on their enthusiasm, until by their own consent, hereditary crowns and distinctions are fixed, and some scion of royal descent is entailed upon them forever."[41]

The threat was clear enough as Warren outlined it. But what could be done to reverse the pernicious tendencies to which she pointed? Gordon S. Wood has argued that in the 1780s different solutions to America's ills came from two emerging schools of thought. One, eventually associated with Federalist political sociology, argued that the remedy for avarice and corruption was to arrange the institutions of government in a way that minimized the potential for social "viciousness." The other, more loosely identified with Antifederalist theory, argued that only a kind of education aimed at the moral regeneration of the people and their social institutions could reinfuse virtue into the republic.[42] The former view held that Amer-

---

[40] *Ibid.*, III, 424, 429. See Ramsay, *American Revolution*, II, 354.

[41] Warren, *American Revolution*, III, 324-326. See MOW to Macaulay, July 1789, "Letter-Book," MS, 28.

[42] Wood, *Creation*, 428-429; see generally chaps. 11 and 12. I do not agree that the emerging opposition between ethical and institutional interpretations can be resolved into "the evangelical scheme and the legal scheme," or "unenlightened" versus "enlightened," or "Calvinist" versus "Liberal," for the contrast implies that members of the "evangelical," "unenlightened," "Calvinist" group based their interpretation of politics and society on a theory of human nature, thus precluding to them an environmentalist analysis (*ibid.*, 428). But Wood insightfully identifies the competing political sociologies and argues later that the Federalists (by whom he now means the exponents of the Federalist party as well as the supporters of the

ica could avoid the failures of past republics by adopting a properly mixed mode of government, thereby overcoming institutional weaknesses by erecting more perfect institutions. This, in fact, was one means of avoiding the inexorable logic of nature, for it substituted a political framework and language for the then conventional natural ones. No less an optimist about man's educability than Thomas Jefferson, comparing man's potential for self-control with his need for external political constraints, held that the latter were imperative. To Edmund Pendleton he wrote: "The fantastical idea of virtue and the public good being a sufficient security to the state against the commission of crimes, which you say you have heard insisted on by some, I assure you was never mine." Nor would it have been for the man who argued for the institutionalization of the future now, once for all, "while our rulers are honest and ourselves united."[43]

John Adams was, with James Madison, the greatest exponent of mixed government and the political constraints that he thought inhered in it. In a letter to Mercy Warren he argued, as he did throughout his political writings, that the only way for America to avoid the decline of earlier republics was to establish a properly mixed and balanced government: "My pictures of the confusions and dissolutions [of past republics] were of republics ill constituted, improperly mixed, or not mixed at all; and this with the single view of convincing my countrymen of the necessity and duty of constituting their republics with such balances as would protect them from tyranny in every form. . . . Republics well constituted have been the best governments in the world, but republics ill-constituted have been the worst."[44] Adams and Jefferson were concerned with virtue, for they believed that the well-ordered republic gained strength from the voluntary self-discipline of its citizens. Nevertheless, as Jefferson's letter to Randolph and Adams's many writings on government make clear, one could more securely depend upon external political controls than on the people's virtue.[45]

As a student of political philosophy, Warren was thoroughly imbued with enlightened social and political theories that recognized the importance of a properly mixed republican government. Indeed, she made plain to Adams that a properly constituted republic did more than merely guard

---

Constitution) "hoped to create an entirely new and original sort of republican government—a republic which did not require a virtuous people for its sustenance" (*ibid.*, 475).

[43] Jefferson to Pendleton, Aug. 26, 1776, in Merrill D. Peterson, ed., *The Viking Portable Jefferson* (New York, 1975), 357.

[44] John Adams to MOW, Aug. 19, 1807, "Adams-Warren Letters," 472-473.

[45] As Adams wrote in his *Defence of the Constitutions of Government in the United States of America*, "Happiness, whether in despotism or democracy, in slavery or liberty, can never be found without virtue. The best republics will be virtuous, and have been so; but we may hazard a conjecture, that the virtues have been the *effect* of the well ordered constitution, rather than the *cause*" (Charles Francis Adams, ed., *The Works of John Adams* [Boston, 1850-1856], VI, 219; emphasis added).

the people against their own excesses. It actually produced "many excellent qualities, and heroic virtues in human nature—which often lie dormant for want of opportunities for exertion." "Yet," she added in a crucial qualifying statement that reasserted the priority of ethics over institutions, "I have my *fears*, that American virtue has not yet reached that sublime pitch which is necessary to baffle the designs of the artful, to counteract the weakness of the timid, or to resist the pecuniary temptations and ambitious wishes that will arise in the breast of many."[46] Adams, of course, had the same fears, which was precisely why he turned to governmental form as a remedy. But implicit in Warren's statement is her belief that, while the form of government is of obvious importance, a republic is impossible without a virtuous people. She took Montesquieu's injunction seriously: "There is no great share of probity necessary to support a monarchical or despotic government. The force of laws in one, and the prince's arm in the other, are sufficient to direct and maintain the whole. But in a popular state, one spring more is necessary, namely, virtue."[47] The ideal government was a republic in which the people were virtuous: thus the form would reflect and be strengthened by the people's virtue, and the virtue of the people would be enhanced and perpetuated by the form, people and institutions reflecting one another, as in parallel mirrors, to infinity. But, as Warren saw it, it was chimerical to believe that America could avoid the failures of past republics merely by creating a mixed form of government. While the politicians addressed themselves to matters of statecraft, the historian would use her writings to inculcate that virtue which she saw as the mainspring of the republic.

Warren's project is simplicity itself. Her fusion of ethical and ideological interpretation to make historical writing useful as explanation of the past and exhortation for the future reasserted the primacy of the people's responsibility for their future. This was the lesson of the Revolutionaries who, she insisted, "procured their own emancipation from foreign thraldom, by the sacrifice of their heroes and their friends." It was "the wise and patriotic" who had "by inconceivable labor and exertion obtained the prize."[48] Warren sought no guarantees for the people's future conduct—not in nature (the logic of which pointed to decline and decay in any case), nor in overarching principles like progress, nor in government itself. There was, as she saw it, no way to institutionalize the future. It would have to be lived, as the Revolutionaries had lived it, as strenuous republicans in the face of contingency.

[46] MOW to John Adams, Mar. 1776, "Letter-Book," MS, 164.
[47] *The Spirit of the Laws*, trans. Thomas Nugent (New York, 1962), 20.
[48] Warren, *American Revolution*, III, 309, 322.